MODELS OF TEACHING

Third Edition

Bruce Joyce

Marsha Weil

Prentice-Hall, Inc., Englewood Cliffs, New Jersey 07632

Library of Congress Cataloging-in-Publication Data

Joyce, Bruce R.
  Models of teachings.

  Bibliography: p.
  Includes index.
  1. Educational innovations.   I. Weil, Marsha.
II. Title.
LB1027.J64 1986   371.3   86–588
ISBN 0–13–586348–1

Editorial/production supervision and
      interior design: *Lori L. Baronian*
Cover design: *Karen Stevens*
Manufacturing buyer: *Harry P. Baisley*

To
Kevin, Brendan, Seamus,
Cynthia, and Lisa

ISBN 0-13-586348-1   01

ACKNOWLEDGMENTS

Excerpts from *Teaching Strategies and Cognitive Functioning in Elementary School Children* by Hilda Taba, 1966, San Francisco State College, Cooperative Research Project No. 2404, San Francisco. Reprinted by permission.

(Acknowledgments continue on page 518)

Prentice-Hall International (UK) Limited, *London*
Prentice-Hall of Australia Pty. Limited, *Sydney*
Prentice-Hall Canada Inc., *Toronto*
Prentice-Hall Hispanoamericana, S.A., *Mexico*
Prentice-Hall of India Private Limited, *New Delhi*
Prentice-Hall of Japan, Inc., *Tokyo*
Prentice-Hall of Southeast Asia Pte. Ltd., *Singapore*
Editora Prentice-Hall do Brasil, Ltda., *Rio de Janeiro*
Whitehall Books Limited, *Wellington, New Zealand*

CONTENTS

1 THE THINKING, FEELING STUDENT
Alternative Models of Learning, *1*

When we teach well, we help students learn well. A good model of teaching, in other words, helps learning. Powerful learners have repertoires of powerful strategies for acquiring educations. Models of teaching are designed to impart those repertoires while helping students learn information, ideas, and academic skills, develop social skills and values, and understand themselves and their environments.

Part I The Information-Processing Family ———————————— *23*
    INTRODUCTION: Models of Teaching Designed to Affect Information Processing

2 ATTAINING CONCEPTS
The Basic Skills of Thinking, *25*

Concepts are our tools for organizing information and approaching problems. This model is designed to teach concepts and to help students become more efficient at learning and creating them.

3 THINKING INDUCTIVELY
Collecting, Organizing, and Manipulating Data, *40*

A fundamental method of science is also one of the important skills of daily life. Hilda Taba developed the Inductive Thinking Model presented here, designed to help students work together to learn information, build concepts, and solve problems.

4 INQUIRY TRAINING
From Facts to Theories, *55*

This model is the core of a program to train students to engage in causal reasoning. The training is built around problems and a process of inquiry designed to lead the students to collect and verify information, develop concepts, and build and test hypotheses.

5 LEARNING FROM PRESENTATIONS
Advance Organizers, *70*

Psychologist David Ausubel has developed a theory of meaningful verbal learning on which a technology has been developed for structuring courses and presentations to increase the mental activities of the students.

Recent research on memory has resulted in the development of techniques for organizing material and teaching students how to master new information. Michael Pressley, Joel Levin, and their associates have explored the use of the link-word method with a wide range of subject matters and students.

Jean Piaget has stimulated the study of intellectual growth. A number of models have been developed to help us adjust instruction to the stages of growth of the students and to attempt to increase their rates of development.

The "model" for Scientific Inquiry Models is the practice of academic research. The student is introduced to the disciplines by analyzing problems and conducting research.

All learning ultimately depends on the focused education of the individual student and has its expression in the enhancement of the self. Personalists have developed a variety of powerful models that focus on the individual and on the shaping of human groups that support one another's struggles to achieve meaning and strength for self-responsible self-determination.

Psychologist Carl Rogers has been the leading spokesperson for teaching oriented around the student's perceptual world. In Nondirective Teaching Models the teacher operates as a counselor, helping the students understand themselves, clarify their goals, and accept responsibility for their growth and the direction of their activities. Designed to enhance the growing self, the model is an important tool to help us understand our students and to enlist them in a teaching-learning partnership.

Designed to help people break set and generate fresh ideas and solutions to problems, synectics has a wide range of applications. It is used to widen perspectives on problems, generate more lucid and creative writing and speaking, and induce cooperative problem solving. Skillfully used, it has the important side effects of increasing empathy and group cohesion.

Gestalt therapists have adapted a number of models to fit the classroom situation and the needs of typical students. Sets of exercises have been crafted to increase understanding of human potential and of how to behave to increase the development of self and others.

William Glasser has developed a way of helping students share in the creation of a positive learning environment. The teacher and the students establish the norms by which they provide support to one another and the space for individuals to flourish.

Part III The Social Family ————————————————— 215
INTRODUCTION: Cooperative Learning Models

We are social creatures and any group of human beings is more than the sum of its parts. In this family, models create education by confronting students with problems that they must solve together, by leading students to analyze their values and the public policies that shape justice in our society, and by introducing students to increasing their social skills and understanding.

13 GROUP INVESTIGATION
Building Education through the Democratic Process, *219*

Democracy is a way of solving problems through collective learning. John Dewey suggested that group investigation should be the basic model for social and academic education in a democratic society. Herbert Thelen extended and refined group investigation theory and practice. Recent research by Shlomo Sharan and his colleagues affirms and illuminates this broad, complex model.

14 ROLE PLAYING
Studying Social Behavior and Values, *239*

To stand back from oneself and think about one's social behavior and values is an extremely complex process, but a rewarding and essential component of education. Fannie and George Shaftel have become the architects of a model designed around the analysis of enactments of problem situations. The model is intended to open values to study and to improve social skills and increase cooperative behavior and empathy.

15 JURISPRUDENTIAL INQUIRY
Learning to Think about Social Policy, *258*

The making of social policy is a basic need in small groups, communities, and nations. Built around case studies of problems which can only be resolved by clarifying values and resolving conflicts among interests and values, the Jurisprudential Inquiry Model introduces students to policy analysis. As developed by James Shaver and Donald Oliver, the model can be used to design entire social studies courses or to illuminate policy questions in science, athletics, and many other curriculum areas.

16 LABORATORY TRAINING
Developing Interpersonal Skill, *275*

Beginning with the observation, during World War II, that both informal and formal leadership depended on the interpersonal skills of both leaders and group members a series of models were developed to teach people to analyze interpersonal situations and to generate productive methods for working together. These models have been extended to a variety of organizational settings. They provide a direct avenue both for educating students to use productive interpersonal styles and also for improving the social climates of the schools themselves.

17 SOCIAL SCIENCE INQUIRY
Studying Human Behavior on Spaceship Earth, *292*

In a fashion similar to the way we use natural science inquiry models, we can use the methods of social science to teach the social studies. The model presented here was designed by Byron Massialas and Benjamin Cox to teach information about social, economic, and political life.

Drawing particularly on the work of B. F. Skinner a large number of models have been designed to take advantage of the human being's capacity to learn and modify behavior by responding to tasks and feedback. These models are used to teach information, concepts, and skills, to increase comfort and relaxation and reduce phobias, to change habits, and to help students engage social and academic tasks appropriately.

18 MASTERY LEARNING AND DIRECT INSTRUCTION
Social Learning Theory, *317*

One of the important applications of behavioral systems theory is in the development of instructional systems that enable learners to adjust the pace of instruction and to record their own progress. Often these systems organize material to be learned in relatively small, sequenced instructional modules that are presented to the students with assessments of progress embedded in them. These "mastery learning" or "direct-instruction" systems have been employed successfully in a wide variety of areas involving academic and physical and mental skills.

19 LEARNING SELF-CONTROL
Using Feedback to Modify Behavior, *337*

This model is designed to help students understand their personal and social situations and to manage their behavior productively.

20 LEARNING FROM SIMULATIONS
From the Basic Skills to the Exploration of Space, *367*

The principles of cybernetics have been employed to design learning environments—from board games to computer simulations to elaborate laboratories for learning. Students are presented with tasks and then receive feedback about their performances. They teach themselves by observing the results of their actions.

21 ASSERTIVE TRAINING
Toward Integrative Communication, *383*

Designed specifically to help students analyze communication tasks and problems and to develop a repertoire of social skills for handling ordinary and stressful situations, this model is being used increasingly in both elementary and secondary schools. A nice side effect is that increases in social competence frequently improve both feelings about self and academic performance.

Models of teaching are designed to bring about learning. In these chapters we examine the evidence about their effectiveness and discuss how to select and combine them for maximum effect.

22 THE EFFECTS OF MODELS OF TEACHING
Academic, Personal, and Social Objectives, *401*

Educational environments are designed to increase the probability that certain kinds of learning will take place and that their effects will be durable. We examine the argument that they will succeed and some of the evidence that has been accumulated about their warrants.

23 THE SKILLS OF THINKING
Teaching Students How to Learn, *420*

The repertoire of models is most useful in teaching if we plan ahead and design courses and units of instruction to make maximum use of their potential.

24 THE CONDITIONS OF LEARNING
Focusing Instruction, *427*

Robert Gagné has provided us with a paradigm for organizing instruction, ensuring that prerequisites are identified and taught as the basis for advanced material and skills.

Individual differences can either make teaching delightful or confound it. The productive use of individual differences requires both the adaptation of instruction and the development of the students' abilities to adapt productively in the learning environment.

25 LEARNING STYLES AND MODELS OF TEACHING
Making Discomfort Productive, *435*

We select and adapt models so that the students can function effectively but are stretching the range of environments from which they can profit.

26 A MODEL FOR MATCHING ENVIRONMENT TO PEOPLE
Conceptual Systems Theory, *449*

David Hunt's adaptation of the system for analyzing learning styles and educational environments that he developed with Harold Schroder and O. J. Harvey gives us a method for predicting student preferences and accommodating them without sacrificing their needs to expand their learning repertoires.

The storehouse of educational models has power only if we learn to use the models effectively. Held rigidly, they have mechanical power only. Fluid control requires practice and a spirit of lifelong experimentation with teaching.

27 HOW TO LEARN A TEACHING REPERTOIRE
Training Ourselves, *469*

Recent research has given us a clearer picture of how we acquire the skill to use models of teaching that are new to us. In this chapter we explore how to use that research to increase our learning power.

28 EDUCATIONAL THEORY, RESEARCH, AND PRACTICE
Creating an Art and Science of Education, *490*

Professional knowledge comes from the analysis of clinical practice with teaching and the operation of schools; from research; and from the building of theory. Their proper use depends on a perspective about what each contributes and how we can draw on the knowledge of others and make it contribute to our own practices.

FOREWORD

In writing a foreword to the first edition of *Models of Teaching* I observed, with delight, that this is a book for all seasons. Clearly, for those in the springtime of their careers, it affords a lively and provocative introduction to the complexities of teaching. It is equally apparent, however, that educators of all levels of experience—provided only that they retain an interest in strengthening their instructional skills and broadening their repertoires of instructional styles and strategies—will find this book an invaluable resource and a highly-prized reference. I could imagine no teacher, whatever the season of his career, who would not covet such a wide-ranging and sensitively described array of alternate models of learning and teaching.

As I read this 1986 edition of *Models of Teaching* I am again impressed by its inclusiveness and by its pertinence to all educators, irrespective of tenure, who remain fascinated by the myriad ways students learn and teachers teach. But my dominant reaction in 1986 is that *Models of Teaching* speaks not only to seasons but to motives. Certainly, it resonates nicely with the basic perspectives teachers bring to pedagogical studies.

Ordinarily, teachers respond to discussions of method that are seen as relevant and applicable in their own classrooms. No model is described that has not been tested in actual learning situations, and each is illustrated from model-in-use experience. At the same time, teachers demand intellectually stimulating pedagogical studies—analyses which excite both their liberal and professional interests in education. Each model incorporates the theoretical considerations upon which it is based; each includes reports of the empirical research which supports it; and each acknowledges unresolved issues in its optimal use. Finally, understanding the uniqueness of particular teaching–learning interactions, and the individuality of the participants, teachers seek pedagogical studies that are flexible and allow for their active involvement. No model, fortunately, is presented didactically as a rigid and static prescription. Each clearly requires persistent sensitivity and continuous inquiry by teachers.

Models of Teaching implicitly recognizes the perspectives teachers bring to the study of their craft. To the degree that it manages to draw more teachers toward the serious analysis of pedagogy, all—students, teachers and so-ciety—will be well-served.

Robert J. Schaefer

PREFACE

We dream of schools that combine technical power and humanity. In those schools students thrive as individuals, growing in personal strength and sensitivity to others. They are members of a cooperative community where each works for the benefit of the others, and they develop the social skills and values that enable them to participate fully and responsibly in their society. They master academic substance to understand the nature of organized knowledge. They learn the literatures of their culture and build the speaking, writing, and technical skills to communicate powerfully and sensitively.

In our schools students embrace the many models of learning that give them the tools to grow. Their teachers have great breadth of repertoire, and through their own continuous study of educational process and academic and social substance, they are a clear model of the educated person for their students—ever growing and always curious.

We humbly give thanks to all the educators through the centuries and in our own decades who have provided us with the wonderful storehouse of models of teaching that we are privileged to describe in this book.

1

THE THINKING, FEELING STUDENT

Alternative Models of Learning

In this book we describe a variety of approaches to teaching, discuss their underlying theories, examine the research that has tested them, and illustrate how to use them. There are many powerful models of teaching designed to bring about particular kinds of learning and to help students become more effective learners. As educators we need to be able to identify these models and to select the ones that we will master in order to develop and increase our own effectiveness. To become competent to use these teaching strategies comfortably and effectively requires much further study and practice. (Chapter 27 describes the process of acquiring the necessary teaching skills.)

Although written from a perspective on teaching, in a real sense this book is about models of *learning*. As we help students acquire information, ideas, skills, values, ways of thinking, and means of expressing themselves, we are also teaching them how to learn. In fact, the most important long-term outcome of instruction may be the students' increased capabilities to learn more easily and effectively in the future. How teaching is conducted has a large impact on students' abilities to educate themselves.

Imagine a school where the variety of models of teaching is not only intended to accomplish a range of curriculum content goals (learning to read; to compute; to understand mathematical systems; to comprehend literature, science, and the social world; and to engage in the performing arts and

1

athletics) but is also designed to help the students increase their power as learners. Thus, as students master information and skills, the result of each learning experience is not only the content they learn, but the greater ability they acquire to approach future learning tasks.

In our school the students learn a range of learning strategies because their teachers use the models of teaching that require them. Our students learn models for memorizing information (described in Chapter 6). They learn how to attain concepts (Chapter 2) and how to invent them (Chapter 3). They practice building hypotheses and theories (Chapter 4) and using the tools of science to test them (Chapters 8, 13, and 17). They learn how to extract information and ideas from lectures and presentations (Chapters 5 and 6), how to study social issues (Chapter 15), and how to analyze their own social values (Chapters 13 and 14).

Our students also know how to profit from training and how to train themselves in athletic, performing arts, mathematical, and social skills (Chapters 18, 19, and 20). They know how to make their writing and problem solving more lucid and creative (Chapter 10). Perhaps most important, they know how to take initiative in planning personal study (Chapter 9), and they know how to work with others to initiate and carry out cooperative programs of inquiry (Chapters 12 and 13).

These students are both challenging and exhilarating to teach, because their expanded learning styles enable us to teach them in the variety of ways that are appropriate for the many goals of education. The most direct route to effectiveness in teaching is to teach the students how to fight effectively for an education. The stronger they are, and the more tools they possess, the more effective we are as teachers.

The core of the process of teaching is the arrangement of environments with which the student can interact (Dewey, 1918). A model of teaching is a plan or pattern that we can use to design face-to-face teaching in classrooms or tutorial settings and to shape instructional materials—including books, films, tapes, and computer-mediated programs and curriculums (long-term courses of study). Each model guides us as we design instruction to help students achieve various objectives.

SOURCES OF MODELS OF TEACHING

For the last twenty years we have conducted a continuous search for promising approaches to teaching. We visit schools and classrooms, examine curriculums, and study research on teaching. We also look at the work of therapists and industrial, military, and athletic trainers. We have found models of teaching in abundance. Some have broad applications while others are designed for very specific purposes. They range from simple, direct procedures that get immediate results to complex strategies that students can acquire only after patient and skillful instruction.

For inclusion in this book we have selected models that constitute a basic repertoire for schooling—that is, with them we can accomplish most of the common goals of schools. Also, they represent a broad range of approaches to education. They include many, but not all, of the major philosophical and psychological orientations toward teaching and learning. Each of them has a coherent theoretical basis—that is, their creators provide us with a rationale that explains why we expect them to achieve the goals for which they were designed. The selected models also have long histories of practice behind them: They have been refined through experience so that they can be used comfortably and efficiently in classrooms and other educational settings. Furthermore, they are adaptable: They can be adjusted to the learning styles of students and to the requirements of subject matter.

Finally, there is evidence that they work. In addition to experience, all of them are backed by some amount of formal research that tests their theories and their abilities to gain effects. The amount of related research varies from model to model: Some are backed by a few studies while others have a history of literally hundreds of studies. Some of the more important studies are discussed in this text; thorough discussions are provided in Chapters 22, 23, and 28.

In assessing the research we are concerned with the general educative effects of each model and the specific, "model-relevant" effects for which it was designed. For example, the "Scientific Inquiry" Models (Chapters 8 and 17) were designed to teach students the methods of science. That is their primary, direct mission. Research clearly indicates that those models achieve those effects very well, but that "traditional," "chalk-and-talk" methods of teaching science are very poor instruments for teaching the scientific method (Bredderman, 1983; El Nemr, 1979). Just as important, scientific inquiry increased the amount of information students learned, encouraged their development of concepts, and improved their attitudes toward science. What is of interest to us is that those models both achieved their primary goals and also had general educational benefits with respect to these important acquisitions and developments.

We are satisfied when some models achieve small but consistent effects that accumulate over time. The Advance Organizer Model (Chapter 5), which is designed to increase the acquisition and retention of information from lectures and other kinds of presentations—such as films and readings—achieves its results when the "organizers" are properly used (Joyce, Showers, Dalton, and Beaton, 1985). Lectures, written assignments, and films and other media are so pervasive as educational tools that even relatively modest increments of knowledge from specific uses of organizers can add up to impressive increases in learning: Consider the thousands of hours of presentations and readings to which a group of students is exposed as part of its education.

Perhaps the most interesting research has resulted when several models have been combined to attack multifaceted educational problems. Robert L. Spaulding, for example, developed a program for economically poor, socially disruptive, low-achieving children that used social learning theory (Part 4), techniques based on knowledge from developmental psychology (Chapter 7), and Inductive Teaching Models (Chapter 3). That program succeeded in improving students' social skills and cooperative learning behavior, induced students to take more responsibility for their education, substantially increased students' learning of basic skills and knowledge, and even improved students' performances on tests of intelligence (Spaulding, 1970).

Spaulding's work illustrates the importance of combining models in an educational program to pyramid their effects and achieve multiple objectives. Effective education requires combinations of personal, social, and academic learning that can best be achieved by using several appropriate models.

Also, although many models have been designed to promote specific kinds of learning, they do not necessarily inhibit other objectives. For example, inductive teaching methods (Chapter 3) are designed to teach students how to form concepts and test hypotheses. Tests of these models have found that they are also excellent ways of helping students learn information. In addition, the information so learned is likely to be retained longer than that learned by the recitation and drill-and-practice methods that are so common in schools (Worthen, 1968).

Methods designed for particular kinds of content can often be adapted successfully for others. Inductive methods, for example, were designed for academic content in the sciences and social sciences, but they can also be used for studying literature and social values.

However, it would be a mistake to assume that because a particular model is effective, it should be used exclusively. Inductive models illustrate this point also. If they are used relentlessly for all purposes, they achieve less than optimal results (see Shulman and Keislar, 1966). Creativity is valuable and the creative spirit should pervade our lives. But much learning requires noncreative activity. Memorization is important too, but to build all of education around memorization would be a serious mistake.

A few models of learning can have dramatic effects in specific applications. The "link-word" method, one of several models that assist memorization, has increased learning two to three times in a series of experiments. Essentially, this means that students learned given amounts of material two to three times more rapidly when they used the link-word methods than they would have if they had used customary procedures for memorizing words (Pressley and Levin, 1982). However, such dramatic effects should not lead us to attempt to achieve all objectives with the link-word method. It is one of the models of choice when rapid acquisition of information is concerned, but it is not the sole answer to the problems of education.

Thus, as we study the tested alternative models of teaching, we find no easy route to a single model that is superior for all purposes, or even that should be the sole avenue to any given objective. However, we do find powerful options that we can link to the multiple educational goals that constitute a complete educational diet. The message is that the most effective teachers (and designers) need to master a range of models and prepare for a career-long process of adding new tools and polishing and expanding their old ones. Spaulding's (1970) work contains many relevant and important lessons, especially that combinations of models can have a more dramatic effect on learning than any one could have alone.

FAMILIES OF MODELS

We have grouped the models of teaching that we have discovered into four families that share orientations toward human beings and how they learn.

THE INFORMATION-PROCESSING FAMILY

Information-processing models emphasize ways of enhancing the human being's innate drive to make sense of the world by acquiring and organizing data, sensing problems and generating solutions to them, and developing concepts and language for conveying them. Some models provide the learner with information and concepts; some emphasize concept formation and hypothesis testing; and still others generate creative thinking. A few are designed to enhance general intellectual ability. In general, as we see, many information-processing models are useful for studying the self and society, and thus for achieving the personal and social goals of education.

The following information-processing models are described in Part One:

CONCEPT ATTAINMENT

This model, built around the studies of thinking conducted by Bruner, Goodnow, and Austin (1967), is designed to help students learn concepts for organizing information and to help them become more effective at learning concepts. It includes an efficient method for presenting organized information from a wide range of areas of study to students of every stage of development.

INDUCTIVE THINKING

The ability to create concepts is generally regarded as one of the basic thinking skills. The model presented here is from the work of Hilda Taba (1966). Its tasks induce students to find and organize information; to create names for concepts; and to explore ways of becoming more skillful at discovering and organizing information and at creating and testing hypotheses describing relationships among sets of data. The model has been used in a wide variety of curriculum areas and with students of all ages.

INQUIRY TRAINING

Designed to teach students to engage in causal reasoning and to become more fluent and precise in asking questions, building concepts and hypotheses, and testing them, this model was first formulated by Richard Suchman (1962). Although originally used with the natural sciences, it has also been applied in the social sciences and in training programs with personal and social content.

ADVANCE ORGANIZERS

During the last twenty years this model, formulated by David Ausubel (1963), has become one of the most researched in the information-processing family. It is designed to provide students with a cognitive structure for comprehending material presented through lectures, readings, and other media. It has been employed with almost every conceivable content and with students of every age. It can be easily combined with other models—for example, when presentations are mixed with inductive activity.

MEMORIZATION

Mnemonics are strategies for memorizing and assimilating information. Teachers can use mnemonics to guide their presentations of material (teaching in such a way that students can easily absorb the information), and they can teach devices that students can use to enhance their individual and cooperative study of information and concepts. This model has also been tested over many curriculum areas and with students of many ages and characteristics. As indicated previously, some of the applications of memorization strategies have had dramatic effects. We include variations developed by Pressley and Levin (1981) and popular applications by Lucas and Lorayne (1974).

THE DEVELOPING INTELLECT

Models based on studies of students' intellectual development (Piaget, 1952; Kohlberg, 1976; Sullivan, 1967; and Sigel, 1969) are used to help us adjust instruction to the stage of maturity of an individual student and to design ways of increasing the student's rate of development. The model can be used in all types of educational settings and with all types of content. Curiously, the bulk of such development models are used with young children, particularly environmentally disadvantaged children, especially when the educational goal is to accelerate their growth (Spaulding, 1970). The applications for older students are, nevertheless, just as important (Purpel and Ryan, 1976).

SCIENTIFIC INQUIRY

As indicated earlier, a number of models have been developed to teach academic content with the methods by which it was created. The purpose of such models is to teach the scientific method in a straightforward manner, and to teach the fundamental concepts of the disciplines and the basic information necessary to understand the area (Bruner, 1960).

Applied particularly to the sciences and social sciences, information-processing models, with appropriate modifications, have been used successfully with both older and younger students. We illustrate with a model for the study of biology (Schwab, 1965).

The long-term goal of all information-processing models is to teach students how to think effectively (see Chapter 22 for an explicit discussion of this goal); all rest on the thesis that students learning more complex intellectual strategies will have greater ability to learn and will absorb more concepts and information if they are taught with complex models for handling information.

THE PERSONAL FAMILY

Ultimately the human reality resides in our individual consciousnesses. We develop unique personalities and see the world from perspectives that are the products of our experiences and positions. Common understandings are a product of the negotiation of individuals who must live and work and create families together.

The personal models of learning begin from the perspective of the selfhood of the individual. They attempt to shape education so that we come to understand ourselves better, take responsibility for our educations, and learn to reach beyond our current development to become stronger, more sensitive, and more creative in our search for high quality lives.

The cluster of personal models pays great attention to the individual perspective and seeks to encourage productive independence, so that people become increasingly self-aware and responsible for their own destinies.

The following personal models are described in Part Two:

NONDIRECTIVE TEACHING

Psychologist and counselor Carl Rogers (1983) has for three decades (Rogers, 1951) been the acknowledged spokesperson for models in which the teacher plays the role of counselor. Developed from counseling theory, the model emphasizes a partnership between students and teacher. The teacher endeavors to help the students understand how to play major roles in directing their own educations—for example, by behaving in such a way as to clarify goals and participate in developing avenues for reaching them. The teacher provides information about how much progress is being made and helps the students solve problems. The nondirective teacher has to actively build the partnerships that are required and provide the help needed as the students try to work our their problems.

The model is used in several ways. At the most general level (and the least common), it is used as the basic model for the operation of entire educational programs (Neill, 1960). Second, it is used in combination with other models to ensure that contact is made with the students. In this role, it moderates the educational environment. Third, it is used when students are planning independent and cooperative study projects. Fourth, it is used periodically when counseling the students, finding out what they are thinking and feeling, and helping them understand what they are about.

The model has been used with all types of students and across all subjects and teaching roles. Although it is designed to promote self-understanding and independence, it has fared quite well as a contributor to a wide range of academic objectives (see Aspy and Roebuck, 1973; Chamberlin and Chamberlin, 1943).

SYNECTICS

Developed first for use with "creativity groups" in industrial settings, synectics was adapted by William Gordon (1961) for use in elementary and secondary education. Synectics is designed to help people "break set" in problem-solving and writing activities and to gain new perspectives on topics from a wide range of fields. In the classroom it is introduced to the students in a series of workshops until they can apply the procedures individually and in cooperative groups. Although it is designed as a direct stimulus to creative thought, synectics has the side effect of promoting collaborative work and study skills and a feeling of warmth among the students.

AWARENESS TRAINING

Helping students expand their awareness of self and their capacity for feeling and thinking is the direct purpose of awareness training (Brown, 1964;

Perls, 1968; Schutz, 1958, 1967). The model consists of sets of workshop activities that induce reflection about interpersonal relations, self-image, experimentation, and presentation of self. Aspects of the model have been used with students of all ages, but the major experience is with secondary students.

THE CLASSROOM MEETING

William Glasser (1965) adapted a counseling process designed to help students take responsibility for their behavior and for their social situations so that it could be used with classroom groups. In the classroom the model takes the form of a meeting in which the group is responsible for establishing a social system appropriate to academic tasks but with room for individual differences and respect for the common tasks and the rights of others.

Used with students of all ages, the model provides a direct method for managing the instructional setting and for organizing the students to take responsibility for the social situation of the classroom. Hence, it is often referred to as a classroom management model. It provides instruction on personal and social development and social skills. It also develops a setting in which other models can be employed to achieve academic goals.

The personal, social, and academic goals of education are compatible with one another. The personal family of teaching models provides the essential part of the teaching repertoire that directly addresses the students' needs for self-esteem and self-understanding and for the support and respect of other students.

THE SOCIAL FAMILY

When we work together we generate a collective energy that we call "synergy." The social models of teaching are constructed to take advantage of this phenomenon. A number of recent studies have put the thesis of the family to the test. David and Roger Johnson and their associates (1974, 1981) and Robert Slavin (1983) have worked with teachers to explore the use of cooperative rewards (pairs or groups rather than individuals receive feedback, test scores, or praise) and cooperative task structures (students work in pairs or small groups on academic tasks). The general message is affirmative: Cooperative study helps many kinds of learning. Again, we stress that the results do not mean that individual or large group task structures should never be used. But synergy pays off, and the social models are an important part of our learning repertoires.

The following models are described in Part Three:

GROUP INVESTIGATION

John Dewey (1917) developed the idea—extended and refined by a great many teachers and theorists, and shaped into powerful definition by Herbert Thelen (1960)—that education in a democratic society should teach democratic process directly. Thus, at least part of the students' education should be by cooperative inquiry into important social and academic problems. The resulting model has been used in all subject areas, with children of all ages, and even as the core model for entire schools (Chamberlin and Chamberlin, 1943). The model is designed to lead students to define problems, explore various perspectives on the problems, collect relevant data, develop hypotheses, and test them. The teacher organizes the group process and disciplines it, helps the students find and organize information, and ensures that there is a vigorous level of activity and discourse. Recently Sharon and his associates (1980) explored the dynamics and the effects of the model, and they learned that rigorous implementation can have very positive effects not only on the high-level social and academic goals for which it is designed, but on traditional learning outcomes as well.

ROLE PLAYING

Designed by Fannie and George Shaftel (1984) specifically to help students study their social values and reflect on them, role playing also helps students collect and organize information about social issues, develop empathy with others, and attempt to improve their social skills. The model asks students to "act out" conflicts, to learn to take the roles of others, and to observe social behavior. With appropriate adaptation, role playing can be used with students of all ages.

JURISPRUDENTIAL INQUIRY

Created especially for secondary students in the social studies, the Jurisprudential Inquiry Model brings the case-study method, reminiscent of legal education, to the process of schooling. Donald Oliver and James Shaver (1966, 1980) devised the model specifically for citizenship education. Students study cases involving social problems in areas where public policy needs to be made (on issues of justice and equality, poverty and power, for example). The students analyze the cases and identify the public policy issues and the options that are available for dealing with them.

Although developed for the social studies this model can be used in any area where there are public policy issues, and most curriculum areas abound with them (athletics, science, business subjects, etc.).

LABORATORY TRAINING

During and after World War II it became evident that both personal and group success in all sorts of work situations, from factories to offices to supermarkets, depended to a remarkable degree on social understanding and skills and the ability of all personnel to develop a setting where differences can be tolerated and accommodated and tasks can be coordinated. The National Training Laboratory was organized and evolved a number of models for appropriate training (Benne, Gibb, and Bradford, 1964). Now, sets of workshop activities are designed to help groups analyze social process, work on their skills, and build group cohesion. Large organizations (notably the Hewlitt Packard corporation) have picked up elements of the model and have incorporated it into their operations with great success. Much of the recent publicity given to "Theory Z" is an acknowledgment of foreign development of organizational techniques.

For the most part, the laboratory method is used with older students but modified versions are used with younger children in the fashion of the classroom meeting model.

SOCIAL SCIENCE INQUIRY

Developed from the same frame of reference as the scientific inquiry models based on the methods of the natural sciences, social science inquiry models teach students using the methods of the social sciences. Massialas and Cox (1966) have presented the general orientation. Specific models have been developed from the methods of anthropology, history, geography, social psychology, and sociology. They have been used with students from the first grade through college.

Although the social models of teaching are designed to use social process for social goals, they also exercise the intellect and result in the learning of information and the building of concepts. The Jurisprudential Inquiry model includes some of the most difficult intellectual tasks of any model of teaching. Their base, however, is the process of social negotiation. They require students to examine themselves, behavior in groups, and the larger social process. They welcome differences in perspective and try to use those differences as sources of the social energy on which they depend.

THE BEHAVIORAL SYSTEMS FAMILY

A common theoretical base—most commonly called social learning theory, but also known as behavior modification, behavior therapy, and cybernetics—guides the design of the models in this family. The stance taken is that human beings are self-correcting communication systems that modify behavior in response to information about how successfully tasks are navigated. For example, imagine a human being who is climbing (the task) an unfamiliar staircase in the dark. The first few steps are tentative as the foot reaches for the treads. If the stride is too high, feedback is received as the foot encounters air and has to descend to make contact with the surface. If a step is too low, feedback results as the foot hits the riser. Gradually behavior is adjusted in accordance with the feedback until progress up the stairs is relatively comfortable.

Capitalizing on knowledge about how people respond to tasks and feedback, psychologists (see especially Skinner, 1953) have learned how to organize task and feedback structures to make it easy for the human being's self-correcting capability to function. The result is, for example, programs for reducing phobias, learning to read and compute, developing social and athletic skills, replacing anxiety with relaxation, and learning the complexes of intellectual, social, and physical skills necessary to pilot an airplane or a space shuttle. Because these models concentrate on observable behavior and clearly defined tasks and methods for communicating progress to the student, this family of teaching models has a very large foundation of research.

Behavioral techniques are amenable to learners of all ages and to an impressive range of educational goals. Part Four describes four models that, together, represent a considerable part of the spectrum and provide considerable power to teachers and program and media designers.

MASTERY LEARNING, DIRECT INSTRUCTION, AND SOCIAL LEARNING THEORY

The most common application of behavioral systems theory for academic goals takes the form of what is called mastery learning (Bloom, 1971) or direct instruction (Becker, 1981; Glaser, 1968). This model has several characteristics that are similar to Skinner's design for programmed instruction. First, material to be learned is divided into units ranging from the simple to the complex. The material is presented to the students, generally working as individuals, through appropriate media (readings, tapes, activities). Piece by piece, the students work their way successively through the units of materials, after each of which is a test designed to help them find out what they have learned. If they have not mastered any given unit, they can repeat it or an equivalent version until they have mastered the material.

Instructional systems based on this model have been used to provide instruction to students of all ages in areas ranging from the "basic skills" to highly complex material in the academic disciplines. With appropriate adaptation they have also been used with gifted and talented students, students with emotional problems, and athletes and astronauts.

LEARNING SELF-CONTROL

B. F. Skinner is the parent theorist of modern behavioral management and his concept of operant conditioning has given rise to an entire school of psychological thought. Skinner himself has applied the theory to many educational problems. Many other scholars, developers, and teachers have applied the concept to therapy (Rimm and Masters, 1974) and to education (Thoresen and Mahoney, 1974). The self-control management model relies on teaching students that their behavior is learned, that they should study the effects of their behavior, and that they should manage their environments so that their own behavior becomes more productive. Students are taught, in other words, that they are responsible for their personal and social environments and that they can learn more productive behavior by understanding themselves more fully. For example, a student who is afraid of snakes or is anxious in examinations learns how to change his or her own behavior so that snakes and examinations lose some or all of their menacing quality.

This model is used to teach students to create productive learning environments and to free themselves from aversions and engage positively with the opportunities that education and life in general offer. Disruptive students learn more productive ways of relating to others. Students who have developed fears about various pursuits (mathematics, athletics, reading) learn to replace those fears with affirmative feelings.

Used with people of all ages the model blends with others in teaching students to take charge of their behavior and approach academic and social tasks positively.

TRAINING FOR SKILL
AND CONCEPT DEVELOPMENT

Two approaches to training have been developed from the cybernetic group of behavior theorists. One is a theory-to-practice model and the other is simulation. The former mixes information about a skill with demonstrations, practice, feedback, and coaching until the skill is mastered. For example, if an arithmetic skill is the objective, it is explained and demonstrated, practice is given with corrective feedback, and the student is asked to apply it with coaching from peers or the instructor. This variation is commonly used for athletic training.

Simulations are constructed from descriptions of real-life situations. A less-than-real-life environment is created for the instructional station. Sometimes the renditions are quite elaborate (for example, flight and space flight simulators or simulations of international relations). The student engages in activity to achieve the goal of the simulation (to get the aircraft off the ground, perhaps, or to redevelop an urban area), and has to deal with realistic factors until the goal is mastered.

These models, employed in all areas where skills need to be acquired, are especially useful for the mastery of teaching strategies (see Chapter 27). With appropriate modification, they can be used with learners of all ages.

ASSERTIVE TRAINING

Honest, integrative communication is the objective of this model (Alberti and Emmons, 1978). Used both in the classroom and in therapy, the model begins with communication problems. Students learn how to produce communications that give others information about their feelings and goals while leaving room for the other participants to negotiate their needs without feeling attacked. The model can also be used to help create a productive classroom climate. Most applications of the model have been with secondary students, but it has also been adapted for use with younger children.

One of the common characteristics of these behavioral models is that they break down learning tasks into a series of small, sequenced behaviors. Although either student or teacher may have control of the learning situation, in education we have been more familiar with behavioral models in which the control is in the teacher's hands. In this edition, however, we also include less familiar uses of behavior theory, especially models based on the premise of self-control.

The behavioral systems models are well studied and highly polished. They add significantly to the repertoires of teachers and the makers of instructional materials. As is the case with the other families, however, the models in this family do need to be used with discretion. Overuse of the behavioral systems models can be avoided especially if they are combined with the other families of models we have discussed.

COMMON AND UNIQUE FEATURES

The four families of teaching models we have discussed are by no means antithetical or mutually exclusive, although each represents a distinctive approach to teaching. Whereas debates about educational method have seemed to imply that schools and teachers should choose a single approach, students need growth in all areas. To tend the personal, but not the social, or the informational but not the personal, simply does not make sense in the life of the growing student.

Thus, models from the four families can be combined to increase their effects. Cooperative learning can be used with inductive strategies and with simulations. Concept attainment can structure a unit so it can then be explored with group investigation. A study of content with advance organizers followed by presentations can be succeeded with an analysis of the value issues using role playing or jurisprudential inquiry model. This available storehouse of models is indeed a flexible resource we can use to organize courses, learning centers, or media-based education. We can amplify the effects of each of them by using them in harmony with the others.

Growth in teaching skill is the increasing mastery of a variety of models of teaching and the ability to use them effectively. Some philosophies of teacher education maintain that a teacher should master a single model and use it well. We believe that very few teachers are so limited in capacity. Most can quite easily develop a basic repertoire of six or eight models of teaching, which can meet the needs generated by any teaching assignment, and can add to that repertoire regularly. Of course, certain models are more appropriate for some curriculums than for others—that is, the curriculum helps define the teacher's role and the kinds of competencies that the teacher needs. For example, a secondary school biology teacher who is using Biological Sciences Study Committee materials will want to master the particular kind of inductive approach that fits best with those materials. Or, an elementary school social studies teacher who is helping children study values will want to master one of the models appropriate to clarifying values and analyzing public issues.

Once a teacher masters the "basic" repertoire of appropriate models, though, he or she can then expand it by learning new models and by combining and transforming the basic ones to create new ones. In the midst of a social studies unit, a teacher may use one model (say, Inductive Thinking) to help children master map skills, and may combine this model with group-dynamic models that help students attack social issues (for example, Group Investigation). A highly skilled teaching performance blends the variety of models appropriately and embellishes them. Master teachers create new models of teaching and test them in the course of their work, drawing on the models of others to combine ideas in various ways. Mastery takes hard work, but poorly implemented models will not produce the effects they should.

DESCRIBING THE MODELS

Each of the following chapters in this text includes four main sections: an orientation to the model, the model of teaching, its application, and its instructional and nurturant effects. We begin with a scenario of the model in use. Then we describe the goals of the model, its theoretical assumptions, and the principles and major concepts underlying it. In the second section, we analyze each model in terms of four concepts: syntax, social system, principles of reaction, and support system. These descriptions are the operational heart of each model: They tell us what activities should occur and, when appropriate, in what sequence. The third section, application, provides information about the use of the model in the classroom. Sometimes this information is an illustration for various subject areas, a guide for age-level adaptations or for curriculum design or suggestions for combining the model with other models of teaching. Sometimes it is a discussion of particular points that seem to cause teachers difficulty when they implement the model. Finally, a section on the instructional and nurturant effects that can be expected from the model identifies some of the research on the model.

Note that we invented the four concepts used to describe the operations of the model itself (syntax, social system, principles of reaction, and support system) as a way of communicating the basic procedures involved in implementing any instructional model.

SYNTAX

The syntax or phasing of the model describes the model in action—for example, as we use it. How do we begin? What would happen next? We describe syntax in terms of sequences of activities we call *phases*; each model has a distinct flow of phases.

For example, one model begins with a presentation to the learner of a concept called an *advance organizer*, which the leader presents to the student verbally, in either written or oral form. In the second phase, data are presented to the learner. He or she reads them, watches a film, or is exposed to the data in some other way. This phase is followed by another in which the learner is helped to relate the material to the organizing concept. In a different model, the first phase of a typical activity includes data collection by the student. The second phase involves organization of the data under concepts the student forms himself or herself, and the third, a comparison of the concepts developed with those developed by other people. As shown in Table 1-1, these two models have very different structures or sets of phases, even though the same type of concept might emerge from both models, and they were in fact designed for somewhat different purposes. The first was designed to encourage mastery of material, and the second, to teach students inductive thinking processes.

Comparing the phasing of the two models in Table 1-1 reveals the practical differences between them. An inductive strategy has different activities and a different sequence than a deductive one.

Table 1-1   Phasing in Two Models

	PHASE ONE	PHASE TWO	PHASE THREE
Model 1	Presentation of concept	Presentation of data	Relating data to concept
Model 2	Presentation of data	Development of categories by student	Identification and naming of concepts

THE SOCIAL SYSTEM

The social system describes student and teacher roles and relationships and the kind of norms that are encouraged. The leadership roles of the teacher vary greatly from model to model. In some models the teacher is a reflector or a facilitator of group activity, in others a counselor of individuals, and in others a taskmaster. In some models the teacher is the center of activity, the source of information, and the organizer and pacer of the situation (high structure). Some models distribute activity equally between teacher and student (moderate structure), whereas others place the student at the center, encouraging a great deal of social and intellectual independence (low structure).

One way to describe a model of teaching, then, is in terms of the degree of structure in the learning environment. As roles, relationships, norms, and activities become less externally imposed and more within the students' control, the social system becomes less structured. As we see, some models are inherently more structured than others. However, the structure of all models can be varied greatly to adapt to the skill personality of the students. We can tighten or loosen the structure considerably.

PRINCIPLES OF REACTION

Principles of reaction tell the teacher how to regard the learner and how to respond to what the learner does. In some models the teacher overtly tries to shape behavior by rewarding certain student activities and maintaining a neutral stance toward others. In other models, such as those designed to develop creativity, the teacher tries to maintain a nonevaluative, equal stance so that the learner becomes self-directing. Principles of reaction provide the teacher with rules of thumb by which to tune in to the student and select model-appropriate responses to what the student does.

SUPPORT SYSTEM

We use this concept to describe not the model itself so much as the supporting conditions necessary for its existence. What are the additional requirements of the model beyond the *usual* human skills and capacities and technical facilities? For example, the laboratory model may require a trained leader; the Nondirective Model may require an exceedingly patient, supportive personality. Suppose a model postulates that students should teach themselves, and that the roles of teachers should be limited to consultation and facilitation. What support is necessary? Certainly a classroom filled only with textbooks would be limiting and prescriptive. Rather, support in the form of books, films, self-instructional systems, and travel arrangements is necessary, or the model will be empty.

A few examples of the use of the model are given—usually in classroom settings. The examples are not exhaustive, but are selected to make real some of the possibilities.

APPLICATION
INSTRUCTIONAL AND NURTURANT
EFFECTS

The effects of an environment can be *direct*—designed to come from the content and skills on which the activities are based. Or, effects can be *implicit* in the learning environment. One fascinating question about models is the implicit learnings they engender. For instance, a model that emphasizes academic discipline can also (but need not) emphasize obedience to authority. Or one that encourages personal development can (but need not) beg questions about social responsibility. The examination of latent functions can be as exciting and important as the examination of direct functions.

Hence, the description of the effects of models can validly be categorized as the direct or *instructional* effects and the indirect or *nurturant* effects. The instructional effects are those directly achieved by leading the learner in certain directions. The nurturant effects come from experiencing the environment created by the model. High competition toward a goal may directly spur achievement, for example, but the effects of living in a competitive atmosphere may alienate people from each other. In choosing a model for teaching, for curriculum building, or as a basis for materials, the teacher must balance instructional efficiency, or directness, with the predictable nurturant effects, as shown in Figure 1–1.

FIGURE 1-1   Instructional and nurturant effects.

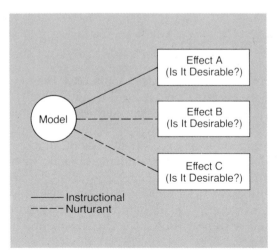

If we have two models whose instructional effects are both appropriate for our goal, we may choose one over the other because its nurturant effects further other goals or because they reinforce the direct instructional effects. Three models might be considered, as shown in Figure 1–2. If we assume equal efficiency, we might choose model 1 because its instructional and nurturant effects reinforce one another, and there are no undesirable nurturant side effects. (Model 3 does not reinforce goal A, and model 2 nurtures an undesirable effect.)

It is possible to defend the selection of a model chiefly on the basis of its nurturant effects, even though it might not have high direct efficiency. The progressive movement, for example, emphasized teaching academic subjects through democratic process skills less because it would be an efficient way to teach content (although many believed it would be) than because it would be likely to *nurture* later democratic behavior and citizen involvement and would *instruct* citizens in democratic skills. Figure 1–3 illustrates these instructional and nurturant effects.

Educators must choose among models that differ considerably from one another. And the models they choose create a certain kind of reality for their students.

FIGURE 1–2

MODEL 1

```
Instructs  ──────────▶ A (Desirable)
Nurtures   ----------▶ A (Desirable)
Nurtures   ----------▶ B (Acceptable)
```

MODEL 2

```
Instructs  ──────────▶ A (Desirable)
Nurtures   ----------▶ B (Acceptable)
Nurtures   ----------▶ C (Undesirable)
```

MODEL 3

```
Instructs  ──────────▶ B (Acceptable)
Nurtures   ----------▶ A (Desirable)
Nurtures   ----------▶ B (Acceptable)
```

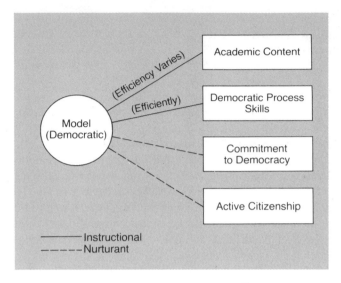

FIGURE 1-3   Instructional and nurturant effects: sample model.

DEVELOPING A REPERTOIRE OF MODELS

Some view teaching as an exceedingly personal art; to them, the available models of teaching represent the *arts* of master teachers—a collective wisdom on which to build one's personal art.

The teacher should view these models of teaching as ways of accomplishing a wide variety of purposes. Since no single teaching strategy can accomplish every purpose, the wise teacher will master a sufficient repertoire of strategies to deal with the specific kinds of learning problems he or she faces. For example, the Nondirective Model is especially useful in helping people to become more open and aware of their feelings, to free their inquisitiveness and initiative, and to help them develop the drive and the sensitivity to educate themselves. Similarly, the Laboratory Method Model can greatly improve human-relations skills.

The teacher's repertoire of models is particularly important if he or she is responsible for teaching many children in several curriculum areas. But even the subject-matter specialist, whose responsibilities may be confined to teaching a single discipline to fairly mature students, faces teaching tasks for which no one single model can be completely adequate. For instance, the secondary teacher of English can draw on several models. Synectics may be used to teach creative writing, Skinnerian techniques to teach skills, and behavioral/nondirective methods to help students develop a sense of their own potentialities and a willingness to capitalize on them.

Teams of teachers working together can discover the models most amenable to each member of the team. Some teachers will use the counseling models effectively, while others will use the behavior modification strategies, and so on. Together, a large team of teachers, able to draw on teacher aides and other support systems, should be able to create a fine spectrum of opportunities for children.

To develop a repertoire means to develop flexibility. Part of this flexibility is professional. Every teacher faces a wide range of problems, and if he or she has an equally wide range of teaching models from which to draw, he or she can generate more creative and imaginative solutions to those problems. On the personal side, having a repertoire requires the ability to grow and expand one's potential, and the capacity to teach oneself more varied and interesting ways of coping with one's own need to develop. The environment for personal growth is greatly enhanced when people can define their present situations and see the alternatives. The growing, developing teacher can embrace more forms of experience, explore more aspects of his or her students, and find more ways of helping them grow.

This satisfaction of growth and exploration should be reason enough for the teacher to set as a goal not one or two basic models to use for all purposes but a variety which he or she explores for the potential they hold for pupils and teacher alike.

FOR THE TEACHER:
SELECTING MODELS TO LEARN

Which models should a teacher learn? We suggest that a beginning be made with one model from each of the four families, and that others be added as they become useful to one's particular teaching specialty. Preservice teachers should master four or five as a beginning repertoire. Note that the first two or three models are more difficult to learn than subsequent ones. Increasingly, one can learn new models efficiently and rapidly (see Chapter 28).

These models of teaching are designs for creating environments—they provide rough specifications for designing and constructing learning situations. We believe that the four families of models provide a current repertoire for teachers and curriculum makers, and the range of models is broad enough to be useful for many educational purposes. The most creative educators, however, rarely take their repertoires only from what exists. They use these models not as recipes but as stimulators to their own activities.

The information-processing, personal, social, and behavioral systems families of models focus on characteristic types of goals and means. The informational models depend on activities that carry content and skills. The personal models emphasize personal relationships and see growth resulting from them. The social models depend on the energy of the group and the process of group interaction. Behavioral systems models focus on specific behavior change and emphasize contingencies, behavioral specification, substitution, and rehearsal. To choose certain models and not others is partly a matter of efficiency (picking the models most likely to get the job done) and partly a matter of considerable philosophical import. The models that are chosen gently and subtly create the world of the learner. That world is learned, along with its values.

The world we hope to see is one in which children (and older students) will experience many models of teaching and learn to profit from them. As teachers increase their repertoires, so will students increase *theirs* and become more powerful and multifaceted learners. *That* is the raison d'etre of *Models of Teaching.*

Part I

The Information-Processing Family

INTRODUCTION
Models of Teaching
Designed to Affect Information Processing

Although all attempts to educate students influence their information processing, many methods and theories are designed specifically to help students acquire and operate on data. To many people, conveying information is the primary business of the school; such widespread interest in information-processing models is certainly one reason why there are so many of them.

Each model discussed in this section has a distinct point of view about how people think and about how to affect the ways they operate on information. Do not assume that all of these models are built on mechanistic theories about the human mind. On the contrary, some of them have rather unstructured views of information handling. They vary, too, in the breadth of their approach. Some focus on narrow aspects of information processing (for example, how to memorize) or on specific types of inductive thinking. Others are designed to influence basic thought patterns.

Models focusing on information processing come from several sources:

1. *Studies of thinking.* From the days of the earliest Greeks, philosophers have theorized about how the mind works, and about how inductive and

deductive thinking function. During this century studies of thinking have been carried on using laboratory experiments and observations of individuals in problem-solving situations. Computer simulations of mental processes have been developed, and a whole science of information theory has grown up to assist in the study of thinking and problem solving.

It is but a short leap from a description of a mental process to a model of teaching designed to improve thinking. Many examples of models for teaching are built around mental processes, ranging from systems for teaching general problem-solving ability to procedures for teaching specific thinking processes, such as the Inductive Teaching Model of the late Hilda Taba and the Inquiry Training Model of Richard Suchman.

2. *Learning theorists.* Many theorists are concerned with developing models for teaching concepts because, they feel, the student uses the concepts he or she learns to process information. To teach a set of concepts would be, by this view, to change a portion of the individual's thinking processes. Theorists such as David Ausubel have confined themselves primarily to verbal learning. Others have dealt with experiential learning. We have included here Ausubel's (1963) model and a creation of our own, generated from studies constructed by Jerome Bruner and his associates (Bruner, Goodnow, and Austin, 1967), in our selection of strategies people use to learn concepts.

3. *The scholarly disciplines.* Many models have been developed to teach either the major concepts or the systems of inquiry used by the disciplines, with the assumption that as students learn the processes and ideas of the discipline, they incorporate them into their own systems and behave differently as a result. We have included a teaching model developed by Joseph Schwab and his associates of the Biological Sciences Curriculum Study committee (1965). The committee developed this model as one of the chief methods for a biology course for secondary schools.

4. *Developmental studies of the human intellect.* Investigators have also studied the development of intellectual processes in the child and adolescent. These studies provide what is still, for the most part, a fairly tentative map of intellectual development, but they can be used to generate theories about how to increase intellectual development. To illustrate them, we have chosen models developed from the work of Jean Piaget.

We begin with a specific method for teaching concepts with precision (concept attainment), because it explores the nature of thinking. We proceed to two models designed to teach students how to develop concepts and how to inquire and theorize (inductive thinking and inquiry training). These are followed by a model designed to teach systems of information and ideas (advance organizer) and another to enhance memorization (Memory Model). Next we present a model developed from Piaget's work—one that tries to increase the rate of intellectual development (cognitive growth). A model for teaching the research methods and flavor of a specific academic discipline (Biological Science Inquiry Model) concludes the section.

2

ATTAINING CONCEPTS
The Basic Skills
of Thinking

SCENARIO

Mrs. Stern's eighth grade class in Houston, Texas, has been studying the characteristics of the fourteen largest cities in the United States. They have collected data on size, ethnicity of population, types of industry, location, and proximity to natural resources.

Working In committees the students have collected information and summarized it on a series of charts now pasted up around the room. One Wednesday in November, Mrs. Stern says, "Today let's try a series of exercises designed to help us understand these cities better. I have identified a number of concepts that help us compare and contrast them. I am going to label our charts either *yes* or *no.* If you look at the information we have and think about the populations and the other characteristics, you will identify the ideas that I have in mind. I'm going to start with the city that's a yes and then one that's a no, and so forth. Think about what the yeses have in common. Then write down after the second yes the idea that you think connects those two places, and keep testing those ideas as we go along. Let's begin with our own city," she says. "Houston is a yes."

The students look at the information about Houston, its size, industries, location, ethnic composition. Then she points to Baltimore, Maryland.

"Baltimore is a no," she says. Then she points to San Jose, California. "Here is another yes," she comments.

The students look for a moment at the information about San Jose. Two or three raise their hands.

"I think I know what it is," one offers.

"Hold on to your idea," she replies. "See if you're right." She then selects another yes—Seattle, Washington. Detroit, Michigan, is a no. Miami, Florida, is a yes. She continues until all students think they know what the concept is, and then they begin to share concepts.

"What do you think it is, Jill?"

"The yeses all have mild climates," says Jill. "That is, it doesn't get very cold in any of them."

"It gets pretty cold in Salt Lake City," objects another.

"Yes, but not as cold as in Chicago, Detroit, or Baltimore," another student counters.

"I think the yeses are all rapidly growing cities. Each one of them increased more than 10 percent during the last ten years." There is some discussion about this.

"All the yeses have lots of different industries," volunteers another.

"That's true, but almost all these cities do," replies another student.

Finally the students decide the yeses are all cities that are growing very fast and have relatively mild climates.

"That's right," agrees Mrs. Stern. "That's exactly what I had in mind. Now let's do this again. This time I want to begin with Baltimore, Maryland, and now it is a yes."

The exercise is repeated several times. Students learn that Mrs. Stern has grouped the cities on the basis of their relationship to waterways, natural resources, ethnic composition, and several other dimensions.

The students are beginning to see patterns in their data. Finally she says, "Now, each of you try to group the cities in a way that you think is important. Then take turns and lead us through this exercise, helping us to see which ones you place in which category. Then we'll discuss the ways we can look at cities and how we can use different categories for different purposes."

In this scenario Mrs. Stern is teaching her students how to think about cities. At the same time she is teaching them about the process of *categorizing*. This is their introduction to the model of teaching we call *concept attainment*.

CATEGORIZING, CONCEPT FORMATION, AND CONCEPT ATTAINMENT

All categorizing activity involves identifying and placing events into classes by using certain cues (criteria) and ignoring others. Suppose that a female college senior is describing her ideal man to someone who is trying to get her a blind date. She tries to communicate her concept, and her friend tries to *attain* the concept. Our senior communicates by identifying to her friend several men who do and do not fit her concept. Finally, in the middle of her description, her friend interrupts:

"Ah, I see!" she says. "You like short men who laugh a lot, and you tend to avoid men who are very good students."

"You've got it, but how did you know?"

"All the time you were talking, I kept thinking about why you put each man on the preferred list. Gradually, I began to get the idea that those were the reasons why you did it. All of the preferred men laugh a lot and are short. Only one is a good student, and he gets his grades by working hard and selecting his courses carefully."

The process used by the matchmaker was one of concept attainment, "the search for and listing of attributes that can be used to distinguish exemplars from nonexemplars of various categories" (Bruner, Goodnow, and Austin, 1977, p. 233). The distinguishing features of the concept in this case were "laughing a lot" and "short." In concept attainment the concept already exists. In the case of the preferred and not-preferred men, the task is to determine the basis of the "yes" and "no" examples. *Concept formation*, in contrast, is the act by which *new* categories are formed; it is an act of invention. If the two seniors had listed the names of all the men they knew and had then grouped them according to similarities, they would have been involved in concept *formation*. This would have been a useful thing to do if a third friend from another college had written asking, "What are the men like at your place?" To come up with the concept, the women would try to determine how the men were alike. The task of identifying a suitable blind date, however, called for concept attainment, a second person's trying to determine the category that was already formed in another person's mind.

TEACHING CONCEPT ATTAINMENT

This model is designed to lead students to a concept by asking them to compare and contrast examples (called exemplars) that contain the characteristics (called attributes) of the concept with examples that do not contain those attributes. We need to have a concept clearly in mind. As an example let us consider the concept *adjective*. Adjectives are words, so we select some words that are adjectives (these become the positive exemplars) and some that are not (these become the "negative" exemplars—the ones that do not have the attributes of the category *adjective*). We present the words to the students in pairs. Consider the following four pairs:

triumphant	triumph
large	chair
broken	laugh
painful	pain

It is probably best to present the words in sentences to provide more information, because adjectives function in the context of sentences. For example:

YES: Our triumphant team returned home after winning the state championship.
NO: After his triumph, Senator Jones gave a gracious speech.
YES: The broken arm healed slowly.
NO: His laugh filled the room.
YES: The large truck backed slowly into the barn.
NO: He sank gratefully into the chair.
YES: The painful separation had to be endured.
NO: He felt a sharp pain in his ankle.

To carry on the model we need about twenty pairs in all—we would need more if the concept were more complex than our current example, *adjectives.*

We begin the process by asking the students to scrutinize the sentences and to pay particular attention to the underlined words. Then we instruct them to compare and contrast the functions of the positive and negative exemplars. "The positive exemplars have something in common in the work they do in the sentence. The negative exemplars do different work."

We ask the students to write down what they believe the exemplars have in common. Then we present more sets of exemplars and ask them whether they still have the same idea. If not, we ask what they now think. We continue to present exemplars until most of the students have an idea they think will withstand scrutiny. At that point we ask one of the students to share his or her idea and how he or she arrived at it. One possible response is as follows: "Well, at first I thought that the positive words were longer. Then some of the negatives were longer so I gave that up. Now I think that the positive ones always come next to some other word and do something to it. I'm not sure just what."

Then other students share their ideas. We provide some more examples. Gradually the students agree that each positive exemplar adds something to the meaning of a word that stands for an object or a person, or qualifies it in some way.

We continue by providing some more sentences and by asking the students to identify the words that belong to our concept. When they can do that, we provide them with the name of the concept (*adjective*) and ask them to agree on a definition.

The final activity is to ask the students to describe their thinking as they arrived at the concepts and to share how they used the information that was given.

For homework we ask the students to find adjectives in a short story we assign them to read. We will examine the exemplars they come up with to be sure that they have a clear picture of the concept.

This process ensures that the students learn the attributes that define a concept (the defining attributes) and can distinguish those from other important attributes that do not form the definition. All the words, for example, are composed of letters. But the presence of letters does not define the parts of speech. The students learn that it is the function of the word that is the essence of the concept, not what it denotes. Pain and painful both refer to trauma, but only one is an adjective.

As we teach the students with this method, we help them become more efficient in attaining concepts. They learn the rules of the model.

Let us look at another example, this time language study for beginning readers.

TEACHER: (Presents 6-year-old students with the following lists of words labeled yes or no.)

FAT   Yes
FATE   No
MAT   Yes
MATE   No
RAT   Yes
RATE   No

I have a list of words here. Notice that some say "yes" by them and some say "no" by them. (Children observe and comment on the format. Teacher puts the list aside for a moment.) Now, I have an idea in my head, and I want you to try to guess what I'm thinking of. Remember the list I showed you. (Picks up the list.) This will help you guess my idea because each of these is a clue. The clues work this way. If a word has a *yes* by it (points to first word), then it is an example of what I'm thinking. If it has a *no* by it, then it is not an example.

(The teacher continues to work with the students so that they understand the procedures of the lesson and then turns over the task of working out the concept to them.)

TEACHER: Can you come up with the name of my idea? Do you know what my idea is?
(The students decide what they think the teacher's idea is. She continues the lesson.)

TEACHER: Let's see if your idea is correct by testing it. I'll give you some examples, and you tell me if they are a *yes* or a *no,* based on your idea. (She gives them more examples. This time the students supply the *nos* and *yeses.*)

KITE _____ (No)
CAT   _____ (Yes)
HAT   _____ (Yes)

Well, you seem to have it. Now think up some words you believe are *yeses.* The rest of us will tell you whether your example is right. You tell us if we guessed correctly.

(The exercise ends with the students generating their own examples and telling how they arrived at the concept.)

In this lesson if the children simply identified the concept as the *at* vowel-consonant blend and correctly recognize *cat* and *hat* as a yes, they had attained the concept on a simple level. If they verbalized the distinguishing features (essential attributes) of the *at* sound, they attained the concept on a harder level. Bruner outlines these different levels of attainment; correctly distinguishing examples from nonexamples is easier than verbalizing the attributes of the concept. Students will probably be able to distinguish examples correctly before they will be able to explain verbally either the concept name or its essential characteristics.

Concept teaching provides a chance to analyze the students' thinking processes and to help them develop more effective strategies. The approach can involve various degrees of student participation and student control, and material of varying complexity.

THEORY OF CONCEPTS

We have used terms such as *example, exemplar,* and *attribute* to describe categorizing activity and concept attainment. Derived from Bruner's work on concepts, each term has a special meaning and function in all forms of conceptual learning, especially concept attainment.

A concept has four elements: (1) a name; (2) examples; (3) attributes (essential and nonessential); and (4) attribute values. Understanding a concept means knowing all of its elements.

The *name* is the term given to a category. Fruit, dog, government, ghetto are all names given to a class of experiences, objects, configurations, or processes. Although the items commonly grouped together in a single category may differ from one another in certain respects (dogs, for example, vary greatly), the common features cause them to be referred to by the same general term. Often we teach ideas that students already know intuitively without knowing the name itself. For instance, young children often put pictures of fruit together for the reason that they are "all things you can eat." They are using one characteristic to describe the concept instead of the name or label. If students know a concept, however, they can easily learn the name for it, and their verbal expressions will be more articulate.

The second element, *examples,* refers to instances of the concept. In the concept-attainment exercise described earlier, two words (*cat, hat*) were positive examples of the concept. The negative exemplars are not instances of the concept. Part of knowing a concept is recognizing positive instances of it and also distinguishing closely related but negative examples.

The third and fourth elements of a concept are *attributes* and *attribute value. Essential* attributes are the common features or characteristics that cause us to place examples in the same category. Exemplars contain *nonessential* attributes as well. Although in the supermarket we often see a sign with the price per pound beside each type of fruit, we know that this sign does not play a role in distinguishing fruit from other foods or objects. We can refer to cost as a nonessential attribute of fruit as it appears in the market. Most concepts have attributes that are often associated with them, but are not essential to them (women's tennis socks, for example, frequently have tassels). Again, part of knowing a concept is distinguishing its essential attributes from its nonessential ones.

MULTIPLE ATTRIBUTES
AND ATTRIBUTE VALUES

As we categorize things, we also have to deal with the fact that some attributes are present to various degrees. We have to decide whether any amount of presence of an attribute is sufficient to place something in a particular category and what the range of density is that qualifies something to belong to a category. For example, consider the category *poisonous*. We put chlorine in water precisely because chlorine is poison. Yet, we judge the amount that will kill certain bacteria and still not harm us. So tap water in a city is not an exemplar of poisonous water because it does not contain enough poison to harm us. But, if we added enough chlorine, it would affect us. In this case, if the value of the attribute is low enough, its presence does not give the water membership in the category *poisonous to humans*.

Now consider the category *short person*. How short is short enough to be so categorized? People generally agree on a relative value, just as they do for *tall*. When is something cold? Hot? When is a person friendly? Hostile? These are all useful concepts, yet the categorization issue turns on matters of degree, or what we call *attribute value*.

In other cases, value is not a consideration. To be a telephone an instrument simply must have certain characteristics. Yet, there are degrees of quality. A question such as, "When is a sound machine a high-fidelity instrument?" puts us back into the consideration of attribute values.

The matter is further complicated because concepts range from cases in which the mere presence of a single attribute is sufficient for membership in a category to those in which the presence of several attributes are necessary for categorization. Membership in the category *red-haired boys* requires the presence of maleness and red hair. *Intelligent, gregarious, athletic red-haired boys* is a concept that requires the presence of several attributes simultaneously. In literature, social studies, and science we deal with numerous concepts that are defined by the presence of multiple attributes, and sometimes attribute value is a consideration also. Consider the theatrical concept *romantic comedy*. A positive exemplar must be a play or film, must have enough humorous values to qualify as a comedy, and must be romantic as well. Negative exemplars include plays that are neither funny nor romantic, are funny but not romantic, and are romantic but not funny.

To teach a concept we have to be very clear about its defining attributes and about whether attribute value is a consideration. We must also select our negative exemplars so that items with some but not all of the attributes can be ruled out.

We call concepts defined by the presence of one or more attributes *conjunctive* concepts. The exemplars are joined by the presence of one or more characteristics. Two other kinds of concepts need to be considered. *Disjunctive* concepts are defined by the presence of some attributes and the absence of others. Inert gases, for example, have the properties of all other gases but are missing the property of being able to combine with other elements. Bachelors, for example, have the characteristics of other men and women, but are identified by the absence of something—a spouse. Lonely people are defined by an absence of companionship. Prime numbers are defined by the absence of a factor other than one and the number itself.

Finally, some concepts require connection between the exemplar and some other entity. Parasites, for example, have hosts, and the relationship between the parasite and its host is crucial to its definition. Many concepts of human relationships are of this type: There are no uncles without nephews and nieces, no husbands without wives, and no executives without organizations to lead.

STRATEGIES FOR CONCEPT ATTAINMENT

What goes on in the minds of students when they are comparing and contrasting sets of exemplars? What kinds of hypotheses occur to them in the early stages and how do they modify and test them? To answer these questions, three factors are important to us. First, we can construct the concept attainment exercises so that we can study how our students think. Second, the students can not only describe how they attain concepts but they can learn to be more efficient by altering their strategies and learning to use new ones. Third, by changing the way we present information and by modifying the model slightly we can affect how students will process information.

The key to understanding the strategies students use to attain concepts is to analyze how they approach the information that is available in the exemplars. In particular, do they concentrate on just certain aspects of the information (partistic strategies) or do they keep all or most of the information in mind (wholistic strategies)? To illustrate, suppose we are teaching concepts for analyzing literary style by comparing passages from novels and short stories. The first set of positive exemplars includes the following passage:

> A new country seems to follow a pattern. First come the openers, strong and brave and rather childlike. They can take care of themselves in a wilderness, but they are naive and helpless against men, and perhaps that is why they went out in the first place. When the rough edges are worn off the new land, businessmen and lawyers come in to help with the development—to solve problems of ownership, usually by removing the temptations to themselves. And finally comes culture, which is entertainment, relaxation, transport out of the pain of living. And culture can be on any level, and is.
>
> (Steinbeck, *East of Eden* 1952, p. 249)

The students know that this passage will be grouped with the others to come on the basis of one or more attributes pertaining to style.

Some students will concentrate on just one kind of attribute, say the use of declarative sentences, or the juxtaposition of contrasting ideas about the opening of the frontier. Others will scan the details of the passage, noting the presence or absence of metaphors, the use of evocative language, the author's stance of being an observer of the human scene, and so on.

When comparing this passage with another positive one, a partist, someone who focuses on just one or two aspects of the use of language, will in some senses appear to have an easier task—just looking to see if the attribute present in the first is also present in the second, and so on. However, if the student's focus does not work out, he or she must return to the earlier examples and scan them for something else on which to concentrate. A wholist, on the other hand, has to keep many attributes in mind and has to eliminate nondefining elements one at a time. However, the wholistic strategy places the learner in a good position to identify multiple-attribute concepts and the loss of a single attribute is not as disruptive to the overall strategy.

There are two ways that we can obtain information about the way our students attain concepts. After a concept has been attained we can ask them to recount their thinking as the exercise proceeded—by describing the ideas they came up with at each step, what attributes they were concentrating on, and what modifications they had to make. ("Tell us what you thought at the beginning, why you thought so, and what changes you had to make.") This can lead to a discussion in which the students can discover one another's strategies and how they worked out.

Older students can write down their hypotheses, giving us (and them) a record we can analyze later. For example, in a study of the classification of plants conducted by Baveja, Showers, and Joyce (1985) students worked in pairs to formulate hypotheses as pairs of exemplars (one positive and one negative) were presented to them. They recorded their hypotheses, changes they made, and the reasons they made them. The students who operated wholistically painstakingly generated multiple hypotheses and gradually eliminated the untenable ones. The students who selected one or two hypotheses in the early stages needed to review the exemplars constantly and revise their ideas in order to arrive at the multiple-attribute concept that was the goal. By sharing their strategies and reflecting on them the students were able to try new ones in subsequent lessons and to observe the effect of the changes.

If we provide students with a large number of labeled exemplars (ones identified as positive and negative) to commence a lesson, they are able to scan the field of data and select a few hypotheses on which to operate. If we provide the exemplars pair by pair, however, the students are drawn toward wholistic, multiple-attribute strategies.

Many people, on first encountering the Concept Attainment Model, ask about the function of the negative exemplars. They wonder why we should not simply provide the positive ones. Negative exemplars are very important because they help the students identify the boundaries of the concept. For example, consider the concept *impressionism* in painting. Impressionistic styles have much in common with other painting styles. It is important for students to "see" examples which have no traces of impressionism for them to be absolutely certain about the defining attributes. Likewise, to identify a group of words as a prepositional phrase we need to be able to tell it from a clause. Only by comparing exemplars which contain and do not contain certain attributes can we identify the characteristics of the attributes precisely, and over time. The Concept Attainment Model is designed to produce long-term learning. Having struggled our way, for example, to precise definitions of *prime number, element, developing nation, irony,* and so on, we should recognize members of their categories positively and surely when we encounter them in the future.

THE MODEL OF TEACHING

The phases of the Concept Attainment Model are outlined in Table 2–1.

SYNTAX

Phase one involves presenting data to the learner. Each unit of data is a separate example or nonexample of the concept. The units are presented in pairs. The data may be events, people, objects, stories, pictures, or any other

Table 2–1   Syntax of the Concept Attainment Model

PHASE ONE: PRESENTATION OF DATA AND IDENTIFICATION OF CONCEPT	PHASE TWO: TESTING ATTAINMENT OF THE CONCEPT
Teacher presents labeled examples. Students compare attributes in positive and negative examples. Students generate and test hypotheses. Students state a definition according to the essential attributes.	Students identify additional unlabeled examples as yes or no. Teacher confirms hypotheses, names concept, and restates definitions according to essential attributes. Students generate examples.

PHASE THREE: ANALYSIS OF THINKING STRATEGIES
Students describe thoughts. Students discuss role of hypotheses and attributes. Students discuss type and number of hypotheses.

discriminable units. The learners are informed that there is one idea that all the positive examples have in common; their task is to develop a hypothesis about the nature of the concept. The instances are presented in a prearranged order and are labeled "yes" or "no." Learners are asked to compare and justify the attributes of the different examples. (The teacher or students may want to maintain a record of the attributes.) Finally, they are asked to name their concepts and state the rules or definitions of the concepts according to their essential attributes. (Their hypotheses are not confirmed until the next phase; students may not know the names of some concepts but the names can be provided when the concepts are confirmed.)

In phase two, the students test their attainment of the concept, first by correctly identifying additional unlabeled examples of the concept and then by generating their own examples. After this the teacher (and students) confirm or disconfirm their original hypotheses, revising their choice of concepts or attributes as necessary.

In phase three, students begin to analyze the strategies by which they attain concepts. As we have indicated, some learners initially try broad constructs and gradually narrow the field; others begin with more discrete constructs. The learners can describe their patterns: whether they focused on attributes or concepts, whether they did so one at a time or several at once, and what happened when their hypotheses were not confirmed. Did they change strategies? Gradually, they can compare the effectiveness of different strategies.

SUMMARY

Data is presented to the students in the form of sets of items called "exemplars," for example, a set of poems. These are labeled "positive" if they have characteristics or attributes of the concept to be taught, (for example, the sonnet form). The exemplars are labeled "negative" if they do not contain the attributes of the concept, (for example, poems that do not have all the attributes of "sonnet").

By comparing the positive and negative exemplars the students develop hypotheses about the nature of the category. They do not, however, share their hypotheses at this point. When most of the students have developed a hypothesis some unlabeled exemplars are presented to them and they indicate whether they think those additional exemplars are positive or negative. When they can successfully identify positive exemplars they may be asked to produce some of their own (as by scanning a set of poems and picking out some positive and negative ones).

Then they are asked to share their hypotheses and describe the progression of their ideas during the process. When they have agreed on the hypotheses that appear most likely, they generate labels for them. Then the teacher supplies the technical label, if there is one, (sonnet, for example).

To consolidate and apply the concept the students then search for more items of the class (poems in this case) and find which ones most closely match the concept they have learned.

SOCIAL SYSTEM

Prior to teaching with the Concept Attainment Model, the teacher chooses the concept, selects and organizes the material into positive and negative examples, and sequences the examples. Most instructional materials, especially textbooks, are not designed in a way that corresponds to the nature of concept learning as described by educational psychologists. In most cases teachers will have to prepare examples, extract ideas and materials from texts and other sources, and design them in such a way that the attributes are clear and that there are, indeed, both positive and negative examples of the concept. When using the Concept Attainment Model, the teacher acts as a recorder, keeping track of the hypotheses (concepts) as they are mentioned and of the attributes. The teacher also supplies additional examples as needed. The three major functions of the teacher during concept-attainment activity are to record, prompt (cue), and present additional data. In the initial stages of concept attainment, it is helpful for the examples to be very structured. However, cooperative learning procedures can also be used successfully (see Part 3).

PRINCIPLES OF REACTION

During the flow of the lesson the teacher needs to be supportive of the students' hypotheses—emphasizing, however, that they are hypothetical in nature—and to create a dialogue in which students test their hypotheses against each others'. In the later phases of the model, the teacher must turn the students' attention toward analysis of their concepts and their thinking strategies, again being very supportive. The teacher should encourage analysis of the merits of various strategies rather than attempt to seek the one best strategy for all people in all situations.

SUPPORT SYSTEM

Concept attainment lessons require that positive and negative exemplars be presented to the students. It should be stressed that the students' job in concept attainment is not to invent new concepts, but to attain the ones that have previously been selected by the teacher. Hence, the data sources need to be known beforehand and the attributes visible. When students are presented with an example, they describe its characteristics (attributes), which can then be recorded.

SOCIAL SYSTEM

The model has moderate structure. Teacher controls action, but it may develop into free dialogue within phase. Student interaction encouraged. Relatively structured with students assuming more initiative for inductive process as they gain more experience with the model (other Concept Attainment Models are lower in structure).

PRINCIPLES OF REACTION

---

1. Give support but emphasize hypothetical nature of discussion.
2. Help students balance one hypothesis against another.
3. Focus attention on specific features of examples.
4. Assist students in discussing and evaluating their thinking strategies.

SUPPORT SYSTEM

Support consists of carefully selected and organized materials and data in the form of discrete units to serve as examples. As students become more sophisticated, they can share in making data units, just as in phase two they generate examples.

APPLICATION

The use of the Concept Attainment Model determines the shape of particular learning activities. For instance, if the emphasis is on acquiring a new concept the teacher will emphasize through his or her questions or comments the attributes in each example (particularly the positive examples) and the concept label. If the emphasis is on the inductive process, the teacher might want to provide fewer clues and reinforce students for participating and persevering. The particular content (concept) may be less important than participation in the inductive process; it may even be a concept the students already know (as it was in Bruner's original experiments). If the emphasis is on the analysis of thinking, a short sample concept attainment exercise might be developed so that more time can be spent on the analysis of thinking.

The Concept Attainment Model may be used with children of all ages and grade levels. We have seen teachers use the model very successfully with kindergarten children, who love the challenge of the inductive activity. For young children the concept and examples must be relatively simple, and the lesson itself must be short and heavily teacher-directed. The typical curriculum for young children is filled with concrete concepts that readily lend themselves to concept attainment methodology. The analysis of thinking phase of the strategy (phase three) is not possible with very young children, though most upper elementary students will be responsive to this kind of reflective activity.

When the model is used in early childhood education, the materials for examples are often available and require little transformation for their use as examples. Classroom objects, cuisinaire rods, pictures, and shapes can be found in almost any early childhood classroom. Although helping children work inductively can be an important goal in itself, the teacher should also have more specific goals to obtain by using this model.

As with all models, we encourage teachers to take the essence of this model and incorporate its features into their natural teaching styles and forms. In the case of concept attainment, it is relatively easy (and intellectually powerful) to incorporate Bruner's ideas about the nature of concepts into instructional presentations and assessment activities. We have seen our own students make these ideas a natural part of their concept teaching.

The Concept Attainment Model is an excellent evaluation tool when teachers want to determine whether important ideas introduced earlier have been mastered. It quickly reveals the depth of students' understanding and reinforces their previous knowledge.

The model can also be useful in opening up a new conceptual area by initiating a sequence of individual or group inquiries. For example, a unit exploring the concept of culture could begin with a series of concept attainment lessons followed by a simulation activity in which students experience the problems that persons of one culture have when they are first introduced to members of a different culture. From this experience, students would be prepared to read about different cultures.

Thus, the Concept Attainment Model can not only introduce extended series of inquiries into important areas, but it can also augment ongoing inductive study. Concept attainment lessons providing important concepts can be interspersed throughout more inductive activity. For example, in social studies units, concepts such as *democracy, socialism, capitalism,* and *due process* can be interjected periodically into units that otherwise depend on student reading and reporting. If a concept is controversial, the teacher can present several interpretations of it, which the students can then debate. Debates are usually great motivators for further inquiry into any subject matter in question.

INSTRUCTIONAL AND NURTURANT EFFECTS

The concept attainment strategies can accomplish several instructional goals, depending on the emphasis of the particular lesson. They are designed for instruction on specific concepts and on the nature of concepts. They also provide practice in inductive reasoning and opportunities for altering and im-

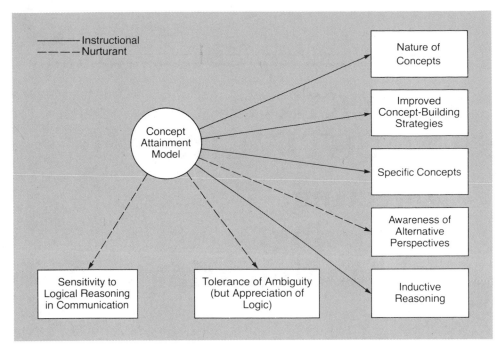

FIGURE 2–1   Instructional and nurturant effects: Concept Attainment Model.

proving students' concept-building strategies. Finally, especially with abstract concepts, the strategies nurture an awareness of alternative perspectives, a sensitivity to logical reasoning in communication, and a tolerance of ambiguity (see Figure 2–1).

   Robert Gagne's 1965 article discusses a similar approach to concept attainment thoroughly. Merrill and Tennyson describe a similar approach without, however, the extensive analysis of the thinking processes that is included in the model in this chapter. McKinney, Larkins, Ford and Davis (1983) have reported a series of interesting studies comparing the Merrill/Tennyson approaches with that of Gagne's and a recitation procedure. Their work illustrates the complexity of designing studies to meaningfully compare sets of models built on the same premises but differing in details of execution.

3

THINKING INDUCTIVELY

Collecting, Organizing, and Manipulating Data

SCENARIO I

At the Motilal Nehru School of Sports in the state of Haryana, India, two groups of tenth grade students are engaged in the study of a botany unit that focuses on the structure of plant life. One group is studying the textbook with the tutorial help of their instructor, who illustrates the structures with plants found on the grounds of the school. We will call this group the presentation cum illustration group. The other group, which we will call the inductive group, is taught by Bharati Baveja, an instructor at Delhi University. This group is presented with a large number of plants that are labeled with their names. Working in pairs, the students build classifications of the plants based on the structural characteristics of their roots, stems, and leaves. Periodically, the pairs share their classifications and generate labels for them. Occasionally, Mrs. Baveja employs concept attainment to introduce a concept designed to expand the students' frame of reference and induce more complex classification. She also supplies the scientific names for the categories the students invent. Eventually Mrs. Baveja presents the students with some new specimens and asks them to see if they can predict the structure of one part of the plant from the observation of another part (as predicting the root structure from the observation of the leaves). Finally, she asks them to collect some more specimens and fit them to the categories they have developed so they can determine how comprehensive their categories have become. They discover that most of the new plants will fit into existing categories but that new categories have to be invented to hold some of them.

After two weeks of study, the two groups take a test over the content of the unit and are asked to analyze some more specimens and name their structural characteristics.

The inductive group has gained twice as much on the test of knowledge and can correctly identify the structures of eight times more specimens than the presentation cum illustration group.

SCENARIO II

Jack Wilson is a first grade student teacher in Lincoln, Nebraska. He meets daily for reading instruction with a group of children who are progressing quite well. He is concerned, however, that they have no trouble attacking new words unless they are unable to figure out the meaning from context. If they are able to figure out what the word means from the rest of the sentence, they seem to have no difficulty using principles they have learned to sound the words out. He has concluded that they have learned a number of concepts but don't have real control over them.

He plans the following activity, which is designed to help them develop concepts of how words are structured and to use that knowledge in attacking words unknown to them.

Jack prepares a deck of cards with one word on each card. He selects words with particular prefixes and suffixes, and he deliberately puts in words that have the same root words but different prefixes and suffixes. Jack plans a series of learning activities over the next several weeks using only the deck of cards as a data base.

When the small group of students convenes on Monday morning, Jack gives several cards to each student. He keeps the remainder, counting on gradually increasing the amount of information students get. Jack has each student read a word on one of the cards and describe something about the word. Other students can add to the description. In this way the structural properties of the word are brought to the students' attention.

After the students have familiarized themselves with the assortment of words, Jack asks them to put the words into groups. "Put the words that go together in piles," he instructs. The students begin studying their cards, passing them back and forth as they sort out the commonalities. At first the students' card groups reflected only the initial letters or the meanings of the words, such as animals and nonanimals. With increased prompting and carefully worded instruction, the students gradually sorted the words according to the prefixes and suffixes. "Okay, this time I want you to have four groups and use the first two or more letters as the reason for your group."

When the students finished sorting the words, Jack asked them to talk about each group, telling what the cards had in common. Gradually, because of the way Jack had selected the data, the students should discover on their own all the major prefixes and suffixes and reflect on their meaning. His approach is to allow the students to form their own groups out of the deck of cards. If he did a good job of selecting the cards, the grouping should emerge naturally.

Probably nothing has been more consistently pursued yet remained more elusive than has the teaching of thinking. From the earliest days of educational writing, philosophers, social reformers, and educators have tried to improve the ways humans process information and solve problems. Thus, there are many models for teaching thinking. In this chapter, we consider part of the sophisticated work of the late curriculum theorist Hilda Taba, who developed a series of teaching strategies designed to help develop inductive mental processes, especially the ability to categorize and to use categories. Taba's models explore some of the same territory as Bruner's Concept Attainment Model, and his notions about the nature of concepts are fundamental to Taba's Concept Formation Model.

ORIENTATION TO THE MODEL

Hilda Taba is largely responsible for popularizing the term *teaching strategy*, and her work in the Contra Costa School District provides a first-rate example of a teaching strategy designed to improve the student's ability to handle information. In fact, her strategy formed the backbone of an entire social studies curriculum (Taba, 1966).

THINKING PROCESSES

Taba analyzes thinking from psychological and logical points of view and concludes:

> While the processes of thought are psychological and hence subject to psychological analysis, the product and the content of thought must be assessed by logical criteria and evaluated by the rules of logic. (Taba, 1966, p. 36)

She identifies three postulates about thinking:

1. *Thinking can be taught.* There is evidence for and against this postulate, but we do not debate it here.
2. *Thinking is an active transaction between the individual and data.* This means that in the classroom setting, the materials of instruction become available to the individual when he or she performs certain cognitive operations on them—organizing facts into conceptual systems; relating points in data to each other and generalizing from these relationships; making inferences and generalizing from

known facts to hypothesize, predict, and explain unfamiliar phenomena. Mental operations cannot be taught directly in the sense of being "given by a teacher" or being acquired by absorbing someone else's thought products. The teacher can, however, *assist* the processes of internalization and conceptualization by stimulating the students to perform complex mental processes and by offering progressively less direct support.

3. *Processes of thought evolve by a sequence that is "lawful."* Taba postulates that, in order to master certain thinking skills, certain earlier ones must be mastered first, and this sequence cannot be reversed. Therefore, "this concept of lawful sequences requires teaching strategies that observe these sequences." (Taba, 1966, pp. 34, 35)

In other words, Taba concludes that thinking skills should be taught using specific teaching strategies designed for those thinking skills. Furthermore, these strategies need to be used sequentially because one thinking skill builds on the other. One can argue with this assumption also, but for the sake of simplicity we accept it, so we can explore the model.

THREE TEACHING STRATEGIES

Taba identifies three inductive thinking tasks and then develops three teaching strategies to induce those tasks. Each task represents a stage in the inductive thinking process as Taba describes it. The first is *concept formation* (the basic teaching strategy), the second is *interpretation of data,* and the third is the *application of principles.*

CONCEPT FORMATION This stage involves (1) identifying and enumerating the data that are relevant to a problem; (2) grouping those items according to some basis of similarity; and (3) developing categories and labels for the groups. To engage students in each of these activities, Taba invented teaching moves in the form of questions. These *eliciting questions* are matched to particular types of activities. For example, the question, "What did you see?" might induce the student to enumerate a list. The question, "What belongs together?" is likely to cause people to group those things that have been listed. The question, "What would we call these groups?" would be likely to induce people to develop labels or categories.

An illustration of the concept-formation strategy is the second grade unit of Taba's Contra Costa social studies curriculum. The unit attempts to develop the main idea that a supermarket needs a place, equipment, goods, and services (Taba, 1967). The unit opens with the following hypothetical situation: "Mr. Smith wants to open a supermarket. What will he need?" The eliciting question might be phrased, "What do you see when you go to the supermarket?" The children can be expected to identify individual food, items, stock people, cashiers, equipment, a building (or place), deliveries of food. Their responses can be recorded and the listing continued until several categories are represented. After the enumerated list has been completed, the children are asked, perhaps on another day, to group the items on the basis of similarity. "What belongs together?" Presumably, if the enumeration is rich enough, the children will identify "things the market sells" and "things done for the supermarket owner." These concepts can then be labeled *goods* and *services*.

The purpose of this strategy is to induce students to expand the conceptual system with which they process information. In the first phases, they are required to group the data, an activity requiring them to alter or expand their capacity for handling information. In other words, they have to form concepts they subsequently can use to approach new information they encounter.

Each overt activity elicited by the teaching strategy reflects mental operations that are hidden from view, which Taba refers to as "covert." Table 3-1 illustrates the relationship between the overt activities in the concept-formation model, the mental operations that the students presumably perform during the activity, and the eliciting questions teachers use to lead the students through each activity.

INTERPRETATION OF DATA   Taba's second teaching strategy (interpretation of data) is built around the mental operations she refers to as *interpreting, inferring,* and *generalizing.* Table 3-2 shows the overt and covert activities involved in the interpretation of data and the questions a teacher can use to elicit the activities.

In the first phase, the teacher's questions lead students to identify critical aspects of the data. For example, after students have completed reading about the economic systems of the Union of South Africa, Great Britain, and Germany, the teacher might ask, "What are the important aspects of the economic systems of these three countries?"

Second, students are to explore relationships. Here the teacher asks questions concerning causes and effects. For example, he or she might simply ask, "Do you think the economic systems of the three countries are very

Table 3-1   Concept Formation

OVERT ACTIVITY	COVERT MENTAL OPERATIONS	ELICITING QUESTIONS
1. Enumeration, listing	Differentiation (identifying separate items)	What did you see? hear? note?
2. Grouping	Identifying common properties, abstracting	What belongs together? On what criterion?
3. Labeling, categorizing	Determining the hierarchical order of items super- and subordination.	How would you call these groups? What belongs to what?

SOURCE: Hilda Taba, *Teacher's Handbook for Elementary Social Studies* (Reading, Mass.: Addison-Wesley Publishing Co., Inc., 1967), p. 92.

Table 3-2   Interpretation of Data

OVERT ACTIVITY	COVERT MENTAL OPERATIONS	ELICITING QUESTIONS
1. Identifying critical relationships	Differentiating	What did you notice? see? find?
2. Exploring relationships	Relating categories to each other Determining cause-and-effect relationships	Why did this happen?
3. Making inferences	Going beyond what is given Finding implications, extrapolating	What does this mean? What picture does it create in your mind? What would you conclude?

SOURCE: Hilda Taba, *Teacher's Handbook for Elementary Social Studies* (Reading, Mass.: Addison-Wesley Publishing Co., Inc., 1967), p. 101.

similar or different? Why?" or "Describe a product and show the ways in which they might handle that product, similarly and differently?" The teacher might even say, "Are the economic systems of the three countries based on the value of the same metal? If so, how does this make them similar to and different from each other?"

In the third phase, making inferences, the teacher in our example might say, "What effect does the economic system have on the relative position of a country?" or "If the currency of all three countries is based on the value of gold, what does this mean for the relative position of the countries?" No one could be certain of a "correct" answer to this question, but it could give rise to conjectures and inferences that would require the students to go beyond the given data to arrive at some conclusions based on inferences about them.

APPLICATION OF PRINCIPLES   The third cognitive task around which Taba builds a teaching strategy is that of applying principles to explain new phenomena (predicting consequences from conditions that have been established). This strategy follows the first two; a unit or course would lead the students from concept-formation activities to activities requiring interpretation of data, and then to activities requiring application of principles. At each stage, students would be required to expand their capacities to handle information, first developing new concepts, then developing new ways of applying established principles in new situations. Table 3-3 describes the overt activities, covert mental operations, and the eliciting questions for this teaching strategy.

The first phase of the strategy requires students to predict consequences, explain unfamiliar data, or hypothesize. We might continue our previous example by asking students, "How would it change the picture if the value of currency were based on iron ore?" Or the teacher might change the emphasis by asking students for various hypotheses about things that might

Table 3-3   Application of Principles

OVERT ACTIVITIES	COVERT MENTAL OPERATIONS	ELICITING QUESTIONS
1. Predicting consequences, explaining unfamiliar phenomena, hypothesizing	Analyzing the nature of the problem or situation, retrieving relevant knowledge	What would happen if . . . ?
2. Explaining and/or supporting the predictions and hypotheses	Determining the causal links leading to prediction or hypothesis	Why do you think this would happen?
3. Verifying the prediction	Using logical principals or factual knowledge to determine necessary and sufficient conditions	What would it take for this to be generally true or probably true?

SOURCE: Hilda Taba, *Teacher's Handbook for Elementary Social Studies* (Reading, Mass.: Addison-Wesley Publishing Co., Inc., 1967), p. 109.

stabilize the international monetary situation as exemplified by the currencies of the three countries.

In the second phase, students attempt to explain or support the predictions or hypotheses. For example, if someone feels that a fixed currency rate for all countries should be established and held for a long time, he or she would attempt to explain why he or she thought this system would work, and how he or she thought it would fare with such factors as the relative prosperities or production ratios within the countries. In the third phase, students verify these predictions or identify conditions that would verify the predictions.

ILLUSTRATIONS OF THE STRATEGIES   Taba's Contra Costa social studies curriculum incorporates her Inductive Teaching Model. Both content and activities in her curriculum are carefully sequenced. As the learning tasks call for students to form concepts, interpret data, generalize, or apply principles, the teacher calls on the appropriate teaching strategy. Taba's *Teacher's Handbook for Elementary Social Studies* provides several illustrations of these strategies in action as well as some useful interpretive comments and cautions. (It should be noted that although Taba's basic developmental work was in social studies, these strategies are useful in many subject areas.)

The first example is one of enumeration and grouping that took place in a second grade class.

DISCUSSION EXCERPT:
ENUMERATION AND GROUPING (GRADE TWO)

1. TEACHER: Let's start listing things on the board that you would buy if you went to the store.
2. DAVID: Apples.
3. PAUL: I'd buy steak.

4. **RANDY:** Shrimp.

5. **DENNY:** I'd buy a puppy.

6. **TEACHER:** A puppy is different, isn't it?

7. **MIKE:** Watermelon.

8. **CARLA:** Candy bar.

9. **ANN:** Scooter.

10. **TEACHER:** Scooter, that's something different again, isn't it?

11. **TEACHER:** We've almost filled up our board with things that we would buy. What can we do with these things? Do some of them belong together? Which ones could you find in the same place?

12. **DENNY:** You can buy a doll and a scooter in the same place.

13. **TEACHER:** You would buy one of them in a toy shop, wouldn't you? Let's pick out the ones that we might buy in a toy shop. You might buy the scooter and the doll. What else would you buy in the toy shop?

14. **RICKY:** Squirt gun.

15. **TEACHER:** All right, we would buy a squirt gun in the toy shop. What else would we buy in the toy shop? (Taba, 1967, p. 95)

Taba makes several points about helping students enumerate. When working in groups, students tend to persist on the theme established by the first speaker (for example, in the listing of food, the first student may begin with canned vegetables). If the concepts to be developed are goods and services, a one-dimensional list would not be as productive for grouping as a more inclusive one. In the preceding excerpt, if the teacher's ultimate objective were to induce the concept of goods and services, a broader opening question would be more likely to elicit a multidimensional list. By requesting students to list "things you would buy if you went to the store," the teacher is in effect providing one category for the children to which they merely add the appropriate items. Taba also points out another problem inherent in categorizing—the provision of such a broad category that it encompasses items in the other groups. For instance, suppose a teacher calls for category labels and is given "facilities and conditions," "education," and "transportation." The item "pavement" could be put under both "transportation" and "facilities and conditions" (Taba, 1967, p. 96).

Taba gives the following suggestions for directing discussion when problems of grouping and categorizing arise:

1. Generally, when a category is given, proceed to identify any other items which belong to it. In the case of "facilities and conditions" it would be possible to do some double categorization, grouping "pavement" under "facilities and conditions" and also under "transportation."

2. When one category is of a different order from the others, it can sometimes be eliminated once the other categories are established. Items of the eliminated category can be subsumed under those remaining.

3. When the meaning of the category is not clear, clarification should be sought from the contributor. That person should either explain what he or she means or name items which he or she thinks belong to the category.

4. In many cases, it is not necessary to press for a final decision, since the emphasis is on the process rather than the content. An open procedure will encourage students to offer items which are too difficult to deal with for the time being. In other instances, the category or item in question may even be irrelevant to the content of the unit. (Taba, 1967, p. 96)

For the interpretation of data strategy to be meaningful, the inferences must be within the confines of the data. Often students will either make inferences totally apart from supporting information or they will use prior knowledge in making their interpretations of data. The teacher can increase the soundness of the inferences by following up student responses with questions that cull unprocessed information.

In the following excerpt the teacher's focusing questions are primarily responsible for sustaining the discussion at a general level:

DISCUSSION EXCERPT:
INTERPRETING DATA (GRADE SIX)

1. **TEACHER:**   Now let's get back to intermarriage. You said that intermarriage was so important. What about that?

2./3. **SETH:**   They marry freely, whoever they want to. They just pick. If they want to marry a Black, an Indian, or a white person, they just do. It doesn't seem to bother them.

4. **TEACHER:**   What do you have to say about that?

5. **CATHY:**   In Argentina they marry very young, and they are restricted and can't go out on dates. I mean free dates.

6. **TEACHER:**   Let's get back to this intermarriage. What does that show about the country of Brazil?

7. **TOM:**   People aren't prejudiced or segregated.

8. **TEACHER:**   Why do you suppose they are not prejudiced?

9. **BOB:**   I think because they did it before.

10. **AMY:**   And there are more percentage of Indian and Negro than there are in different countries.

11. **TEACHER:**   All right, do you want to carry that a little further? You thought that was a good idea, didn't you, when we talked about it?

12. **KARL:**   When the Portuguese came over to colonize, they married. They found out that the Indians were there many hundreds of years before and they married them freely, and then there was an intermingling of bloods.

13. **TEACHER:**   A melting pot, isn't it? All these different peoples and they seem to get along together, which is wonderful.

14. **AMY:**   In Argentina there are not many Indians because of the war of 1888.

15. **TEACHER:**   What happened to the Indians then?

16. **AMY:**   They were almost wiped out because of the war. They were against the people and they were almost wiped out.

17. **KARL:**   The intermarriage came in places that are lightly settled.

18. **TEACHER:**   Why is that?

19. **SETH:**   Because there is not very many to pick from.

20. **KARL:** They used what is around.

21. **TOM:** Another thing about intermarriage is that they have married freely, but they didn't lose the language.

22./23. **TEACHER:** That's a good thing. What language? Where did this happen?

24. **GWEN:** Well, intermarriage shows that everybody is created equal. (Taba, 1967, pp. 106–107)

In the third teaching strategy, *application of principles,* the student must apply known principles and facts either to explain unfamiliar phenomena or to predict consequences. The alternating movement between prediction and explanation as the class builds to a more complete explanation (or prediction) is demonstrated in the following excerpt:

DISCUSSION EXCERPT:
APPLICATION OF PRINCIPLES (GRADE FIVE)

Focus of Content and Operation: "Suppose that America suddenly discovered a large, beautiful island out in the Pacific Ocean close to California. Also suppose that this island was inhabited by non-literate people who were farmers. What would happen?

OPERATIONS	CONTENT	SPEAKER	
Prediction	Tools	Carla	They would have to import tools.
Reason		Ned	They don't know how to make tools.
Informational support		Teacher	All right. How are most of our tools made?
		Ned	By machines.
Prediction	Machines	Teacher	Do you think that they would have machinery as we have it?
		Ned	No.
		Teacher	Why do you think that they wouldn't?
Support by logical reasoning		Ned	Because they wouldn't have schools.
		John	Electricity would run the machines.
Prediction	Electricity		They probably wouldn't have electricity over there.
		Teacher	Why do you think they wouldn't have electricity?
Support by logical reasoning		John	Well, they wouldn't know about electricity.
		Rita	But they could still have machines if they knew how to use water power.

(Continued)

OPERATIONS	CONTENT	SPEAKER	
Prediction	Water Power	Teacher	Do you think that perhaps they would know how to use water power?
Support by logical reasoning		Rita	Maybe. (Taba, 1967, p. 110)

The third step of the strategy involves verifying the prediction or hypothesis by checking its probability or universality. In one class students were asked what would happen if the desert had water. If the students had reached the conclusion that the presence of water makes the soil productive and that water would transform the desert way of life, the teacher could move the discussion to questioning whether the presence of water is the only condition that would make the soil productive and transform the way of life—for example, what about the need for a transportation system? How will the products be distributed (Taba, 1967, p. 111)?

THE MODEL OF TEACHING

SYNTAX

These three teaching strategies strongly resemble each other. Each is built around a mental operation: concept formation, interpretation of data, application of principles or ideas. In each case, the strategy involves overt activities that assume students must go through certain covert operations to perform the activities. Thus, the sequence of activities forms the syntax of the teaching strategies and is presumably accompanied by underlying mental processes. In each case, the teacher moves the strategy along by means of eliciting questions to guide the student from one phase of activity into the next, at the appropriate time. In the case of concept-formation strategy, for example, the grouping of data would be premature if the data had not been identified and enumerated. But to delay too long before moving to the next phase would be to lose opportunities and interest.

SOCIAL SYSTEM

In all three strategies, the atmosphere of the classroom is cooperative, with a good deal of pupil activity. Since the teacher is generally the initiator of phases, and the sequence of the activities is determined in advance, he or she begins in a controlling, though cooperative, position. However, as the students learn the strategies, they assume greater control.

PRINCIPLES OF REACTION

Taba provides the teacher with rather clear guidelines for reacting and responding within each phase. In matching the eliciting questions or moves to the specific cognitive tasks within each strategy, the teacher must be sure that the cognitive tasks occur in optimum order, and also at the right time. As mentioned earlier, the teacher should not direct a grouping question to a person who has not yet enumerated or listed, and if the teacher is working with a large group, he or she must be sure that the enumeration and listing activity is completed and understood by all before proceeding to the grouping questions. The most prominent moves by the teachers are questions, and the eliciting questions are modeled after the cognitive functions. The teacher's primary mental task in the course of the strategies is to monitor how students are processing information, and then to use appropriate eliciting questions. The important task for the teacher is to sense the students' readiness for new experience and new cognitive activity with which to assimilate and use those experiences.

SUPPORT SYSTEM

These strategies can be used in any curricular area that has large amounts of raw data that need to be organized. For example, in studying the economic aspects of various nations, students would need large quantities of data about the economics of those countries and statistics about world affairs. Then the teacher's job would be to help them process the data in increasingly complex ways, and at the same time to increase the general capacities of their systems for processing data.

APPLICATION

Since each of Taba's teaching strategies is built on a particular mental, or cognitive, task, the primary application of the model is to develop thinking capacity. However, in the course of developing thinking capacity, the strategies obviously require students to ingest and process large quantities of information. Furthermore, although the strategies were developed specifically during the construction of a social studies curriculum, they could easily be applied to a very large number of other curricula. In fact, there are a great many examples of inductive strategies in science curricula, English curricula, and many other courses that are not based on specific subject areas. In addition, the third strategy, by inducing students to go beyond the given data, is a deliberate attempt to increase productive or creative thinking. Inductive processes thus include the creative processing of information, as well as the convergent use of information to solve problems.

Taba's concept-formation strategy is especially applicable to the education of young children. Although many early childhood teachers have their students engage in grouping activities, few understand this process from the points of view of Taba and Bruner (concept formation and concept attainment). Concept formation, like concept attainment, can be a vehicle for helping students understand the nature of a concept. It is a strategy especially suited to philosophies of education and instruction that call for *active* learning and require manipulable materials. The strategy is also beneficial to students in upper grades who must learn and process masses of information. Concept formation is a means of pulling discrete items together into larger conceptual schemes.

The model causes students to collect information and examine it closely, to organize it into concepts, and to learn to manipulate those concepts. Used regularly, the strategy increases the students' abilities to form concepts efficiently and also the perspectives from which they can view information.

For example, if a group of students regularly engages in inductive activity, it can be taught increasing numbers of sources for the data. The students can learn to examine data from many sides, and to scrutinize all aspects of objects and events. For example, imagine students studying communities. We can expect that at first their data will be superficial, but their increasingly sophisticated inquiry will turn up more and more attributes that they can use for classifying the data. Also, if a classroom of students works in groups to form concepts and data and then the groups share the categories they develop, they will stimulate each other to look at the information from different perspectives. The instructor can use the concept-attainment strategy to open up still more perspectives to them.

Also, the students can learn to categorize categories. Imagine students who have classified poems or short stories. They can build concepts that further cluster those categories.

The research on the effects of inductive-teaching strategies has explored, first, whether students can learn inductive processes, and, second, what are the effects of these processes on the acquisition of information and concepts. The answer to the first question appears to be affirmative (Bredderman, 1981; El Nemr, 1979). Also, when compared to drill-and-practice methods that typify instruction in most schools, induction appears to increase both the amount of information learned and the concepts that are developed to organize it. Worthen (1968) hypothesized that inductive processes would increase the retention of information and found that it did. Apparently the process of forming concepts enabled the students to develop mental structures that "held" the information better than structures that were provided to them. Hunt and Joyce (1981) explored inductive processes with both relatively rigid and flexible students (See Chapter 26); they found that both groups were able to engage in the inductive process but that the more flexible students made the greatest gains initially. More important, they found that practice and training increased effectiveness and that the students could learn to carry on inductive activity independently.

The accompanying summary chart outlines elements of the concept-formation strategy. All the strategies have relatively clear syntaxes, with the reactions of the teachers coordinated with the phases, a cooperative but (at first) teacher-centered social system, and support systems that require ample sources of raw ungrouped data. Their applicability is extremely wide, and the classroom teacher should consider a repertoire of basic inductive strategies such as these to be an essential tool.

Summary Chart: Inductive-Thinking Model

SYNTAX

Strategy One:
Concept Formation

Phase One: Enumeration and listing
Phase Two: Grouping
Phase Three: Labeling, categorizing

Strategy Two:
Interpretation of Data

Phase Four: Identifying critical relationships
Phase Five: Exploring relationships
Phase Six: Making inferences

Strategy Three:
Application of Principles

Phase Seven: Predicting consequences, explaining unfamiliar phenomena, hypothesizing
Phase Eight: Explaining and/or supporting the predictions and hypotheses
Phase Nine: Verifying the prediction

SOCIAL SYSTEM

The model has high to moderate structure. It is cooperative, but the teacher is initiator and controller of activities.

PRINCIPLES OF REACTION

Teacher matches eliciting questions to students' level of cognitive activity, determines students' readiness.

SUPPORT SYSTEM

Students need raw data to organize and analyze.

INSTRUCTIONAL AND NURTURANT EFFECTS

The Inductive Thinking Model (Figure 3–1) is designed to instruct students in concept formation and, simultaneously, to teach concepts. It nurtures attention to logic, to language and the meaning of words, and to the nature of knowledge.

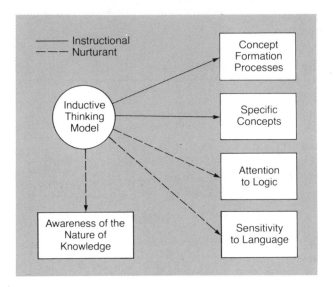

FIGURE 3–1   Instructional and nurturant effects: Inductive Thinking Model.

4

INQUIRY TRAINING
From Facts
to Theories

SCENARIO

One morning, as Mrs. Harrison's fourth grade class is settling down to their arithmetic workbooks, she calls their attention. As they raise their eyes toward her, a light bulb directly over Mrs. Harrison's desk blows out, and the room darkens.

"What happened?" asks one child.

"Can't you see, dopey?" remarks another. "The light bulb blew out."

"Yeah," inquires another, "but what does that mean?"

"What do you mean, 'What does that mean?'"

"Just that. We have all seen a lot of light bulbs blow out, but what does that really mean? What happens?"

Mrs. Harrison unscrews the light bulb and holds it up. The children gather around, and she passes it among them. After she receives it, she says, "Well, why don't you see if you can develop a hypothesis about what happened?"

"What's inside the glass?" asks one of the children.

"I'm afraid I can't answer that," she replies. "Can you put it another way?"

"Is there air inside the glass?" one questions.

"No," says Mrs. Harrison.

"Is there a gas inside?" asks another.

"No," says Mrs. Harrison. The children look at one another in puzzlement. Finally, one asks, "Is it a vacuum?"

"Yes," nods Mrs. Harrison.

"Is it a complete vacuum?" someone inquires.

"Almost," replies Mrs. Harrison.

"What is that little wire made of?" asks another student.

"I can't answer that," says Mrs. Harrison. "Can you put it another way?"

"Is the little wire made of metal?"

"Yes," she agrees.

Asking questions such as these, the children gradually identify the materials that make up the light bulb and the events that took place. Finally, they begin to venture hypotheses about what happened. After they have generated four or five of these, they search through reference books in an effort to verify them.

Mrs. Harrison's class has been prepared to carry out a model of teaching that we call *inquiry training*. Normally, the class uses inquiry training to explore preselected areas. That is, either Mrs. Harrison organizes a unit of instruction or the children identify a topic that they are going to explore. In this case, the children used the techniques of inquiry training to formulate theories about an unanticipated event that was familiar to all of them, and yet puzzled them, for none of them had previously developed ideas about what really went on when a light bulb blew out.

Inquiry training was developed by Richard Suchman to teach students a process for investigating and explaining unusual phenomena. Suchman's model takes students through miniature versions of the kinds of procedures that scholars use to organize knowledge and generate principles. Based on a conception of scientific method, it attempts to teach students some of the skills and language of scholarly inquiry (Suchman, 1962).

Suchman developed his model by analyzing methods employed by creative research personnel, especially physical scientists. As he identified the elements of their inquiry processes, he built them into the instructional model called inquiry training.

RESEARCH

Inquiry training is designed to bring students directly into the scientific process through exercises that compress the scientific process into small periods of time. What are the effects? Schlenker (1976) reported that inquiry training resulted in increased understanding of science, productivity in creative thinking, and skills for obtaining and analyzing information. He reported that it was not more effective than conventional recitation methods of teaching in the acquisition of information, but that it was as efficient as recitation or lectures accompanied by laboratory experiences. Ivany (1969) and Collins (1969) reported that the method works best when the confrontations are strong, arousing genuine puzzlement, and when the materials the students use to explore the topics under consideration are especially instructional. Both elementary and secondary students can profit from the model (Voss, 1982). In an intriguing study, Elefant (1980) successfully carried out the model with deaf children, which suggests that the method can be powerful with students who have severe sensory handicaps.

ORIENTATION TO THE MODEL

GOALS AND ASSUMPTIONS

Inquiry training originated in a belief in the development of independent learners; its method requires active participation in scientific inquiry. Children are curious and eager to grow, and inquiry training capitalizes on their natural energetic explorations, giving them specific directions so that they explore new areas more forcefully. The general goal of inquiry training is to help students develop the intellectual discipline and skills necessary to raise questions and search out answers stemming from their curiosity. Thus, Suchman is interested in helping students inquire independently, but in a disciplined way. He wants students to question why events happen as they do and to acquire and process data logically, and he wants them to develop general intellectual strategies that they can use to find out why things are as they are.

Inquiry training begins by presenting students with a puzzling event. Suchman believes that individuals faced with such a situation are *naturally motivated* to solve the puzzle. We can use the opportunity provided by natural inquiry to teach the procedures of disciplined searching.

Like Bruner and Taba, Suchman believes that students can become increasingly conscious of their process of inquiry, and that they can be taught scientific procedures directly. All of us often inquire intuitively; however, Suchman feels we cannot analyze and improve our thinking unless we are conscious of it.

Suchman believes, further, that it is important to convey to students the attitude that *all knowledge is tentative.* Scholars generate theories and explanations. Years later, these are pushed aside by new theories. There are no permanent answers. We can always be more sophisticated in our explanations, and most problems are amenable to several plausible explanations. Students should recognize and be comfortable with the ambiguity that genuine inquiry entails. They should also be aware that the point of view of a second person enriches our own thinking. The development of knowledge is facilitated by help and ideas from colleagues if we can learn to tolerate alternative points of view. Thus, Suchman's theory is that:

1. Students inquire naturally when they are puzzled.
2. They can become conscious of and learn to analyze their thinking strategies.
3. New strategies can be taught directly and added to the students' existing ones.
4. Cooperative inquiry enriches thinking and helps students to learn about the tentative, emergent nature of knowledge and to appreciate alternative explanations.

OVERVIEW OF THE TEACHING STRATEGY

Following Suchman's belief that individuals have a natural motivation to inquire, the Inquiry-Training Model is built around intellectual confrontations. The student is presented with a puzzling situation and inquires into it. Anything that is mysterious, unexpected, or unknown is grist for a discrepant event. Because the ultimate goal is to have the students experience the creation of new knowledge, the confrontation should be based on discoverable ideas. In the following example, bending a metallic strip held over a flame begins the inquiry cycle.

> The strip is made of a lamination of unlike strips of metal (usually steel and brass) that have been welded together to form a single blade. With a handle at one end it has the appearance of a narrow knife or spatula. When this apparatus is heated, the metal in it expands, but the rate of expansion is not the same in the two metals. Consequently, half of the thickness of this laminated strip becomes slightly longer than the other half and since the two halves are attached to each other the internal stresses force the blade to assume a curve of which the outer circumference is occupied by the metal which has expanded the most. (Suchman, 1962, p. 28)

Suchman deliberately selects episodes that have sufficiently surprising outcomes to make it difficult for students to remain indifferent to the encounter. Usually things that are heated do not bend into a big curve. When this metal strip does, the students *naturally* want to know *why*. The learners cannot dismiss the solution as obvious; they have to work to explain the situation, and the product of that work is a new insight, concepts, and theories.

After the presentation of the puzzling situation, the student asks the teacher questions. The questions, however, must be answered by yeses or nos. Students may not ask the teacher to explain the phenomenon to them. They have to focus and structure their probes to solve the problem. In this sense, each question becomes a limited hypothesis. Thus, the student may not ask, "How did the heat affect the metal?" but may ask, "Was the heat greater than the melting point of the metal?" The first question is not a specific statement of what information is wanted; it asks the teacher to do the conceptualizing. The second question requires the student to put several factors together—heat, metal, change, liquid. The student had to ask the teacher to verify the hypothesis that he or she has developed (the heat caused the metal to change into a liquid).

The students continue to ask questions. Whenever they phrase one that cannot be answered by a yes or no, the teacher reminds them of the rules and waits until they find a way of stating the question in proper form. Comments such as, "Can you restate this question so that I can answer it with a yes or a no?" are common teacher responses when students slip out of the inquiry mode.

Over time, the students are taught that the first stage in inquiry is to verify the facts of the situation—the nature and identity of the objects, the events, and the conditions surrounding the puzzling event. The question "Was the strip made of metal?" helps verify the facts—in this case, a property of the object. As the students become aware of the facts, hypotheses should come to mind and guide further inquiry. Using their knowledge about the behavior of the objects, students can turn their questions to the relationships among the variables in the situation. They can conduct verbal or actual experiments to test these causal relationships, selecting new data or organizing the existing data in new ways to see what will happen if things are done differently. For example, they could ask, "If I turn the flame down, will the bending still occur?" Better yet, they could actually do this! By introducing a new condition or altering an existing one, students isolate variables and learn how they affect one another.

It is important for students and teachers to recognize the difference between questions that attempt to verify "what is" and questions or activities that "experiment" with the relationships among variables. Each of these is essential to theory development, but fact gathering should precede hypothesis raising. Unless sufficient information about the nature of the problem situation and its elements is verified, students are likely to be overwhelmed by the many possible causal relationships.

> If the child immediately tries to hypothesize complex relationships among all the variables that seem relevant to him, he could go on testing indefinitely without any noticeable progress, but by isolating variables and testing them singly, he can eliminate the irrelevant ones and discover the relationships that exist between each relevant independent variable (such as the temperature of the blade) and the dependent variable (which in this case is the bending of the blade). (Suchman, 1962, pp. 15–16)

Finally, the students try to develop hypotheses that will fully explain what happened. (For instance, "The strip was made of two metals that were fastened together somehow. They expand at different rates, and when they were heated, the one that expanded the most exerted pressure on the other one so that the two bent over together.") Even after lengthy and rich verification and experimentation activities, many explanations may be possible, and the students are encouraged not to be satisfied with the first explanation that appears to fit the facts.

Inquiry cannot be programmed, and the range of productive inquiry strategies is vast. Thus, students should

> experiment freely with their own questions, structuring and sequencing [the inquiry session]. . . . Nevertheless, inquiry can be divided into broad phrases which, on the whole, should be taken in logical order simply because they build upon one another. Failure to adhere to this order leads either to erroneous assumptions or to low efficiency and duplication of effort. (Suchman, 1962, p. 38)

The emphasis in this model is clearly on becoming aware of and mastering the inquiry process, not on the content of any particular problem situation. Although the model should also be enormously appealing and effective as a mode of acquiring and using information, the teacher cannot be too concerned with subject-matter coverage or "getting the right answer." In fact, this would violate the whole spirit of scientific inquiry, which envisions a community of scholars searching together for more accurate and powerful explanations for everyday phenomena.

THE MODEL OF TEACHING

SYNTAX

Inquiry training has five phases (see Table 4-1). The first phase is the student's *confrontation* with the puzzling situation. Phases two and three are the *data-gathering* operations of *verification* and *experimentation*. In these two phases students ask a series of questions to which the teacher replies yes or no, and they conduct a series of experiments on the environment of the problem situation. In the fourth phase students *organize* the information they obtained during the data gathering and try to *explain* the discrepancy. Finally, in phase five, students *analyze* the problem-solving strategies they used during the inquiry.

Phase One requires that the teacher present the problem situation and explain the inquiry procedures to the students (the objectives and the procedure of the yes-no question). The formulation of a discrepant event such as the bimetallic strip problem requires some thought, although the strategy can be based on relatively simple problems—a puzzle, riddle, or magic trick—that do not require much background knowledge. Of course, the ultimate goal is to have students, especially older students, experience the creation of new knowledge, much as scholars do. However, beginning inquiries can be based on very simple ideas.

Table 4-1   Syntax of the Inquiry Training Model

PHASE ONE: CONFRONTATION WITH THE PROBLEM	PHASE TWO: DATA GATHERING— VERIFICATION
Explain inquiry procedures. Present discrepant event.	Verify the nature of objects and conditions. Verify the occurrence of the problem situation.
PHASE THREE: DATA GATHERING— EXPERIMENTATION	PHASE FOUR: ORGANIZING, FORMULATING AN EXPLANATION
Isolate relevant variables. Hypothesize (and test) causal relationships.	Formulate rules or explanations.
PHASE FIVE: ANALYSIS OF THE INQUIRY PROCESS	
Analyze inquiry strategy and develop more effective ones.	

The distinguishing feature of the discrepancy is that it involves events that conflict with our notions of reality. In this sense, not every puzzling situation is a discrepant event. It may be puzzling because we do not know the answer, but we do not need new concepts to understand it and therefore we do not need to conduct an inquiry. We mention this because occasionally teachers do not pick problems that are truly puzzling to the student. In these cases, the learning activity does not progress beyond a "twenty-questions" format. Even though the questioning activity has value for its own sake, it should not be confused with the notion of scientific inquiry.

Phase Two, verification, is the process whereby students gather information about an event they see or experience. In experimentation, phase three, students introduce new elements into the situation to see if the event happens differently. Although verification and experimentation are described as separate phases of the model, the students' thinking and the types of questions they generate usually alternate between these two aspects of data gathering.

Experiments serve two functions: *exploration* and *direct testing*. Exploration—changing things to see what will happen—is not necessarily guided by a theory or hypothesis, but it may suggest ideas for a theory. Direct testing occurs when students try out a theory or hypothesis. The process of converting a hypothesis into an experiment is not easy and takes practice. Many verification and experimentation questions are required just to investigate one theory. We have found that even sophisticated adults find it easier to say, "I think it has something to do with . . ." than to think of a series of questions that will test the theory. Also, few theories can be discarded on the basis of one experiment. Although it is tempting to "throw away" a variable if the first experiment does not support it, it can be very misleading to do so. One of the teacher's roles is to restrain students whenever they assume that a variable has been disproven when it has not.

A second function of the teacher is to broaden the students' inquiry by expanding the type of information they obtain. During verification they may ask questions about objects, properties, conditions, and events. *Object* questions are intended to determine the nature or identity of objects. (Is the knife made of steel? Is the liquid water?) *Event* questions attempt to verify the occurrence or nature of an action. (Did the knife bend upward the second time?) *Condition* questions relate to the state of objects or systems at a particular time. (Was the blade hotter than room temperature when he held it up and showed that it was bent? Did the color change when the liquid was added?) *Property* questions aim to verify the behavior of objects under certain conditions as a way of gaining new information to help build a theory. (Does copper always bend when it is heated?) Because students tend not to verify all aspects of the problem, teachers can be aware of the type of information they seek and work to change the questioning pattern.

In phase four the teacher calls on the students to organize the data and to formulate an explanation. Some students have difficulty making the intellectual leap between comprehending the information they have gathered and constructing a clear explanation of it. They may give inadequate explanations omitting essential details. Sometimes several theories or explanations are possible based on the same data. In such cases, it is often useful to ask students to state their explanations so that the range of possible hypotheses becomes obvious. Together the group can shape the explanation that fully responds to the problem situation. Finally, in phase five, the students are asked to analyze their pattern of inquiry. They may determine the questions that were most effective, the lines of questioning that were productive and those that were not, or the type of information they needed and did not obtain. This phase is essential if we are to make the inquiry process a conscious one and systematically try to improve it.

SOCIAL SYSTEM

Suchman's intention is that the social system be cooperative and rigorous. Although the Inquiry Training Model can be quite highly structured, with the social system controlled largely by the teacher, the intellectual environment is open to all relevant ideas; teachers and students participate as equals where ideas are concerned. Moreover, the teacher should encourage students to initiate inquiry as much as possible. As the students learn the principles of inquiry, the structure can expand to include the use of resource material, dialogue with other students, experimentation, and discussion with the teacher.

After a period of practice in teacher-structured inquiry sessions, students can undertake inquiry in more student-controlled settings. A stimulating event can be set up in the room, and students can inquire on their own or in informal groups, alternating between open-ended inquiry sessions and data gathering with the aid of resource materials. In this way, the students can move back and forth between inquiry sessions and independent study. This utilization of the Inquiry Training Model is especially suited to the open-classroom setting, where the teacher's role is that of instructional manager and monitor.

In the initial stages of inquiry the teacher's role is to select (or construct) the problem situation, to referee the inquiry according to inquiry procedures, to respond to students' inquiry probes with the necessary information, to help beginning inquirers establish a focus in their inquiry, and to facilitate discussion of the problem situation among the students.

PRINCIPLES OF REACTION

The most important reactions of the teacher take place during the second and third phases. During the second phase the teacher's task is to help the students to inquire, but not to do the inquiry for them. If the teacher is asked questions that cannot be answered by a yes or no, he or she must ask the students to rephrase the questions so as to further their own attempts to collect data and relate them to the problem situation. The teacher can, if necessary, keep the inquiry moving by making new information available to the group and by focusing on particular problem events or by raising questions. During the last phase, the teacher's task is to keep the inquiry directed toward the process of investigation itself.

SUPPORT SYSTEM

The optimal support is a set of confronting materials, a teacher who understands the intellectual processes and strategies of inquiry, and resource materials bearing on the problem.

APPLICATION

Although inquiry training was originally developed for the natural sciences, its procedures are usable in all subject areas; any topic that can be formulated as a puzzling situation is a candidate for inquiry training. In literature, murder mysteries and science fiction stories or plots make excellent puzzling situations. Newspaper articles about bizarre or improbable situations may be used to construct stimulus events. One of the authors was at a Chinese restaurant not too long ago and puzzled over the question, "How is the fortune put into the fortune cookie, since it does not appear burned or cooked in any way?" It occurred to us that this would make an excellent inquiry-training topic for young children. The social sciences also offer numerous possibilities for inquiry training.

The construction of puzzling situations is the critical task, because it transforms curriculum content into problems to be explored. When objects and other materials are not available or appropriate to the problem situation, we recommend that teachers make up a *problem statement* for students and a *fact sheet* for themselves. The problem statement describes the discrepant event and provides the information that is shared initially with the students. The fact sheet gives the teacher further information about the problem, and the teacher draws on it to respond to the students' questions. Two examples of this process follow.

EXAMPLE ONE

In anthropology students have the problem of reconstructing cultural events. For a social studies class an instructor composed a problem statement and a student fact sheet based on an anthropological issue. The teacher passed the following statement out to his students:

PROBLEM STATEMENT

This map shows an island in the middle of a lake. The island is connected to the shore by a causeway made of stones piled on the bottom of the lake until the pile reached the surface. Then smoothed stones were laid down to make a road. The lake is surrounded by mountains, and the only flat land is near the lake. The island is covered with

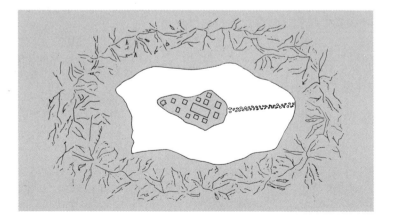

buildings whose walls are still standing although the roofs are now gone. It is completely uninhabited.

Your task is to discover what happened to the people who lived there. What caused the place to be empty of human beings?

As the students conducted their inquiry the instructor drew on the following fact sheet for his responses:

INSTRUCTOR FACT SHEET

1. The lake is 500 feet deep, 600 feet across.
2. The lake is 6,500 feet above sea level. The mountains rise to 11,000 feet.
3. The causeway is made of dumped rocks.
4. The houses are close together. Each one is about 20 by 25 feet and has more than one room. They are made of limestone blocks.
5. Some broken tools and pottery have been found in the homes.
6. The edifice in the center is made of marble and has three levels. At the bottom it is six times larger than the houses. At the top level of the edifice, you can sight the planets and stars through a hole slit in a stone. You can sight Venus at its lowest rise, which occurs on December 21.
7. There is evidence that the islanders fished with traps. They also had livestock such as sheep, cows, and chickens.
8. Apparently, there was no art, but evidence of graphic writing has been found.
9. Cisterns have been found under limestone streets.
10. There is no habitation within 80 miles.
11. The island has been uninhabited for about 300 years.
12. The area was discovered in 1900.
13. It is located in a subtropical area of South America where there is plenty of drinking water and where every available area was farmed. There is evidence of irrigation but no evidence of crop rotation. In general, the land is marginal for farming.
14. There is a thin layer of topsoil over a limestone shelf.
15. About 1,000 to 1,500 people lived on the island.
16. The mountains around the island can be crossed, but with difficulty.
17. There is a stone quarry in nearby mountains and a burial ground across the lake.
18. Dead bodies with hands folded have been found.
19. There is no evidence of plague, massive disease, or war.

EXAMPLE TWO

An English teacher using inquiry training based a discrepant event on Chapter 6 of Kurt Vonnegut's *Venus on the Half-Shell* (published under the pen name of Kilgore Trout). She formulated the following problem situation and then read a short excerpt from the book:

Simon, a space traveler from Earth, visited the planet Shaltoon. He was disconcerted to find that the Shaltoonians had different voices and personalities every day. Apparently they were different people every day, except for their physical appearance, which remained unchanged.

The students were asked to explain the principle behind the unusual phenomenon.

AGE-LEVEL ADAPTATION

Inquiry training can be used with children of all ages, but each age group requires adaptation. We have seen the method be successful with kindergarten children but encounter difficulty with third graders. As with many other aspects of teaching, each group and each student are unique. However, there are several ways to simplify the model until students are able to engage in all phases.

For very young children it is best to keep the content of the problems simple, perhaps with more emphasis on discovery than on a principle of causation. Problem situations like "What is in this box?" or "What is this unusual thing?" or "Why does one egg roll differently from the other?" are appropriate. One teacher we know showed her students a picture of a flying squirrel from a magazine for science teachers. Since most of us believe animals do not fly, this was truly a discrepant event. She asked the students to come up with an explanation for this phenomenon using inquiry procedures.

Numerous children's science books are filled with simple science experiments, many of them suitable for primary grades. Mystery stories and riddles work well as stimuli for young children. Another way to adapt inquiry training to young children is to use visual material—props giving clues—which simplifies the stimuli and lessens the requirements for memory. It is useful to aim for only one or two specific objectives in a single inquiry training session. Initially (with students of all ages) it is good to start off with a simple game that requires yes-no questions. This game will give students confidence that they can formulate questions and avoid direct theory questions. Some teachers we know use the mystery bag; others play "I'm thinking of something I'm wearing. Guess what it is?" Simple guessing games like this also give the students practice in distinguishing theory questions (Is it your shirt?) from attribute questions (Is it made of cotton?). We recommend that teachers introduce and stress each element of inquiry separately. At first the teacher could pose all yes-no questions. Then they can ask students to convert their theory questions to experiments. One by one the teachers can tighten the constraints of the inquiry as they teach the students each of the elements. Trying to explain and enforce all of the elements at once will only frustrate both students and teachers.

Older students are better able to handle the inquiry process itself, and their subject matter—especially science—more readily lends itself to inquiry training. On the other hand, age and sex may be inhibiting factors in the process. Although there are more suitable discrepant events in the upper elementary and secondary curricula, it is usually necessary for the teacher to convert available materials from an expository mode into the inquiry mode—that is, to create a discrepant event.

LEARNING ENVIRONMENT ADAPTATIONS

Like many other models, especially Information-Processing Models, inquiry training can be taught in a teacher-directed setting or incorporated into more self-directed, learning-center environments. Discrepant events can be developed through print, film, or audio means, and task cards directing students to respond according to the model can be developed. The inquiry can be conducted over a period of several days, and the results of other students' inquiries can be shared. Students should have access to appropriate resources, and they may work together in groups. Students may also develop discrepant events and conduct inquiry sessions for peers.

INSTRUCTIONAL AND NURTURANT EFFECTS

The model promotes strategies of inquiry, and the values and attitudes that are essential to an inquiring mind, including:

> Process skills (observing, collecting, and organizing data; identifying and controlling variables; formulating and testing hypotheses and explanations; inferring);
> Active, autonomous learning;
> Verbal expressiveness;
> Tolerance of ambiguity, persistence;
> Logical thinking;
> Attitude that all knowledge is tentative.

The chief learning outcomes of inquiry training are the processes involved—observing, collecting and organizing data, identifying and controlling variables, making and testing hypotheses, formulating explanations, and drawing inferences (see Figure 4–1). The model splendidly integrates these several process skills into a single, meaningful unit of experience.

The format of the model promotes active, autonomous learning as the students formulate questions and test ideas. It takes courage to ask questions, but it is hoped that this type of risk will become second nature to the students. They will also become more proficient in verbal expression as well as in listening to others and remembering what has been said.

Although its emphasis is on process, inquiry training also results in the

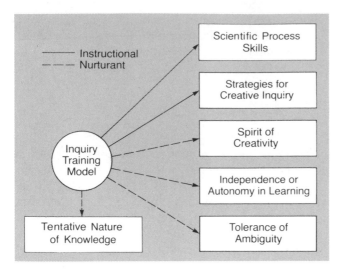

FIGURE 4-1   Instructional and nurturant effects: Inquiry Training Model.

learning of content in any curriculum area from which problems are selected. For example, Suchman developed entire curricula in economics and geology. In our opinion, it is adaptable to all elementary and secondary curriculum areas.

Summary Chart: Inquiry Training Model

SYNTAX

Phase One:
Confrontation with the Problem
Explain inquiry procedures.
Present discrepant event.

Phase Two:
Data Gathering—Verification
Verify the nature of objects and conditions.
Verify the occurrence of the problem situation.

Phase Three:
Data Gathering—Experimentation
Isolate relevant variables.
Hypothesize (and test) causal relationships.

Phase Four:
Organizing, Formulating an Explanation
Formulate rules or explanations.

Phase Five:
Analysis of the Inquiry Process
Analyze inquiry strategy and develop more effective ones.

SOCIAL SYSTEM

The Inquiry Training Model can be highly structured, with the teacher controlling the interaction and prescribing the inquiry procedures. However, the norms of inquiry are those of cooperation, intellectual freedom, and equality. Interaction among students should be encouraged. The intellectual environment is open to all relevant ideas, and teachers and students should participate as equals where ideas are concerned.

PRINCIPLES OF REACTION

1. Ensure that questions are phrased so they can be answered with yeses or nos, and that their substance does not require the teacher to do the inquiry.
2. Ask student to rephrase invalid questions.
3. Point out unvalidated points—for example, "We have not established that this is liquid."
4. Use the language of the inquiry process—for instance, identify student questions as theories and invite testing (experimenting).
5. Try to provide a free intellectual environment by not evaluating student theories.
6. Press students to make clearer statements of theories and provide support for their generalization.
7. Encourage interaction among students.

SUPPORT SYSTEM

The optimal support is a set of confronting materials, a teacher who understands the intellectual processes and strategies of inquiry, and resource materials bearing on the problem.

5

LEARNING FROM PRESENTATIONS
Advance Organizers

A guide, beginning a tour of an art museum with a group of high school students, says, "I want to give you an idea that will help you understand the paintings and sculpture we are about to see. The idea is simply that art, although it is a personal expression, reflects in many ways the culture and times in which it was produced. This may seem obvious to you at first when you look at the differences between Oriental and Western art. However, it is also true that, within each culture, as the culture changes, so the art will change—and that is why we can speak of *periods* of art. The changes are often reflected in the artists' techniques, subject matter, colors, and style. Major changes are often reflected in the forms of art that are produced." The guide then points out examples of one or two changes in these characteristics. She also asks the students to recall their elementary school days and the differences in their drawings when they were 5 and 6, and when they were older. She likens the different periods of growing up to different cultures.

In the tour that follows, as the students look at paintings and sculpture, the guide points out to them the differences that result from changing times. "Do you see here," she asks, "that in this painting the body of the person is almost completely covered by his robes, and there is no hint of a human inside his clothes? In medieval times, the church taught that the body was unimportant and that the soul was everything." Later she remarks, "You see in this painting how the muscularity of the man stands out through his clothing and how he stands firmly on the earth. This represents the Renaissance view that man was at the center of the universe and that his body, his mind, and his power were very important indeed."

The art teacher is using an *advance organizer*—in this case, a powerful concept used by art historians. This organizer contains many subordinate ideas that can be linked to the particular characteristics of the art objects being viewed. In this scenario, the teacher has thus provided students with what David Ausubel calls an "intellectual scaffolding" to structure the ideas and facts they encounter during their lesson.

David Ausubel is an unusual educational theorist. First, he directly addresses the goal of learning subject matter. Second, he advocates the improvement of *presentational* methods of teaching (lectures and reading) at a time when other educational theorists and social critics are challenging the validity of these methods and finding fault with the "passiveness" of expository learning. In contrast to those who advocate discovery methods of teaching, "open education," and experience-based learning, Ausubel stands unabashedly for the mastery of academic material.

Ausubel is also one of the few educational psychologists to address himself simultaneously to learning, teaching, and curriculum. His theory of meaningful verbal learning deals with three concerns: (1) how knowledge (curriculum content) is organized; (2) how the mind works to process new information (learning); and (3) how teachers can apply these ideas about curriculum and learning when they present new material to students (instruction).

Many of us have been frustrated by theorists who can explain how learning occurs but do not help us teach and organize curriculum. The theory of meaningful verbal learning and its derivative, the Advance Organizer Model of teaching, provide recommendations for selecting, organizing, *and* presenting new information.

ORIENTATION TO THE MODEL

GOALS AND ASSUMPTIONS

Ausubel's primary concern is to help teachers convey large amounts of information as meaningfully and efficiently as possible. He believes that the acquisition of information is a valid, indeed an essential, goal of schooling, and that certain theories can guide teachers in their job of transmitting bodies of knowledge to their students. His own ideas of how this learning takes place are embodied in his theory of meaningful verbal learning.

This theory applies to situations in which the teacher plays the role of lecturer or explainer. Its major purpose is to help students acquire subject matter. The teacher is responsible for presenting what is to be learned. The learner's primary role is to master ideas and information. Whereas inductive approaches lead the students to discover or rediscover concepts, the advance organizers provide concepts and principles to the students directly.

The Advance Organizer Model is designed to strengthen students' *cognitive structures,* a term Ausubel uses for a person's knowledge of a particular subject matter at any given time and how well organized, clear, and stable it is (Ausubel, 1963; p. 27). In other words, cognitive structure has to do with what kind of knowledge of a field is in our minds, how much of it there is, and how well it is organized.

Ausubel maintains that a person's existing cognitive structure is the foremost factor governing whether new material will be meaningful and how well it can be acquired and retained. Before we can present new material effectively, we must increase the stability and clarity of our students' prior knowledge. Strengthening students' cognitive structure in this way facilitates their acquisition and retention of new information and is one of the model's primary goals.

In recent years there has been much criticism of expository learning. Reception (or expository) learning has been accused of leading to rote memorization, fostering intellectual passivity rather than curiosity, and inherently lacking meaning for the student. Ausubel rejects the notion that expository teaching (or learning) is necessarily rote, passive, or nonmeaningful and has addressed these issues in his writings.

THE ROTE-LEARNING ISSUE *Meaningful learning* is intellectually linked to what we have learned previously. We must be able to transform this new knowledge and to apply it creatively in novel situations. *Rote learning,* in contrast, typically lacks conceptual and critical approaches to the information we acquire. It usually does not prepare us to transform this knowledge or to apply it in new contexts. Furthermore, material learned by rote is highly subject to forgetting. However, the precise learning of facts is absolutely essential for certain tasks. It is crucial to the medical student who must memorize the names and functions of the various parts of the body. Discrimination learning is also essential in learning the letters of the alphabet.

Ausubel points out the need for many types of learning designed to promote different educational objectives. Discovery-learning procedures, for example, are designed to achieve some objectives (learning how to discover) and not others (learning how to master material). Problems arise with many approaches not so much because they are inherently bad, but more because they are used for the wrong purposes (Ausubel 1968, pp. 83–84).

Any poorly executed teaching methods can lead to rote learning. Expository teaching is no exception. Well-done, it promotes complex rather than rote learning.

WHAT IS MEANINGFUL?   Ausubel disagrees with the belief that meaningful material cannot be "presented" but must come through independent problem-solving and manipulative experience. According to Ausubel, whether or not material is meaningful depends on the learner and on the material, not on the method of presentation. If the learner begins with the right "set," and if the material is potentially understandable, then meaningful learning can occur. The key to meaning involves solidly connecting the new learning material with existing ideas in the learner's cognitive structure. In other words, we must relate and reconcile what we know with what we are learning. A meaningful learning set implies that the learner must be ready to comprehend and relate what is being presented, rather than to memorize it verbatim.

IS RECEPTION LEARNING PASSIVE?   Finally, and not unrelated to the question of meaningfulness, is the assumption that the learner's role in reception learning is a passive one. On the contrary, during a lecture or other form of expository teaching, the listeners' or watchers' minds can be quite active. But they must relate the new material to existing knowledge, and judge how to catalog the new knowledge. Ausubel speaks about the learner's struggle with the material—looking at it from different angles, reconciling it with similar or perhaps contradictory information, and finally translating it into his or her own frame of reference and terminology. Each of these mental activities increases the meaning and internalization of new information. Learners who passively receive new material, not realizing that they must engage in these activities, learn relatively little. Ausubel assumes that for meaningful verbal learning to occur, the learner must play an active role, whether covert or overt. However, this does not happen automatically. The teaching model for reception learning must be designed to facilitate these active mental operations. Ausubel suggests specific procedures for promoting what he calls active reception learning, which are discussed in the section "The Model of Teaching."

ORGANIZING INFORMATION: THE STRUCTURE OF THE DISCIPLINE AND COGNITIVE STRUCTURE

According to Ausubel there is a parallel between the way subject matter is organized and the way people organize knowledge in their minds (their cognitive structure). He expresses the view that each of the academic disciplines has a structure of concepts (and/or propositions) that are organized hierarchically (Ausubel, 1963, p. 18). That is, at the top of each discipline are a number of very broad, abstract concepts that include the more concrete concepts at lower stages of organization. Figure 5-1 illustrates the hierarchical structure of the discipline of economics, with the more abstract concepts at the top of the pyramid of concepts.

Like Jerome Bruner, Ausubel believes that the structural concepts of each discipline can be identified and taught to students, which then become an information-processing system for them—that is, they become an intellectual map that students can use to analyze particular domains and to solve problems within those domains. For example, students can use economic concepts to analyze events from an economic point of view. Suppose we present filmed case studies depicting activities on a farm, in a grocery store, in a suburban household, and in a brokerage house. Each case contains many pieces of information; the students see people engaged in various activities, observe many behaviors, and listen to several conversations. If the students were then to make an economic analysis of these cases, they would catalog the behaviors and activities of the people in terms of such concepts as: supply and demand, wants and needs, goods and services, consumers and producers. These concepts help in several ways. They enable students to make sense of large amounts of data and to compare the four case studies, discovering the underlying commonalities in the apparent differences.

FIGURE 5-1   Structure of the discipline of economics. Based on Clinton Boutwell, *Getting It All Together* (San Rafael, Calif.: Leswing Press, 1972).

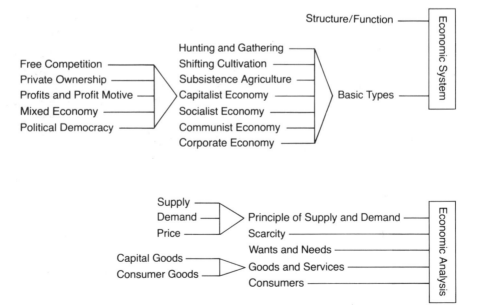

Ausubel describes the mind as an information-processing and information-storing system that can be compared to the conceptual structure of an academic discipline. Like the disciplines, the mind is a hierarchically organized set of ideas that provides anchors for information and ideas and that serves as a storehouse for them. Figure 5–2 shows the hierarchy of cognitive structure in the discipline of economics. The shaded concepts are the most inclusive: They have been "learned" and exist presently in a hypothetical learner's cognitive structure. The unshaded concepts are potentially meaningful because they can be *linked* to the existing concepts. The black circles are not yet potentially meaningful concepts because suitable anchors for them are not yet incorporated into the cognitive structure. As this information-processing system acquires new information and new ideas, it reorganizes itself to accommodate those ideas. Thus, the system is in a continuous state of change.

Ausubel maintains that new ideas can be usefully learned and retained only to the extent that they can be related to already available concepts or propositions that provide ideational anchors. If the new material conflicts too strongly with the existing cognitive structure *or* is so unrelated that no linkage is provided, the information or ideas may not be incorporated or retained. To

FIGURE 5-2 An individual's cognitive structure with respect to economics. Based on Clinton Boutwell, *Getting It All Together* (San Rafael, Calif.: Leswing Press, 1972, pp. 180–280).

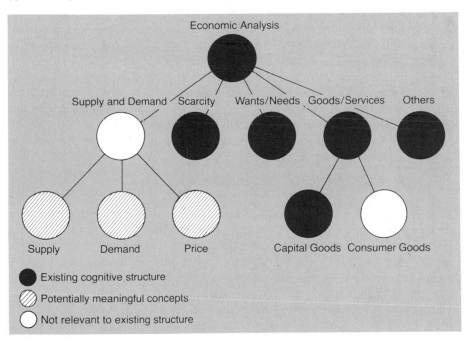

prevent this from occurring, the teacher must organize a sequence of knowledge and present it in such a way that the ideational anchors are provided. In addition, the learner must actively reflect on the new material, think through these linkages, reconcile differences or discrepancies with existing information, and note similarities.

IMPLICATIONS FOR CURRICULUM

Ausubel's ideas about subject matter and cognitive structure have important and direct implications for the organization of curriculum and for instructional procedures. He uses two principles, *progressive differentiation* and *integrative reconciliation,* to guide the organization of content in the subject fields in such a way that the concepts become a stable part of a student's cognitive structure and to describe the student's intellectual role.

Progressive differentiation means that the most general ideas of the discipline are presented first, followed by a gradual increase in detail and specificity. *Integrative reconciliation* simply means that new ideas should be consciously related to previously learned content. In other words, the sequence of the curriculum is organized so that each successive learning is carefully related to what has been presented before. If the entire learning material has been conceptualized and presented according to progressive differentiation, then integrative reconciliation follows naturally, though it requires the learner's active cooperation. Gradually, as a result of both principles, the discipline is built into the mind of the learner.

It must be remembered that both the discipline and the sequence of instruction are built from the top down, with the most inclusive concepts, principles, and propositions presented first. Ausubel points out that the organization of most textbooks puts each topic into a separate chapter or subchapter, all at the same level of abstraction and generality. "Thus, in most instances students are required to learn the details of new and unfamiliar disciplines before they have acquired an adequate body of relevant subsumers at an appropriate level of inclusiveness" (Ausubel, 1968, p. 153).

IMPLICATIONS FOR TEACHING

Advance organizers are the primary means of strengthening cognitive structure and enhancing retention of new information. Ausubel describes advance organizers as introductory material presented ahead of the learning task and at a higher level of abstraction and inclusiveness than the learning task itself. Its purpose is to explain, integrate, and interrelate the material in the learning task with previously learned material (and also to help the learner discriminate the new material from previously learned material) (Ausubel, 1968, p. 148). The most effective organizers are those that use concepts, terms, and propositions that are already familiar to the learner, as well as appropriate illustrations and analogies.

Suppose, for example, a teacher wants students to acquire information about current energy problems. The teacher provides learning material containing data about possible power sources, general information about United States economic growth and technology, and alternative policies on the energy crisis and future planning. The learning material is in the form of newspaper articles, a lecture, and perhaps a film. The learning task for the students is to internalize the information—that is, to remember the central ideas and perhaps the key facts. Before introducing students to the learning material, however, the teacher provides introductory material in the form of an advance organizer to help them relate to the new data.

In this example, the concept of energy might be used as the basis of the organizer, and related concepts such as energy efficiency and energy conservation can provide auxiliary organizers. Another potential set of organizers would be the concept of ecology and its various subsystems dealing with the environment, the economy, the political arena, social structures, and patterns of behavior. This second set of organizers would focus students' attention on the *impact* of old and new energy sources on the subsystems of our ecological system, whereas the first set would encourage them to process the data through a consideration of energy efficiency and energy conservation.

The organizer is important content in itself and needs to be taught. It may be a concept or a statement of relationship. In either case, time must be taken to explain and develop the organizer, because only when it is fully understood can it serve to organize the subsequent learning material. For example, students must fully understand the concept of *culture* before the teacher can use it effectively to organize factual information about different culture groups. Advance organizers are generally based on the major concepts, propositions, generalizations, principles, and laws of a discipline. For example, a lesson or text describing the caste system in India might be preceded by an organizer based on the concept of social stratification. Similarly, the generalization, "Technological changes can produce major changes in society and culture," could be the *basis* for an organizer preceding the study of several historical periods and places.

Usually, the organizer is tied closely to the material it precedes. However, the organizer can also be conceptually distant in order to provide a new perspective. For instance, the concept of balance or form, though generic to the arts, may be applied to literature, to mathematics, to the functioning of the branches of government, or even to our daily activities. A study of churches can be viewed under the rubric of many different organizers: those focusing on the economic implications of the church, cultural or sociological perspectives, or architectural perspectives. In other words, the significance of the learning material can vary with the organizers or perspectives applied to it.

There are two types of advance organizers—*expository* and *comparative*.

Expository organizers provide a basic model of class relationship as a general subsumer for a new class, subclass, and species before more limited subsumers (classes) are provided for the particular subclass or species. Thus, varying kinds of forest are first distinguished from one another before the component sub-forests and trees are differentiated. Before discussing specific types of mechanical energy, such as potential and kinetic, an instructor would build an expository organizer around the concept of mechanical energy, describing what it is and how it functions and providing several examples. Expository organizers are especially helpful because they provide ideational scaffolding for *unfamiliar* material.

Comparative organizers, on the other hand, are used most with relatively familiar material. They are designed to integrate new concepts with basically similar concepts existing in the cognitive structure; yet they are also designed to discriminate between the old and new concepts in order to prevent confusion caused by their similarity. For example, when the learner is being introduced to long division, a comparative organizer might be used to point out the similarities, and differences, between division facts and multiplication facts. Whereas in multiplication, the multiplier and multiplicand can be reversed without changing the product—that is, 3 times 4 can be changed to 4 times 3—the divisor and dividend cannot be reversed in division without affecting the quotient—that is, 6 divided by 2 is not the same as 2 divided by 6. The comparative organizer can help the learner see the relationship between multiplication and division, and therefore anchor the new material on division in the old material on multiplication.

Ausubel and others have conducted a variety of studies exploring the effectiveness of the meaningful learning theory, especially the use of advance organizers. The investigations by Ausubel, Ausubel and Fitzgerald, and Kuhn and Novak have supported the theory, whereas a series of investigations reported in the early 1970s produced mixed results (Ausubel, 1960, pp. 267–72. Ausubel and Fitzgerald, 1962, pp. 243–49. Ausubel, Stager, and Gaite, 1968, pp. 250–55. Barron, 1971. Clawson and Barnes, 1973, 11–15. Lucas, 1972).

In 1977 Joseph T. Lawton reported a very careful and complex investigation of whether the use of advance organizers would affect the learning of social studies materials and also facilitate logical thinking in 6- and 10-year-old children (see the Developmental Model for a more complete discussion of children's development and thinking) (Lawton, 1977, pp. 25–43). The investigation provides support for a theory of meaningful verbal learning, both with respect to learning and retention of material, and also with respect to its potential for influencing logical operations—that is, thinking in general. However, the effects are much stronger for the older children, especially with regard to transfer of thinking ability.

In general Lawton's study seems to support the notion that what is taught will be learned. If we present material to students, some of it will be learned. If it is presented with an organizing structure, somewhat more will be learned. If we use a process that helps students develop certain ways of thinking, then some of those ways of thinking will be learned. Thus, if we avoid using those models of teaching that provide certain intellectual structures and employ certain thinking processes, we decrease the chances of those structures and thinking processes being acquired. Generally speaking, the development of an *intellectual structure*—whether through presentational or inductive methods—increases the probability that students will learn those structures and the thinking processes associated with them, and that they will retain material more fully.

THE MODEL OF TEACHING

The model of teaching developed here is based on Ausubel's ideas about subject matter, cognitive structure, active reception learning, and advance organizers.

SYNTAX

The Advance Organizer Model has three phases of activity. Phase one is the presentation of the advance organizer, phase two is the presentation of the learning task or learning material, and phase three is the strengthening of cognitive organization. Phase three tests the relationship of the learning material to existing ideas to bring about an active learning process. A summary of the syntax appears in Table 5-1.

The activities are designed to increase the clarity and stability of the new learning material so that fewer ideas are lost, confused with one another, or left vague. The students should operate on the material as they receive it by relating the new learning material to personal experience and to their existing cognitive structure, and by taking a critical stance toward knowledge.

Phase one consists of three activities: clarifying the aims of the lesson, presenting the advance organizer, and prompting awareness of relevant knowledge.

Clarifying the aims of the lesson is one way to obtain students' attention and to orient them to their learning goals, both of which are necessary to facilitate meaningful learning. (Clarifying aims is also useful to the teacher in planning a lesson.)

As mentioned earlier, the organizer is not just a brief, simple statement; it is an idea in itself and, like the learning material, must be explored intellectually. It must also be distinguished from introductory comments, which are useful to the lesson but are not advance organizers. For instance, when we teach, many of us begin our instruction by asking students to recall what we

Table 5-1   Syntax of the Advance Organizer Model

PHASE ONE: PRESENTATION OF ADVANCE ORGANIZER	PHASE TWO: PRESENTATION OF LEARNING TASK OR MATERIAL

Clarify aims of the lesson.
Present organizer
    Identify defining attributes.
    Give examples.
    Provide context.
    Repeat.
Prompt awareness of learner's relevant knowledge
and experience.
	Present material.
	Maintain attention.
	Make organization explicit.
	Make logical order of learning
	material explicit.

PHASE THREE: STRENGTHENING COGNITIVE ORGANIZATION
Use principles of integrative reconciliation. Promote active reception learning. Elicit critical approach to subject matter. Clarify.

did last week or last year or by telling them what we are going to do tomorrow. In this way, we give them a context or orientation for our presentation. Or we may ask students to recall a personal experience and then acknowledge that what we are about to say resembles that situation or will help students understand a previous experience. We may also tell them the objectives of the session—what we hope they will get out of the presentation or discussion. *None of the just-described techniques are advance organizers.* However, all of them are part of a well-organized presentation, and some of them reflect principles that are central to Ausubel's theory of meaningful verbal learning and are part of the model of teaching.

The actual organizer, however, is built around the major concepts and/or propositions of a discipline or area of study. First, the organizer has to be constructed so that the learner can perceive it for what it is—an idea distinct from and more inclusive than the material in the learning task itself. The chief feature of an organizer is thus that it is at a higher level of abstraction and generality than the learning material itself. This higher level of abstraction is what distinguishes organizers from introductory overviews, which are written (or spoken) at the same level of abstraction as the learning material because they are, in fact, previews of the learning material.

Second, whether the organizer is expository or comparative, the essential features of the concept or proposition must be pointed out and carefully explained. (Definitional statements do not always point out the essential features of the term being defined.) Thus, the teacher and students must explore the organizer as well as the learning task. To us, this means citing the essential features, explaining them, and providing examples. The presentation of an organizer need not be lengthy, but it must be perceived (the learner must be aware of it), clearly understood, and continually related to the material it is organizing. This means the learner must already be familiar with the language and ideas in the organizer. It is also useful to illustrate the organizer in multiple contexts and to repeat it several times, particularly any new or special terminology.

Finally, to develop an integrative cognitive structure, it is especially important to prompt awareness of the learner's prior knowledge and experiences that might be relevant to this learning task and organizer.

Following the presentation of the advance organizer in phase one, phase two presents the learning material (learning task) in the form of lectures, discussions, films, experiments, or reading. Two procedures are important here. The first is to maintain students' attention (see memory learning, Chapter 6). Another task is to make the organization of the learning material explicit to the students so that they have an overall sense of direction. Related to this is the need to make the logical order of the material explicit throughout the presentation so that students can see how the ideas relate to each other.

The purpose of phase three is to anchor the new learning material in the student's existing cognitive structure—that is, to strengthen the student's cognitive organization. In the natural flow of teaching, some of these procedures may be incorporated into phase two; however, we want to emphasize that the reworking of new material is a separate teaching task with its own set of activities and skills. Ausubel identifies four activities: (1) promoting integrative reconciliation; (2) promoting active reception learning; (3) eliciting a critical approach to subject matter; and (4) clarification.

There are several ways to facilitate reconciliation of the new material with the existing cognitive structure. The teacher can: (1) remind students of the ideas (the larger picture); (2) ask for a summary of the major attributes of the new learning material; (3) repeat precise definitions; (4) ask for differences between aspects of the material; and (5) ask students to describe how the learning material supports the concept or proposition that is being used as a subsumer.

Active learning can be promoted by: (1) asking students to describe how the new material relates to a single aspect of their existing knowledge; (2) asking students for additional examples of the concept or propositions in the learning material; (3) asking students to verbalize the essence of the material, using their own terminology and frame of reference; (4) asking students to examine the material from alternative points of view; and (5) relating the material to contradictory material, experience, or knowledge.

A critical approach to knowledge is fostered by asking students to recognize assumptions or inferences that may have been made in the learning material, to judge and challenge these assumptions and inferences, and to reconcile contradictions among them.

Finally, students will probably have questions about parts of the learning material or task (the observation, film, or reading) that are unclear to them. The teacher can clarify by giving additional new information, rephrasing previously given information, or applying the ideas to a new problem or example.

It is not possible or desirable to use all these techniques in one lesson. Constraints of time, topic, and relevance to the particular learning situation will guide their use. However, it is important to keep in mind the four goals of this phase and specific techniques for effective expository teaching.

Ideally, the initiation of phase three is shared by teachers and students. At first, however, the teacher will have to respond to the students' need for clarification of some area of the topic and for integration of the new material with existing knowledge.

In addition to presenting the learning material, the teacher has several other functions to perform when using advance organizers. He or she must decide under what concept, proposition, or issue to catalog the new learning material and must, over the course of instruction, continually reorganize knowledge in relation to more inclusive concepts. In other words, the teacher designs the hierarchy of knowledge in a subject area and also makes decisions about definitions and meanings. Based on these definitions, the teacher must point out discrepancies, conflicts, and similarities between existing knowledge and new knowledge. Finally, the teacher must translate the new material into a frame of reference that has personal meaning for the student—that is, the material must reflect the student's experiential and intellectual background.

Essentially, Ausubel has provided us with a method for improving not only presentations, but also students' abilities to learn from them. The more we teach students to become active—to *look* for organizing ideas, reconcile information with them, and generate organizers of their own (engaging in inductive activity while reading or watching)—the greater their potential for profiting from presentations becomes.

SOCIAL SYSTEM

In this model the teacher retains control of the intellectual structure, as it is continually necessary to relate the learning material to the organizers and to help students differentiate new material from previously learned material. In phase three, however, the learning situation is ideally much more interactive, with students initiating many questions and comments. The successful acquisition of the material will depend on the learners' desire to integrate it with prior knowledge, on their critical faculties, and on the teacher's presentation and organization of the material.

PRINCIPLES OF REACTION

The teacher's solicited or unsolicited responses to the learners' reactions will be guided by the purpose of clarifying the meaning of the new learning material, differentiating it from and reconciling it with existing knowledge, making it personally relevant to the students, and helping to promote a critical approach to knowledge. Ideally, students will initiate their own questions in response to their own drives for meaning.

SUPPORT SYSTEM

Well-organized material is the critical support requirement of this model. The effectiveness of the advance organizer depends on an integral and appropriate relationship between the conceptual organizer and the content. This model provides guidelines for building (or reorganizing) instructional materials.

APPLICATION

INSTRUCTIONAL USES

The Advance Organizer Model is especially useful to structure extended curriculum sequences or courses and to instruct students systematically in the key ideas of a field. Step by step, major concepts and propositions are explained and integrated, so that at the end of a period of instruction, the learners should gain perspective on the entire area being studied.

We would expect an increase, too, in the learners' grasps of factual information linked to and explained by the key ideas. For example, the concept of socialization can be drawn on recurrently in the study of socialization patterns in different cultures and subcultures. This advance organizer thus aids in expanding students' knowledge about cultures.

The model can also be shaped to teach the *skills* of effective reception learning. Critical thinking and cognitive reorganization can be explained to the learners, who receive direct instruction in orderly thinking and in the notion of knowledge hierarchies. Ultimately, they can apply these techniques independently to new learning. In other words, this model can increase effectiveness in reading and watching films, and in other "reception" activities.

Whenever ideas or information needs to be presented, renewed, or clarified, the advance organizer is a useful model. For example, in phase two of the Simulation Model, the advance organizer can present a conceptual over-view of the processes being simulated (see Chapter 20). It can also be used after the simulation activities for review. Similarly, in the process of long-term inquiry training activities, the teacher might introduce new ideas using the Advance Organizer Model.

Other models are also useful for evaluating or applying the material presented by the advance organizer. For example, the Advance Organizer Model, after introducing new material in a deductive, presentational way, can be followed by inductive concept attainment activities that reinforce the material or that informally evaluate students' acquisition of the material.

Finally, the activities designed to strengthen cognitive organization can be spontaneously applied to the clarification of ideas in whatever instructional context they appear, as can the technique of an organizer.

DESIGNING LEARNING MATERIAL AND CURRICULUM

The Anthropology Curriculum Project developed at the University of Georgia was based on presentational methods of teaching and designed with the inclusion of advance organizers and other principles of meaningful verbal learning theory. For example, the learning material on an explanation of ac-culturation in Kenya was preceded by the following organizer:

> Acculturation takes place when the people of one culture acquire the traits of another culture as a result of contact over a long period of time. The British governed Kenya for about 80 years. During this period, the direction of cultural change was largely one way. (Clauson and Rice, 1972, p. 56)

The acculturation process and specific forms of acculturation taken on by the Kenyans are described in the learning material itself, which is reprinted here in part:

> African traits were replaced or modified by European traits. Almost all African traits have been influenced by European culture, especially in the cities. The people in the cities have been most affected by modernization in Kenya.
>
> In 1886, Kenya came under the control of the British. Kenya was ruled by the British for almost 80 years. British laws became the law of Kenya. English became the official language. The schools that were started were taught in English.
>
> Contact with the British brought many changes to African culture. This con-tact with the British is an example of innovations coming from outside the culture. Look at the Cultural Change Model in Chapter 2, Figure 5. This kind of innovation is called acculturation, because Africans and British came into direct contact. Acculturation is the change that takes place in a culture over a period of time as a result of contact between different cultures.
>
> In Kenya there were European settlers and British officials. Kenyans came into contact with Europeans in government work, in factories, and on the farms. Many new traits came to Kenya through acculturation.

Why have Africans wanted to change? If you can ride in a car to work, would you want to walk? If you can have a refrigerator, would you want to cool meat in a spring? If you can have a pair of shoes, would you want to always go barefooted? People everywhere want to live better. Living better is related to making and having more things. People all over the world want to have enough food to eat, enough clothes to wear, and more time to have fun. Africans are no different from other people. They want many of the same things other people want.

The direction of acculturation was largely one way; European traits replaced or changed African traits, but African traits had little impact on European traits. The new traits have helped in the modernization of Kenya. Modernization in Kenya has resulted in the replacement of African traits by European traits. Table 1 summarizes some of these changes. On the left of this table is the "Cultural Universal" column. A cultural universal is a trait that is found in all cultures. The second column shows the "African Trait," and the third column shows the "European Trait" that is replacing or changing the African Trait. Acculturation has been strongest in the urban areas. Here the three major forces, nationalism, urbanization, and industrialization, have affected more people for the longest length of time.

TRAIT CHANGES: A RESULT OF ACCULTURATION

Cultural Universal	African Trait	Replaced by or Changing to European Trait
Social organization	Tribe and smaller kin groups	National government
Family	Extended; man has more than one wife	Nuclear; man has only one wife
Children	Many	Fewer
Dress	Unfitted dress	Cut and fitted pants, shirts, coats, dresses
Housing	Round and square huts with thatched roofs; no water and electricity	Shantytowns and modern housing with water and electricity
Settlement	Small family groups; kinship, clan, village	Villages, towns, cities; pull of urbanization
Making a living	Subsistence agriculture and nomadic herding	Crops to export for foreign exchange
Cultivation of soil	Hoe, hand tools	Plows, pulled by animal or tractor
Work	For self or in exchange for work	Day laborers for wages
Power	Man and animal	Steam, diesel, gasoline, electricity (machine)
Manufacturing	Handcrafts and hand tools	Light and heavy industries with assembly lines
Material goods	Few material goods	Related to income; wealthier government workers and businessmen have many modern goods

Cultural Universal	African Trait	Replaced by or Changing to European Trait
Exchange system	Barter in weekly markets	Money and banks; importers and exporters
Language	Tribal language and Swahili	In government, business, schools, the national language is English; Swahili
Education	Learning the customs of the tribe	Primary, secondary, university education
Medicine	Magic, herbs	Doctors, nurses, hospitals
Population growth	Low: high infant death rates, short life expectancy	High: decreased infant death, longer life expectancy
Transportation	Safari, caravan, man, and animals	Railroads, roads, airplanes
Communication	Messenger, drums	Newspapers, radio, television, telephone, telegraph, post office
Cultural stability	Few innovations; highly stable culture	Many innovations; many cultural changes (Clauson and Rice, 1972, p. v)

The Anthropology Curriculum Project illustrates well the use of advance organizers in the design of curriculum or text material. As far as we know, the project is the only curriculum developed to make use of the strategy in the design of learning materials.

Although the organizers we have considered so far have been based on single concepts, generalizations, principles, and propositions also serve as organizers. A unit of study called *Life Cycle* from the Anthropology Curriculum Project at the University of Georgia is built around a set of propositions:

> Some of the major ideas of anthropology emphasized in the unit on the life cycle include: (1) life as a biological continuum that begins at birth and ends with death; (2) biological life cycle; (3) universals in the life cycle growing out of the limits imposed by adjusting to the universals in the life cycle; (4) childhood as a period of slow biological development which facilitates enculturation or the learning of basic culture traits; (5) achieving self-identity and personal responsibility during adolescence or the transition from childhood to adulthood; (6) work and family obligations as a continuing responsibility of adulthood; (7) decline in physical ability and shift in social position with advancing years or old age; and (8) how changes in the patterning of the total culture bring about changes in the life cycle. (Persing, Bailey, and Kleg, 1969, p. v)

The eight major ideas that form the life cycle are what we call *expository organizers*. Each organizer is presented to the learner prior to the study of four cultures: (1) middle-class United States; (2) Balkans; (3) Chinese; and (4) Tiv. For example, the first organizer (life as a biological continuum that begins at birth and ends with death) is presented to the learner with necessary clarifying information. The student is subsequently presented with specific information about how life begins and ends in the four subcultures. Each of the eight organizers listed in the quotation is presented in sequence for each of the four subcultures.

SELECTING AN ADVANCE ORGANIZER

In our experience the most difficult problem for teachers in applying this teaching strategy surrounds the formulation and selection of the advance organizer. One needs to become very familiar with the subject area and conceptualize the discipline as a series of hierarchically organized concepts or propositions. Most textbook series and teacher-training experiences do not facilitate the ability—we have to do it for ourselves!

In using the model it is also necessary to be aware that simple introductory comments do not function as organizers because they are usually not built around powerful concepts or propositions. We have found it helpful to view the presentation of the organizer as a separate phase of activity that includes certain characteristics. It is a distinct teaching episode apart from the usual introductions or transitions that take place in any teaching transaction.

INSTRUCTIONAL AND NURTURANT EFFECTS

The probable instructional values of this model seem quite clear, and Ausubel does not make any claims beyond them. However, an interest in inquiry and precise habits of thinking are likely effects (see Figure 5-3).

FIGURE 5-3 Instructional and nurturant effects: Advance Organizer Model.

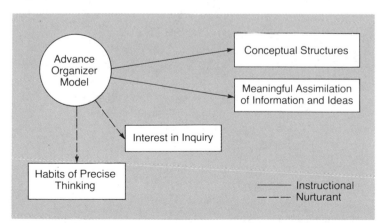

Summary Chart: Advance Organizer Model

SYNTAX

Phase One:
Presentation of Advance Organizer
Clarify aims of the lesson.
Present organizer:
   Identify defining attributes.
   Give examples.
   Provide context.
   Repeat.
Prompt awareness of learner's relevant knowledge and experience.

Phase Two:
Presentation of Learning Task or Material
Present material.
Maintain attention.
Make organization explicit.
Make logical order of learning material explicit.

Phase Three:
Strengthening Cognitive Organization
Use principles of integrative reconciliation.
Promote active reception learning.
Elicit critical approach to subject matter.
Clarify.

6

MEMORIZATION
Getting the Facts Straight

SCENARIO

Imagine a group of students who are presented with the task of learning the names of the presidents of the United States and the order in which they served. Previously the students have learned to count from 1 to 40 mnemonically. That is, each number is represented by a rhyming word that has an image attached to it. "One" is "bun," "two" is "shoe," and so on. Also, each set of number decades (1 to 10, 11 to 20) is connected to a location or setting. The decade 1 to 10 is represented by a spring garden scene, 10 to 20 by a summer beach scene, 21 to 30 by a fall football scene, and 31 to 40 by a winter snow scene.

Now, capitalizing on this system of number associations, the name and order of each president is presented to the students in terms of the scene, the mnemonic for the number, and a word, called a *link-word,* associated with the president's name. Thus Lincoln (link), number sixteen (sticks), is presented with an illustration of a sand castle on a beach encircled by a set of sticks which are linked together. Similar illustrations are used for the other presidents. The students study the pictures and the words. They are given a test right after they study and again sixty days later.

How effective was this experience? Did the students learn more than other students who tried to memorize the names and their order using the usual procedures for the same length of time? The answer is "yes." In this and other studies, students are being taught unfamiliar material much more quickly than usual through the application of various mnemonic devices (Pressley, Levin, and Delaney, 1982, p. 83).

The humble task of memorizing is with us throughout our lives. From the moment of birth a world of new artifacts and events is presented to us and has to be sorted out. Moreover, many of the elements of our world have been named by those who have come before us. We have to learn large quantities of words and we have to learn to connect them to the objects, events, actions, and qualities that they represent. In other words, we have to learn a meaningful language.

In any new area of study, a major task is learning the important words and definitions—the languages, if you will—that pertain to the area. To deal with chemistry we have to learn the names of the elements and their structural properties. To study a continent we have to learn the names of its countries, its major geographical features, the important events in its human history, and so on. Initial foreign language learning involves developing a vocabulary of words that look and sound unfamiliar.

The study of memory has a long history. Although "the goal of a unified coherent and generally satisfying theory of human memory" (Estes, 1976, p. 11) has not yet been achieved, progress has been made. A number of instructional principles are being developed whose goals are both to teach memorization strategies and to help students study more effectively.

For instance, the material on which a particular teacher chooses to focus will affect what information the students retain. "Many items are presented to an individual in a short time and only those to which attention is directed enter into memory, and only those receiving rehearsal are maintained long enough to secure the processing necessary to establish a basis for long-term recall" (Estes, 1976, p. 7). In other words, if we do not pay attention to something, we are not likely to remember it. Second, we need to attend to it in such a way that we are rehearsing later recall of it. For example, as we wander through a forest, if we do not look carefully at the tree trunks, we are unlikely to remember them, although some visual images may be retained in a haphazard fashion. Second, even if we notice them, we need to use the information, for example by comparing different trees, in order to remember it. When we rehearse we develop *retrieval cues,* which are the basis for sorting through our memories at later times and locating information.

Short-term memories are often associated with *sensory* experiences of various kinds. When we are exposed to the wine called *Chablis,* we may remember it as straw-colored and tasting a certain way. For long-term recall we may associate things according to *episodic* cues—that is, those having to do with the sequences of experience to which we have been exposed. We may remember Andrew Johnson, for example, as the president who followed Abraham Lincoln. They are connected in time and their episodes in history are connected to one another. *Categorical* cues, on the other hand, involve conceptualizations of the material. When we compare tree trunks, for example, we form concepts that provide a basis for describing the individual trunks in relation to one another. In other words, we replace specific items with categories, and this categorization provides us with the basis for memory.

Both scholarly and popular sources agree that the ability to remember is fundamental to intellectual effectiveness. Far from being a passive, trivial activity, memorizing and remembering are active pursuits. The capacity to take in information, to integrate it meaningfully, and later to retrieve it at will is the product of successful memory learning. Most important, individuals can improve this capacity to memorize material so that they can recall it later. That is the objective of this model.

ORIENTATION TO THE MODEL

GOALS AND ASSUMPTIONS

Our recollections of our early years in school usually include an image of struggles to master lists of unstructured material such as new words, new sounds, the days of the week, the fifty states, and the nations of the world. Some of us became effective at memorizing. Some did not. As we look back, it is easy to dismiss much of this information as trivial. However, imagine for a moment what our world would be like without the information we acquired in those years of school. We *need* information.

One of the most effective forms of personal power comes from competence based on knowledge; it is essential to success and a sense of well-being. Throughout our lives, we need to be able to memorize skillfully. To improve this ability increases learning power, saves time, and leads to a better storehouse of information.

THE LINK-WORD METHOD

Over the last ten years an important line of research has been conducted on what is termed the link-word method. The result is a considerable advance in knowledge about memorization as well as the development of a system that has practical implications for the design of instructional materials, for classroom teaching and tutoring, and for students.

The method has two components, assuming that the learning task is to master unfamiliar material. The first component provides the students with familiar material to link with the unfamiliar items. The second provides an association to establish the meaning of the new material. For example, when the task involves new foreign-language words, one link ties the sounds to those of words in English. The second ties the new word to a representation of its meaning. For example, the Spanish word carta (postal letter) might be linked to the English word "cart" and a picture showing a letter inside a shopping cart (Pressley, Levin, and Delaney, 1982, p. 62).

An important finding from the research is that people who master material more quickly and who retain it longer generally use more elaborate strategies for memorizing material. They use mnemonics—assists to memorization. The less effective memorizers generally use "rote" procedures. They "say" what is to be memorized over and over again until they believe it is implanted in their memories.

A second important finding is that devices like the *"link-word"* method are even more elaborate than the methods used by the better "natural" memorizers—that is, they require more mental activity than do the rote procedures. When first confronted by the presidential illustrations discussed earlier, many teachers respond, "But why add all that extra stuff? Isn't it hard enough to master the names of the presidents and their order? Why add words like "link" and "stick" and pictures of sand castles on a summer beach?"

The answer is that the additional associations provide a richer mental context and the linking process increases the cognitive activity. The combination of activity and associations provides better "anchors" within our information-processing systems.

Does the key-word method help students who are ordinarily good, poor, and average memorizers? Apparently so (Pressley and Dennis-Rounds, 1980). Further, it appears to help students who are below average in verbal ability, who might have been expected to have greater difficulty with complex learning strategies. In addition, as students use the method they seem to transfer it to other learning tasks. In other words, mnemonics can be taught so that students can use them independently of the teacher. The students, in other words, can develop systems for making up their own links.

Finally, even young (kindergarten and first grade) students can profit from mnemonics (Pressley et al., 1981). Obviously, they have greater difficulty generating their own links, but they can benefit when links are provided to them.

The "effect sizes" from this research is impressive. Even in Atkinson's (1985) early studies the link-word method was about 50 percent more effective than conventional rote methods. In some of the later studies it has been twice as efficient or more (Pressley, 1977; Pressley, Miller, and Levin, 1981).

As we stated earlier, there are two obvious uses of this research in teaching. The first is to arrange instruction so as to make it as easy as possible for students to make associations and to discourage isolated rote drill. The second is to teach students to make their own links when they are studying new material.

Some of the other models can help us here. Concept attainment provides categories that associate examplars on the basis of attributes and induce students to make contrasts with the nonexemplars. Inductive teaching causes students to build associations on the basis of common characteristics. Advance organizers provide an "intellectual scaffolding that ties material together and comparative organizers link the new with the old. The scientific inquiry methods provide an experiential base for terms and an intellectual structure to "glue" material together.

For the teacher, the major labor for this method is in its preparation. Generating the links, and in some cases creating visual materials or working with students to create them, are the chief activities involved. Once the presentations have been prepared, the delivery is rather straightforward.

OTHER MEMORY SYSTEMS

A number of popular "memory systems" have been developed, none of them backed by the research that Pressley, Levin, and their associates have generated. However, some of these systems use sensible principles that are congruent with that research. Lorayne and Lucas's *The Memory Book* (1974) is one such, and we have drawn on it for some suggestions of procedures to use with children.

We repeat first the important maxim that before we can remember something we must first attend to it. An effective memory model must induce attention to what is to be learned. Because entities we can see, feel, touch, smell, or taste generate powerful associations for remembering, we remember best those ideas that are represented to several of our sensory channels. Each channel contains old material we can associate with the new. If we "see" a flower, for example, as a visual image, something that feels a certain way, has a distinctive smell, and makes a crunchy noise when its stem is cut, we are linked to it through several types of perception. The likelihood of remembering it (or its name) is greater than if we observe it through one sense only. Lorayne and Lucas quote Aristotle:

> It is the image-making part of the mind which makes the work of the higher processes of thought possible. Hence the mind never thinks without a mental picture. The thinking faculty thinks of its form in pictures. (Lorayne and Lucas, 1974, p. 22)

Lorayne and Lucas build their model to increase: (1) *attention* to what is to be learned; (2) the *senses* involved in attending; and (3) the *associations* we make between the new material and things that have previously been learned. A sense of how this is done can be seen in the following vignette:

Boris, who is running for student body president of the elementary school, has prepared a speech to deliver before his schoolmates. But he is having difficulty remembering his speech, so he appeals to his teacher for help and support. The teacher encourages him to use the memory strategies they have applied to other seemingly more simple learning tasks: learning new words and the names of African and Spanish American countries. Informally, she guides him through the stages of the model much the same way Lorayne and Lucas do with their clients.

First the teacher has Boris identify (attend to) the main thoughts of his speech. He carefully numbers each different and main idea. Next she has him identify one word from each main idea that reminds him of the entire thought. One by one Boris isolates ideas and underlines a *key word* (one that can stand for the point to be made).

Next the teacher has Boris identify familiar words that have vivid meanings for him and connect those words with the key words. He picks his sister Kate for the term *qualifications* and *pear* for peer. To help him remember those two ideas she asks him to imagine them in any silly way he can. Boris thinks for a minute and then relays the picture of a gigantic pear chasing his sister Kate. He is on his way to remembering! With each pair of key words and substitute words, Boris imagines some outrageous event combining the two.

After he has gone through all of the key thoughts and generated appropriate images, the teacher has Boris repeat words and describe the images several times. Then she asks him to test his memory by giving the whole speech. He is able to go through it comfortably. He has *attended* to his major points, *visualized* the key words and substitutes, and *associated* the key points with vivid sensory images.

If Boris had been learning a new vocabulary or important science concepts the teacher would have asked him to relate the new material to other *related* material he had learned previously, and she would have suggested that he put the new material to use immediately. This active repetition in a natural setting would assist Boris in retaining the material over the long term. However, Boris's speech is a one-time activity requiring only short-term retention, so it is necessary only to review the associations and test his memory by giving the speech several times.

CONCEPTS ABOUT MEMORY

These six concepts are essentially principles and techniques for enhancing our memory of learning material.

AWARENESS   Before we can remember anything we must give attention to, or concentrate on, the thing or idea to be remembered. "Observation is essential to original awareness" (Lorayne and Lucas, 1974, p. 6). According to Lorayne and Lucas, anything of which we are originally aware cannot be forgotten.

ASSOCIATION   The basic memory rule is, "You Can Remember Any New Piece of Information if It is Associated to Something You Already Know or Remember" (Lorayne and Lucas, 1974, p. 7). Lorayne and Lucas give two examples of the Basic Memory Rule that most of us will probably recognize. The lines of the music staff, EGBDF, are often taught by asking students to remember the sentence, "Every good boy does fine." To help students remember the spelling of *piece*, teachers will give the cue a *piece* of *pie*.

The major limitation of these devices is that they apply only to one specific thing. We can't use the phrase *a piece of pie* for more than the spelling of *piece*. In addition, we usually need to remember a number of ideas. To be broadly applicable a memory system should apply more than once and should link several thoughts or items.

LINK SYSTEM   The heart of the memory procedure is connecting two ideas, with the second idea triggering yet another one, and so on. Suppose, for example, you want to remember the following five words: *house, glove, chair, stove, tree.* You should imagine an unusual picture, first with a house and a glove, then with a glove and a tree. For example, in the first picture you might imagine a glove opening the front door of a house greeting a family of gloves. The second picture might be a tree with gloves hanging like fruit. Taking the time to concentrate making up these images and then to visualize them will force original awareness.

Most memory problems break down into entities of two: We often want to associate names and dates or places, names and ideas, words and their meaning, or a fact that establishes a relationship between two ideas.

RIDICULOUS ASSOCIATION   Even though it is true that association is the basis of memory, the strength of the association is enhanced if the image is vivid and ridiculous, impossible, or illogical. A tree laden with gloves and a family of gloves are examples of ridiculous association.

There are several ways to make an association ridiculous. The first is to apply the rule of substitution. If you have a car and a glove, picture the glove riding along instead of the car. Second, you can apply the out-of-proportion rule—make small things gigantic or large things miniature—for example, a gigantic baseball glove driving along. The third means is the rule of exaggeration, especially by number. Picture millions of gloves parading down the street. Finally, get action into the association. In the examples discussed earlier, the glove is *ringing* the doorbell and *parading* down the street.

Imagining ridiculous associations is not at all difficult for us when we are young children, but making these images gets harder for us as we get older and more logical.

The basic memory rule now needs to be revised slightly to incorporate the role of the absurd. It should read:

In Order to Remember Any New Piece of Information, It Must Be Associated to Something You Already Know or Remember in *Some Ridiculous Way.* (Lorayne and Lucas, 1974, p. 9)

SUBSTITUTE-WORD SYSTEM   The substitute-word system is a way of making "an intangible, tangible and meaningful" (Lorayne and Lucas, 1974, p. 21). It is quite simple. Merely take any word or phrase that seems abstract and "think of something . . . that sounds like, or reminds you of, the abstract material and can be pictured in your mind" (Lorayne and Lucas, 1974, p. 22). Remember when you used to say "I'll ask her" in order to remember the state of Alaska. If you want to remember the name *Darwin* you might visualize a dark wind. The concept of force can be represented by a fork. The pictures you construct represent words, thoughts, or phrases.

KEY WORD   The essence of the key-word system is to selecct one word to represent a longer thought or several subordinate thoughts. Boris's speech is an example of one word's being used to trigger many verbal statements. Boris chose key word qualifications to represent a list of his superior qualities. If, as in his case, the key word is abstract, is it necessary to use the substitute-word system before inventing a memorable image.

The key-word system is most useful for lengthy phrases as in a speech or text material. Together with the substitute-word system and the link system, this system is all you need for remembering any material, however lengthy, abstract, or complex.

THE MODEL OF TEACHING

The model of teaching that we have developed from Lorayne and Lucas's work includes four phases: attending to the material; developing connections; expanding sensory images; and practicing recall. These phases are based on the principle of attention and the techniques for enhancing recall (see Table 6–1).

SYNTAX

Phase one calls for activities that require the learner to concentrate on the learning material and organize it in a way that helps that learner remember it. Generally this includes focusing on what needs to be remembered—the major ideas and examples. Underlining is one way to do this. Listing the ideas separately and rephrasing them in one's own words is another task that forces attention. Finally, reflecting on the material, comparing ideas, determining the relationship among the ideas is a third attending activity.

Once the material to be learned has been clarified and evaluated, several

Table 6-1   Syntax of Memory Model

PHASE ONE: ATTENDING TO THE MATERIAL	PHASE TWO: DEVELOPING CONNECTIONS
Use techniques of underlining, listing, reflecting.	Make material familiar and develop connections using key-word, substitute-word, and link-word system techniques.

PHASE THREE: EXPANDING SENSORY IMAGES	PHASE FOUR: PRACTICING RECALL
Use techniques of ridiculous association and exaggeration. Revise images.	Practice recalling the material until it is completely learned.

memory techniques should be used to develop connections with what is to be learned. Phase two includes using such techniques as the link words, substitute words (in the case of abstractions), and key words for long or complex passages. The notion is to connect the new material to familiar words, pictures, or ideas, and to link images or words together.

Once the initial associations have been identified, the images can be enhanced (phase three) by asking the student to associate with more than one sense and by generating humorous dramatizations through ridiculous association and exaggeration. At this time the images can be revised for greater recall power.

In phase four the student is asked to practice recall of the material.

SOCIAL SYSTEM

The social system is cooperative; the students and teacher work as a team to shape the new material for commitment to memory.

PRINCIPLES OF REACTION

The teacher's role in this model is to help the student work the material. Working from the student's frame of reference, the teacher assists him or her to identify key items, pairs, and images.

SUPPORT SYSTEM

Pictures, concrete aids, films, and other audiovisual materials are especially useful for increasing the sensory richness of the associations. However, no special support system is required for this model.

APPLICATION

The Memory Model is applicable to all curriculum areas where material needs to be memorized. It can be used with groups (a chemistry class mastering the table of elements) or individuals (a student learning a poem, story, speech, or part in a play).

Although it has many uses in teacher-led "memory sessions," it has its widest application after students have mastered it and can use it independently. Thus, the model should be taught so that dependence on the teacher is decreased and students can use the procedures whenever they need to memorize.

INSTRUCTIONAL AND NURTURANT EFFECTS

The Memory Model is specifically designed to increase the capacity to store and retrieve information. It should nurture a sense of intellectual power—a growing consciousness of the ability to master unfamiliar material, as well as imagery skills and attention to one's environment (See Figure 6–1).

One of the most important outcomes of the model is the students' recognition that learning is not a mysterious, innate process over which they have no control. As Ian Hunter (1964) points out:

> The mastery of some simple mnemonic system may lead some people to realize, for the first time, that they can control and modify their own mental activities.

FIGURE 6-1   Instructional and nurturant effects: Memory Model.

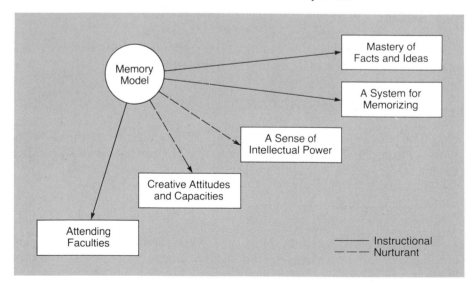

And this realization may encourage them to undertake that self-critical experimentation with their own learning and remembering procedures which is such an important part of intellectual development. (p. 302)

Thus, awareness of how to learn and how to improve learning results in a sense of mastery and control over one's future.

A second outcome is the improvement of imaging capacity and the realization that creative forms of thinking are an essential part of more convergent, information-oriented learning. In training for imagery, creativity is nourished, and ease with playful, creative thought is encouraged.

Imaging requires that we observe and attend to the world around us. Consequently, the use of imaging as part of memory work disciplines us to attend to our surroundings automatically.

Finally, of course, our capacity for remembering particular material is strengthened by this model—we become more effective memorizers.

Summary Chart: Memory Model

SYNTAX

Phase One:
Attending to the Material
Use techniques of underlining, listing, reflecting.

Phase Two:
Developing Connections
Make material familiar and develop connections using key-word, substitute-word, and link-word system techniques.

Phase Three:
Expanding Sensory Images
Use techniques of ridiculous association and exaggeration.
Revise images.

Phase Four:
Practicing Recall
Practice recalling the material until it is completely learned.

SOCIAL SYSTEM

The social system is cooperative. Teacher and students become a team working the new material together. The initiative should increasingly become the students' as they obtain control over the strategy and use it to memorize ideas, words, and formulas.

PRINCIPLES OF REACTION

The teacher helps the student identify key items, pairs, and images, offering suggestions but working from the students' frames of reference. The familiar elements must be primarily from the students' storehouse of material.

SUPPORT SYSTEM

All of the customary devices of the curriculum areas can be brought into play. Pictures, concrete aids, films, and other audiovisual materials are especially useful for increasing the sensory richness of the associations.

7

THE DEVELOPING INTELLECT
Models from Cognitive Psychology

SCENARIO

A high school in Seattle, Washington, has arranged a mini-course to help junior students identify the higher education options available and learn how to apply to junior colleges, business schools, colleges, and universities.

The mini-course has included discussions with college admissions officers, and the reading of *Barron's Guide to Colleges.* In addition, representatives of local business and trade schools have spoken to the group.

In the course of their exploration, the students have discovered that some colleges give preferential treatment to minority persons to increase the racial and ethnic balances at their schools. One of the students, however, has brought in a newspaper clipping about deliberations in the Bakke case in which an applicant to law school has challenged whether a school has the right to admit students who belong to racial and ethnic minorities while denying admission to Caucasian students whose credentials may exceed those of the admitted students.

This precipitates a discussion about the problems entailed in differential admissions policies. Some students feel that the issue should be decided strictly on the basis of achievement in high school and test scores.

"That's the only way," says one. "Anything else is unfair. What the heck are we working for anyway?"

Some students feel that the only way to bring about a better balance in the professions is to have admissions quotas. Others feel that the problem is one of economic opportunity and that there would be plenty of qualified minority students if there were enough scholarships to go around.

Mr. Jones, the guidance counselor, concludes that although many students are arguing from a "right-and-wrong" orientation, a few students seem to have the attitude that if the system works for them they are not going to worry about the issues involved. Some students feel that prior achievement ought to be enough for admission regardless of the social consequences, while others feel that equality must be achieved regardless of the feelings of individuals who believe they are victims of "reverse discrimination."

Since he has responsibility for a weekly seminar on general issues of adjustment and personal development, Mr. Jones decides to use this opportunity to help students develop a more complex view of the moral issues involved. He comments, "I'd like to see if each of you can think this problem out in terms of principles you're willing to live with for a long time to come. Let's suppose that you are responsible for the admission of students to colleges. As a group, let's decide on the issues. Then each of you, as an admissions officer, will prepare an argument about the issues—you will decide where you stand on the issues *and* you will develop admissions principles with which you think you can live."

Mr. Jones has used the framework developed by Lawrence Kohlberg to analyze the stages of students' moral development. He is applying the model to help students rise toward the next, more complex, level of development.

One of the most important areas of psychology is devoted to the study of how humans learn to think. It focuses on the question of development—that is, on what kinds of thinking characterize us as infants and on what changes occur as we mature. Especially important for teachers is the study of how we can influence the development of thinking and how we can match instruction to the developmental levels of our students.

In this chapter we concentrate on the work of Swiss psychologist Jean Piaget (Piaget, 1952) who published his first studies in the mid-1920s and whose active work spanned fifty years. Recently Piaget's philosophy of development has gained increasing popularity with educators. Currently, the most widespread applications of Piaget are in the areas of curriculum for young children and in the organization of the educational environment for students of all ages. Two strategies are used to apply developmental psychology to teaching. One strategy matches the curriculum to the student's level of development, which necessarily involves accurately assessing the student's stage of growth. Another calls for instruction that accelerates intellectual development, making it occur more rapidly than if teaching did not take place. The model of teaching presented here adjusts instruction to the learner's stage of development.

In our discussion about Piaget we draw heavily on the work of those who have summarized Piaget's theory and have explained its application, especially Flavell (1963), Hunt (1961), Furth (1969), Sigel and Hooper (1968), and Wadsworth (1978).

ORIENTATION TO THE MODEL

THEORY OF DEVELOPMENT: INTELLECTUAL STAGES

Piaget believes that human beings develop increasingly more complex levels of thinking in definite stages. Each stage is characterized by the possession of certain concepts or intellectual structures, which he refers to as *schemas*. Schemas organize the world in some way (the early schemas, for example, are very egocentric and place the student at the center of the universe); schemas are programs or strategies that the individual uses as he or she interacts with the environment.

In the course of life, students acquire experience. They assimilate this experience into their present patterns of behavior. After awhile, however, their present patterns become inadequate to explain their new experiences, and then they develop new schemas by accommodating to the new information. The process of *assimilation* is the incorporation of new experience. *Accommodation* is changing one's structure to fit the new experiences that occur.

The schemas mediate between the child and his or her environment. Hans G. Furth uses the example of a baby who has acquired the ability to grasp objects. The baby moves about the environment relating to many things by grasping them—that is, by simply reaching out a hand and closing it over them. Thus, much experience that the baby receives during a cetain period is in terms of grasping behavior, which is his or her schema, or strategy, for relating to his or her surroundings. The child's intellectual capacities grow through the development of more complex schemas for assimilating the environment. The major mechanism by which this occurs is accommodation.

Experience slowly supplies the child with information that cannot be handled adequately through the existing structures; the schemas gradually accommodate, and new ones develop. For example, children shopping with their mothers in the supermarket gradually learn that there is an order to the aisles in which the goods are stacked. Encountering this order again and again, and learning that certain objects are always in the same places are likely, together with other experiences, to result in an understanding of order. Prior to acquiring such an appreciation, the child sees any collection of objects as unordered. After that he or she is able to perceive their order. He or she is now intellectually able to assimilate new information, such as that baseball players run to first base first, whereas before that he or she did not have the schema to assimilate that information.

At each stage of development the human organism is, for a while, in a state of equilibrium—that is, the experiences that are assimilated are compatible with the schemas in operation. After a certain period the child has assimilated new experiences that cannot be handled by the existing schema, and this sets up an imbalance between the data being assimilated from the environment and the existing cognitive structure. When this point is reached a cognitive reorganization is necessary. In a sense, pressure has built up, and intellectual movement must take place: a new shape of development is entered.

Piaget's stance is that the development of the schemas or structures occurs in the same order in all of us and furthermore at a relatively predetermined rate—a rate governed by our physiological maturation. Until the requisite neurological structures are developed, these schemas cannot appear.

Piaget thus classifies intellectual development in terms of stages that are characterized by the way the schemas permit the organism to relate to the world. At any given stage one is able to perform certain kinds of thinking and not others. The earlier stages, however, lay the basis for future development. The stages are:

1. Sensorimotor stage (0 to 2 years);
2. Preoperational stage (2 to 7 years):
   a. Preconceptual thought (2 to 4 years);
   b. Intuitive thought (4 to 7 years);
3. Operational stage (7 to 16 years):
   a. Concrete operational thought (7 to 11 years);
   b. Formal operational thought (11 to 16 years).

According to Edmund Sullivan:

Sensorimotor thought (birth to about 2 years) refers to those behaviors which are preverbal and are not mediated by signs or symbols. At birth the child mediates with the world with inborn reflex schemas and has no conception of object permanence. During this period the child is concerned with objects as objects. Thus, when a toy is hidden from his view, he shows no searching movements, since he has no internal representation of the objective world (i.e., object schemas) when not perceiving it. Gradually object permanence develops through repeated experiences with the world. As the child constructs object permanence through experience, primitive concepts of space, time, causality, and intentionality, which were not present at birth, develop and are incorporated into present patterns of behavior.

The second of Piaget's stages is preoperational thought (about age 2 to 7 years). This stage is further divided into two substages: preconceptual thought (transductive), which extends from age 2 to about 4, and intuitive thought, which extends from about age 4 to 7.

(a) The substage of preconceptual thought marks the beginning of what Piaget (1960) calls conceptual intelligence. In contrast to sensorimotor intelligence, adaptations are now beginning to be mediated by signs and symbols, particularly words and images. During this period, the child develops what Piaget calls the "symbolic function," or imagery. The main concern during this period will be with such activities as imitation, play, and the preconcepts shown in language behavior.

(b) The substage of intuitive thought appears at approximately age 4 and marks the halfway house between preconceptual thought and the more advanced stage of concrete operations. The thought exemplified in this stage is illustrated in the following problem. The child is presented with two small glasses, A1 and A2, which are identically the same in height and width dimensions. The child places one bead in each glass alternatively until both are filled. Glass A2 is emptied into a taller but thinner glass B. The child in the preconceptual stage thinks that the amount of beads has changed in the process, even though he says no beads were removed or added. The child says that there are more beads in B, since it is taller than A, or that there are more beads in A1, since it is wider than B. The child is centered on one aspect of the situation, "height" or "width." Because the child cannot hold the centerings simultaneously, he is unable to solve the conservation problem. The child in the intuitive stage still remains prelogical, but decenterings occur where previous centerings led to absurd conclusions. Thus the child who estimated that there are more beads in the taller glass because the level has been raised centers his attention on height and ignores width. If the experimenter continues to empty the beads into the thinner and taller glass, there will be a time when the child replies that there are fewer beads in the taller glass, since it is too narrow.

The stage of operational thought marks the advent of rational activity in the child. Up to this time the child demonstrates a logic (transductive) which is quite different from that of the adult members of his species (i.e., inductive and deductive).

(a) Concrete operational thought. The first substage of operational thought is labelled "concrete operations." Piaget (1960) defines an operation as an internalized action which can return to its starting point, and which can be integrated with other actions also possessing this feature of reversibility. Operations are "mental acts" which were formerly actions with reversible properties. Piaget calls the operational structures between the ages of 7 and 11 years "concrete" because their starting point is always some real system of objects and relations that the child perceives; that is, the operations are carried out on concrete objects. The emergence of concrete operations is often a sudden phenomenon in development. Piaget (1960) attributes their emergence to a sudden thawing of intuitive structures which were up to now more rigid, despite their progressive articulation.

(b) Formal operational thought. The substage of formal operations (11 to 16 years) marks the emergence of *vertical decalages,* that is, the ability to make vertical separations by solving problems at a level which transcends concrete experience (the area of *horizontal decalages*). Formal thinking marks the completion of the child's emancipation from reliance on direct perception and action. In contrast to the concrete action-oriented thought of the child, the adolescent thinker goes beyond the present and forms theories about everything. This thought is considered "reflective" since the adolescent reasons on the basis of purely formal assumptions. He can consider hypothesis as either true or false and work out inferences which would follow if the hypotheses were true. (Sullivan, 1967, pp. 4-9)

To summarize the major points covered so far: (1) Intelligence is defined as operations for transforming data from the environment. These operations change with age and are described as logical structures (or schemas) for processing information. (2) Development is associated with passage from one stage of operation to another. (3) Development is a function of experience and maturation.

PRINCIPLES OF LEARNING AND TEACHING

Whereas Piaget has concentrated his work on describing the stages of intelligence, American educators have been interested in the factors that might affect development. Barry Wadsworth has provided a summary of their ideas on teaching and learning, which we review here.

The first notion is that *teaching is the creation of environments* in which students' cognitive structures can emerge and change. The goal is to provide learning experiences that give the student practice with particular operations. Piaget believes that cognitive structures will grow only when students initiate their own learning experiences; learning must be *spontaneous*. The assumption is that students will initiate learning experiences that optimally match their cognitive structures, provided the opportunity exists in the environment, because students intuitively know what activities they need. Piaget believes that if we teach too far above the students, learning is not possible. Each person must construct his or her own knowledge, which cannot be absorbed ready-made from adults. He feels that we may alter students' verbal responses and behaviors as a result of direct teaching and reinforcement, but he does not consider verbal fluency to be "real knowledge" that can occur only as a result of development—that is, when the task is useful to the student and when he or she is psychologically ready.

The student's role in the learning experience must be an active, self-discovering one, and the experiences themselves must be inductive. In learning new operations children must be given extensive opportunity to manipulate the environment. For young children the materials we use should be concrete instead of symbolic representations (for example, blocks or bottle caps instead of numbers). The environment should be rich in sensory experiences. Piaget sees important symbolic meaning in the manipulation, play, and aesthetic behaviors of children, activities that have much to tell us about children's intellectual development. The teacher's function is to arrange for learning experiences that facilitate stage-relevant thinking, and to organize instruction so that students can initiate the activity and discover for themselves the logical connections between objects or events (for example, three marbles plus two marbles equals two marbles plus three marbles).

The second principle is based on Piaget's distinction among three types of knowledge: physical, social, and logical. The demands of the learning situation are different for the three types of knowledge. Physical knowledge refers to learning about the nature of matter (for example, cotton is soft, metal is hard and often unbendable, balls drop to the ground when you release them). Social knowledge is obtained through feedback from other people. It provides a framework for determining the effects of social actions and social connections (for example, most people say hello when they first see each other, and celebrate their birthdays each year). Social knowledge must come through free interaction with other people in the environment. We need to hear other people's views, have different role models available, and make choices for ourselves. Logical knowledge is concerned with mathematics and logic. It is constructed by processes of reflection and abstraction. The teacher's role in physical and logical knowledge is to provide a setting in which students construct this knowledge for themselves through questioning and experimenting. Teachers should refrain from giving answers directly but may use prompting questions that encourage further thought and exploration. For example, suppose a child is playing with two eggs—one hard-boiled—near a bowl of water. The teacher might ask, "What happens if you put the eggs in the water?" Or the teacher might be serving juice to the students and ask, "How many juices do we need?" It is important to establish a climate in which wrong answers are perfectly acceptable, even valued, because they reveal what we know and how we think.

With respect to moral development, Piaget describes children as moving in a general direction away from egocentric and individualized ways of thinking to more socially centered, publicly validated ways of thinking. In the egocentric stages, the children tend to judge actions solely by their consequences. For example, if someone bumps into them, they usually judge the act by whether they are hurt. An intentional "hurt" is judged to be "bad." As people move toward a more sociocentric organization, they begin to judge acts by intentions, and become concerned not only with whether injury was justified but also with whether perhaps anyone intended to hurt them. Participation with others is more on a basis of equality and mutual respect. The opportunity to exchange viewpoints and share personal experiences produces the cognitive conflict that is fundamental to intellectual development. Teachers can foster social knowledge by providing many opportunities for students to interact with each other, especially by sharing their views and cooperating on tasks. In addition, teachers themselves must provide structured social feedback (for example, "John, we can only have one person sharing at a time. Can you wait until Kevin is finished?") so that social conventions are conveyed.

The last principle of teaching and learning has to do with the role of the social environment. Piaget maintains that especially logical and social knowledge are best learned from other children. They provide a source of motivation and information in a linguistic form that matches each other's cognitive structures. The peer group is also a reliable source of disequilibrium.

Given these principles, Wadsworth (1978) outlines three roles for teachers who operate from a Piagetian orientation: (1) organizer of the learning environment; (2) assessor of children's thinking; and (3) initiator of group activities, especially play, games, and discussions.

During the past ten years, three Piaget-derived educational models have become prominent, particularly among early childhood educators. Each places a different amount of emphasis on each of the three roles identified by Wadsworth.

The first model was developed by Celia Lavatelle and is referred to as a packaged Piaget-based curriculum for children 4 to 7 years old (Lavatelle, 1970). It consists of 100 activities occurring over a thirty-week period. Lavatelle recommends that the activities be completed in 10- to 15-minute periods with small groups of five to six children. She also outlines other activities, especially self-directed play. The objective of Lavatelle's curriculum is to develop children's intellectual processes through self-directed activity. The topics include classification; number, measurement, and space operations; and seriation operations. A typical early activity might have the children identify all squares that are blue (object matching on bases of two or more properties).

While Lavatelle accents the curriculum, in his program *Project Follow-Through: The Cognitively Oriented Curriculum,* David Weikart (1971) includes the entire learning environment. The curriculum is similar to Lavatelle's, with the core areas being classification (grouping), seriation (ordering), spatial relations, and temporal relations. Weikart's activities stress experiencing concepts first on a motoric (physical manipulation) level and then gradually adding the verbal level—first the sign (objects from pictures) and then the symbol (words alone). Each goal is implemented along all three levels.

Weikart organizes the day into: planning time (20 minutes), work time (40 minutes), group meetings for evaluation (10 minutes), clean-up (15 minutes), juice and group time (30 minutes), activity time (20 minutes), and dismissal (10 minutes). A rich array of field trips and sociodramatic play are interspersed throughout the schedule. Lavatelle's curriculum is highly sequenced. Many of Weikart's learning activities, in contrast, are developed by the teachers. Weikart focuses on socioemotional development as well as on the cognitive.

The third educational model is that of Kamii and DeVries (1974). Their current model represents a shift away from specific objectives and a sequenced curriculum. The new program is based on Piaget's ideas about the nature of knowledge and teachers' special role in relationship to each type of knowledge.

In Kamii and DeVries's program, the long-term objectives are general ones: intellectual inventiveness, critical thinking, and autonomous judgment. The focus is on both cognitive and socioemotional development, because they are interdependent in the learning process. Content serves as a motivator, capturing children's interest enough to act upon it as they discover the three basic kinds of knowledge. The program developers identify this knowledge in general terms. *Physical knowledge* refers to knowledge about such attributes of everyday objects, as weight, texture, and size, and knowledge about a repertoire of actions, such as folding, cutting, squeezing. *Social knowledge* refers to knowledge of social information—for example, about occupational roles—and to knowledge of norms for social conduct and social regularities. *Logicomathematical knowledge* includes knowledge of classification, seriation, number, space, and time concepts. Kamii and DeVries believe strongly that the child must construct his or her own knowledge but that the teacher can, through appropriate questions or comments, facilitate this process. Finally, Kamii and DeVries stress the importance of children's play as a learning medium and include a set of games.

Despite clear differences among these Piagetian model-builders, they generally agree about the value of concrete experiences, of play, and of problem-solving. They also all deemphasize didactic instruction. Although they disagree about how, specifically, learning experiences should be designed, they do not dispute the need for active, inquiry-oriented experiences.

One of the issues that has surrounded the consideration of Piaget's ideas has been the extent to which any outside influence can alter development. Until a few years ago it was thought that little could be done. We now know, however, that development is not automatic; for example, not all individuals reach the stage of formal operations. We also know that we can affect development because we can create in schools richer social, physical, and intellectual environments to which children can adapt. But Piaget cautions against acceleration lest we produce readers who decode but cannot comprehend and students who pass math tests but do not understand math.

Another related issue concerns the use of any developmental framework in constructing a model for teaching. Some people believe that developmental schemas such as Piaget's have little to tell us about the teaching act. On the other hand, others believe that this knowledge about the nature of development offers strong guidelines for what and how to teach. David Olson (1970) has identified three modes of instruction that can be built around Piaget's model. The first is to develop situations that pull the students toward a more complex level of thinking. The second is a language-oriented teaching style in which the student is presented with rules that require a more complex level of thinking. In a sense, the teacher provides the next step of thinking to the child with the assumption that if the child can grasp what is being said, he or she will take on the more complex way of operating. The third strategy can be described as modeling. Essentially one demonstrates the performance of the operation for the student either in person, or through a film or television. For example, to teach the concept of reversibility as it is represented in the commutative property of multiplication ($a / b = b / a$), a teacher might set up a three-by-four matrix and count off concrete aids such as checkers. Then the teacher would count the material first by threes and then by fours, thus modeling the proposition that the product is the same regardless of whether the three or the four takes the first position.

Olson's research clearly indicates that the indiscriminate use of these models does not necessarily have any effect and that psychologists are a long way from establishing the precise instructional conditions under which development can be facilitated (Olson, 1970, p. 118).

Psychologist Irving Sigel has developed and studied the use of a model resembling the first of Olson's alternatives. That is, the student is set up with a situation that does not make sense at his or her level of thinking. The idea is that, confronted with clear evidence that his or her thinking is not adequate, the student will reach toward another level of development. For Sigel, teaching involves providing experiences which will produce a deep disequilibrium so that the child will have to develop a new kind of logic to deal with the experiences he or she is having. In other words, the teacher must set up confrontations that are well matched to the child's stage of development (Sigel, 1969, p. 473). According to Sigel the form of the confrontation as well as its nature depend on the developmental level of the child: "Verbal and/or nonverbal techniques ranging from questions, demonstrations and/or environmental manipulations can be employed in the service of confrontation" (Sigel, 1969, p. 173). Thus, like Olson, Sigel acknowledges alternative instructional approaches for setting up situations that require of students slightly higher levels of thinking.

Lavatelle, Weikart, Kamii and DeVries, Olson, and Sigel are only a few of the individuals who have worked to apply Piaget's ideas to the teaching situation. Regardless of their differences, all of the adaptations depend on a means of assessing the child's level of intellectual development. Diagnosis is not easy, however; Sigel points out that diagnosis relying on verbal behavior is often misleading because children use terms before they can understand the logical bases of the terms. For example, the concrete-stage child understands "brother" as "the boy who lives in my house" rather than as someone related to him. The idea of kinship is a concept understood at a more complex stage of development. Effective assessment, then, requires procedures that reveal the actual cognitive structure beneath the student's verbalization. Piaget describes such a process, which he refers to as the *methode clinique* (the clinical method). The principles and procedures of the clinical method as used in assessment are also applicable to the instructional setting, when it is geared to promote development. Teaching that has a developmental framework as its intellectual basis and development as its aim is inherently "clinical." By clinical we mean that the teacher is constantly "assessing." He or she selects the learning task in relation to development, reads the students' responses in terms of development, and reacts to the students in a way to promote (ascertain) development. The guidelines for these activities are found in Piaget's original writings about the clinical method (and later those of other psychologists and educators). We consider the clinical interview to be the basis for developmental instruction.

THE CLINICAL METHOD

Piaget's development of the clinical method grew out of his dissatisfactions with pure observation and with the validity of most standardized testing. He wanted to develop a structured yet fluid procedure, one allowing the child to move spontaneously in directions congruent with his or her reasoning and at the same time yielding definitive information about the level of reasoning.

> The essential feature of the test method . . . is that it falsifies the natural mental inclination of the subject or at least risks doing so . . . . The only way to avoid such difficulties is to vary the questions, to make counter-suggestions, in short, to give up all idea of a fixed questionnaire.
> . . . The skill of the practitioner consists not in making the child answer questions but in making him talk freely and thus engaging the flow of his spontaneous tendencies instead of diverting it into the artificial channels of set questions and answers. (Piaget, 1960, pp. 3–4)

Piaget refers to this procedure as the *clinical interview*.

The goal of the clinical interview is to determine the nature (stage) of the child's reasoning by "testing the limits" of the child's capabilities. In a one-to-one situation a student is presented with a task that typically is geared to assess one area of thinking, such as classification or conservation of number. The interviewer asks questions. As the child responds, the interviewer listens to and observes the child's behaviors. Based on a hypothesis about the level of thinking, the interviewer asks more questions until he or she is convinced that the requirements for the level of thinking have been met. In this situation both wrong and right answers provide useful information to the interviewer. The interviewer must be careful not to predetermine the child's responses by formulating questions in such a way that they cue the child:

> The clinical examination is experimental in the sense that the practitioner sets himself a problem, makes hypotheses, adapts the conditions to them and finally controls each hypothesis by testing it against the reactions he stimulates in conversation.
> . . . It is so hard not to talk too much . . . . It is so hard not to be suggestive! And above all, it is hard to find a middle course between systematization due to preconceived ideas and incoherence due to the absence of any directing hypothesis. (Piaget, 1960, pp. 8–9)

As Piaget implies, student responses during the clinical interview are not all equally useful. Sometimes when students are uninterested in the question, they answer at random. Sometimes they romance, inventing an answer they don't really believe. Occasionally they respond to an implied suggestion by the interviewer, trying to satisfy him or her. The most valid reflections are those based on conviction given either after reflection or spontaneously:

> Even when the solution is invented by the child during the interview, it is not invented from nothing. It implies previously formed schemes, tendencies of mind, intellectual habits, etc. (Piaget, 1960, p. 13)

The major means of separating useful from worthless answers is to make countersuggestions, probing the student's answers to see if they are firmly rooted. One might also let the student think for a while and then ask the question again in several different guises.

If a student is at a specific reasoning level, he or she can (1) make a correct judgment; (2) offer a logical justification for that judgment; (3) successfully resist a verbal countersuggestion; and (4) complete a successful performance on a related task (Wadsworth, 1978, p. 225). For example, on a term-to-term correspondence task the student is given sixteen blocks, eight of one color and eight of another. They are placed in two rows by color, spaced equally. The child is asked whether the rows have the same number or whether one has more. (If beginning with an open-ended probe, the child will first be asked to describe what he or she sees.) After the child acknowledges that both rows are the same, the rows are collapsed and reset; this time one is spread out farther than the rest. Again the equivalence question is asked. The reasons for the child's responses are probed. If the answer and reasoning are correct, a countersuggestion is made—for example, by removing one block from the longer row and saying, "If I remove one block from this row, each will still have the same number of blocks, won't they?" After the countersuggestion the rows are moved back to their original positions and the equivalence question is asked again. Finally, the child is presented with a different but related task, perhaps this time using erasers or triangles. This is because what is possible in one situation (one set of stimuli) may not be possible in another. In other words, the level of reasoning may be apparent but not firmly established.

Wadsworth provides a sample interview of such an assessment task:

> The examiner arranges a row of nine blue blocks, each about an inch apart, between himself and the child.
>
> **EXAMINER:** "Will you make a row of blocks using the red ones just like my row, and right in front of you?" The child makes a row below the examiner's row by first placing two end blocks in position, then placing eight blocks between those two without any careful comparison.
>
> **EXAMINER:** Does one row of blocks have more blocks than the other, or do they both have the same number?
>
> **CHILD:** They're the same.
>
> **E:** Are you sure?

C: Yes.

E: How do you know they're the same number of blocks? (request for reasoning)

C: I can count them. (Child proceeds to count the blocks in each row. He counts nine for the blue row and ten for the red row.) They're different. There are more reds.

E: Can you make them so they have the same number? (Child removes one of the red blocks from the middle of the row and lines the other red ones up according to the blue ones.)

E: Now both rows have the same number of blocks?

C: Yes.

E: Okay, I'm going to move my blue blocks together like this. (The row of blue blocks is collapsed so that they are about one-half inch apart.) Now, are there more blocks in my row or in your row, or do we both have the same number of blocks?

C: I have more.

E: How can you tell? (request for reasoning)

C: My row sticks out more. (preoperational reasoning)

E: Okay, I'm going to make my row just like your row again. Who has more blocks now, or do we have the same number of blocks? (Examiner makes his row of blocks as long as Child's.)

C: Same.

E: How do you know? (request for reasoning)

C: See, they both come out to here and here. (The child points to the ends of each row.)

E: Now if I move your blocks closer together (Child's row of blocks is collapsed the way Examiner's row was previously), do we both have the same number of blocks or does one of us have more blocks than the other?

C: You have more.

E: How do you know I have more? (request for reasoning)

C: Same as before; your row is bigger.

E: Why don't you count the number of blocks in each row? (suggestion is made to determine whether counting influences reasoning) (Child counts nine blocks for each row)

E: How many blocks in your row?

C: Nine.

E: How many blocks in my row?

C: Nine.

E: Which row has more blocks or do they both have the same number of blocks?

C: You have more.

E: Tell me why I have more blocks than you have. (request for reasoning)

C: You have more blocks. They come out more. (pointing to the ends of Examiner's row)

At this point the interview could have been terminated, and one would conclude that the child had not yet developed, or was still preoperational with respect to, term-to-term correspondence. The interview was extended in the following way to assess number concepts further.

E: Okay, I'm going to take one block out of my row like this (see figure)

E $\quad$ ☐ ☐ ☐ ☐ ☐ ☐ ☐ ☐ ☐

C

Who has more blocks now, or do we still have the same number?

C: Same.

E: How do you know? (request for reasoning)

C: I can see it.

E: Why don't you count the number in each row again? (Child counts both rows. For Examiner's row Child counts eight. For Child's row Child counts nine. After counting Child looks puzzled. (Wadsworth, 1978, p. 236)

Wadsworth points out that on the basis of this task it is fairly clear that the child cannot conserve number. "When faced with a conflict between perception and reasoning the child still made a perceptual judgment" (Wadsworth, 1978, p. 238).

The Piagetian tasks based on logico-mathematical knowledge are well known to many educators. Less familiar are those in the social/moral development area. While conducting some research several years ago, one of the authors used a task adapted from the work of William Damon. Damon (1977) focuses on three conceptual areas: (1) concerns of "positive justice"—for example, fair distribution of property, sharing, treatment of friends; (2) concerns of authority, such as whom to obey under what conditions, the meaning of power; (3) concerns of responsibility and blame, such as what is a bad act, extent of obligations to others, retribution. A typical positive justice task—the one we used in our study—is as follows:

> One day a teacher lets his class spend the whole afternoon making paintings and crayon drawings. The teacher thinks these pictures are so good that the class can sell them at the school fair, so the children set up a stand and sell the pictures to their parents, and together the class makes a lot of money.
>
> Now all the children gather the next day and try to decide how to split up the money. What do you think they should do with it? Why? Kathy says that the kids in the class who made the most pictures should get most of the money. Andy says the kids who made the best ones should get the most. What do you think? There are some lazy children in the class who didn't draw very much in comparison to the others. What about them?
>
> Jim says that the best behaved kids should get more than the rest. Lisa says that the poor kids should get the money, because they don't have much. Someone says that the teacher should get the money, because it was his idea to sell the pictures. What do you think? Why?

Our procedures consisted of reading the problem situation aloud, then asking in open-ended fashion what the student would do. After this we showed pictures representing each of the children in the problem situation, and we told the student what each child thought according to the problem story. In essence, these characterizations represented countersuggestions concerning issues of poverty, welfare, merit, and equality. At each point we probed the student's thinking. We also prepared a list of countersuggestions at each level of Damon's developmental scale that might be used as necessary in the interview (see Table 7-1). Since this is a task that might draw the full developmental range, it was important to have countersuggestions at each level to be sure of the student's predominant stage of reasoning.

Damon's task is similar to those used by Lawrence Kohlberg, whose work on moral development is discussed later in this chapter. Problem situations based on stories are frequently found in the classrooms of young children. Once a teacher is familiar with a developmental framework such as Damon's or Kohlberg's, it is relatively easy to design instruction so that the level of reasoning is assessed and challenged.

Table 7-1   Responding to Stage Behavior

STAGE	STAGE LEVEL COUNTERSUGGESTIONS
"I Want"	But what if there is a disagreement?
	How do you think all the other kids would feel if you got all the prize money?
	What if someone else wanted it just as badly as you?
"After the Fact Justification"	What does Kathy's being pretty have to do with money earned for the paintings?
	What would you do if someone in the class thought the best should get it instead of the most?
"Equal Action"	But what about Jane? She was absent.
	What if Kathy did one painting and Andy did ten paintings?
	What would happen if you didn't share the money equally?
"Merit and Fair Exchange"	How will you measure? Who will measure? Should you consider the one who was best behaved?
	What about Andy who does not get any allowance?
	Is that important?
"Equal Persons" (need plus merit)	Is it a difficult decision? Why?
	But what if the poor person needs the money and the one who did the best is rich?
"Justifiable"	How will you decide?
	Kathy says the best. Andy says the one who did the most. Jim says the one who is best behaved. Lisa says the one who gets the least allowance.
	Which is the best reason?

Source: William Damon, "Studying Early Moral Development: Some Techniques for Interviewing Young Children and for Analyzing Results" (unpublished paper, Worcester, Mass., Clark University, n.d.).

ASSESSMENT TASKS   Over the years collections of assessment tasks based on Piaget's writings have been developed, particularly in the logico-mathematical area. In his book Wadsworth presents descriptions of twenty-nine tasks based on the work of Beth Stephens. These include the areas of classification, conservation, concrete reasoning, symbolic imagery, spatial orientations, and formal reasoning. Each task is described along with the purpose procedures, countersuggestions, and level of performance (typical age acquisition). The list of tasks and corresponding cognitive abilities appears in Table 7-2. Wadsworth believes that five to ten assessments are sufficient to determine a child's level of development. The tasks also yield information about the student's reasoning with respect to a particular concept (Wadsworth, 1978, pp. 242-243).

THE MODEL OF TEACHING

Derived from the principles of the clinical interview, the model of teaching requires teachers to give tasks, notice how the student interacts with the tasks, and respond in accordance with the student's actions—for example, by asking for justification, or offering stage-appropriate countersuggestions. The teacher, based on his or her assessment, must determine the general range of developmental stages of the students so that inappropriate tasks are not incorporated into the curriculum. (Elementary school teachers do this when they select a range of basic readers or math series for their classrooms. Providing fifth-level readers when the range is level one to four will be of no value.) For this purpose the teacher may choose to assess students individually. Once the individual developmental levels are determined, the teacher can use the model as part of the instructional process with small or large groups. Of course, in a group situation it is not possible to tell for certain the level of reasoning of any one student. Instead the goal is to prompt development by exposure to other levels of reasoning.

SYNTAX

The model consists of three phases: confrontation with stage-relevant task; inquiry; and transfer (see Table 7-3). In phase one the students are presented with a situation that confronts them with the illogic of their thinking or that is puzzling to them. The confronting situation must be relatively well matched, both in its substance and form, to the learners' developmental stages. There must be enough familiarity in the confronting situation to permit assimilation, yet enough newness to require accommodation. The choice of form for the confrontation (verbal, nonverbal, or environmental manipulations) also depends on the learners' developmental stages.

Table 7-2   Developmental Sequence and Mental Ages for Achievement of Piagetian Reasoning Assessments

ASSESSMENT NUMBER	NAME OF TASK	MENTAL AGE	COGNITIVE ABILITY
1	Intersection of classes	6	Classification
2	Rotation of beads	6	Symbolic imagery
3	Euclidean space*	7	Spatial reasoning
4	One-for-one exchange	7	Concrete reasoning
5	Term-to-term correspondence	7	Concrete reasoning
6	Conservation of length	7	Conservation
7	Conservation of liquids	7	Concrete reasoning
8	Conservation of length—rod sections	7	Concrete reasoning
9	Conservation of substance	7	Conservation
10	Dissolution of sugar—substance	7	Concrete reasoning
11	Conservation of weight	7	Conservation
12	Class inclusion—beads	7	Classification
13	Class inclusion—animals (1)	7	Classification
14	Relationships—right and left	7	Classification
15	Class inclusion—animals (2)	8	Classification
16	Relationships—brothers and sisters	8	Classification
17	Spatial coordinates*	9	Spatial reasoning
18	Dissolution of sugar—weight	9	Concrete reasoning
19	Dissolution of sugar—volume	10	Concrete reasoning
20	Changing perspectives—stationary	11	Symbolic imagery
21	Changing perspectives—mobile	12	Symbolic imagery
22	Conservation of volume—solids	12	Formal reasoning
23	Combination of liquids	12	Formal reasoning
24	Probability*	12	Formal reasoning
25	Dissociation of weight and volume	13	Formal reasoning
26	Conservation of volume (1-3)	14	Conservation
27	Conservation of volume (4)	15	Conservation
28	Class inclusion—animals (3)	15	Classification
29	Class inclusion—animals (4)	16	Classification

This table is adapted from W. Beth Stephens, "The Development of Reasoning, Moral Judgment and Moral Conduct in Retardates and Normals: Phase II" (unpublished manuscript, Temple University, May 1972); we have added the starred assessments. Mental ages (MA) were determined for the nonstarred items by the Wechsler Intelligence Scale for Children (WISC) and the Wechsler Adult Intelligence Scale (WAIS). Mental ages for the starred items and some of the nonstarred items have been established through a research program at Mount Holyoke College (S. Heard and Barry Wadsworth, "The Relationship between Cognitive Development and Language Complexity" [unpublished manuscript, Mount Holyoke College, May 1977]).

In phase two the students' responses are elicited and probed to determine their levels of reasoning. Generally, probing consists of asking for justifications and offering countersuggestions. Depending on the nature of the task the initial question may be open, such as "What do you think?" or "What do you see?" as it was in the positive justice task, or closed, such as "Does one row have more blocks than the other, or do they have the same

Table 7-3   Syntax of Development Model

PHASE ONE: CONFRONTATION WITH STAGE-RELEVANT TASK	PHASE TWO: INQUIRY
Present puzzling situation well matched to learner's developmental stage.	Elicit student responses and ask for justifications. Offer countersuggestions, probe student's responses.

	PHASE THREE: TRANSFER
	Present related task and probe student's reasoning. Offer countersuggestions.

number?" as it was in the correspondence task. The reason for probing is to try to obtain the correct response, if there is a correct response. (If a closed question is asked it is important that all options, such as "more" or "the same," are included in the question. This prevents the student from simple agreement with the questioner.) The next step is to ask the student to justify the response by showing his or her reasoning, such as "How do you know they are the same number of blocks?" After the reasoning is pursued, one or more countersuggestions are made. In the correspondence task this involved moving the blocks apart, making them even again, then collapsing them. Each time the student's reasoning was probed. At one point it was suggested the student count again and respond to the question of sameness. In the positive justice task several considerations were mentioned—for example, merit: "What if Sue painted more?"; and need: "What about Sam? He really needs the money." Each of these served as a countersuggestion to check the solidity of the student's reasoning.

Phase three is the transfer phase. The objective here is to see if the student will reason similarly on a related task. Once again the teacher presents a problem; the students make judgments; the teacher requests to know the reasons and then offers countersuggestions.

SOCIAL SYSTEM

The social system can range from minimally structured to highly structured. The teacher can provide an environment of activities and materials that induce student-guided inquiry. For the most part, however, we have described a fairly structured teaching model with the teacher initiating and guiding the inquiry in a free intellectual and social atmosphere. The highly structured approach may be more suitable for certain age-stage levels and to particular problem areas.

For moral development Lawrence Kohlberg stresses the importance of an atmosphere in which open and searching discussion is the norm. In addition, he recommends that the classroom and, whenever possible, the school model a just society in which the value of moral inquiry is strongly nurtured. His research, in the United States and abroad, indicates that home and school atmosphere are critically important to moral development.

PRINCIPLES OF REACTION

The teacher must create a facilitating atmosphere so that students feel free to respond naturally. He or she must be careful to avoid leading or cuing questions. It is as important to inquire into (request the reasoning of) "wrong" responses as into "correct" ones. Sometimes it is useful, depending on the nature of the task, to ask students if they can recall a similar real situation in their lives. The teacher must constantly test students' thinking with counter-suggestions until he or she is satisfied as to the level of reasoning, if that is the goal of the activity.

SUPPORT SYSTEM

The optimal support system is a teacher well grounded in developmental theory and an environment that includes structured or unstructured stage-appropriate tasks. The teacher must also be equipped with relevant counter-suggestions. In the case of Piagetian educational models a rich object and resource environment is needed, as is a free social environment that permits the student to work out the cognitive problems developed in the confrontation. The teacher can be a useful facilitator offering appropriate stimulating comments at the right moment.

Summary Chart: Developmental Model

SYNTAX

Phase One:
Confrontation with Stage-Relevant Tasks
Present puzzling situation well matched to learner's developmental stage.

Phase Two:
Inquiry
Elicit student responses and ask for justifications.
Offer countersuggestions, probe student's responses.

Phase Three:
Transfer
Present related task and probe student's reasoning. Offer countersuggestions.

SOCIAL SYSTEM

Minimal structure is needed for establishing educational environment. High structure is required for assessment interview. Teacher initiates and guides inquiry. The intellectual and social climate is free and open.

PRINCIPLES OF REACTION

Teacher, as environmental provider: (1) creates setting, rich physically and free socially; (2) selects learning activities according to student's developmental level.
Teacher, as assessor: (1) creates facilitating atmosphere; (2) avoids leading or cuing questions; (3) inquires into student's reasoning; (4) offers countersuggestions; (5) continues until requirements for level of reasoning are satisfied.

SUPPORT SYSTEM

Instructor should be well acquainted with developmental sequence and equipped with stage-relevant tasks and countersuggestions. A rich setting of inviting tasks is developed.

APPLICATION

The developmental model drawn from Piaget's notions on the clinical interview is applicable to both cognitive and social development. It cuts across all areas in which illogic or problems in thinking arise, and it can be used for diagnosis and evaluation as well as for instructional purposes. The model, inherently interwoven with developmental considerations, can be employed to ensure that a child can operate smoothly in his or her environment or to specify activities that will accelerate the child's cognitive growth.

Although our illustrations thus far have referred to Piaget's schema for logico-mathematical development and to Damon's developmental schema for positive justice, the model is applicable to any developmental schema. Probably the most well known next to Piaget's is Lawrence Kohlberg's framework for moral development.

MORAL DEVELOPMENT

Kohlberg's work on moral development is especially descriptive of older students. He identifies three major levels of moral development: preconventional, conventional, and postconventional (principled or autonomous). Each level has two stages. These are described next:

A. *Preconventional level.* At this level, the child is responsive to cultural rules and labels of good and bad, right and wrong, but interprets these labels in terms of either the physical or the hedonistic consequences of action (punishment, reward, exchange of favors) or in terms of the physical power of those who enunciate the rules and labels. The level is divided into the following two stages:

   1. *The punishment and obedience orientation.* The physical consequences of action determine its goodness or badness regardless of the human meaning or value of these consequences. Avoidance of punishment and unquestioning deference to power are valued in their own right, not in terms of respect for an underlying moral order supported by punishment and authority (the latter being stage four).

   2. *The instrumental relativist orientation.* Right action consists of that which instrumentally satisfies one's own needs and occasionally the needs of others. Human relations are viewed in the terms of the marketplace. Elements of fairness, of reciprocity, and of equal sharing are present, but they are always interpreted in a physical, pragmatic way. Reciprocity is a matter of "you scratch my back and I'll scratch yours," not of loyalty or justice.

B. *Conventional level.* At this level, maintaining the expectations of the individual's family, group, or nation is perceived as valuable in its own right, regardless of immediate and obvious consequences. The attitude is not only one of *conformity* to personal expectations and social order, but of loyalty to it—of actively maintaining, supporting, and justifying the order and of identifying with the persons or group involved in it. At this level, there are the following two stages:

   1. *The interpersonal concordance or "good boy–nice girl" orientation.* Good behavior is that which pleases or helps others and is approved by them. There is much conformity to stereotypical images of what is majority or "natural" behavior. Behavior is frequently judged by intention—"he means well" becomes important for the first time. One earns approval by being "nice."

   2. *The "law and order" orientation.* Orientation at this stage is toward authority, fixed rules, and the maintenance of the social order. Right behavior consists of doing one's duty, showing respect for authority, and maintaining the given social order for its own sake.

C. *Postconventional, autonomous, or principled level.* At this level, there is a clear effort to define moral values and principles that have validity and application apart from the authority of the groups or persons holding these principles and apart from the individual's own identification with these groups. This level again has two stages.

   1. *The social-contract, legalistic orientation.* Generally this stage has utilitarian overtones. Right action tends to be defined in terms of general individual rights and in terms of standards that have been critically examined and agreed on by the whole society. There is a clear awareness of the relativism of personal values and opinions and a corresponding emphasis on procedural rules for reaching consensus. Aside from what is constitutionally and democratically agreed on, the right is a matter of personal values and opinion. The result is an emphasis on the "legal point of view," but with the possibility of changing law in terms of rational considerations of social utility (rather than freezing it in terms of stage 4 "law and order"). Outside the legal realm, free agreement and contract are the binding elements of obligation. This is the "official" morality of the American government and Constitution.

2. *The universal ethical principle orientation.* Right is defined by the decision of conscience in accord with self-chosen *ethical principles* appealing to logical comprehensiveness, universality, and consistency. These principles are abstract and ethical (the Golden Rule, or a categorical imperative); they are not concrete moral rules like the Ten Commandments. At heart, these are universal principles of *justice,* of the *reciprocity* and *equality* of human *rights,* and of respect for the dignity of human beings as *individual persons.* (Kohlberg, 1976, pp. 215–216)

Kohlberg believes it is possible to influence a student's level of thinking and that it is important to organize instruction with development as a guiding principle. The important conditions appear to be: (1) exposure to the next higher stage of reasoning; (2) exposure to situations posing problems and contradictions for the child's current structure, leading to dissatisfaction with his or her current level; and (3) an atmosphere of interchange and dialogue combining the first two conditions, in which conflicting moral views are compared in an open manner (Kohlberg, 1976, p. 190). For example, suppose the student is involved in an argument and cannot make judgments based on general moral grounds. The teacher would try to confront him or her with the need to operate on a more general moral level. If the student reacted to city council action only in terms of "I like that" or "I don't like that," the task would be to help him or her try to find whether general principles underlie his or her judgment and to move toward a more general basis of judgment. Teachers need to be familiar with the development hierarchy and have probing questions and countersuggestions ready.

Kohlberg stresses that matching teaching to moral levels is not a minor point. To provide a stage-one child with stage-five tasks would be unproductive. Teaching should aim about one level above the student's level of functioning. The optimal grouping pattern is probably one that spans two, perhaps three stages.

In terms of specific educational practice the first task, of course, is to learn about the children's level of moral judgment. This can be done through the use of carefully selected tasks or more informally through observing students' behavior in conflict situations. For example, if students learning about the patterns of bills passed by a legislature find that pressure groups have been getting their own way by lobbying, we can expect that the students' responses will vary substantially in terms of moral judgment. Some may be reluctant to believe that council members are anything but wise and just (probably an indication of stage-four orientation: authority and maintaining social order). Others may be quick to condemn, especially if the majority leans that way (orientation to pleasing). In these cases the teacher can introduce them to a more complex analysis by getting them to look at the general implications of their position. ("Should we say a pressure group should *never* have access to lawmakers—what are the pros and cons?" "What are the positions of other groups in the community who have not been able to lobby successfully?") Teachers should not preach a set of principles for the behavior of lawmakers, however. This both denies the student the new elements he or she needs for development *and* is ineffective as a method.

Much research describes the stages of moral development, and the findings are relatively consistent in confirming the progression through stages and the movement from the relatively egocentric toward the less self-centered views of moral development. However, it should not be assumed that all persons progress naturally through the higher stages of development. Many persons appear to be arrested in their development before or at the stage of the "good boy" orientation. Thus, the attempt to increase moral development is relatively critical.

Treatment studies are relatively few. Kohlberg's thesis is quite clear, and his model has been used extensively, but the majority of the studies are short-term and show changes on pencil-and-paper tests rather than in actual moral behavior. The results of the research in general are promising, but much remains to be done (see Adkins, Payne, and O'Malley, 1974, pp. 108–144).

EVALUATION OF DEVELOPMENTAL MODELS

Over the last twenty years there has been a considerable amount of research to determine the effectiveness of the various models built on developmental psychology, and there are a number of excellent summaries of this work. The reader is referred to (1) Myron Rosskopf and others, *Piagetian Cognitive Development Research in Mathematical Education* (Washington, D.C.: National Council of Teachers in Mathematics, 1971); (2) a review by Herbert J. Klausmier and Frank H. Hooper, "Conceptual Development on Instruction," chapter 1, *Review of Research in Education*, ed. Fred N. Kerlinger and John B. Carroll (Itasca, Ill.: F. E. Peacock Publisher, Inc., 1974), pp. 3–54; (3) a very thorough review by F. H. Hooper, "An Evaluation of Logical Operations in Instruction in the Preschool," in *The Preschool in Action: Exploring Early Childhood Education Programs*, rev. ed., ed. R. K. Parker (Boston: Allyn & Bacon, 1974), pp. 134–86; and (4) *Recent Research in Moral Development*, ed. Lawrence Kohlberg (New York: Holt, Rinehart & Winston, 1977). Taken together these sources provide a very thorough analysis.

The results of short-term studies are generally positive. That is, directly targeted instruction such as that advocated by Sigel, Olson, and Kohlberg results in the particular types of learning desired. Interestingly enough, some of the more general approaches—putting the student in a rich environment (Kamii and DeVries; Weikart) and modeling generally more complex logical operations—appear to have much the same result as the more narrowly focused models. We are just beginning to see the results of the first long-term studies, which should indicate whether teaching during the early years results in lasting increments in logical operations. (Research from the Weikart program discussed earlier in the chapter indicates that students now in high school show high achievement and low deviancy rates.)

DEVELOPMENTAL PSYCHOLOGY
AND OTHER MODELS OF TEACHING

One of the important uses of developmental psychology is a framework for adjusting instruction with any model of teaching to the developmental level of the students. We can seek to adjust instruction to the present stage of development or we can seek the "optimal mismatch" by pitching intruction slightly above the current operating level of the students. (See Chapters 25 and 26 for an introduction to and thorough discussion of a model designed to guide the coordination of instruction with development.)

Robert Spaulding (1970) reported a study that dramatically illustrates the effects that can be gained by combining several models of teaching and governing them with developmental theory. He designed a curriculum for economically poor, low-achieving, socially disruptive primary students. A number were in such serious trouble with their school districts that they had already been expelled from school at ages 6 or 7!

Spaulding taught teachers to assess the students' cognitive development and to adjust instruction appropriately. He made extensive use of inductive models, built a cooperative learning environment (see Part 3), and used social learning theory (see Part 4) to teach independent study habits. The curriculum was much more complex in both intellectual and social demands than the rote-learning environments in which the students had been unsuccessful.

Spaulding demonstrated that the students could work cooperatively, could learn inductive procedures, and could learn to govern their behavior. Their achievement rose substantially and even their scores on intelligence tests showed considerable improvement. All of the models contributed to the

FIGURE 7-1 Instructional and nurturant effects: Developmental Model.

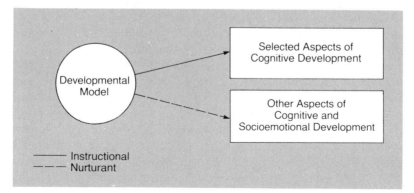

effects. The role of the developmental model, which enabled the teachers to understand student performance from a developmental point of view, was less visible to observers than the cooperative inductive projects and independent study. It quietly made its solid contribution by facilitating the continuous modulation of the environment and providing the teachers with a way of assessing the students' cognitive growth.

Nearly all current research is with relatively young children. Improving the cognitive development model of older children has not been explored fully, but we feel the probability is that the older, generally more able, learner will probably profit even more than the younger child from effective methods.

INSTRUCTIONAL AND NURTURANT EFFECTS

To bring about cognitive development in the Piagetian sense means to affect all aspects of functioning. Thus, concentration on one aspect of cognition (such as moral development) means to nurture development in all other areas (see Figure 7–1).

8

BIOLOGICAL SCIENCE INQUIRY MODEL
Approaches Built on the Researcher's Tools

SCENARIO

In London, Ontario, Mr. Hendricks's fourth grade students enter their classroom after lunch to find an array of glasses, bottles, bells, wooden boxes of different sizes (with holes in them), tuning forks, xylophones, and small wooden flutes. These objects are spread about the room, and the students spend a few minutes playing with them, creating a most horrendous sound. Mr. Hendricks watches.

After a few minutes the students begin to settle down and one of them asks, "What's going on here, Mr. Hendricks? It looks like you've turned the place into an orchestra."

"Well, in a way," he smiles. "Actually, for the next few weeks this is going to be our sound laboratory." He moves across the room and picks up an instrument made of wood and wires and plucks one of the wires. At the same time he uses a spoon to strike a soft drink bottle on the desk next to him. "Do you notice anything about these sounds?" he asks, and repeats his plucking and striking.

"Hey," says one of the girls, "they sound the same, but different."

"Do it again," suggests one of the students, and Mr. Hendricks obliges. Soon all of the students have noticed that the sound is at the same pitch or level.

"Your problem," explains Mr. Hendricks, "is to find out what makes sound vary and to describe that variation. Given the limitations of the devices we have in this room, I want you to organize yourselves to conduct some experiments and present me with sets of principles that you think describe the variations. When you're finished, I want you to be able to describe to me how you would design an instrument with certain capabilities. I'll tell you what I want the instrument to be able to do and you can tell me how to make it. Then we'll begin to test your ideas. Now, I think we ought to organize ourselves into groups and decide how we're going to go about this. Does anybody have any ideas?"

"Well," Sally ventures, "I've noticed that the things are made out of five different kinds of materials. Maybe we could get into five groups, and each group would experiment with those for awhile. Then we could share what we've learned and trade around and check out the thinking of the other groups. After that we could decide what to do next."

Someone joins in with another suggestion, and the class spends the next half hour planning how the study will begin.

From the early 1950s to the late 1960s, innovation in American education was propelled mainly by the Academic Reform movement, an effort to revise the conventional curriculum areas of the school around conceptions of the major ideas and research methods of the academic disciplines. In the area of mathematics, for example, the curriculum designers attempted to influence the way students would think about mathematics, both the major ideas and the methods they would use to inquire into mathematics. Similarly, the science curriculums reflected both the major ideas of the sciences and the research methods and attitudes of the scientific community. In other words, curriculums were built around the information-processing systems of the academic disciplines.

Two straightforward examples were the Biological Sciences Curriculum Study (BSCS) (Schwab, 1965), which produced curricular and instructional patterns for use in high school biology, and the Social Science Curriculum project, which teaches the use of social psychology methods to study human relations (Lippitt, Fox, and Schaible, 1969). In this chapter we use the BSCS model to represent the group of models.

ORIENTATION TO THE MODEL

The essence of the BSCS approach is to teach students to process information using techniques similar to those of research biologists—that is, by identifying problems and using a particular method to solve them. BSCS emphasizes content and process. The first emphasis is on human behavior in the ecology of earth: "The problems created by growing human populations, by depletion of resources, by pollution, by regional development, and the like, all require intelligent government or community action. These are, in part at least, biological-ecological problems, and every citizen should have some awareness of their background" (Schwab, 1965, p. 19). The second emphasis is on scientific investigation:

> Although one of the major aims of this version [of the course] is to describe the major contributions modern molecular biology has made to the general understanding of scientific problems, a second aim will also be apparent. Measured by almost any standard, science has been and continues to be a powerful force in our society. A difficulty has arisen, however. This difficulty, expressed by C. P. Snow in his book, *Two Cultures*, arises from the fact that although many people may understand the *products* of science, at the same time they may be very ignorant of the nature of science and its methods of inquiry. It is probably a safe generalization to say that the understanding of the *products* of science cannot be attained unless the process is also understood. It is apparent that in a free society such as ours, much will depend on the average citizen's evaluation of science. (Schwab, 1965, pp. 26–27).

To help students understand the nature of science, the strategies developed by the BSCS committees introduce students to the methods of biology at the same time that they introduce them to the ideas and facts. The committee put it rather pungently:

If we examine a conventional high school text, we find that it consists mainly or wholly of a series of unqualified, positive statements. "There are so many kinds of mammals." "Organ A is composed of three tissues." "Respiration takes place in the following steps." "The genes are the units of heredity." "The function of A is X."

This kind of exposition (the statement of conclusions) has long been the standard rhetoric of textbooks even at the college level. It has many advantages, not the least of which are simplicity and economy of space. Nevertheless, there are serious objections to it. Both by omission and commission, it gives a false and misleading picture of the nature of science.

By commission, a rhetoric of conclusions has two unfortunate effects on the student. First, it gives the impression that science consists of unalterable, fixed truths. Yet, this is not the case. The accelerated pace of knowledge in recent years has made it abundantly clear that scientific knowledge is revisionary. It is a temporary codex, continuously restructured as new data are related to old.

A rhetoric of conclusions also tends to convey the impression that science is complete. Hence, the fact that scientific investigation still goes on, and at an ever-accelerated pace, is left unaccounted for to the student.

The sin of omission by a rhetoric of conclusions can be stated thus: It fails to show that scientific knowledge is more than a simple report of things observed, that it is a body of knowledge forged slowly and tentatively from raw materials. It does not show that these raw materials, data, spring from planned observations and experiments. It does not show that the plans for experiments and observation arise from problems posed, and that these problems, in turn, arise from concepts which summarize our earlier knowledge. Finally, of great importance, is the fact that a rhetoric of conclusions fails to show that scientists, like other men, are capable of error, and that much of inquiry has been concerned with the correction of error.

Above all, a rhetoric of conclusions fails to show that our summarizing concepts are tested by the fruitfulness of the questions that they suggest, and through this testing are continually revised and replaced.

The essence, then, of a teaching of science as inquiry, would be to show some of the conclusions of science in the framework of the way they arise and are tested. This would mean to tell the student about the ideas posed, and the experiments performed, to indicate the data thus found, and to follow the interpretation by which these data were converted into scientific knowledge (Schwab, 1965, pp. 39–40).

The BSCS uses several techniques to teach science as inquiry. First, it uses many statements that express the tentative nature of science, such as, "We do not know." "We have been unable to discover how this happens." and "The evidence about this is contradictory" (Schwab, 1965, p. 40). Current theories, it is pointed out, may be replaced by others as time goes by. Second, in place of a rhetoric of conclusions, BSCS uses what is called a "narrative of inquiry" in which the history of major ideas in biology is described and the course of inquiry in that area is followed. Third, the laboratory work is arranged to induce students to investigate problems, rather than just to illustrate the text. As they put it, "They [scientists] treat problems for which the text does not provide answers. They create situations in which the students can participate in the inquiry" (Schwab, 1965, p. 40). Fourth, the laboratory programs have been designed in blocks that involve the student in an investigation of a real biological problem. At first students may be presented with materials already familiar to scientists and problems whose solutions are already disclosed, but "as the series of problems progresses, they come nearer and nearer to the frontier of knowledge" (Schwab, 1965, p. 41). Thus, the student simulates the activity of the research scientist. Finally, there is the use of what are called "Invitations to Enquiry." Like the functioning of the laboratory, the Invitations to Enquiry involve the student in activities that enable him or her to follow and participate in the reasoning related to a frontline item of investigation or to a methodological problem in biology.

In this chapter we present the Invitations to Enquiry as the model of teaching drawn from the BSCS materials.

INVITATIONS TO ENQUIRY

Credited to Schwab, this strategy was designed:

To show students how knowledge arises from the interpretation of data . . . to show students that the interpretation of data—indeed, even the search for data—proceeds on the basis of concepts and assumptions that change as our knowledge grows . . . to show students that as these principles and concepts change, knowledge changes too . . . to show students that though knowledge changes, it changes for a good reason—because we know better and more than we knew before. The converse of this point also needs stress: The possibility that present knowledge may be revised in the future does *not* mean that present knowledge is false. Present knowledge is science based on the best-tested facts and concepts we presently possess. It is the most reliable, rational knowledge of which man is capable (Schwab, 1965, p. 46).

Each Invitation to Enquiry (or lesson) is a case study illustrating either a major concept or method of the discipline. Each invitation "poses example after example of the process itself. Second, *it engages the participation of the student in the process*" (Schwab, 1965, p. 47).

In each case a real-life scientific study is described. However, omissions, blanks, or curiosities are left uninvestigated, which the student is invited to fill. "This omission may be the plan of an experiment, or a way to control one factor in an experiment. It may be the conclusion to be drawn from given data. It may be an hypothesis to account for data given" (Schwab, 1965, p. 46). In other words the format of the invitation ensures that the student sees biological inquiry in action and is involved in it, because he or she has to perform the missing experiment or draw the omitted conclusion.

The sets of invitations are sequenced in terms of difficulty to gradually lead the students to more sophisticated concepts. We can see this sequencing in the first group of Invitations to Enquiry, which focus on topics related to methodology—the role and nature of general knowledge, data, experiment, control, hypothesis, and problems in scientific investigation. The subjects and topics of the invitations in Group 1 appear in Table 8–1.

Invitation 3 in Group 1, an example of this model, leads students to deal with the problem of misinterpretation of data.

INVITATION 3
(Subject: Seed Germination)
(Topic: Misinterpretation of Data)

(It is one thing to take a calculated risk in interpreting data. It is another thing to propose an interpretation for which there is no evidence—whether based on misreading of the available data or indifference to evidence. The material in this Invitation is intended to illustrate one of the most obvious misinterpretations. It also introduces the role of a clearly formulated *problem* in controlling interpretation of the data from experiments to which the problem leads.)

To the student: (a) An investigator was interested in the conditions under which seeds would best germinate. He placed several grains of corn on moist blotting paper in each of two glass dishes. He then placed one of these dishes in a room from which light was excluded. The other was placed in a well-lighted room. Both rooms were kept at the same temperature. After four days the investigator examined the grains. He found that all the seeds in both dishes had germinated.

What interpretation would you make of the data from this experiment? Do not include facts that you may have obtained elsewhere, but restrict your interpretation to those from *this experiment alone.*

(Of course, the experiment is designed to test the light factor. The Invitation is intended, however, to give the inadequately logical students a chance to say that the experiment suggests that moisture is necessary for the

Table 8-1 Invitations to Enquiry, Group 1, Simple Enquiry: The Role and Nature of General Knowledge, Data, Experiment, Control, Hypothesis, and Problems in Scientific Investigation

INVITATION	SUBJECT	TOPIC
1	The cell nucleus	Interpretation of simple data
2	The cell nucleus	Interpretation of variable data
3	Seed germination	Misinterpretation of data
4	Plant physiology	Interpretation of complex data
Interim Summary 1, Knowledge and Data		
5	Measurement in general	Systematic and random error
6	Plant nutrition	Planning of experiment
7	Plant nutrition	Control of experiment
8	Predator-prey; natural populations	"Second-best" data
9	Population growth	The problem of sampling
10	Environment and disease	The idea of hypothesis
11	Light and plant growth	Construction of hypotheses
12	Vitamin deficiency	"If . . . , then . . . ." analysis
13	Natural selection	Practice in hypothesis
Interim Summary 2, The Role of Hypothesis		
14	Auxins and plant movement	Hypothesis; interpretation of abnormality
15	Neurohormones of the heart	Origin of scientific problems
16	Discovery of penicillin	Accident in inquiry
16A	Discovery of anaphylaxis	Accident in inquiry

Source: Joseph J. Schwab, supervisor, BSCS, *Biology Teachers' Handbook* (New York: John Wiley & Sons, Inc., 1965), p. 52. By permission of the Biological Sciences Curriculum Study.

sprouting of grains. Others may say it shows that a warm temperature is necessary. If such suggestions do not arise, introduce one as a possibility. Do so with an attitude that will encourage the expression of unwarranted interpretation, if such exists among the students.)

(If such an interpretation is forthcoming, you can suggest its weakness by asking the students if the data suggest that corn grains require a glass dish in order to germinate. Probably none of your students will accept this. You should have little difficulty in showing them that the data some of them thought were evidence for the necessity of moisture or warmth are no different from the data available about glass dishes. In neither case are the data evidence for such a conclusion.)

To the student: (b) What factor was clearly *different* in the surroundings of the two dishes? In view of your answer, remembering that this was a deliberately planned experiment, state as precisely as you can the specific problem that led to this particular plan of experiment.

(If it has not come out long before this, it should be apparent now that the experiment was designed to test the necessity of light as a factor in germination. As to the statement of the problem, the Invitation began with a very general question: "Under what conditions do seeds germinate best?" This is not the most useful way to state a problem for scientific inquiry, because it does not indicate where and how to look for an answer. Only when the "question" is made specific enough to suggest what data are needed to answer it does it become an immediately useful scientific problem. For example, "Will seeds germinate better with or without light?" is a question pointing clearly to what data are required. A comparison of germination in the light with germination in the dark is needed. So we can say that a general "wonderment" is converted into an immediately useful problem when the question is made sufficiently specific to suggest an experiment to be performed or specific data to be sought. We do not mean to suggest that general "wonderments" are bad. On the contrary, they are indispensable. The point is only that they must lead to something else—a solvable problem.)

To the student: (c) In view of the problem you have stated, look at the data again. What interpretation are we led to?

(It should now be clear that the evidence indicates that light is *not* necessary for the germination of *some* seeds. You may wish to point out that light is necessary for some other seeds [for example, Grand Rapids Lettuce] and may inhibit the germination of others [for example, some varieties of onion].)

(N.B.: This Invitation continues to deal with the ideas of data, evidence and interpretation. It also touches on the new point dealt with under paragraph (b), the idea of a *problem*. It exemplifies the fact that general curiosity must be converted into a specific problem.)

(It also indicates that the problem posed in an inquiry has more than one function. First, it leads to the design of the experiment. It converts a wonder into a plan of attack. It also guides us in interpreting data. This is indicated in (c), where it is so much easier to make a sound interpretation than it is in (a), where we are proceeding without a clear idea of what problem led to the particular body of data being dealt with.)

(If your students have found this Invitation easy or especially stimulating, you may wish to carry the discussion further and anticipate to some extent the topic of Invitation 6 [planning an experiment]. The following additions are designed for such use) (Schwab, 1965, p. 57–58.)

The format of this investigation is fairly typical. The students are introduced to the problem the biologist is attacking and they are given some information about the investigations that have been carried on. The students are then led to attempt to interpret the data and to deal with the problems of warranted and unwarranted interpretations. Next, the students are led to try to design experiments that would test the factor with less likelihood of data misinterpretation. This syntax—to pose a problem about a certain kind of investigation, and then to induce students to attempt to generate ways of inquiring that will eliminate the particular difficulty in the area—is used throughout the program.

Let's look at another Invitation to Enquiry—this time, with a more concept-oriented topic. The following illustration is from the Invitation to Enquiry group dealing with the concept of *function*. The topic has been structured so that it is approached as a methodological problem: How can we infer the function of a given part from its observable characteristics (what is the evidence of function)? In this model the question is not posed directly. Rather the student is guided through an area of investigation, which in this invitation has been framed to embed the methodological concern and the spirit of in-quiry. Questions are then posed so that the student himself or herself iden-tifies the difficulty and later speculates on the ways to resolve it.

INVITATION 32
(Subject: Muscle Structure and Function)
(Topic: Six Evidences of Function)

(We concluded Interim Summary 3 by pointing out that the concept of causal lines has no place for the organism as a whole. Instead, the concept treats the organism simply as a collection of such causal lines, not as an organization of them. Each causal line, taken separately, is the object of in-vestigation. The web formed by these lines is not investigated. The concep-tion of function is one of the principles of inquiry which brings the web, the whole organism, back into the picture.)

(This Invitation introduces the student to the idea of *function*. This concept involves much more than the idea of causal factor. It involves the assumption that a given part (organ, tissue, and so on) encountered in an adult organism is likely to be so well suited to the role it plays in the life of the whole organism that this role can be inferred with some confidence from observable characteristics of the part (its structure, action, and so on). As we shall indicate later, this assumption, like others in scientific research, is a *working* assump-tion only. We do not assume that organs are invariably perfectly adapted to their functions. We do assume that most or many of the organs in a living organism are so well adapted (because of the process of evolution) that we proceed farther in studying an organ by assuming that it is adapted to its func-tion than by assuming that it is not.)

To the student: (a) Which of the various muscle masses of the human body would you say is the strongest?

(Students are most likely to suggest the thigh muscles, or the biceps, on the grounds that they are the largest single muscle in the body. If not, suggest the thigh muscle yourself, and defend your suggestion on grounds of size.)

To the student: (b) We decided that the thigh muscle was probably the strongest of our body muscles, using *size* as our reason for choosing it. Hence size seems to be the datum on which we base this decision. But why size, rather than color or shape? Behind our choice of size as the proper criterion, are there not data of another sort, from common experience, that suggest to us that larger muscles are likely to be stronger muscles?

(In considering this question students should be shown that their recogni-tion and acceptance of this criterion of muscle strength is derived from associations from common experience: A drop-kick sends a football farther than a forward pass, a weight lifter has bulkier musculature than a pianist, and so on.)

To the student: (c) Now a new point using no information beyond common ex-perience. What can you say happens to a *muscle* when it contracts?

(The question here is *not* what a muscle does to other parts of the body, but what the muscle itself does—its change of shape in a certain way—becoming shortened, thicker, firmer by contraction. Have the students feel their arm muscles as they lift or grasp.)

To the student: (d) To the fact that the motion of a muscle is as you have found it to be, add two further facts: Many muscles are attached to some other parts of the body, and many such muscles are spindle-shaped, long, narrow, and tapering. From these data alone, what do you think muscles do?

(The motion, attachment, and shape taken together suggest that muscles in general move one or all of the other parts of the body to which they may be attached. Such inferences about function are only probable. But so are practically all inferences in science. In (e) and later queries, we shall make a point of the doubtful character of functional inference) (Schwab, 1965, pp. 174–76).

The example continues in this vein.

THE MODEL OF TEACHING

The essence of the model is to involve students in a genuine problem of inquiry by confronting them with an area of investigation, helping them identify a conceptual or methodological problem within that area of investigation, and inviting them to design ways of overcoming that problem. Thus, they see knowledge in the making and are initiated into the community of scholars. At the same time, they gain a healthy respect for knowledge and will probably learn both the limitations of current knowledge and its dependability.

SYNTAX

The syntax takes a number of forms. Essentially it contains the following elements or phases, although they may occur in a number of sequences (also see Table 8–2): In phase one, an area of investigation is posed to the student, including the methodologies used in the investigation. In phase two, the problem is structured so that the student identifies a difficulty in the investigation. The difficulty may be one of data interpretation, data generation, the control of experiments, or making inferences. In phase three, the student is asked to speculate about the problem, so that he or she can identify the difficulty involved in the inquiry. In phase four, the student is then asked to speculate on ways of clearing up the difficulty, either by redesigning the experiment,

Table 8–2   Syntax of Biological Science Inquiry Model

PHASE ONE	PHASE TWO
Area of investigation is posed to student.	Students structure the problem.
PHASE THREE	PHASE FOUR
Students identify the problem in the investigation.	Students speculate on ways to clear up the difficulty.

organizing data in different ways, generating data, developing constructs, and so on.

SOCIAL SYSTEM

A cooperative, rigorous climate is desired. Because the student is to be welcomed into a community of seekers who use the best techniques of science, the climate includes a certain degree of boldness as well as humility. The students need to hypothesize rigorously, challenge evidence, criticize research designs, and so on. In addition to the necessity for rigor, students must also recognize the tentative and emergent nature of their own knowledge as well as that of the discipline, and in doing so develop a certain humility with respect to their approach to the well-developed scientific disciplines.

PRINCIPLES OF REACTION

The teacher's task is to nurture the inquiry by emphasizing the process of inquiry, and inducing the students to reflect on it. The teacher needs to be careful that the identification of facts does not become the central issue and should encourage a good level of rigor in the inquiry. He or she should aim to turn the students toward the generation of hypotheses, the interpretation of data, and the development of constructs, which are seen as emergent ways of interpreting reality.

SUPPORT SYSTEM

A flexible instructor skilled in the process of inquiry, a plentiful supply of "real" areas of investigation and their ensuing problems, and the necessary data sources from which to conduct inquiry into these areas provide the necessary support system for this model.

APPLICATION

A number of models for teaching the disciplines as processes of inquiry exist, all built around the concepts and methods of the particular disciplines.

The Michigan Social Science Curriculum Project, directed by Ronald Lippitt and Robert Fox, is based on an approach that is potentially very powerful but is startling in its simplicity. The strategy is to teach the research techniques of social psychology directly to children using human relations content, including their own behavior. The result presents social psychology as a living discipline whose concepts and method emerge through continuous application to inquiry into human behavior. Another result is a direct demonstration of the relevance of social science to human affairs. This curriculum illustrates how elementary school children can use scientific procedures to examine social behavior.

Both the conception of social psychology held by these curriculum makers and their teaching strategy, which is essentially to lead the children to practice social psychology, are probably best illustrated by looking at their materials and the activities they recommend. They have prepared seven "laboratory units" developed around a resource book or text and a series of project books. The seven units begin with an exploration of the nature of social science. "Learning to Use Social Science," and proceed to a series of units in which the students apply social science procedures and concepts to human behavior: "Discovering Differences," "Friendly and Unfriendly Behavior," "Being and Becoming," "Influencing Each Other."

The first unit is structured to introduce students to social science methods such as:

1. "What is a behavior specimen?" (How do we obtain samples of behavior?)
2. "Three ways to use observation" (Introduces the children to description, inference, and value judgment, and the differences among them.)
3. "Cause and Effect" (Introduces the inference of cause, first in relation to physical phenomena, then in relation to human behavior.)
4. "Multiple Causation" (Teaches how to deal with several factors simultaneously. For example, the children read and analyze a story in which a central character has several motivations for the same action.) (Lippitt, Fox, and Schaible, 1969, pp. 24–25)

The children compare their analyses of the samples so that they check observations and inferences against one another and come to realize problems of obtaining agreement about observations. They also learn how to analyze interaction through the technique of circular analysis.

Finally, a series of activities introduces the children to experiments by social psychologists that have generated interesting theories about friendly and unfriendly behavior and cooperation and competition.

This approach focuses the children's study on human interaction, provides an academic frame of reference and techniques for delineating and carrying out inquiry, and involves the student in the observation of his or her own behavior and that of those around him. The overall intention is that he or she will take on some of the characteristics of the social scientist. Thus, the instructional values are in the interpersonal as well as the academic domain.

This model has wide applicability, but unfortunately it is dependent on inquiry-oriented materials (areas of investigation), which are rare in most classrooms, since the didactic text is the standard. However, every subject area has at least one text series that is inquiry-oriented or one that is easily adapted to this model. The instructor with a clear understanding of the model will easily discern instructional material that, with a little rearrangement, might provide suitable areas for investigation. Instructors who are quite knowledgeable in their particular disciplines can probably construct their own materials.

INSTRUCTIONAL AND NURTURANT EFFECTS

The Biological Science Inquiry Model (Figure 8–1) is designed to teach the processes of research biology, to affect the ways that students process information, and to nurture a commitment to scientific inquiry. It probably also nurtures open-mindedness, and an ability to suspend judgment and balance alternatives. Through its emphasis on the community of scholars, it also nurtures a spirit of cooperation and an ability to work with others in scientific inquiry.

Scientific-inquiry models have been developed for use with students of all ages, from preschool through college. The core purpose is to teach the essential process of science and, concurrently, major concepts from the disciplines and the information from which these have been developed.

Research on these models has usually focused on entire curriculums that have been implemented for one or more years, using the models consistently with appropriate materials of instruction. Two types of findings are of particular interest to us. The first is that teachers who would use them need to

FIGURE 8-1　Instructional and nurturant effects: Biological Science Inquiry Model.

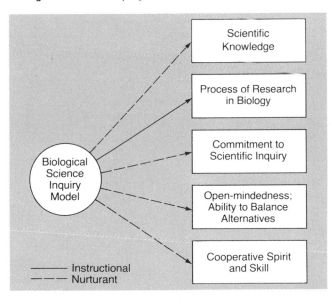

engage in intensive study both of the academic substance and of these models of teaching. Otherwise, they tend to withdraw from the models. The second is that where these models have been well implemented with adequate attention to the teachers' study of academic content and teaching process, the results have been impressive (Bredderman, 1981; El Nemr, 1979). The students have learned the scientific processes, have mastered the major concepts of the disciplines, have acquired basic information about science, and developed positive views toward science.

Summary Chart: Biological Science Inquiry Model

SYNTAX (FLOATS)

Phase One
Area of investigation is posed to student.

Phase Two
Students structure the problem.

Phase Three
Students identify the problem in the investigation.

Phase Four
Students speculate on ways to clear up the difficulty.

SOCIAL SYSTEM

The model has moderate structure, and a cooperative, rigorously intellectual climate.

PRICIPLES OF REACTION

Teacher nourishes inquiry, turning students toward inquiry process rather than identification efforts.

SUPPORT SYSTEM

The model requires a flexible instructor skilled in the process of inquiry and a supply of problem areas of investigation.

Part II
The Personal Family

The rich texture of human life lies in the individual consciousness we all have. Our personal qualities act on the world, substantially affecting the environments in which we live. Reciprocally, we are acted on by the world. Our social environment gives us our language and the other facets of culture. It teaches us how to behave and affects how we feel. Our personalities have remarkable continuity from early in life (White, 1980), and yet we have great capacity to change. We can adapt to a wide range of climates and physical environments but, paradoxically, we also have the capacities to pursue unadaptive behaviors—as if to force the world to yield and make our incompetencies productive.

Personal models of teaching refer to approaches that share one or more of the following purposes: One is to lead the student toward greater and greater mental and emotional health by improving the concept of self, increasing realism, creating self-confidence, and extending sympathetic and empathetic reactions to others. A second is to increase the proportion of education that emanates from the needs and aspirations of the students themselves, taking each student as a partner in determining what he or she will learn and how he or she will learn it. In other words, the students are taught to take charge of their own educations. A third is to develop specific kinds of qualitative thinking, such as creativity and personal expression.

These models can be used in several ways. First, they can be used to moderate the entire learning environment. For example, we can "carry around with us" concern for the students' self-concepts and we can think carefully about how to shape everything we do to maximize their positive feelings about self and to minimize the likelihood that our teaching will diminish them as people. In other words, we can use these models to attend to the personal qualities and feelings of our students and to look for opportunities to make them partners with us and to communicate affirmatively with them.

Second, we use these models when we wish to achieve specific goals for which they are uniquely designed. We use nondirective techniques when we are counseling the students, synectics to enhance creativity, classroom meetings to build the community of learners.

Finally, some of the personal models can be used as general models of teaching. Some schools have adopted a nondirective philosophy as the core of their approaches to education (e.g., Aspy and Roebuck, 1973; Neill, 1960) or as a major component (Chamberlin and Chamberlin, 1943). In addition, certain approaches to teaching academic subjects have been developed around personal models. The "experience" methods for teaching reading, for example, use student-dictated stories as the initial reading materials and student-selected literature as the chief materials once initial competence has been established.

In addition to the belief that enhancing the learner as a person is a worthwhile educational goal in its own right, a major thesis of this family of models is that the better-developed, more affirmative, self-actualizing learners have increased learning capabilities. Thus, personal models will increase academic achievement by tending the learners. This thesis is supported by a number of studies (Roebuck, Buhler, and Aspy, 1976) that indicate that the students of teachers who incorporate personal models into their repertoires increase their achievement.

From the range of personal models we have selected several to illustrate the genre. The chapter on Carl Rogers's Nondirective Teaching Model illustrates the philosophy and technique of the major spokesperson for the family; that on synectics illustrates models designed to enhance creativity and problem solving; that on awareness training illustrates the use of gestalt psychology to enhance the self; and that on the classroom meeting illustrates personalistic approaches to the organization of the classroom as a self-disciplining community of learners.

9

NONDIRECTIVE TEACHING
The Learner at the Center

SCENARIO

John Denbro, a 26-year-old high school English teacher in suburban Chicago, is very concerned about Mary Ann Fortnay, one of his students. Mary Ann is a compulsive worker who does an excellent job with literature assignments and writes excellent short stories. She is, however, reluctant to share those stories with other members of the class and declines to participate in any activities in the performing arts.

Mr. Denbro recognizes that the issue cannot be forced, but he wants Mary Ann to understand why she is reluctant to allow any public display of her talents. She will make her own decisions about participation that involves sharing her ideas.

One afternoon she asks him to read some of her new pieces and give her his opinion.

MARY ANN: Mr. Denbro, could you take a look at these for me?

DENBRO: Why sure, Mary Ann. Another short story?

MARY ANN: No, some poems I've been working on. I don't think they're very good, but I'd like you to tell me what you think.

DENBRO: When did you write them?

MARY ANN: One Sunday afternoon a couple of weeks ago.

DENBRO: Do you remember what started you thinking that you wanted to write a poem?

MARY ANN: I was feeling kind of sad and I remembered last month when we tried to read "The Waste Land," and it seemed to be trying to say a lot of things that we couldn't say in the usual way. I liked the beginning lines, "April is the cruelest month, breeding lilacs out of the dead land."[1]

DENBRO: And is this what you wrote down?

MARY ANN: Yes. It's the first time I've ever tried writing anything like this.

DENBRO: (reads for a few minutes and then looks up) Mary Ann, these are really good.

MARY ANN: What makes a poem good, Mr. Denbro?

DENBRO: Well, there are a variety of ways to judge poetry. Some methods are technical and have to do with the quality of expression and the way one uses metaphors and analogies and other literary devices. Others are subjective and involve the quality of expression, the real beauty of the words themselves.

MARY ANN: I felt very good when I was writing them, but when I read them over, they sound a little dumb to me.

DENBRO: What do you mean?

MARY ANN: Oh, I don't know. I guess the main thing is that I feel ashamed if anybody else sees them.

DENBRO: Ashamed?

MARY ANN: I really don't know. I just know that if these were to be read aloud, say to my class, I would die of mortification.

DENBRO: You really feel that the class would laugh at these?

MARY ANN: Oh sure, they wouldn't understand.

DENBRO: How about your short stories? How do you feel about them?

MARY ANN: You know. I don't want *anybody* to see what I write.

DENBRO: You really feel that you want to put them away somewhere so nobody can see them?

MARY ANN: Yes, I really think so. I don't exactly know why, but I'm pretty sure that no one in my class would understand them.

DENBRO: Can you think of anybody else that might understand them?

MARY ANN: I don't know. I kind of think there are people out there who might, but nobody around here, probably.

DENBRO: How about your parents?

MARY ANN: Oh, they like everything I write.

DENBRO: Well, that makes three of us. Can you think of anybody else?

MARY ANN: I guess I think adults would, but I'm not really so sure about other kids.

DENBRO: Kids are somehow different from adults in this respect?

MARY ANN: Well, kids just don't seem to be interested in these kinds of things. I think they put down anybody who tries to write anything.

DENBRO: Do you think they feel that way about the authors we read in class?

MARY ANN: Well sometimes they do, but I guess a lot of the time they really enjoy the stories.

---

[1] T. S. Eliot, "The Waste Land," in *Collected Poems 1909–1962.*

DENBRO: Well then, why do you think they wouldn't like what you write?

MARY ANN: I guess I really don't know, Mr. Denbro. I guess I'm really afraid, but I can't put my finger on it.

DENBRO: Something holds you back.

MARY ANN: In a lot of ways, I really would like to find out whether anybody really would appreciate what I write. I just don't know how to go about it.

DENBRO: How would you feel if I were to read one of your short stories but not tell them who wrote it?

MARY ANN: Would you promise?

DENBRO: Of course I would. Then we could talk about how everybody reacted. You would know that they didn't know who had written it.

MARY ANN: I don't know, but it sounds interesting.

DENBRO: Depending on what happened, we could cook up some kind of strategy about what to do next.

MARY ANN: Well, I guess you've got me right where I don't have anything to lose.

DENBRO: I hope we're always where you don't have anything to lose, Mary Ann; but there's always a risk in telling about ourselves.

MARY ANN: What do you mean, telling about ourselves?

DENBRO: I think I should go now—but let me pick one of your stories and read it next week, and then let's get together on Wednesday and talk about what happened.

MARY ANN: OK, and you promise not to tell?

DENBRO: I promise. I'll see you next Wednesday after school.

MARY ANN: OK. Thanks a lot, Mr. Denbro. Have a good weekend.

The Nondirective Teaching Model is based on the work of Carl Rogers (1951, 1983) and other advocates of nondirective counseling. Rogers extends his view of therapy as a mode of learning to education: He believes that positive human relationships enable people to grow, and, therefore, instruction should be based on concepts of human relations in contrast to concepts of subject matter or thought processes. The teacher's role in nondirective teaching is that of a facilitator who has a personal relationship with students and who guides their growth and development. In this role, the teacher helps students explore new ideas about their lives, their schoolwork, and their relations with others. The model assumes that students are willing to be responsible for their own learning, and its success depends on the willingness of student and teacher to share ideas openly and to communicate honestly with one another.

In general, the personal family models of teaching describe learning environments that hope to nurture students rather than to control student learning. These models are more concerned with long-term learning styles and with developing individual personalities than they are with short-term instructional or content objectives. The nondirective teacher is patient and does not sacrifice the long view by forcing immediate results.

ORIENTATION TO THE MODEL

GOALS AND ASSUMPTIONS

The Nondirective Teaching Model focuses on *facilitating* learning. The primary goal of nondirective teaching is to assist students in attaining greater personal integration, effectiveness, and realistic self-appraisal. A related goal is to create a learning environment conducive to the process of stimulating, examining, and evaluating new perceptions. A reexamination of needs and values—their sources and outcomes—is crucial to personal integration. Students do not necessarily need to change, but the teacher's goal is to help them understand their own needs and values so that they can effectively direct their own educational decisions.

The model draws on Rogers's stance toward nondirective counseling, in which the client's capacity to deal constructively with his or her own life is respected. Thus, in nondirective teaching the teacher respects the students' ability to identify their own problems and to formulate solutions.

Nondirective teaching is student-centered in that the facilitator attempts to see the world as the student sees it. This creates an atmosphere of empathetic communication in which the student's self-direction can be nurtured and developed. The primary means used is the nondirective interview strategy, a mode in which the teacher mirrors students' thoughts and feelings. By using reflective comments, the teacher raises the students' consciousness of their own perceptions and feelings, thus helping them clarify their ideas. The facilitative counseling style results in the strengthened understanding and knowledge of oneself and others that develops within the security of an empathetic relationship.

The teacher also serves as a benevolent alter ego, one who accepts all feelings and thoughts, even those the students may be afraid of or may view as wrong, or perhaps even punishable. In being accepting and nonpunitive, the teacher indirectly communicates to the students that all thoughts and feelings are acceptable. In fact, recognition of both positive and negative feelings is essential to emotional development and positive solutions.

The nondirective interview, a series of face-to-face encounters between teacher and student takes place with individuals or groups. During the interview, the teacher serves as a collaborator in the process of student self-exploration and problem solving. The interview itself is designed to focus on the uniqueness of the individual and the importance of emotional life in all human activity. Although the interview technique is borrowed from counseling, the technique is not the same in the classroom as it is in the clinical setting.

Within the classroom, the interview is used as a learning experience, but its content is not confined solely to personal problems—a common focus of counseling. A teacher using the nondirective interview strategy can counsel students about class-assignment progress, evaluate the progress of individual students in their work, and help students explore new topics that may be of interest to them. Although the nondirective strategy is appropriate for dealing with students who are having personal or academic problems, it is equally appropriate to use the technique with successful, happy students. In general, nondirective interview techniques help students strengthen their self-perceptions and evaluate their own progress and development.

During the interview the teacher gives up the traditional decision-making role, choosing instead the role of a facilitator who focuses on student feelings. Also, the teacher as counselor is not an advisor. The relationship between student and teacher in a nondirective interview is best described as a *partnership*. Thus, if the student complains of poor grades and an inability to study, the teacher does not attempt to resolve the problem simply by explaining the art of good study habits. Instead, the teacher encourages the student to express those feelings about school, himself or herself, and other persons that may surround the inability to concentrate. When these feelings are fully explored and perceptions are clarified, the student himself or herself tries to identify appropriate changes and bring them about.

According to Rogers, the best interview atmosphere has four definite qualities. First, the teacher shows warmth and responsiveness, expressing genuine interest in the student and accepting him or her as a person. Second, the counseling relationship is characterized by permissiveness in regard to the expression of feeling; the teacher does not judge or moralize. Because of the importance of emotions, much content is discussed that would normally be guarded against in more customary student relationships with teachers or advisors. Third, the student is free to express feelings symbolically, but is not free to control the teacher or to carry impulses into action. The counseling situations have definite limitations in terms of responsibility, time, affection, and aggressive action. Fourth, the counseling relationship is free from any type of pressure or coercion. The teacher avoids showing personal bias or reacting in a personally critical manner to the student during the interview.

In the nondirective interview, the teacher wants the student to experience four stages: (1) a release of feelings; (2) insight followed by (3) action; and (4) integration that leads to a new orientation. Figure 9–1 illustrates this process.

The teacher depends on the three concepts for assessing the direction and progress of the counseling process that takes place in the nondirective interview: (1) release of feelings (or catharsis); (2) insight; and (3) integration. These concepts are interrelated here in that they all stress the feeling or emotional elements of the situation. Each concept functions separately, but unity of the three is essential for a successful counseling experience. These concepts are equally important in counseling for classroom problems and for personal problems.

The release of feelings (catharsis) involves the breaking down of the emo-

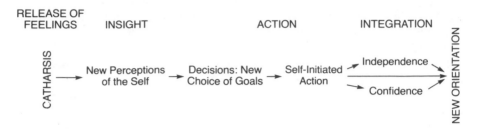

FIGURE 9-1   Phases of personal growth in the nondirective interview process.

tional barriers that often impair a person's ability to solve dilemmas. By discharging the emotions surrounding a problem, a person paves the way for developing a new perspective or insight into the problem. Usually, people are not conscious of these emotional barriers and are afraid to search for, express, and acknowledge their existence. The function of catharsis in nondirective counseling is to expose feelings so that more constructive emotional attitudes may emerge that will facilitate decision making, new behaviors, and new actions.

According to Rogers, responding on a purely intellectual basis to students' problems inhibits the expression of feelings, which are, after all, at the root of the problems. For example, if a student is struggling with writing, an intellectual response would be, "Start by making an outline." An empathetic response would be "When I get stuck I often feel panicky. How do you feel?" Without the release and exploration of these feelings, students will reject suggestions and be unable to sustain real behavior changes. On the other hand, catharsis, with its therapeutic effects, permits a solid working through of a problem.

Typically the problem-solving process proceeds as follows: At first, the students have pent-up feelings. They are tense, defensive, and as a result, unable to see the problem and themselves clearly. The student-centered counseling situation presents an opportunity for free personal expression. The students become less tense by experiencing the release that comes with the expression of pent-up feelings. Free of these feelings, the students become more comfortable and explore more aspects of themselves. Gradually, they become aware of and accept more sides of themselves—strengths as well as weaknesses.

Insight is the short-term goal of the cathartic processes. Students involved in nondirective counseling experience more than the release of feelings. They experience the insight that leads to a reorganization of the self and to increased understanding of one's emotions and patterns of behavior. Indications of insight come from statements by the students that describe behavior in terms of cause and effect, or in terms of personal meaning. As they begin to understand the reasons for their behaviors, they begin to see other, more functional ways of satisfying their needs. Through the release of emotions, the students can perceive options more clearly. New insights enable the students to select delayed goals that are more satisfying than goals that give immediate but only temporary satisfaction.

Ultimately, the test of personal insight is the presence of actions that motivate the students toward new goals. At first, these positive actions may concern minor issues, but they create a sense of confidence and independence in the student. Gradually, the students' positive actions, at first sporadic and disparate in focus, begin to accumulate around a single problem area, thereby leading to a new, more comprehensive orientation. This is the integration phase.

These three goals of the nondirective interview—catharsis, insight, and integration—are the same for counseling with an individual or with a small group. In school use of the counseling relationship, the nondirective interview is a technique by which teachers can help students focus the direction of their own learning. In accomplishing this end, the teacher may consider personal problems, but the model does not deal exclusively with such problems and is not intended to supplant counseling from other sources.

The nondirective approach maintains that the most effective means of uncovering the emotions underlying a problem is to follow the pattern of the students' feelings as they are freely expressed. Instead of asking direct questions for the purpose of eliciting feelings, the teacher lets the students direct the flow of thoughts and feelings. If the students express themselves freely, the problems and their underlying emotions will emerge. This process is facilitated by reflecting the students' feelings, thereby bringing them into awareness and sharper focus.

This is a difficult skill for most of us because we are more attuned to the content of what people are saying than to their emotional attitudes. Unlike other kinds of teacher-student relationships, nondirective counseling focuses on the emotional element of the students' behavior. The nondirective strategy usually looks to three sources of student problems: (1) present feelings; (2) distorted perceptions; and (3) alternatives that have been unexplored because of an emotional reaction to them. Elimination of these difficulties is brought about, not by direct solutions (deciding what to do), but by getting rid of negative feelings and distorted perceptions (dealing with the emotional content of decision making and thought processes).

TEACHER RESPONSES FOR
THE NONDIRECTIVE INTERVIEW

In the nondirective interview, the student and teacher share the responsibility for the discussion; however, at times the teacher must make "lead-taking" responses to direct or maintain the conversation (see Table 9–1). Ap-

Table 9-1   Nondirective Responses in Interview

A. NONDIRECTIVE RESPONSES TO FEELINGS	B. NONDIRECTIVE LEAD-TAKING RESPONSES
1. Simple acceptance	1. Structuring
2. Reflection of feelings	2. Directive questioning
3. Paraphrasing of content	3. Forcing student to choose and develop a topic
	4. Nondirective leads and open questions
	5. Minimal encouragements to talk

propriate nondirective lead-taking responses are statements by the teacher that help start the interview, or establish the direction in an open manner, or that give the student some indication as to what he or she should discuss, either specifically or generally. They may also be statements that explain what counseling is all about, or remarks that set the time and other limits of the interview. The essential skill in using this technique is to lead-take without assuming the basic responsibility for maintaining the interview. Nondirective lead-taking remarks are stated directly in a pleasant, positive, and amiable manner. Some examples are:

> "What do you think of that?"
> "Can you say more about that?"
> "How do you react when that happens?"

Nondirective responses to feelings are attempts to respond either to the feelings the student expresses or to the content of the expressions (see Table 9-2). In making these comments, the teacher does not interpret, evaluate, or offer advice, but reflects, clarifies, accepts, and demonstrates understanding. The purpose of these comments is to create an atmosphere in which the student is willing to expand the ideas he or she is expressing. Usually, the responses are short statements that are supportive and enable the student to continue the discussion. Some examples are:

> "Mm-hm." (nods)
> "I see."
> "It's especially hard to be alone."
> "Sort of like it doesn't matter what you do, it will still go on the same way."

Semidirective responses to feelings can be thought of as directive, but they are used to a certain extent by nondirective counselors. There are two types of semidirective response: *interpretation* and *approval*. Both are used

Table 9-2   Sequence of the Nondirective Interview

PHASE ONE: DEFINING THE HELPING SITUATION	PHASE TWO: EXPLORING THE PROBLEM
Teacher encourages free expression of feelings.	Student is encouraged to define problem. Teacher accepts and clarifies feelings.
PHASE THREE: DEVELOPING INSIGHT	PHASE FOUR: PLANNING AND DECISION MAKING
Student discusses problem. Teacher supports student.	Student plans initial decision making. Teacher clarifies possible decisions.
PHASE FIVE: INTEGRATION	ACTION OUTSIDE THE INTERVIEW
Student gains further insight and develops more positive actions. Teacher is supportive.	Student initiates positive actions.

sparingly because they intrude on the nondirective style, but occasionally they are useful in moving the interview forward.

An interpretation by the teacher can often promote further discussion by a student who is unable to offer any explanation for his or her behavior. Interpretative responses are attempts to suggest to the student his or her reasons for being unable to continue the discussion. But interpretation is given only to those feelings that can definitely be accepted by the student. The decision to use interpretation is made cautiously by the teacher and is used only in situations in which the teacher feels confident that interpretation will advance rather than close a dialogue. Some examples of interpretative openers are:

"You do this because . . ."
"Perhaps you feel you won't succeed."
"It sounds like your reasons for your actions this week are . . ."
"You are saying to me that the problem is . . ."

Approval is usually given only when genuine progress has been achieved. It must be used sparingly, or the nondirective relationship is likely to drift rapidly into the traditional teacher-student relationship. Approval as a closure technique must be used carefully, or it may become a signal to the student that the interview is over. Other techniques, such as summarizing or recapping the session using the student's own words, are more appropriate to the nondirective strategy. In making approval statements, the teacher might say:

"That's right."
"That's a very interesting comment and may well be worth considering again."
"That last idea was particularly strong. Could you elaborate on it some more?"
"I think we are really making progress together."

Directive counseling moves imply a relationship in which the teacher attempts to change the ideas of the student or influence his or her attitudes. The teacher does this by giving support, expressing disapproval and criticism, giving information or explanations, proposing a solution, or attempting to convince the student. For example, "Don't you think it would be better if . . ." directly suggests a choice to the student. Attempts to support the student directly are usually made to reduce apparent anxiety, but they do not contribute to the nondirective problem-solving technique. Directive counseling moves should be used sparingly; otherwise, they can defeat the nondirective interview strategy. When using directive counseling moves, the teacher maintains a more traditional role and does not help the student as an equal. The relationship remains traditional, and the teacher can easily become an authority figure rather than a partner.

These responses are supported by specific skills that enable the nondirective interviewer to act as a facilitator during the interview. The skills, which encourage the development of a direction to the interview or maintain the student's initiative in the interview, can be divided into two categories: (1) nondirective responses to feelings, by which the teacher reacts to the student's feelings; and (2) nondirective lead-taking responses, by which the teacher takes on leadership without removing the student's responsibility for initiative. These techniques develop from the nondirective view of the relationship between student and teacher. (For further discussion of these skills, see Weil, Joyce and Kluwin, 1978.)

THE MODEL OF TEACHING

The nondirective stance presents some interesting problems. First, the responsibility for the initiation and maintenance of the interview is shared. In most models of teaching, the teacher actively shapes events and can picture the pattern of activities that lies ahead; but in most counseling situations, events emerge and the pattern of activities is more fluid. Second, from the teacher's point of view counseling is made up of a series of responses that occur in an unpredictable sequence. This is unlike most teacher-controlled teaching strategies, where the activities are broad and sequential yet distinct from one another, as in presenting information and then analyzing it. As teaching becomes more student-centered, it becomes less a sequence of activities and more a series of principles for reacting that the teachers use to guide their responses to the needs of the situation.

Since nondirective teaching assumes that every student, every situation, and every teacher are unique, the specific events in a nondirective interview situation cannot be anticipated. To master nondirective teaching, teachers learn general principles, work to increase their sensitivity to others, master the nondirective skills, and then practice making contact with students and responding to them, using skills drawn from a repertoire of nondirective counseling techniques.

SYNTAX

Despite the fluidity and unpredictability of the nondirective strategy, Rogers points out that the nondirective interview has a sequence. We have divided this sequence into five phases of activity, as shown in Table 9–2.

In phase one, the helping situation is defined. This includes structuring remarks by the counselor that define the student's freedom to express feelings, an agreement on the general focus of the interview, an initial problem statement, some discussion of the relationship if it is to be ongoing, and the establishment of procedures for meeting. Phase one generally occurs during the initial interview in an ongoing relationship; however, some structuring or definition by the teacher may be necessary for some time, even if this consists only of occasional summarizing moves that redefine the problem and reflect progress. Naturally, these structuring and definitional comments vary considerably with the type of interview, the specific problem, and the student. Negotiating academic contracts will likely differ from working with behavioral problem situations. Voluntary and involuntary counseling situations are likely to be shaped differently.

In phase two, the student is encouraged, by the teacher's acceptance and clarification, to express negative and positive feelings, to state and explore the problem.

In phase three, the student gradually develops insight: He or she perceives new meaning in his or her experiences, sees new relationships of cause and effect, and understands the meaning of his or her previous behavior. In most situations, the student seems to alternate between exploring the problem itself and developing new insight into his or her feelings. Both activities are necessary for progress. Discussion of the problem without exploration of feelings would indicate that the student him- or herself was being avoided.

In phase four, the student moves toward planning and decision making with respect to the problem. The role of the teacher is to clarify the alternatives.

In phase five, the student reports the actions he or she has taken, develops further insight, and plans increasingly more integrated and positive actions.

The syntax presented here could occur in one interview or in a series of interviews. In the latter case, phases one and two could occur in the first few interviews, phases three and four in the next, and phase five in the last interview. Or, if the interview consists of a voluntary meeting with a student who has an immediate problem, phases one through four could occur in only one meeting, with the student returning briefly to report his or her actions and insights. On the other hand, the interviews involved in negotiating academic contracts are sustained for a period of time, and the context of each meeting generally involves some kind of planning and decision making, although several interviews devoted entirely to exploring a problem might occur.

The five phases of the nondirective interview provide the teacher with an overview of the process being engaged in, though the specific flow is only minimally in the teacher's control. The syntax varies with different functions, problems, and personalities.

SOCIAL SYSTEM

The social system of the nondirective strategy requires the teacher to assume the roles of facilitator and reflector. The student is primarily responsible for the initiation and maintenance of the interaction process (control); authority is shared between student and teacher. The norms are those of open expression of feelings and autonomy of thought and behavior. Rewards, in the usual sense of approval of specific behavior—and particularly punishment— do not apply in this strategy. The rewards in a nondirective interview are more subtle and intrinsic—acceptance, understanding, and empathy from the teacher. The knowledge of oneself and the psychological rewards gained from self-reliance are generated by the student himself or herself.

PRINCIPLES OF REACTION

The principles of reaction for the teacher are based on nondirective responses. The teacher reaches out to the students, empathizes with their personalities and problems, and reacts in such a way as to help them define their problems and feelings, take responsibility for their actions, and plan objectives and how to achieve them.

SUPPORT SYSTEM

The support system for this strategy varies with the function of the interview. If the interview is to negotiate academic contracts, then the necessary resources for self-directed learning must be made available. If the interview consists of counseling for a behavioral problem, no resources beyond the skills of the teacher are necessary. In both cases, the one-to-one situation requires spatial arrangements that allow for privacy, removal from other classroom forces and activities, and time to explore a problem adequately and in an unhurried fashion. For academic curriculum areas—reading, writing, literature, science, and social science—rich arrays of materials are necessary.

APPLICATION

The Nondirective Teaching Model may be used for several types of problem situations: personal, social, and academic. In the case of personal problems the individuals explore feelings about self. In social problems, students explore their feelings about relationships with others and investigate how feelings about self may influence these relationships. In academic problems, students explore their feelings about their competence and interests. In each case, however, the interview content is always personal rather than external; it centers on each individual's own feelings, experiences, insights, and solutions.

To use the Nondirective Teaching Model effectively, a teacher must be willing to accept that a student can understand and cope with his or her own life. Belief in the student's capacity to direct himself or herself is communicated through the teacher's attitude and verbal behavior. The teacher does not attempt to judge the student. Such a stance indicates limited confidence in the student's capabilities. The teacher does not attempt to diagnose problems. Instead, the teacher attempts to perceive the student's world as he or she sees and feels it. And, at the moment of the student's self-perception, the teacher reflects the new understanding to him or her. In this model, the teacher temporarily sets aside personal thoughts and feelings and reflects the student's thoughts and feelings. By doing this, the teacher conveys understanding and acceptance of the feelings.

The theory behind the teacher's role in the nondirective interview is that people deny feelings that they perceive as incongruous or incompatible with their views of themselves. If we perceive ourselves as kind, sympathetic individuals, we usually repress feelings of anger and hostility, for these contradict our views of ourselves. Yet when we do this, the problems surrounding these feelings fail to be resolved and we continue to occupy less effective states of being. What we need, the theory holds, is an alter ego who can bring these feelings into our awareness in an atmosphere of safety and acceptance.

To function in an alter-ego role, the teacher needs to develop an *internal* frame of reference—the ability to perceive as the student perceives. Expressing the student's feelings in terms of "you" rather than "he" or "I" demonstrates the use of an internal frame of reference. Rogers points out that some situations are genuinely difficult to perceive from the student's perspective, especially if the student is confused. At times all teachers will experience evaluative and diagnostic thoughts, but teachers beginning to use the nondirective interview are often concerned with themselves and concentrate on thinking about what they should do. They do not listen to the student. The strategy works only if the teacher enters the perceptual world of the student and leaves behind the more traditional external frame of reference. Developing an internal frame of reference is not easy to do at first, but it is essential if the teacher is to understand *with* the student, not merely *about* the student.

Nondirective counseling stresses the emotional elements of the situation more than the intellectual. That is, nondirective counseling strives for reorganization through the realm of feeling rather than through purely intellectual approaches. Often, this view leads teachers who are considering adopting the nondirective stance to question the possibility of conflicting roles. How, they reason, can I be a disciplinarian, a referee, an instructor, and a friend—and also be a counselor implementing nondirective principles?

In elementary schools the establishment of "open" classrooms reflects the adoption of nondirective principles. An open classroom typically has the following characteristics: First, its *objectives* include affective development, growth of student self-concept, and student determination of learning needs. Second, its *methods* of instruction are directed toward student flexibility in learning. Group work that concentrates on creativity and self-knowledge is the main instructional technique. Third, the *teacher's role* is that of a facilitator, resource person, guide, and advisor. Fourth, *the students determine what is important* to learn. They are free to set their own educational objectives and to select the method(s) for attaining their goals. Fifth, the *evaluation* of progress in the classroom consists more of student self-evaluation than of teacher evaluation. Progress is measured qualitatively rather than quantitatively.

One of the important uses of nondirective teaching occurs when a class becomes "stale" and the teacher finds himself or herself just "pushing" the students through exercises and subject matter. One sixth grade teacher, exhausted by the failure of more traditional attempts to cope with the discipline problems and the lack of interest on the part of her class, decided to experiment with student-centered teaching. She turned to nondirective approaches to help her students take more responsibility for their learning and to ensure that the subject matter would be related to their needs and learning styles. She has provided an account of that experience, from which excerpts are presented here:

MARCH 5, WE BEGIN

A week ago I decided to initiate a new program in my sixth grade classroom, based on student-centered teaching—an unstructured or non-directive approach.

I began by telling the class that we were going to try an "experiment." I explained that for one day I would let them do anything they wanted to do—they did not have to do anything if they did not want to.

Many started with art projects; some drew or painted most of the day. Others read or did work in math and other subjects. There was an air of excitement all day. Many were so interested in what they were doing that they did not want to go out at recess or noon!

At the end of the day I asked the class to evaluate the experiment. The comments were most interesting. Some were "confused," distressed without the teacher telling them what to do, without specific assignments to complete.

The majority of the class thought the day was "great," but some expressed concern over the noise level and the fact that a few "goofed off" all day. Most felt that they had accomplished as much work as we usually do, and they enjoyed being able to work at a task until it was completed, without the pressure of a time limit. They liked doing things without being "forced" to do them and liked deciding what to do.

They begged to continue the "experiment" so it was decided to do so, for two more days. We would then re-evaluate the plan.

The next morning I implemented the idea of a "work contract." I gave them ditto sheets listing all our subjects with suggestions under each. There was a space provided for their "plans" in each area and for checking upon completion.

Each child was to write his or her contract for the day—choosing the areas in which he would work and planning specifically what he would do. Upon completion of any exercise, drill, review, etc., he was to check and correct his own work, using the teacher's manual. The work was to be kept in a folder with the contract.

I met with each child to discuss his plans. Some completed theirs in a very short time; we discussed as a group what this might mean, and what to do about it. It was suggested that the plan might not be challenging enough, that an adjustment should be made—perhaps going on or adding another idea to the day's plan.

Resource materials were provided, suggestions made, and drill materials made available to use when needed.

I found I had much more time, so I worked, talked, and spent the time with individuals and groups. At the end of the third day I evaluated the work folder with each child. To solve the problem of grades, I had each child tell me what he thought he had earned.

MARCH 12, PROGRESS REPORT

Our "experiment" has, in fact, become our program—with some adjustments.

Some children continued to be frustrated and felt insecure without teacher direction. Discipline also continued to be a problem with some, and I began to realize that, although the children involved may need the program more than the others, I was expecting too much from them, too soon—they were not ready to assume self-direction yet. Perhaps a gradual weaning from the spoon-fed procedures was necessary.

I regrouped the class—creating two groups. The largest group is the nondirected. The smallest is teacher-directed, made up of children who wanted to return to the former teacher-directed method, and those who, for varied reasons, were unable to function in the self-directed situation. I would have waited longer to see what would have happened, but the situation for some disintegrated a little more each day—penalizing the whole class. The disrupting factor kept everyone upset and limited those who wanted to study and work. So it seemed to me best for the group as a whole as well as the program to modify the plan.

Those who continued the "experiment" have forged ahead. I showed them how to program their work, using their texts as a basic guide. They have learned that they can teach themselves (and each other) and that I am available when a step is not clear or advice is needed.

At the end of the week they evaluate themselves in each area—in terms of work accomplished, accuracy, etc. We have learned that the number of errors is not a criterion of failure or success. Errors can and should be part of the learning process; we learn through our mistakes. We also discussed the fact that consistently perfect scores may mean that the work is not challenging enough and perhaps we should move on.

After self-evaluation, each child brings the evaluation sheet and work folder to discuss with me.

Some of the members of the group working with me are most anxious to become "independent" students. We will evaluate together each week their progress toward that goal.

I have only experienced one parental objection so far. A parent felt her child was not able to function without direction.

Some students (there were two or three) who originally wanted to return to the teacher-directed program are now anticipating going back into the self-directed program. (I sense that it has been difficult for them to readjust to the old program as it would be for me to do so.)

INSTRUCTIONAL
AND NURTURANT EFFECTS

Since the activities are not prescribed but are determined by the learner as he or she interacts with the teacher and other students, the nondirective environment depends largely on its nurturant effects, with the instructional effects dependent on its success in nurturing more effective self-development (Figure 9–2). The model thus can be thought of as entirely nurturant in character, dependent for effects on experiencing the nondirective environment rather than carrying content and skills through specifically designed activity.

In the introduction to Part Two we stated that there are three ways that the personal models are used: first, as a general moderating influence on our

FIGURE 9-2 Instructional and nurturant effects: Nondirective Teaching Model.

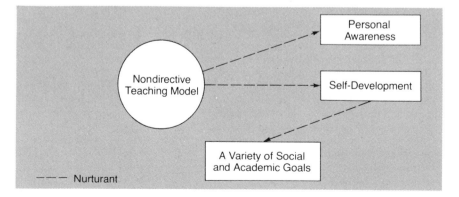

teaching; second, in intensive applications for specific purposes; third, as a general model of teaching. When we add nondirective teaching to our repertoire, all three applications are possible.

As a moderating influence, elements of the approach can be used to help us keep contact with the students' self-concepts and feelings. For example, when students are struggling with a learning task we can remember that frustration often accompanies struggle. We can be understanding and accepting of the frustration, legitimize the students' expression of their feelings, and help them recognize the frustration and find ways to deal with it.

With respect to the second use, we can employ the model intensively for those activities for which partnership and initiative are essential. For example, when we are guiding independent study projects we can help the students identify their goals and decide how to achieve them. When teaching writing we can help the students analyze their feelings and learn to put them into written form. When working with failure we can help the students define reasonable goals and support them as they work their way toward success.

Finally, when this model is used as the dominant one we can organize the classroom or learning center so that the students take a major share in determining their activities. In one of the preceding examples we described teachers who teach reading through literature, helping students to select books and to analyze their own progress.

Summary Chart: Nondirective Teaching Model

SYNTAX

Phase One:
Defining the Helping Situation
Teacher encourages free expression of feelings.

Phase Two:
Exploring the Problem
Student is encouraged to define problem.
Teacher accepts and clarifies feelings.

Phase Three:
Developing Insight
Student discusses problem.
Teacher supports student.

Phase Four:
Planning and Decision Making
Student plans initial decision making.
Teacher clarifies possible decisions.

Phase Five:
Integration
Student gains further insight and develops more positive actions.
Teacher is supportive.

SOCIAL SYSTEM

The model has little external structure: teacher facilitates; student initiates, and the discussion is problem-centered. Rewards, in the usual sense of approval of specific behavior, and punishment do not apply in this strategy. The rewards are intrinsic and include acceptance, empathy, and understanding from the teacher.

PRINCIPLES OF REACTION

Teacher reaches out to students, empathizes, reacts to help students define problems and take action to achieve solutions.

SUPPORT SYSTEM

Teacher needs quiet, private place for one-to-one contacts, resource center for conferences on academic contracts.

10

SYNECTICS
Enhancing
Creative Thought

SCENARIO

A junior high school class is creating a book of short stories and poems.
Their English teacher, Martin Abramowitz, has gradually become aware that
some stories and many of the poems are hackneyed and ordinary. He has
been helping individuals rewrite their poems and stories, and some of them
have been improved, but on the whole he is disappointed with the work.

Then Abramowitz runs across the work of William Gordon of
Cambridge, Massachusetts, who believes that creativity can be enhanced by
a series of group exercises that help individuals to understand the process
of creativity more completely and to use new metaphors and analogies to
"break set" and generate new alternatives. Abramowitz decides to try
Gordon's methods. One morning, he has each of his students read a poem
and a short story. He then says, "Today we're going to try something new
that I hope will help us see our stories and poems in a different light. For the
next fifteen or twenty minutes I want to play with ideas with you and then
have you come back to your work and see what you can do to improve it. At
the end of this exercise I'm going to ask you to rewrite part or all of your
poems and stories." He begins by asking what a poem is. The children give a
variety of answers, from which Abramowitz selects key words and writes
them on the board.

"It doesn't have to rhyme."

"It lets your feelings come out."

"It uses different kinds of words."

He then asks, "How is a poem like an automobile?" The children are puzzled. Then one ventures. "It takes you on a trip. It's a word trip, and you have to have the road in your imagination."

Someone else observes, "It is self-propelled—you just get in it and it goes."

Another student comments, "When you're writing one, sometimes you have trouble getting the motor started."

After a time, Abramowitz says, "Pick an animal—any animal." "How about a giraffe?" someone suggests. "OK," the teacher asks, "how is a poem like a giraffe?"

"It has a lot of parts fastened together in funny ways," one student laughs.

"It kind of stands above everything else and looks at things in a different way," another adds.

The exercise goes on. After a time, Abramowitz asks the students to select one of the words that they have dealt with in discussing a poem. They select the word *above.*

"How does it feel," he asks, "to be above?"

"You feel different," replies one. "You can see things you don't ordinarily even notice," says another.

"You'll start feeling superior if you don't watch out," says a third student.

And so it goes. Finally, Abramowitz asks the students to make lists of words they have been dealing with that seem to be opposites in some fashion—words that apply tension to each other. The students pick *giraffe* and *snail,* for they feel that both are animals but that they are very different in the way they live and move.

"Well," Abramowitz says, "let's come back to your poems and short stories. Think of them as giraffes and snails together; write your poems or stories as if they were a giraffe and a snail holding hands, going through the woods together."

Here are two of the products of that exercise.

THE MOTORCYCLE

It sounds like an enraged mountain lion.
It looks like a steel horse.
It shifts gear and changes notes.
It goes very fast.
The sound of the motorcycle
    breaks the stillness
        of the night.

THE ADVENTURES OF SAMUAL O'BRIAN, SECRET SPY

It all happened when Samual Watkins O'Brian, an average blonde-haired thirty-five-year-old chemist, was working in Laboratory 200, Hartford,

Connecticut for the government. While mixing chemicals in a beaker, the substance started glowing strangely. It also became very hot. At that moment he dropped it to the floor. He turned to run, but before he had time to take a step it crashed to the floor followed by a blinding explosion! As he started to run, he felt his skin shrinking. As he ran he shrank to a height of 5.5 inches, one-tenth of his normal height!!

His superior ran in with a fire extinguisher yelling, "What happened in here, Sam?"

While jumping up and down, Sam yelled, "I've shrunk! I've shrunk!" His superior made no reply. He again yelled out his cry for help. Then Sam, realizing that his yelling was useless over the roar of the fire that had now started, tugged at his superior's giant shoelace. His superior bent down to see what was happening with his shoelace and he saw a very small and scared Samual O'Brian.

Samual yelled, "Hey Jack, pick me up *carefully!*"

His superior's reply was "*Cripes!* What happened to you?" Sam explained the story in Jack's ear while Jack ran swiftly with Sam in the palm of his hand to the guard on the second floor.

Jack said (when they got there), "Seal off the building! I have Top Secret government personnel and *speed it up!!!*" Because of the excitement, Sam fainted.

The next thing he knew he was in the Central Security President's office lying in a marble ashtray, filled with warm water (and plenty of bubbles, of course). He found himself staring into the face of David Shields, President of C.S.

Sam stated that he was so sorry to clutter up the President's desk but. . . . Then David broke in "Oh, it's nothing, people shrink every day around here, but I guess you wouldn't know because you can't see the rings around the bathtub . . . er, uh, ashtray."

David presented Sam with a small box of cigars and a custom-fitted suit, James Bond style (if you know what I mean). Sam got dressed and David said, "We'd like you to work for us, Sam."

Martin Abramowitz has induced metaphoric thinking, a type of creativity, in his students. Synectics is an interesting approach to the development of creativity designed by William J. J. Gordon and his associates (1961). Gordon's initial work with synectics procedures was to develop "creativity groups" within industrial organizations—that is, groups of persons trained to work together to function as problem solvers or product developers. In recent years, Gordon has adapted synectics for use with school children, and materials containing many of the synectics activities are now being published.[1] The chief element in synectics is the use of analogies. In synectics exercises

[1] For a complete list of synectics materials write to Synectics Education Systems, 121 Brattle Street, Cambridge, Mass. 02138.

students "play" with analogies until they relax and begin to enjoy making more and more metaphoric comparisons, as did Abramowitz's students. Then they use analogies to attack problems or ideas.

Ordinarily, when we are confronted with a task, say a problem to be solved or a piece of writing to be produced, we consciously become logical. We prepare to write by making an outline of the points to be made. We analyze the elements of a problem and try to think it through. We use our existing storehouse of words and phrases to set down our ideas; we use our storehouse of learned solutions to face a problem.

For most problems and tasks of expressing ourselves our logic works well enough. What do we do when our old solutions or ways of expressing ourselves are not sufficient to do the job? That is when we use synectics. It is designed to lead us into a slightly illogical world—to give us the opportunity to invent new ways of seeing things, expressing ourselves, and approaching problems.

For example, school officials struggle with the problem of how to deal with absenteeism. When a student repeatedly fails to come to school, what do they do? Frequently, they turn to punishment. And what punishment is available? Frequently, suspension. That is logical, isn't it—to choose a severe punishment to match what is regarded as a severe infraction? The trouble with the solution is that it imposes on the student as a penalty exactly the same condition that the student had chosen in lieu of school. Synectics is used to help us develop fresh ways of thinking about the student, the student's motives, the nature of penalties, our goals, and the nature of the problem. We have to deliberately avoid logical thought because it leads us to an inadequate conception of the problem and, thus, an absurd (if logical) solution. We have to develop empathy with someone who is in conflict with us.

Through analogies we might conceive of our absentee as an "unhappy lark," as on a "destructive vacation," and the problem as one of ending an "empty feast." Our own needed behaviors may be ones of "seductive strictness," "strong lovingness," and "dangerous peacemaking."

If we can relax the premises that have blocked us, we can begin to generate new solutions. We can consider that we have been taking responsibility for the students in areas where they may need to be responsible for themselves. We can wonder whether the solution lies as much in our administration of the rules as it does in how we teach. We may wonder whether communities of peers might not create the energy and sense of belongingness that would attack the problem from a different perspective.

The social and scientific world in which we live abounds with problems for which new solutions are needed. Problems of poverty, international law, crime, just taxation, and war and peace would not exist if our logic did not fail us.

Striving for appropriate self-expression—trying to learn how to write and speak lucidly and compellingly—bedevils all of us. Two problems are persistent: grasping the subject clearly and comprehensively and generating appropriate forms of expression.

Let us consider another example from Martin Abramowitz's classroom in New York City:

Now, Martin Abramowitz's seventh grade class, which we met earlier, is preparing a campaign in opposition to a change in Forest Service regulations that would permit a large part of a grove of redwood trees to be cut down as part of a lumbering operation. They have made posters that they intend to display around their community and send to the members of the state legislature. They have the rough sketches for the posters and their captions, and they are examining them.

"Well, what do you think?" asks Priscilla.

"Well, they're OK," says Tommy. "They sure say where we stand. Actually, though, I think they're a little dull."

"So do I," adds Maryann. "A couple of them are OK, but the others are real preachy and stiff."

"There's nothing really wrong with them," chimes in another, "they're just not very zingy."

After some discussion it is obvious that nearly everybody feels the same way. They decide that two or three of the posters are well designed and convey their message, but they need some others that would be more poignant.

"Let's try synectics," suggests one of the children.

"With pictures and captions?" asks one of the other children. "I thought we could only use synectics with poetry. Can we use synectics with stuff like this?"

"Why sure we can," says Priscilla. "I don't know why I didn't think of it. We've been doing it with our poetry all year long."

"Well, we sure have nothing to lose," adds Tommy. "How would it work?"

"Well," says Priscilla, "we could see these posters we've done as the beginning point and then go through a synectics training exercise and see if it gives us some ideas for pictures and captions. We could think of redwood trees in terms of various personal and direct analogies and compressed conflicts."

"Well let's try it," chimes in George.

"Let's start right now," says Sally. "We could go through our exercises and then have lunch time to think about the posters."

"Can I be the leader?" asks Marsha. "I've got some super ideas for some stretching exercises."

"Is that OK?" says Priscilla.

The children agree and Marsha begins.

"How is a redwood tree like a toothpick?" she asks.

"You use them to pick the teeth of the gods," laughs George. Everyone joins in the laughter and they are off.

It's clear that Mr. Abramowitz has spent enough time using synectics that the students internalized the process and purpose enough to proceed on their own, drawing on the model when they find it helpful.

One of the present authors struggled for a month to write a single page that would introduce a book on school improvement. The introduction had to express the complexity of the situation the school occupies in society and to convey that it needs improvement, but it had to do so in an upbeat and not discouraging fashion. Finally, after an afternoon of synectics, he produced the following passage:

Richly connected to its social milieu, tightly clasped by tradition and yet the medium of modern ideas and artifacts, the school floats paradoxically in its ocean of social forces. It is a cradle of social stability and the harbinger of cultural change. Throughout history its critics have found it both too backward and too advanced. It falls behind the times and fails to keep us in simultaneous cadence.

Its missions are elusive. Basic education is prized but so are creativity, problem solving, academic excellence, and vocational skills, sometimes by the same people, sometimes not. Liberals and conservatives alike seek to make the school the instrument of social policy. It is the sword of the militant and the warm bosom of the humanist. Its students are varied. Talents and handicaps mingle, sometimes in the same minds and bodies.

The inner city and rural hinterland make their claims on creaky old schoolhouses while shiny suburban schools grope for a coherent mission. Powerful self-concepts march through the front door of the school while timid souls slip in by the back stairs. Cultural differences are mixed together, with problems of identity and adaptation surfacing chaotically to be dealt with.

Technologies strengthen the school's potential and threaten to replace it. Its personnel receive very little training but are asked to manage one of the most complex professional tasks in our society. They have little status but awesome responsibility both for individual children and for the health of the society as a whole.

Because education exerts great influence on the young, society places great constraints on its schools so that they will reflect the prevailing social attitudes and will fit current views about how its children should be trained. Its very size draws attention. (In the United States there are more than 2,000,000 education professionals and about 8 percent of the gross national product is directly or indirectly consumed by the enterprises of education.) The public watches its investment carefully, scrutinizing educational practices, both traditional and innovative (Joyce & Morine, 1976).

Efficiency is highly prized, but innovations are watched with apprehension. Our societal patterns of schooling, established in the early 1800s, have become familiar and comfortable, and we want our children to have an education that has continuity with our own. Thus most citizens are cautious about educational innovation. People like the familiar old schoolhouse as much as they criticize it. They tend to believe that current problems in education are caused by changes (perceived as a "lowering of standards") rather than because the old comfortable model of the school may be a little rusty and out-of-date. In fact, our society has changed a great deal since the days when the familiar and comfortable patterns of education were established, and many schools have become badly out of phase with the needs of children in today's world (Joyce, Hersh, and McKibbin, 1983, pp. 3–4).

This passage is by no means perfect, but it is much better than the prosaic passages that were its early drafts (e.g., "The public is somewhat ambivalent about the schools. In some ways they want a forward-looking education for their children and in others they want a familiar, stable education.")

ORIENTATION TO THE MODEL

GOALS AND ASSUMPTIONS

Gordon grounds synectics in four ideas that challenge conventional views about creativity. First, creativity is important in everyday activities. Most of us associate the creative process with the development of great works of art or music, or perhaps with a clever new invention. Gordon emphasizes creativity as a part of our daily work and leisure lives. His model is designed to increase problem-solving capacity, creative expression, empathy, and insight into social relations. He also stresses that the meanings of ideas can be enhanced through creative activity by helping us see things more richly.

Second, the creative process is not at all mysterious. It can be described, and it is possible to train persons directly to increase their creativity. Traditionally, creativity is viewed as a mysterious, innate, and personal capacity that can be destroyed if its processes are probed too deeply. In contrast, Gordon believes that if individuals understand the basis of the creative process, they can learn to use that understanding to increase the creativity with which they live and work, independently and as members of groups. Gordon's view that creativity is enhanced by conscious analysis led him to describe it and create training procedures that can be applied in schools and other settings.

Third, creative invention is similar in all fields—the arts, the sciences, engineering—and is characterized by the same underlying intellectual processes. This idea is contrary to common belief; in fact, to many people creativity is confined to the arts. In engineering and the sciences, however, it is simply called by another name: *invention*. Gordon maintains that the link between generative thinking in the arts and that in the sciences is quite strong.

Gordon's fourth assumption is that individual and group invention (creative thinking) are very similar. Individuals and groups generate ideas and products in much the same fashion. Again, this is very different from the stance that creativity is an intensely personal experience, not to be shared.

THE CREATIVE STATE AND THE SYNECTICS PROCESS

The specific processes of synectics are developed from a set of assumptions about the psychology of creativity. First, by bringing the creative process to consciousness and by developing explicit aids to creativity, we can directly increase the creative capacity of both individuals and groups.

A second assumption is that the "emotional component is more important than the intellectual, the irrational more important than the rational" (Gordon, 1961, p. 6). Creativity is the development of new mental patterns. Nonrational interplay leaves room for open-ended thoughts that can lead to a mental state in which new ideas are possible. The basis for decisions, however, is always the rational; the irrational state is the best mental environment for exploring and expanding ideas, but it is not a decision-making state. Gordon does not undervalue the intellect; he assumes that a logic is used in decision making and that technical competence is necessary to the formation of ideas in many areas. But he believes that creativity is essentially an *emotional* process, one that requires elements of irrationality and emotion to enhance intellectual processes. Much problem solving is rational and intellectual, but by adding the irrational we increase the likelihood that we will generate fresh ideas.

The third assumption is that the "emotional, irrational elements must be understood in order to increase the probability of success in a problem solving situation" (Gordon, 1961, p. 1). In other words, the analysis of certain irrational and emotional processes can help the individual and the group to increase their creativity by using irrationality constructively. Aspects of the irrational can be understood and consciously controlled. Achievement of this control, through the deliberate use of metaphor and analogy, is the object of synectics.

METAPHORIC ACTIVITY

Through the metaphoric activity of the Synectics Model, creativity becomes a conscious process. Metaphors establish a relationship of likeness, the comparison of one object or idea with another object or idea by using one in place of the other. Through these substitutions the creative process occurs, connecting the familiar with the unfamiliar or creating a new idea from familiar ideas.

Metaphor introduces conceptual distance between the student and the object or subject matter and prompts original thoughts. For example, by asking students to think of their textbook as an old shoe or as a river, we provide a structure, a metaphor, with which the students can think about something familiar in a new way. Conversely, we can ask students to think about a new topic, say the human body, in an old way by asking them to compare it to the transportation system. Metaphoric activity thus depends and draws from the students' knowledge, helping them connect ideas from familiar content to those from new content, or view familiar content from a new perspective. Synectics strategies using metaphoric activity are designed, then, to provide a structure through which persons can free themselves to develop imagination and insight into everyday activities. Three types of analogies are used as the basis of synectics exercises: personal analogy, direct analogy, and compressed conflict.

PERSONAL ANALOGY   To make personal analogies requires students to empathize with the ideas or objects to be compared. Students must feel they have become part of the physical elements of the problem. The identification may be with a person, plant, animal, or nonliving thing. For example, students may be instructed, "Be an automobile engine. What do you feel like? Describe how you feel when you are started in the morning; when your battery goes dead; when you come to a stop light."

The emphasis in personal analogy is on empathetic involvement. Gordon gives the example of a problem situation in which the chemist personally identifies with the molecules in action. He might ask, "How would I feel if I were a molecule?" and then feel himself being part of the "stream of dancing molecules."

Personal analogy requires some loss of self as one transports oneself into another space or object. The greater the conceptual distance created by loss of self, the more likely it is that the analogy is new and that the students have created or innovated. Gordon identifies four levels of involvement in personal analogy:

1. *First-person description of facts.* The person recites a list of well-known facts but presents no new way of viewing the object or animal and shows no empathetic involvement. In terms of the car engine, the person might say, "I feel greasy" or, "I feel hot."
2. *First-person identification with emotion.* The person recites common emotions but does not present new insights. "I feel powerful" (as the car engine).
3. *Empathetic identification with a living thing.* The student identifies emotionally and kinesthetically with the subject of the analogy.
4. *Empathetic identification with a nonliving object.* This level requires the most commitment. The person sees himself or herself as an inorganic object and tries to explore the problem from a sympathetic point of view. "I feel exploited. I cannot determine when I start and stop. Someone does that for me" (as the car engine).

The purpose of introducing these levels of personal analogy is not to identify forms of metaphoric activity but to provide guidelines for how well conceptual distance has been established. Gordon believes that the usefulness of analogies is directly proportional to the distance created. The greater the distance, the more likely the student is to come up with new ideas.

DIRECT ANALOGY   Direct analogy is a simple comparison of two objects or concepts. The comparison does not have to be identical in all respects. Its function is simply to transpose the conditions of the real topic or problem situation to another situation in order to present a new view of an idea or problem. This involves identification with a person, plant, animal, or nonliving thing. Gordon cites the experience of an engineer watching a shipworm tunneling into a timber. As the worm ate its way into the timber by constructing a tube for itself and moving forward, the engineer, Sir March Isumbard Brunel, got the notion of using caissons to construct underwater tunnels (Gordon, 1961, pp. 40–41). Another example of direct analogy occurred when a group was attempting to devise a can with a top that could be used to cover the can once it had been opened. In this instance, the analogy of the pea pod gradually emerged, which produced the idea of a seam placed a distance below the top of the can, thus permitting a removable lid.

COMPRESSED CONFLICT   The third metaphorical form is compressed conflict, generally a two-word description of an object in which the words seem to be opposites or contradict each other: *Tiredly aggressive* and *friendly foe* are two examples. Gordon's examples are *life-saving destroyer* and *nourishing flame.* He also cites Pasteur's expression, *safe attack.* Compressed conflicts, according to Gordon, provide the broadest insight into a new subject. They reflect the student's ability to incorporate two frames of reference with respect to a single object. The greater the distance between frames of reference, the greater the mental flexibility.

STRETCHING EXERCISES: USING METAPHORS

The three types of metaphors form the basis of the sequence of activities in this model of teaching. They can also be used separately with groups, as a warm-up to the creative process—that is, to problem solving; we refer to this use as *stretching exercises.*

Stretching exercises provide experience with the three types of metaphoric activity, but they are not related to any particular problem situation nor do they follow a sequence of phases. They teach students the process of metaphoric thinking before asking them to use it to solve a problem, create a design, or explore a concept. They are simply asked to respond to ideas such as the following:

DIRECT ANALOGIES

An orange is like what living thing?
How is a school like a salad?
How are polar bears like frozen yogurt?
Which is softer—a whisper or a kitten's fur?

PERSONAL ANALOGIES

Be a cloud. Where are you? What are you doing?
How do you feel when the sun comes out and dries you up?
Pretend you are your favorite book. Describe yourself.
What are your three wishes?

COMPRESSED CONFLICTS

How is a computer shy and aggressive?
What machine is like a smile and a frown?

THE MODEL OF TEACHING

SYNTAX

There are actually two strategies or models of teaching based on synectics procedures. One of these (*creating something new*) is designed to make the familiar strange, to help students see old problems, ideas, or products in a new, more creative light. The other strategy (*making the strange familiar*) is designed to make new, unfamiliar ideas more meaningful. Although both strategies employ the three types of analogy, their objectives, syntax, and principles of reaction are diferent. We refer to creating something new as *strategy one*, and making the strange familiar as *strategy two*.

Strategy one helps students see familiar things in unfamiliar ways by using analogies to create conceptual distance. Except for the final step, in which the students return to the original problem, they do not make simple comparisons. The objective of this strategy may be to develop a new understanding; to empathize with a show-off or bully; to design a new doorway or city; to solve social or interpersonal problems, such as a garbage strike or two students fighting with each other; or to solve personal problems, such as how to concentrate better when reading. The role of the teacher is to guard against premature analyses and closure. The syntax of strategy one appears in Table 10–1.

The following transcript of a synectics session shows a teacher helping students to see a familiar concept in fresh ways. At the beginning, the students pick the concept of "The Hood," to be described later in a writing composition. The lesson illustrates the six phases of the model:

TEACHER:	Do you have any ideas?
STUDENT:	Charlie Brown! (Groans from the class.)
STUDENT:	Prince Valiant! (Groans from the class.)
STUDENT:	How about a hood? A gangster? (Class likes the idea.)

Table 10–1 Syntax for Creating Something New, Strategy One

PHASE ONE: DESCRIPTION OF PRESENT CONDITION	PHASE TWO: DIRECT ANALOGY
Teacher has students describe situation or situation as they see it now.	Students suggest direct analogies, select one, and explore (describe) it further.
PHASE THREE: PERSONAL ANALOGY	PHASE FOUR: COMPRESSED CONFLICT
Students "become" the analogy they selected in phase two.	Students take their descriptions from phases two and three, suggest several compressed conflicts, and choose one.
PHASE FIVE: DIRECT ANALOGY	PHASE SIX: REEXAMINATION OF THE ORIGINAL TASK
Students generate and select another direct analogy, based on the compressed conflict.	Teacher has students move back to original task or problem and use the last analogy and/or the entire synectics experience.

TEACHER: Where?

STUDENT: Cincinnati.

1. TEACHER: Now the problem is how to present this hood so that he's the hoodiest of hoods; but also a special, individualized person.

STUDENT: He robs the Rabbinical School.

STUDENT: Let's name him.

STUDENT: Trog.

STUDENT: Al.

STUDENT: Slash.

STUDENT: Eric.

TEACHER: His names don't matter all that much. Let's call him Eric. What can we say about Eric?

STUDENT: Black, greasy hair. They all have black, greasy hair.

STUDENT: Long, blonde hair—bleached—peroxided—With baby-blues. Eyes, I mean.

STUDENT: Bitten fingernails.

STUDENT: He's short and muscular.

STUDENT: Maybe he should be scrawny.

STUDENT: Bow-legged and yellow teeth and white, tight Levis.

2. TEACHER: Is there anything here that's original? If you wrote that and backed off and read it, what would you think?

CLASS: No! Stereotyped! Standard! No personality! Very general! Same old stuff!

TEACHER: I agree. Eric, so far, is like every other hood. Now we have a problem to attack!

TEACHER: We must define a personality for this hood, for Eric.

STUDENT: He's got to be individualized.

STUDENT: He has to have a way of getting money.

3. TEACHER: That's still an overgeneral idea of Eric. Let's put some strain into this idea. Hold it. Suppose I ask you to give me a Direct Analogy, something like Eric, but it's a machine. Tell me about a machine that has Eric's

1. *Phase One:* Describing the Problem or Present Condition. Teacher asks students to discuss the familiar idea.

2. Teacher has students state the problem . . .

and define the task.

3. *Phase Two: Direct Analogy.* Teacher moves the students into analogies. He asks for a direct analogy. He also specifies the nature of the analogy—that is, a machine—in order to assure

qualities as you see him. Not a human being, a machine.

STUDENT: He's a washing machine. A dishwasher.

STUDENT: An old beat-up car.

STUDENT: I want him to be a rich hood.

STUDENT: A beer factory.

STUDENT: A pinball machine in a dive.

STUDENT: Roulette.

4. TEACHER: You're focusing on the kinds of machines that Eric plays with. What is the thing that has his qualities in it?

STUDENT: An electric can opener.

STUDENT: A vacuum cleaner.

STUDENT: A neon sign.

STUDENT: A jello mold.

5. TEACHER: What is the machine that would make the strangest comparison between it and Eric? Go ahead and vote. (The class voted for the dishwasher.)

6. TEACHER: First of all, how does a dishwasher work?

STUDENT: People put in the dirty dishes and the water goes around and around and the dishes come out clean.

STUDENT: There's a blower in the one that's in the common room.

STUDENT: It's all steam inside. Hot!

STUDENT: I was thinking that if you want to make an analogy between the washer and the joy . . .

7. TEACHER: Hold it. Just stay with me. Don't look backward and make an analogical comparison too soon . . . and now is probably too soon.

8. TEACHER: OK. Now, try being the dishwasher. What does it feel like to be a dishwasher? Tell us. Make yourself the dishwasher.

STUDENT: Well, all these things are given to me. Dishes are dirty. I want to get them clean. I'm trying. I throw off some steam and finally I get them clean. That's my duty.

getting one of some distance (organic-inorganic comparison).

4. Teacher reflects to students what they are doing so that they can be pushed to more creative analogies.

5. Teacher lets students select the analogy to develop, but he provides the criterion for selection: "strangest comparison."

6. Teacher moves students simply to *explore* (describe) the machine they selected before making comparisons to their original source.

7. Teacher controls responses to keep students from pushing to a comparison too soon. No comparisons to original source are made before moving on to another analogy.

8. *Phase Three: Personal Analogy.* Teacher asks for personal analogy.

9. TEACHER: Come on now people! You've got to put yourselves into the dishwasher and be it. All Lee's told us is what we already know about a dishwasher. There's none of *Lee* in it. It's hard, but try to *be* the dishwasher.

STUDENT: It's very discouraging. You're washing all day long. I never get to know anybody. They keep throwing these dishes at me, and I just throw the steam at them. I see the same type of dishes.

STUDENT: I get mad and get the dishes extra hot, and I burn people's fingers.

STUDENT: I feel very repressed. They keep feeding me dishes. All I can do is shut myself off.

STUDENT: I get so mad at everybody maybe I won't clean the dishes and then everybody will get sick.

STUDENT: I just love garbage. I want more and more. The stuff that falls off the dishes is soft and mushy and good to eat.

9. Teacher reflects to students the fact that they are describing the dishwasher, not what it *feels* like to be a dishwasher.

10. TEACHER: Let's look at the notes I've been making about your responses. Can you pick two words that argue with each other?

STUDENT: "Used" vs. "clean."

STUDENT: "Duty" vs. "what you want to do."

TEACHER: How can we put that more poetically?

STUDENT: "Duty" vs. "inclination."

STUDENT: "Duty" vs. "whim."

STUDENT: "Discouraging fun."

STUDENT: "Angry game."

10. *Phase Four: Compressed Conflict.* Teacher asks for compressed conflict as outgrowth of the personal analogy: "Can you pick two words that argue with each other?

11. TEACHER: All right. What one do you like best? Which one has the truest ring of conflict?

CLASS: "Angry game."

11. Teacher ends enumeration of possible compressed conflicts and asks them to select one. The teacher furnishes the criterion: "Which has the truest ring of conflict?"

12. TEACHER: All right. Can you think of a direct analogy, an example from the animal world, of "angry game?"

STUDENT: A lion in the cage at the circus.

STUDENT: Rattlesnake.

STUDENT: A pig ready for slaughter.

12. *Phase Five: Direct Analogy.* Recycling the analogies; compressed conflict is not explored but serves as the basis of the next direct analogy, an example from the animal world of "angry game." There is no mention of the original.

STUDENT: A bear when it's attacking.

STUDENT: Bullfrog.

STUDENT: A bird protecting its young.

STUDENT: Bullfight.

STUDENT: A fish being caught.

STUDENT: A skunk.

STUDENT: A horse.

STUDENT: A charging elephant.

STUDENT: A fox hunt on horseback.

STUDENT: Rodeo.

STUDENT: Porcupine.

TEACHER: Does anyone know where we are?

STUDENT: We're trying to put personality into Eric, trying to make him more original.

13.   TEACHER: All right. Which of all the things you just thought of do you think would make the most exciting direct analogy?
(Class chooses the bullfight.)

TEACHER: Now we go back to Eric. How can we get the bullfight to describe Eric for us. Does anyone know what I mean by that?

14.   (Class doesn't respond.)

15.   TEACHER: All right. What do we know about a bullfight?

STUDENT: He'll have to be the bull or the matador. I say he's the bull.

STUDENT: Bull runs into the ring and he's surrounded by strangeness.

STUDENT: They stick things into him and goad him . . .

STUDENT: . . . from horses and from the ground.

STUDENT: But sometimes he doesn't get killed.

STUDENT: And everytime the bull is downgraded the crowd yells.

16.   TEACHER: What happens at the end?

STUDENT: They drag him off with horses.

STUDENT: How do they finish him off?

STUDENT: A short sword.

13.   Teacher ends the enumeration of direct analogies. Again, he has the students select one but he gives the criterion: "Which of all the things you just thought of do you think would make the most *exciting* direct analogy?"

14.   Students are not into the analogy of the bullfight yet.

15.   Teacher gets students to explore the characteristics of the bullfight, the analogy.

16.   Teacher tries to obtain more information about the analogy.

17. **TEACHER:** How can we use this information to tell us something about Eric? How will you talk about Eric in terms of the material we've developed about a bullfight?

STUDENT: He's the bull.

STUDENT: He's the matador.

STUDENT: If he's the bull, then the matador is society.

TEACHER: Why don't you write something about Eric in terms of the bullfight? Talk about his personality and the outward signs of it. The reader opens your story about Eric, and he reads. It is your reader's first introduction to Eric. (A pause while the students write.)

TEACHER: All finished? All right, let's read your stuff, from left to right.

17. *Phase Six: Reexamination of the Task.* Getting students to make comparisons; return to the original problem or task.

Here are a few examples of the students' writing.

In rage, running against a red neon flag and blinded by its shadow, Eric threw himself down on the ground. As if they were going to fall off, blood throbbed in his ears. No use fighting anymore. The knife would in this side; the metallic jeers that hurt worse than the knife; the flash of uniforms and the flushed faces of the crowd made him want to vomit all over their clean robes.

He stood there in the middle of the street staring defiantly at the crowd. Faces leered back at him. Scornful eyes, huge red mouths, twisted laughs; Eric looked back as the crowd approached and drew his hand up sharply as one man began to speak. "Pipe down kid. We don't want any of your nonsense."

He was enclosed in a ring, people cheering all around for his enemy. He has been trained all his life to go out and take what he wanted and now there was an obstacle in his course. Society was bearing down and telling him he was all wrong. He must go to them and he was becoming confused. People should cheer at the matador.

The matador hunts his prey. His claim to glory is raised by the approaching approval of the crowd. For although they brought all their holiday finery, the bull is goaded, and the matador smiles complacently. You are but my instrument and I hold the sword. (Gordon, 1970, pp. 7–11)

The Synectics Model has stimulated the students to see and feel the original idea (a gangster or hood, described in stereotypic terms) in a variety of fresh ways. If they had been solving a problem, we would expect that they would see it more richly and increase the solutions they could explore.

By contrast, strategy two, making the strange familiar, seeks to increase the students' understanding and internalization of substantially new or difficult material. In this analogy, metaphor is used for *analyzing,* not for creating conceptual distance as in strategy one. For instance, the teacher might present the concept of culture to her class. Using familiar analogies (such as a stove or a house), the students begin to define the characteristics that are present and those that are lacking in the concept. The strategy is decidedly analytical, and convergent: Students constantly alternate between defining the characteristics of the more familiar subject and comparing these to the characteristics of the unfamiliar topic.

In phase one of this strategy, explaining the new topic, the students are provided with information. In phase two the teacher, or the students, suggest a direct analogy. Phase three involves "being the familiar" (personalizing the direct analogy). In phase four, students identify and explain the points of similarity between the analogy and the substantive material. In phase five, students explain the differences between analogies. As a measure of their acquisition of the new information, students can suggest and analyze their own familiar analogies in phases six and seven. The syntax of strategy two appears in Table 10–2.

The following is an illustration of strategy two as it has been used in a programmed workbook. The students are asked to make a comparison between democracy (new topic) and the body (familiar topic). The sample presented here does not include the personal analogy phase (phase three), which we recommend as part of the strategy. We feel that asking the students to "be the thing" before asking them to make intellectual connections will increase the richness of their thinking.

Table 10–2   Syntax for Making the Strange Familiar, Strategy Two

PHASE ONE: SUBSTANTIVE INPUT	PHASE TWO: DIRECT ANALOGY
Teacher provides information on new topic.	Teacher suggests direct analogy and asks students to describe the analogy.
PHASE THREE: PERSONAL ANALOGY	PHASE FOUR: COMPARING ANALOGIES
Teacher has students "become" the direct analogy.	Students identify and explain the points of similarity between the new material and the direct analogy.
PHASE FIVE: EXPLAINING DIFFERENCES	PHASE SIX: EXPLORATION
Students explain where the analogy does not fit.	Students reexplore the original topic on its own terms.
PHASE SEVEN: GENERATING ANALOGY	
Students provide their own direct analogy and explore the similarities and differences.	

In this example the student first is presented with a short, substantive paragraph:

Democracy is a form of government that is based on the highest possible respect for the individual. All individuals have equal rights, protected by law. Since each person has a vote, when the people so desire they can change the law to further protect themselves. The role of education in a democracy is critically important because the right to vote carries with it the responsibility to understand issues. An uneducated voting public could be led by a power-hungry political group into voting away their right to freedom. Thus democracy puts all its faith in the individual, in all the people . . . democracy's respect for the individual is expressed in the right of individuals to own property such as industries whose purpose is to make profit in competition with others.

Next the student is told:

List the connections you see between the description of democracy and the human body. Certain elements of the human body are written in the left-hand column. In the right-hand column jot down the elements in the paragraph on democracy that you think are parallel.

Body	*Democracy*
each cell	each individual
muscles	education
brain	law
body as whole	democratic country
disease	loss of freedom

After the student has filled in his connection list he is asked to "Write a short paragraph showing your analogical connections. Be sure to point out where you think the body analogue fits and where it doesn't."

A sample response:

Each body cell is an individual. It may not look like it to the naked eye, but that's how it looks under a microscope. The muscles are education because they must be taught (except for automatic things such as blinking and digestion and there may be teaching here that we don't know about) to do certain acts; walking, games, knitting, etc. The brain is the law. If I do something wrong my mind tells me and my brain is in my mind. The body as a whole is democratic because it depends on the health of all the cells. When there is disease the body loses freedom and a power-hungry disease takes over. The body dies when the disease takes over all the cells.

Non-fit. In democracy the people control the government by voting, and then they can always repair bad laws. You can't always repair a body that is growing older . . . it will finally die.

So far in this sample exercise the student has been held by the hand. An analogue was presented to him, and all he had to do was make the connections as he saw them. The final skill taught in this exercise is *application*. The student's program tells him:

Now think up your own analogue for democracy. Draw on the non-living world to make sure that your analogue is not like the body analogue. Write your choice of analogue on the line below. If your analogue doesn't fit, pick a new one. REMEMBER that analogues never fit exactly, they are just a way of thinking.

Use this list form to get you going. Fill in the elements of your analogue and add more elements about democracy if you want.

Your Analogue	Democracy
automobile	democracy
each part	each individual
education	design of parts
car itself	democracy
no gas	loss of freedom

In the final phase of the programmed exercise he is told:

> Now write your connections in the best prose you can. First get your connective thoughts down; then go back and worry about grammar. Don't let grammar get in your way while you are trying to say what you mean. Grammar is a skill that makes it easier for your reader; so do it later. Try *not* to write more than the following lines allow. QUALITY not QUANTITY: Remember, show the fits and the non-fits.

The student writes:

> All parts of a car are like the individuals in a democracy. When they are all in good shape they are free and the car runs well. The way each part was made was its education. God gave men the right to be free and God gave the car's engine the right to run—how the gases explode in the engine is God's gift. If democracy is neglected, then no freedom. If the car runs out of gas then no freedom.

> . . . One further small phase is necessary to make sure the students realize that analogues are not exact parallels. . . . The student is told: "on the lines below explain where your analogue doesn't fit."

A sample response follows:

> In a democracy, all the people must not neglect the country. In a car it is the owner who neglects when he forgets to fill her up. Also I tried to find "profit" in a car—and couldn't. Any competition is a race in a car—not like competition in a democracy. Also, there are so many freedom laws in a democracy and the only law I can think of for a car is the science law that makes the engine run.

The major difference between the two strategies lies in their use of analogy. In strategy one, students move through a series of analogies without logical constraints; conceptual distance is increased, and imagination is free to wander. In strategy two, students try to connect two ideas and to identify the connections as they move through the analogies. The strategy the teacher selects depends on whether he or she is trying to help students create something new or to explore the unfamiliar.

SOCIAL SYSTEM

The model is moderately structured, with the teacher initiating the sequence and guiding the use of the operational mechanisms. He or she also helps the students intellectualize their mental processes. The students, however, have freedom in their open-ended discussions as they engage in the metaphorical problem solving. Norms of cooperation, "play of fancy," and intellectual and emotional equality are essential to establishing the setting for creative problem solving. The rewards are internal, coming from students' satisfaction and pleasure with the learning activity.

PRINCIPLES OF REACTION

The instructor notes the extent to which individuals seem to be tied to regularized patterns of thinking, and he or she tries to induce psychological states likely to generate a creative response. In addition, the teacher himself or herself must use the nonrational to encourage the reluctant student to indulge in irrelevance, fantasy, symbolism, and other devices necessary to break out of set channels of thinking. Because the teacher as model is probably an essential of the method, he or she has to learn to accept the bizarre and the unusual. The instructor must accept all student responses to ensure that students feel no external judgments on their creative expressions. The more difficult the problem is, or seems to be, to solve, the more it is necessary for the teacher to accept far-fetched analogies so that individuals develop fresh perspectives on problems.

In strategy two the teacher should guard against premature analyses. He or she also clarifies and summarizes the progress of the learning activity and hence, the students' problem-solving behavior.

SUPPORT SYSTEM

The group needs most of all facilitation by a leader competent in synectics procedures. It also needs, in the case of scientific problems, a laboratory in which it can build models and other devices to make problems concrete and to permit practical invention to take place. The class requires a work space of its own, and an environment in which creativity will be prized and utilized.

A typical classroom can probably provide these necessities, but a classroom-sized group may be too large for many synectics activities, and smaller groups would need to be created.

APPLICATION

USING SYNECTICS IN THE CURRICULUM

Synectics is designed to increase the creativity of individuals and groups. Sharing the synectics experience can build a feeling of community among students. Students learn about their fellow classmates as they watch them react to an idea or problem. Thoughts are valued for their potential contribution to the group process. Synectics procedures help create a community of equals in which simply having a thought is the sole basis for status. This norm and that of playfulness quickly give support to even the most timid participant.

Synectics procedures may be used with students in all areas of the curriculum, the sciences as well as the arts. They can be applied to both teacher-student discussion in the classroom and to teacher-made materials for the students. The products or vehicles of synectics activity need not always be written: They can be oral, or they can take the form of role plays, paintings and graphics, or simply changes in behavior. When using synectics to look at social or behavior problems, you may wish to notice situational behavior before and after synectics activity and observe changes. It is also interesting to select modes of expression that contrast with the original topic, such as having students paint a picture of prejudice or discrimination. The concept is abstract, but the mode of expression is concrete.

Some possible uses of the creative process and its accompanying emotional states are discussed in the following paragraphs:

CREATIVE WRITING   Strategy one of the Synectics Model is an excellent instructional strategy for developing creative writing abilities. Writing, either expository writing about a particular concept (such as friendship) or more personalized writing (regarding an emotion or an experience), is an area of the language arts program where synectics can help students develop highly creative styles of expression. The metaphoric activity stimulates their imaginations and helps them record their thoughts and feelings.

EXPLORING SOCIAL PROBLEMS   Strategy one is excellent for exploring social and disciplinary problems. The metaphor creates distance, so the confrontation does not threaten the learner, and discussion and self-examination are possible. The personal analogy phase is critical for developing insight.

PROBLEM SOLVING   Problem solving concerned with social issues, interpersonal relations, or personal problems is amenable to synectics. The objective of strategy two is to break set and conceptualize the problem in a new way in order to suggest fresh approaches to it. An example of a social issue would be how to better relations between the police and the community. Reducing family spending is an example of an interpersonal relations problem. Personal problems might include how to stop fighting with a friend, how to do math lessons, how to feel better about wearing glasses, or how to stop making fun of people.

CREATING A DESIGN OR PRODUCT   Synectics can also be used to create a product or design. A product is something tangible, such as a painting, a building, or a bookshelf, whereas a design is a plan, such as an idea for a party or a new means of transportation. Eventually, designs or plans become real, but for the purposes of this model they remain as sketches or outlines.

BROADENING OUR PERSPECTIVE OF A CONCEPT Abstract ideas such as culture, prejudice, and economy are difficult to internalize because we cannot see them in the same way we can see a table or building, yet we frequently use them in our language. Synectics is a good way to make a familiar idea "strange" and thereby obtain another perspective on it.

We have found that synectics can be used with all ages, though with very young children it is best to stick to stretching exercises. Beyond this the adjustments are the same as for any other approach to teaching—care to work within their experience, rich use of concrete materials, attentive pacing, and explicit outlining of procedures.

The model often works effectively with students who withdraw from more "academic" learning activities because they are not willing to risk being wrong. Conversely, high-achieving students who are only comfortable giving a response they are sure is "right" often feel reluctant to participate. We believe that for these reasons alone, synectics is valuable to everyone.

Synectics combines easily with other models. It can stretch concepts being explored with the information-processing family, open up dimensions of social issues explored through role playing, group investigation, or jurisprudential thinking, and expand the richness of problems and feelings opened up by other models in the personal family.

The most effective use of synectics is over time. It has short-term results in stretching views of concepts and problems, but when students are exposed to it repeatedly they can learn how to use it with increasing skill, and they learn to enter a metaphoric mode with increasing ease and completeness.

Gordon, Poze, and their associates have developed a wide assortment of materials for use in schools, especially in the language development areas (Gordon and Poze, n.d.). The strategy is universally attractive, and its fortunate combination of enhancing productive thinking and nurturing empathy and interpersonal closeness finds it many uses with all ages and most curriculum areas.

INSTRUCTIONAL AND NURTURANT EFFECTS

As shown in Figure 10-1, the Synectics Model contains strong elements of both instructional and nurturant values. Through his belief that the creative process can be communicated and that it can be improved through direct training, Gordon has developed specific instructional techniques. Synectics is applied, however, not only to the development of general creative power but also to the development of creative responses over a variety of subject-matter domains. Gordon clearly believes that the creative energy will enhance learn-

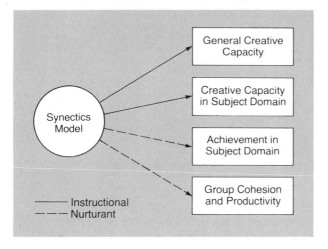

FIGURE 10-1   Instructional and nurturant effects:
Synectics Model.

ing in these areas. To this end, he emphasizes a social environment that encourages creativity and uses group cohesion to generate energy that enables the participants to function interdependently in a metaphoric world.

The method of synectics has been explicitly designed to improve the creativity of individuals and of groups. However, the implicit learning from this model is equally vivid. Participation in a synectics group invariably creates a unique shared experience that fosters interpersonal understanding and a sense of community. Members learn about one another as each person reacts to the common event in his or her unique way. Individuals become acutely aware of their dependence on the various perceptions of other group members. Each thought, no matter how prosaic, is valued for its potential catalytic effect on one's own thoughts. Simply having a thought is the sole basis for status in this community, and the playfulness of synectics activities encourages even the most timid participant.

Another approach to the stimulation of creativity through metaphoric activity is presented by Judith and Donald Sanders (1984). Their book is particularly useful for the range of explicit applications that are included. We have noticed that many educators are not automatically aware of the spectrum of useful applications for models designed to induce divergent thinking. For some reason, many people think of "creativity" as an aptitude that defines talent in the arts, especially writing, painting, and sculpture, whereas the creators of these models believe that this aptitude can be improved and that it has applications in nearly every human endeavor and, thus, in every curriculum area. By providing illustrations in the setting of goals, development of empathy, the study of values, a variety of areas of problem solving, and the increase of perspectives for viewing topics, the Sanders make a clear and convincing case for the power of these models.

Summary Chart: Synectics

SYNTAX OF STRATEGY ONE: CREATING SOMETHING NEW

Phase One:
Description of Present Condition
Teacher has students describe situation or topic as they see it now.

Phase Two:
Direct Analogy
Students suggest direct analogies, select one, and explore (describe) it further.

Phase Three:
Personal Analogy
Students "become" the analogy they selected in phase two.

Phase Four:
Compressed Conflict
Students take their descriptions from phases two and three, suggest several compressed conflicts, and choose one.

Phase Five:
Direct Analogy
Students generate and select another direct analogy, based on the compressed conflict.

Phase Six:
Reexamination of the Original Task
Teacher has students move back to original task or problem and use the last analogy and/or the entire synectics experience.

SOCIAL SYSTEM

The model is moderately structured. Teacher initiates phases, but students' responses are quite open. Norms of creativity and "play-of-fancy" are encouraged. Rewards are internal.

PRINCIPLES OF REACTION

Encourage openness, nonrational, creative expression. Model, if necessary.
Accept all student responses.
Select analogies that help students stretch their thinking.

SUPPORT SYSTEM

No special support system.

SYNTAX OF STRATEGY TWO: MAKING THE STRANGE FAMILIAR

Phase One:
Substantive Input
Teacher provides information on new topic.

Phase Two:
Direct Analogy
Teacher suggests direct analogy and asks students to describe the analogy.

Phase Three:
Personal Analogy
Teacher has students "become" the direct analogy.

Phase Four:
Comparing Analogies
Students identify and explain the points of similarity between the new material and the direct analogy.

Phase Five:
Explaining Differences
Students explain where the analogy does not fit.

Phase Six:
Exploration
Students reexplore the original topic on its own terms.

Phase Seven:
Generating Analogy
Students provide their own direct analogy and explore the similarities and differences.

11

INCREASING AWARENESS
Expanding Personal and Social Horizons

SCENARIO

"I want you to form a circle." Mr. Homulka's request is aimed at a group of six junior high school students standing in the middle of the classroom. The desks have been pushed aside to make an open space. The boys and girls join hands. "Now, Tommy and Marion, try to get inside the circle, and the rest of you try to keep them out. You have to keep your hands joined, and the idea is for you to keep a chain strong enough that they can't get in."

Everyone looks a little puzzled.

"OK, now," he says to Tommy and Marion, "let's start."

Tommy and Marion begin tentatively. They get on opposite sides of the ring and begin to push at the other students. When the ring stays strong they begin to push more firmly. As they meet with resistance, they push even stronger, and they succeed in bending the chain back upon itself, but the students in the circle hold firm and crowd in toward one another so that there is actually no place on the inside. Tommy tries to duck under their arms, but there is no place to go in the crowd at the center. The struggle goes on for a couple of minutes. Then Mr. Homulka calls time.

Tommy and Marion have expressions of anger on their faces, and the other students look a little puzzled but very determined.

"Let's begin with some of the observers," Mr. Homulka suggests. "What did you see?"

"Well, of course, we saw them try to get in," volunteers one.

"It began gently at first, but they were all really pushing at the end."

"Toward the end everybody looked mad or at least determined."

"How did you feel?" asks one of the students in the circle.

"How did *you* feel, Jane?" Mr. Homulka directs this question at one of the girls in the circle.

"Well, at first I thought it was kind of silly, but then I began to push harder and I really didn't want them to get inside. I thought it was none of their business to get inside this group."

Marion agrees. "That's what I thought you felt. We've been friends all through school and I couldn't understand why you wanted to keep me out."

"Neither could I," Sally says, shaking her head. "It was kind of as we did this the feelings came along with it."

"That's what I felt," nods Tommy. "At first I thought it was just silly and then I couldn't understand why you wanted to keep me out. I still feel mad about that."

These students are exploring human relations. Mr. Homulka is using one of a series of awareness-training exercises designed to help students explore feelings of exclusiveness and belonging and the kinds of human behaviors that make other people feel more and less welcome. Many of the exercises, as in this case, are simulations of what happens in the real world. Interestingly, feelings commonly experienced in normal social situations arise in the simulations too.

The purpose of awareness training is to increase self-understanding and awareness of one's own behavior and that of others, and also to help students develop alternative patterns for their personal and social development.

Recent years have seen an explosion of interest in freeing the human being to develop more fully, particularly by helping people achieve fulfilling interpersonal relations. For many, this quest begins with a recognition that most of us are only shadows of what we could be, and that somehow we have surrounded ourselves with invisible barriers that keep us from reaching out and becoming more than we are. Although there has been much attention to physical development, emotional development, personal expression, and other forms of individual development, it is in the interpersonal realm that the human-potential movement has found its fullest expression. We have chosen to focus on a model described by William Schutz, especially in *FIRO: A Three-Dimensional Theory of Interpersonal Behavior; Joy: Expanding Human Awareness;* and *Elements of Encounter* (Schutz, 1958, 1967, 1973, respectively). Schutz's writings emphasize interpersonal training as a means of increasing personal awareness and joy, which he defines as the feeling that one is fulfilling one's potential. We also draw on the work of other practitioners in the human-potential movement, notably Howard Lewis, Harold Streitfeld, and George Brown. The version we present here is built on the encounter or "exploratory game," which we believe is especially suited to the classroom.

ORIENTATION TO THE MODEL

GOALS AND ASSUMPTIONS

FULFILLMENT OF PERSONAL POTENTIAL   Schutz leaves no doubt about the mission of his work:

> The theme of this book is Joy. The theories and methods presented here are aimed at achieving joy. Joy is the feeling that comes from the fulfillment of one's potential. Fulfillment brings to an individual the feeling that he can cope with his environment; the sense of confidence in himself as a significant, competent, loveable person who is capable of handling situations as they arise, able to use fully his own capacities, and free to express his feelings. (Schutz, 1967, p. 15)

Schutz believes there are four types of development necessary to the realization of an individual's full potential. One is bodily functioning. Another is personal functioning (including the acquisition of knowledge and experience, the development of logical thinking and creative thinking, and the integration of intellectual development). The third is interpersonal development. And the fourth is the individual's relationships to societal institutions, social organizations, and culture. It is on the third of these, the personal awareness of interpersonal needs, that we concentrate in this chapter.

AWARENESS   One of the main obstacles to fulfillment in interpersonal relations (and in other areas) is people's inability to be aware of their own needs and feelings. Traditional psychotherapists have long argued that most people have not only great capacity for feeling, but a real capacity for being out of touch with their emotions. We push them away (suppression, repression), turn them around (projection), and masquerade them as something else. Sometimes these devices, designed to protect us from our feelings, are useful and necessary, but in their extreme they lead to unrewarding life patterns. Schutz and others believe that it is necessary for people to free their emotions from these psychological devices. We need to become more in touch with our feelings, experience more of our own sensations. In addition, we must also be aware of what we are feeling.

Aside from having a generalized sense of like or dislike most people do not know precisely what they feel. Nor do they observe how they actually behave (Lewis and Streitfeld, 1970). If this is an accurate characterization, the task for Schutz and others is to design learning activities that facilitate people's emotional responses. In this case, useful situations enable people to call up familiar feelings and typical behavior patterns in response to those feelings. Through these experiences, people become aware how they react to and handle situations: What scares them and how do they express this fright? What is pleasurable and how do they communicate their pleasure? Schutz's encounter model (or exploratory game) is designed to elicit feelings and to help people recognize them.

According to Schutz one of the primary ways feelings are revealed is through the body—our tones of voice, gestures, postures, facial expressions, and muscles. These indicators are as important to the expression of emotions as are words and behaviors. In fact, Schutz believes that these bodily manifestations are often closer to revealing genuine feelings than are verbal expressions. It is also true that sometimes if we want to repress a feeling we adopt an opposite body posture. We assume an air of confidence or cockiness to cover our fears of inadequacy; we smile constantly to mask our deep sadness. One goal of this model is to help people become aware of their body mannerisms and the emotions behind them. A related goal is to become a keen observer of other people's behavior so that we can discriminate a rigid smile that holds back sadness from one revealing joy and pleasure. The ability to read our feelings through our bodies will put us in deeper touch with our own interpersonal needs and the needs of others.

BASIC INTERPERSONAL NEEDS   Schutz maintains that a person's self-concept is derived from relations with others. In these relationships the individual has three basic needs: for inclusion, control, and affection. *Inclusion* refers to one's need to be perceived, attended to, and given reasonable attention by others. Part of this need is manifested by one's need for identity, to know that one is distinct from other persons, to feel justified in one's uniqueness, and at the same time to feel that others identify and empathize with him or her as a fellow being. *Control* is the second basic need: "The need for control varies along a continuum from the desire for power, authority and control over others (and therefore over one's future) to the need to be controlled and have responsibility lifted from oneself" (Schutz, 1967, p. 118). There is no necessary relationship between one's desire to control and one's desire to be controlled. One may combine both or tend toward only one. *Affection*, the third basic need, "refers to close personal feelings between two people, especially love and hate in their various degrees" (Schutz, 1967, p. 119). All of us have a powerful need to feel affection and to express and receive it whenever we are with other people.

Each person must come to terms with these basic needs. They are the means by which full human potential between individuals is developed (Schutz, 1967, p. 11). Failure to satisfy one or more needs creates a problem area. Usually the behavior chosen to meet the need results in less than satisfactory social relations. Underlying these dysfunctional behavior patterns are deep fears. For each of the interpersonal needs Schutz outlines the typical concerns and ineffective coping behaviors. His comments are useful in helping us better understand our students' areas of difficulties and select appropriate teaching situations.

People who want attention and interaction are reflecting their basic need to be included. In an attempt to satisfy this need they may exhibit behavior that is asocial, social, or oversocial. Asocial and oversocial people both have a fear or being ignored and left behind. Asocial people prefer to be alone, distant, introverted, and withdrawn, while oversocial people are extroverts who seek out people and cannot stand to be alone. They may be exhibitionistic to gain attention, or they may try to be powerful (for control) or well liked (for affection). People without inclusion problems are comfortable being alone or with others. They can be active or retiring participants in a group and can experience high involvement and commitment or withhold commitment. These people feel worthwhile; consequently, they do not experience anxiety about exclusion or inclusion.

People who have problems with control are not comfortable with power and decision making. Underlying their difficulty is a fear of being incompetent, helpless, or irresponsible. The need varies from the need to control others to the need to be controlled by others. Independence and rebellion can represent a lack of willingness to be controlled, while compliance, submission, and following directions indicate willingness to accept control. Power struggles reflect control issues, as does leadership style. Autocrats, for example, have high control needs, whereas abdicrats habitually refuse to take responsibility for making decisions. Thus, some people overcompensate by taking too much responsibility, and others will not risk taking any control. People who have resolved their control problems are comfortable giving and taking orders. They feel competent.

Affection, the third basic need, refers to emotional closeness between two people, especially degrees of love and hate. All of us have a powerful need to feel affection and to express and receive it whenever we are with other people. People who are afraid of affection remain distant and superficial in their relations with others. They view themselves as unlovable and fear rejection. On the surface they claim to want to remain uninvolved emotionally. Other people with the same fear are overpersonal; they try to become close to everyone hoping to gain approval and intimacy. People who have come to terms with their needs for affection are comfortable with relations that are close or distant. They do not believe that dislike is the result of being unlovable, but that it is a product of the relationship. Table 11-1 summarizes the three interpersonal needs and their underlying issues and behavior patterns.

Schutz's methods of encounter and awareness training are designed to help individuals recognize their feelings and modes of behavior with respect to inclusion, control, and affection. They also aim to help people cope with their own states of development and their participation in social groups in relation

Table 11-1   Basic Interpersonal Needs

BASIC NEED	UNDERLYING FEELING ISSUES	SOCIAL INTERACTION
Inclusion	Worthwhileness Significance Importance	Noninvolvement High and low group participation Strong commitment with groups
Control	Responsibility Competence Confidence Intelligence	Power relations Competition Abdicrat/autocrat
Affection	Acceptance Lovability Likability	Superficial distant relationships Search for approval Extremely personal and confiding relationships

to these three basic needs—particularly, to increase awareness, to experience telling the truth, and to understand self-responsibility and choice.

THE ENCOUNTER STRATEGY: EXPLORATORY GAMES

Schutz describes his series of concepts and procedures as *encounter theory*. He borrows liberally from other theorists, most notably Fritz Perls, Freud, Bion, and body theorists such as Alexander Lowen, I. Rolf, and M. Feldenkrais. He places special emphasis on "interaction" with others and on the group:

> Encounter is a method of human relating based on openness and honesty, self-awareness, responsibility, awareness of the body, attention to feelings and an emphasis on the here-and-now. It usually occurs in a group setting. Encounter is therapy insofar as it focuses on removing blocks to better functioning. Encounter is education and religion in that it attempts to create conditions leading to the most satisfying use of personal capacities. (Schutz, 1973, p. 3)

Schutz does not describe a general format for the activities used for encounters: They are depicted in specific rather than generic terms. Nearly all are group activities that emerge into various forms depending on what happens in a specific group. We refer here to the activities or tasks as *exploratory games,* which are devices for creating social situations typical to those most people encounter and find stressful. In this gamelike situation people are given the chance to enact their usual behavioral patterns and experience the accompanying emotions. The "game" generates the content for later discussion when participants can share their thoughts and feelings. They also receive feedback from others and, through the rules of encounter, are assisted in the direct expression of their feelings.

We distinguish here between *awareness groups* and *encounter groups*. In an awareness group the exploratory game generates the content for discussion, which is primarily a sharing of awareness. In an encounter group the social contact is less structured. Members gather together and react to each other or to issues brought by individuals to the group. When suitable, one, two, or more people may gradually experiment with an appropriate exploratory game. In general, awareness groups begin with a move by the teacher (counselor, therapist, group leader), who poses a problem or gives a task. This provides the whole group or, perhaps, selected individuals with an opportunity to encounter the interpersonal area in which growth is desired (inclusion, control, or affection). All members are expected to engage either in the activity or in the subsequent discussion of it and to help one another deal with the area. In both awareness and encounter groups the leader (or therapist) may play an important part. However, both emphasize group responsibility and the obligation of each individual to open up before the group to the extent that he or she is able.

AN ILLUSTRATION   Recently we visited a classroom in which the teacher was using the Awareness Training Model. We observed the following sequence of events:

> In an average-sized classroom twelve students were silently milling about with their eyes closed, alternately making contact with one person and then shifting to another, all without words. Occasionally students would stay with the person they touched. More often they communicated nonverbally, tapping the person's back, connecting hands, pounding the other's fist, and then moving on to another person. Sometimes they "introduced" two people to each other. It was difficult to do without words. Gradually, we found small lines forming, connecting two, three, four people. When we returned to the room twenty minutes later, the group was arranged almost in a circle. Most people were connected to people on either side. Some were not. There were places in the circle with large gaps.
>
> Moments later an inconspicuous leader-facilitator asked everyone to open his or her eyes and sit on the floor in a small circle. She began by sharing some observations with the group. We learned that everyone had been given a secret number and that the task was to find the "numbers" that went on either side of them. They were also given the constraint that this must be accomplished without words.
>
> The leader observed that some people were very energetic in seeking out other people and in "matchmaking." Other people stood around waiting to be found. She then asked everyone to describe his or her experience in the exploratory game. Some people talked about feeling shy and awkward. Other people felt angry when they were interrupted by another participant while "communicating" with someone else. Still others expressed contentment once they found their pairs. Some people liked meeting many people; others lost interest as soon as the second party proved to be "of no value." Soon people talked back and forth to each other, commenting how a particular contact felt, what certain

gestures meant and how they were interpreted. Some members in the circle were very articulate about their experiences. Others were general and vague; the leader-facilitator prompted them to describe feelings or to be more specific. Gradually most people had identified their behavioral styles, especially in response to certain feelings. Everyone seemed to make connections between his or her responses in this exploratory game and other typical social situations.

The rough sequence of activities that we observed in this classroom is typical of the Awareness Training Model. First, participants engage in a task or exploratory game; then they discuss their reactions to the activity. In the discussion they are encouraged to take responsibility for their feelings and behaviors, to stay with the description of feelings, and to give each other feedback on what they experience and hear in the discussion itself as well. These three guidelines—take *responsibility* for yourself; *focus on feelings*; and *engage in feedback*—form the basic ground rules for encounter sessions (Lewis and Streitfeld, 1970, pp. 13–22). These concepts recur often in humanistic psychology.

TAKING RESPONSIBILITY   The notion of responsibility has implications for how people describe their problems and solutions. When people take responsibility for themselves, they acknowledge that they are the source of their difficulties (not others) and that they are responsible for doing something about them. They do not wait for others to tell them what to do but are willing to make decisions for themselves and support themselves emotionally. It is important that the teacher-facilitator be alert to the way students frame their problems, and point out when they are not accepting responsibility for themselves. Does the student blame others or see the problem as someone else's? Does he or she wait for that person to change his or her behavior or break the impasse? Is the student waiting for other people to take charge of his or her life?

The language people use is very reflective of their inner experiences, of how they see themselves. People who do not acknowledge responsibility for themselves tend to say "I can't" when they mean "I won't." The words we choose are not just a matter of semantics; they reflect our senses of personal power and strength. Lewis and Streitfeld believe that taking responsibility is a large part of fulfilling one's potential. People who do this feel more strength and confidence (Lewis and Streitfeld, 1970, p. 14). Teacher-facilitators need to be aware of the connections between students' language and their concepts of responsibility.

FOCUSING ON FEELINGS   A second rule of encounter concerns the emphasis on feelings. The broad purpose of exploratory games is to involve people in situations that normally provoke emotional reactions and to have people be aware of those feelings. Consequently, discussion should focus on feelings and direct experience rather than on thoughts and reasons. Teacher-facilitators need to be alert to intellectualizations, prompting students to return to their feelings. Again, language is one indicator whether people are in touch with their feelings: One way people avoid their feelings is to use the term *it* or *we* instead of *I*. Phrases such as *it seems to me* and *most people feel* actually mean *I feel*, but the speaker is avoiding responsibility for his or her feelings by using impersonal pronouns. Adolescents often have favorite phrases that actually cover up their feelings about a particular incident: *That's cool; What a high; I'm into myself.*

FEEDBACK   The third rule of encounter involves both giving and receiving feedback. Feedback provides information about how others experience you and how you experience them. The latter requires you to be in touch with your own feelings. You may want to tell someone that you are angry with him or her or that you like him or her. Effective feedback requires that you be specific and direct. Avoid generalizations and accusations such as, "You're shy." Instead you might say, "When someone new comes into the room, you stop talking." Feedback is not arguing or defending yourself. It is a statement about how *you* are feeling toward someone or something or about how you see them *behaving*. You cannot know for sure how someone else is feeling or whether he or she fits some general personality trait, like shy or crazy. However, you can point out to a person what you observe happening in his or her interactions with others; you might observe, "When someone tells you how much they like you, you put yourself down," for example. Lewis and Streitfeld refer to two kinds of feedback: *leveling* (letting someone know how you are feeling) and *confronting* (telling someone what you did or did not like, such as, "When I was talking you interrupted me."). Both are important for honest communication.

THE MODEL OF TEACHING

The Awareness Training Model varies from one leader (or therapist) to another and from one group to another. Most of its advocates would resent its being stereotyped or confined into any given formula, and despite our interest in clarifying and coding teaching models we would not want to subvert their interest in keeping the process open and flexible. However, there are many similarities in techniques among awareness training advocates, particularly in presenting a group with a task that involves exploration of an area in a warm emotional way, and in the extensive use of discussion where frankness and open expression of affect are encouraged. The models also use a common storehouse of exploratory games. Regardless of style, they emphasize unlocking the potential of each individual and capitalizing on the unique possibilities of the group.

SYNTAX

Although there is seldom a clear structure to encounter-group sessions, they generally consist of two phases: first, posing and completing the task and second, discussing or analyzing what has gone on. For example, with respect to the area of inclusion, Schutz describes the following activity:

> All members of the group are asked to gather close together, either sitting on the floor (which is preferable) or sitting in chairs. Then they are asked to close their eyes and stretch out their hands, "feel their space"—all space in front of them, over their heads, behind their backs, below them—and then be aware of their contact with others as they overlap and begin to touch each other. This procedure is allowed to continue for about five minutes.
>
> Usually there are a variety of clear reactions. Some people prefer to stay in their own space and resent as an intrusion anyone coming into it. Others feel very chary about introducing themselves into another's space for fear that they are not wanted. Still others seek out people and enjoy the touch contact. Where one person is inviting, another may be forbidding and simply touch and run. Discussion following this activity is usually very valuable in opening up the whole area of feelings about aloneness and contact (Schutz, 1967, p. 123).

The activity, in short, begins with the arrangement of the people and the instructions to them. Then they engage in the activity, generating experience. Next, discussion identifies the different types of reactions, and the participants are encouraged to analyze their reactions and those of others and to begin to probe into the area under concern and generate some ideas about their development in that area.

The leader presents the task, of course, but does not attempt to influence what the group members do with the task. He or she participates in the discussion, usually in a nondirective role, attempting to get others to explore their reactions and noticing their reactions as they compare with others. The activities from this point emerge from the encounter and are controlled largely by the interactions of the group, rather than being imposed by the moves of the leader (See Table 11–2.)

SOCIAL SYSTEM

The encounter group is really a social encounter that is all-dependent on the social climate generated—a willingness to explore onself; a sense of responsibility in assisting others to explore themselves; an openness to interact over issues, however intimate they may turn out to be; a considerateness of one's own need for growth and others' needs for growth; and above all, a recognition of the shared need for people to work together to improve their possibilities as individuals and groups.

Table 11-2   Syntax of Awareness Training Model

PHASE ONE POSING AND COMPLETING THE TASK	PHASE TWO DISCUSSION OR ANALYSIS OF PHASE ONE
Give directions. Ensure safe environment for participants.	Emphasize responsibility, feelings, and feedback. Focus on here and now. Promote honesty and openness.

PRINCIPLES OF REACTION

The leader guards vulnerable group members against overintense exchanges or overexposure to the rest of the group. However, in general he or she helps individuals obtain insights into their own behavior and develop conceptual tools for describing their behavior so that they can manipulate it if they choose. The leader works to maintain openness at all times, both with respect to his or her own acceptance of feelings and ideas from others and the other group members' acceptance of feelings and ideas from their fellows. He or she attempts to communicate a climate of directness and honesty and of an uninhibited exploration of one's feelings and reactions. The leader is alert to both verbal and nonverbal expressions of feeling, pointing these out and inquiring about them. The facilitator is also alert to the use of language, particularly when it reveals lack of responsibility, intellectualization, and avoidance of feeling.

SUPPORT SYSTEM

For this model the leader needs access to or familiarity with a variety of exploratory games that relate to the interpersonal areas of inclusion, control, and affection. He or she also needs competence in recognizing feelings (and the avoidance of feelings) and in facilitating an open, accepting social climate.

APPLICATION

Until recently few schools considered personal awareness and interpersonal success as serious missions of the school, although some paid lip service to it. In the last ten years educational designers, curriculum developers, and teachers have explored ways of incorporating so-called affective education into the school curriculum and activities (Lederman, 1973). The methods vary. An elementary level K–6 curriculum developed by Harold Bessell and Jack Palomares, the Human Development curriculum, provides activities and a method that can be used in the classroom for a short time each day (Palomares, Ball, and Bessell, 1972–1976). Although it is not based specifically on the Awareness Training Model, they share certain features, and it has as its primary goal the emotional education of students. It is one of the few theoretically based, systematic curriculum efforts in the area of affective education.

Another well-known effort is a project on humanistic education, undertaken by George Brown of the University of California and Esalen Institute, which examined affective approaches to education and analyzed their potential for integration into the conventional curriculum (Brown, 1968). In addition to inventorying suitable awareness experiences and encounter-group techniques, Brown and his staff trained five elementary and secondary school teachers and assisted them in developing and trying out lessons and units based on these techniques. The project report is replete with their annotated accounts of classroom experiences spanning all subjects, grade levels, and special learning situations. We can illustrate only a few of these accounts here.

The first two exercises actually take place with one of the five teachers acting as trainer for other inservice teachers unfamiliar with encounter group activities. However, in both instances the teacher-trainer describes how he has utilized this procedure with his own high school English class:

Mr. Hillman asked the members of the group to get up and mill about in the center of the room and, without talking, end up in groups of exactly four people. If there were five, one had to leave, if three, someone had to be found to join the group. The participants then discussed the process by which the groups were formed—what caused them to choose the group they chose, etc. Mr. Hillman related this procedure to his English classes' discussion of Crane's *Red Badge of Courage*. The protagonist of the novel enters and leaves several groups during the course of the story, encountering both acceptance and rejection. The use of this technique enables students to get more in touch with the hero's feelings. It was used again in connection with the grouping of the boys in the novel *Lord of the Flies*, illustrating how grouping is often unconscious. Becoming aware of what causes us to choose certain groups can give us some insight into ourselves.

The group was asked to complete, in turn, the statement, "It takes courage for me to . . ." (". . . look people in the eyes"; ". . . to have any one touch me.") Mr. Hillman related this to his classes' discussion of *Red Badge of Courage* as a means for helping students understand the meaning of courage, and to personalize and humanize the struggle going on in the mind of Henry Fleming, the hero of the novel.

Mr. Hillman continued the session with a "touch conversation." Grouped in dyads, the participants closed their eyes and carried on a conversation with their hands. They said hello, got acquainted, took a walk together, danced, got into a fight, made up, and said good-bye. He then explained how he had used this technique in the discussion of the lack of communication between the members of the Loman family in *Death of a Salesman*, showing the class through experience, that people can communicate in other ways than talking, and often much more effectively. (Brown, 1968, pp. 4–9)

Another core-staff teacher describes an account of the blind walk with her first grade class: "In the blind walk, one person closes his eyes and is led around by the other who tries to give the blind one many different kinds of sensory experiences. After about twenty minutes, the partners switch roles, the leader becoming blind and vice versa" (Brown, 1968, p. 10). The teacher used the technique to build trust and to help students discover things other than through sight. Excerpts from her report follow:

> We're trying to get the children to the point of taking a meaningful blind walk. I'm beginning to think the experience itself won't be nearly as meaningful as all the learning that will build up to it. We may not even get that far.

STEP ONE: INTRODUCE BLINDFOLDS

After much consideration, I made blindfolds for the whole class. We have discovered great difficulty in keeping eyes closed.

On the first day, Peggy instructed the class to put the blindfolds on and to explore first only the rug. There was a lot of chaos, bumping each other, much more fun to explore each other than the room. There was a lot of peeking. Many wore their blindfolds slightly too high so that they could see well enough to run around. We let them try to explore the whole room and then let them go outside to the grass by our room. I would say about 5 children seemed to be really exploring the world without sight. About half were running around (most of the boys). About five girls did not like to wear the blindfolds at all. These girls were mainly the ones who always had to be "right." In their words, "good students." They seemed very afraid of the uncertain experience without their eyes. After about 20 minutes of exploring, we called them back in and talked a while about the experience. It seemed that most of the children did not like it. Many found the blindfolds uncomfortable.

I feel that many negative responses were of a "me too" type—especially since verbal and physical response was very different in many cases. And the girls who really did not enjoy the experience are "stars" whose reactions are closely attended to by others in the class. I recommended more structure and a safer environment for the next lesson.

The following comes from that and again, Peggy is the teacher. I told the children to bring things the next day to "share and tell," things they could share while all of the class had on their blindfolds. That day we decided to start with a kind of structured experience before the sharing, which is usually first. I've forgotten exactly what I did; however, most of the kids did not like the experience (I think I was trying to give them "mystery sounds.") Most of them peeked to see what I was doing rather than using their ears. By the time it was sharing time many of them did not want to wear their blindfolds any longer. I permitted them to take them off and not play if they didn't want to. About six started the sharing period with their blindfolds on. Some dropped out and others joined in as the period went on. After about 10 minutes the disorganization was too much for me to bear, so I collected all of the blindfolds and we went on with sharing without the blindfolds.

Insights: First of all, we're having trouble timing this new—maybe fearful—experience. I feel much was lost today on two counts. First, the period should have started out with them feeling, smelling and listening to the sharing objects, and then gone into mystery sounds if they were still with it. Second, the items shared should have been handled in a structured way—such as sitting in a circle and passing items from hand to hand, rather than one child doing it. Some of the problems were those of control. Perhaps items should be teacher-chosen at first. Another insight in regard to children bringing things: be sure to include a teacher preview of the items so that they really do have a tactile quality to them.

I would like to try this: Have the children sit in the circle blindfolded. Give each child an item. Set up a sound signal. When they hear the sound they are to pass the object to the next child. Do this only for about 5 minutes.

After the first two days, we just let the blindfolds sit. We left them out so the kids could play with them if they wanted. All during this time I saw evidence that they had been used during indoor recesses on rainy days.

JAN. 15.

Today, Peggy used the blindfolds again in a lesson. Most of the children wanted to take them. Only about three said they didn't want to use them. These three were easily persuaded to try them. I had the kids find their own space, lie down on their backs on the lawn, and put on their blindfolds and listen to the sounds around them. Except for about five or six who had difficulty, most of the classes enjoyed the experience.

Insights: Steps still needed. More experience with wearing the blindfolds and taking directions at the same time. More trust in moving about without using their eyes. Perhaps instruction about how to move when you can't see. Finding and practicing a way of selecting a partner—someone you really trust. Demonstrating and practicing how to be a leader in a blind walk, how to protect and guide and show your partner what you want him to attend to.

JAN. 23: BLINDFOLDS

We're still trying to get the children used to wearing the blindfolds long enough to experience feeling more intently.

I sat all the children around in a circle wearing blindfolds. I gave each child an item from the classroom—scissors, brushes, ball, pencil, chalk, eraser, etc. I asked them to feel each object. Try not to worry about what it is. Try to experience the feel of each thing. I clicked sticks when they were to pass the object to their right. (A good lesson in directions.) I continued to do it until each object was passed all the way around.

I was very impressed at how quiet the children were. The lesson was about twenty-five minutes, and they were interested and in good control the whole time. I whispered any direct statements to individual children. At first a few could not resist saying out loud what they had. This stopped after about the fifth object.

I stayed pretty busy picking up "lost" items. I was happy that the children waited until I could get them back to them rather than taking off their blindfolds to find them themselves. After that we discussed how some of the items felt, rather than how they look.

JAN. 24: RED LETTER DAY! ACCIDENTAL BLIND WALK

Since Monday several children have asked if they could do what Kathy and I had done, I sat, she was blindfolded, and I took her hand exploring.

Today we took the children out on the grass after asking them to choose someone they could trust. They went out in groups of two or three. Peggy instructed us to sit close to our partners. One put on the blindfold, the other directed his hand. I was working with two girls. They both put on blindfolds. I began moving their hands on things around us. Out of the corner of my eye I saw some movement. Upon looking up, I saw one girl begin to lead another on a blind walk. Others, who were sitting on the grass with "blind" partners, saw this, got up, and led their partners around. The area we were in was rather confined and not at all the area I would have chosen for this experience, and yet here it was happening. My mind raced through all the "little steps" I had thought to be prerequisites before we could do this, and yet here they were, leading each other all around—to the fence, to the pillars, walls, trees, drinking fountains, even back into the room and out again. I couldn't believe it. After about 10 minutes, Peggy instructed the children to change—those wearing blindfolds were to give them to their partners.

Away they went again. . . .

SELECTING EXPLORATORY GAMES

Some of the best exploratory games are those that people make up themselves. However, over the last ten years many books of growth games have been published. In addition to Schutz's book, Lewis and Streitfeld's *Growth Games* is one of the more popular ones. Games can be very simple and short or complex, as in the example presented earlier. They can encompass a wide range of issues. We are concerned with interpersonal games that call forth feelings surrounding issues of inclusion, control, and affection. The following games from Lewis and Streitfeld's book seem to concern themselves with interpersonal issues:

LIST OF GROWTH GAMES

Games for Building Warmth and Trust
  What Makes Groups Tick
    Getting Acquainted
    Conversations
    Touching Experiences
  Getting Closer
    First Impressions
    Silent Language
    Straight Talk
  Building Trust
    Big Lifts
    Back Fall
    Teeter-Totter
    Rock-a-by-Baby
Games for Breaking Through Blocks
  Ice Cubes in Your River
  Rejection
    Castaway

Without Self-Consciousness
Selling Yourself
(Brown, 1971, 143–45, 150–51).

In his book *Joy*, Schutz describes the game of *First Impression*. We present his description here to illustrate how simple activities lead to rich emotional experiences:

> First impression. Specifically focusing on another individual while using many senses helps a person to make contact. Ordinarily we are either oblivious to many cues the other person gives us or we are reacting to them unconsciously rather than consciously. One way of exploring these cues is to begin a new group by having each member stand in front of the whole group. The group is instructed to give a first impression, perhaps a few adjectives, based entirely on appearance, preferably even before the person speaks. "Watch the structure of the body, the way the body is held, look carefully at the expression on the face, at the way he moves, at the tension and relaxation reflected in movement and positioning. Then go up and touch him, note the feel of the skin—the firmness or softness; the size, firmness and tension of the muscles; the quality of the hair. Now push him or have him push you and see the resistance or compliance. Then add more adjectives or reinforce or amend the first ones. Now smell him." How rarely we deliberately use smell, but it is often the repository of memories (who can forget the Prom gardenia smell), and may affect or impress in a way of which we are not aware.
>
> After this first contact, group members may be allowed some time together, perhaps half an hour, and then be asked to continue giving their first impressions. This time several new features are added. First, group members are brought into direct interaction with each other. Each person is asked to give his first impressions of each of the other group members, not only verbally, but by standing directly in front of the person to get a much more direct awareness of his presence, looking him straight in the eye so that his attention is more easily directed to the person, and touching him in whatever way best expresses the toucher's feelings while he describes his impression. This procedure makes the reality of the other person much greater.
>
> This experience is usually a very emotionally involving one for both the teller and the told, and typically brings the group members much closer together. Often there is resistance to the touching. This follows from the meaning given to it in our society, which interprets touch as basically aggressive or sexual. Such an interpretation, of course, need not be the case, but it does prevent warmer direct expression of feeling. A group context can frequently release people to feel more comfortable about touching. If the resistance to actual contact is too great, a person may give his impression without touching (Schutz, 1967, pp. 126–27).

RESEARCH INTO AFFECTIVE EDUCATION

Awareness training is only one of the approaches to teaching that focuses on affective behavior and approaches to emotional development. In his review of literature pertinent to the training of teachers for affective roles,

George I. Brown identifies a number of interrelated constructs in affective education, "including humanistic education, affective education, psychological education, self-science education and confluent education" (Brown, 1975, pp. 173–203). Schutz's description of human beings' need for inclusion, control, and affection also have their parallels in Weinstein and Fantini's (1970) "identity connectedness and potency."

Affective education has proven exceptionally difficult to study. Kahn and Weiss's (1973) review of research into affective education is laced with concern about the areas in which research tools have not been developed and the existence of a great many important concepts still waiting to be tested. Most affective education models are not backed by the precision and experimental quality of the research devoted to the information-processing and behavior-modification families. Nonetheless, sufficient work is being done to establish quite clearly the importance of the teacher's role in determining the affective responses of students and the potential strength of affectively oriented models. These models focus on the human emotions, which are generally only a side effect of other models, or are ignored or repressed by them.

INSTRUCTIONAL
AND NURTURANT EFFECTS

Awareness training is specifically designed to help people realize themselves more fully. The type of group encounter model described here is similar to laboratory method or T-group work, and some practitioners use methods from each interchangeably. However, the primary purpose of awareness training is to open up to individuals their possibilities for development, for increasing awareness of the universe and their possibilities in it as well as the interpersonal relations they might have with other people.

Although very few awareness trainers would want to employ their models to teach school subjects, most would admit that awareness training would probably lead to increased school learning in addition to its other beneficial effects. However, the model's aim is to focus on opening people up for greater personal development, and the subject-matter agenda would subvert this purpose.

The awareness training does not avoid direct instruction deliberately, but he or she uses training devices that are extremely nondirective. As illustrated in Figure 11-1, encounters open up to the "student" the possibility of development, but they do not lead him or her precisely toward preselected goals—the individual grows as he or she can, in directions greatly determined by personal readiness and wishes.

Organizations characterized by awareness-training activities would be

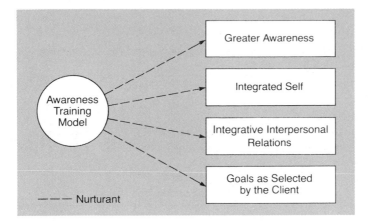

FIGURE 11-1 Instructional and nurturant effects: Awareness Training Model.

likely to be more effective, as well as more humane, for the individuals in it would be assisted in working out their problems. Awareness trainers on the whole are frankly messianic. As Schutz says in the closing of *Joy:*

> More and more we can enjoy other people, learn to work and play with them, to love and fight with them, to touch them, to give and take with them, to be with them contentedly or to be happily alone, to lead or to follow them, to create with them. In our institutions, our organizations, the establishment—even these we are learning to use for our own joy. Our institutions can be improved, can be used to enhance and support individual growth, can be reexamined and redesigned to achieve the fullest measure of human realization. All these things are coming. None are here, but they are closer. Closer than ever before (Schutz, 1967, p. 233).

Summary Chart: Awareness Training Model

SYNTAX

Phase One:
Posing and Completing the Task
Give directions.
Ensure safe environment for participants.

Phase Two:
Discussion or Analysis of Phase One
Emphasize responsibility, feelings, and feedback.
Focus on here and now.
Promote honesty and openness.

SOCIAL SYSTEM

The model is characterized by norms of mutuality, trust, and openness. Low to moderate external structure is provided by the task sequences.

PRINCIPLES OF REACTION

Guards against overintensity.

Help individuals gain insight into their own behavior and develop conceptual tools.

Attempts to maintain openness and honesty at all times with respect to oneself and group-member feelings.

Alert to verbal and nonverbal manifestations of feelings.

Assist students in taking responsibility and focusing on feelings.

SUPPORT SYSTEM

The teacher should be an open person who has the requisite interpersonal and intrapersonal skills.

12

THE CLASSROOM MEETING
Sharing Responsibility for the Environment

SCENARIO

A teaching team in a Kansas City school has been concerned about the relationships between the younger and older children in their cluster. Children from 7 to 9 are grouped with the six teachers, and many of the activities are developed around learning centers where the children are organized for work in the various curriculum areas. Some of the younger children have been complaining that they are not getting a fair share of the materials and that the older children, instead of helping them, often engage in activities by themselves.

This teaching team meets regularly with its students in what is called a classroom meeting. At that time they air problems, discuss them, identify the values that are involved, and then make commitments to try various courses of action.

One of the teachers approaches the problem directly in the daily classroom meeting.

"How are things going in the learning centers?"

No one says anything.

"Is everything going all right?"

Again there is silence.

"Let's talk about one of the centers in particular. How are things going in the science center?"

Finally one of the smaller children speaks up. "I like the science center a lot," she says, "but sometimes I feel crowded out."

"What does 'crowded out' mean?"

"Well, sometimes I can't get the stuff I need. I feel like the big kids—well—they don't exactly push us around, but often I can't get what I want and I find that somebody's been there before me."

"Is this a general problem? Who thinks so? Just raise your hands."

Nearly everybody in the room raises a hand.

"Well, it seems like it is something of a problem. Can anybody tell me what's going on?"

One of the older children explains, "Well, I think science is one of the areas where having older and younger kids together just doesn't work very well. I know I'm supposed to help the other kids, but I get involved in what I'm doing and then it seems like I have to stop all the time and help somebody else fix something."

"Well, how do you feel about that?"

Someone else speaks up, "Well, we should help each other. We can't get along in here if we don't work together."

"Yeah, but Amy's right," another protests. "We can't be interrupted all the time either."

"How can we approach this problem?" their teacher asks. "We need to figure out how we can do the best thing possible for everybody and then make a commitment to try that. Does anybody have any ideas?'

William Glasser's *Reality Therapy* (1965) challenges the fundamentals of personality theory as well as the basic conception of the traditional therapeutic and teaching relationships. Glasser believes that most individual problems do not constitute mental illness and do not need the attention of highly trained specialists. Skilled laypeople, especially parents and teachers, are quite capable of handling the majority of human problems. He also feels that individuals fail because of their interpersonal relations. Therefore, "therapy" or help must be channeled through a social medium such as the group.

Glasser applies his principles to the classroom through the mechanism of the classroom meeting, a thirty- to forty-five-minute period when students and teachers set aside their ongoing curricular activities to engage in open-minded, nonjudgmental discussions of problems (personal, behavioral, or academic) of concern to them in an effort to find collective solutions. The model of teaching we discuss in this chapter is based on Glasser's classroom meeting strategy.

ORIENTATION TO THE MODEL

GOALS AND ASSUMPTIONS

Glasser's contention that most human problems are failures of social functioning is based on his belief that each of us has two basic needs: love and self-worth. Both of these needs are rooted in our relationships with other people or in the norms of our social group. Individuals have problems because they have failed to satisfy their basic needs for relatedness (love) and respect (self-worth).

> From birth to old age we need to love and be loved. Throughout our lives our health and happiness depend on our ability to do so. . . . When we cannot satisfy our total need for love, we will suffer and react with many psychological symptoms from mild discomfort through anxiety and depression to complete withdrawal from the world around us.
>
> Equal in importance to the need for love is to feel that we are worthwhile both to ourselves and to others. (Glasser, 1965, pp. 9–10)

In the classroom love takes the form of a social responsibility to help and care for one another. He believes that schools fail, not in promoting academic performance, but in fostering the warm, constructive relationships essential for success. This is a failure caused by loneliness. "Those who fail in our society are lonely. In their loneliness they grope for identity but the pathways to success are closed: only anger, frustration, withdrawal—a failure in identity—are open" (Glasser, 1965, p. 17). If children lack good, close relationships with other people outside of school, they need to get them in school.

For most of us, loving and being loved will produce a feeling of being worthwhile. However, as Glasser states, this is not always true. An overindulged child may feel loved but not worthwhile. His or her parents have set no limits and have not distinguished correct and incorrect behavior:

> To be worthwhile we must maintain a satisfactory standard of behavior. To do so we must correct ourselves when we do wrong and credit ourselves when we do right. If we do not evaluate our own behavior, or having evaluated it, we do not act to improve our conduct where it is below our standards, we will not fulfill our need to be worthwhile and we will suffer as acutely as when we fail to love or be loved. Morals, standards, values, or right and wrong behavior are all intimately related to the fulfillment of our need for self-worth. (Glasser, 1965, p. 17)

Glasser believes that it is impossible to form a successful identity without the fulfillment of love and self-worth.

A second assumption of reality therapy is reflected in its commitment to action and to behavioral change. Traditional therapies rely on insight to change behavior. Reality therapy, on the other hand, is not interested in insights as to why something happened but in *what is done*. It teaches patients better *ways* to fulfill needs *now* and in the future.

Traditional therapies have often viewed unrealistic aims as a cause of dysfunctional behavior. Glasser, in contrast, finds not that aims are too high but that performance is too low. He seeks to improve peformance and satisfy basic needs by helping people do what is (1) real (reality); (2) responsible (responsibility); and (3) right (morality).

The goals of reality therapy are the ability to fulfill a commitment to behavioral change, and by doing this to fulfill one's emotional needs for self-worth, love, and identity. These goals are brought about by emotional involvement, a caring relationship that is a combination of love and discipline. "In essence, we gain self-respect through discipline and closeness to others through love. Discipline must always have within it the element of love" (Glasser, 1965, p. 17). The overindulgent parent whose love does not include discipline stifles the child from acquiring responsibility and the ultimate ability to fulfill his or her needs.

MAJOR CONCEPTS

Three general requirements of reality therapy are: (1) having an intense personal involvement; (2) facing reality and rejecting irresponsible behavior; and (3) learning better ways to behave.

REALITY   The quality of reality is an important criterion in establishing a standard of behavior. An action can be called realistic or unrealistic when its remote and immediate consequences are considered and compared. Individuals need to assess their behavior in terms of its consequences to themselves and to others. By doing this they are likely, according to Glasser, to choose realistic behaviors.

RESPONSIBILITY   Responsibility, along with reality and morality, is indicative of behavior capable of fulfilling our need for self-worth. Responsibility is defined as "the ability to fulfill one's needs, and to do so in *a way that does not deprive others of the ability to fulfill* their needs" (Glasser, 1965, p. 13). It also involves the attempt to fulfill the commitments one has made. Irresponsible people may or may not meet their obligations depending on their mood at the time, the amount of work involved, and the personal gain.

MORALITY   Although traditional psychotherapy avoids issues of right and wrong, Glasser is clear that individuals must do what is "right" in order to attain a measure of self-worth. By this he means that individuals themselves must maintain a standard of behavior which *they* set and evaluate.

INVOLVEMENT   The key to success in reality therapy is the process of involvement, the love of a parent or personal involvement of a teacher. Often for the first time, the student will realize the someone cares "enough about him not only to accept him but to help him fulfill his needs in the real world" (Glasser, 1965, p. 13). Emotional involvement requires more than caring and being cared for; involvement, according to Glasser, is a combination of love and discipline. Thus, the overindulgent parent whose love does not include discipline stifles the child from acquiring responsibility and the ultimate ability to fulfill his or her needs. According to Glasser, "to begin to be successful, children must receive at school what they lack: a good relationship with other people, both children and adults" (Glasser, 1969, p. 16). In isolation, children cannot develop the capacities to fulfill their needs for a successful identity. A teaching strategy based on reality therapy would thus aim at reducing this loneliness.

More traditional views of the school (and of therapy) have fashioned the role of the teacher as an objective, distant one, not an emotional one. Glasser's principles attempt to make schooling a personal experience for both student and teacher.

THE CLASSROOM MEETING

The classroom meeting is Glasser's mechanism for developing a caring social group, self-discipline, and behavioral commitment. The meeting is a time when students and teachers join, preferably daily, in an open-ended, non-judgmental discussion of behavioral problems, personal problems, and academic or curriculum issues. Glasser distinguishes three types of meeting, each with a slightly different focus. In this model we focus on the *social problem-solving meeting,* which is usually concerned with behavioral and social problems. The classroom meeting is thus a time when students attempt to share the responsibility for learning and behaving by resolving their problems within the classroom. Glasser would like to see the whole disciplinary structure of the school revolve around classroom meetings.

The orientation of the meeting is always positive—that is, toward a solution rather than toward fault finding. Obviously many problems do not have a single answer. For example, in the case of coping with a bully, the solution is often in the discussion itself, which serves to decrease the intimidation of other students and increase their strength. If this is the case, further discussion of the bully should be avoided unless he or she does something constructive (Glasser, 1969, p. 129).

In the *open-ended meeting,* students discuss thought-provoking questions related to their lives. The teacher might begin with "What's interesting to you?" Frequently students initiate the discussion by eagerly sharing something they read or saw. Glasser gives the example of an elementary class that responded to this question with an interest in eyes and ears, which led to a discussion of their function and also of blindness. Having stimulated the students' involvement, the teacher introduced a problem for solution, "Could a blind man read?" After some experimentation, hypothesizing, and guidance from the teacher, the students expressed the idea that a blind man could read if he could feel the letters on the page. But how might this be done? Once again the children thought, experimented, and formulated a Braille-type system (Glasser, 1969, pp. 134–135). The third type of meeting is similar to the open-ended meeting but is tied directly to what the class is studying.

In the strategy of the classroom meeting distinctions between the interpersonal and the academic blur. The atmosphere of the meeting, which is its distinctive feature, is the same for all types of meetings. It is brought about by an honest sharing of feelings and opinions, noncompetitiveness, thought-provoking questions (as opposed to factual ones), student-inititated discussions, and nonevaluative responses. In addition, social problem solving includes assessing the reality of an idea and of the personal choice and commitment to a new behavior.

The flavor of a classroom meeting can be seen in the following account of an elementary school class:

> For weeks two students in an open-plan second grade classroom had been arguing, fighting, and generally disrupting their own work and that of others in the classroom. Finally, one student brought the issue up, describing the most recent incident. Others echoed their complaints. Occasionally each of the two disruptive students started recounting previous times the other had transgressed or explaining the emotions (anger, hurt) that propelled these incidents. The teacher listened in a calm, nonjudgmental way but made it clear that the group was not interested in explanations or excuses for the behavior. Instead, sufficient examples were encouraged so that everyone could understand when these incidents occurred, their effect on the participants and bystanders, and what the classroom norm was under these circumstances.
>
> The two students were asked to participate in these descriptions, and they did. Anger and tensions didn't mount to unbearable proportions in this classroom. Infractions and issues were talked out readily and regularly. Those whose behavior was "deviant" were not mortified with fear or shame when they were questioned. They understood that this group problem solving occurred routinely, and, in fact, that they had some power in it. It was important to hear from them what was happening, and it was important that they view their fighting as a legitimate social problem. Nothing much could happen if the parties involved in violating the norm did not acknowledge what behavior had occurred and that its existence was in fact a problem.
>
> Once the problem had been clearly, matter-of-factly described and acknowledged by everyone, the teacher asked the two students to make personal value judgments about their behavior. How was this behavior helping and hurting them? They described what acceptable behavior might be and its advantages. They also explored the consequences of their former behavior. With the help of the teacher they labeled the underlying values in their choices of behavior. Finally, the teacher asked the students to choose, hoping they would commit themselves to more realistic behaviors. The students both agreed that they would refrain from tormenting each other. The next question was, How?

Everyone suggested specific ways the two students might avoid their clashes, including rescheduling, reseating, signaling each other when they were getting angry, and walking away. The two students selected one or two of the behaviors they would be willing to follow and agreed to report at successive class meetings how they had implemented their contract with the group.

At the next meeting several classmates eagerly volunteered that they had observed the two students successfully avoid a confrontation by using the new procedures.

Glasser explains how this classroom meeting strategy is aimed at reducing loneliness and prompting a success identity:

Today increasing numbers of students fail to gain a successful identity and react illogically and emotionally to their failure. Because they are lonely, they need involvement with educators who are warm and personal and who will work with their behavior in the present. They need teachers who will encourage them to make a value judgment of their behavior rather than preach or dictate; teachers who will help them plan behavior and who will expect a commitment from the students that they will do what they have planned. They need teachers who will not excuse them when they fail in their commitments, but who will work with them again and again as they commit and recommit until they finally learn to fulfill a commitment. When they learn to do so, they are no longer lonely; they gain maturity, respect, love and a successful identity. (Glasser, 1969, pp. 23–24)

To some people, reality therapy may seem harshly unsympathetic to students' feelings. It contrasts sharply with Carl Roger's premise that the underlying feeling must be released *before* new solutions can be envisioned and acted on. Glasser believes that emotion is the *result* of behavior; good behavior results in good feeling (Glasser, 1969, pp. 20–21). Emotions cannot be improved directly, only indirectly by improving one's behavior.

THE MODEL OF TEACHING

The Classroom Meeting Model for social problem solving includes six phases: (1) establishing a climate of involvement; (2) exposing the problem for discussion; (3) making a personal value judgment; (4) identifying alternative courses of action; (5) making a commitment; and (6) behavioral follow-up (see Table 12–1). These phases may take place during one or more meetings or they may be quickly accomplished in a single meeting, even for several problems. The main emphasis is on the style of problem solving, not the duration.

SYNTAX

Phase one is a prerequisite for all classroom meetings. It is not established anew each meeting but is a quality that permeates all the relationships in the classroom. A climate of involvement is one of warm, personal, con-

Table 12-1   Syntax of Classroom Meeting Model

PHASE ONE: ESTABLISHING A CLIMATE OF INVOLVEMENT	*PHASE TWO:* EXPOSING THE PROBLEM FOR DISCUSSION
Encourage everyone to participate and speak for himself or herself. Share opinions without blame or evaluation.	Students and/or teacher bring up issue or problem. Give examples. Describe problem fully. Identify consequences. Identify social norm.
PHASE THREE: MAKING A PERSONAL VALUE JUDGMENT	*PHASE FOUR:* IDENTIFYING ALTERNATIVE COURSES OF ACTION
Identify values behind problem behavior and social norm. Students make personal judgments about norms to follow and articulate their values.	Students discuss specific behavioral alternatives. Students agree on which ones to follow.
PHASE FIVE: MAKING A COMMITMENT	*PHASE SIX:* BEHAVIORAL FOLLOW-UP
Students make a public commitment.	After a period of time, students assess effectiveness of commitment and new behaviors.

cerned relationships. It is one in which people bring up problems or differences in a matter-of-fact, business-as-usual manner. Feelings and opinions are given without blame, and they are received without fear, judgment, or evaluation. Each person speaks for himself or herself, and all persons are encouraged to participate. It is clear that everyone's views are equally valued and respected. The emphasis is on description and solution, and the preferred mode is directness and honesty.

Phase two, exposing the problem for discussion, may be initiated by either students or teachers. It may take the form of a confronting situation or simply a question. In either case an honest discussion clarifying and reacting to the problem should follow. The teacher should solicit from the students examples of incidents when the problem occurred. As group facilitator, the teacher should avoid asking for justifications of the behavior and should intervene if students in their descriptions begin to blame and criticize. Students often offer excuses. The teacher may accept them but quickly remind the group that the task is to describe what happened. After the problem has been described, the students should identify (1) the consequences if the situation continues and (2) the social norm that usually governs the situation.

The purpose of phase three is to have the students make personal value judgments about their behavior. To do this they need to identify the values behind their behavior and behind those identified as the social norm. Then they will be asked to choose between behaviors and summarize the values they see for themselves in the behaviors they have chosen.

In phase four the students further specify the behavioral alternatives and agree on specific ones. This is followed, in phase five, by a public commitment to carry out the specific behaviors.

Finally, in phase six, a later meeting, the teacher asks the students to examine the effectiveness of the new behaviors and reinforces them for future action.

SOCIAL SYSTEM

The classroom meeting is moderately structured. Leadership—that is, responsibility for guiding the interaction through the phases—ultimately resides with the teacher. However, it is hoped that the students will initiate topics for discussion too; after many experiences, the whole behavioral-change process may establish itself on its own. Although leadership remains with the teacher, moral authority rests with the students. The students express value judgments and make decisions; the teacher is nonjudgmental.

PRINCIPLES OF REACTION

The teacher's behavior is governed by three principles. First is the principle of involvement; he or she must develop a warm, personal, interested, and sensitive relationship with the students (as opposed to an objective and detached view of them). Second, the teacher, though nonjudgmental himself or herself, must prod students to accept responsibility for diagnosing their own behavior, rejecting irresponsible behavior in themselves and their classmates: "It is important, therefore, in class meetings for the teacher, but not the class to be nonjudgmental. The class makes judgments and from these judgments works toward positive solutions. The teacher may reflect class attitudes but she should give opinions sparingly and be sure the class understands that her opinions are not law" (Glasser, 1969, p. 13). Third, the classroom group as a whole identifies, selects, and follows through with alternative courses of behavior.

SUPPORT SYSTEM

The optimal support for this strategy is a classroom teacher who has a warm personality and is skilled in interpersonal relations as well as group discussion techniques. He or she must be able to create a climate of openness and nondefensiveness, yet at the same time guide the group toward behavioral evaluation, commitment, and follow-up.

APPLICATION

We have seen classrooms in which classroom meetings occur as often as three times a day. In others it happens only once a day. Generally, the meeting is a time when teachers and students sit informally in a circle, close to one another. The morning classroom meeting often involves organizing for the day's activities, sharing events that occurred outside of school since the previous day, and, perhaps, reflecting on world events. Anyone can bring up a thought, and there is no attempt to evaluate anyone's idea. It is enough to want to share. Some students respond with questions for that person; others may volunteer opinions on the same topic. Issues needing solutions are put forth for the group to solve. Students suggest alternative courses of actions for evaluation by the group. They are encouraged to express their feelings openly and honestly. Finally, when a commitment to action is made, everyone expects it to be taken seriously. If it is not, it will be brought up before the group at the next classroom meeting.

Major individual problems come up less frequently as the social structuring of the classroom becomes established. More and more, the classroom meeting deals with planning curriculum activities and managing the logistics of the classroom.

It also becomes a time for sharing something with the group, an important piece of work that day, a new idea, or an exciting event that has happened in one's life. The group listens intently, asking questions to indicate its involvement. Students know they will have an opportunity to participate. A student may comment on how much he or she liked the contribution or the improvement he or she notices. The atmosphere is clearly not one of academic competitiveness. Unspoken rewards are the skills of being a good listener, an interesting contributor, an emotionally open and honest person, and a cooperative problem solver. The classroom group becomes a supportive, interested family for each student.

After awhile, the students enforce the norms themselves, comfortably confronting one another if suggestions are not realistic or if their feelings and opinions are different. The classroom meeting has the feeling of a very mild encounter group that relies on honest communication of feelings and differences without the need to win or criticize.

In one class we visited, a second grade student commenting on the importance of the Middle East talks gave the example of dropping the atomic bomb on Japan as a less desirable way to end war. This provoked a stimulating, sophisticated discussion among the group on U.S. alternatives for ending World War II.

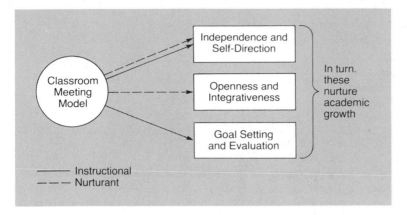

FIGURE 12-1   Instructional and nurturant effects: Classroom Meeting Model.

Even though none of this may sound terribly unique, the classroom tends to be so culture-bound to norms of competing, evaluating, and goal setting that apparently only the creation of a special mechanism, the classroom meeting, set apart in time and space, can induce a different social system.

INSTRUCTIONAL AND NURTURANT EFFECTS

This model is specifically designed to help individuals understand themselves and take responsibility for their own development. This process would obviously have latent benefits for all kinds of social and academic functioning; however, its primary application is to further personal functioning. Glasser is primarily concerned with the general development of students—toward more responsible, integrated, responsive persons who can direct and monitor their own growth. While the individual students plan some activities, they depend on the development of a climate that nurtures responsibility, openness, and self-directedness. The Classroom Meeting Model (Figure 12-1) is thus primarily a nurturant model.

Summary Chart: Classroom Meeting Model

SYNTAX

Phase One:
Establishing a Climate of Involvement
Encourage everyone to participate and speak for himself or herself.
Share opinions without blame or evaluation.

Phase Two:
Exposing the Problem for Discussion
Students and/or teacher bring up issue or problem.
Give examples.
Describe problem fully.
Identify consequences.
Identify social norm.

Phase Three:
Making a Personal Value Judgment
Identify values behind problem behavior and social norm.
Students make personal judgments about norms to follow and articulate their values.

Phase Four:
Identifying Alternative Courses of Action
Discuss specific behavioral alternatives.
Students agree on which ones to follow.

Phase Five:
Making a Commitment
Students make a public commitment.

Phase Six:
Behavioral Follow-Up
After period of time, students assess effectiveness of commitment and new behaviors.

SOCIAL SYSTEM

The model has moderate structure: The teacher controls much of the action, but in certain phases he or she shares the initiation or closure of activity with the students.

PRINCIPLES OF REACTION

Teacher behavior is governed by three principles:
1. Involvement;
2. Nonjudgmental attitude;
3. The classroom group as a whole identifies, selects, and follows through with alternative courses of behavior.

SUPPORT SYSTEM

Chief qualities of the classroom teacher are warm personality and skill in interpersonal and discussion techniques.

Part III
The Social Family

The social models combine a belief about learning and a belief about society. The belief about learning is that cooperative behavior is stimulating not only socially but also intellectually and, hence, that tasks requiring social interaction will stimulate learning. The belief about society is that a central role of education is to prepare citizens to perpetuate a democratic social order.

The combination of these two beliefs has resulted in the development of a large number of models that have great potential for our teaching repertoires. Also, many of the social theorists have not only built rationales for their models, but have raised serious questions about the adequacy of the current dominant patterns of schooling. In most schools the majority of learning tasks are structured by teachers for individuals. Most interaction between teachers and students is in the pattern of recitation—the teacher directs questions about what has been studied, calls on an individual who responds, and then affirms the response or corrects it (Sirotnik, 1983).

Many developers of the cooperative learning models thus believe not only that they have developed important additions to the storehouse of models but also that teacher-dominated recitation is actually bad for society.

RESEARCH ON COOPERATIVE MODELS

The social models received much attention in the 1930s and 1940s, when a number of studies were conducted of the effects of the schools that used democratic-process models as their cores. Many of the studies were in response to serious questions raised by concerned citizens about whether such a degree of reliance on social purposes would retard the students' academic development. The studies generally indicated that social and academic goals are not at all incompatible. The students from those schools were not disadvantaged; in many respects, in fact, they outperformed the others (Chamberlin and Chamberlin, 1943).

Recently, interest has been renewed in research on the cooperative learning models. The more sophisticated research procedures that now exist have enabled better tests to be made of the basic assumptions of these models. Work by three groups of researchers is of particular interest. One is led by David and Roger Johnson of the University of Minnesota (Johnson and Johnson, 1974, 1981). Another is led by Robert Slavin (1983) of Johns Hopkins University, and the third by Shlomo Sharan of Israel (1980). We discuss these studies more extensively in Chapter 13, but some of the key directions of the work have implications for the entire family of models and so we touch on them here. Using somewhat different strategies, the teams of both the Johnsons and Slavin have conducted sets of investigations that closely examine the assumptions of the social family of teaching models. Specifically, they have studied whether cooperative tasks and reward structures affect learning outcomes positively. Also, they have asked whether group cohesion, cooperative behavior, and intergroup relations are improved through cooperative learning procedures. In some of their investigations they have examined the effects of cooperative task and reward structures on "traditional" learning tasks, in which students are presented with material to master. Important for us is the question of whether cooperative groups do in fact generate the energy that results in improved learning. The evidence is largely affirmative. Classrooms organized so that students work in pairs and larger groups, tutor each other, and share rewards are characterized by greater mastery of material than the common individual-study cum recitation pattern. Also, the shared responsibility and interaction produce more positive feelings toward tasks and others, generate better intergroup relations, and result in better self-images for students with histories of poor achievement. In other words, the results generally affirm the assumptions that underlie these models.

Sharan and his colleagues have studied the most comprehensive and complex social model, group investigation, and have learned much both about how to make the dynamics of the model work and about its effects on cooperative behavior, intergroup relations, and lower- and higher-order achievement. Thus, he has investigated classroom situations that are much different from the conventional patterns, for in group investigation the teachers and students form a partnership to determine goals and procedures—the cooperative aspects of the classroom are pervasive. Sharan's team has confirmed the results of the Johnson and Slavin teams, but it has also learned that the stronger the model implemented—the more that cooperative endeavor replaced directive recitation and individual study—the more positive the results. He has also demonstrated that cooperative learning is appropriate for a broad range of learning objectives: the "basic skills" as well as the more complex cognitive and social goals of schooling.

An exciting use of the social models is in combination with models from the other families, in an effort to combine the effects of several models. For example, Baveja, Showers, and Joyce (1985) conducted a study in which concept and inductive procedures were carried out in cooperative groups. The effects fulfilled the promise of the marriage of the information-processing and social models, and the treatment generated gains twice those of a comparison group that received intensive individual and group tutoring over the same material.

The models we have selected to illustrate this family include the classic Group Investigation Model, several similar models that emphasize social values and policies (the Role Playing Model and the Jurisprudential Inquiry Model), and a model for teaching group dynamics and social skills (The Laboratory Method). We conclude with a social science based model.

13

GROUP INVESTIGATION
Building Education Through the Democratic Process

SCENARIO

Our fifth grade class is studying India. The textbook deals with all of the orthodox content areas that texts are obliged to deal with, such as geographic location, population density, agriculture, industry, major cities, and products. A second textbook briefly describes important historical developments, the four divisions of the caste system, and the beneficence of the British during their 300-year rule. These topics suffice for a starting point. But to achieve an understanding of the feeling and flavor of the Indian culture, we need to go beyond the textbooks. Our study includes such topics as the British East India Company; the maharajas and the untouchables; the meanings of Buddhism and Hinduism; literature and art; contributions to human knowledge; Gandhi and passive resistance; customs and beliefs; daily life; partition and independence; major problems, and the historical, religious, political, and social forces that bear on those problems. In summary, we are seeking to enter the lives of the people who are part of this distant and different culture.

We begin the study by outlining areas of interest that indicate the distinctiveness of India, focusing on the people in relation to the various topics of the outline. The class decides that they will select one topic at a time and work independently to gather relevant information from sources in and out of school. Students will then bring the information to class for discussion, raise and answer questions, seek and analyze implications, trace causal relationships, and so on.

However, the children bring in more than information; they also contribute their reactions to their discoveries about this vastly different culture. For example, Student A, whose emotional honesty prohibits him from squelching anything he feels, on hearing of the sacrosanct position of the cow in Indian society expresses the opinion, "That's stupid! Why would people treat a cow that way?" As the severe hardships of life in India come to light, the attitude also emerges that it is stupidity on the part of the people that perpetuates their difficulties. The underlying reason for the impatience and derision of these students is due, of course, to their ethnocentric attitudes toward the information they are gathering: In these beginning discussions, it is apparent that the class is having difficulty in understanding ways of life so different from their own. Their judgment of what is good, bad, or "stupid" in that society is based almost entirely on the degree to which Indian customs, beliefs, and values are similar to our own. The discussions provide an opportunity to place the various aspects of Indian life into the social, historical, religious, or political contexts of the Indian culture, not the American culture. Derision gradually diminishes and a rather sympathetic, accepting attitude develops with the students' growing understanding of the forces that shape the lives and dictate the customs of the people of India.

Classroom procedure is now going along smoothly. There are activities such as bulletin board displays, additional reports on the philosophy of the major religions, picture displays of famous places and art objects, and biographies of famous people. Although not one of these activities is particularly spectacular, they are sufficient evidence to me that the class is interested in the study. They are deriving meanings that are among my goals.

We have arrived at the topic of major problems of India, which is last on our outline. The children have long since ceased viewing the different cultural behaviors of the Indian people as "stupid." Considerable understanding by the class has evolved concerning the overwhelming forces that create and perpetuate hardship in the lives of these people. Several children have just reported on news articles about the drought in Kerala and the impending famine. There is considerable discussion about this situation as an historic problem and as a current emergency. Our class is very moved by one report that 150 million people—20 million of whom are children—are expected to perish. Student B, very knowledgeable about such matters, reminds us that these figures represent total populations of some countries. As the discussion proceeds, there is a mounting intensity of feeling from many children. At first I think the excitement is because a bit of history is coming alive before them. Perhaps this reasoning does explain, in part, the events that follow.

As the discussion continues, the words *famine in India* disappear. Instead, the children speak in terms of people being hungry and in danger of starvation. The shift in language probably represents a humanizing of the problem, a recognition of an intensely human tragedy happening to a people they have come to feel they know. Unable to contain himself, Student C ignores the usual procedure of class discussion and shouts out, "Why don't we send food there?" The idea catches on immediately. Out of the excitement and exuberance a plan emerges. Student A adds, "We could get all the other schools in town to collect food too." Students D and E think we can submit information to a local radio station so that perhaps other communities will follow suit. It is even suggested that perhaps we publicize our idea on a major television network and encourage children all over the country to collect food for India.

We discuss the details. There is the question of how to contact the other schools and coordinate our efforts, the problems of where to store the canned and dried foods we collect and how to pick up the food we collect and deliver it to the ship. But what ship? At this point we realize that finding an agency that will ship the food free of charge is the starting point for our project. It is decided that I will not request official permission from the principal to carry out our plans until we secure information about shipping.

Students E, D, and A volunteer to call such agencies as CARE, the Indian Consulate, and UNICEF. Plans are made to ask several store owners in the area if posters advertising the campaign may be placed in their windows. We are not certain at this point whether to make the posters in the homeroom or to ask the art teacher if it can be done during her class. We make a note to ask her advice.

Student F's father owns a truck, and Student D's father has a friend who owns a truck. The students will speak to their parents about helping us with transportation arrangements. Student G suggests that we send a flier to parents and all people in the neighborhood describing our food campaign and informing them when they should expect collectors. The date is not yet decided. Several parents will be asked to mimeograph fliers for us.

Within forty-five minutes the children have outlined the major aspects of their plan. In that short period of time, history and world events have reached into the classroom and touched them, and they have responded. The response is entirely their own.

The volunteers who have agreed to find out about shipping arrangements report to the class within the next few days. CARE cannot ship for us. They will accept a donation of money and send their own food packages. This proposal is rejected definitely by the class. They say they want to send food, not money. The children express some doubt as to whether, under such an arrangement, all of the money will be used as they direct. There seems to be some cynicism regarding charitable organizations. I comment that perhaps this isn't a fair attitude, but I don't pursue my feeling further as the shipping problem seems of more immediate concern. At any rate, it is firmly established that food is to be sent, as that is the most direct expression of their concern. UNICEF cannot help either; they know of no agency that can ship for us. We also asked UNICEF if they would contribute money containers because the children have decided to give people a choice of donating food or money. With money collected, we plan to shop for food. UNICEF has no containers for us, and so we will have to make our own.

Student E, with the help of her father, contacts someone at the Indian Consul General's office who says they will ship for us. We are all delighted that we can begin to put our plans into operation. We are ready to ask the principal's permission to carry out the project. I have also intended to ask his advice on how we can get other schools in the community involved in our plans. I am uncertain how the project will be received since it will entail considerable disruption of school routine. I am not unaware that it is rather late for that reality to have dawned. With as much confidence in the desirability and plausibility of our project as I can muster, I prepare to meet with the principal.

After listening to our plan, the principal informs me that we will have to get permission from the superintendent of schools for a project of this nature. A meeting with the superintendent is arranged. He thinks the idea is good but suggests that carrying out the plan on a citywide basis is perhaps too ambitious. He suggests that before starting on our original plan we try it first in our own school with several classes participating. If that plan succeeds, he will assign us an administrator to help coordinate the efforts on a broader scale. Finally, he suggests that we locate the name of a school in the famine area where the food and letters will be sent to the children. The project will thus be carried out on a very personal level between the children of both countries.

Although the class is very pleased with the suggestion that we send food to a particular school, they are extremely annoyed that we cannot conduct the campaign on a citywide basis. They consider this decision an unjust interference with our plans. I try to placate the class by reminding them that if we are successful, we will be given an administrator to assist us. Somehow they are not as impressed with that explanation as I seem to be.

The modification of plans reveals some attitudes that have to be dealt with immediately. Of course I realize that I have contributed to the problem by not explaining more carefully to the class on that first day the plan was formed that our project must remain tentative until official permission was granted. If that point had been made clear, the modification of plans would not have produced as much resentment. It might also have been wiser not to have proceeded so far with the plans before permission had been secured. However, the feelings that initiated the plan were so spontaneous and so full of conviction that both the children and I were swept along with little thought to possible impediments.

One of the attitudes I observe in addition to the resentment of the "interference" and the feeling of injustice is a pessimism on the part of quite a few children that our plans will not come to fruition since we cannot act autonomously. It is apparent that many children cannot manage their frustrations in the situation. As a consequence, we have several class discussions emphasizing the need for us to remain flexible in our thinking to achieve our purpose. We even predict the possibility of having to modify our plans in other respects if necessary. We have to learn that modifying our plans does not mean failure, as long as our goals are achieved.

For a few days this week, we think our plans will not succeed. We are unable to locate the person at the Consul General's office who has said that they will take care of shipping for us. When I call the consul (the only phone call *I* make in the project), the consul representative tells me that his office is definitely not prepared to ship food for us and that he can't imagine who might have told us otherwise. He tells me that the U.S. government shipment of food to India is carried out by American shipping lines but is paid for by the Indian government. I ask him if he thinks we can simply send our food along with the government's shipments. He explains that it will not be possible unless I receive special permission from the Indian government. At that point I don't understand the reasons for such rigid procedures, but the thought of negotiating with a government as a solution to the problem seems more than I can handle.

Despite our setback regarding shipping, we have been proceeding with other aspects of the campaign. An ample supply of one-pint milk containers has been accumulated for money collecting and is decorated in the art class. It is decided that the large posters we want will be designed by the more artistic class members and given to Student C's mother, who has volunteered to have them duplicated at her place of business by silk-screen process. We have approached individual parents and the PTA to mimeograph our fliers, but because so many are needed and the expenditures will be beyond their budgets, we are turned down. Instead, I ditto them. They are then distributed to each child in the fifth and sixth grades (five other classes totally), who will put them into mailboxes and under doors throughout the neighborhood. The children arrange among themselves to divide the district into areas so that duplication of effort will be avoided. The same arrangements will be used for the food collection.

All fifth and sixth grade children are ready to start the collection. We have stresed the need for dried foods on our fliers and posters, but the class decides to accept any kind of food donated. Whatever foods can't be sent to India because of the dietary needs there will be converted to cash, and then we will buy food that can be sent. I feel somewhat uneasy about the indefiniteness of this decision, but the children do not share my doubts. They feel quite sure that when the problem arises, they will handle it. And so the neighborhood is descended upon by 180 children determined to take part in the prevention of a tragic reality so far away.

We are inundated with cans and packages of food! Each morning and afternoon, participating children and little brothers and sisters who have worked at collecting come to our room burdened with heavy packages and containers of money. They obviously have worked hard at their collecting and deliver their contributions with pride. We are kept very busy counting, stacking, sorting, and recording all contributions. Tables, bookshelves, and windowsills are stacked high with canned goods. The local newspaper sends a photographer to take a picture of the collection. We have accumulated more than 1,000 pieces, including canned goods, dry milk, and dried beans.

As we sit amid this display of abundance, the reality dawns that we can't send most of the food we have collected as the Indians do not eat such foods. What to do now? Student A proposes an idea that we think has excellent possibilities. April 18 is parents' visiting day. Student A thinks that when they come into the classroom to observe, a small committee of children might invite parents to do some shopping among our goods, thereby donating to our cause. We think we will use the money to buy rice wholesale. We are at least certain that rice is eaten in that part of the world.

Dolores Greco developed this unit when teaching in the Mt. Vernon (New York) schools, while she was a graduate student at Teachers College, Columbia University. This description is presented with her permission.

CREATORS

Educational models derived from a conception of society usually envision what human beings would be like in a very good, even utopian, society. Their educational methods aim to develop ideal citizens who could live in and enhance that society, who could fulfill themselves in and through it, and who would even be able to help create and revise it. We have had such models from the time of the Greeks. Plato's *Republic* is a blueprint for an ideal society and the educational program to support it (Cornford, 1945). Aristotle also dealt with the ideal education and society (Smith and Ross, 1912). Since their time, many other utopians have produced educational models, including Augustine (*The City of God*, 1931), Sir Thomas More (*Utopia*, 1965), Comenius (*The Great Didactic*, 1907), and John Locke (1927).

It was natural that attempts would be made to use teaching methods to improve society. In the United States, extensive efforts have been made to develop classroom instruction as a model of democratic process; in fact, variations on democratic process are probably more common than any other general teaching method as far as the educational literature is concerned. In terms of instructional models, *democratic process* has referred to organizing classroom groups to do any or all of the following tasks:

1. Develop a social system based on and created by democratic procedures.
2. Conduct scientific inquiry into the nature of social life and processes. In this case the term *democratic procedures* is synonymous with the scientific method and inquiry.
3. Engage in solving a social or interpersonal problem.
4. Provide an experience-based learning situation.

The implementation of democratic methods of teaching has been exceedingly difficult. They require the teacher to have a high level of interpersonal *and* instructional skills. Also, democratic process is cumbersome and frequently slow; parents, teachers, and school officials often fear that it will not be efficient as a teaching method. In addition, a rich array of instructional resources is necessary, and these have not always been available. Probably the most important hindrance is that the school simply has not been organized to teach the social and intellectual processes of democracy. Instead, it has been directed toward and organized for basic instruction in academic subjects, and school officials and patrons have, for the most part, been unwilling to change that direction or organization.

THE PHILOSOPHICAL UNDERPINNINGS

The dominating figure in the effort to develop models for democratic process has been John Dewey, who wrote *How We Think* in 1910. Nearly all of the theoreticians dealing with reflective thinking since that time have acknowledged their debt to him. However, those who have emphasized democratic process have by no means been homogeneous, nor have they followed Dewey in the same ways or even directly. For example, in the 1920s Charles Hubbard Judd emphasized academic scholarship (Judd, 1934). William Heard Kilpatrick, for many years a major spokesperson for the Progressive movement, emphasized social problem solving (Kilpatrick, 1919). George Counts stressed not only problem solving but also reconstruction of society (Counts, 1932). Boyd Bode emphasized the general intellectual processes of problem solving (Bode, 1927).

A well-known statement of this group's concern with the democratic process and societal reconstruction was made in 1961 by Gordon H. Hullfish and Phillip G. Smith in *Reflective Thinking: The Method of Education*. These authors stress the role of education in improving the capacity of individuals to reflect on the ways they handle information, on their concepts, their beliefs, their values. A society of reflective thinkers would be capable of improving itself and preserving the uniqueness of individuals. This philosophy contains many ideas or propositions common to democratic-process philosophies. It carefully delineates the ties among the personal world of the individual, his or her intellect, social processes, and the functioning of a democratic society.

Hullfish and Smith see intellectual development and social process as inextricably related. For example, the development of skill in social process requires skill in synthesizing and analyzing the viewpoints of those engaged in social interaction.

Next, they believe that knowledge is constructed and continuously reconstructed by individuals and groups. They stress that knowledge is not conveyed to us merely through our sensory interactions with our environment, but that we must operate on experience to produce knowledge. As a result, knowledge has a personal quality and is unique for each individual. For example, a few hours before writing this, one of the authors stood on a rocky point looking at the Pacific Ocean against the brown of the California coast. He felt a quiet excitement and an appreciation of the sea and the rocks and the great peace of the scene about him. Yet the concept *sea*, the concept *rock*, the concept *wave*, and the excitement, peace, and appreciation he felt were not inherent in the experience themselves. These were constructed by the author in relation to that experience and to others he has had. He created some concepts and borrowed some from others. He generated some feelings and some beliefs and had been given some by imitating other people (the vast majority were borrowed in this way).

Thus, individuals' ways of reflecting on reality are what make their world comprehensible to them and give them personal and social meaning. Therefore, the quality of an individual's ability to reflect on experience becomes a critical factor in determining the quality of the world he or she will construct about him or her. Someone who is insensitive to much of his or her experience and does not reflect on it will have a far less richly constructed world than someone who takes in a good deal of experience and reflects fully on it. It becomes critical for education to sensitize the individual to many aspects of his or her physical and social environment and to increase his or her capacity to reflect on the environment.

The individual quality of knowledge creates some difficulties, especially when it comes to constructing a society. Nevertheless, Hullfish and Smith maintain that individual differences are the strength of a democracy, and negotiating among them is a major democratic activity. The more an individual learns to take responsibility for reflecting on experience and developing a valid view of the world and a valid set of beliefs, the more it is likely that the resulting network of information, concepts, and values will be unique to the individual. In other words, the more fully reflective an individual is, the more he or she will develop a personal processing system. A democratic society requires that we work together to understand each other's worlds and develop a shared perspective that will enable us to learn from each other and govern ourselves while preserving a pluralistic reality.

The perception of alternative frames of reference and alternative courses of action is essential to social negotiations. But one must have very great personal development to understand other people's viewpoints. This sharing of perceptions is necessary, however, if a mutual reality is to be constructed (see Berger and Luckman, 1966).

The essence of a functioning democracy is the negotiation of problem definitions and problem solutions. This ability to negotiate with others also helps each person negotiate his or her own world. Maintaining a sense of meaning and purpose depends on developing a valid and flexible way of dealing with reality. Failure to make life comprehensible or to negotiate reality with others will result in a feeling of chaos. The ability to continually reconstruct one's value stances, and the ability to create value systems that are compatible are both essential to mature development.

Most models of teaching assume that one does something in particular to get a specific outcome from the learner. *On the contrary, models that emphasize democratic process assume that the outcome of any educational experience is not completely predictable.* The democratic-model makers reason that if they are successful in persuading students to inquire into the nature of their experiences, and to develop their own ways of viewing the world, it will be impossible to predict just how they will face any given situation or solve any particular problem. Hence, if the student is taught an academic discipline, it is not so that he or she will know *exactly* the discipline known by others, but so that this exposure will help him or her create a frame of reference and a unique way of ordering reality.

ORIENTATION TO THE MODEL

GOALS AND ASSUMPTIONS

In *Democracy and Education,* John Dewey (1916) recommends that the entire school be organized as a miniature democracy. Students participate in the development of the social system and, through experience, gradually learn how to apply the scientific method to improve human society. This, Dewey feels, is the best preparation for citizenship in a democracy. John U. Michaelis (1980) has extracted from Dewey's work a formulation specifically for teaching the social studies at the elementary level. Central to his method of teaching is the creation of a democratic group that defines and attacks problems of social significance.

Herbert Thelen is one of the founders of the National Training Laboratory. In many respects Thelen's Group-Investigation Model resembles the methods Dewey and Michaelis recommend. Group investigation attempts to combine in one teaching strategy the form and dynamics of the democratic process with the process of academic inquiry. Thelen is reaching for an experienced-based learning situation, easily transferable to later life situations, and characterized by a vigorous level of inquiry.

Thelen begins with a conception of a social being: "A man [woman] who builds with other men [women] the rules and agreements that constitute social reality" (Thelen, 1960, p. 80). Any view of how people should develop has to refer to the inescapable fact that life is *social*—and a social being cannot act without reference to his or her companions on earth; otherwise in the quest for self-maintenance and autonomy each person may well conflict with other people making similar efforts. In establishing social agreements, each individual helps to determine both prohibitions and freedom for action. Rules of conduct operate in all fields—religious, political, economic, and scientific—and constitute the culture of a society. For Thelen, this negotiation and renegotiation of the social order are the essence of social process:

> Thus in groups and societies a cyclical process exists: individuals, interdependently seeking to meet their needs, must establish a social order (and in the process they develop groups and societies.) The social order determines in

varying degrees what ideas, values and actions are possible, valid and "appropriate"! Working within these "rules" and stimulated by the need for rules the culture develops. The individual studies his reactions to the rules and reinterprets them to discover their meaning for the way of life he seeks. Through this quest, he changes his own way of life, and this in turn influences the way of life of others. But as the way of life changes, the rules must be revised, and new controls and agreements have to be hammered out and incorporated into the social order. (Thelen, 1960, p. 80)

The classroom is analogous to the larger society; it has a social order and a classroom culture, and its students care about the way of life that develops there—that is, the standards and expectations that become established. Teachers should seek to harness the energy naturally generated by the concern for creating the social order. The model of teaching replicates the negotiation pattern needed by society. Through negotiation the students study academic knowledge and they engage in social problem solving. According to Thelen, one should not attempt to teach knowledge from any academic area without teaching the social process by which it was negotiated.

Thelen rejects the normal classroom order that develops around the basic values of comfort and politeness or of keeping the teacher happy. Rather, the classroom group should take seriously the process of developing a social order:

> "The teacher's task is to participate in the activities of developing the social order in the classroom for the purpose of orienting it to inquiry, and the "house rules" to be developed are the methods and attitudes of the knowledge discipline to be taught. The teacher influences the emerging social order toward inquiring when he "brings out" and capitalizes on differences in the way students act and interpret the role of investigator—which is also the role of member in the classroom." (Thelen, 1960, p. 81)

Life in classrooms takes the form of a series of "inquiries." Each inquiry starts with a stimulus situation to which students

> can react and discover basic conflicts among their attitudes, ideas, and modes of perception. On the basis of this information, they identify the problem to be investigated, analyze the roles required to solve it, organize themselves to take these roles, act, report and evaluate these results. These steps are illuminated by reading, by personal investigation, and by consultation with experts. The group is concerned with its own effectiveness, and with its discussion of its own process as related to the goals of investigation. (Thelen, 1960, p. 82)

In their concentration on the overt activities of democratic process, many followers and interpreters of Dewey overlook the underlying spirit that brings the democratic process to life. The activities, if followed by rote, provide only lifeless applications quite unlike the democratic process and scientific method Dewey and Thelen have in mind. The class should become a miniature democracy that attacks problems and, through problem solving, acquires knowledge and becomes more effective as a social group. Many attempts to use democratic process did little to change educational practice because the implementation was superficial, following the form but not the substance of democracy.

BASIC CONCEPTS

The three concepts of (1) inquiry; (2) knowledge; and (3) the dynamics of the learning group are central to Thelen's strategy.

INQUIRY Inquiry is stimulated by confrontation with a problem, and knowledge results from the inquiry. The social process enhances inquiry and is itself studied and improved. The heart of group investigation lies in its formulation of inquiry. According to Thelen (1960), the concern of inquiry is "to initiate and supervise the processes of giving attention to something; of interacting with and being stimulated by other people, whether in person or through their writing; and of reflection and reorganization of concepts and attitudes as shown in arriving at conclusions, identifying new investigations to be undertaken, taking action and turning out a better product" (p. 85).

The first element of inquiry is an event the individual can react to and puzzle over—a problem to be solved. In the classroom the teacher can select content and cast it in terms of problem situations—for example, "How did our community come to be the way it is?" Simply providing a problem, however, will not generate the puzzlement that is a major energy source for inquiry. The students must add an awareness of self and a desire for personal meaning; in addition, they must assume the dual roles of participant and observer, simultaneously inquiring into the problem and observing themselves as inquirers. Because inquiry is basically a social process, students are aided in the self-observer role by interacting with, and by observing the reactions of, other puzzled people. The conflicting viewpoints that emerge also energize the students' interest in the problem.

Although the teacher can provide a problem situation, it is up to the students as inquirers to identify and formulate the problem and pursue its solution. Inquiry calls for firsthand activity in a real situation and ongoing experience that continually generates new data. The students must thus be conscious of method so that they may collect data, associate and classify ideas recalling past experience, formulate and test hypotheses, study consequences, and modify plans. Finally, they must develop the capacity for reflection, the ability to synthesize overt participative behavior with symbolic verbal behavior. The students are asked to give conscious attention to the experience—to formulate explicitly the conclusions of the study and to integrate them with existing ideas. In this way thoughts are reorganized into new and more powerful patterns.

Let us examine a few examples that Thelen gives us to illustrate the flavor of inquiry and to point out the difference between inquiry and activity. The first example is drawn from a second grade social studies class dealing with the question, "How do different people live?" The teacher proposed that the students select some group, find out how they live, and put this information in a play they would write themselves. After some discussion the students selected prairie dogs as a focus for their study. Here is an account of their inquiry:

> They started their study by naming the characters for the play they would write, and of course the characters turned out to be baby, chicken, mother, father, farmer's boy, snake, etc. They made lists of questions to be answered: What do prairie dogs eat? Where do they live? What do they do with their time? How big are their families? Who are their enemies? etc. Individuals sought answers to questions from science pamphlets, books, the science teacher, officials of the local zoo, and I have no doubt at least a few of them talked to their parents to be taken to see the Disney opus. They reported their findings in compositions during the writing lessons. The plot of the play gradually took shape and was endlessly modified with each new bit of information. The play centered around family life, and there was much discussion and spontaneous demonstrations of how various members of the family would act. Most of these characterizations actually represented a cross-section of the home lives of seven-year-old children, as perceived by the children. But each action was gravely discussed and soberly considered, and justified in terms of what they knew about the ecology of prairie dogs.
>
> They built a stage with sliding curtains and four painted backdrops—more reference work here to get the field and farm right. The play itself was given six times, with six different casts, and each child played at least two different parts. There was never any written script; only an agreement on the line of action and the part of it to occur in each scene. And after each presentation the youngsters sat around and discussed what they had been trying to communicate, how it might be improved. (Thelen, 1960, pp. 142–143)

Thelen contrasts this example with one drawn from a high school social studies class in which the students were to put on a series of television programs on the history of the community. As preparation, the students looked up information and visited historical sites, taking pictures of important evidence:

> Harry and Joe took pictures of an Indian mound, left there by original settlers. They took it from the south because the light was better that way; and they never discovered the northern slope where erosion had laid bare a burrow full of Indian relics. Mary and Sue spent two afternoons on a graph of corn production in the region; the graph was in a geography book the teacher gave them and the time was mostly spent in making a neat elaborately lettered document for the camera. The narrators were chosen for their handsome appearance, and much of the staging of the show (which used reports mostly) centered around deciding the most

decorative way to seat the students. A lot of old firearms and household im-
plements were borrowed from a local museum and displayed, a sentence or two
of comment for each. (Thelen, 1960, pp. 143–144)

In this latter instance, Thelen acknowledges that the students have
learned something about the region, but he points out that most of the energy,
the measure of success, was the effectiveness of the television as a blend of
entertainment and information giving. The roles in which the students inquired "were those of a reporter with a keen eye for human interest angles,
rather than the sociologist's or historian's with a disciplined concern for the
course of human events" (Thelen, 1960, p. 144).

These two examples illustrate the distinction between activity and inquiry. The actions of the second grade class investigating prairie dogs contained the elements of inquiry: puzzlement, self-awareness, methodology, and
reflection. In looking at the two examples given, we may ask ourselves: Were
there questions? Who formulated them? Who sought their answers? How was
this information obtained? Was the information applied? Were the conclusions drawn, and who drew them? Activities are potential channels for inquiry,
but inquiry must emanate from the motivations and curiosity of the students.
Activities cease to be inquiry when the teacher is the sole source of the problem identification and the formulation of plans, or when the end-product of
inquiry takes precedence over the inquiry process. That is what happened to
the high school group—they attained production, but lost the process on the
way.

KNOWLEDGE   The development of knowledge is the goal of inquiry,
but Thelen uses knowledge in a special way: as the application of the univer-
sals and principles drawn from past experience to present experience. In the
prairie dog example the process of discovering knowledge was on center stage
at all times; the principles of inquiry were what counted:

> Knowledge is unborn experience; it is the universals incorporated into the ner-
> vous system; it is a predisposition to approach the world with inquiry; it is mean-
> ingful past experience living within oneself; it is the seed of potential internal
> reorganization through which one keeps in touch with the changing world.
> Knowledge lies in the basic alternative orientations and the proposition through
> which new orientations can be built. (Thelen, 1960, p. 51)

In other words, we "try on" various ways of looking at experience, continually
reinterpreting experience into workable principles and concepts.

Why should inquiry take place in groups? In addition to the application
of scientific method, inquiry has emotional aspects—emotions arising from involvement and growing self-awareness, the seeking of personal meaning and
the affect that accompanies conscious reflective behavior. Thus, Thelen
views a learning situation as "one which involves the emotions of the learner"

(Thelen, 1954, p. 47). The group is both an arena for personal needs as in-dividuals deal with their anxieties, doubts, and private desires, and an instru-ment for solving social problems. As conflicting views impinge on individuals, they find themselves inescapably involved in the social and academic dimen-sions of the inquiry. "[The individual] is driven by very profound and very per-vasive psyche needs for the kind of classroom in which he can survive as a per-son and find a place for himself in the organization. Algebra may mean less than nothing initially, but self-esteem, freedom of sorts, feelings of growing adequacy and stimulation that provoke him into rewarding activity are impor-tant" (Thelen, 1960, p. 147). The social aspects of group investigation provide a route, therefore, to disciplined academic inquiry.

As a group confronts a puzzling situation, the reactions of individuals vary widely, and the assumptive worlds that give rise to these varied reactions are even more different than the reactions themselves. The need to reconcile this difference generates a basic challenge. The newly perceived alternatives extend the student's experience by serving both as a source of self-awareness and as a stimulant to his or her curiosity. Engaged in inquiry with a group, in-dividuals become aware of different points of view that help them find out who they are by seeing themselves projected against the views of others. It also stimulates them: They want to know *why* differences exist and how they af-fect them.

DYNAMICS OF THE LEARNING GROUP   Thelen feels that having a "teachable group" is a prerequisite for conducting any productive group in-vestigation. Ideally about ten to fifteen students should comprise the in-vestigating group. This number is large enough for diversity of reactions and small enough for individual participation. There should be enough com-monality of values that communication is easy and ways of working are similar, but enough differences to generate alternative reactions. Finally, group members should possess a common level of sophistication and orientation toward the knowledge area to be investigated. If the range is too great, the levels of conceptualization will very likely be too far apart to enable the group to relate productively (Thelen, 1960, p. 157).

OVERVIEW OF THE
TEACHING STRATEGY

Thelen provides the example of a group of eleven adult women prepar-ing to be elementary school teachers. This group has enough in common to facilitate close relationships but contains enough diversity to generate the dif-fering reactions that energize inquiry. These women were investigating the skills, attitudes, and knowledge necessary to be effective teachers. The initial confrontation centered on seven elementary school classes that the teachers had observed. They were given no instructions as to what to observe but were simply told to report their findings to the group. Soon, heated arguments developed over the interpretation of a kindergarten teacher's behavior. The discussion revealed a great many attitudes and ideas about teaching and learning as well as many submerged personal concerns about the course.

At that point the discussion dissolved into arguments and ceased being informative. Hence, the instructors broke in with the suggestion that the group accept the difference of opinion and more systematically examine the factors that influence classroom activities. Short filmstrip samples of classroom activities were then presented. The group listed all the factors they could think of to account for the differences among the samples. The purposes of the teacher seemed central. The next task was to relate the observed behavior of children to the motivations of the teacher. Out of this task grew a checklist for studying the behavior and roles of the students. In other words, the original emotional conflict had led to the collection of new information, more disciplined analysis, and finally the development of an instrument for making judgments more objectively. The group continued to make and compare its observations. From these discussions individuals were stimulated to pursue aspects of teaching that interested them; then they met on a private, personal basis with each person and developed further individual goals.

But what were to be the next activities of the group as a whole? On the basis of their discussion with their students, the instructors were able to identify broad questions about child development that interested the group. Accordingly, they made a proposal to study the skills, attitudes, and orientations of children at different ages. The group called in resource people, evaluated the children's progress gradually, and took over responsibility for guiding its own action. The original inquiry into different reactions to the behavior of a teacher had been "recycled" into an inquiry into child development.

THE MODEL OF TEACHING

SYNTAX

The model begins by confronting the students with a stimulating problem. The confrontation may be presented verbally, or it may be an actual experience; it may arise naturally, or it may be provided by a teacher. If the students react, the teacher draws their attention to the differences in their reactions—what stances they take, what they perceive, how they organize things, and what they feel. As the students become interested in their differences in reaction, the teacher draws them toward formulating and structuring the problem for themselves. Next students analyze the required roles, organize themselves, act, and report their results. Finally, the group evaluates its solution in terms of its original purposes. The cycle repeats itself, either

Table 13-1   Syntax of Group Investigation Model

PHASE ONE:	PHASE TWO:
Students encounter puzzling situation (planned or unplanned).	Students explore reactions to the situation.
PHASE THREE:	**PHASE FOUR:**
Students formulate study task and organize for study (problem definition, role, assignments, etc.).	Independent and group study.
PHASE FIVE:	**PHASE SIX:**
Students analyze progress and process.	Recycle activity.

with another confrontation or with a new problem growing out of the investigation itself (see Table 13-1).

SOCIAL SYSTEM

The social system is democratic, governed by decisions developed from, or at least validated by, the experience of the group—within boundaries and in relation to puzzling phenomena identified by the teacher as objects to study. The activities of the group emerge with a minimal amount of external structure provided by the teacher. Students and teacher have equal status except for role differences. The atmosphere is one of reason and negotiation.

PRINCIPLES OF REACTION

The teacher's role in group investigation is one of counselor, consultant, and friendly critic. He or she must guide and reflect the group experience over three levels: the problem-solving or task level (What is the nature of the problem? What are the factors involved?); the group management level (What information do we need now? How can we organize ourselves to get it?); and the level of individual meaning (How do you feel about these conclusions? What would you do differently as a result of knowing about . . . ?)(Thelen, 1954, pp. 52–53). This teaching role is a very difficult and sensitive one, because the essence of inquiry is student activity—problems cannot be imposed. At the same time the instructor must (1) facilitate the group process; (2) intervene in the group to channel its energy into potentially educative activities; and (3) supervise these educative activities so that personal meaning comes from the experience (Thelen, 1960, p. 136). Intervention by the instructor should be minimal unless the group bogs down seriously. Chapters 16, 17, and 18 of

Leadership of Discussion Groups by Gertrude K. Pollack (1975) provide an excellent advanced discussion of leadership in groups. Although the material was prepared for persons leading therapy groups, it is written at a very general level and provides much useful advice for persons wishing to build classrooms around group inquiry.

SUPPORT SYSTEM

The support system for group investigation should be extensive and responsive to the needs of the students. The school needs to be equipped with a first-class library that provides information and opinion through a wide variety of media; it should also be able to provide access to outside resources as well. Children should be encouraged to investigate and to contact resource people beyond the school walls. One reason cooperative inquiry of this sort has been relatively rare is that the support systems were not adequate to maintain the level of inquiry.

APPLICATION

Group investigation requires flexibility from the teacher and the classroom organization. Although we assume that the model fits comfortably with the environment of the "open" classroom, we believe it is equally compatible with more traditional classrooms. We have observed successful group-investigation teachers in a context in which other subjects, such as math and reading, are carried out in more structured, teacher-directed fashion. If students have not had an opportunity to experience the kind of social interaction, decision making, and independent inquiry called for in this model, it may take some time before they function at a high level. On the other hand, students who have participated in classroom meetings and/or self-directed, inquiry-oriented learning will probably have an easier time. In any case it is probably useful for the teacher to remember that the social aspects of the model may be as unfamiliar to students as the intellectual aspects and may be as demanding in terms of skill acquisition.

Although the examples of the model described here tend to be intellectually and organizationally elaborate, all investigations need not be so complex. With young children or students new to group investigation, fairly small-scale investigations are possible; the initial confrontation can provide a narrow range of topics, issues, information, and alternative activities. For example, providing an evening's entertainment for the school is more focused than resolving the energy crisis. Deciding who will care for the classroom pet and how is even narrower. Of course, the nature of the inquiry depends on the interests and ages of the students. Older students tend to be concerned with more complex issues. However, the skillful teacher can design inquiries appropriate to the students' abilities and to his or her own ability to manage the investigation.

As we indicated in the introduction to the social family of models, three recent lines of research by three teams (lead by David and Roger Johnson, Robert Slavin, and Shlomo Sharan) have contributed a good deal of knowledge about how to engineer social models and what their effects are likely to be.

The Johnsons have concentrated on cooperative tasks, cooperative rewards, and peer tutoring. They have made extensive reviews of studies with students of all ages working in many substantive areas. As mentioned earlier, their reviews and studies support the contention that working together increases student energy and that rewarding teams of students for performance is effective, appearing to increase the energy of the teams. (Johnson, D., Maruyana, G., Johnson, R., Nelson, D., and Skon, L., 1981). In addition, their work with peer tutoring appears positive as well, and heterogeneous teams (composed of high and low achievers) appear to be the most productive (Johnson and Johnson, 1977).

Slavin's work (Slavin, 1983) generally confirms that of the Johnson's and he has added some interesting variations. He has explored ways of differentiating tasks when groups are working on projects and has found that differentiating tasks increases the energy of the students. For example, when students are studying a topic in history, individuals can become "specialists" in certain areas of the topic, with the responsibility of mastering certain information and conveying it to the other students. In addition, he has looked at the effects of team composition on learning and attitudes toward self and others. Generally, the more heterogeneous groups learn more, form more positive attitudes toward the learning tasks, and become more positive toward one another (Slavin, 1983).

Sharon has studied group investigation per se. His team has reported that the more pervasive the cooperative climate, the more positive the students toward both the learning tasks and toward each other (Sharon and Hertz–Lazarowitz, 1980). In addition he has hypothesized that the greater social complexity would increase achievement of more complex learning goals (concepts and theories) and both confirmed his hypothesis and found that it increased the learning of information and basic skills as well.

The purpose of cooperative inquiry is to combine complex social and academic tasks to generate academic and social learning. Properly implemented, it appears to achieve its goals.

INSTRUCTIONAL AND NURTURANT EFFECTS

This model is highly versatile and comprehensive; it blends the goals of academic inquiry, social interaction, and social process learning. It can be used in all subject areas, with all age levels, when the teacher desires to emphasize

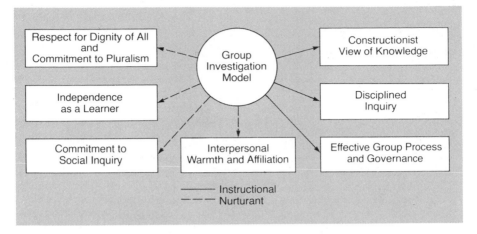

FIGURE 13-1 Instructional and nurturant effects: Group Investigation Model.

the formulation and problem-solving aspects of knowledge rather than the intake of preorganized, predetermined information.

Provided that one accepts Thelen's view of knowledge and its reconstruction, the Group Investigation Model (Figure 13-1) can be considered a very direct and probably efficient way of teaching academic knowledge as well as social process. It also appears likely to nurture interpersonal warmth and trust, respect for negotiated rules and policies, independence in learning, and respect for the dignity of others.

In deciding whether to use the model, considering the potential nurturant effects may be as important as analyzing the likely direct instructional effects. Another model might be as appropriate for teaching academic inquiry, but a teacher may prefer group investigation for what it might nurture.

Summary Chart: Group Investigation Model

SYNTAX

Phase One:
Encounter puzzling situation (planned or unplanned).

Phase Two:
Explore reactions to the situation.

Phase Three:
Formulate study task and organize for study (problem definition, role, assignments, etc.).

Phase Four:
Independent and group study.

Phase Five:
Analyze progress and process.

Phase Six:
Recycle activity.

SOCIAL SYSTEM

The system is based on the democratic process and group decisions, with *low* external structure. Puzzlement must be genuine—it cannot be imposed. Authentic exchanges are essential. Atmosphere is one of reason and negotiation.

PRINCIPLES OF REACTION

Teacher plays a facilitative role directed at group process (helps learners formulate plan, act, manage group) and requirements of inquiry (consciousness of method). He or she functions as an academic counselor.

SUPPORT SYSTEM

The environment must be able to respond to a variety of learner demands. Teacher and student must be able to assemble what they need when they need it.

14

ROLE PLAYING
Studying
Social Behavior
and Values

SCENARIO

We are in a seventh grade classroom in East Los Angeles, California. The students have returned to the classroom from a recess period and are complaining excitedly to one another. Mr. Williams, the teacher, asks what the matter is and they all start in at once, discussing a series of difficulties that lasted throughout the recess period. Apparently, two of the students began to squabble about who was to take the sports equipment outside. Then all of the students fought about what game to play. Next, there was an argument about choosing sides for the games. This included a dispute over whether the girls should be included with the boys, or whether they should play separately. The class finally began to play volleyball, but very shortly there was a dispute over a line call and the game was never completed.

At first, Mr. Williams displays his displeasure toward the class. He is angry, not simply over the incidents, but because these arguments have been going on since the beginning of the year. At last he says, "OK, we really have to face this problem. You must be as tired of it as I am, and you really are not acting maturely. So we are going to use a technique that we have been using to discuss family problems to approach our own problems right here in this classroom: we're going to use role playing. Now, what I want you to do is divide into groups and try to identify the types of problems that we've been having. Just take today, for example, and outline the problem situations that got us into this fix."

The students begin with the argument over taking the sports equipment outside, and then outline other arguments. Each is a typical situation that people face all the time and that they must learn to take a stand on. After the separate groups of students have listed their problems, Mr. Williams appoints one of the students to lead a discussion in which each group reports the kinds of problem situations that have come up; the groups agree on a half-dozen problems that have consistently bothered the class.

The students then group the problems according to type. One type concerns the division of labor. A second type deals with deciding principles for selecting teams. A third type focuses on resolving disputes over the particulars of games, such as whether balls have been hit out of bounds, whether players are out or safe, and so on. Mr. Williams then assigns one type of problem to each group and asks the groups to describe situations in which the problems come up. When they have done this, the class votes on which problem to start with. The first problem they select is disputes over rules; the actual problem situation they select is the volleyball game in which the dispute over a line call occurred.

Together, the class talks about how the problem situation develops. It begins when a ball is hit close to the boundary line; one team believes it is in and the other believes it is out of bounds. The students then argue with one another, and the argument goes on so that the game cannot continue.

Several students are selected to enact the situation. Others gather around and are assigned to observe particular aspects of the role playing that follows. Some students are to look for the particulars of how the argument develops. Some are to study one role player and others another, to determine how they handle the situation.

The enactment is spirited. The students select as role players those who have been on opposite sides during the game, and they become as involved in the argument during the role playing as they were during the actual situation. Finally, they are standing in the middle of the room shouting at one another. At this point, Mr. Williams calls, "Time!" and asks the students to describe what has gone on.

Everyone is eager to talk. The discussion gradually focuses on how the attitude of the participants prevented resolving the problem. No one was listening to the other person. And no one was dealing with the problem of how to resolve honest disputes. Finally, Mr. Williams asks the students to suggest other ways that people could behave in this kind of conflict. Some students suggest giving in gracefully. But others object that if someone believes he or she is right, that is not an easy thing to do. Finally, the students identify an important question to focus on: "How can we develop a policy about who should make calls, and how should others feel about those calls?" They decide to reenact the scene by having all the participants assume that the defensive team should make calls only when they see clear evidence that a ball is out and the other team has not seen the evidence.

The enactment takes place. This time, the players attempt to follow the policy that the defensive team has the right to make the call, but the offensive team has the right to object to a call. Once again, the enactment results in a shouting match; however, after it is over, the students who have watched the enactment point out that the role players have not behaved as if there is a resolution of the situation. They recognize that if there are to be games, there has to be agreement about who can make calls, and a certain amount of trust on both sides.

They decide to try a third enactment, this time with two new role players inserted as dispute referees. The introduction of referees completely changes the third enactment. The referees insist that the other players pay attention to them, which the players do not want to do. In discussing this enactment, the students point out that there has to be a system to ensure reasonable order and the resolution of disputes. The students also agree that as things stand, they probably are unable to resolve disputes without including a referee of some sort, but that no referee will be effective unless the students agree to accept the referee's decisions as final. They finally decide that in future games, two students will be referees. Those students will not be chosen by any side prior to the game; their function will be to arbitrate and to make all the calls relevant to the rules of the game, and their decisions will be final. The students agree that they will see how that system works.

The next day Mr. Williams opens up the second issue, and the students repeat this process. The exploration of other areas of dispute continues over the next few weeks. At first, many of the notions that are clarified are simply practical ones about how to solve specific problems. Gradually, however, Mr. Williams directs the discussion to a consideration of the basic values governing individual behavior. The students begin to see the problems of communal living; and they develop policies for governing their own behavior, as individuals and as a group. They also begin to develop skills in negotiating. The students who were locked in conflict gradually learn that if they behave in a slightly different way, others may also modify their behavior, and problems become easier to solve.

In role playing, students explore human-relations problems by enacting problem situations and then discussing the enactments. Together, students can explore feelings, attitudes, values, and problem-solving strategies. Several individuals have experimented with role playing, and their treatments of the strategy are remarkably similar. The version we explore here was formulated by Fannie and George Shaftel (1967). We have also incorporated ideas from the work of Mark Chesler and Robert Fox (1966).

Role playing as a model of teaching has roots in both the personal and social dimensions of education. It attempts to help individuals find personal meaning within their social worlds and to resolve personal dilemmas with the assistance of the social group. In the social dimension, it allows individuals to work together in analyzing social situations, especially interpersonal problems, and in developing decent and democratic ways of coping with these situations. We have placed role playing in the social family of models because the social group plays such an indispensable part in human development and because of the unique opportunity that role playing offers for resolving interpersonal and social dilemmas.

ORIENTATION TO THE MODEL

GOALS AND ASSUMPTIONS

On its simplest level, role playing is dealing with problems through action; a problem is delineated, acted out, and discussed. Some students are role players; others observe. A person puts himself or herself in the position of another person and then tries to interact with others who are also playing roles. As empathy, sympathy, anger, and affection are all generated during the interaction, role playing, if done well, becomes a part of life. This emotional content, as well as the words and the actions, become part of the later analysis. When the acting out is finished, even the observers are involved enough to want to know why each person reached his or her decision, what the sources of resistance were, and whether there were other ways this situation could have been approached.

The essence of role playing is the involvement of participants and observers in a real problem situation and the desire for resolution and understanding that this involvement engenders. The role-playing process provides a live sample of human behavior that serves as a vehicle for students to: (1) explore their feelings; (2) gain insights into their attitudes, values, and perceptions; (3) develop their problem-solving skills and attitudes; and (4) explore subject matter in varied ways.

These educational goals reflect several assumptions about the learning process in role playing. First, role playing implicitly advocates an experience-based learning situation in which the "here and now" becomes the content of instruction. The model assumes that it is possible to create authentic analogies to real-life problem situations and that through these recreations students can "sample" life. Thus, the enactment elicits genuine, typical emotional responses and behaviors from the students.

A related assumption is that role playing can draw out students' feelings, which they can recognize and, perhaps, release. This *catharsis,* or release of feeling, is an especially important goal when role playing is used in therapeutic settings in a variation known as *psychodrama.* In psychodrama, the enactment and its emotional and behavioral confrontations are the central activities; discussion and analysis are minimal. Educational uses of role playing, in contrast to therapeutic uses, are oriented to the generation and recognition of feelings. The Shaftels' version of role playing emphasizes the intellectual content as much as the emotional content; analysis and discussion of the enactment are as important as the role playing itself. We, as educators, are concerned that students recognize and understand their feelings and see how their feelings influence their behavior.

Another assumption, similar to an assumption of the Synectics Models, is that emotions and ideas can be brought to consciousness and enhanced by the group. Problem solving is not stifled by the activity of an overt, public situation, nor is an expert necessary to solve dilemmas or to teach everything. On the contrary, the collective reactions of the peer group can bring out new ideas and provide directions for growth and change. The model deemphasizes the traditional role of teacher and encourages listening and learning from one's peers.

A final assumption is that covert psychological processes involving one's own attitudes, values, and belief system can be brought to consciousness by combining spontaneous enactment with analysis. Furthermore, individuals can gain some measure of control over their belief systems if they recognize their values and attitudes and test them against the views of others. Such analysis can help them evaluate their attitudes and values and the consequences of their beliefs, so that they can revise them if necessary.

THE CONCEPT OF ROLE

Each individual has a unique manner of relating to people, situations, and objects. One person may feel that most people are dishonest and cannot be trusted; someone else may feel that everyone is interesting and may look forward to meeting new people. People also evaluate and behave in consistent ways toward themselves, seeing themselves as powerful and smart, or perhaps afraid and stupid. These feelings about people and situations and about themselves influence people's behavior and determine how they will respond in various situations. Some people respond with aggressive and hostile behavior, playing the part of a bully. Others withdraw and remain alone, playing the part of a shy or sulking person.

These parts people play are called *roles*. A role is "a patterned sequence of feelings, words and actions. . . . It is a unique and accustomed manner of relating to others" (Chesler and Fox, 1966, pp. 5, 8). Unless people are looking for them, it is sometimes hard to perceive consistencies and patterns in behavior. But they are usually there. Terms such as *friendly, bully, snobby, know-it-all,* and *grouch* are convenient for describing characteristic responses or roles.

The roles individuals play are determined by several factors over many years. The kinds of people someone meets determine his or her general feelings about people. How those people act toward the individual and how the individuals perceive their feelings toward them influence their feelings about themselves. The rules of one's particular culture and institutions help to determine which roles a person assumes and how he or she plays them.

People may not be happy with the roles they have assumed. And they may misperceive the attitudes and feelings of others because they do not recognize *their* role and *why* they play it. Two people can share the same feelings but behave in very different ways. They can desire the same goals, but if one person's behavior is misperceived by others, he or she may not attain that goal.

For a clear understanding of oneself and of others, it is thus extremely important that a person be aware of roles and how they are played. To do this, each person must be able to put himself or herself in another's place, and to experience as much as possible that person's thoughts and feelings. If someone is able to empathize, he or she can accurately interpret social events and interactions. Role playing is a vehicle that forces people to take the roles of others.

The concept of role is one of the central theoretical underpinnings of the Role Playing Model. It is also a major goal. We must teach students to use this concept, to recognize different roles, and to think of their own and other's behavior in terms of roles. At the same time, there are many other aspects to this model, and many levels of analysis, which to some extent compete with one another. For example, the content of the problem, the solutions to the problem, the feelings of the role players, and the acting itself all serve to involve students in the role play. Therefore, to be a salient part of the role-playing experience, the concept of role must be interwoven, yet kept in the fore throughout all the role-playing activities. It also helps if, prior to using the model, students have been taught this concept directly.

THE MODEL OF TEACHING

SYNTAX

The benefits of role playing depend on the quality of the enactment and especially on the analysis that follows. They depend also on the students' perceptions of the role as similar to real-life situations. Children do not necessarily engage effectively in role playing or role analysis the first time they try it. Many have to learn to engage in role playing in a sincere way so that the content generated can be analyzed seriously. Chesler and Fox suggest pantomimic exercises as a way of freeing inexperienced students (Chesler and Fox, 1966, pp. 64–66). Role playing is not likely to be successful if the teacher simply tosses out a problem situation, persuades a few children to act it out, and then conducts a discussion about the enactment.

The Shaftels suggest that the role playing activity consist of nine steps: (1) warm up the group; (2) select participants; (3) set the stage; (4) prepare observers; (5) enact; (6) discuss and evaluate; (7) reenact; (8) discuss and evaluate; and (9) share experiences and generalize. Each of these steps or phases has a specific purpose that contributes to the richness and focus of the learning activity. Together, they ensure that a line of thinking is pursued throughout the complex of activities, that students are prepared in their roles, that goals for the role play are identified, and that the discussion afterwards is not simply a collection of diffuse reactions, though these are important too. Table 14–1 summarizes the phases and activities of the model, which are discussed and illustrated in the remainder of this section.

Table 14-1 Syntax of Role Playing

PHASE ONE: WARM UP THE GROUP	*PHASE TWO:* SELECT PARTICIPANTS
Identify or introduce problem. Make problem explicit. Interpret problem story, explore issues. Explain role playing.	Analyze roles. Select role players.
PHASE THREE: SET THE STAGE	*PHASE FOUR:* PREPARE THE OBSERVERS
Set line of action. Restate roles. Get inside problem situation.	Decide what to look for. Assign observation tasks.
PHASE FIVE: ENACT	*PHASE SIX:* DISCUSS AND EVALUATE
Begin role play. Maintain role play. Break role play.	Review action of role play (events, positions, realism). Discuss major focus. Develop next enactment.
PHASE SEVEN: REENACT	*PHASE EIGHT:* DISCUSS AND EVALUATE
Play revised roles; suggest next steps or behavioral alternatives.	As in phase six.

PHASE NINE: SHARE EXPERIENCES AND GENERALIZE
Relate problem situation to real experience and current problems. Explore general principles of behavior.

Based on Fannie Shaftel and George Shaftel, *Role-Playing for Social Values* (Englewood Cliffs, N.J.: Prentice-Hall, Inc., 1967).

Phase one, warm up the group, involves introducing students to a problem so that they recognize it as an area with which everyone needs to learn to deal. The warm-up can begin, for example, by identifying a problem within the group.

> **TEACHER:**   Do you remember the other day we had a discussion about Janey's lunch money? Because she had put her money in her pocket and had not given it to me when she came into the room, it was lost. We had quite a talk about finding money: whether to keep it or turn it in. Sometimes it's not easy to decide what to do. Do you ever have times when you just don't know what to do? (Shaftel and Shaftel, 1967, p. 67)

The teacher sensitizes the group to a problem and creates a climate of acceptance, so that students feel that all views, feelings, and behaviors can be explored without retribution.

The second part of the warm-up is to express the problem vividly through examples. These may come from student descriptions of imaginary or real situations that express the problem, or from situations selected by the teacher and illustrated by a film, television show, or problem story.

In *Role-Playing for Social Values,* the Shaftels provide a large selection of problem stories to be read to the class. Each story stops when a dilemma has become apparent. The Shaftels feel that problem stories have several advantages. They focus on a particular problem and yet ensure that the children will be able to disassociate themselves from the problem enough to face it. Incidents that students have experienced in their lives or that the group has experienced as a whole, though visually and emotionally involving, can cause considerable stress and therefore be very difficult to analyze. Another advantage of problem stories is that they are dramatic and make role playing relatively easy to initiate. The burden of involving the children in the activity is lightened.

The last part of the warm-up is to ask questions that make the children think about and predict the outcome of the story: "How might the story end?" "What is Sam's problem and what can he do about it?" The teacher in the preceding illustration handled this step as follows:

> **TEACHER:**   I would like to read you a story this afternoon about a boy who found himself in just such a spot. His parents wanted him to do one thing, but his gang insisted he do something else. Trying to please everybody, he got himself into difficulty. This will be one of those problem stories that stop, but are not finished.
>
> **PUPIL:**   Like the one we did last week?
>
> **TEACHER:**   Yes.
>
> **PUPIL:**   Oh! But can't you give us one with an ending?
>
> **TEACHER:**   When you get into a jam, does someone always come along and tell you how your problems will end?
>
> **PUPIL:**   Oh no! Not very often.
>
> **TEACHER:**   In life, we usually have to make our own endings—we have to solve our problems ourselves. That's why I'm reading you these problem stories—so that we can

practice endings, trying out many different ones to see which works the best for us. As I read this story, you might be thinking of what you would do if you were in Tommy Haines's place. (Shaftel and Shaftel, 1967, p. 67)

The story is about a boy caught between his father's views and those of his club. He has committed himself financially to a club project his father does not approve of and would not support. Tommy does not have the money and resorts to somewhat devious means of getting it. The problem centers on Tommy's opportunity to clear the debt with his gang. He delivers a package for the druggist and is overpaid $5—enough to clear the debt. Tommy stands outside the customer's door, trying to decide whether to return or keep the money. After reading the story, the teacher focuses the discussion on what might happen next, thus preparing for different enactments of the situation:

TEACHER: What do you think Tommy will do?
PUPIL: I think he'll keep the money.
TEACHER: Oh?
PUPIL: Because he needs to pay the club.
PUPIL: Oh no he won't. He'll get found out, and he knows it. (Shaftel and Shaftel, 1967, p. 69).

In phase two, select participants, the children and the teacher describe the various characters—what they are like, how they feel, and what they might do. The children are then asked to volunteer to role play; they may even ask to play a particular role. The Shaftels caution us against assigning a role to a child who has been suggested for it, because the person making the suggestion may be stereotyping the child or putting him or her in an awkward situation. A person must want to play a role. Although he or she takes into account the children's preferences, the teacher should exercise some control in the situation.

We can use several criteria for selecting a child for a role. Roles can be assigned to those children who appear to be so involved in the problem that they identify with a specific role, those who express an attitude that needs to be explored, or those who should learn to identify with the role or place themselves in another person's position. The Shaftels warn the teacher not to select children who would give "adult-oriented, socially acceptable" interpretations to the role, because such a quick and superficial resolution of the problem dampens discussion and exploration of the basic issues (Shaftel and Shaftel, 1967, p. 67).

In our illustration, the teacher asks a student to be Tommy and then asks the student what roles need to be filled. He answers that he'll need someone to be the customer and some students to be the gang. The teacher asks several children to fill these roles.

In phase three, set the stage, the role players outline the scene but do not prepare any specific dialogue. They simply sketch the setting and perhaps one person's line of action. The teacher may help set the stage by asking the students a few simple questions about where the enactment is taking place, what it is like, and so on. It is necessary only that a simple line of action be identified and a general setting clarified so that participants feel enough security in the roles to begin to act.

In our illustration, the setting is arranged so that one corner of the classroom becomes the school where the gang is waiting for Tommy to bring the money; in another corner, a chair is used to represent the door of the customer's house. The teacher asks the boy playing Tommy where in the action he wants to begin, and the boy decides to start with the scene where he is delivering the packages.

In phase four, prepare the observers, it is important that the observers become actively involved so that the entire group experiences the enactment and can later analyze the play. The Shaftels suggest that the teacher involve observers in the role play by assigning them tasks, such as evaluating the realism of the role playing, commenting on the effectiveness and the sequences of the role players' behavior, and defining the feelings and ways of thinking of the persons being portrayed. The observers should determine what the role players are trying to accomplish, what actions the role players took that were helpful or not helpful, and what alternative experiences might have been enacted. Or they can watch one particular role to define the feelings of that person. The observers should understand that there will be more than one enactment in most cases, and if they would have acted out a certain role in a different way, they may have a chance to do so.

In our illustration, the teacher prepares the observers as follows:

TEACHER: Now, you people, as you watch, consider whether you think Jerry's way of ending the story could really happen. How will people feel? You may want to think of what will happen next. Perhaps you'll have different ideas about it; and when Jerry's finished, and we've talked about it, we can try your ideas. (Shaftel and Shaftel, 1967, p. 69)

At phase five, enact, the players assume the roles and "live" the situation spontaneously, responding realistically to one another. The role playing is not expected to be a smooth dramatization, nor is it expected that each role player will always know how to respond. This uncertainty is part of life, as well as part of feeling the role. A person may have a general idea of what to say or do but not be able to enact it when the time comes. The action now depends on the children and emerges according to what happens in the situation. This is why the preparatory steps are so important.

The Shaftels suggest that enactments be short. The teacher should allow the enactment to run only until the proposed behavior is clear, a character has developed, a behavioral skill has been practiced, an impasse is reached, or the action has expressed its viewpoint or idea. If the follow-up discussion reveals a lack of student understanding about the events or roles, the teacher can then ask for a reenactment of the scene.

The purpose of the first enactment is simply to establish events and roles, which in later enactments can be probed, analyzed, and reworked. In our illustration, the boy playing Tommy chooses not to tell the customer that he has overpaid. During the initial enactment, the players of the major role can be changed to demonstrate variety of the role and to generate more data for discussion.

In phase six, discuss and evaluate, if the problem is an important one and the participants and the observers are intellectually and emotionally involved, then the discussion will probably begin spontaneously. At first, the discussion may focus on different interpretations of the portrayal and on disagreements over how the roles should have been carried out. More important, however, are the consequences of the action and the motivations of the actors. To prepare for the next step, a teacher should focus the discussion on these aspects.

To help the observer think along with the role players, the teacher can ask questions such as, "How do you suppose John felt when he said that?" The discussion will probably turn to alternatives, both within the roles and within the total pattern of action. When it does, the stage is set for further enactments in which role players change their interpretations, playing the same roles in a different way.

In our illustration, the discussion of the first enactment goes like this:

TEACHER: Well, Jerry has given us one solution. What do you think of it?

PUPIL: Uh-uh! It won't work!

JERRY: Why not?

PUPIL: That man is going to remember how much money he had. He'll phone the druggist about it.

JERRY: So what? He can't prove anything on me. I'll just say he didn't overpay me.

PUPIL: You'll lose your job.

JERRY: When they can't prove it?

PUPIL: Yes, even if they can't prove it!

TEACHER: Why do you think so, John?

PUPIL: Because the druggist has to be on the side of his customer. He can fire Tommy and hire another boy. But he doesn't want his customers mad at him.

PUPIL: He's going to feel pretty sick inside, if he keeps the money.

TEACHER: What do you mean?

PUPIL: Well, it bothers you when you know you've done something wrong.

TEACHER: Do you have any other way to solve this problem?

PUPIL: Yes. Tommy should knock on the door and tell the customer about being overpaid. Maybe the man'll let Tommy keep the money.

TEACHER: All right, let's try it your way, Dick. (Shaftel and Shaftel, 1967, p. 71)

In phase seven, reenact, the reenactment may take place many times. The students and the teacher can share new interpretations of roles and decide whether new individuals should play them. The activity alternates between discussion and acting. As much as possible, the new enactments should explore new possibilities for causes and effects. For example, one role may be changed so that everyone can observe how that change causes another role player to behave. Or at the critical point in the enactment, the participants may try to behave in a different way and see what the consequences are. In this way, the role playing becomes a dramatic conceptual activity.

In our illustration, a second enactment produces the solution in which Tommy alerts the man to his overpayment and gets to keep the money for being so honest.

In the discussion that follows the second enactment, phase eight, discuss and evaluate, students are willing to accept the solution, but the teacher pushes for a realistic solution by asking whether they think this ending could really happen. One student has had a similar experience but was overpaid only $1.25, which he was allowed to keep. The teacher asks the class whether they think it might be different with $5. She asks for another solution, and it is suggested that Tommy consult his mother. There follows some discussion of Tommy's father, concepts about family, and parental roles. The teacher suggests that this third solution be enacted. Here's what happens in the third enactment:

> TOMMY: Mom, I'm in an awful jam!
> MOTHER: What's the trouble, Tommy?
> TOMMY: (tells his mother the whole story)
> MOTHER: Why, Tommy, you should have told me sooner. Here, you pay the money (opens purse) and we'll talk this over with Dad when he comes home. (Shaftel and Shaftel, 1967, p. 73)

During the discussion of this enactment, the teacher asks what will happen next, and someone suggests that Tommy will get a licking. The students feel that his punishment will relieve Tommy's guilt.

Phase nine, share experiences and generalize, should not be expected to result immediately in generalizations about the human-relations aspects of the situation. Such generalizations require much experience. The teacher should, however, attempt to shape the discussion so that the children, perhaps after long experience with the role-playing strategy, begin to generalize about approaches to problem situations and the consequences of those approaches. The more adequate the shaping of the discussion, the more general will be the conclusions reached, and the closer the children will come to hypothetical principles of action they can use in their own lives.

The initial goal, however, is to relate the problem situation to the children's experiences in a nonthreatening way. This goal can be accomplished by asking the class members if they know someone who has had a similar experience. In our illustration with Tommy and the money, the teacher asks if anyone in the class knows of an instance in which a boy or girl was in a situation like Tommy's. One student describes an experience with his father. The teacher then asks about parental attitudes and the role of fathers with respect to their children's money.

From such discussions emerge principles that all students can articulate and use. These principles may be applied to particular problems, or they can be used by the children as a springboard for exploring other kinds of problems. Ideally, the children will gradually master the strategy so that when a problem comes up, either within their group or from a topic they have studied, they will be able to use role playing to clarify and gain insight into the problem. Students might, for example, systematically use role playing to improve the quality of classroom democracy.

THE SOCIAL SYSTEM

The social system in this model is moderately structured. Teachers are responsible, at least initially, for starting the phases and guiding students through the activities within each phase; however, the particular content of the discussions and enactments is determined largely by the students.

The teachers' questions and comments should encourage free and honest expression of ideas and feelings. Teachers must establish equality and trust between themselves and their students. They can do this by accepting all suggestions as legitimate and making no value judgments. In this way, they simply reflect the children's feelings or attitudes.

Even though teachers are chiefly reflective and supportive, they assume direction as well. They often select the problem to be explored, lead the discussion, choose the actors, make decisions about when the enactments are to be done, help design the enactments, and most significant, decide what to probe for and what suggestions to explore. In essence, the teachers shape the exploration of behavior by the types of questions they ask and, through questioning, establish the focus.

PRINCIPLES OF REACTION

We have identified five principles of reaction that are important to this model. First, teachers should accept student responses and suggestions, especially their opinions and feelings, in a nonevaluative manner. Second, teachers should respond in such a way that they help the students explore various sides of the problem situation, recognizing and contrasting alternative points of view. Third, by reflecting, paraphrasing, and summarizing responses, the teacher increases students' awareness of their own views and feelings.

Fourth, the teacher should emphasize that there are different ways to play the same role and that different consequences result as they are explored. Fifth, there are alternative ways to resolve a problem; no one way is correct. It is important to look at the consequences to evaluate a solution.

THE SUPPORT SYSTEM

The materials for role playing are minimal but important. The major curricular tool is the problem situation. However, it is sometimes helpful to construct briefing sheets for each role. These sheets describe the role or the character's feelings. Occasionally, we also develop forms for the observers that tell them what to look for and give them a place to write it down.

Films, novels, and short stories make excellent sources for problem situations. Problem stories or outlines of problem situations are also useful. Problem stories, as their name implies, are short narratives that describe the setting, circumstances, actions, and dialogue of a situation. One or more of the characters faces a dilemma in which a choice must be made or an action taken. The story ends unresolved.

Many resource materials now commercially available include stories or problem stories whose endings can be omitted or changed. Books by the Shaftels and by Chesler and Fox each contain a section of problem stories.

APPLICATION

The Role Playing Model is extremely versatile, applicable to several important educational objectives. Through role playing students can increase their abilities to recognize their own and other people's feelings, they can acquire new behaviors for handling previously difficult situations, and they can improve their problem-solving skills.

In addition to its many uses, the Role Playing Model carries with it an appealing set of activities. Because students enjoy both the action and the acting, it is easy to forget that the role play itself is only a vehicle for developing the content of the instruction. The stages of the model are not ends in themselves, but they help expose students' values, feelings, attitudes, and solutions to problems, which the teacher must then explore.

ROLE PLAYING
AND THE CURRICULUM

There are two basic reasons why a teacher might decide to use role playing with a group of children. One is to begin a systematic *program of social education* in which a role-playing situation forms much of the material to be discussed and analyzed; for this purpose, a particular kind of problem story might be selected. The second reason is to counsel a group of children to deal with an *immediate human-relations problem*; role playing can open up this problem area to the students' inquiry and help them solve the problem.

Several types of social problems are amenable to exploration with the aid of this model, including:

1. *Interpersonal conflicts.* A major use of role playing is to reveal conflicts between people so that students can discover techniques for overcoming them.
2. *Intergroup relations.* Interpersonal problems arising from ethnic and racial stereotyping or from authoritarian beliefs can also be explored through role playing. These problems involve conflict that may not be apparent. Role playing situations of this type might be used to uncover stereotypes and prejudices or to encourage acceptance of the deviant.
3. *Individual dilemmas.* These arise when a person is caught between two contrasting values or between his or her own interests and the interests of others. Such problems are particularly difficult for young children to deal with, since their moral judgment is still relatively egocentric. Some of the most delicate and difficult uses of role playing make this dilemma accessible to the child and help him or her understand why it occurs and what to do about it. Individual dilemmas that might be explored are ones in which a person is caught between the demands of the peer group and those of his or her parents, or between the pressures of the group and his or her own preferences.
4. *Historical or contemporary problems.* These include critical situations, past or present, in which policy makers, judges, political leaders, or statespeople have to confront a problem or person and make a decision.

Regardless of the particular type of social problem, students will focus naturally on the aspects of the situation that seem important to them. The students may concentrate on the feelings that are being expressed, the attitudes and values of the role players as seen through their words and actions, the problem solution, or the consequences of behavior. It is possible for the teacher to emphasize any or all of these areas in the enactments and discussions. In-depth curriculum sequences can be based on each of the following focuses:

Exploration of feelings;
Exploration of attitudes, values, and perceptions;
Development of problem-solving attitudes and skills;
Subject-matter exploration.

We have found that a single role-playing session is often extremely rich. Discussion can go in many directions—toward analyzing feelings, consequences, the roles themselves and ways to play them, and alternative solutions. After several years of working with this model, we have come to believe that if any one of these ideas, or objectives, is to be developed adequately, the teacher must make a concerted effort to explore one particular emphasis. Because all these aspects tend to emerge in the role-playing process, it is easy to consider them only superficially. One difficulty we are faced with, then, is that an in-depth treatment of any one focus requires time. Especially in the beginning, when students are getting accustomed to the model and to exploring their behavior and feelings, we feel it is important to select one major focus, or perhaps two, for any one session. Other aspects, of course, may also need to be considered in the development of ideas, but their place should be secondary. For example, the feelings of the characters will be discussed even when the teacher is trying to get the students to concentrate on alternative solutions to the problem, but in this case the feelings will tie in to a consideration and evaluation of the solutions.

By choosing one or perhaps two emphases for the role play, carefully questioning and responding to students' ideas, and building on the ideas of the previous phases, the teacher gradually develops each phase so that it supports the particular objectives that have been selected for that session. This is what we mean by developing a focus (see Table 14–2).

SELECTING A PROBLEM SITUATION

The adequacy of the topic depends on many factors, such as the age of the students, their cultural background, the complexity of the problem situa-

Table 14-2   Possible Focuses of a Role Playing Session

I. Feelings
   A. Exploring one's own feelings
   B. Exploring others' feelings
   C. Acting out or releasing feelings
   D. Experiencing higher-status roles in order to change the perceptions of others and one's own perceptions
II. Attitudes, values, and perceptions
   A. Identifying values of culture or subculture
   B. Clarifying and evaluating one's own values and value conflicts
III. Problem-solving attitudes and skills
   A. Openness to possible solutions
   B. Ability to identify a problem
   C. Ability to generate alternative solutions
   D. Ability to evaluate the consequences to oneself and others of alternative solutions to problems
   E. Experiencing consequences and making final decisions in light of those consequences
   F. Analyzing criteria and assumptions behind alternatives
   G. Acquiring new behaviors
IV. Subject matter
   A. Feelings of participants
   B. Historical realities: historical crises, dilemmas, and decisions

tion, the sensitivity of the topic, and the students' experience with role playing. In general, as students gain experience with role playing and develop a high degree of group cohesiveness and acceptance of one another, as well as a close rapport with the teacher, the more sensitive the topic can be. The first few problem situations should be matters of concern to the students but not extremely sensitive issues. Students themselves may develop a list of themes or problems they would like to work on. Then, the teacher can locate or develop specific problem situations that fit the themes.

The sex of the students and their ethnic and socioeconomic backgrounds influence their choice of topic and, according to Chesler and Fox (1966), their expectations for the role play. Different cultural groups experience different sets of problems, concerns, and solutions. Most teachers account for these differences in their curricula all the time. Problems that are typical for a particular ethnic or age group, sex, or socioeconomic class can become the basis of problem situations.

Other ideas for problem situations can be derived from (1) the age and developmental stage of the student, such as personal and social concerns; (2) value (ethical) themes, such as honesty, responsibility; (3) problem behaviors, such as aggression, avoidance; (4) troublesome situations—for example, making a complaint at a store, meeting someone new; and (5) social issues, such as racism, sexism, labor strikes. These various sources of problem situations are summarized in Table 14-3.

Another consideration in choosing a problem situation is its complexity, which may be a result of the number of characters or the abstractness of the issues. There are no definite rules about levels of difficulty in problem situations, but intuitively it seems that the following sequence is a reasonable guide: (1) one main character; (2) two characters and alternative solutions; (3) complex plots and many characters; (4) value themes, social issues, and community issues.

INSTRUCTIONAL
AND NURTURANT EFFECTS

Role playing is designed specifically to foster: (1) the analysis of personal values and behavior; (2) the development of strategies for solving interpersonal (and

Table 14-3   Sources of Problem Situations

1. Issues arising from developmental stages
2. Issues arising from sexual, ethnic, or socioeconomic class
3. Value (ethical) themes
4. Difficult emotions
5. Scripts or "games people play"
6. Troublesome situations
7. Social issues
8. Community issues

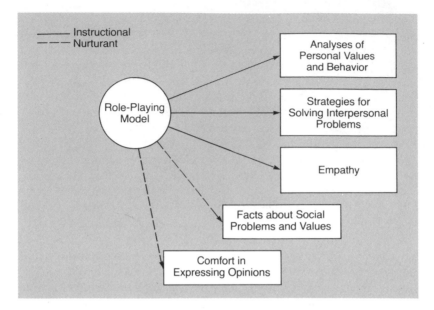

FIGURE 14-1   Instructional and nurturant effects: Role Playing Model.

personal) problems; and (3) the development of empathy toward others. Its nurturants are the acquisition of information about social problems and values, and comfort in expressing one's opinions (see Figure 14-1).

Summary Chart: Role Playing Model

SYNTAX

Phase One:
Warm Up the Group
Identify or introduce problem.
Make problem explicit.
Interpret problem story, explore issues.
Explain role playing.

Phase Two:
Select Participants
Analyze roles.
Select role players.

Phase Three:
Set the Stage
Set line of action.
Restate roles.
Get inside problem situation.

Phase Four:
Prepare the Observers
Decide what to look for.
Assign observation tasks.

Phase Five:
Enact
Begin role play.
Maintain role play.
Break role play.

Phase Six:
Discuss and Evaluate
Review action of role play (events, positions, realism).
Discuss major focus.
Develop next enactment.

Phase Seven:
Reenact
Play revised roles; suggest next steps or behavioral alternatives.

Phase Eight:
Discuss and Evaluate
As in phase six.

Phase Nine:
Share Experiences and Generalize
Relate problem situation to real experience and current problems.
Explore general principles of behavior.

SOCIAL SYSTEM

The model is moderately structured. The teacher is responsible for initiating the phases and guiding students through the activities within each phase. The particular content of the discussions and enactments is determined largely by the students.

PRINCIPLES OF REACTION

Accept all student responses in a nonevaluative manner.

Help students explore various sides of the problem situation and compare alternative views.

Increase students' awareness of their own views and feelings by reflecting, paraphrasing, and summarizing their responses.

Use the concept of role, and emphasize that there are different ways to play a role.

Emphasize that there are alternative ways to resolve a problem.

SUPPORT SYSTEM

Role playing is an experience-based model and requires minimal support material outside of the initial problem situation.

15

JURISPRUDENTIAL INQUIRY

Learning to Think About Social Policy

SCENARIO

Mrs. Giaretto's senior civics class is examining current cases before the United States Supreme Court. One morning one of the students brings in an article from the *New York Times* discussing the Bakke case. (This case dealt with admission to higher education institutions. Bakke claimed that special preference given to minority candidates had discriminated against him.)

"This case bothers me personally," comments Tammy. "You know, a number of us are applying for colleges, and my college board scores aren't too high. It seems to me, though, the important thing is that the actual scores I have are changed depending on how I'm looked at. If I'm looked at just as an anonymous person then my scores are what they are. In some colleges I would be looked at as a woman, and the scores would be higher if they wanted to increase the number of women. In some other places they would be lower because I don't belong to any minority group."

"Wait a minute," says one of the other students, "the Bakke case involved a law student. Are the same kind of issues involved in undergraduate college admissions?"

"You bet they are," comments one of the black students. "We've been shut out of a lot of private universities for years."

"Do medical schools do this kind of thing?" asks another. "Do they admit unqualified doctors?"

"Now just a minute," says one of the other students, "just because some groups are given a break doesn't mean that they're unqualified."

"Well, what *is* the story on test scores?" asks another.

"OK, OK," says Mrs. Giaretto. "This is obviously going to be a complicated case. It's so important in so many ways. I think we'd better sort out the public issues and see where we stand on them."

"Well, how do we begin?" asks Miguel.

"I think we begin by collecting some information. Let's have one group find an abstract of the case to see how it was argued in the lower courts. You can go up to the law library at the university, and I'll call the reference librarian before you get there. Then let's have another group collect what the newspapers have said about it since the case first came to public attention. A third group can collect editorials from the newspapers. I think it would be worthwhile if a fourth group talked to the counselors to find out what information they have about college admissions. Another group might arrange to have one of the college admissions officers talk with us about how they handle scores. Can anybody think of anything else?"

"Yes," adds Sally. "Do the people who sell tests have representatives we can talk to?"

"That's a wonderful idea," says Mrs. Giaretto. "Now let's organize ourselves into those groups and begin to get the facts. Then each group can take the material they've collected and start identifying some of the issues. I think it's going to take us quite a long time just to get the issues identified. Then we can proceed to identify the value questions that underlie those issues. Finally we can look at the implications for public policy and try to come up with a statement about where we stand as individuals and possibly as a group."

For the senior civics class at Mervyn Park High School, this discussion initiates exposure to jurisprudential inquiry, which the class later used to resolve their differences over the dance program. During the intervening months, Mrs. Giaretto exposed the class to several important public issues and taught them the framework for jurisprudential inquiry.

Donald Oliver and James P. Shaver (1966/1974) created the Jurisprudential Inquiry Model to help students learn to think systematically about contemporary issues. It requires them to formulate these issues as public policy questions and to analyze alternative positions about them. Essentially, it is a high-level model for citizenship education.

As our society undergoes cultural and social changes, the Jurisprudential Inquiry Model is especially useful in helping people rethink their positions on important legal, ethical, and social questions. The citizenry needs to understand the current critical issues and share in the formulation of policy. By giving them tools for analyzing and debating social issues, the jurisprudential approach helps students participate forcefully in the redefinition of social values.

ORIENTATION TO THE MODEL

GOALS AND ASSUMPTIONS

This model is based on a conception of society in which people differ in their views and priorities and in which social values legitimately conflict with one another. Resolving complex, controversial issues within the context of a productive social order requires citizens who can talk to one another and successfully negotiate their differences.

Such citizens can intelligently analyze and take a stance on public issues. The stance should reflect the concepts of justice and human dignity, two values fundamental to a democratic society. Oliver and Shaver's image of a skillful citizen is very much that of a competent judge. Imagine for a moment that you are a Supreme Court justice hearing an important case. Your job is to listen to the evidence that is presented, analyze the legal positions taken by both sides, weigh these positions and the evidence, assess the meaning and provisions of the law, and finally, to make the best possible decision. This is the role students are asked to take as they consider public issues.

To play the role, three types of competence are required. The first is familiarity with the values of the American creed, as embedded in the principles of the Constitution and the Declaration of Independence. These principles form the *values framework*—the basis for judging public issues and for making legal decisions. If policy stances are to be truly derived from ethical considerations, one must be aware of and understand the key values that form the core of our society's ethical system.

The second area of competence is a set of skills for clarifying and resolving issues. Usually, a controversy arises because two important values conflict or because public policies, when examined closely, do not adhere to the core values of our society. Whenever a conflict of value arises, three kinds of problems are likely to be present:

> The first kind of problem (*value problem*) involves clarifying which values or legal principles are in conflict, and choosing among them. The second kind of problem (*factual problem*) involves clarifying the facts around which the conflict has developed. The third kind of problem (*definitional problem*) involves clarifying the meanings or uses of words which describe the controversy. (Oliver and Shaver, 1966/1974, p. 89)

The process of clarifying and resolving issues involves clarifying definitions, establishing facts, and identifying the values important to each issue.

The third area of competence is knowledge of contemporary political and public issues, which requires that students be exposed to the spectrum of political, social, and economic problems facing American society. Although a broad understanding of the history, nature, and scope of these problems is very important, in the Jurisprudential Inquiry Model, students explore issues in terms of a specific legal case rather than in terms of a general study of values.

OVERVIEW OF THE TEACHING STRATEGY

Oliver and Shaver's work encompasses many ideas: They present us with a model of society, a conception of values, and a conception of productive dialogue. They also detail curriculum and pedagogical considerations (see Oliver and Shaver, 1971, p. 7). It is possible to extrapolate several models of teaching from their work. However, to us the strategy that seems most reflective of their goals and thinking is one built around a confrontational, or Socratic, mode of discussion. In Socratic dialogue, the students take a position, and the teacher challenges the position with questions. The teacher's questions are designed to push students' thinking about their stance and to help them learn: Does it hold up well against positions reflecting alternative values? Is it consistent across many situations? Are the reasons for maintaining the position relevant to the situation? Are the factual assumptions on which the position is based valid? What are the consequences of this position? Will the student hold on to this stance in spite of its consequences?

In the sample Socratic discussion that follows, students have been examining a voting rights issue. The policy question is: Should the federal government compel southern states to give Negroes equal voting rights? The setting for this session is a ninth grade public school classroom in Philadelphia in 1962. The teacher has oriented the class to the case and the students have identified the values in conflict as states' rights versus equality of opportunity. One student, Steve, has volunteered to state his position and defend it. His position is that blacks should have the right to vote. The teacher and students are exploring Steve's stance; throughout the discussion the teacher uses several patterns of reasoning to challenge his position. (See page 269 for a description of the patterns.)

T: What do you think, Steve?

S: I think that the police power of local government can go only so far, that the constitutional rights of voting—maybe the Negroes should have them.

Steve takes a position.

T: Negroes should have the right to vote even though there may be all kinds of violence and resistance? We should send troops into the South and protect every individual's right to vote?

Teacher explores the stance by pointing out undesirable consequences of the position (Pattern 3).

S: I'm not saying that. I don't think that we would have to send down troops.

Steve qualifies his position.

T: But what if it did go that far?

S: Probably, yes.

Teacher continues probing.

T: Suppose people called Negroes who intended to vote on the phone and said, "If you vote tomorrow, something might very well happen to your kids." Do you think we should send the FBI down there to investigate these intimidations?

Teacher checks to determine the point at which the value is violated (Pattern 1).

S: No.

T: Why not?

S: If the threat is carried out, then I would send down troops or the FBI.

Steve establishes the point at which the value is violated.

T: After something has happened to the courageous Negro's family, then you would send someone down to stop it? You don't go along with the notion that, if there is an atmosphere of fear and intimidation, we should do something to change the atmosphere so that people will be free to vote? We shouldn't do anything until there is actual violence?

Teacher checks consistency of Steve's position (Principle of Reaction).

S: In the case of Negroes, yes.

T: Why?

S: Because I don't want to give them complete power to vote. This is taking a little of it away.

Steve changes his position.

T: You want to deny some Negroes the right to vote, a right you are willing to give to whites?

Teacher tests the new position for consistency (Principle of Reaction).

S: Yes.

T: Why?

S: Because I feel that Negroes are inferior to whites.

Steve give underlying assumption for his position.

T: In what respect?

S: In intelligence, in health, in crime rates.

T: You are suggesting that if a person is tubercular or sick, you should deny him the right to vote?

Teacher uses an analogy to test Steve's position (Pattern 2).

S: No.

T: But if a Negro is sick, we don't let him vote?

S: Let him vote, sure. It is just that I think they are inferior for these reasons. I'm not saying because of these reasons I'm not going to let him vote.

T: Then for what reasons aren't you going to let him vote?

S: Because I think they are inferior
because of these reasons. (Student then
laughs, self-consciously, aware of his
inconsistency.) (Oliver and Shaver,
1966/1974, pp. 150–152)

By having to take a stand and defend a position, students usually become
emotionally involved in the analysis, making the discussions intense and personal. It is hoped that with more practice, their positions will become more
complex and well formulated.

MAJOR CONCEPTS

SOCRATIC DIALOGUE   In the Socratic style, the teacher asks the
students to take a position on an issue or to make a value judgment, and then
he or she challenges the assumptions underlying the stand by exposing its implications. For example, if a student argues for freedom in some situation,
the teacher will test whether the argument is meant to apply to *all* situations.
The function of the teacher is to probe the students' positions by questioning
the relevance, consistency, specificity, and clarity of the students' ideas until
they become more clear and more complex.

Most characteristic of the Socratic style is the *use of analogies* as a means
of contradicting students' general statements. For example, if a student argues
that parents should be fair with children, the teacher may wonder if the
parents' function is being compared to that of a court. Analogous situations
that test and define the logic and limits of positions are chosen.

PUBLIC POLICY ISSUES   Public controversies tend to fill many pages of
our newspapers and many hours of television coverage. A public policy issue is
a way of synthesizing a controversy or case in terms of a decision for action or
choice.

A PUBLIC POLICY ISSUE is a question involving a choice or a decision for action by citizens or officials in affairs that concern a government or community.
Policy issues can be phrased as general questions: "Should the United States
stay in Vietnam?" "Should capital punishment be abolished?" "Should Government regulate automobile design?"
Public policy issues can also be phrased as choices for personal action: "Should
I write my Congressman to protest draft laws?" "Should I petition the Governor
to commute a criminal's death sentence?" "Should I write a candidate asking
him to pledge support for auto design regulations?" (Oliver and Newman, 1967,
p. 29)

One of the most difficult tasks for the teacher is to assist students in integrating the details of a case into a public policy question.

A FRAMEWORK OF VALUES   Political and social values, such as personal freedom, equality, and justice, concern Oliver and Shaver in their strategy because these are "the major concepts used by our government and private groups to justify public policies and decisions" (Oliver and Shaver, 1966/1974, p. 64). When we speak of a framework of values for analyzing public issues, we imply the *legal-ethical* framework that governs American social policies and decisions. A partial list of these principles of American government (as found in the Declaration of Independence and the Constitution of the United States) is shown in Table 15–1.

Resolving a controversy involves screening the details of the case through this legal-ethical framework, identifying the values and policies in question. Social values help us to analyze controversial situations because they provide a common framework that transcends any one particular controversy. However, in most controversial situations, two general rules of ethical conduct conflict with each other. Thus although a framework of social values permits us to speak of diverse conflict situations in common terms, it does not tell us how to go about resolving controversies.

Recent years have witnessed many social problems, frequently involving conflicting values. Some of these problem areas and their underlying value conflicts are listed in Table 15–2. As you read over these topics, note that although the values are identified, the controversies remain. Alternative policy stances are possible on any topic, and most issues can be argued on a number of grounds.

DEFINITIONAL VALUE, AND FACTUAL PROBLEMS   Most arguments center on three types of problems: definitional, value, and factual. Participants in a discussion need to explore these three kinds of assumptions in

Table 15–1   The Legal-Ethical Framework: Some Basic Social Values

Rule of law.   Actions carried out by the government have to be authorized by law and apply equally to all people.

Equal protection under the law.   Laws must be administered fairly and cannot extend special privileges or penalties to any one person or group.

Due process.   The government cannot deprive individual citizens of life, liberty, or property without proper notice of impending actions (right to a fair trial).

Justice.   Equal opportunity.

Preservation of peace and order.   Prevention of disorder and violence (reason as a means of dealing with conflict).

Personal liberty.   Freedom of speech, right to own and control property, freedom of religion, freedom of personal associations, right of privacy.

Separation of powers.   Checks and balances among the three branches of government.

Local control of local problems.   Restriction of federal government power and preservation of states' rights.

Table 15-2 Some General Problem Areas

PROBLEM AREAS	SAMPLE UNIT TOPICS	CONFLICTING VALUES [a]
Racial and Ethnic Conflict	School Desegregation Civil Rights for Nonwhites and Ethnic Minorities Housing for Nonwhites and Ethnic Minorities Job Opportunities for Nonwhites and Ethnic Minorities Immigration Policy	Equal Protection Due Process Brotherhood of Man v. Peace and Order Property and Contract Rights Personal Privacy and Association
Religious and Ideological Conflict	Rights of the Communist Party in America Religion and Public Education Control of "Dangerous" or "Immoral" Literature Religion and National Security: Oaths, Conscientious Objectors Taxation of Religious Property	Freedom of Speech and Conscience v. Equal Protection Safety and Security of Democratic Institutions
Security of the Individual	Crime and Delinquency	Standards of Freedom Due Process v. Peace and Order Community Welfare
Conflict among Economic Groups	Organized Labor Business Competition and Monopoly "Overproduction" of Farm Goods Conservation of Natural Resources	Equal or Fair Bargaining Power and Competition General Welfare and Progresss of the Community v. Property and Contract Rights
Health, Education, and Welfare	Adequate Medical Care: for the Aged, for the Poor Adequate Educational Opportunity Old-Age Security Job and Income Security	Equal Opportunity Brotherhood of Man v. Property and Contract Rights
Security of the Nation	Federal Loyalty-Security Programs Foreign Policy	Freedom of Speech, Conscience, and Association Due Process Personal Privacy v. Safety and Security of Democratic Institutions

[a] The *v.* in the listing of values suggests that the top values conflict with the bottom values. Although this is generally true, there are, of course, many exceptions. One can argue, for example, that a minimum wage law violates property and contract rights and that it is also against the general welfare. *Source:* Donald Oliver and James P. Shaver, *Teaching Public Issues in the High School* (Boston: Houghton Mifflin Company, 1966), pp. 142–143.

one another's position to assess the strength of alternative stances. The process of clarifying and resolving issues by solving these problems is called *rational consent*.

A basic problem in discussions of social issues is the ambiguous or confusing use of words. Unless we recognize common meaning in the words we use, discussion is very difficult, and agreement on issues, policies, or actions is virtually impossible. To resolve these definitional disagreements, it is necessary first to determine whether participants in a discussion are using the same term in a different way or different terms for the same referent, and second to establish a common meaning for terms. Then, to clarify communication, participants may: (1) appeal to common usage by finding out how most people use a word or by consulting a dictionary; (2) stipulate the meaning of the word for purposes of discussion by listing the agreed criteria; (3) obtain more facts about an example to see if it meets the agreed criteria for a definition.

Valuing means classifying things, actions, or ideas as good or bad, right or wrong. If we speak of something as a value (such as honesty), we mean that it is good. As people make choices throughout their lives, they are constantly making value judgments, even if they cannot verbalize their values. The range of items or issues over which each of us makes value judgments is vast—art, music, politics, decoration, clothes, and people. Some of these choices seem less important than others, and the degree of importance has something to do with what we mean by a value. Choices that are not so important are personal preferences, not values. Value issues such as art or the physical environment involve artistic taste or judgment of beauty, and many such choices of ideas, objects, or actions do become subjects of discussion in our society and communities.

People make decisions on issues involving values because they believe (1) certain consequences will occur; (2) other consequences will be avoided; or (3) important social values will be violated if the decision is not made. In a values conflict there is often disagreement about the predicted consequences, which can be partially resolved by obtaining evidence to support the prediction; however, to some extent it is always a matter of speculation. "Affirmative action laws will equalize employment opportunity" is an example of predicted consequences. Although there is some evidence that equal employment opportunity results from affirmative action, this is partly a prediction based on logical grounds.

When two *values* conflict, Oliver and Shaver suggest that the best solution is one in which each value is compromised somewhat, or, put another way, each value is violated only minimally (see the following section on balancing values). When the value issues conflict because of predicted consequences, then the disagreement becomes a *factual* problem.

The reliability of a factual claim can be established in two ways: (1) by evoking more specific claims, and (2) by relating it to other general facts accepted as true (Oliver and Shaver, 1966/1974, pp. 103–104). In both approaches, evidence is used to support the truth of a factual claim. For example, suppose we claim that lowering the speed limit will reduce accidents and save gas. The first way we might support the statement is to look at more *specific* claims. We might find that:

1. In cities that have adopted the fifty-five miles per hour speed limit, accidents have decreased.
2. Gasoline consumption decreased under the fifty-five miles per hour speed limit, while the number of miles driven remained the same.

The greater number of specific claims we can identify to support the conclusion we are trying to prove, the more reliable the conclusion becomes.

A second way to support the claim is to relate it to other general facts accepted as true. In this example, we might find that cars traveling at fifty-five miles per hour can stop 25 percent faster than cars traveling at sixty-five miles per hour.

BALANCING VALUES: THE BEST POLICY STANCE Oliver and Shaver emphasize that values can be used on a *dimensional* as well as an *ideal* basis. If social values are construed as ideals, they have to be dealt with on an *absolute* basis; either one lives up to a value or one does not. For example, if you approve of equality of all races before the law in the ideal sense, you feel it either has or has not been achieved. If you see values on a dimensional basis, then you judge *degrees* of desirable conditions on a continuum. For example, you can accept a compromise that ensures some, but not all, possible racial equality. Politically, you might choose such a position, hoping to gain more in the future.

Using the example of free speech, Oliver and Shaver suggest that if we see free speech as a total ideal—something to be preserved at all costs and in all situations—then we are unable to cope with situations in which it might be desirable to abrogate free speech temporarily in deference to public safety. For instance, a speaker might be prevented from continuing a speech before a hostile crowd about to turn on him violently. In such a case, one might restrict his free speech to provide for his safety and prevent the crowd from destructive action. The *dimensional* basis enables such a policy to be considered, although citizens may well prefer an ideal basis.

Oliver and Shaver feel that the best stance on an issue is to maintain a *balance of values* in which each value is only minimally compromised. To achieve such a balance, each party in a controversy should try to understand the reasons and assumptions behind the other's position. Only by rational consent can useful compromises be reached.

THE MODEL OF TEACHING

SYNTAX

Although the exploration of students' stances through confrontational dialogue is the heart of the Jurisprudential Inquiry Model, several other activities are especially important, such as helping students *formulate* the stance they eventually defend and helping them *revise* their position after the argumentation. The basic model includes six phases: (1) orientation to the case; (2) identifying the issues; (3) taking positions; (4) exploring the stances underlying the positions taken; (5) refining and qualifying positions; and (6) testing assumptions about facts, definitions, and consequences (see Table 15–3).

Table 15-3   Syntax of Jurisprudential Inquiry Model

PHASE ONE: ORIENTATION TO THE CASE	PHASE TWO: IDENTIFYING THE ISSUES
Teacher introduces materials. Teacher reviews facts.	Students synthesize facts into a public policy issue(s). Students select one policy issue for discussion. Students identify values and value conflicts. Students recognize underlying factual and definitional questions.

PHASE THREE: TAKING POSITIONS	PHASE FOUR: EXPLORING THE STANCE(S), PATTERNS OF ARGUMENTATION
Students articulate a position. Students state basis of position in terms of the social value or consequences of the decision.	Establish the point at which value is violated (factual). Prove the desirable or undesirable consequences of a position (factual). Clarify the value conflict with analogies. Set priorities. Assert priority of one value over another *and* demonstrate lack of gross violation of second value.

PHASE FIVE: REFINING AND QUALIFYING THE POSITIONS	PHASE SIX: TESTING FACTUAL ASSUMPTIONS BEHIND QUALIFIED POSITIONS
Students state positions and reasons for positions, and examine a number of similar situations. Students qualify positions.	Identify factual assumptions and determine if they are relevant. Determine the predicted consequences and examine their factual validity (will they actually occur?).

In phase one, the teacher introduces the students to case materials by reading a story or historical narrative out loud, watching a filmed incident depicting a value controversy, or discussing an incident in the lives of the students, school, or community. The second step in orienting students to the case is to review the facts by outlining the events in the case, analyzing who did what and why, or acting out the controversy.

In phase two, the students synthesize the facts into a public policy issue, characterize the values involved (for example, freedom of speech, protecting the general welfare, local autonomy, or equal opportunity), and *identify conflicts between values*. In the first two phases, the students have not been asked to express their opinions or take a stand.

In phase three, they are asked to articulate positions on the issue and state the basis for their positions. In a school finance case, for example, a student might take the position that the state should not legislate how much each school district can spend on each pupil because this would constitute an unacceptable violation of local autonomy.

In phase four, the positions are explored. The teacher now shifts to a confrontational style as he or she probes the students' positions. In enacting the Socratic role, the teacher (or a student) may use one or more of four patterns of argumentation.

1. Asking the students to identify the point at which a value is violated.
2. Clarifying the value conflict through analogies.
3. Asking students to prove desirable or undesirable consequences of a position.
4. Asking students to set value priorities: asserting priority of one value over another *and* demonstrating lack of gross violation of the second value.

Phase five consists of refining and qualifying the positions. This phase often flows naturally from the dialogue in phase four, but sometimes the teacher may need to prompt students to restate their positions.

While phase five clarifies the reasoning in a value position, phase six further tests the position by identifying the factual assumptions behind it and examining them carefully. The teacher helps the students to check whether their positions hold up under the most extreme conditions imaginable.

The six phases of the Jurisprudential Inquiry Model can be divided into analysis (phases one, two, and three) and argumentation (phases four, five, and six). The analysis activities, which occur in the form of careful discussion of values and issues, prepare the material for exploration. The argumentation, carried out in a confrontational style, seeks to produce the strongest possible stance.

SOCIAL SYSTEM

The structure in this model ranges from high to low. At first, the teacher initiates the phases; moving from phase to phase, however, is dependent on the students' abilities to complete the task. After experience with the model the students should be able to carry out the process unassisted, thereby gaining maximum control of the process. The social climate is vigorous and abrasive.

PRINCIPLES OF REACTION

The teacher's reactions, especially in phases four and five, are not evaluative, in the sense of being approving or disapproving. They probe substance: The teacher reacts to students' comments by questioning relevance, consistency, specificity or generality, and definitional clarity. The teacher also enforces continuity of thought, so that one thought or line of reasoning is pursued to its logical conclusion before other argumentation begins.

To play this role well, the teacher must anticipate student value claims and must be prepared to challenge and probe. In the Socratic role, the teacher probes one student's opinion at length before challenging other students. Because a Socratic dialogue can easily become a threatening cross-examination or a game of "guess what the teacher's right answer is," the teacher must make it clear that the clarification of issues and the development of the most defensible position are the objectives. The questioning of evidence and assumptions must be tempered with supportiveness. The merits of the case, not of the students, are the basis for evaluation.

SUPPORT SYSTEM

The major material support for this model is source documents that focus on a problem situation. There are some published case materials, but it is relatively easy to develop one's own case materials. The distinguishing feature of this approach is that the cases are accounts of real or hypothetical situations. It is essential that all pertinent facts of the situation be included in the case material so the case will not be vague and frustrating.

A controversial case describes a specific situation that has conflicting ethical, legal, factual, or definitional interpretations. The case may consist of a classic historical or legal situation, such as *Plessy v. Ferguson* in race relations, or the Wagner Act or the Kohler strike in labor relations; or it may be a short story or fictionalized account of a societal controversy, such as Orwell's *Animal Farm*. Generally, each page of the daily newspaper contains three or four articles that either explicitly or implicitly present an important public policy question. Usually some facts of the situation are presented, but the original situation that provoked the controversy is not described in full detail.

APPLICATION

In developing their alternative framework for teaching social studies courses in high schools, Oliver and Shaver were concerned with both the *substance* of what was taught and the *methods* of teaching it. Consequently, the model provides a framework for developing contemporary course *content* in public affairs (cases involving public issues) and for developing a *process* to deal with conflict in the public domain, leading students to an examination of values.

The model is tailored to older students and must be modified considerably for use at the junior high school and middle school levels even with the most able students. We have successfully carried out the model with extremely able seventh and eight grade students but have had little success with younger children.

The confrontational dialogue that surrounds the argumentation of social issues is apt to be very threatening at first, especially to less verbal students. We have had small groups (three or four students) formulate a stand and collectively argue the stand with another small group. The format allows for time out, reevaluating the stance with one's group, and discussing the issue again. Initially, we presented the case, and after students had selected the policy issue we asked them to take an initial stand. On this basis we divided them into small groups and told each group to come up with the strongest possible case. The students understood that, regardless of the group they were in at first, they might well choose a different stance at the end of the discussion.

Neither the skills of reasoning nor the confidence to take a stance and discuss it are acquired easily or quickly. Teachers should let a single case continue for a long period of time, giving students the opportunity to acquire information, reflect on their ideas, and build their courage. It is self-defeating to set up short, one-time debates over complex questions. Formal instructional sessions teaching students directly about analytic and argumentative techniques may be useful, but these should be introduced naturally and slowly. The initial case materials should be relatively simple and require little previous background. Some should be drawn from the students' experiences, perhaps in the classroom or at home.

For many years instructors have organized social studies courses around cases; the Jurisprudential Inquiry Model heightens the vigor and intensity with which such cases are studied. Of course, cases must have public issues or value conflicts embedded in them to lend themselves readily to the jurisprudential approach. But unless social studies courses deal with values, both personal and public, they will have missed the vital mainstream of social concern.

Once students become fluent in the use of the Jurisprudential Inquiry Model, they can apply it to conflicts that occur in and around their own lives. The scenario at the beginning of this chapter is an example of students' exploration of an issue that touched their own concerns. Without such application, we speculate that the study of public issues, even vigorously pursued, can seem abstract and irrelevant to the lives of students. Because students live in communities where issues abound, their study of values should not be confined to cases far removed from them, but should be applied to the dynamics of their own lives and the community around them.

AGE-LEVEL ADAPTATION

This model is not easily applied below the junior high level. It does seem possible to introduce some highly verbal upper elementary students to aspects of the model, such as identifying issues and alternative value positions.

LEARNING ENVIRONMENT ADAPTATIONS

Initially, the Jurisprudential Inquiry Model requires a fair amount of teacher-directed activity and direct instruction. Gradually, as students become competent the phases of the model should blend into student-directed discussions.

INSTRUCTIONAL AND NURTURANT EFFECTS

Mastery of the framework for analyzing issues is the major direct learning outcome. This includes skill in identifying policy questions; application of social values to policy stances; the use of analogies to explore issues, and ability to identify and resolve definitional, factual, and value problems.

The ability to carry on forceful dialogue with others is another important outcome. It nurtures the capacity for social involvement and arouses the desire for social action.

Finally, the model nourishes the values of pluralism and a respect for the point of view of others. It also advocates the triumph of reason over emotion in matters of social policy, although the strategy itself strongly brings into play the students' emotional responses. (See Figure 15-1.)

At the Ontario Institute for Studies in Education a number of faculty, particularly Malcolm Levin and John Isenberg, have developed interesting cases for use with the Jurisprudential Inquiry Model. Many of these cases are set in Canada and can be quite exciting for students not only because the issues are excellent but because of the somewhat different context and legal system. In addition, their publication, *Ethics in Education* covers a large

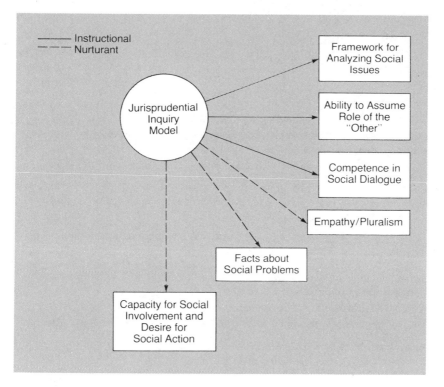

FIGURE 15-1 Instructional and nurturant effects: Jurisprudential Inquiry Model.

number of issues which can stimulate the development of cases and the study of public issues.

Summary Chart: Jurisprudential Inquiry Model

SYNTAX

Phase One:
Orientation to the Case
Introduce materials.
Review facts.

Phase Two:
Identifying the Issues
Synthesize facts into a public policy issue(s).
Select one policy issue for discussion.
Identify values and value conflicts.
Recognize underlying factual and definitional questions.

Phase Three:
Taking Positions
Articulate a position. State basis of position in terms of the social value or consequences of the decision.

Phase Four:
Exploring the Stance(s), Patterns of Argumentation
Establish the point at which value is violated (factual).
Prove the desirable or undesirable consequences of a position (factual).
Clarify the value conflict with analogies.
Set priorities. Assert priority of one value over another *and* demonstrate lack of gross violation of second value.

Phase Five:
Refining and Qualifying the Positions
State position and reasons for position, and examine a number of similar situations.
Qualify position.

Phase Six:
Testing Factual Assumptions behind Qualified Positions
Identify factual assumptions and determine if they are relevant.
Determine the predicted consequences and examine their factual validity (will they actually occur?).

SOCIAL SYSTEM

The model has moderate to high structure, with the teacher initiating and controlling the discussion; however, an atmosphere of openness and intellectual equality prevails.

PRINCIPLES OF REACTION

Maintain a vigorous intellectual climate where all views are respected; avoid direct evaluation of students' opinions.
See that issues are thoroughly explored.
Probe the substance of students' thinking through questioning relevance, consistency, specificity, generality, definitional clarity, and continuity.
Maintain dialectical style: use confrontational dialogue, questioning students' assumptions and using specific instances (analogies) to contradict more general statements.
Avoid advocating a stand.

SUPPORT SYSTEM

Source documents that focus on a problem situation are needed.

16

LABORATORY TRAINING
Developing Interpersonal Skill

SCENARIO

Mr. Marks's twelfth grade social studies class is studying the government of a medium-sized city in Connecticut. He and the students have worked together to plan a series of interviews, observations of city council meetings, discussions with employees in the city manager's office, and a questionnaire survey of community members' attitudes toward certain aspects of city government. During the planning process it became apparent that there were a number of struggles for leadership, and the class appeared to contain several cliques that operated as factions as the more extensive and important activities were being planned. A number of times he noticed that power seemed more important than substance, and individuals frequently defended their suggestions heatedly regarding any alternative ideas. He decides that the process itself presents an opportunity to help the students learn about their social behavior and to develop skills for mediating conflict.

He begins by asking the groups that are planning various activities to make tape recordings of their discussions. He plays several of the recordings back to the entire class, at first simply asking them to listen to them. The class reacts somewhat angrily. Several members feel that they are being "put on the spot." He replays the tapes for them, this time asking them to concentrate on the communications that occur just after a suggestion is made. They list the suggestions and then list the responses. By this time the class is thoroughly uncomfortable, but Mr. Marks persists with a firm but amiable manner. "Now," he says, "I want you to identify each of the responses that you think would be likely to make the people being spoken to feel pretty good about themselves, as if they're being taken care of by the person who is speaking." The students are shocked. The list contains forty responses to suggestions, and the students identify only six of them as statements likely to make the person being spoken to feel positive. For example, a couple of items on the list of comments following suggestions are "Annie, don't you ever have any practical ideas?" and "*Bo-ring!*" More than twenty contain what the students call "put downs," seem to be expressions of anger, or reject the suggestion without explanation or acknowledgment that there might be some merit to it.

"Now how do you feel about what we're doing?" asks Mr. Marks. "Lucy?"

"Well," responds Lucy, "it makes me feel terribly uncomfortable."

"Me too," adds Sally. "I didn't realize we were so bitchy."

Everybody laughs, and the tension eases.

"Well," says George, "I don't think we have to spend an awful lot of time deciding that we want to do something about this."

There are general murmurs of agreement.

"Yes," says Mr. Marks, "I really don't want to beat this into the ground. So let me tell you what I have in mind. Even though you could see very quickly that there are some problems in the way we've been relating, changing patterns of behavior is not easy simply because they *are* patterns and they tend to perpetuate themselves. You become accustomed to relating in a certain kind of way, even uncomfortable ways. I want to ask you to make recordings of most of our planning sessions over the next few weeks. Then we'll play some of them back, and we'll concentrate on one kind of pattern at a time, trying to select some goals to change and working together to make those changes happen. I also want to warn you that you're going to find some of this to be very uncomfortable, and I hope you'll express that when it happens. Even though we spend time looking at our process, you'll find that we will become more efficient and probably get more done because we were spending so much energy trying to cope with each other."

"Is that why we get so tired sometimes?" asks Lucy. "Sometimes we'll have just a fifteen or twenty minute meeting and I feel exhausted. I didn't realize that you spend more energy doing something when it's emotional."

"Right on, Lucy," says Mr. Marks. "It will really wear you out. Well," he adds, "I think that's enough for now. I'll see you tomorrow and I hope you have a good day."

The class exits. As they leave, Mr. Marks overhears two of the students talking to each other.

"I'm not sure I'm going to like this," complains Gordon.

"I'm not sure any of us are," says George, "but you know I feel better that we have it out in the open."

Laboratory training, also referred to as *T-group* and *process analysis*, was accidentally hit upon in 1947 in Bethel, Maine. At that time a group of social psychologists, including Kurt Lewin, were concerned with the rapid personal and social changes taking place in modern society. They believed that human beings were subject to new and increasingly fragmented roles that made it impossible to establish identity and personal wholeness; people were working in or relating to complex bureaucratic organizations that also produced a sense of helpless isolation. The social psychologists were hoping to design an action model using group dynamics to influence in positive ways the process of social change. Out of a series of meetings and activities in Maine the notion of the T-group emerged.

The T-group, the heart of the Laboratory Training Model, confronts participants with an unstructured learning situation. With the help of a facilitator, group members struggle to create a meaningful task and agenda for themselves. As they do this they encounter many patterns of human relationships and experience a myriad of feelings, which then form the basis for the learning that occurs during laboratory training. Briefly stated, "Laboratory training is an educational strategy which is based primarily on the experiences generated in the various social encounters by the learners themselves and which aims to influence attitudes and develop competencies toward learning about human interaction" (Schein and Bennis, 1965, p. 4). It rests on the assumption that the skills of participating in social groups and organizations can be learned through the process of participation. Learning, in this model, rests on personal experience as it is later integrated with ideas.

The T-group focuses on individual behaviors as well as on group dynamics and development. Although the original intent of the T-group method was to make large-scale organizations more humane, a new field of ideas and procedures known as organizational development has developed, taking over the function of organizational improvements. Currently, laboratory training (and the T-group) is devoted primarily to helping *individuals* function more effectively in groups and organizations.

ORIENTATION TO THE MODEL

THE T-GROUP

Laboratory training is more than the T-group; it also includes didactic experiences and focused exercises. However, the T-group is the core of the learning experience.

A T-group, normally comprised of ten to twelve persons, spends anywhere from eight to forty hours together in a face-to-face group situation. Individuals participate as learners at the same time they are helping others in their quest for understanding. The information for learning comes from the

immediate group experience, and the experienced behavior, feelings, perceptions, and reactions of individual group members. Also present is a trainer,
who intervenes to facilitate the development of valid communication and to
help members make explicit the process of that development (Shepard, 1964,
p. 637). The trainer, however, does not serve as a leader or authoritative
person.

At the beginning of the T-group participants are given the vague task of
"constructing a group which will meet the requirements of all its members for
growth" (Bradford, Gibb, and Benne, 1964, p. viii). There are virtually no
agenda, no clear expectations, and no guidelines for behavior; instead there is
a vacuum that forces participants to react and to respond.

The following passages present an excellent description of the initiation
and evolution of a T-group:

A typical T-group might begin with the "trainer" saying that he imagines that the group
members have come to learn about how people behave in groups by learning from their
own experience of becoming group members. He offers neither agenda nor any suggestions as to how to proceed. In the vacuum that is created, group members begin to act
in characteristic ways; some may try to provide structure by suggesting the formulation
of an agenda or the election of a chairman, others may complain about the leader's
failure to lead, while still others may comment about the anxiety that the lack of structure creates in them. These comments are likely to be interspersed with periods of
silence. Group members experience considerable tension as they attempt to cope with
the ambiguity of the situation. Although a number of suggestions may be offered by
group members as to how to proceed, none is followed up. The group looks to the
trainer for guidelines, and the trainer in turn reflects back the group's desire for
guidelines. Finally a member suggests some easily agreed to action, such as all of the
members introducing themselves, and the group, seizing on it, agrees to proceed in this
manner. The first session typically ends with members feeling confused and bewildered
about what happened during the session and about how they ought to proceed next.

The succeeding few sessions provide further evidence of group members' efforts to
cope with the frustration of ambiguity and lack of structure. Abortive attempts at
leadership develop; the group may become divided into two camps—those who very
much want leadership and structure and those who are opposed to organizing until the
group decides what it wants to do. The trainer's suggestion that the members explore
their feelings of frustration at their inability to get the group going is typically ignored.
There may be a variety of other abortive attempts to organize, set up committees, elect
chairmen, and the sense of frustration grows. Eventually the group responds to the
trainer's comment suggesting that it examine the members' contributions to the lack of
group progress.

At this point focus shifts to an examination of member behavior and interpersonal
style. Attention might be first directed to a member who has been particularly active in
an earlier effort to elect a chairman. Let us say that Alex, a hard-driving, production
manager, has played this role in the group. He begins to get feedback about the bossy
and authoritarian way in which he insists his procedure is correct, his inability to consider alternatives once he has formed an opinion, and his open attack on those who
stand in the way of his drive for leadership. He initially reacts defensively, unwilling to
consider the comments, but several warmly concerned members convince him that
their comments are meant to help in exploration, and are not the cruel attack Alex
believes them to be. Slowly he begins to look at his over-concern with performance,

with getting the job done properly, his distrust of others' capabilities, and his consequent inability to share responsibility. In a similar fashion the characteristics of other members are explored, sometimes at the person's own initiation, at other times with assistance, prodding, or feedback from other members or the trainer. Don, another member, who had vacillated among supporting a number of alternative ways to proceed earlier, spontaneously begins talking about his inability to take responsibility and his constant hedging and avoiding, touched off by the stark contrast with Alex's account. Others chime in with concerns about being too aggressive or too passive, too involved or too cool, too emotional or too stolid. Finally Ned, a member who has been quite inactive, is turned on by the group for not wanting to reveal his feelings, not letting other people know him.

The mutual support members have given each other during the period of feedback may lead to a great deal of expression of positive feeling between members; for example, Don may be lavishly praised for his willingness to take a good hard look at himself. Group cohesiveness is now at its height. The concern of the group may then turn to comparing individual members in terms of their degree of involvement and efforts are made to "bring in" those who seem insufficiently involved. Ned is again focused on in an effort to make him feel more a part of the group. As the time draws to a close, attention is turned to evaluation and examination of what the members have gained from the group both in terms of greater awareness of the nature of their impact on others, and knowledge about how group process works. (Shaffer and Galinsky, 1974, pp. 194–195)

The setting is an important feature of laboratory training. To the extent possible, participants should be in a new place, removed from their day-to-day work and familiar context. This permits their energies to focus completely on the work of the group and opens them to new experiences. It also removes old expectations and norms, thus increasing uncertainty about one's behaviors. Because of the newness and unfamiliarity, participants are able to experience more fully their emotional selves and at the same time achieve an objectivity that is often lost in routine contexts. As a result, they become keen observers of their own and other's behaviors, an important learning outcome of the model.

GOALS AND ASSUMPTIONS

The potential learnings from laboratory training are many and varied. The T-group experience may be designed to emphasize one or more of four areas—intrapersonal, interpersonal, group dynamics, and self-direction—and thus promote particular goals. When the intrapersonal is stressed, the primary goal is *self-knowledge*. Gaining insight into one's behaviors and reactions, especially through feedback from others, is the learning task. For example, individuals might want to deal first with factors that cause them stress and then with how they react to them; with how they manage hostility and tension; with what goals they have; and with how they can better integrate their emotional selves and their work selves.

Interpersonal learning focuses on the dynamics of relations among per-

sons—relationships of influence, feedback, leadership, communication, conflict resolution, trust formation, leadership, giving and receiving help, power
and control. Understanding these potentially problematic aspects of relationship will increase one's ability to experience events more fully and to be more
responsive to others. The goal here is developing more effective membership
in group function, meeting one's own needs as well as the needs of other
members of the group.

A third learning goal is understanding the conditions that facilitate or inhibit group functioning. It is well established that the group as a medium,
apart from the collection of individuals that comprise it, possesses its own
unique characteristics that distinguish it from other groups. Properties of the
group include its particular norms and standards, its role for participants, its
communication patterns and processes, its power and sociometric structures,
its cohesiveness, and its goals. Becoming aware of these dimensions is part of
developing leadership skills that can eventually establish a group that meets
the needs of all its members and that rests on the value of concern for others.

Finally, the fourth learning goal is self-direction. By this is meant that
participants learn how to learn by using their observational skills. They
develop skills for diagnosing and for increasing their behavioral competency in
group situations—"the ability not only to act but also to monitor the action
and accurately assess its consequences for the actor in relation to others; and
for the group in relation to its goals" (Shepard, 1964, p. 637).

All of these goals may be accomplished in terms of increased awareness,
changed attitudes, and new behaviors. Individuals may increase their
awareness (and acceptance) of their own feelings and the feelings of others; of
the complexity of the communication process; of the genuine differences in
members needs, goals, and styles of approaching problems; of their own impact on others; of how groups function; of the consequences of certain kinds
of group action; of learning how to learn (as observation analysis). Increased
awareness may result in changed *attitudes* toward self, others, and groups.
Finally, new *behavior* in the form of greater diagnostic and social skill competence may be built on the previous levels.

It is difficult to speak of the goals of laboratory training without identifying its implicit values: the spirit of inquiry (an orientation toward truth and
discovery), commitment to the democratic process, and concern for others.

The spirit of inquiry involves a feeling of tentativeness and of
hypothesizing. The ambiguity of the laboratory situation creates a need to
define and organize the environment, naturally generating hypotheses about
group process. A second component of a spirit of inquiry is expanded consciousness. The laboratory situation brings into analysis social processes usually taken for granted. Finally, a spirit of inquiry requires an authenticity in interpersonal relations and an openness of communication.

Acceptance of democratic values and adherence to its processes do not mean blind acceptance of democratic shibboleths. Commitment to democratic values involves mutual collaboration and interdependence as opposed to authoritarian interaction. It also requires conflict resolution through rational means and problem solving rather than through bargains, power plays, and compromise. Problem solving in this case includes recognition and acknowledgment of conflict, full understanding of its causes and consequences, and exploration of all possible alternatives in an atmosphere of mutual trust. It also involves the element of choice, a recognition that there are circumstances when even authenticity is inappropriate or dysfunctional (Schein and Bennis, 1965, pp. 30–35). Choice involves autonomy of judgment instead of slavish adherence to a formula.

Increasing genuine concern for others was one of the original intents of the founders of laboratory training. They believed that enhancing the humanness of organizations would add to, not detract from, their work.

MAJOR CONCEPTS

Groups have been part of instructional methodology for many years, but their value has been as an organizational setting rather than as a medium for learning. As such, their structure, agenda, norms, and goals are usually prescribed either by habit or authority. The group can serve as a learning medium, according to laboratory method theorists, only when these forces are absent and ambiguity is present. Besides this fundamental condition, Schein and Bennis have identified six necessary conditions that distinguish training groups from other learning groups.

The first is a *here-and-now* focus. That is, the content of laboratory training is the immediate feelings and behaviors of the participants as they interact with each other. "In other words, here and now learning is based on experiences which are shared, public, immediate, direct, first-hand, unconceptualized and self-acknowledged" (Schein and Bennis, 1965, p. 39). In contrast, the traditional sharing of past behavior—such as what happened in our jobs or our families—is vicarious, detached, and filtered. Participants are encouraged to share their immediate reactions without reference to past events or intellectual labels. One assumption of the here-and-now focus is that participants are motivated to share their reactions and feelings with one another. The norm of disclosure is thus powerful in the T-group, and learning is based on concrete behavior to which words and concepts can be related.

If here-and-now learning establishes reality, the second condition, *feedback*, provides a mechanism to recognize it. Without open and authentic communication, we cannot have adequate and trustworthy feedback mechanisms from which to obtain information about our behavior. *Feedback* means that the members of the group interpret each other's reactions and feelings in an open, descriptive, nonevaluative way. Occasionally this condition is misinterpreted. Participants fall into mechanical turn taking or politeness, neither of which provides honest feedback.

A third learning condition involves a period of *unfreezing* or unlearning old ways of perceiving and behaving in interpersonal situations. The purpose of unfreezing is to create a desire and ability to learn. The unfamiliar setting of laboratory training and the T-group's ambiguous situation stemming from unclear goals, norms, and lack of structure make it difficult for individuals to use past habits to resolve the discomfort they feel in the situation. It provides an incentive for exploring their reactions and behaviors and for learning new ones.

Unfreezing can lead to anxiety instead of a desire to learn if the fourth condition, *psychological safety*, is not also present. Psychological safety refers to the creation of a supportive environment and a climate of trust. Group members have concern for one another and tolerance for each other's flaws. They encourage each other in risk taking with new behaviors because they are reasonably confident that the group will be supportive even if the behavior is a mistake. The climate of the group thus helps the participants feel comfortable and supported, despite the ambiguity and frustration in the situation.

A fifth condition requires participants to engage in the role of observant participant—that is, they must act, diagnose, and behave. Such a position blends the worlds of action and analysis. "To be detached without losing commitment is the aim of laboratory training" (Schein and Bennis, 1965, p. 45).

Finally, laboratory learning, if it is to be successful in supplying a mastery over previously perplexing phenomena, must provide an *intellectual framework* for our emotional experience, making our feelings understandable and manageable (Schein and Bennis, 1965, p. 46). Such a framework helps us to make finer emotional discriminations.

PATTERNS OF T-GROUP PROCESS

Despite the unplanned, evolving nature of the T-group, certain regularities characterize its dynamics and its content. The Dilemma-Invention-Feedback-Generalization (D-I-F-G) Model developed by Blake and Mouton addresses the cyclical processes found in the T-group (Schein and Bennis, 1965, pp. 47, 145). According to the model, the dilemma, created primarily by the participants, generates the anxiety or discomfort that is the main source of energy for the learning laboratory. The state for the dilemma is set by bringing the group together without specifying goals or content. Tension develops as individuals attempt to structure the situation. They conflict, and each individual finds that his or her perceptions of the situation are not confirmed by all of the others. The dilemma arises from the lack of structure compounded by the lack of confirmation, and it provides most of the here-

and-now content for the group. By analyzing the dilemma, the trainee can specify the appropriate subjects for the theory sessions and exercises that take place in addition to and outside of the basic T-group meeting.

In the beginning, solutions to the dilemma exhibit habitual patterns, but when these fail the need to invent becomes apparent, creating even more anxiety. In this emotional contest, analysis of the forces operative in the dilemma begins, and this analysis leads to search thinking and creative behavior. At this point the participants supply emotional and conceptual evaluations of their own actions and reactions to others. On a group level, members may reflect on the direction and goal of the group. Finally, out of the feedback come generalizations. Delegates and trainer theorize together, formulate hypotheses, retest them, and recycle into the next learning phase.

Similarly, despite the absence of a planned agenda the content also exhibits predictable qualities. According to T-group theory the major obstacles to the development of honest, direct communication are the orientations toward authority and intimacy that people bring to groups. Thus, people will respond with rebelliousness, submissiveness, or withdrawal toward authority figures. To peers, people exhibit destructive competitiveness, emotional exploitiveness, or withdrawal (Bennis and Shepard, 1964, p. 323). The problems of dependence (authority relations) and interdependence (personal relations) occur in a predictable sequence. The group will devote the initial D-I-F-G cycles to questions of broad role distinctions (concern with power) and after some resolution of these problems spend the remaining D-I-F-G cycles discussing such personality issues as reaction to failure, warmth, and anxiety (concern with affection). Warren Bennis identifies the development of content in a T-group in terms of these two major phases (dependence and interdependence), and each phase has three subphases. The subphases and their major issues appear in Table 16-1.

FORMAT OF A TRAINING GROUP

Laboratory training may be designed in many ways, but it is usually comprised of four major training activities that may be integrated into the structure of the basic activity or handled outside the T-group:

1. The first training activity is the *T-group* itself, the basic learning group described earlier, in which self-observation and diagnosis of the group's growth and development are the primary means of training.
2. *Theory sessions* that provide a conceptual framework for group experiences are the second major training activity. Such a framework might include the notion of group goals; norms; cohesiveness; power structure; sociometric structure; and role functions, including the various group task roles, group building and maintenance roles, and individual roles (see Bany and Johnson, 1964; Bennis and Shepard, 1964, pp. 747–752).

Table 16-1   Phases in the Development of a T-Group

PHASE	ISSUES
Dependence	Relations with authority as major issue.
1. Dependence/Flight	Wish for structure and for a leader. Also a flight from structure and blocking leadership attempts.
2. Counterdependence/Flight	Avoidance of leader. Emergence of two subgroups, one desiring structure and agenda, another opposing it.
3. Resolution-Catharsis	Emergence of desire to use the time more fully— i.e., better use of it. Resentment toward trainer as authority figure increases. Growing recognition of various attitudes toward authority and of member responsibility. Some sense of trust and cooperation.
Interdependence	Concern for the another and for working together are major issue.
4. Enchantment/Flight	Group solidarity. Focus on positive feelings toward each other. Sense of relaxation.
5. Disenchantment/Flight	Concern with differences over desired amount of involvement with one another. Issue is how much to disclose of oneself. Fear of being attacked.
6. Consensual Validation	Preparation for end of group. Evaluation of each member's contribution to group. Awareness of responses to others. Dealing with separation.

Source: Warren G. Bennis, "Patterns and Vicissitudes in T-Group Development," in *T-Group Theory and Laboratory Method,* ed. Leland P. Bradford, Jack R. Gibb, and Kenneth D. Benne (New York: John Wiley & Sons, Inc., 1964); Warren G. Bennis and Herbert A. Shepard, "A Theory of Group Development," in *The Planning of Change: Readings in the Applied Behavioral Sciences,* ed. Warren G. Bennis, Kenneth D. Benne, and Robert Chin (New York: Holt, Rinehart & Winston, 1964), pp. 331–339; and John B. Shaffer and M. David Galinsky, *Models of Group Therapy and Sensitivity Training* (Englewood Cliffs, N.J.: Prentice-Hall, Inc., 1974), pp. 202–204.

3. *Focused exercises* with specifically enumerated learning goals are another important activity. For example, role-playing may be used to enact group role problems, or listening skills may be improved with tape listening using various rating scales. Other skill practices may include an observation task using various instruments, decision-making tasks, and feedback tasks. Consultation skills may be improved by having one group list its problems and discuss them with another group. Similarly, practice in giving and receiving help may include division into a four-person group in which one person presents a problem to two individuals who are already briefed by him or her. One raises questions (redefines) and probes for information while the other recommends an action. The observer keeps notes on the reactions to the two styles. Learning about larger systems can be accomplished by designing tasks that include intergroup competition.

4. Finally, there may be *experimentation* with a common real-life problem, especially if the group shares a work setting or profession.

Other activities designed to supplement the T-group structure may be seminars on a particular topic, two-person interviews, or trials in which a smaller group facilitates bringing more sensitive problems into the open, informal sessions.

THE MODEL OF TEACHING

There are four basic elements in the Laboratory Training Model. First is a situation lacking goals, leadership, and agenda. The ambiguity of the situation produces stress, enabling participants to respond at first inadequately and dependently but ultimately with self-direction. Second is an orientation toward group growth and development; although individual learning is the common goal, its realization involves concern and collaboration among all members of the group. Third, the data for analysis are the experiences and feedback of the participants while they are together; actual past experiences are put aside. In this way learning is active and direct, allowing concepts to follow from experience. Finally, members and trainer must take the roles of observant participant, which includes collecting and analyzing information as well as experimenting and generalizing.

SYNTAX

A precise sequencing of the structure of trainer-group, member-member, or trainer-member interaction cannot be specified for several reasons. First, as mentioned earlier, the overall design of laboratory training is adjusted to the development of the group. Focused exercises, theory sessions, and supplemental activities may occur within or outside the context of the T-group, and they may vary in their nature. The syntax including all these experiences thus differs depending on the training design. Second, even though the actual T-group experience does have a theoretical structure, it is an approximate account of events. Each group is unique in its growth and development and, more importantly, is self-evolving. In other words, after the initial presentation of an ambiguous situation by the trainer, the nature and structure of interaction is emergent. Insofar as the basic T-group is concerned, no *planned* pattern of interaction moves the group through the predictable phases. However, the phases in their probable order of occurrence are (1) dependence/flight (desire for and resistance to structure); (2) counterdependence/flight (avoidance of leader and subgroup emergence); (3) resolution-catharsis (desire for more productive use of time and recognition of responses to authority); (4) enchantment/flight (group solidarity and emphasis on positive feelings); (5) disenchantment/flight (discomfort over closeness and self-disclosure); (6) consensual validation (awareness of responses to each other, constructive evaluation of each member's contribution, preparing for separation. With each phase a cycle of dilemma, invention, feedback, and generalization appears to operate.

SOCIAL SYSTEM

After establishing the initial ambiguous situation, the trainer makes it clear that he or she will not serve as leader and takes a place as a group member. Structure is nonexistent, and the group must take responsibility for directing its own growth. Inherent, however, in the nature of the T-group experience is a climate of supportiveness and collaborative relationships for learning, along with a climate of permissiveness (nonevaluation). The group norms and a spirit of inquiry support open, authentic communication and individuality.

PRINCIPLES OF REACTION

The trainer functions in several roles in the T-group (and throughout the training laboratory). As an observant participant, the trainer is like the other group members in terms of his or her interventions and openness. With his or her established skills, the trainer provides a model of the observant participant. Much of the teaching is mediated through modeling good group behavior—openness, honesty and directness, desire to learn from the situation, giving and receiving feedback, supportiveness, and concern for others (Shaffer and Galinsky, 1974, p. 205). Finally, as laboratory training designer, the trainer provides additional concepts and skill-building exercises.

SUPPORT SYSTEM

The optimal support system is, of course, an experienced trainer and, ideally, a haven in the woods where the group can meet, away from established patterns. However, laboratory training procedures can take place within institutional settings and can be incorporated into the ongoing life of any group, such as a class.

APPLICATION

Any or all of the elements from laboratory training—basic T-group, theory sessions, or focused exercises—can be used by teachers to help individuals study their own behavior and their relations with others and to help groups of children work together more effectively. In a project supported by the United States Office of Education, Springport High School developed a human-relations handbook for high school students based on laboratory method (*Human Relations Laboratory Training Student Notebook*, 1961). The manual provides theoretical information on the basic concepts of laboratory training and a set of activities or focused exercises. We include the task on feedback here, which begins with a description:

WHAT IS FEEDBACK?

Feedback is communicating to a person or group about how their behavior has affected us or other people. The communication can be in the form of a spoken word, a gesture, or an action. If a person says or does something that makes me angry, I can give him feedback as to the effect of his behavior on me by (1) telling him about my angry feelings, (2) frowning or looking mad at him, or (3) punching him in the nose. As you can see, feedback can be either constructive or destructive, depending on whether it stems from the receiver's needs or the giver's needs.

One function of feedback is to make a person aware of the effects of his behavior on other people so that he may change or discard ineffective modes of behavior, or support certain kinds of behavior that are effective. Feedback lets a person know where he stands in the group and how he is seen by other members. It helps the person answer the question, "who am I?" Finally, feedback helps the individual evaluate his progress toward his goals and how closely his behavior is related to his intentions.

To be useful to the person receiving the feedback, the giver should be able to (1) describe his *own reaction* to the behavior, (2) describe the specific behavior or incident that evoked the reaction, (3) give the feedback as soon as possible after the behavior occurred, and (4) take into consideration the needs of the person on the receiving end of the feedback. Feedback that is given out of anger or hostility is useless and only makes the receiver defensive and unable to benefit by it.

CONSTRUCTIVE USE OF FEEDBACK

The next important goal for your group is to discover the use of constructive *feedback* in small group interaction. *Feedback* is reporting to an individual the kind of impressions he is making on you or reporting your reactions to him. Constructive feedback is rarely effectively used in interpersonal communication. Our society puts a great deal of emphasis on the value of honesty. Children are taught in their homes and schools that it is bad to lie about their behavior. Stealing, lying, cheating, and other dishonest acts are denounced in every aspect of life. Yet all of us are guilty of a great deal of dishonesty in interpersonal relationships all of the time. (Since children are often very aware of this it makes the learning of the value of honesty very complex.) We rarely express our honest feelings toward others in home or in school. Often this involves simply avoiding the expression of reactions which we feel would be detrimental to others or ourselves. Often it involves what we call "little white lies" when we tell people something positive or reassuring rather than be direct, honest, or critical.

People often feel threatened by the introduction of feedback exercises. The notion that people will be hurt by criticism is very prevalent. Yet think of how many people you know who have good intentions but irritate, embarrass, or behave in ways which diminish their effectiveness. The range of operating efficiently and productively in many areas in life is seriously hampered if we never have a chance to become aware of our impact on others. Most of us are quite capable of improving our styles on interpersonal communication and becoming much more effective as people—parents, teachers, whatever—when we really become aware of our impact on others.

Before going on to an exercise designed to give and receive feedback to others in the group, it is useful to think about destructive versus constructive feedback. Feedback is destructive when it is given only to hurt or to express hostility without any goal of improving the communication between people. It may also be destructive when only derogatory or extremely critical statements are given without any balance of positive evaluation.

Feedback is useful to a person when:

1. It describes what he is doing rather than placing a value on it. Example: "When you yell at me it makes me feel like not talking to you any more." Rather than: "It's awful of you to yell at me."
2. It is specific rather than general.
3. It is directed toward behavior which the receiver can do something about.
4. It is well-timed.
5. It is asked for rather than imposed.
6. It is checked to insure clear communication. (*Human Relations Laboratory Training Student Notebook*, 1961)

After explaining the function of feedback and the characteristics of constructive feedback, the manual gives the students a task:

FEEDBACK TASK FOR THE GROUP

Your group should now divide into triads. Each triad should have paper and pencil and go to separate corners of the room. Each triad should then list all the members of the group on the paper. The task for the triad is to discuss each member of the entire group (exclude yourselves) in terms of what would be the most useful positive and negative feedback statements to give each member. You will probably find considerable disagreement in your triads about your reactions to the various members. You must develop the positive and negative feedback statements which include the reactions of everyone in your triad. The triad should think about how to state the feedback so it will be very clear, direct, and useful to the recipient. Each triad should complete two statements for each member.

Example:

The most negative behavior that Member A exhibits in this group is _____.

The most valuable behavior that Member A exhibits in this group is _____.

At the end of twenty minutes the group will reform and each triad will give each member of the group their joint feedback report *verbally*.

After the feedback report of each triad to the entire group is completed, the group should spend time comparing reports of different triads.

Were the triad's reports similar or quite different? Why? or Why not?

Were some triads more critical? Why?

Were some reports more useful? Why? Why not?

Learning to give constructive feedback to others is only one part of the process. Learning how to receive feedback from others is equally important. Two extreme reactions to receiving feedback are (1) to ignore the feedback and devalue it as being unimportant, hostile, or useless or (2) to pay too much attention to all feedback and to try to change in accordance with all feedback received. Neither reaction is constructive. It is important to learn to deliberately weigh feedback from others in terms of the motivation of the sender, the correctness of the sender's perceptions, and the appropriateness of the behavior when it occurred even if the consensus of the feedback received is negative. (An effective group leader or teacher must sometimes behave in a manner to which he will receive only negative feedback. However, consistently dismissing it is a different situation.) While people generally have the most difficulty with critical feedback it is important to be aware that some people under-react or over-react to positive feedback also.

RECEIVING FEEDBACK TASK

The group members should return to triads and discuss how the members of the triad felt about the feedback they received. (1) Discuss the feelings about the feedback. Were you hurt, did you feel attacked, pleased, or what? (2) Are there ways of changing your behavior that would be appropriate or possibly related to the feedback received? Members of the triads should help each other in turn to evaluate and suggest ways of effectively utilizing (or ignoring if appropriate) the feedback. (*Human Relations Laboratory Training Student Notebook,* 1961)

In another exercise the students are asked to reach a decision by consensus over the rank ordering of the importance of a list of items. They must pretend they are part of a space flight in trouble, and the listed items represent available equipment, of which only the most critical pieces can be taken on the special 200-mile survival trip. Initially, the students make their own individual rankings. Later they are asked to use the consensus method and then to compare the scores of the two methods by a procedure that is specified. (The hunch is that the group method will be better.) Following are the instructions for the group-consensus section of the students' task:

DECISIONS BY CONSENSUS

Instructions: This is an exercise in group decision-making. Your group is to employ the method of *Group Consensus* in reaching its decision. This means that the prediction for each of the 15 survival items *must* be agreed upon by each member before it becomes a part of the group decision. Consensus is difficult to reach. Therefore, not every ranking will meet with everyone's *complete* approval. Try, as a group, to make each ranking one with which all group members can at least partially agree. Here are some guides to use in reaching consensus:

1. Avoid arguing for your own individual judgments. Approach the task on the basis of logic.
2. Avoid changing your mind only in order to reach agreement and avoid conflict. Support only solutions with which you are able to agree somewhat, at least.
3. Avoid "conflict-reducing" techniques such as majority vote, averaging, or trading in reaching decisions.
4. View differences of opinion as helpful rather than as a hindrance in decision-making.

On the "Group Summary Sheet" place the individual rankings made earlier by each group member. Take as much time as you need in reaching your group decision. (*Human Relations Laboratory Training Student Notebook,* 1961, p. 7)

Because of its lack of structure and its varied activities, laboratory training is perhaps more difficult than most models to understand and to use.

Several sources of information may be helpful, especially for their examples of actual T-group experiences. The best general introduction is *T-Group Theory and Laboratory Method* (Bradford, Gibb, and Benne, 1964). Another source, a general book of readings about the laboratory method, is *Sensitivity Training and the Laboratory Approach* (Golembiewski and Blumberg, 1970). This volume contains many essays by persons who founded and extended the method. Its final five chapters introduce the problems of researching the laboratory method.

An excellent recent book by John B. P. Shaffer and M. David Galinsky (1974) explores models of group therapy and sensitivity training. Chapter 10 specifically treats T-groups and the laboratory method, but many other chapters provide helpful explanations of the foundations of the movement that led to the laboratory method, other methods of interpersonal training, and the variety of models available within that field. The authors deal in some detail with eleven models that differ from one another in a variety of ways but that have many common features focused especially on helping individuals lead more productive lives in group settings.

INSTRUCTIONAL AND NURTURANT EFFECTS

Laboratory training methods are specifically designed to improve interpersonal relations and, by doing so, to increase flexibility and the ability to respond to change. Every setting in which people live and work together can

FIGURE 16-1   Instructional and nurturant effects: Laboratory Training Model.

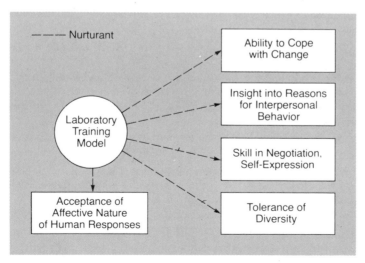

potentially be improved through interpersonal relations training, and every organization that is involved with change is a potential site for laboratory training. It is hoped that one of the major results of this process will be that the student can help organize human groups and organizations to function more effectively and humanely. Although the major purposes are primarily social, a powerful by-product of this kind of training should be an improvement in self-concept, confidence, and personal skills for stating needs and for making effective contributions that will be satisfying on the personal as well as the social level.

The Laboratory Training Model (Figure 16–1) is so unstructured that it hardly seems proper to say that it operates at all directly, in the sense, for example, that the Jurisprudential Inquiry Model *teaches* the jurisprudential framework. However, the environment generated in training groups can be extremely powerful. Hence, we feel that its primary mechanisms are nurturant in character, but the effects are by no means side effects. The effects vary, depending on the nature of the group and the direction of the trainer.

Summary Chart: Laboratory Training Model

SYNTAX

The phases vary, depending on the design of the laboratory training sessions. Usually the T-group structure is entirely emergent, but in focused exercises this may be less true.

SOCIAL SYSTEM

The model has low to moderate external structure. Norms are those of supportiveness, and the climate is permissive.

PRINCIPLES OF REACTION

Training agent (1) assumes role of observer and assumes memberlike role in terms of his or her interventions and opinions; (2) provides a model and interprets group behavior, calling attention to critical events or motivations in the group.

SUPPORT SYSTEM

An experienced trainer is needed.

17

SOCIAL SCIENCE INQUIRY
Studying Human Behavior on Spaceship Earth

SCENARIO

Pete Mesa's 10:00 A.M. eleventh grade social studies class in a Los Angeles high school is studying the formation of ethnic neighborhoods in Los Angeles. They are especially interested in learning how persons who are recent arrivals to Los Angeles become distributed geographically. After looking at large quantities of census tract data they are concerned about the recent formation of a new series of what appear to be "ethnic ghettos." In concentrating on people entering the community the students begin to form a series of hypotheses about why people live in certain neighborhoods. Some hypotheses turn on racial prejudice—people avoid places where they might be exposed to the prejudice of others. Some turn on the ability to find housing—certain racial and ethnic groups are excluded by landlords and banks. Some hypotheses deal with knowledgeability—people coming into a new area make contacts through other people who lead them only into certain areas. Some hypotheses have to do with social comfort—people seek out others with whom they have a common background.

Mr. Mesa helps the group organize their hypotheses. They are now trying to figure out how to test them. One of the students comes up with an idea based on some of the research he has been doing. "I've noticed," he says, "that a good number of people from Vietnam have come into the area recently, and they appear to be moving into certain neighborhoods. I wonder if we could get into contact with any of the Vietnamese who are just coming into the country and talk to them. Maybe we could find out how they are going to make decisions about where to live and where they get their information."

"That's a wonderful idea," says Miguel.

"How would we find people?" he asks.

"Well," says Mr. Mesa, "everybody entering the country has to get an alien registration card from the Department of Justice, and we could go down there and get information about where the Vietnamese are moving to. We also might be able to use that to make contact with some people who are just entering."

"How will we use that to test our hypotheses?" asks Margie.

"Why, I think we ought to take each hypothesis and then decide what kind of information we could ask the people that would relate to the different hypotheses. For example, when we find out how they find housing, we might be able to find out whether they expect to find prejudice, whether they only hear about certain neighborhoods, and other kinds of information that would relate to each of the ideas we've come up with."

"Yes, and maybe some of them would let us keep in touch with them. Suppose somebody tries to find an apartment; we can find out whether he or she is denied it, and so forth," adds another student.

In subsequent sessions the class proceeded to organize their hypotheses more completely and began to make contact with sources that could lead them to recently arriving Vietnamese. As time went on some of their hypotheses seemed to check out and others did not, and they began to generate yet other notions that would help explain the formation of ghettos.

For more than a decade, "inquiry" has been one of the rallying cries of educational reformers. However, the term has actually had different meanings to its users. To some, inquiry has meant a general position toward child-centered learning and has referred to building most facets of education around the natural inquiry of the child. To others, it has meant the use of the modes of inquiry of the academic disciplines as teaching models. Many of the approaches to teaching described in this book share more or less academic definitions of inquiry: the Inductive Model developed by Hilda Taba (Chapter 3), the procedures for inquiry training developed by T. Richard Suchman (Chapter 4), and the Scientific Inquiry model built on the practice of biology by makers of the Biological Sciences Study Committee curriculum (Chapter 8). Still others are concerned with developing student capacity to inquire into and reflect on the nature of social life, particularly the course of their own lives and the direction of their society. This stance toward inquiry is generated from a philosophical belief that the promotion of a reflective and inquiring frame of reference will improve the quality of personal and social existence. Thelen, Oliver, and Shaver share many of these concerns, although they have worked them out differently in the operational sense.

Byron Massialas and Benjamin Cox (1966) are also representatives of the social science inquiry approach as it applies to the social studies. Their concern is primarily with the improvement of society—the solution of societal problems: "It is our contention that in view of the prevailing conditions in our culture, the single most important goal of education should be the reflective examination of values and issues of current import" (Massialas and Cox, 1966, p. 12).

Massialas and Cox take the position that the school has to be an active participant in what they call the "creative reconstruction" of the culture. The school has no business maintaining only one set of values reflecting a single segment of U.S. society. It does not have the right to avoid the value controversies that are necessary in a pluralistic democracy, nor can it reasonably avoid the difficulties in the culture and the problems that require systematic cooperation of all citizens. On the contrary, they believe that the school must deal actively with the serious and critical areas of public controversy; the school must make a solid effort to teach citizens to reflect on values and to participate with others in the creative reconstruction of the society. The method of inquiry they recommend bears some resemblance to the general methodologies described by Hullfish, Smith, and Thelen, but it also has a number of unique aspects that are worth noting, especially when we consider the popularity of "inquiry" today, and the number of people who are attempting to explore it as an educational method.

ORIENTATION TO THE MODEL

GENERAL CONDITIONS OF INQUIRY

There are three essential characteristics of the reflective classroom, as explored by Massialas and Cox. They stress first that the social aspects of the classroom are especially important, and an open climate of discussion is required. "All points of view and statements are solicited and accepted as propositions that merit examination" (Massialas and Cox, 1966, p. 12).

An emphasis on hypotheses as the focus of inquiry is the second characteristic of the reflective classroom. The discussion revolves around hypothetical solutions of problem situations and the nature of the hypotheses themselves. Knowledge is viewed as hypotheses that are continually tested and retested. This focus requires a continual negotiation as the members of a class and their teacher collect data relevant to the hypotheses, revise their notions, and try again. The atmosphere then becomes one of negotiation, and students are willing to modify their ideas in the face of evidence. Hypothesizing requires skills of logic, because of logical formulation and implication of the hypothesis are as much a part of inquiry as are experimentation and observation (Massialas and Cox, 1966, pp. 92–193).

The third distinguishing aspect of the reflective classroom is the use of fact as evidence. "The classroom is recognized as a form where scientific inquiry is engaged" (Massialas and Cox, 1966, p. 115). In the classroom, the validity and reliability of facts are considered as the hypothesis is tested. The validation of facts is given the greatest consideration.

OVERVIEW OF THE TEACHING STRATEGY

Massialas and Cox describe phases for carrying out inquiry in the social studies classroom. They also provide a hypothetical illustration that we follow through its phases.

ORIENTATION   Orientation is simply the sensitization of the teachers and students to a problem in the social domain. It may arise from a real-life contemporary situation, from reflection on reading, from a conflict within the classroom itself, or from any number of other sources. The important criterion is that all concerned consider it a problem, and that it can be summarized as a genuine problem. For example, it should not simply be an obstacle to "good behavior" for which a predetermined solution will be sought. There must be a genuine puzzlement about the problem, or a genuine conflict with respect to any quick solution. The teacher should work to help the group become sensitized and also to help the group develop a general statement of the problem that defines its elements and can be accepted by all as a starting point for the inquiry. The starting point can be a question that calls for an explanatory relationship, solution, or policy.

> In our hypothetical illustration of the process, the orientation is achieved through the use of a passage from a high school text. The springboard passage appears in Canfield and Wilder's text for high school United States history. It may be thought of as having constituted a part of a class's reading assignment, now to be focused on more directly (Massialas and Cox, 1966, pp. 116–117).

>> During the next two centuries, however, trade was revived in an unusual way. From Western Europe whole armies, led by noblemen in armor, journeyed by land and sea to the Holy Land in Asia Minor. There they fought battle after battle with the Mohammedans in heroic attempts to rescue the Holy Land and bring it again under Christian control. These religious expeditions were known as the Crusades.
>> People who took part in the Crusades became acquainted with eastern luxuries that they had never dreamed existed. They brought home from the Orient spices, rare drugs, brilliant dyes, perfumes, jewels, ivory, glassware, fine silks, and gorgeous tapestries. More and more Europeans longed to possess such luxuries, so that the demand for them grew rapidly. The merchants of the Italian cities, especially those of Venice, were quick to see the importance of meeting that demand.

These merchants set out on buying trips to the ports of the eastern Mediterranean, returning to Europe with spices, perfume, and other items. For centuries some goods had been trickling from many parts of Asia along land and water routes to the cities of the eastern Mediterranean. Now the trade routes became crowded as the riches of Asia began to flow to the Mediterranean Sea, to be shipped by Italian merchants to all parts of Europe . . . .

While Europeans were learning to enjoy new physical comforts, they were also waking up to new ideas. For centuries, under feudalism, people's interests had been limited to the simple affairs of the small estates on which they lived. They had almost completely lost the desire to educate themselves. Few men had written books or produced works of art.

Now the relations with the East were bringing about a new interest in learning. Europeans not only came in contact with the rich culture of the Mohammedans but also rediscovered the advanced learning of the Greeks and Romans. The booming trade relations which grew out of the Crusades also stirred up an exciting exchange of ideas between Europe and the East. The result was a great revival of learning and of the arts.

This revival took many forms. Universities were founded and grew. Scholars began to study and enjoy certain literature and art of Greece and Rome which had been neglected or forgotten. Architecture and painting flourished. Stories and travelers' tales were written in the simple languages which common people understood instead of in Latin. By the time of Columbus, this great intellectual movement was on the march. The movement is called the *Renaissance*, which means rebirth (Canfield and Wilder, 1966, pp. 116–17).

These passages constitute the springboard about which the teacher asks the following kinds of questions: How would you summarize the point of view the author is suggesting here? Or more specifically, How do you explain the fact that these Europeans in this episode were in the process of changing their values and cultural orientation?

The forming of the summarizing statement is the result of discussing the above questions: European contact with the Orient as a consequence of the Crusades resulted in the buying trips of Italian merchants to eastern Mediterranean ports for the acquisition of Eastern products with the effect of the infusion of new ideas and values. This summary statement then serves as the basis for the hypothesizing phase of the process. (Massialas and Cox, 1966, p. 116–117)

HYPOTHESIS   The second stage of the inquiry is the development of a hypothesis that expresses as clearly as possible the antecedents and consequents of the proposed explanation, policy, or solution to the phenomenon. The hypothesis will serve as a guide to the inquiry that follows, where students attempt to verify the elements of the problem, to see whether those elements do indeed relate to the proposed solution, and to determine whether the solution holds up or others need to be generated. There can be more than one hypothesis advanced at this stage in the model, and in fact many of the most interesting applications of the model occur when there appears to be more than one competing solution to the same problem.

From the summary statement in our example it is hypothesized that contact with different cultures results in changed values and desires. This hypothesis is now tested by the teacher and class in terms of (1) its validity as an explanation of the springboard episode; (2) its compatibility with previously devised generalizations and the experiences of the pupils and teacher; and (3) the existence of other historical facts and evidence which are relevant to its proof or disproof (Massialas and Cox, 1966, p. 117). Before validating a hypothesis, however, the members of the group should make sure it is clear to them that the terms have been defined adequately. Hence, the next phase.

DEFINITION   In this stage the terms of the hypothesis are clarified and defined until all members of the group are able to communicate about the problem situation, and the language that each of them uses in relation to the problem situation is made clear and pinned down to verifiable experience.

> For example, with reference to our illustration it may have been hypothesized to begin with that contact with different cultures results in progress. Here an ambiguous term, *progress*, requires either clarification and definition or substitution by another term or terms, the meaning of which has more specific connotations to the teacher and class. (Massialas and Cox, 1966, p. 118)

EXPLORATION   During this phase the hypothesis is extended in terms of its implications, its assumptions, and the deductions that can be made from it. It is qualified and limited, and examined for logical validity and internal consistency.

In our example a logical implication could be stated as follows:

> If contact with different cultures in changed values and desires, then people involved in trade outside their own territory are more likely to undergo cultural change. Or to state another possible implication, If a people live in isolation, then their culture will remain relatively static. The statement of implications leads directly to the searching for evidence to support the original hypothesis. (Massialas and Cox, 1966, p. 118)

EVIDENCING   In this stage, facts and evidence needed to support the hypothesis are gathered in terms of the conditions that have been hypothesized and defined.

> In pursuing the implications made in our illustrative case, questions like the following are asked: Do you know of people who trade(d) extensively and who in the process of exchanging goods also trade(d) ideas and cultural patterns? Or, with reference to the second implication, Do you know of any such isolated people; and is it true that their culture has (did) not change(d) over a long period of time?
> As evidence relevant to these deductions the early feudal experience of Europe presents a clear case of isolation whereas the Crusades and the Renaissance in Europe are examples and results of intercultural exchange. The transformation that took place in Japan following its opening to the Western trade in the mid-nineteenth century offers additional evidence applicable to both deduc-

tions. Other historical, anthropological, sociological and social science data relevant to these and other deductions are brought to bear on the hypothesis to prove or refute its validity in all times and places. In many cases, of course, insufficient data preclude any pursuit of the inquiry beyond this phase. In such an instance students and teachers should recognize that further examination without available evidence is not warranted. (Massialas and Cox, 1966, p. 119)

GENERALIZATION   The sixth and last phase of inquiry is an expression of the solution of the problem. More than likely if an honest problem has been approached, defined carefully, related well to evidence, and culled with sufficient complexity, no absolute general solution will be found. The generalization is simply the best possible statement. If two or three hypotheses seem equally tenable at the conclusion of an investigation, they should be maintained together, with their alternative advantages and disadvantages identified as carefully as possible.

If we assume that in the example sufficient evidence for its support, and no evidence leading to its refutation or major reconstruction is found, the warrantable conclusion to be drawn from the reflective procedure may be stated as follows: If a people of one culture contact a people of another culture, then a culture different from either of these but characterized by identifiable elements of each emerges. (Massialas and Cox, 1966, p. 119)

THE MODEL OF TEACHING

SYNTAX

The six phases of the model, then, are: (1) orientation—sensitization to a dilemma or problem and development of a general statement of the problem as a starting point for inquiry; (2) hypothesis—development of a hypothesis or hypotheses that can serve as guides to inquiry and can be tested; (3) definition—clarification and definition of terms in the hypotheses; (4) exploration—examination of the hypotheses in terms of their logical validity and internal consistence, on the basis of this examination; (5) evidencing—the gathering and reconciliation of facts in terms of the hypotheses to be tested; and (6) generalization—expression of solutions or statements about the problems.

SOCIAL SYSTEM

The social system is moderately structured. The teacher initiates the inquiry and sees that it moves from phase to phase. Students, depending on their inquiry abilities, should take major responsibility for the inquiry itself, and should even carry it through the phases if they are able. The norms of inquiry call for free and open discussion among a body of equals.

Table 17-1   Syntax of Social Inquiry Model

PHASE ONE	PHASE TWO
Present and clarify puzzling situation.	Develop hypotheses from which to explore or solve problem.
PHASE THREE	**PHASE FOUR**
Define and clarify hypothesis.	Explore hypothesis in terms of its assumptions, implications, and logical validity.
PHASE FIVE	**PHASE SIX**
Gather facts and evidence to support hypothesis.	Form generalized expression or solution.

PRINCIPLES OF REACTION

During all phases the teachers are counselors to inquiry, helping the students clarify their positions, improve the process of study, and work out their plans. They help the students clarify language, improve logic, become more objective, understand their assumptions, and communicate more effectively with one another. Consequently, the teachers' role is reflective; they help students understand themselves and find their own ways. The teachers are, then, sharpeners, focusers, and counselors, rather than instructors.

SUPPORT SYSTEM

The means needed to carry out the model are, primarily, a teacher who believes in the development of a leisurely, problem-solving approach to life, open-ended library resources, and access to expert opinion and other sources outside the school itself. A very rich environment of information is necessary to maintain an honest inquiry; this is particularly difficult to provide because one cannot tell in advance what problems will be identified, or exactly what kinds of evidence will be considered relevant to them.

APPLICATION

One of the interesting aspects of this model is that it lends itself well to building on the prescribed course of study and the mechanics of the "traditional" classroom. Ironically, the textbook is one of the most fertile sources of dilemmas for inquiry. These dilemmas can be created out of textbook generalizations, which often warrant further examination or statements of fact. Massialas and Cox provide us with the following examples:

> The class may encounter the generalization in its government text: The orderly conduct of a society is dependent upon an accepted system of law. This statement expresses a relationship between constitutional government and an orderly society. A legitimate doubt could be raised, however, over the nature of this relationship. Do constitutions *cause* societies to behave in an orderly fashion? Do orderly societies insure tranquility *via* constitution—as suggested by one well-known statement of the relationship? Or is there a functional relationship between these two, both phenomena, perhaps, being the effects of the third factor? . . .
>
> A social studies class might become oriented to a problem by the way of a statement of fact like the following: The Spanish conquistadors, and the colonists who followed, brought with them their religion, art, architecture, law and customs, and left the indelible mark of their culture in Mexico. A fact, as we have stated, is primarily used as evidence in the reflective classroom. So, in this case, the students must move inductively from the single episode to the statement of a hypothesis which explains the process of cultural infusion in a given region. (Massialas and Cox, 1966, p. 120)

It may be helpful at this point to examine some transcripts and anecdotal records of social inquiry discussion to see the flow of inquiry as it moves from phase to phase as well as to conceptualize better the phases themselves.

In the earlier example, the first transcript captures the class in the orientation phase as it was just beginning to formulate the hypothesis that in order to adjust to a cultural region a state has to be like its neighbors (Massialas and Cox, 1966, p. 122).

In another situation, students are directed to interpret a passage in a paperback book being used in class. The students in this case are becoming aware of the problem of Israel's accommodation to Arab-Islamic culture. The passage reads as follows:

> The influx of immigrants from Yemen, Iraq, and other non-Western areas means that today 40 percent of Israel's population is non-Western in origin. It is predicted that within a decade the population of the country will be 60 percent non-Western. The more non-Western Israel becomes the sooner and more effectively it will fit into the Middle East, and we must remember that, whatever may be the intellectual and spiritual attachments of Israel's European-born population, the new state, for better or for worse, must live in the Middle East, and not in Europe or in the United States. (Dean, 1960, p. 65)

TEACHER: Who would like to interpret the passage?

KATHY: Well, it tells us about the immigration of non-Western Jews to Israel, and predicts that they will soon outnumber the European or Western Jews. I am not sure of this, but the author seems to be saying that as Israel's people become more Oriental so will Israel, and that this will help the country fit into the Middle East better.

STEVE: I think this is a terrible passage.

TEACHER: Why so?

STEVE: Because it is wrong.

TEACHER: Why?

STEVE: Well, for one thing, how can Israel fit into the Middle East if the Arabs do not want it to happen? Maybe the author thinks they should become Arabs.

RANDY: Also, as far as I know, the Arabs are having a great deal of trouble westernizing. Why should Israel become like them? That would be a step backward for Israel.

HELEN: Well, maybe the author means that Israel should develop its own special brand of life that combines Western life with that of its Arab neighbors.

STEVE: That might be, but she does not really say so. She says that as Israel becomes less Western, the better it will become a part of the Middle Eastern way of life.

BOB: I have something to add. (pause) How can Israel fit in with its neighbors if they are at war with her? That is pretty hard to do, isn't it?

MARY: What is Israel supposed to fit in with? Since we have been studying something about the Middle East, I know that all those neighbors of Israel are not the same at all. Lebanon, I think, is more Christian than Moslem; whereas most Arabs are supposed to be Moslem. What exactly is Israel going to fit in with? (Massialas and Cox, 1966, pp. 125–27)

Once a hypothesis has emerged, it is up to the students to explore its validity. There are several ways to approach that task. The first is simply to look at the hypothesis logically. Does it make sense on its own terms? What assumptions does the hypothesis make? What are the implications of the hypothesis if it were true? Are the implications reasonable? The second step is to verify the hypothesis in terms of supporting information. What facts and evidence are available that support (or contradict) the hypothesis? How good (accurate) are the sources of supporting or contradicting evidence? The following excerpt shows a world history class considering the issue of evidence for the topic of nationalism:

Chapter fourteen dealt with the development of nationalism in England and France in the thirteenth and fourteenth centuries and with the Protestant Reformation. In an earlier classroom discussion when we talked about William the Conqueror, the Capetian kings in France, certain political developments in Spain under Ferdinand and Isabella, and the fight of the Spanish people against the Moors, we made some causal generalizations concerning national consciousness. Students easily recalled the generalizations and the supporting material. For example, they said that *if an aggregate of individuals speaks a common language, have the same religion, the same customs, the same enemies, identify themselves with the same heroes and symbols, and have one historic background, then national consciousness will emerge.* The author, in the beginning of the chapter, provided a definition of a nation which was consistent with the definition that we had given to the term except for the addition of independent government as a characteristic factor. When Bob raised the question of how the Jews would be classified before they gained independence in 1948, much discussion followed. The general consensus was that the Jewish population justifiably could have been called a nation; but this would have required a reconstruction of the definition provided by the authors since the Jews did not have an independent government prior to 1948. Many students referred to the dictionary in an attempt to get a more adequate definition of a nation. However, several said that the dictionary provided circular definitions which did not really explain or illuminate the phenomenon. I brought in the notion of operational definitions and definitions by stipulation. From there, I asked how we knew when we had nationalism. Could we see it, feel it, measure it, etc.? This again, brought about much discussion. Lorraine said that the feeling of nationalism was the feeling of oneness, that of being related to other people. Jack said that all we could depend on was the declaration of a person purporting to be a national of a country, or claiming to have national feelings. This brought about the idea that national consciousness amounted to the conception that a person has of himself in relation to other persons. If the relationship is a positive one, then the people involved can identify themselves as a nation. I observed that my pupils were moving to another, higher level of analysis. Now they talked in terms of measuring the level of intensity of sentiments on the basis of overt behavior, they talked about identifying and isolating social phenomena, and they talked about variable analysis. (Massialas and Cox, 1966, pp. 126–127)

Exploration and evidencing with a more concrete phenomenon can be found in the following example:

Peter had prepared what he called the pattern of revolution from *The Anatomy of Revolution*. He had identified six steps in the revolutionary pattern, the first of which was the breakdown of the financial system of the country. After discussing the meaning of this financial aspect of the hypothesis the class developed this deduction: *If it is true that there is a breakdown of the financial system of a state preceding a revolution, then we should find in the period preceding the American Revolution (1750–1775) events which show the government (England) unable to cope with tax, trade, money, and debt problems, in ways satisfactory to the colonies.* (Massialas and Cox, 1966, p. 127)

The definition phase can be a frustrating experience. However, in addition to its logical importance, defining terms reflects the process of inquiry. This can be seen in the following excerpt in which the word *environment* is used in relation to early colonial settlements in America (Massialas and Cox, 1966, p. 127).

TEACHER: I think you have got a problem on your hands here. Who sees a logical way out of it? Now, as I interpret it, Clara Sue was attempting to say that environment is a very broad concept. The people along with the climate, the land, the minerals, the buildings, and the production of the people become environment. And if you have a brother and sister, these people are part of this environment.

CLARA: Isn't that true?

TEACHER: Now, that is certainly one kind of definition. But over on this side, George says that environment as he has been thinking about it, is principally climate and land.

GEORGE: I did not say that it was principally climate and land, I said that I do not think that that would affect that type of environment where you would have just physical environment. What she was talking about would not affect physical environment.

TEACHER: Well, that could be. I would not argue with that. What are you thinking of Clara? What happens within this family to change the environment?

CLARA: I do not know. Anything could happen, I guess.

TEACHER: What?

CLARA: Anything could happen. But I thought environment was everything about you. But, I was not thinking of physical environment. I do not know.

TEACHER: Let us determine some kind of meaning here. I do not think we are going to have any luck at all in this enterprise until we do.

STEVE: Well, I want to go back to the colonists.

TEACHER: All right.

STEVE: I think it definitely meant a change in physical environment, meaning a change in the land and climate and possibly also the people in the colony and other things like this. I think it is the second thing.

TEACHER: The second thing being what?

STEVE: Things other than just the land, the climate, the people, ideas and all this.

TEACHER: Here is a new dimension. The ideas which the society holds comprise a part of the environment. (Massialas and Cox, 1966, pp. 130–131)

Finally, generalizations should be thought of as open-ended statements subject to change. Following are some examples developed by a world history class discussing the rise of civilization in India and China:

1. If a religion meets the needs and wants of the people better than the present religion, then the new religion will be adopted.
2. If the system of writing in a country is hard to understand and is difficult for the common people to use, then it will be changed or revised.
3. If the people have a relatively long period of peace and a government which does not change, then these people will advance the arts.
4. If a strong ruler dies or is overthrown and there is no strong ruler to succeed him, then the country will decline or fall. (Massialas and Cox, 1966, p. 132)

INSTRUCTIONAL AND NURTURANT EFFECTS

The primary purpose of the Social Science Inquiry Model is to teach students how to reflect on significant social problems. Through genuine inquiry, they should learn how to define these problems, how to work with others in exploring different ways of looking at them, and how to conclude on the basis of the data as much as possible. No claim is made that the model will be more efficient for learning facts than any other given method. However, the authors of the model clearly believe that learning facts in isolation is not a very productive enterprise and that the social sciences should be learned by developing solutions to significant social problems, so that the structure and modes of inquiry of the disciplines will be seen as they apply to the arena of human concern.

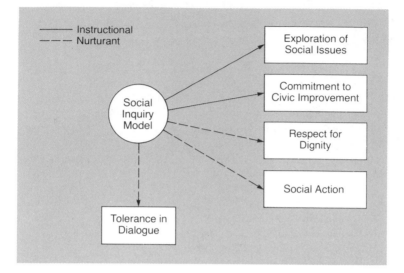

FIGURE 17-1   Instructional and nurturant effects: Social Science Inquiry Model.

The Massialas and Cox model (Figure 17-1) is specifically designed to teach students to explore social issues and to develop a commitment to civic improvement. It stops short of social action, although it clearly hopes to nurture such action. Respect for the dignity of all people and tolerance in dialogue with differing people also seem to be nurtured in the environment of the model.

Summary Chart: Social Science Inquiry Model

SYNTAX

Phase One:
Present and clarify puzzling situation.

Phase Two:
Develop hypotheses from which to explore or solve problem.

Phase Three:
Define and clarify hypothesis.

Phase Four:
Explore hypothesis in terms of its assumptions, implications, and logical validity.

Phase Five:
Gather facts and evidence to support hypothesis.

Phase Six:

Form generalized expression or solution.

SOCIAL SYSTEM

The model is moderately structured. The teacher is generally initiator of the inquiry and sees that it moves from phase to phase. Students, however, carry the responsibility for its development. The social norms call for open discussion among equals.

PRINCIPLES OF REACTION:

Teacher acts as sharpener, focuser, and counselor to inquiry. He or she helps students to clarify their positions and improve the process of study.

SUPPORT SYSTEM

The teacher needs patience to carry out a problem-solving approach and the resourcefulness to locate the necessary information for which the inquiry may call. Open-ended library resources and access to expert opinion are also required.

Part IV

The Behavioral Systems Family

INTRODUCTION
Behavior Theory

Behavioral models of learning and instruction have their origins in the classical conditioning experiments of Pavlov (1927), the work of Thorndike on reward learning (1909, 1911, 1913), and the studies of Watson and his associates (Watson, 1916; Watson and Rayner, 1921), who applied Pavlovian principles to the psychological disorders of human beings. In the past twenty years behavior (learning) theory, systematically applied in school settings, has been greatly influenced by B. F. Skinner's *Science and Human Behavior* (1953) and J. Wolpe's *Psychotherapy by Reciprocal Inhibition* (1958). Wolpe's influence also stems from his descriptions of specific therapeutic procedures for dealing with human problems (for example, in systematic desensitization and assertiveness training).

In the late 1950s educators began to employ behavioral techniques, particularly forms of contingency management and programmed learning materials, in school settings. For some types of learners these have had great success. For example, some youngsters who previously had made no progress in language development and social learning are now trainable, and often able to mix with normal individuals. Milder forms of learning problems have responded to behavior models as well (Becker, 1977, 1980, 1981.)

During the past ten years there has been an impressive amount of research demonstrating the effectiveness of behavioral techniques with a wide range of problems, from snake phobias to social skill deficits, behavioral problems, and test anxiety. The research also indicates that these procedures can be used effectively in group settings and by laypeople. We believe that behavior theory presently offers an array of procedures that are extremely useful to teachers and curriculum planners. Many of them are not widely known or used in school settings; others are frequently used by some practitioners but too often dismissed by others, perhaps for lack of genuine understanding.

The models we have developed or borrowed from behavior theory include one for mastery learning and direct instruction, another for achieving self-control, another for learning from simulations, and another for assertiveness training.

These models are all drawn from the body of knowledge we call *behavior therapy*. Other terms such as *learning theory, social learning theory, behavior modification,* and *behavior therapy* have been used by various leaders in this field to refer to the models we discuss here. (Bandura, 1969; Lazarus, 1971; Salter, Wolpe, and Reyna, 1964; Wolpe, 1969; see also Estes, 1975). Because each term is generally associated with one particular form of the basic theory, we prefer to use the more neutral term *behavior theory* to cover those procedures emanating from both operant and counterconditioning principles, which have been useful in educational and psychological settings. Although there have been many school applications of models based on operant principles, we find less use of the counterconditioning models discussed in psychotherapy references, especially relaxation, desensitization, and assertiveness training. We believe that these models, too, are valuable for educational purposes, are applicable in school settings, and can easily be transferred to them.

ASSUMPTIONS OF MODERN BEHAVIORAL THEORY

BEHAVIOR IS LAWFUL AND SUBJECT TO VARIABLES IN THE ENVIRONMENT

People respond to variables in their environment. These external forces stimulate individuals to act in certain ways: either to exhibit or avoid behaviors. According to the principle of operant conditioning, once a behavior has been manifested the probability that it will occur again can be strengthened or decreased by responses from the environment. Thus, if a 2 year old sees a table in the room (stimulus), points to it, and verbalizes the word "table" (response behavior), he or she is responding to external forces. If, after the child says the word "table," the child's mother picks him or her up, gives him or her a big hug, and repeats, "Table, that's right." (reinforcing stimuli), the child is likely to say the word again (response behavior). On the other hand, suppose the child sees a rattlesnake curled nearby (stimulus), and experiences a sudden surge of anxiety and fear (response behaviors). If the child runs away (another response behavior) and thereby avoids the snake, that act reduces his or her anxiety (reinforcing stimulus). The reinforcement increases the likelihood that the child will try to avoid snakes. Both of these examples illustrate the basic behavioral notion that behavior is acquired or enacted through external variables that serve either as the original stimulus or as the reinforcing stimulus. In one case we are learning to do something; in the other case, to avoid something.

Counterconditioning is related, but slightly different; in counterconditioning, a new behavior that is incompatible with the old behavior is substituted, such as relaxation for anxiety. To cure a phobia toward snakes, the individual substitutes positive feelings for anxiety.

From this stance the task of the psychologist is to discover what kinds of environmental variables affect behavior in which ways. The educator ascertaining these relationships can apply the findings directly to his or her work—changing variables to change behavior. The leverage of external control can also be given to the individual. If the teacher can, by appropriate techniques, ascertain and control the external variables, so can the student. Thus, what appears at first to be a technique for controlling others can be used to free people by increasing *their* capabilities for self-control.

BEHAVIOR IS AN OBSERVABLE, IDENTIFIABLE PHENOMENON

Behavior theory concentrates on the behavior itself, and takes an optimistic view. Given the right conditions and enough time we can (and will) succeed.

Original Stimulus	→	Response Behavior	→	Reinforcing Stimuli

Behavior theorists believe that even internal responses (such as anxiety in the presence of snakes), which mediate our observable responses (such as running away), can be changed. For example, biofeedback represents a successful attempt to alter so-called internal states such as anxiety, tension, or stress, (Rimm and Masters, 1974).

MALADAPTIVE BEHAVIORS ARE ACQUIRED THROUGH LEARNING AND CAN BE MODIFIED THROUGH LEARNING PRINCIPLES

Many people have assumed, quite erroneously, that many children have "blocks to learning" (internal states that cannot be changed). Yet in recent years, we have seen numerous examples of growth through the systematic application of learning principles. Other more typical, but frustrating, behavioral problems of normal children have been handled successfully with behavioral techniques. Perhaps more than any other school of thought, behavior theorists have documented their effectiveness simply by manipulating the stimulus conditions in the environment (operant principles), or by substituting the behavioral response (counterconditioning). Maladaptive behavior can be changed, often producing changes in feelings and attitudes.

BEHAVIORAL GOALS ARE SPECIFIC, DISCRETE, AND INDIVIDUALIZED

It is assumed that all behavioral problems, however globally presented, can be described in specific, concrete terms, given enough probing or observation. Another assumption is that two externally similar responses do not necessarily proceed from the same original stimulus. Conversely, no two people will respond to the same stimulus in the same way. Consequently, the procedures for encouraging new behaviors involve setting specific, individualized behavioral goals. This does not mean that some group training (as in programmed instruction or assertiveness groups) is not possible. On the contrary, group training for assertiveness, reading instruction, and even the elimination of phobias has been quite effective. It does mean that the goals for each student may differ and that the training process will need to be individualized in terms of pacing or content.

BEHAVIORAL THEORY FOCUSES ON THE HERE-AND-NOW

The role of the past in shaping a person's behavior is deemphasized. The conditions stimulating the behavior are ascertainable through observation or interviewing. What is crucial is determining (describing) the functional relationship currently operating in producing or maintaining the behavior. Once this is done the best procedure for altering the behavior can be selected and implemented.

Behavioral practitioners have often reported that they have been able to alter maladaptive behaviors in a short time, even in the case of severe phobias or long-term withdrawal patterns. Many people have felt relaxed and socially effective in a short time, and students who had remained virtually illiterate have progressed quickly (Resnick, 1967).

OPERANT CONDITIONING AND COUNTERCONDITIONING

The procedures or models evolving from behavior theory fall into two general categories: those emphasizing the principle of operant conditioning (Skinner) and those using principles of counterconditioning (Wolpe). Operant principles stress the role of reinforcement (particularly reward and punishment): Counterconditioning emphasizes procedures for substituting an adaptive for a maladaptive response— for example, substituting tapping on the table with one's fingers for nail biting. Programmed instruction and training (operant-based models) and desensitization (a counterconditioning model) all rely heavily on stimulus control. Table 1 shows the six models and their theoretical emphases.

The first two models, drawn from operant conditioning, are more familiar to educators than the last four. The Contingency Management Model, discussed in Chapter 19, is widely used with students who have major learning and behavior problems. However, many school administrators now believe it is essential for all teachers to possess the knowledge and skills of this model, which they regard as the heart of effective classroom management. Knowing how to conceptualize and describe behavior in discrete, observable terms, noticing when and under what conditions it usually occurs, identifying more appropriate behaviors and suitable reinforcers, and finally instituting a reinforcement program may soon be standard requirements for many teachers. Programmed instruction, a variant of contingency management, has found its way into numerous basic skills curricula in reading and math;

Table 1   Behavioral Models

MODEL	MAJOR PRINCIPLE	PRIMARY EMPHASES
Mastery Learning and Quest Instruction	Operant Conditioning	Reinforcement Stimulus Control Immediate feedback
Self-Control	Operant Conditioning	Reinforcement
Training: Observation and Practice	Operant Conditioning	Stimulus control
Relaxation	Counterconditioning	Response substitution Reciprocal inhibition
Desensitization	Counterconditioning	Response substitution Reciprocal inhibition
Assertiveness Training	Counterconditioning	Response substitution Reciprocal inhibition

even elementary school classrooms representing an open-education environment frequently have these materials. The approach is thought to be important to youngsters who need a high degree of success and immediate reinforcement or feedback about their progress. The Training Model relies on modeling through observation and practice as the means of obtaining new behaviors or eliminating old ones, although it also uses stimulus control and feedback.

Three related models that come from counterconditioning principles of behavior theory are relaxation, desensitization, and assertiveness training. [The first is a general model for helping students to relax. The second increases students' control over the ability to reduce anxiety in stressful situations (like speaking to a group and dealing with conflict)]. The third focuses on improving social communication.

The focus of these models is on the maladaptive behavior patterns of the individual, including those nonvisible states that—contrary to many opinions—can be described fairly accurately. Anxiety is the common example. Although anxiety occurs *inside* the individual, it has visible physiological symptoms, especially tension in the muscles and changes in the skin. Thus, one can "see" anxiety (infer its existence) in a variety of symptoms. All three models are directly focused on the reduction of anxiety. The first model depends on learning physical—that is, muscle—relaxation. The techniques of progressive muscle relaxation provide an individual with control over his or her ability to relax and thus inhibit anxiety. The second model applies the relaxation techniques to the reduction of anxiety about certain objects (tests, social situations, snakes, and rodents). The third model deals with the acquisition of a general social skill that can decrease anxiety and increase authenticity of communication in social situations.

Most behavior therapy procedures involve the establishment of very specific, often quite limited goals, although the patterns of behavior may be quite complex in themselves. Anxiety, for example, is a relatively complex syndrome, yet it is possible, through the application of learning principles, to teach individuals to control anxiety by substituting relaxation, which is physiologically incompatible with anxiety. By learning to relax one's body in situations in which one is usually anxious, the feelings of anxiety are reduced! As in other applications of behavioral techniques, a baseline of present behavior is established. Then exercises are introduced during which the student learns new patterns.

There is a vast amount of conceptual and empirical literature on behavior therapy, much of which is summarized in David C. Rimm and John C. Masters, *Behavior Therapy: Techniques and Empirical Findings* (1974). We draw heavily from their work. Rimm and Masters encourage the use of behavioral procedures by laypeople and by teachers in the classroom, particularly the latter because they feel that many school-related problems could benefit from it. Many educators, too, believe that one purpose of schooling is to increase students' self-esteem and life skills. These models offer one way of addressing preventive mental health as well as basic intellectual knowledge and skills.

MAJOR CONCEPTS

The key ideas in behavior theory are based on the stimulus-response-reinforcement paradigm in which human behavior is thought to be under the control of the external environment. A *stimulus* is "any condition, event or change in the environment of an individual which produces a change in behavior" (Taber, Glaser, and Halmuth, 1967, p. 16). It may be verbal (oral or written) or physical. A response may be defined as a unit of behavior. It is the basic unit upon which complex performances or response repertoires are built. Responses may be covert, as anxiety or tension, or overt, as talking, hitting the ball, or marking a paper. Complex behaviors are made up of response repertoires consisting of many kinds of responses that are functionally related (as in the solution of a long-division problem).

The condition upon which reinforcement will occur depends on the standard set by the teacher. In skill development, what is acceptable for the beginner may be less than adequate for the advanced student. Thus, as practice increases, the teacher expects better performance and so will reward only more advanced responses. In mathematics the teacher may on one occasion accept the response *triangle* and later accept only *isosceles triangle* as a response to the same stimulus. Obviously, the behavior ultimately desired does not come forth in the first stages but is the result of a continuous *shaping* process executed by changing stimuli and conditions of reinforcement. A person's initial response must exist in some strength in his or her repertoire; the task of the instructor is to build more complex patterns of responses from this initial response by changing the demands and rewards in the environment. The essence of operant conditioning is to have reinforcement contingent only on emission of the desired behavior. This process is known as *contingency management*.

According to behavioral theorists, the most effective reinforcement immediately follows a response. Delayed reinforcement is much less powerful in modifying behavior. *Reinforcement* is at the heart of the behavioral model, for without it behavior (responses) cannot be brought under the control of particular environmental stimuli. A *reinforcer* always increases the frequency of a response on which it is contingent.

Reinforcers may be either *positive* or *negative*. *Positive reinforcers* are those events whose presentation increases response. Money, affection, approval, smiles, and attention are examples of positive reinforcers. When they appear the contingent responses usually occur. Another positive reinforcer familiar to educators is *confirmation* or knowledge of results. Knowing that you have behaved correctly or adequately is highly reinforcing. Self-instructional programmed material is sequenced by such small steps as to virtually ensure correct responses and the subsequent reinforcement the learner derives from knowledge of his correctness. This is why highly sequenced programmed materials often work well with students who previously experienced little success. Biofeedback is another illustration of the value of knowledge of results.

Finally, students are also reinforced by controlling their environments. Such simple activities as turning a page after reading its contents stimulate continued activity. Part of the attraction of self-instructional computer programs is the reinforcement quality of mechanical manipulation. One can design a program to encourage many satisfying actions. Simulators often provide opportunities for similar pleasurable activities.

The range of naturally occurring positive reinforcers available to teachers is broad—for example, a smile, enthusiasm, show of interest, attention, physical contact, enjoyment, and casual conversation. Most often their use is not monitored carefully, and this increases students' maladaptive behaviors. How many times have teachers called on the student who interrupts others because he or she catches their eyes and ears first?

Negative reinforcement, on the other hand, removes something from the situation (possibly by adding something disagreeable). Punishment, such as threats that decrease response probability, is an example of a negative reinforcer (aversive stimulus). The management mode in many classrooms is based on aversive control; students are threatened with reprisals if they do not learn. Many years ago the birch rod was used; today the aversive stimuli are less physical (poor grades, disapproval). According to behavior theorists, punishment suffers from several drawbacks. First, its effects are temporary; punished behavior is likely to reoccur. Second, the aversive stimuli used in punishment may generate unwanted emotions, such as predispositions to escape or retaliate, and disabling anxieties (Skinner, 1956, p. 183). Wherever possible, positive rather than negative reinforcements should be used.

The effectiveness of reinforcement programs is determined not only by establishing close temporal relation between reinforcement and behavior and by the type of reinforcement selected, but also by the scheduling or frequency of reinforcement (*reinforcement schedule*). In Skinner's opinion, reinforcement should be as continuous as possible, occurring after every response. Research on reinforcement schedules shows that although continuous reinforcement contributes to the most rapid acquisition of behavior, it does not bring about the strongest retention rate. A *variable* ratio schedule in which reinforcement is contingent on the number of responses and is administered irregularly creates the most durable response levels. One of the most difficult skills for teachers, or anyone, to master is to be consistent, immediate, and frequent in rewarding the desired responses when they occur. Often contingency management programs break down because the reinforcement is not consistent. If a response goes unreinforced it will become less and less frequent until it is extinguished.

In many classrooms the primary instructional objective is to bring the students' behavior under the control of subject-matter stimulus (stimulus control). The learner connects appropriate responses to various stimuli (as words for objects). *Stimulus discrimination* is particularly important in the learning situation. When we respond differently to different stimuli, we are distinguishing or discriminating between their properties. Most subject matter is brought to control behavior through discrimination training. For example, suppose we have previously conditioned the response *ball* to the spherical object, ball, and *ring* for an enclosed circular band. To ensure that the new response *ring* is not called forth in the presence of a ball, we must present the ball and extinguish the response *ring* if it is made. In this manner, the control of the response *ring* to the appropriate stimulus is sharpened. Or a child may have learned to respond to the letter *d* and may then need to distinguish *d* from *b* and learn not to give the *d* response when *b* is the stimulus.

A related process is known as *stimulus generalization*, or extension of stimulus control. In this case, several stimuli possessing similar properties share the response control. The response *animal* is shared with many discriminative stimuli. The child learns to apply it to a few animals, then more, then all. In this way concepts are acquired that refer to classes of objects and events.

Desensitization procedures make use of stimulus control by gradually enlarging the range of stimuli to which individuals can respond without anxiety. Stress-reduction models depend on people's recognizing a range of cues indicating body tension or mental stress.

Training models using observation and practice illustrate the basic behavioral concepts. For example, when one goes to a hotel, the registration desk is a stimulus to the patterns of behavior one uses to obtain a room. Seeing someone else ask for a room gives one a model to follow. Hearing the correct pronunciation of foreign words functions in the same way. Thus, an instructional pattern can take the form of:

1. Presenting a stimulus;
2. Observing or modeling a response (optional);
3. Providing practice in responding to the stimulus;
4. Reinforcing appropriate responses as immediately as possible.

Imagine a teacher whose objective is to help a class read a section of one of Shakespeare's plays in an appropriate way. He or she might

1. Present the written passage.
2. Demonstrate some ways of reading it.
3. Induce the students to practice reading the passage.
4. Reinforce performance selectively. (For some, participation might be rewarded. For others, high standards of reading and performing would be applied.)

As we explore the models derived from the behavioral stance we find each of these elements (stimulus control; generalization and discrimination; response repertoires and response substitution; reinforcers and reinforcement schedules; observation, modeling, and practice) present in various combinations and with different amounts of emphasis.

18

MASTERY LEARNING AND DIRECT INSTRUCTION
Social Learning Theory

MASTERY LEARNING

In recent years much attention has been given to an approach for organizing instruction termed *mastery learning,* formulated by John B. Carroll (1971) and Benjamin Bloom (1971). Mastery learning provides a compact and interesting way of increasing the likelihood that more students will attain a satisfactory level of performance in school subjects. Many of its elements are not new: Both Bloom and Carroll cite practices developed by Carlton Washburn and Henry Morrison in the 1920s. But recent work has sharpened the idea, and contemporary instructional technology has made it more feasible. A strong body of research supports the application of the approach.

A CONCEPT OF APTITUDE

The core theoretical idea in mastery learning is based on John Carroll's interesting perspective on the meaning of aptitude. Traditionally aptitude has been thought of as a characteristic that correlates with a student's achievement. (The more aptitude one has, the more he or she is likely to learn.) Carroll, however, views aptitude as the *amount of time* it takes someone to learn any given material, rather than his or her capability to master it. By Carroll's view, students with very low aptitude with respect to a particular kind of learning simply take a much longer time to reach mastery than students with a higher aptitude.

This view is optimistic in the sense that it suggests that it is possible for nearly all students to master any given set of objectives, if sufficient time (the opportunity to learn) is provided, along with appropriate materials and instruction. Thus viewed, aptitude becomes primarily a guide to how much time a learner will need. Aptitude also suggests *how* to instruct because learners of different aptitudes will learn more efficiently if the style of instruction is suited to their configurations. (In *our* terms, some aptitudes are model-relevant—they help us choose and adapt models.) For any given objective, according to Carroll, the degree of learning achieved by any given student will be a function of time allowed, the perseverance of the student, the quality of instruction, the student's ability to understand instruction, and his or her aptitude. The problem in managing instruction is deciding how to organize the curriculum and the classroom so that students will have optimal time, benefit from good instruction, be induced to persevere, and receive assistance in understanding the learning tasks.

Bloom transformed Carroll's stance into a system with the following characteristics:

1. Mastery of any subject is defined in terms of sets of major objectives which represent the purposes of the course or unit.
2. The substance is then divided into a larger set of relatively small learning units, each one accompanied by its own objectives, which are parts of the larger ones or thought essential to their mastery.
3. Learning materials are then identified and the instructional strategy selected.
4. Each unit is accompanied by brief diagnostic tests to measure the student's developing progress (the formative evaluation) and identify the particular problems each student is having.
5. The data obtained from administering the tests is used to provide supplementary instruction to the student to help him overcome his problems. (Bloom, 1971, pp. 47–63)

If instruction is managed in this way, Bloom believes, then time to learn can be adjusted to fit aptitude. Students of lesser aptitude can be given more time and more feedback while the progress of all is monitored with the assistance of the tests.

INDIVIDUALLY PRESCRIBED INSTRUCTION (IPI)

Bloom, Block, and the other advocates of mastery learning believe that it can be implemented simply by modifying traditional group instructional procedures to ensure that some students have more time and that they receive appropriate additional instruction according to the results of the formative evaluation (Carroll, 1971, pp. 37–41). We are not so sure that mastery learning can be easily and simply implemented in the usual classroom.

However, modern instructional technology, especially the development of self-administering multimedia units and the application of programmed learning procedures, has encouraged curriculum developers to invent comprehensive curricular systems and to reorganize schools to provide for a much greater degree of individualized instruction than is generally possible under conventional school organizations.

A prominent example of an application of systems planning to elementary and secondary school instruction is the Individually Prescribed Instructional Program (IPI), developed by the Learning Research and Development Center of the University of Pittsburgh, in collaboration with the Baldwin-Whitehall School District. The system, originally designed for the Oakleaf School in suburban Pittsburgh, now operates in more than 100 schools across the country and includes instructional materials in five curriculum areas: mathematics, reading, science, handwriting, and spelling. A student receiving IPI usually works independently on the materials prescribed daily (or every few days) for him or her, depending on his or her demonstrated level of competence, learning style, and particular learning needs.

STEPS IN THE PROGRAM

IPI illustrates a modular curriculum developed by applying systems analysis procedures to curriculum materials development. It is a particularly useful case study because it readily demonstrates the steps the IPI planners took in creating the system. As we examine these steps, we stop briefly to show how each reflects the inner workings of the performance model.

First, in conceptualizing a performance model the planners operate with a set of goals and assumptions about the learner, the learning process, and the learner vis-à-vis the system in which he or she will work. The goals with respect to the learner are:

1. To enable each pupil to work at his own rate through units of study in a learning sequence.
2. To develop in each pupil a demonstrable degree of mastery.
3. To develop self-initiation and self-direction of learning.
4. To foster the development of problem-solving through processes.
5. To encourage self-evaluation and motivation for learning. (*Individually Prescribed Instruction*, 1966, p. 5)

The assumptions regarding the learning process and the related learning environment are as follows:

1. One obvious way in which pupils differ is in the amount of time and practice that it takes to master given instructional objectives.

2. One important aspect of providing for individual differences is to arrange conditions so that each student can work through the sequence of instructional units at his own pace and with the amount of practice he needs.

3. If a school has the proper types of study materials, elementary school pupils, working in a tutorial environment that emphasizes self-learning, can with a minimum amount of direct teacher instruction, learn.

4. In working through a sequence of instructional units, no pupil should be permitted to start work on a new unit until he has acquired a specified minimum degree of mastery of the material in the units identified as prerequisite to it.

5. If pupils are to be permitted and encouraged to proceed at individual rates, it is important for both the individual pupil and the teacher that the program provide for frequent evaluations of pupil progress which can provide a basis for the development of individual instructional prescriptions.

6. Professionally trained teachers are employing themselves most productively when they are performing such tasks as instructing individual pupils or small groups, diagnosing pupil needs, and planning instructional programs rather than carrying out such clerical duties as keeping records, scoring tests, and so on. The efficiency and economy of a school program can be increased by employing clerical help to relieve teachers of many non-teaching duties.

7. Each pupil can assume more responsibility for planning and carrying out his own program of study than is permitted in most classrooms.

8. Learning can be enhanced, both for the tutor and the one being tutored, if pupils are permitted to help one another in certain ways. (Lindvall and Bolvin, 1966, pp. 3–4)

The second step is to analyze the performance model into a set of sequentially organized behavioral objectives. IPI planners believe that such a listing is fundamental to other aspects of the program and must have the following characteristics:

a. Each objective should tell exactly what a pupil should be able to do to exhibit his mastery of the given content and skill. This should typically be something the average student can master in such a relatively short period as one class period. Objectives should involve such action verbs as solve, state, explain, list, describe, etc., rather than general terms such as understand, appreciate, know and comprehend.

b. Objectives should be grouped in meaningful streams of content. For example, in arithmetic the objectives will be grouped (typically) into such areas as numeration, place, value, addition, subtraction, etc. Such grouping aids in the meaningful development of instructional materials and in the diagnosis of pupil achievement. At the same time, this grouping does not preclude the possibility of having objectives that cut across areas.

c. Within each stream or area the objectives should to the extent possible, be sequenced in such an order that each one will build on those that precede it, and, in turn, be a prerequisite to those that follow. The goal here is to let the objectives constitute a "scale" of abilities.

d. Within the sequence of objectives in each area the objectives should be grouped into meaningful subsequences or units. Such units can be designated as representing different levels in progress and provide break-points so that when a student finishes a unit in that area, he may either go on to the next unit in that area or may switch to a unit in another area. (For example, upon completing

Level B Addition the pupil may either go on to Level C Addition or move on to Level B Subtraction.) (*Individually Prescribed Instruction*, 1966, p. 3)

Over 400 specific behavioral objectives are included in the thirteen topics of the mathematics curriculum. The following excerpt, one small series from the sequence, illustrates the minute detail of the plan:

LEVEL E   *LEVEL F*

Addition and Subtraction

1. Given any two whole numbers, the student adds or subtracts using the short algorithm.

2. Given an addition problem with ≤ 5 addends, the student solves using the short algorithm.

3. Given multiple step word problems requiring addition and subtraction skills mastered to this point, the student solves them.

1. Given any two numbers ≤ 9,999.99 and an operation of addition or subtraction, the student solves. LIMIT: Answers must be positive numbers.

2. Given ≤ 5 addends which are mixed decimals with ≤ 7 digits, the student adds. LIMIT: Decimals to millionths.

3. Given two mixed decimals, the student subtracts. LIMIT: ≤ 7 digits, decimals to millionths.

4. Solves multiple step word problems using addition and subtraction skills mastered to this point.

Multiplication

1. Given a two digit number and a one digit number, the student multiplies in horizontal form by using the distributive principle.

2. Given a problem with a three digit multiplicand and a one digit multiplier, the student solves using partial products.

3. Given a multiplication problem whose multipliers and multiplicands are whole numbers ≤ 10 times a multiple of ten, the student solves. LIMIT: Factors ≤ 9,000.

4. Given a multiplication problem whose multipliers are whole numbers < 10 times a power of ten, and whose multiplicand is 3 digits, the student solves. LIMIT: Multipliers ≤ 9,000.

5. Given a multiplication problem with a two digit number times a two digit number, the student solves using partial products.

1. Given a two digit number times a two digit number, the student multiplies using the standard algorithm.

2. Given a three digit number times a two digit number, the student multiplies using the standard algorithm.

3. Given a whole number and a mixed decimal to hundredths as factors, the student multiplies. LIMIT: Whole number part ≤ 100.

4. Given two pure decimals ≤ .99, the student multiplies and shows the equivalent problem in fractional form and converts product to decimal notation, compares answers for check.

5. Given a multiple step word problem requiring multiplication skills mastered to this point, the student solves.

LEVEL E

Multiplication

6. Given a two digit number and a one digit number, the student solves by using the multiplication algorithm.
7. Given a multiplication problem for skills to this point, the student checks the multiplication by commuting the factors and solving again.
8. Given a number ≤ 100, the student finds the complete factorization for the number. (*Individually Prescribed Instruction*, 1968)

Each of the thirteen areas has nine levels of difficulty, A through I. Within each level for a given topic area, several behavioral objectives are identified and sequentially organized. The breakdown of the thirteen topics into levels creates certain options for the student and teacher. The student can cover one area in depth before moving to the next or can go from Addition level E to Subtraction level E. We can see that the content for the IPI math program is spelled out in great detail, ordered sequentially, and interrelated well in advance of the time the teachers and students come together.

The third step in the program is to develop the materials that the students use to achieve each objective. These are mostly self-study materials that a student can pursue by himself or herself with minimal assistance from the teacher: in the mathematics curriculum, worksheets, individual pages, or lesson groups of pages. In addition to the self-instruction, the program calls on the teacher to offer some of his or her own instruction to small or large groups and to individuals. For instance, if several students are having difficulty successfully completing a particular objective, the teacher may bring them together for small-group instruction. The mathematics program makes the additional assumption that not all students learn equally well by the same approach. Some students may need more practice in the use of the concept, while others learn the concept more effectively by being given examples in which they must decide what is and what is not an instance of the concept. Still others have difficulty transferring behavior from one situation to another and need experience with a variety of formats for using the concept. For example, students can add two-digit numbers using a number line, an abacus, or memorized addition tables with rulers for carrying! To accommodate these differences, the mathematics materials for a given behavioral objective include a variety of approaches and formats.

The fourth step for the system planner is to bring together the components of the system—student, teacher, materials—so that the behavioral objectives are achieved. One program devoted a portion of the school day at the beginning of the academic year to testing:

It was essential to find out exactly what abilities each pupil had in each of the many areas in reading, arithmetic and science. In arithmetic for example, sequenced materials had been developed for each topic, such as numeration, measurement, addition, and subtraction. Because so many topics were involved and because it was necessary to know where a pupil should start in each of them, several days had to be devoted to diagnosis of pupil abilities.

On the basis of this diagnosis, a "prescription" was developed for each pupil in each subject. This prescription listed the materials that the pupil was to start with, which might be enough for one day, several days, or a week, depending on the ability of the student, and the difficulty of the unit. Evaluation and feedback, then, were built into the ongoing curricular activities. This is in contrast to many educational programs which depend heavily on periods of examination and the like that are separated from other curricular activities.

The faculty also developed a system for guiding the students as they worked. A student was to begin working on his prescribed materials usually by himself at a desk in a study area with eighty or ninety other pupils. In this room there were also two or three teachers to provide instructional assistance, and three or four clerks to distribute materials and grade papers. Most pupils were able to proceed through their study materials with a minimum of help from the teachers. If a teacher found a pupil who needed more help than she could give in this large-group situation, she directed him to a small side room where another teacher gave him more extensive individual help or involved him in small-group instruction. (Joyce and Harootunian, 1967, pp. 83–84)

Lastly comes the creation of a management system for monitoring the student's progress and adjusting prescriptions so that carefully tailored feedback, the heart of the cybernetic approach, can be given.

The materials prescribed for a student at any given time typically would include, as a final exercise, a "check test" or "curriculum embedded" test. This exercise, which the student viewed as just another worksheet, would play a large part in determining what the pupil did next. When a pupil completed his prescribed unit of work, he took it to a clerk for checking and then to the teacher who was developing the prescriptions. This teacher held a brief conference with the pupil, examined the work he had just completed, and then developed the next prescription. As we can see, the learner role variables are carefully defined and provision is made for developing them under this system. (Joyce and Harootunian, 1967, p. 84)

In this case the management system for tracking a pupil's progress and specifying the role of functionaries is embedded in the instructional system. As in business, the teacher-manager has the responsibility for bettering the system and adjusting it to the needs of the individual. The teacher's role in IPI is a crucial one. He or she serves as a "diagnostician (analyzing the IPI diagnostic data about each student in order to tailor a program to meet the individual learning needs), a selector (drawing on the bank of both human and material resources available to the IPI instructional situation), and a tutor (building meaningful and appropriate learning experiences that lead a student to a more independent and responsible role in his IPI learning setting)" (Scanlon and Brown, n.d., p. 1). This represents an organizational approach to teaching quite different from that of the self-contained classroom teacher working with the groups of children he or she sees every day and for whose education he or she maintains total responsibility.

LANGUAGE LABORATORY

Another prominent example of an instructional system, one in which the machine components paved the way for an entirely different learning environment, is the *language laboratory*. Its development represents vivid application of the combined properties of systems analysis, task analysis, and cybernetic principles in the educational setting. Before the language laboratory became commonplace, the classroom teacher served as the model for foreign speech in a classroom of twenty-five to thirty-five students who were trying to reproduce sounds of speech. The individual in such a situation might have a maximum of one minute of speech practice per classroom session, hardly enough to produce fluency or accuracy.

Today in the typical classroom laboratory, learners use electrical equipment to hear, record, and play back spoken materials. The general physical equipment includes student stations and an instructor's control panel. Through this panel, the teacher can broadcast a variety of content materials, new and remedial programs, and instruction to individuals, selected groups, or the entire class. He or she can also monitor the students' performance. The students' stations are often a series of individual, acoustically treated carrels, usually equipped with headphones, a microphone, and a tape recorder. Each student listens through the headphones to live or recorded directions from the instructor to repeat, answer questions, or make other appropriate responses to the lesson. The instructor may also choose to use the chalkboard, textbook, or other visual stimuli to supplement audio inputs. Modern technology has made it possible for almost instantaneous situations in which students might:

1. Hear their own voices more clearly through earphones than they could otherwise;
2. Directly compare their speech with a model's;
3. Provide themselves with immediate feedback;
4. Isolate items for study;
5. Permit pacing for specific drill;
6. Permit more finely sequenced instructional content.

Learning a foreign language requires that the student hear vocabulary and speech patterns repeatedly. The exercises are carefully sequenced and are followed by new combinations of varying complexity. The ultimate goal is to have the student readily comprehend what he or she hears and make immediate and appropriate responses. From the student's viewpoint the language laboratory serves as a base for tireless practicing of finely sequenced behavior, matching aural models, and developing speech fluency; from the instructor's viewpoint the language laboratory provides the facilities (hardware and software) for a more effective language-learning situation.

In systems analysis terminology, the language laboratory represents the development of a human-machine system based on the performance objectives and requirements of foreign language proficiency. Prior to the development of the language laboratory, it was possible to provide reasonably sequenced visual materials. But the critical elements of language training—individualized audial practice and dynamic feedback—far outran the human-management capacities and support facilities of the self-contained classroom teacher with twenty-five students. With electronic hardware and software support subsystems, the instructor can now divide his or her time more effectively between monitoring (management), diagnosis, and instruction. The student is provided immediate, direct sensory feedback so that he or she can compare his or her performance with the desired performance and make the necessary self-corrective adjustments.

DIRECT INSTRUCTION

ORIGINS

Although empirically derived, Direct Instruction has its theoretical origins in the behavioral family, particularly in the thinking of training and behavioral psychologists. Training psychologists have focused on training people to perform complex behaviors that involve a high degree of precision and often coordination with others—for example, being a crew member on a submarine. Their main contributions to learning situations are task definition and task analysis. The instructional design principles they propose focus on conceptualizing learner performance into goals or tasks, breaking these tasks into smaller component tasks, developing training activities that ensure mastery of each subcomponent, and, finally, arranging the entire learning situation into sequences that ensure adequate transfer from one component to another and achievement of prerequisite learning before more advanced learning.

Whereas training psychologists have emphasized the design and planning of instruction, behavioral psychologists address the interaction between teachers and students. They speak of modeling, reinforcement, feedback, and successive approximation, concepts discussed earlier, in the Introduction to the behavioral family of models. Behaviorists sometimes refer to their approach as "modeling with reinforced guided performance." In subsequent sections of this chapter, as we review the major findings regarding direct instruction, the similarity between the theoretical underpinnings of training and behavioral psychology and the empirical results from basic skills research become apparent.

GOALS AND ASSUMPTIONS

Direct instruction plays a limited but important role in a comprehensive educational program. Research on direct instruction indicates that this approach is effective in promoting student learning in reading and math, especially for students from lower socioeconomic backgrounds. In some studies the use of direct instruction also successfully improved students' self-concepts. Critics of direct instruction caution that this approach should not be used all the time, for all educational objectives, nor for all students. Indeed, later studies and reviews of research do point out that other teaching strategies may be more suitable for promoting such educational goals as abstract thinking, creativity, and problem solving (a conclusion entirely consistent with the point of view taken in this book!). In addition, slight variations in implementing the teaching strategy appear to enhance the effect for students of different ability levels.

Despite the cautions and the caveats, this model of teaching stands out as one with a relatively solid empirical track record. Even though the effects may not be large, the research does suggest that students tend to perform better on math and reading achievement tests under direct-instruction conditions. For students of lower ability the difference may be even greater. The Basic Practice Model is certainly one to consider when the goal is basic skills acquisition.

THE LEARNING ENVIRONMENT FOR DIRECT INSTRUCTION

Direct Instruction, like all teaching strategies, occurs within the larger context of the classroom environment. Because the model is highly structured and teacher directed, it would not flourish in an environment that could not support a traditional educational approach. Fortunately, teacher-effectiveness research provides some guidelines as to the environmental variables that promote successful implementation of a direct-instruction teaching strategy. These are academic focus, teacher direction and control, high expectations for pupil progress, time, and nonnegative affect.

Academic focus means one places highest priority on the assignment and completion of academic tasks. During instruction academic activity is emphasized; the use of nonacademic materials—for example, toys, games, and puzzles—is deemphasized or even discouraged, as is nonacademically oriented student-teacher interaction, such as questions about self or discussions of personal concern. Several studies have shown that a strong academic focus produces greater student engagement and, subsequently, achievement (Fisher, 1980; Madaus, Airasian, and Kellaghan, 1980; Rosenshine, 1970, 1979, 1980).

Teacher direction and control occur when the teacher selects and directs the learning tasks, determines grouping patterns, maintains a central role during instruction, keeps student choice and freedom at low levels, and minimizes the amount of nonacademic pupil talk. Teachers who have high expectations for their students and concern for academic progress demand academic excellence and behavior conducive to academic progress. They expect more of their students in terms of quantity and quality of work.

A major goal of direct instruction is the maximization of student learning time. Many teacher behaviors found to be associated with student achievement are in fact associated with student time on task and student rate of success, which in turn are associated with student achievement. Thus, the behaviors incorporated into Direct Instruction are designed to create a structured, academically oriented learning environment in which students are actively engaged (on task) during instruction and are experiencing a high rate of success (80 percent or better). Time spent by pupils in both these conditions is referred to as "academic learning time" (ALT). Since it appears to be highly related to pupil achievement, maximizing ALT is an important aspect of the strategy.

Finally, there is substantial evidence that negative affect inhibits student achievement (Soar and Soar, 1979; Rosenshine, 1980). Teachers who create an academic focus and avoid such negative practices as criticism of student behavior, screaming, sarcasm, and scolding and ridicule facilitate student learning. Research is less clear on the role of positive affect on student outcomes: Some students may benefit more from large amounts of praise than others; some types of praise are more effective than others (Brophy, 1985).

In summary, the direct-instruction environment is one in which there is a predominant focus on learning, and students are engaged in academic tasks a large percentage of time and achieve at a high rate of success. The social climate is positive and free of negative affect.

ORIENTATION TO THE MODEL

The term *direct instruction* has been used by researchers to refer to a pattern of teaching which consists of the teacher's explaining a new concept or skill to a large group of students, having them test their understanding by practicing under teacher direction (i.e., controlled practice), and encouraging them to continue to practice at their seats under teacher guidance (guided practice). More common terms for this pattern might be recitation and seatwork. As intuitive and familiar as this teaching pattern may seem, theory and research have done much to verify its effectiveness and to identify some fine points to better carry out this pattern; these are discussed next.

Before presenting and explaining new material, it is helpful to establish a framework for the lesson and orient the students to the new material. Structuring comments made at the beginning of a lesson are designed to clarify for the students the purposes, procedures, and actual content of the subsequent learning experience. Such comments are associated with improved student engagement during the learning activity and with overall achievement (Block, 1980; Coker, Medley, and Soar, 1980; Fisher et al., 1980; Medley, 1977). These orienting comments can take various forms including: (1) introductory activities that elicit students' relevant existing knowledge structures (Anderson, 1977), such as reviewing the previous day's work (Rosenshine, 1983); (2) discussing the objective of the lesson (Faw and Waller, 1976; Hartley and Davies, 1976); (3) providing clear, explicit directions about work to be done; (4) telling the students about the materials they will use and the activities they will be engaged in during the lesson; and (5) providing an overview of the lesson.

Once the context for learning has been established, instruction can begin with the presentation of the new concept or skill. Students' success in learning the new material has much to do with the thoroughness and quality of the teacher's initial explanation. We know from research that effective teachers spend more time explaining and demonstrating new material than less effective teachers (Rosenshine, 1983). Presentation practices that appear to facilitate learning include: (1) presenting material in small steps so that one point can be mastered at a time; (2) providing many, varied examples of the new skills or concepts; (3) modeling, or giving narrated demonstrations of the learning task; (4) avoiding digressions, staying on topic; and (5) reexplaining difficult points (Rosenshine, 1983). From research on concept learning we also know that when teaching a new concept it is important to clearly identify the characteristics (attributes) of the concept and to provide a rule or definition (or sequence of steps in skill learning). Finally, providing a visual representation of the concept or skill along with the verbal explanation assists students in following the explanation. Later, at other points in the learning process, the visual representation serves as a cue or prompt.

Following the explanation comes the recitation in which the teacher checks for students' understanding of the new concept or skill. A common error is simply to ask students if they understand or have any questions and then to assume that if no one or only a few students respond everyone understands well enough to move on to seatwork. Effective teachers ask more questions that check for student understanding than less effective teachers (Rosenshine, 1983). Such questions call for specific answers or ask for explanations of how answers were found. According to Rosenshine, effective teachers not only asked more questions, but they also spent more time on teacher-led practice and on repeating the new material they were teaching. Other aspects of effective questioning behavior for direct-instruction approaches are: (1) asking convergent, as opposed to divergent, questions (Rosenshine, 1976, 1983); (2) ensuring that all students get a chance to respond—not just those who raise their hands or call out the loudest; this can be accomplished by calling on students in a patterned order, as in reading groups, calling the students' names first, before asking them questions, or calling for a choral response (Gage and Berliner, 1979); (Rosenshine, 1983); (3) asking questions within students' "reach" a high percentage of the time (75 to 90 percent)(Rosenshine, 1983); (4) teacher initiating questions most of the time, not the students (Fisher et al., 1980; Medley, 1977); and (5) avoiding nonacademic questions during direct instruction (Rosenshine, 1979; Soar and Soar, 1979).

Once the teacher has initiated a question and a student has responded, the teacher needs to give the student feedback on his or her response. Research indicates that effective teachers do a better job of providing feedback than do noneffective ones (Rosenshine, 1983). They do not let errors go uncorrected, nor do they simply give the answers to students who have responded incorrectly. They use techniques for correcting responses or they reteach the material. In addition, effective teachers maintain a brisk pace during this recitation activity. When they provide corrective feedback or reteach, they do it efficiently so that many practice opportunities are provided and many students have the opportunity to respond. For example, when a correct answer has been given, the teacher simply asks a new question. In the early stages of learning, when answers may be correct but somewhat tentative, the teacher provides knowledge of results and quick-process feedback ("Very good. You remembered that 'i' goes before 'e' when it comes after 'c.'") If the student has carelessly provided an incorrect answer, the teacher provides corrective feedback and moves on. If the incorrect response indicated lack of understanding, the teacher should provide hints or clues, such as referring back to the visual representation. It is important to probe for clarification and improved answers. Effective feedback is academically oriented, not behaviorally oriented (Berliner, 1980; Fisher et al, 1980). It is also substantive in that it tells students *what* they have done correctly. Feedback may be combined with praise; however, it is important that praise be deserved based on the quality of the response (Gage and Berliner, 1979). Students differ in the amount of praise they need; some students, particularly low-achieving students, need a lot, whereas others do not need as much. Even if a student's need for praise is great, he or she should not be praised for an incorrect response (Brophy, 1985).

To summarize, the kind of feedback students receive during structured practice has much to do with their later success. Feedback helps students find out how well they understand the new material and what their errors are. To be effective, feedback must be academic, corrective, respectful, and deserved.

The need for students to be given thorough explanations and structured practice with feedback before they begin their seatwork seems obvious. However, it is clear both from the research and from the authors' own experiences that students are often asked to work from their texts or workbooks with almost no explanation and/or practice. Students need to have a high degree of success when they are engaged in seatwork. In order for this to occur, they should move from structured practice to seatwork only when they have achieved about 90 percent accuracy on the structured-practice examples.

In the average classroom, students spend between 50 percent and 75 percent of their time working alone on seatwork (Rosenshine, 1983). If this large amount of time is to be productively directed toward learning, then students need to remain engaged in the learning task. What helps most toward engagement is being well prepared, before beginning seatwork, by the teacher's presentation and by teacher-led practice. Seatwork that is directly related to the presentation and that occurs right after teacher-led practice facilitates student engagement. It is also helpful for the teacher to circulate during seatwork, monitoring individual students with relatively short contacts (Rosenshine, 1983).

PRACTICE THEORY

As its name implies, the "heart" of this teaching strategy is its practice activities; three phases of the model deal with practice under varying conditions of assistance. Over the years considerable research has been devoted to studying the role of practice in the acquisition of new knowledge and the conditions of practice which facilitate retention of information. From this literature we have identified six principles of effective practice.

The first principle is that of *shaping*. The goal of all practice is mastery, the ability to perform a skill independently and without error. When the principle of shaping is adhered to, the teacher moves the student through practice with different levels of assistance: lock step or structured, semiindependent or guided, and independent or homework. This practice progression ensures appropriate support for the student to experience success at each practice level until independence is achieved.

The three levels of practice function in the following manner: When the students are first introduced to a new skill or concept, the teacher leads the group through each step in working out the problem. This lock-step method ensures that few errors are produced in the initial learning stages when memory is most vulnerable to remembering incorrect practice and when errors reinforce incorrect information. After lock-step or structured practice, the students practice on their own at their seats while the teacher monitors. During this time the teacher provides corrective feedback for any errors produced as well as reinforcement for correct practice. When students are able to practice with accuracy, they are ready for independent practice—that is, for practice under conditions when assistance is not available in the environment. Homework is an example of independent practice. This last step in the practice progression is the mastery level; students are performing the skill independently with minimal error.

The second practice principle has to do with the length of each practice session. Research indicates that, on the whole, the more a person practices a skill the longer it takes him or her to forget it. However, this relationship is affected by the length of time recommended for practice. The general principle guiding the length of time recommended for practice is: *Short, intense, highly motivated practice periods* produce more learning than fewer but longer practice periods. For example, with younger students, short, five- to ten-minute practice sessions interspersed over the day or a series of days will be more effective than long thirty- to forty-minute sessions. Older students have longer attention spans and are able to handle longer practice sessions; however, all practice sessions should be monitored so that boredom and apathy do not undercut their effectiveness.

The third principle is the need to *monitor the initial stage* of practice because incorrect performance at this stage will interfere with learning. Students need corrective feedback to prevent incorrect procedures from becoming embedded in their memories. Immediate corrective feedback (i.e., information on how to perform correctly) will reverse misconceptions early in the instructional process. It also reduces performance anxiety because students practice with the assurance of immediate feedback. In addition to catching incorrect performance in the early stages, it is also important to reinforce correct performance. This gives students the knowledge of results that stabilizes the new learning more quickly.

Having students achieve an 85 to 90 percent *level of accuracy* at the current practice level before going to the next level is the fourth practice principle. Paying attention to accuracy rates ensures that students experience success and do not practice errors.

The fifth principle is that of *distributed practice,* or multiple practice sessions spread out over a period of time. Research shows that without practice to reinforce it 80 percent of new information is forgotten within twenty-four hours. With periodic reviews spread out over an extended period of time, such as four or five months, nearly all new information can be retained. The effect is cumulative: The more information a person has stored in memory, the easier it is for him or her to learn new information. This is because more items of information are available from which to form memory connections. People with fewer items of information in memory have less capacity to remember new information.

The last principle addresses the issue of the optimal *amount of time between practice sessions.* The general guideline is that practice periods should be close together at the beginning of learning; once learning is at an independent level, then the practice sessions can be spaced farther and farther apart. Thus, guided practice sessions should occur immediately after new learning has been introduced and should continue frequently until independence is achieved. When this has occurred independent practice sessions can be distributed farther apart—that is, one, two, six, and then fifteen days apart.

To summarize, successful practice is founded upon six principles: shaping, short and intense practice sessions, monitoring of practice, requisite accuracy level of 85 to 90 percent, distribution of practice, and appropriate length of time between practice. A practice plan designed upon these principles greatly enhances the chances for mastery of new learning.

THE MODEL OF TEACHING

SYNTAX

The Basic Practice Model consists of five phases of activity: orientation, presentation, structured practice, guided practice, and independent practice (see Figure 18-1). However, the use of this model should be preceded by effective diagnosis of students' knowledge or skills to be sure that they have the prerequisite knowledge or skills to achieve high levels of accuracy in the different practice conditions.

Phase one is the orientation phase in which a framework for the lesson is established. During this phase the teacher's expectations are communicated, the learning task is clarified, and student accountability is established. Three steps are particularly important in carrying out the intent of this phase: (1) the teacher provides the objective of the lesson and the level of performance; (2) the teacher describes the content of the lesson and its relationship to prior knowledge and/or experience; and (3) the teacher discusses the procedures of the lesson—that is, the different parts of the lesson and students' responsibilities during those activities.

Phase two is the presentation phase in which the teacher explains the new concept or skill through demonstrations and examples. If the material is a new concept, it is important that the teacher discuss the characteristics (or *attributes*) of the concept, the rule or definition, and several examples. If the material is a new skill, it is important to identify the steps of the skill with examples of each step. In either case, it is helpful to convey this information both orally and visually so that students will have the visual representation as a reference in the early stages of learning. The latter is sometimes called a *visual representation of the task* (VRT). Another part of this phase is checking to see that students have understood the new information before they apply it in the practice phases. Can they recall the attributes of the concept that the teacher has explained? Can they recall the number and list of steps in the skill they have just been shown? Checking for understanding (CFU) requires that students recall or recognize the information that they have just heard. Next, in structured practice, they will apply it. Several techniques can be used to check for understanding: *sampling,* questions directed toward the entire group but responses given by only a sample of students; *signaling,* questions directed toward the entire group with responses from everyone through signaling agreement or disagreement; *individual private response,* questions directed to

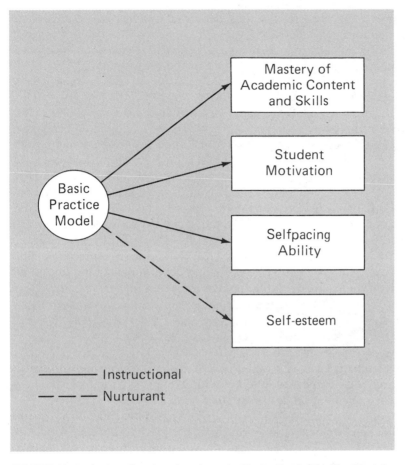

FIGURE 18-1   Instructional and nurturant effects: Basic Practice Model.

everyone with instructions to write responses; then students' responses checked privately. A clear, thorough explanation is crucial to students' success in applying the new information. The three parts of a presentation just described will contribute to an effective explanation.

Structured practice is phase three of the strategy. In structured practice the teacher leads students through practice examples working in a lock-step fashion each step of the problem as it appears on the VRT. The students practice as a group, offering or writing answers. A good way to accomplish the lock-step technique is to use an overhead projector, doing practice examples on a transparency so that all students can see the generation of each step. The teacher's role in this phase is to give feedback on the students' responses, to reinforce accurate responses, and to correct errors. The VRT is available. In referring to it while working the practice examples, the teacher is ensuring that students understand it so that they can use it as a resource during their semiindependent practice phase.

Phase Four, guided practice, presents students the opportunity to practice on their own while the teacher is still in the environment. Most of us recognize this activity as seatwork. Guided practice enables the teacher to make an assessment of the students' abilities to perform the learning task by assessing the amount and types of errors the students are making. The teacher's role in this phase is to monitor students' work, providing corrective feedback when necessary. Although this function might seem self-explanatory, research studies have shown that some teachers perform this role more effectively than others. Common but not optimal monitoring practices include having students come to the teacher and/or having the teacher move around, but help only a few students—the ones who typically get most of the help. A better way to monitor is to use a specific corrective feedback technique called "praise, prompt, and leave." In this technique the teacher moves around the room systematically and efficiently, checking students' work. The teacher tells *each* student whether he or she has done an item or part of a practice correctly; if there are errors, the teacher reteaches to *one* error and refers the student to the VRT. The corrective feedback interaction lasts about a half a minute or less. In a class of thirty students and a practice activity of thirty minutes, every student can receive feedback at least twice!

Independent practice is the last phase of the Basic Practice Model. It begins when students have achieved an accuracy level of 85 to 90 percent in guided practice. The purpose of independent practice is to reinforce the new learning to ensure retention as well as to develop fluency. In independent practice students practice on their own without assistance and with delayed feedback. This can be done in the classroom, if the teacher is not involved, but is usually done at home. The teacher's role in this phase is to make sure the independent practice work is reviewed soon after completion to assess if the students' accuracy level has remained stable and to provide corrective feedback for those who need it. Independent-practice activities can be short in length of time and number of practice items; however, it should not be a one-time venture. As described earlier, five or six practice sessions distributed over a month or more will sustain retention.

APPLICATION

The evidence and examples of direct instruction come from several sources, including the studies of effective teachers mentioned earlier as well as educational programs specifically designed on a direct-instruction model. The evaluation of Project Follow Through, a federal program which extended Head Start into the elementary grades, has much to tell us about the relative effectiveness of different approaches for students from disadvantaged backgrounds. When the evaluation was complete, two programs stood out as promoting greater achievement in reading and math. Both of these programs were based on a direct-instruction approach.

One of these, the University of Oregon's Direct Instruction Model, produced more significant differences on both cognitive and affective measures than any of the other eight major programs (Becker, 1977). Overall, the students in this program went from being well below the 25th percentile in reading, math, and spelling before starting the program, to being in the 50th percentile or above (the national norm) by the third grade. Becker offers the following description of the Oregon program.

> The major goal of the Direct Instruction Model is to improve basic education of children from economically disadvantaged backgrounds and thus increase their life options. Developed by Bereiter and Becker, the model has its roots in Bereiter and Engelman's experimental preschool and in Becker's behavioral research on classroom management. The model emphasizes small-group, face to face instruction by a teacher using carefully sequenced, daily lessons in reading, arithmetic and language. The lessons utilize modern learning principles and advanced programming strategies (Becker, Engelmann & Thomas, 1975a, 1975b)... A positive self-concept was viewed as a by-product of good teaching rather than as a goal that be achieved in the abstract. (Becker, 1977, p. 921–922)

The University of Oregon model reflects nearly all the elements of the Basic Practice Model discussed earlier. Highly structured, teacher-directed lessons begin the learning. Before new material is introduced, previous material is reviewed and/or checked. To ensure appropriate sequencing of material and selection of examples, the teacher presentations have been scripted. Thus, the quality of explanation and the nature and length of structured practice are regulated. Signals (VRTs in our terminology) are provided as part of the script with instructions on how and when to use these cues to prompt students' responses. During structured practice students give a group (or choral) response, alternating occasionally with individual responses. The program outlines specific correction procedures and provides additional teaching (reteaching) material. The main guidelines are to teach new material in small steps, practice to the point of overlearning, and reteach, if necessary.

Student materials form the basis for guided practice. Published under the trade name DISTAR, the student materials coordinate with the teacher materials. They are composed of nine curricular strands covering the areas of reading, mathematics, and language.

Two other elements of direct instruction stand out in the University of Oregon model: reinforcement and review and assessment. Positive reinforcement is strongly encouraged to enhance student motivation; negative behavior is ignored. Generally, reinforcement is in the form of praise, attention, or success; however, if necessary at the beginning of instruction, a token system may be used and later phased out. Becker and his associates have developed training manuals on the principles and procedures of reinforcement.

Periodic reviews and recycling of instruction are also part of the model, as are continuous progress tests. The latter are used to produce biweekly reports of students' progress in reading, math, and language. These reports from the basis for changes in students' instructional groups.

Summary Chart Basic Practice Model

Phase One:
Orientation
Teacher establishes content of the lesson.
Teacher reviews previous learning.
Teacher establishes lesson objectives.
Teacher establishes the procedures for the lesson.

Phase Two:
Presentation
Teacher explains/demonstrates new concept or skill.
Teacher provides visual representation of the task.
Teacher checks for understanding.

Phase Three:
Structured Practice
Teacher leads group through practice examples in lock step.
Students respond to questions.
Teacher provides corrective feedback for errors and reinforces correct practice.
Teacher refers to VRT.

Phase Four:
Guided Practice
Students practice semiindependently.
Teacher circulates, monitoring student practice.
Teacher provides feedback through praise, prompt, and leave.
Teacher refers student to VRT as a resource.

Phase Five:
Independent Practice
Students practice independently at home or in class.
Feedback is delayed.
Independent practices occur several times over an extended period.

19

LEARNING SELF-CONTROL
Using Feedback to Modify Behavior

SCENARIO

John is a bright, verbal, second grader who is perhaps slightly hyperactive. He is popular with his classmates and entertains them with endless stories, some true and some slightly exaggerated. John does pretty well in his studies: He is a good reader but has difficulty with math. For the past few months Jean Meades, John's teacher, has been struggling to encourage John to persist in his schoolwork. John is always up, wandering around the room or going to the pencil sharpener, aquarium, or hamster cage. More often, he is distracting another student. The problem is that when John comes to a math problem he does not understand he complains out loud: "I don't understand," or "This doesn't make sense." Then he calls out for Jean, "Ms. Meades, I don't get this." If Jean is not at his side promptly, showing John how to do the problem, he flips his pencil in the air, whistles, and gazes at the ceiling for awhile, coming to rest by engaging his neighbor in conversation. If that does not work, he is off to the aquarium.

Jean would like John to make more of an attempt to stick with a math problem longer before he calls for assistance. Although John's jumping up and calling for assistance occur throughout the whole day, Jean decides to concentrate on the math situation.

During math the students are grouped roughly according to their abilities. Each child has a set of worksheets. Generally the children work alone more or less at their own pace. A few times each week Ms. Meades or the teacher's aid instructs the group in a new concept or principle. When the students have finished designated segments, their work is checked.

For a few days Ms. Meades pays close attention to John's behavior during math. She observes that on the average he calls out or comes up to her or the aid about ten times during the forty-minute work period. He devotes about ten minutes to actual work on his own. Knowing that John needs and wants a lot of adult reinforcement, Jean makes a deal with him.

She explains her observations to John and says she wants to work out a new system. She asks John to try at least three problems before asking for help. When he does need help he should raise his hand, and either Jean or the aid will come as soon as she can. In the meantime, John can work on a drawing (he is a very good artist and enjoys doodling). Every time John follows the procedure he gets a point. If he actually completes three problems correctly he gets two points. At the end of the week John's points are totaled. Depending on the number accumulated he gets to select activities of his choice. Initially, Jean insists that John work on math for only part of the math period, or on nine problems. As time goes on she adjusts the reward schdule to increase his work time and accomplishment.

Before beginning the program Jean worked with John on how to approach an unfamiliar problem. She gave him a general, three-step sequence to follow for any math problem. One of John's difficulties is that he looks at a problem, goes blank, and gives up. Jean tries to increase his capacity for reflective thought by giving him a general problem-solving approach. In addition, each step in the sequence has a corresponding color-numbered block. For a while John uses these to remind him to do the steps. He starts out with the blocks on the right side, and as he takes each step he moves the block over to the left. The manipulative activity helps ease the anxiety generated by the "blank mind"; it literally takes his mind off his feelings and onto his math and his hands.

Jean does one more thing. She makes sure that at first either she or the aid frequently passes by John's desk to compliment him for attempting the problems (if he is) and to check his work without his asking.

The contingency management program is instituted. It takes a few days for John to follow the procedures agreed upon, but Jean and the aid are very consistent in reminding him of the rules. After a while the distractable (and distracting) becomes less frequent. John's ability to try problems and continue to work at them markedly improves, so much, in fact, that within a few weeks the number of problems solved before John needs assistance increases to five. In addition, when John does need assistance he is not so helpless. He can tell Jean the steps he followed, what he had figured out, and where he is stuck. Jean also notices that John's attention span and ability to sit quietly without talking is maintained in other activities, not just math.

Jean alerts John's parents to the plan so that at the end of the week he will report to them his point count and the rewards. The program gives John's parents a nice way to follow his progress and talk to him about the school day.

Contingency management, which has been used in educational settings more than other applications of behavior theory, can be found in the conceptualizations of entire classroom environments and educational programs, such as Pittsburgh's Primary Education Project, which stresses the behavioral analysis of learning tasks (Resnick, 1967), Bereiter and Englemann's DISTAR program (Bereiter and Englemann, 1966; Englemann, Osborn, and Englemann, 1972), and Bushell's behavior analysis Follow-Through classrooms (Bushell, 1970). In these instances all aspects of the learning environment—physical, material, interactive—are perceived and planned for in terms of behavioral principles. Other applications of behavior theory focus on specific individuals within a classroom and the identification and treatment of specific maladaptive responses. In these instances contingency management stresses tailoring its programs to individuals, placing particular emphasis on reinforcement. Programmed learning is a third application of behavior theory and emphasizes control of the learning stimuli, which are carefully sequenced in relatively small steps. Finally, the use of contingency management for the self-control of behavior is a fourth and increasingly popular use.

ORIENTATION TO THE MODEL

CONCEPTS

Behavior theorists perceive human behavior as a function of the immediate environment—specifically, an eliciting stimulus and a reinforcing stimulus. The essential feature is the relationship between the response and reinforcing stimuli. If the reinforcement is presented when and only when the response appears, we say it is *contingent. Contingency management,* then, is the systematic control of reinforcing stimuli such that it is presented at selected times and only after the desired response has been given. People who set up contingency management programs must be aware of desirable responses as well as undesirable responses. They also must take into account the eliciting stimuli, carefully observing what triggers maladaptive responses. Often the environment can be arranged so that undesirable *cues* are minimized, and cues that facilitate desirable behaviors are enhanced. For example, people who overeat know that they are asking for trouble when they balance their checkbooks in the kitchen. Similarly, teachers know that play stimuli can be distracting to some students while they are accomplishing work-oriented tasks, so they remove these stimuli from the immediate surroundings. Students who need more attention are instructed in smaller groups. Teachers also take advantage of positive cuing when they nonverbally remind students of the appropriate responses. A friend of ours wears a yellow scarf when she is in a bad mood, alerting her husband that this is not a good time to make demands or ask for favors.

Contingency management is based on the operant principle that behavior is influenced by the consequences that follow. For an operant or contingent relationship to be established, *reinforcing consequences* must follow. If a behavior is not reinforced, it will become extinct. A *reinforcer,* then, is a consequence that increases the probability of a particular response. Desirable reponses can be strengthened through both *positive* and *negative* reinforcements. A reinforcement is positive if its addition to the environment, such as a smile, a hug, or a deadline, produces the adaptive responses. A reinforcement is negative if its removal from the situation following a response produces the desirable behavior. Yelling, threatening, and nagging are examples of negative reinforcers. They do work. After a while most of us will respond to requests if only to stop these aversive stimuli. The problem with negative reinforcers, or *punishment,* is that the effects are less predictable than those of positive reinforcement. While they might produce impressive changes at the beginning, the side effects are often undesirable, such as hating school, disliking the punisher, or developing a poor self-concept. Programs based on behavior theory emphasize positive reinforcement, specifically discouraging the use of negative or aversive stimuli except in rare instances (Rimm and Masters, 1974).

Reinforcers can be social, material, and activity. Many of these reinforcers occur naturally in the environment, although not systematically and often for undesirable behavior. For instance, even though, as teachers, we have been told not to respond in a particular way we still laugh at the show off, scowl at the bully, and acknowledge the student who speaks out the quickest and loudest, often ignoring the ones who raise their hands.

Most reinforcing events are social—a smile, a hug, praise, attention, approval, or physical contact. Social reinforcers work especially well with young children. Few children are totally unresponsive to social stimuli, but some are more so than others. In his research using contingency management with autistic children, Lovaas has demonstrated that such asocial individuals will gradually become more sociably responsive by pairing social reinforcers with an existing material reinforcer such as candy. Not all social reinforcers are verbal praise. Facial expressions such as a wink or interested look, nearness to an important person who is sharing time and conversation, and physical contact such as walking arm in arm or sitting on the teacher's lap are all rewarding.

Material reinforcers can be consumable, such as candy and other foods, toys, pictures, or music. Tokens, which can then be exchanged for prizes or privileges, are also given as reinforcers. Gold stars are a classic classroom reinforcer. Money, of course, is always a valued material reinforcer.

The last group of reinforcers is called activity reinforcers. In 1965 Premack made a formal principle called the Premack principle. Essentially it says that you can get people to engage in one activity if you promise them the privilege of engaging in another more desirable activity when they are finished (Premack, 1965). Teachers use this principle all the time when they give students free time after completing their work. Grownups too reward themselves with a big treat when they have worked hard to accomplish a difficult task. Common activity reinforcers for children include being read to, recess, games, going first, and watching television.

Choosing an appropriate reinforcer involves some careful thought and attention to individual preferences. Careful behavioral observation is an indispensable tool to identifying the best reinforcer. Often the stimulus that elicits the maladaptive behavior gives a good clue as to the best reinforcer.

We noted earlier that for a response to be established, it must be followed by a reinforcement. However, reinforcement can be delivered on several bases. Depending on the purpose some *reinforcement schedules* are more advantageous than others. *Continuous reinforcement* is the application of reinforcement after every emission of the desirable response. Although it is often inconvenient, continuous reinforcement is the quickest way to establish a new behavior and is very useful in the initial learning phases. More than likely, reinforcement is *intermittent*—that is, it occurs reliably in relationship to the desirable response either after a period of time (interval schedule) or after a certain number of desirable responses (ratio schedule). Both types of intermittent schedules can be *fixed* or *variable*.

Most naturally occurring reinforcement schedules are variable. Teachers are aware of the student responses they want to establish and periodically reinforce them. For example, when students are completing their seatwork, teachers will often praise on-task behavior or, when gathering a group, the teacher will acknowledge students who are seated and attentive, both reinforcing that behavior and establishing a model for other students. Variable reinforcement produces a moderate response rate, but the respondent behaviors are highly resistant to extinction. It is wise to use continuous reinforcement schedules initially in establishing a behavior and, as the behavior becomes more "intrinsic," to switch to a variable reinforcement schedule to enhance its duration.

A word of caution is in order with respect to the expectations for reinforcement. Although it is true that contingency management has had an impressive, well-documented history (probably more so than most models of instruction), with many facets of learning and many types of learners, reinforcement is not effective all the time with every student. Certain elements contribute to the success of reinforcement (Rimm and Masters, 1974, pp. 177–185). For example, younger children tend to respond more to social reinforcers than do older children or adults. The nature of the reinforcing agent is a factor; high-status adults are more effective reinforcers than low-status adults; an adult with whom someone has a good relationship is a more effective reinforcer than one with whom that person has a poor, discordant relationship. Sometimes there is simply too much reinforcement in the environment, and a saturation point is reached. People deprived of positive reinforcement tend to respond well to it. Finally, people have different personality styles; contingency-management principles may work better with some people's learning styles than with others' (Spaulding and Papageorgio, 1975).

CONTINGENCY-MANAGEMENT PROCEDURES

Contingency management, used either as a basis for organizing the learning environment or for altering the behavior of individuals, consists generally of the same procedures: (1) specifying final performance; (2) assessing entering behavior (establishing baseline); (3) formulating a contingency-management program; (4) instituting the program; and (5) evaluating the program.

Phase one, *specifying the final performance*, entails a general recognition that a behavior needs to be changed or accomplished. The behavior can involve descriptive or maladaptive habits or actions, or the acquisition of particular skills and knowledge. However, before a contingency-management program can be developed it is necessary to (1) specify precisely the behavior to be altered and the responses to be enforced (or the behavioral objectives, in the case of subject-matter acquisition); and (2) develop a procedure for measuring the behavior. Classrooms conducted on a behavioral analysis model normally use highly structured, well-defined educational programs in which progress is monitored continuously as part of the design of the curriculum. Behaviors may be measured by *specimen description*, direct observational reports in which the observer records the time and occurrence of each behavior, or by *time sampling*, observing once every time period—perhaps five minutes—noting whether the behavior has occurred. The important point is that definition of the target behavior and evaluation (or assessment) are part of the same conceptual task.

Phase two, actual *assessment of the entering behavior*, comes after the target behavior has been identified and defined and preliminary plans for measuring it have been developed. Sometimes this phase is referred to as *establishing a baseline*. It is the actual recording of the frequency of behavior; in the case of maladaptive behaviors, its purpose is to confirm the initial diagnosis and give information about the maintaining conditions and stimuli. For this reason it is important to record not only when a behavior occurs but under what conditions and to whom—for example, one might note that one child hits younger children during free play. Academic behaviors are usually assessed by tests so that students can be placed at the appropriate steps in the learning sequence for their skill levels. For example, a student may be given fifteen long-division problems to complete in fifteen minutes. His or her performance can be calculated in terms of the number correct or the number of errors.

Baseline data are useful because they help determine where to begin instruction and the rate of progress or effectiveness of the contingency program. Once the behavior has been recorded, it is best to plot it on a graph (see Figure 19-1). In some classrooms students keep their own progress charts, a procedure that tends to be highly reinforcing.

The third phase is to *formulate a contingency management program* for a particular behavior or set of behaviors. This involves (1) structuring the situation; (2) selecting reinforcers; and (3) formulating behavior-shaping plans. In a classroom, attention must be given to the physical environment, the learning materials, and interactive features, all of which can facilitate the acquisition of responses. We know an enthusiastic teacher who concentrates on managing one or two hyperactive youngsters. She works hard at setting limits and reinforcing their positive behavior, but she has failed to notice that her general manner of speaking is very excitatory, almost like a spell-binding television character. She also asks many rhetorical questions to capture students' interest. When she communicates in this way, the two students become absorbed in the atmosphere and begin to talk out in response to the questions. Other youngsters are easily distracted and need the classroom arranged in a manner that minimizes such distractions.

We have already mentioned the role of some learning materials in presenting discrete, highly sequenced material with provision for immediate feedback. The selection of reinforcers is something that must be tailored for each person, though some reinforcers, particularly activity reinforcers, seem to work for most people. Finally, the planning of the contingency management program must account for gradual progress toward the terminal behavior. A procedure known as *behavior shaping* refers to the reinforcement of responses for behaviors that approximate the desired behaviors. Parents do this by rewarding beginning speech that sounds like the referrent—for in-

FIGURE 19-1 Plotting baseline graph.

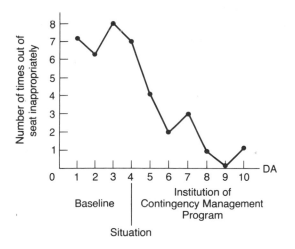

stance *Da* for father. Tennis coaches reward beginners for swinging correctly or simply getting the ball over the net. Teachers praise beginning handwriting that resembles the correct letter. Even more elaborate and systematic shaping is designed for desensitization programs. Sometimes cues are used to help discriminate. One first grade classroom has different colored lines within a single letter to remind students of the different writing strokes and which come first when they print the letter. Gradually behavior-shaping procedures should involve withdrawing the cues.

The fourth phase is to *institute the contingency management program.* This includes actually arranging the environment, making the contingency announcement, and reinforcing the students' responses according to the reinforcement schedule and shaping program that have been selected.

Some behavioral practitioners do not believe it is necessary for the respondent to be aware of the target behavior and reinforcers. This is particularly true with more subtle forms of social reinforcement, such as praise for attentiveness. With other contingency-management programs it is necessary (and useful) to make the student aware of the desirable responses and reinforcers, as in a token environment or the case of free play. Many teachers prefer to have students aware of the desirable behaviors—for example, "I like the way Susan has cleared her desk and is ready for listening." or "Thank you, Brian, for waiting patiently while I helped Donald with his work." The research literature on the role of awareness is not conclusive. However, the importance of cognition in self-control and psychological development is gaining increasing respect among clinical psychologists. Many therapists have come to believe that mediating cognitive responses play a large role in calling forth unpleasant feelings and subsequent behaviors; for example, we tell ourselves that dangerous prowlers are about and imagine such scenes, creating feelings of anxiety and avoidance of going out. When students take exams or practice in their workbooks, they say, "I can't do it," feel discouraged, frustrated, and angry, and stop working. Our tendency is to encourage teachers to discuss the "problem-behavior sequence" with students and inform them, whenever appropriate, of the desirable response, or of the entire contingency management program. We believe that this will foster the students' own cognitive controls, both in terms of the adaptive behavior and their images of themselves. Of course, this depends on the problem behavior, the student, the relationship with the teacher, and the reinforcer. For example, teachers usually do not inform students of social reinforcers, they just supply them.

A technique that is sometimes used quite effectively, especially in the classroom, is called *time-out.* Technically this involves the withdrawal of all reinforcing consequences, usually by having the individual move to a place without objects or people. Sometimes students will ask other students to leave a group until they feel they are ready to come back. Ignoring disruptive behavior (a student who is interrupting others) or taking away a material reinforcer (a pencil with which the student is fiddling) are also forms of time-outs. In our experience this procedure gives students a chance to collect themselves and make the choice to join the group activity. It can be used very punitively and without choice, or very calmly as a mutual decision that helps students take responsibility for their behavior.

The last phase in contingency management is *evaluating the program*. Most behaviorists regard this as validating the program's success. Often this evaluation is built into the program—for example, if people are obviously not fearful in situations that previously made them fearful or if students have maintained a high rate of progress and level of performance in a math program that has frequent evaluation measures. One of the main characteristics of behavioral-analysis environments is the deliberate structuring for and awareness of evaluation. Of course, evaluation is facilitated by initially specifying desirable behaviors in precise terms by devising or identifying measurement procedures. In some cases, particularly in behavioral research, reinforcement is discontinued for awhile and then reinstated. Behavior is recorded under both conditions.

GOALS AND ASSUMPTIONS

The ultimate goal of any contingency management program is transferability of the behaviors to similar new situations. Implicit in this goal is durability; the new adaptive behaviors will become intrinsic and under the individual's self-control and self-monitoring.

Contingency management has many uses, including reducing undesirable behaviors such as those associated with hyperdependency, aggression, passivity, depression, withdrawal, and general off-task activities. Sometimes these behaviors need removal from their reinforcing consequence. Often, however, individuals need to substitute new, more adaptive ways of behaving. Contingency management might well be used to reduce maladaptive behaviors, and other behavioral models employed to develop the new skills. However, this model is also valuable in developing new behaviors, such as academic skills, social skills, and self-management skills, and it is a valuable tool for altering emotional responses, such as reducing fears or eliminating anxiety. Finally, contingency management is effective in strengthening and maintaining existing desirable behaviors (Rimm and Masters, 1974).

THE MODEL OF TEACHING

The Contingency Management Model of teaching follows the five procedures discussed earlier in some detail: specifying a final performance, assessing entering behavior, formulating a program, instituting the program, and evaluating the program. The activities in each are summarized in the following section.

SYNTAX

The objective of phase one is to define the target behavior, the final behavioral outcome desired. Two activities must be accomplished at this point: (1) specifying the actual behavior outcome and (2) developing plans for measuring the behavior. Two relatively simple means of measuring and recording behavior are the *behavior specimen* and the *time sample*. A sample of a behavioral specimen from Rimm and Masters appears in Table 19–1. Another way to record is imply to observe the student once every ten minutes and to record the presence of the targeted behavior—for example, nailbiting. Modifications on the time sample may include noting the activity during the time period and noting the number of occurrences of the behavior in a particular time segment. The choice of measuring schemes depends on the behavior to be observed and other practical considerations. For instance,

Table 19–1   Instances of Tantrum Behavior and Parental Responses to Tantrum over a Seven-Day Period: Sample Behavior Chart

DAYS	TANTRUMS	DURATION (MINUTES)	RESPONSE
1	1	4	Comforted child when he slipped and banged head during crying
2	1	5	Told child to be quiet but finally gave cookie to quiet down
	1	6	Ignored until couldn't stand it, gave cookie
3	1	5	Ignored
	2	6	Ignored
	3	8	Ignored until child took cookie himself, spanked child
4	1	4	Ignored; child stopped spontaneously
5	1	4	Company present; give child cookie to quiet him
	2	5	Ignored; finally gave in
6	1	8	Ignored, went into bathroom, had cigarette, read magazine until child quieted himself
	2	4	Ignored; just as I was about to give in, child stopped
7	1	3	Ignored, child stopped, began to play

Source: David C. Rimm and John C. Masters, *Behavior Therapy: Techniques and Empirical Findings* (New York: Academic Press, Inc., 1974), p. 170.

Rimm's example on tantrum behavior and its duration seems best suited to behavior specimen recording.

Once decisions about the target behavior and measurement have been made the teacher can proceed with the actual assessment (phase two). Recording the frequency of the behavior creates a baseline for later comparison after the institution of the contingency management program. It can also provide additional information about the nature and context of the behavior.

Phase three includes the final planning steps in formulating the contingency program. These are (1) structuring the situation (or environment); (2) selecting the reinforcers and reinforcement schedule; and (3) finalizing the behavior-shaping plans—that is, what will occur when.

After the first three phases have been completed, the contingency management program can be instituted (phase four). This involves actually arranging the environment, informing the student, and maintaining the reinforcement and shaping schedules.

The final phase (five) is evaluating the program. This involves once again measuring the desired response. Some people reinstitute the old reinforcement conditions to see if the original behavior returns and then return to the contingency program.

A summary of the syntax is found in Table 19-2.

Table 19-2   Syntax of the Contingency Management Model

PHASE ONE: SPECIFYING A FINAL PERFORMANCE	PHASE TWO: ASSESSING THE BEHAVIOR
Identify and define target behavior. Specify desired behavioral outcome. Develop plans for measuring and recording behavior.	Observe, record frequency of behavior and, if necessary, nature and context of behavior.
PHASE THREE: FORMULATING THE CONTINGENCY	**PHASE FOUR:** INSTITUTING THE PROGRAM
Make decisions regarding the environment. Select the reinforcers and reinforcement schedule. Finalize behavior-shaping plans.	Arrange the environment. Inform the student. Maintain the reinforcement and behavior-shaping schedules.

PHASE FIVE: EVALUATING THE PROGRAM
Measure desired response. Reinstitute old conditions, measure, and then return to contingency program (optional).

SOCIAL SYSTEM

The social system for the particular behavior under consideration is highly structured, with the teacher controlling the reward system and the environment. Sometimes aspects of the social system can be negotiated, especially as the model moves toward contingency management for self-control. In any case, reinforcers, and occasionally the reinforcement schedule, may be negotiated with the student.

PRINCIPLES OF REACTION

The principles for reacting to the learner are based on the principles of operant conditioning and the specific contingency management that has been developed. In general, inappropriate behaviors are ignored (occasionally restructured), and appropriate ones are positively reinforced. If necessary, time-out may be used.

SUPPORT SYSTEM

The requirements vary with the type of contingency management program. A simple individual behavioral program may not require any special support, or it may require material reinforcers, and rearrangement of schedules or activities. A complex token economy such as the one described in the application section calls for more elaborate preparations. Programmed instructional uses require carefully sequenced material and probably an individualized learning environment. The person developing this program needs to plan carefully and must be patient and—above all—consistent.

APPLICATION

Contingency management finds educational applications in the form of programmed instruction, individual modification programs, and environmental design. Of course, the most common application is the informal use of reinforcement principles for classroom management. Descriptions of several contingency management applications as they have been developed for the classroom are presented in the following pages. In the next section we discuss the use of similar principles for the development of self-control programs.

ENVIRONMENTAL DESIGN
AND BEHAVIOR MANAGEMENT

With the assistance of two inner-city teachers, Michael Orme and Richard Purnell successfully employed contingency management procedures to modify the out-of-control behavior of eighteen students in a combined third and fourth grade classroom. The results were reported in a 1968 study. They describe pupil behavior prior to the contingency management procedures as follows:

> Pupil behavior in the classroom was, for the most part, impulsive, aggressive and destructive. Neither T1 nor T2 was able to prevent pupils from taking apart their slatted wooden desks, tearing up classmates' papers, throwing books, yelling and singing. The noise level in the room was such one could frequently hear the class from any one of the rooms in the three-story building.
>
> Aggressive pupil behavior was of central concern. In one twenty-minute period T2 recorded aggressive acts in the classroom. She found that while not every child had acted as an aggressor, every child in the room had been struck by another one or more times during that period. . . .
>
> Finally, the teachers were not able to stop pupils from running out of the classroom, through the halls, into other classes and offices, or outside of the school. . . . (Orme and Purnell, 1968, p. 4)

Two of the objectives of their program were to reduce the aggressive behavior, by substituting more acceptable responses, and to increase the percentage of time the students spent on educationally related tasks. To accomplish these objectives, the researchers proposed to institute "total milieu control"—that is, to apply teaching techniques that manipulate multiple aspects of both the stimulus conditions and the reinforcing events. The stimulus properties they identified included the surrounding conditions of the room, the curriculum, and the teacher's verbal and nonverbal behavior. The reinforcement program included the teachers' verbal and nonverbal behavior. The reinforcement program included the teachers' verbal and nonverbal responses to student behavior as well as a specially designed, elaborate token (tangible) reinforcement system that was translated into instructional procedures.

STIMULUS PROPERTIES

Surrounding Conditions:	Physical changes in the room were made to (1) encourage teacher movement, (2) facilitate teacher control, and (3) reduce extraneous stimulation. For example, the desks were joined together to form a U-shaped table which was strategically located to enable the teacher to control the door and also to encourage her to move from the blackboard into the U and over to the work table. All books and child art were removed from the room. They were replaced by content-relevant posters that were changed as the curriculum changed.
Teachers' Verbal and Non-Verbal Behavior:	The teachers were acquainted with the stimulus determinants of attention and were taught a variety of verbal and non-verbal techniques designed to elicit attention and curiosity, desirable behaviors that could then be reinforced. Some examples of these techniques are: presenting the content as a problem rather than a statement, rapidly shifting class focus, asking heuristic

questions, enforced debates, non-verbal patterns such as silence or decisive movement patterns when shifting from one activity to another.

Curriculum: The teachers selected either content with an eye to its "control" potential. For instance, choral reading and drama were used to teach English literature. This required a relatively high level of cooperative verbal behavior by the students and provided opportunities for teacher reinforcement. Another teacher selected a math workbook which lent itself easily to the token reinforcement for work completed. In another instance, a game was played with reading flashcards. This set up a quasi-competitive situation which assists in capturing student interest.

REINFORCEMENT SYSTEM

Token
Reinforcement: The authors provide the following description of the reinforcement system study. Unusual problems usually require unusual solutions.

To be sure token reinforcement systems are not a new idea; they are, however, perceived as unusual by a substantial majority of educators. Like other systems, the one in this study was set up in such a way that pupils could "earn" points by emitting certain specified behaviors. The points or tokens earned could then be used to purchase preferred backup reinforcers from the "store." Thus, tangible reinforcers were manipulated in such a way that children's responses became contingent upon their prior behavior. The token system described here differs from those outlined in the previous literature in that the pupils shared actively in the determination of backup reinforcers. In addition, the range of store items available went considerably beyond the usual variety of consumables and manipulables to include educationally relevant reinforcers.

In view of the strength and frequency of disruptive pupil behavior, and the teachers' lack of reinforcement value in the classroom, the store included tangible items such as candy and gum. We could not be sure that the children would find more esoteric "reinforcers" reinforcing. Indeed, there was little or no evidence to indicate that they would be capable of delaying gratification long enough to accumulate any points. In anticipation of this T2 provided herself with a liberal quantity of small candies (they were not needed, as the children immediately set their sights on items requiring fairly large numbers of points).

In addition to several kinds of candy, gum, balloons, baseball cards, and the like, the store also included items such as: comics, selected novels and math puzzles, the opportunity to write poetry, a "conversation" with a computer (feed in disease symptoms for diagnoses), a short series of art lessons from a *real* artist, a model airplane together with instruction on aerodynamics, a ship-building project, science projects and puzzles, field trips to several types of museums and art institutions, and finally an opportunity to attend a *real* lecture at a major university. Apart from the last (for which there were no final takers), each of the "items" above were designed to provide further in-school opportunities for individual or small group study. Thus, the student was given the opportunity to earn the right to select his own curriculum for a part of the school day.

All items were displayed on a table and a large white sheet of cardboard immediately above it. Trips, lessons, and projects were illustrated on colorful cards, together with their prices. Small suckers and taffy twists were priced at 15 points (the cheapest items). From there, point prices rose, with the highest priced items being the field trips and projects leading to preferred study. The latter ranged from 450 to 1000 points.

Upon initial exposure to the room all the pupils were given 25 points to spend immediately. This was done to impress upon them the reinforcement value of the points. Items were priced in such a way that if they purchased an item, they would still have 10 points left over. This meant they had only a few more points to earn before they could purchase another item. This was done to avoid short-term satiation effects, and to maintain a high incentive level.

Each pupil's name was listed on the front board. The recording and decision to give points was controlled by the teacher at all times. As the children came into the room, T2 began selectively dispensing points and continued to do this throughout the experimental period.

The system was explained briefly, and the point-getting rules were outlined on the side blackboard. They were *Keep Busy All the Time, Have Good Manners,* and *Don't Bother Your Neighbor.* The teacher pointed out that these were general rules, and that the next few minutes would be devoted to allowing the pupils to suggest things that they thought should get points. The teacher then proceeded to list the *do* and *don't* behaviors suggested by pupils. Throughout this discussion handraising, questioning (defining terms) and volunteered comments were reinforced verbally, non-verbally and with points.

Both teachers were trained to emit verbal and non-verbal "reinforcement" along with points on the assumption that the teachers' reinforcement value would increase through contiguous association with the point system. At the same time they were told to reinforce only when they really felt the behavior in question was desirable or approximated some desired terminal pupil response.

Teachers' Verbal and Non-Verbal Reinforcement:
The teachers were given training in (1) discriminating the pupil behaviors that would be reinforced (task behavior, silence, hand-raising, pupil attending to another pupil discussing lesson content, pupil-pupil cooperation); (2)

> providing positive and negative verbal and non-verbal
> gestures, teacher change in position reinforcement (The
> teachers were directed to ignore disruptive behavior by
> focusing on an adjacent pupil who modeled desirable
> behavior.); (3) manipulating schedules of reinforcement
> (Orme and Purnell, 1968, pp. 12–15).

The results were very encouraging. The disruptive behavior so prevalent before the behavior-shaping procedures were instituted virtually disappeared, and the pupil time spent on educationally related tasks increased from 50 percent to 80 percent.

PROGRAMMED INSTRUCTION

Programmed instruction is the most direct application of the writings of B. F. Skinner. It provides for highly systematic stimulus control and immediate reinforcement. Although Skinner's initial programmed instruction format has undergone many transformations, most adaptations retain three essential feaures: (1) an ordered sequence of items, either questions or statements to which the student is asked to respond; (2) the student's response, which may be in the form of filling in a blank, recalling the answer to a question, selecting from among a series of answers, or solving a problem; and (3) provision for immediate response confirmation, sometimes within the program frame itself but usually in a different location, as on the next page in a programmed textbook or in a separate window in the teaching machine. (Examples of programmed material appear on the following pages.)

Recent research on programmed instruction shows that considerable deviation from these essentials can be made with no significant difference in the amount of learning that takes place. Programmed lectures with no overt student response are one example. The original linear self-instructional programs in which each student is submitted to the same material though at his own pace were not sufficiently individualized for some educators. Hence, "branching" programs were developed. The idea in branching is that slower students, unable to respond correctly to a particular frame or sequence of frames, may need additional information or review of background information. On the other hand, the more advanced students could benefit by additional and more difficult material. At various points the branching program directs students to the appropriate material depending on their answer to a particular frame or the number of correct responses within a particular frame sequence. Branching programs, like linear ones, have their variations. Some multiple-choice programs will automatically direct the student to a special section depending on his or her choice. If he or she selects any of the wrong responses, the particular mistake in reasoning is pointed out; if he or she chooses the correct response a more difficult example may appear.

Programmed instruction has been successfully employed for a variety of subject matters, including English, math, statistics, geography, and science. It has been used at every school level from preschool through college. Programmed-instructional techniques have been applied to a great variety of behaviors: concept formation, rote learning, creativity, and problem solving, for example. Some programs have even taught by discovery (leading the student to discover, which superficially is often thought to be incompatible with conditioning).

How is programmed instruction different from traditional workbooks that have been used by classroom teachers for years with no startling effects? With workbooks the emphasis is on practice (response maintenance) rather than on behavioral acquisition through carefully sequenced material. Workbooks provide endless "frames" of review material. Obviously, review is of little value unless the behavior has first been successfully established; the traditional workbook is not designed to do this. Second, the reinforcing effect of continuous review is bound to suffer diminishing returns; the learner only goes over material already mastered. Lastly, most workbooks make no provision for immediate feedback, supplying the answer only in the teacher's copy!

On the following pages we have included two examples of programmed materials. The first is an excerpt from a high school English course, and the second is from an elementary school arithmetic book.

PROGRAMMED ENGLISH
M. W. Sullivan

1. Words are divided into classes. We call the largest class nouns.
   Nouns are a class of _____   words

2. In English the class of words called *nouns* is larger than all the other _____ of words combined.   classes

3. We call the largest class of English words
   _____.   nouns

4. You will learn a number of ways to recognize and to use the class of _____ called nouns.   words

5. The words in a class are all alike in some way. All the members of the _____ of words called nouns have characteristics in common.   class

6. You will see that nouns occur in special positions in English sentences. Any word that occurs in a noun position must be a _____.   noun

7. Any word which fits the blank in the sentence
   "I saw the _____."
   occurs in the noun position.
   Can the word DOG occur in the noun position?   yes

8. Any position which is occupied by a noun in English is part of a NOUN PATTERN.
   "I saw the _____(noun)_____."
   This entire sentence is a _____   noun
   pattern.

9. When a word occurs in the noun position in a noun pattern, we say that it fits the
   _____ pattern.   noun

10. When a word fits a noun pattern, we say that it FUNCTIONS as a noun.
    A word which does not fit the noun pattern cannot _____ as a noun.   function

11. When a word functions as a noun, we say it belongs to the class of words called
    _____.   nouns

12. But a word may function as a member of several classes.
    We classify it as a noun only when it _____ as a noun.   functions
    A word functions as a noun only when it occurs in the _____ position in a noun   noun
    pattern.

13. A word which fits the blank in the following sentence occurs in a *noun* position
    "I saw the _____."
    We say that a word which occurs in a noun _____ in a noun pattern functions   position
    as a noun.
    Therefore we will use the above pattern as one test for _____.   nouns

14. "I saw the *book*."
    In this pattern, the word BOOK is in a _____ position.   noun
    We therefore say that the word _____ functions as a noun.   book

15.   "I saw the *airplane*."
    Here the word _____ is in a noun position.   airplane

16. Test the following words in the noun pattern to see whether or not they can function
                                    desk   as nouns:
    "I saw the _____." cat
                                    stone
    Can these three words function as nouns?   yes

17. We use the pattern "I saw the _____" to decide whether or not a
    word functions as a _____.   noun

18. Can the word BOAT function as a noun?   yes
    We know that BOAT functions as a noun because we can say "_____
    _____ boat."   *"I saw the* boat."

From now on, when several words are to be
filled in, we will often indicate this with a
series of dots. For example, instead of writing
"_____ _____ _____ boat,"
we will write
". . . . . boat."

19. Give the pattern which we use to test for nouns.   "I saw the _____."

20.   "I saw the _____."
If a word fits this blank, we say that it can
_____ as a noun.   function

21. Which of these words can function as a noun?
      chair
      cautiously   chair

22. CAUTIOUSLY does not function as a noun
because we do not say ". . . . ."   "I saw the cautiously."

23. Which of these words can function as a noun?
      hat
      usually   hat

(Sullivan, 1963, pp. 1–4)

INTRODUCTION TO SETS

	Some children like to collect stamps.	1
	Charles collects records. John likes to collect pictures of baseball players.	2
	Roger has a collection of model airplanes.	3
	Roger collects model planes. He has a plane	4
col *lec* tion	col_____tion.	
collec*tion*	Dick collects coins. He has a coin collec_____	5
collection	A bunch of flowers is a _____ of flowers	6
	Another word for collection is set. A collection of	7
set	stamps is a _____ of stamps.	
set	A collection of butterflies is a _____ of butterflies.	8
collection	Set and _____ have the same meaning.	9
set	A collection of things is a _____ of things.	10
	Each thing in a set is called an element of the set. Jim has a stamp collection.	11
element	His World's Fair stamp is a thing or e_____ in his collection.	
element	Each roller skate in a set of roller skates is an e_____t of that set.	12
element	In John's set of train cars a flat car is an e_____.	13
car	In a set of cars, an element of this set would be a (car/thing) _____. Choose the better answer.	14

dog	An element of the set of dogs is a(n)	
	_____.	15
element	A cat is a(n) _____ of the set of cats.	16
element	A funny face is a(n) _____ of the	17
	_____ of funny faces.	
	Here is a set of kittens. Pick out an element of this set 18 by drawing a circle around this element.	
element	A cup is a(n) _____ in the set of cups.	19
books	A book is an element in the set of	
	_____.	20
set	An element is one of the things in a(n)	
	_____.	21

(Starr, 1965, pp. 1–3)

INSTRUCTIONAL AND NURTURANT EFFECTS

Contingency management is extremely versatile: Teachers can use it to guide their goals in every domain and to develop their instructional materials (see Figure 19–2).

FIGURE 19-2 Instructional and nurturant effects: Contingency-Management Model.

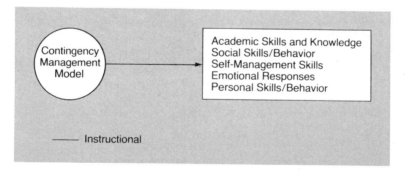

Summary Chart: Contingency Management Model

SYNTAX

Phase One:
Specifying a Final Performance
Identify and define target behavior.
Specify desired behavioral outcome.
Develop plans for measuring and recording behavior.

Phase Two:
Assessing the Behavior
Observe, record frequency of behavior and, if necessary, nature and context of behavior.

Phase Three:
Formulating the Contingency
Make decisions regarding the environment.
Select the reinforcers and reinforcement schedule.
Finalize behavior-shaping plans.

Phase Four:
Instituting the Program
Arrange the environment.
Inform the student.
Maintain the reinforcement and behavior-shaping schedules.

Phase Five:
Evaluating the Program
Measure desired response.
Reinstitute old conditions, measure, and then return to contingency program (optional).

SOCIAL SYSTEM

The model has the high structure. The teacher controls the reward system and the environment. Certain aspects of the social system—for example, reinforcement and schedule—may be negotiated. Eventually, the model is totally in the hands of students, especially for self-control.

PRINCIPLES OF REACTION

Follow principles of operant conditioning, including stimulus control, reinforcement of appropriate behavior according to the behavior-shaping, and reinforcement schedules. Ignore inappropriate behavior or, when necessary, restructure and use time-out.

SUPPORT SYSTEM

Support varies with the type of program, from no special support to elaborate support. Material reinforcers, rearrangement of schedules, activities, seating, and sometimes programmed material are needed.
The greatest human support is accuracy and consistency in applying contingency management.

We now move to a variation that places greater control in the hands of the student.

SCENARIO

Susan had been having a difficult time finishing her homework. Typically, she would relax a little after dinner, then go upstairs to her bedroom and get her books. With her arms full of every textbook she was using that semester and all her notebooks, she would head downstairs to the family room and plop on the soft couch in front of the television set. Usually her younger brother sprawled out on the mounds of pillows on the floor with *his* array of school books. Together they would work on their assignments while watching their favorite television programs, chatting, and eating snacks. The telephone, conveniently located next to the couch, would ring periodically. One or both of them would rush to answer it. They would carry on short conversations in the television room. If it was to be a long, private conversation they would go upstairs to the telephone extension there. Susan's grades began to drop, and one of her teachers became concerned. Jim Long, Susan's English teacher, knew she was both motivated and able to do much better work. He asked her to stay after school to speak with him.

When Jim brought the issue up to Susan, she whispered in a low, careful voice, "I know. I just can't seem to concentrate on my schoolwork. I'm always rushing to get it finished and my ideas don't come easily." Mr. Long was quite familiar with the habits of teenagers (he has two boys himself). He asked Susan some questions about her study habits—where, when, and how she studied. Also, how she organized herself to get ready to study. Detail by detail Susan described her environment during study time. Mr. Long exclaimed, "No wonder you are having difficulty concentrating. You really do yourself in with all these interesting distractions. I don't think there is anything wrong with your ability to concentrate and learn. I do think you've been sabotaging yourself. Not intentionally, of course."

At first Susan thought Mr. Long was blaming her, but he explained what he has to do to get himself organized to grade English papers at night. He talked about all the things he'd rather do than grade papers. He talked about distractions and how he arranges his environment to get a little time each night to give his undivided attention to his work. Susan felt more comfortable and acknowledged that she would like to develop a better system to get her work done. Mr. Long agreed to help her design one for herself—a "self-control" project.

Before they discussed the details of the program, Mr. Long explored some of Susan's other behavior patterns—her need to talk to her friends and to watch certain television programs. He also asked her how long she could read without getting bored. Of course, her interest varied with the subject matter and type of assignment. Together they analyzed her habits for each area. Mr. Long made it clear that Susan should take her interest and needs into account when setting up her program in order to satisfy them in a way that wouldn't interfere with her studying.

Next, Mr. Long explained to Susan some basic principles of behavior, especially how the environment influences behavior. Susan began to see that she had arranged her environment in such a way that studying was almost impossible. It wasn't a character flaw that prevented her from studying, just a normal response to immediate temptations.

Mr. Long and Susan spent several meetings setting up her program. They decided short-term goals and long-term goals. For example, each night before dinner Susan would make a list of the work to do. She would then assign priorities and decide a plan for the evening's work. After dinner Susan was to establish her bedroom desk as the place of study, away from the telephone, television, and her brother. Initially, she was to spend twenty minutes on subjects that were relatively easy to her and fifteen minutes on the more difficult ones. After that time she could take a short break, either watching television or making a quick phone call. Lengthy, important calls were to be made before she began studying at 7:15 P.M., or at the end of the study period. They also worked out other details of the plan, such as what Susan would do if she got bored or frustrated. These were some of the most immediate goals. The long-term goal was to increase the length of her periods of study or amount of material covered.

As they talked, Susan made a list of the steps in her program. She purchased a special notebook in which she could keep track of her progress each day and jot down suggestions for revising the program. These notes would be the basis of her review meetings wih Mr. Long. Susan and Mr. Long agreed to meet briefly twice a week for the first few weeks to discuss Susan's progress and adjust the program.

With Mr. Long's assistance, Susan applied behavioral techniques to establish self-control over her study habits. Gradually she became aware of the role the environment plays in influencing her behavior. She also became aware that she can modify the environment.

B. F. Skinner wrote *Science and Human Behavior* in 1953, inspiring the debate of mind control versus human dignity. During the next ten years behaviorists demonstrated considerable success with the application of contingency management techniques to previously unsolvable educational problems. Still, the community of educators seemed polarized by the freedom/control issue. By the early 1970s the social climate had changed, and behavioral scientists had published major works devoted to self-control through operant methods (Thoreson and Mahoney, 1974). Clinical psychologists moved toward behavioral techniques as a way of helping their patients quickly overcome social and emotional problems associated with self-control. It is now clear that contingency management methods can be used successfully for such problems associated with self-control (Bandura and Perloff, 1967). Several of these methods are particularly relevant to school issues, such as study problems and social problems.

ORIENTATION TO THE MODEL

The principles of operant conditioning used in contingency management are also used here—notably, stimulus control and positive reinforcement. However, in this model these aspects are totally in the hands of the participant. One of the main reasons for moving toward a Self-Control Model is that for many behaviors, the environment is unlikely to provide incentives at the rate and time that the individual actually needs them to establish the new behavior. Studying, exercising, practicing the piano, and more assertive social behavior toward members of the opposite sex are a few examples. Consequently, it is important that the person have ways of rewarding himself or herself. Self-control problems almost always involve situations with short-term positive gratification and long-term negative consequences. Smokers, for example, do not feel the impact of the potential long-term effects as vividly as they experience the short-term satisfaction from one more cigarette. Making people aware of the short-term and long-term response consequences that maintain their behaviors is a first step to helping them select new reinforcements.

Another critical factor hindering changes in self-control patterns is the conditions in the environment that initially stimulate the self-defeating behavior. If a student is distracted by noise but continually studies with the television on, it is likely that his or her study behavior will not be too effective. Or if a student cannot resist having a beer with the group and manages to run into them just before he or she is to go off and study, he or she is being coerced by the environmental stimuli. The ways in which people with weight problems sabotage themselves by arranging their environments with tempting foods and lots of time to eat is well known. Paying attention to and deliberately arranging a better environment is a cornerstone of self-control procedures.

Often the stimulant for self-defeating behavior is covert, a thought such as "I need a little something sweet. I'll have just one cookie." "I don't think I can pass this exam." "Everyone seems to understand this material but me." It is just as possible to rearrange the stimuli in one's mental environment as in one's physical environment for the purposes of lessening the probability of such self-defeating behaviors. This is called *covert control*. In helping people establish a self-control program it is important to check out the thoughts or images that may be part of their behavioral chains.

The key to stimulus control is *changing the environment*. This may be done through physical changes—for example, turning the television off, taking it out of the room, or selecting a different room in which to study. Narrowing the range of stimuli-eliciting behaviors is another way to control the environment. For example, a person with an eating problem may remove food from all rooms except the kitchen and establish a rule that food may only be eaten in the kitchen. Finally, the eliciting stimuli may be altered by substituting a desirable, *competing response* or thought, such as reminding oneself that he or she did well on the last exam or temporarily switching to a routine, accomplishable task instead of building up anxiety by sticking to a momentarily unsolvable problem or writing assignment. When the anxiety has subsided, the person can later come back to the problem or task.

The notion of *shaping* is applicable to self-control programs as well as to contingency-management programs. Individuals often fail in their own self-control efforts because they set their goals too high and thus never obtain positive reinforcement for their efforts. They see tasks as all-or-nothing. If they "fail" one time to control the undesirable behavior, they give up, believing that the program has failed. *Changing attitudes* as to what constitutes success is a third essential feature of self-control programs. Individuals can be assisted in setting up realistic behavioral continuums in which some success is virtually assured.

THE MODEL OF TEACHING

The activities of the Self-Control Model are similar to those of contingency management, with the major differences occurring in the orientation of the learner to the strategy and the social system—that is, in initiating and having responsibility for carrying out the model. The phases of the model include: introduction to behavioral principles; establishing the baseline; setting up the program; and monitoring and modification.

SYNTAX

In phase one the instructor introduces the self-control program, and, in particular, the self-control principles. The objective here is for the student to understand that his or her difficulty in self-control is a function of the environment, not some permanent, unalterable part of her or her character. The instructor then goes over the specific principles discussed here and in Chapter 19. Rimm and Masters summarize the basic operant principles with which the student should be familiar as follows:

1. Self-control is not a matter of will power. Instead, it comes about as a result of judicious manipulation of antecedent and consequent events, in accord with established principles of learning.
2. The client should take advantage of the fact that behavior is under stimulus control by employing any of the following tactics:
   a. Physically changing the stimulus environment.
   b. Narrowing the range of stimuli eliciting undesirable behaviors.
   c. Strengthening the connection between certain stimuli and desirable behaviors.
3. The client should determine events that are potent rewards and administer them immediately after responding appropriately.
4. The client should determine which responses are competing with, and thereby inhibiting, desirable behavior, with the goal of weakening them. He should determine which responses might serve as healthy alternatives to undesirable ways of behaving, with the goal of strengthening them.

5. The client should attempt to interrupt behavior chains leading to undesirable responses as early as possible in the chain.
6. Step-wise behavior goals in a self-control program should always be easily attainable. That is, the client should deliberately plan to achieve his overall goal in a very gradual manner.

Auxiliary Principles

7. Thoughts exert a certain amount of control over behavior. Thoughts may be thought of as internal behaviors subject to the same principles of learning applicable to overt behavior.
8. Contracts involving exchange of reinforcers may be arranged between client and therapist, or between the client and some other party. Such contracts may serve as an additional basis for motivation. (Rimm and Masters, 1974, pp. 284–285)

Of course, the introduction should be made in the context of the problem behavior and not as a formal lecture on behavioral theory. It need not be lengthy, and the manner and extent of this first phase will depend on the individual student. Obviously, the student must indicate a genuine desire to participate or at least a willingness to "give it a try," a factor that must be assessed and agreed on in this first phase.

In phase two, establishing the baseline, the instructor and student agree on the procedures and schedule for collecting the baseline data about the target behavior. This should be a quantitative record including events (and thoughts) prior to and after the target behavior is emitted. The environment should also be noted. In addition to establishing a baseline, the purpose is to ascertain the controlling stimuli, reinforcing consequences, and possible adaptive and maladaptive competing responses and reinforcers. After a week or two of self-monitoring, the student will be in a position to set up a self-control program with the instructor's assistance.

Phase three is setting up the actual program, especially making decisions regarding the stimulus environment and the reinforcers. At this point both short-term and long-term goals are identified. It is important that the program be written down with each short-term goal and target clearly specified. The instructor's role in helping the student draw up a realistic, well-scaled program is essential. Before the student begins the actual self-control program, subsequent meetings with the instructor to review the program should be set up. Finally, the student should be encouraged to continue with the program even if there are "behavioral" lapses. At the time of the meeting the two can review possible unanticipated problems in the original plan.

Finally, in phase four the student begins to undertake the self-control program. Initially, he or she will meet with the instructor to evaluate the progress of the program and make any modifications in schedule, reinforcement, or stimulus control that may be necessary. Gradually, as the student experiences his or her own success, instructor contact will diminish. (The syntax of this model is summarized in Table 19–3.)

Table 19-3   Syntax of the Self-Control Model

PHASE ONE: INTRODUCTION TO BEHAVIORAL PRINCIPLES	PHASE TWO: ESTABLISHING THE BASELINE
Communicate that self-control is a function of the environment. Explain specific self-control principles. Establish willingness to participate.	Specify clearly target behavior. Determine measuring procedures and schedule. Carry out measurement, noting control stimuli, reinforcing consequences, possible competing responses.
PHASE THREE: SETTING UP THE SELF– CONTROL PROGRAM	PHASE FOUR: MONITORING AND MODIFYING THE PROGRAM
Make decisions regarding stimulus environment, reinforcers. Set up short-term and long-term goals, possible target dates. Draw up written program. Agree upon review meetings and times.	Student undertakes program. Periodic meeting with instructor to review progress and modify program as necessary.

SOCIAL SYSTEM

The structure in this model is moderate to low. Although the instructor is important in initiating the possibility of a program, the student ultimately has control over the situation and maintenance of activities, many of which are carried out independent of the joint sessions. Furthermore, all aspects of the self-control program are negotiated with the student.

PRINCIPLES OF REACTION

The instructor has a critical role to play in the success of the self-control program. First, he or she must encourage the student, reminding him or her that behavior is under environmental control and is not a function of personal weaknesses. At first, the instructor is a powerful reinforcer for the student; gradually, this role will diminish. Second, he or she ensures a sense of realism (and specificity) in planning and carrying out the self-control program, seeing to it that reasonable goals are established and that perfection is not demanded. Third, the instructor offers the student intellectual guidance in applying behavioral principles and techniques.

SUPPORT SYSTEM

This model has no special support system.

APPLICATION

One of the best uses of the Self-Control Model is toward the improvement of study habits (Rimm and Masters, 1974, pp. 292–296). Probably the biggest obstacle students have in this area is their tendency to set unrealistic goals. After a long history of failure in a subject area, they may expect themselves to do several hours or many pages of uninterrupted work. Predictably they will fail. Their frustration with the difficulty of the task will mount, and in a short time they will give up, confirming their original assumption, "I'm no good. I can't do it!" One of the most important roles of the instructor is helping the student establish a program with small goals, such as ten to fifteen minutes of study, or a few pages of the textbook. Other self-control techniques for increasing study time are (1) changing the stimulus environment (for example, selecting a quiet place free of distractions and people); (2) cue strengthening (establishing a desk or study area used only for this purpose); (3) reinforcement (limiting the task so that the student can experience success before boredom and frustration set in). After studying for the preselected period of time the student should reward himself or herself. During the rest intervals he or she may engage in the original competing behavior, such as telephoning a friend. Many people find that cleaning the house or other chores are best accomplished as a respite from studying and writing. For others, quick play periods are important. Some people need a longer break than others. In any case, the notion of rest intervals needs to be legitimated.

Besides the problem of time devoted to studying, student may have difficulty because of the quality of their habits. Various methods have been developed to improve study habits, most notably the SQ3R (Robinson, 1946; Wrenn and Larsen, 1955). Other aspects of the studying process include techniques for improving note taking (Bencke and Harris, 1972) and test taking. In the Self-Control Model, the instructor can take the opportunity to introduce students to qualitatively different behaviors that will improve their performance.

INSTRUCTIONAL AND NURTURANT EFFECTS

This model directly instructs for the target behaviors and also eliminates maladaptive behaviors. Almost any behaviors are eligible for this model, especially those requiring large amounts of self-control. The model also has powerful nurturant effects: It teaches individuals that they can control their environments and themselves, and this enhances self-esteem. It also encourages individuals to perceive the world from a behavioral point of view, to notice the stimulus and reinforcements in their interactions with people and things (Figure 19–3).

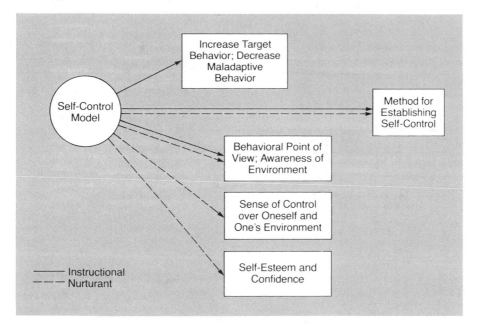

FIGURE 19-3   Instructional and nurturant effects: Self-Control Model.

Summary Chart: Self-Control Model

SYNTAX

Phase One:
Introduction to Behavioral Principles
Communicate that self-control is a function of the environment.
Explain specific self-control principles.
Establish willingness to participate.

Phase Two:
Establishing the Baseline
Specify clearly target behavior.
Determine measuring procedures and schedules.
Carry out measurement, noting control stimuli, reinforcing consequences, possible competing responses.

Phase Three:
Setting up the Self-Control Program
Make decisions regarding stimulus environment, reinforcers.
Set up short-term and long-term goals, possible target dates.
Draw up written program.
Agree on review meetings and times.

Phase Four:
Monitoring and Modifying the Program

Student undertakes program.

Periodic meeting with instructor to review progress and modify program as necessary.

SOCIAL SYSTEM

The model has a moderate to low structure. Instructor is a facilitator helping the student initiate and maintain activities. All aspects of the program are negotiated with the student.

PRINCIPLES OF REACTION

Encourage student, especially in dispelling notion of personal weakness. Reiterate idea of environmental control.

Ensure that student's goals and plans are realistic.

Offer knowledge and guidance in applying behavioral principles and techniques.

SUPPORT SYSTEM

No special support system.

20

LEARNING FROM SIMULATIONS
From the Basic Skills to the Exploration of Space

SCENARIO

Driver education students in a secondary school in Chicago are taking turns driving a simulated car. As the motion picture camera projects an image of the roadway ahead, obstacles appear. A child steps out from behind two parked cars; the "driver" turns the wheel and misses the child. A stop sign appears suddenly beyond a parked truck; the driver slams on the brakes. The driver makes a turn and a roadway narrows suddenly; again the driver brakes. One by one the students experience driving under simulated conditions. As students complete the "course," the instructor and the other students debrief them, questioning their reactions and their defensive driving.

In another classroom, this time in the suburbs of Boston, a class is watching a television show. The actors are portraying the members of the United States cabinet facing a crisis. After examining the issues, the class reaches a conclusion. One student reaches for the telephone in the classroom, dials a number, and speaks to the actors in the studio, suggesting how they might play their roles differently to resolve the crisis. Twenty-five other classrooms are simultaneously debating the issues seen on television and they, too, are communicating their views to the actors in the studio. The next day the show resumes. In various ways, the actors play out the suggestions made by the classes. The other members of the cabinet react. Students in the twenty-five classrooms not only see their ideas brought to life on the television screen, but also see the consequences of their recommendations.

In an inner-city school in Toronto, an elementary school is also watching a television screen. The announcer portrays a countdown as a rocket attempts to break free from the gravity of the moon but fails to do so. Class members then take the role of members of the spaceship crew. Instructions from the Royal Canadian Space Administration divide them into teams, and they prepare to work together to conserve their life-support systems and to manage their relationships in the rocketship until repairs can be made.

In San Antonio, two groups of children enter a room. One group represents the Alpha culture, the other the Beta culture. Their task is to learn how to communicate with others who have learned rules and patterns of behavior from a different society. Gradually, they learn to master communication patterns. Simultaneously, they become aware that, as members of a culture, they have inherited powerful patterns that strongly influence their personalities and their ways of communicating with other people.

In Philadelphia, a class is engaged in a caribou hunt. As they progress through the hunt, which the Netsilik Eskimos operate, they learn behavior patterns of the Netsilik and begin to compare those patterns with the ones they carry on in their everyday lives.

In a San Franciscan suburb, a group of students faces a problem posed by the Secretary of State. Agronomists have developed a nutrient that, when added to the food of beef cattle, greatly increases their weight. Only a limited amount of this nutrient is available, and the students must determine how the nutrient will be divided among the needy nations of the world. Congress has imposed the following restraints: The recipient nations must have a reasonable supply of beef cattle, must not be aligned with the hard-core Communist block of nations, must not be vegetarians, and must have a population that exceeds a certain size. The students debate the alternatives. Some countries are ruled out immediately. Of the remaining countries, some seem attractive at first, yet less attractive later. The students grapple with the problems of humanity and ideology and with practical situations. In simulation they face the problems of the committees of scientists who continually advise the United States government on various courses of action.

These students are all involved in simulations, playing the roles of persons engaged in real-life pursuits. Simulation allows them to face realistic conditions and develop realistic solutions. These elements of the real world are simplified and presented in a form that can be contained inside the classroom.

To progress through the tasks of the simulation, students must develop concepts and skills necessary for performance in the specified area. The young drivers have to develop concepts and skills for driving effectively. The young caribou hunters have to learn concepts about a certain culture.

The young members of the cabinet need to learn about international relations and the problems of conducting a major nation.

In simulation, students learn from the consequences of their actions. The driver who does not turn rapidly enough "hits" the child he or she is trying to avoid; he or she must learn to turn more quickly. Yet if he or she turns too quickly, the car goes out of control and veers to the other side of the street. The driver has to learn to correct his or her initial move while keeping his or her eyes on the road and looking for yet other obstacles. The students who do poorly in the caribou hunt learn what happens if the culture does not function efficiently, or if its members shrink from carrying out its mandates.

In this chapter we explore simulations of various kinds, some of which are goal-oriented games, such as the familiar board game, Monopoly. Monopoly simulates the activity of real estate speculators and incorporates many elements of real-life speculation. In this type of game simulation the players compete; in other simulations players attempt to reach their goals in a noncompetitive way. No score is kept, but interactions are recorded and analyzed later. An example is the Life Career game, in which the students play out the life cycle of a human being: They select mates, choose careers, decide whether to obtain various amounts of education, and learn through the consequences of their decisions how these choices can affect their real lives.

Unlike many other models of teaching, game simulations depend on *software*—that is, the game has paraphernalia of various kinds. Monopoly has a game board, pieces that represent the players, houses, hotels, cards that insert chance events into the situation, and paper money. Without these, the game cannot be played. Similarly, driver simulators, games involving cabinets in crises, human-relations games such as Star Power, and many other simulations all require material to represent the real world to the students in a simulated form. Much of the model of teaching that we call simulation involves learning to use this software effectively. Whereas other models of teaching depend on the interpersonal skill of the teacher (understanding concepts, making skillful moves that help the students explore important ideas), the Simulation Model depends on the teacher's blending the already prepared game or other simulation into the curriculum, highlighting and reinforcing the learning inherent in the game. Because many people do not realize the critical role a teacher can play in enhancing learning from a simulation activity, we believe a model of teaching that describes these activities is especially useful. The game itself is essential, but the teacher's ability to make the activities truly meaningful is critical.

ORIENTATION TO THE MODEL

CYBERNETIC PRINCIPLES

Simulations have been used increasingly in education over the last thirty years, but the Simulation Model did not originate within the field of education. Rather, it is an application of the principles of *cybernetics*, a branch of psychology. Cybernetic psychologists, making an analogy between humans and machines, conceptualize the learner as a self-regulating feedback system. As a discipline, cybernetics "has been described as the comparative study of the human (or biological) control mechanism, and electromechanical systems such as computers" (Smith and Smith, 1969, p. 202). The central focus is the apparent similarity between the feedback control mechanisms of electromechanical systems and human systems. "A feedback control system incorporates three primary functions: it generates movement of the system toward a target or defined path; it compares the effects of this action with the true path and detects error; and it utilizes this error signal to redirect the system (Smith and Smith, 1969, p. 203).

For example, the automatic pilot of a boat continually corrects the helm of the ship, depending on the readings of the compass. When the ship begins to swing in a certain direction and the compass moves off the desired heading more than a certain amount, a motor is switched on and the helm is moved over. When the ship returns to its course, the helm is straightened out again, and the ship continues on its way. The automatic pilot operates in essentially the same way as does a human pilot. Both watch the compass, and both move the wheel to the left or right, depending on what is going on. Both initiate action in terms of a specified goal ("Let's go north"), and depending on the feedback or error signal, both redirect the initial action. Very complex self-regulating mechanical systems have been developed to control devices such as guided missiles, ocean liners, and satellites.

The cybernetic psychologist interprets the human being as a control system that generates a course of action and then redirects or corrects the action by means of feedback. This can be a very complicated process—as when the secretary of state reevaluates foreign policy—or a very simple one—as when we notice that our sailboat is heading into the wind too much and we ease off on our course just a little. In using the analogy of mechanical systems as a frame of reference for analyzing human beings, psychologists came up with the central idea "that performance and learning must be analyzed in terms of the control relationships between a human operator and an instrumental situation. That is, learning was understood to be determined by the nature of the individual, as well as by the design of the learning situation (Smith and Smith, 1969, p. vii).

All human behavior, according to cybernetic psychology, involves a perceptible pattern of motion. This includes both covert behavior, such as thinking and symbolic behavior, and overt behavior. In any given situation, individuals modify their behavior according to the feedback they receive from the environment. They organize their movements and their response patterns in relation to this feedback. Thus, their own sensorimotor capabilities form the basis of their feedback systems. This ability to receive feedback constitutes the human system's mechanism for receiving and sending information. As human beings develop greater linguistic capability, they are able to use indirect as well as direct feedback, thereby expanding their control over the physical and social environment. That is, they are less dependent on the concrete realities of the environment because they can use its symbolic representations. The essence, then, of cybernetic psychology is the principle of sense-oriented feedback that is intrinsic to the individual (one "feels" the effects of one's decisions) and is the basis for self-corrective choices. Individuals can "feel" the effects of their decisions because the environment responds *in full*, rather than simply "You're right" or "Wrong! Try again." That is, the environmental consequences of their choices are played back to them. *Learning in cybernetic terms is sensorially experiencing the environmental consequences of one's behavior and engaging in self-corrective behavior.* Instruction in cybernetic terms is designed to create an environment for the learner in which this full feedback takes place.

SIMULATIONS IN EDUCATION

The application of cybernetic principles to educational procedures is seen most dramatically and clearly in the development of *simulators*. A simulator is a training device that represents reality very closely, but in which the complexity of events can be controlled. For example, a simulated automobile has been constructed in which the driver sees a road (by means of a motion picture), has a wheel to turn, a clutch and a brake to operate, a gearshift, and all the other devices of a contemporary automobile. The driver can start this simulated automobile, and when he or she turns the key he or she hears the noise of a motor running. When the driver presses the accelerator the noise increases in volume, so he or she has the sensation of having actually increased the flow of gas to a real engine. As the person drives, the film shows curves in the road and, as he or she turns the wheel, he or she may experience the illusion that the automobile is turning. The simulator can present the student with learning tasks to which he or she can respond, but the responses do not have the same consequences that they would have in a real-life situation; the simulated automobile does not crash into anything, although it may look like it is crashing from the driver's point of view. And in the manner of training psychology, the tasks presented can be made less complex than those a driver would have to execute in the real world; this way, it is easier for him or her to acquire the skills he or she will need later for actual driving. For example, in a driving simulator the student can simply practice shifting from one gear to another until he or she has mastered the task. The student can also practice applying the brakes and turning the wheel until he or she has a feel for how the automobile responds when he or she does those things.

The advantages of a simulator are several. As we noted earlier, the learning tasks can be made much less complex than they are in the real world, so that the students may have the opportunity to master tasks that would be extremely difficult when all the factors of real-world operations impinge upon them. For example, learning how to fly a complex airplane without the aid of a simulator leaves very little room for error: The student pilot has to do everything adequately the first time, or the plane is in difficulty. With the use of a simulator the training can be staged. The trainee can be introduced to simple tasks, and then more complex ones, until he or she builds a repertoire of skills adequate for piloting the plane. In addition, difficulties such as storms and mechanical problems can be simulated, and the student can learn how to cope with them. Thus, by the time the student actually begins flying he or she has built the repertoire of necessary skills.

A second advantage of simulators is that they permit students to learn from self-generated feedback. As the student pilot turns the wheel of the great plane to the right, for example, he or she can feel the plane bank, he or she can feel the loss of speed in some respects, and he or she can learn how to trim the craft during the turn. In other words, the trainee can learn through his or her own senses, rather than simply through verbal descriptions, the corrective behaviors that are necessary. In the driving simulation, if the driver heads into curves too rapidly and then has to jerk the wheel to avoid going off the road, this feedback permits him or her to adjust his or her behavior so that when he or she is on a real road he or she will turn more gingerly as he or she approaches sharp curves. The cybernetic psychologist designs simulators so that the feedback about the consequences of behavior enables the learners to modify their responses and develop a repertoire of appropriate behaviors.

Some very elaborate applications of cybernetic psychology have been made in military training. For example, in a submarine simulator several members of the crew can communicate with one another by radio and other devices. They are able to take their "submarine" under water, maneuver it against enemy ships, raise their periscope, sight ships through it, and fire torpedoes. The simulator is constructed so it can be attacked by enemy destroyers and can emerge and engage in evasive action; the crew can hear the enemy only over sonar and other undersea listening devices.

Thus far, the applications of cybernetics within normal elementary and secondary education are somewhat less spectacular. Exceptions are an urban simulator, which is being used experimentally with children from the upper elementary grades,[1] and Omar Khayyam Moore's famous talking typewriter,

---

[1]Developed by the Washington Center for Metropolitan Studies, 1717 Massachusetts Ave., Washington, D.C.

which simulates a human being who talks back to the student as he or she presses typewriter keys representing particular words or letters. Most other applications of cybernetics to education are fairly simple. As we describe some of them here, the cybernetic principles become more explicit.

THE LIFE CAREER GAME   This game was developed to assist guidance counselors and students in their mutual task of planning for the future, a task that requires the student to consider many factors, such as job opportunities, labor-market demands, social trends, and educational requirements (Varenhorst, 1968). Vocational and educational guidance personnel seek to help students become aware of these multiple factors, evaluate their significance, and generate alternative decisions. In the *Life Career Game* students make decisions about jobs, further education or training, family life, and the use of leisure time, and they receive feedback on the probable consequences of these decisions. The environment in this case is represented by other persons or organizations. That is, the probable consequences of the students' decisions are represented by responses from persons playing the roles of teachers, college admissions officers, employers, and marriage partners. As the players move through the different environments of school, work, family, and leisure, they are able to see the interrelationships among their decisions and among the components of their lives. The game is played as follows:

> The Life Career Game can be played by any number of teams, each consisting of two to four players. Each team works with a profile or case history of a fictitious person (a student about the age of the players).
> The game is organized into rounds or decision periods, each of which represents one year in the life of this person. During each decision period, players plan their person's schedule of activities for a typical week, allocating his time among school, studying, job, family responsibilities, and leisure time activities. Most activities require certain investments of time, training, money and so on (for example a full-time job takes a certain amount of time and often has some educational or experience prerequisites as well; similarly having a child requires considerable expenditure of time, in addition to financial expenses), and a person clearly cannot engage in all the available activities. Thus, the players' problem is to choose the combination of activities which they think will maximize their person's present satisfaction and his chances for a good life in the future . . . .
> When players have made their decisions for a given year, scores are computed in four areas—education, occupation, family life, and leisure. Calculations use a set of tables and spinners—based upon U.S. Census and other national survey data which indicate the probability of certain things happening in a person's life, given his personal characteristics, past experiences, and present efforts. A chance or luck factor is built into the game by the use of spinners and dice.
> A game usually runs for a designated number of rounds (usually ten to twelve) and the team with the highest total score at the end is the winner.

The variations of the Life Career Game illustrate the educational features of a simulation game as well as the enormous potential of simulation for incorporating several educational objectives into the basic simulation-game design. For instance, every simulation implies a theory about behavior in the area of life being simulated. This theory is implicit in the goal-achievement rules (the objectives of the game) and the rules governing the environmental responses.

One version of the Life Career Game assumes that each person attaches a different amount of importance to the various areas of life. Following this assumption, players determine their own goals by weighing the various areas in terms of their importance to them. At the end of the game, the objective achievements in those areas are converted to subjective satisfaction by means of weighted conversion ratios selected by the player. Alternately, if one of the processes being simulated is the selection and modification of goals contingent on the consequences of one's actions, the player may be asked to weigh the different areas of life at various times during the course of play. In both cases, the student is "playing against" the environment according to a personal criterion rather than an externally determined goal (such as gaining more points in the game than someone else).

The game may also include certain requisite skills, such as actually making formal applications for jobs, setting up interviews, or selecting courses from the college catalog. It can be conducted to allow group discussion at the end of rounds, where students can analyze and challenge each other's decisions and identify the values underlying them.

COMPUTER-BASED ECONOMICS GAMES   The Center for Educational Services and Research, of the Board of Cooperative Educational Services (BOCES) in northern Westchester County, New York, has recently developed two computer-based economics games for sixth graders.[2] The use of the computer makes it possible to individualize the simulation in terms of learning pace, scope, sequence, and difficulty of material. Aside from this feature, the properties of the simulation remain the same as in noncomputer-based simulation games.

The Sumerian Game instructs the student in the basic principles of economics as applied to three stages of a primitive economy—the prevalence of agriculture, the development of crafts, and the introduction of trade and other changes. The game is set during the time of the Neolithic revolution in Mesopotamia, about 3500 B.C. The student is asked to take the role of the ruler of the city-state of Lagash. The ruler must make certain agricultural decisions for the kingdom at each six-month harvest. For example, the ruler is presented with the following problematic situation: "We have harvested 5,000 bushels of grain to take care of 500 people. How much of this grain will be set aside for next season's planting and how much will be stored in the warehouse?"

---

[2]Center for Educational Services and Research, Board of Cooperative Educational Services, 42 Triangle Center, Yorktown Heights, N.Y., 10598.

(Boocock and Schild, 1968, p. 156). The student is asked to decide how much grain to allocate for consumption, for production, and for storage.

These situations become more complex as the game continues, for the student must take into account such circumstances as changes in population, the acquisition of new land, and irrigation. Periodically, technological innovations and disasters alter the outcome of the ruler's decisions. The effect of each decision on the economic condition of the kingdom is shown in an immediate progress report. Students are apprised of certain quantitative changes—for example, in population, in the amount of harvested grain, and in the amount of stored grain—and they are furnished with some substantive analyses of their decisions—for instance, "The quantity of food the people received last season was far too little" (Boocock and Schild, 1968, p. 164). In phase two of the Sumerian Game, the student can apply his or her surplus grain in the development of crafts.

INTERNATIONAL SIMULATION   Harold Guetzkow and his associates have developed a very complex and interesting simulation for teaching students at the high school and upper elementary levels the principles of international relations (Guetzkow and others, 1963). This International Simulation consists of five "nation" units; in each of these nations, a group of participants acts as decision makers and "aspiring decision makers." The simulated relations among the nations are derived from the characteristics of nations and from principles that have been observed to operate among nations in the past. Each of the decision-making teams has available to it information about the country it represents. This information concerns the basic capability of the national economic systems, the consumer capability, force capability (the ability of the nation to develop military goods and services), and trade and aid information. Together, the nations play an international-relations game that involves trading and the development of various agreements. International organizations can be established, for example, or mutual-aid or trade agreements made. The nations can even make war on one another, the outcome being determined by the force capability of one group of allies relative to that of another group.

As students play the roles of national decision makers, they must make realistic negotiations such as those diplomats and other representatives make as nations interact with one another, and they must refer to the countries' economic conditions as they do so. In the course of this game-type simulation, the students learn ways in which economic restraints operate on a country. For example, if they are members of the decision-making team of a small country and try to engage in a trade agreement, they find that they have to give something to get something. If their country has a largely agricultural economy and they are dealing with an industrialized nation, they find that their country is in a disadvantageous position unless the other nation badly needs the product they have to sell. By receiving feedback about the consequences of their decision, the students come to an understanding of the principles that operate in international relations.

THE TEACHER'S ROLE

It is easy to assume that because the learning activity has been designed and packaged by experts, the teacher has a minimal role to play in the learning situation. People tend to believe that a well-designed game will teach itself. But this is only partly true. Cybernetic psychologists find that educational simulations enable students to learn first-hand from the simulated experiences built into the game rather than from teacher's explanations or lectures. However, because of their intense involvement, students may not always be aware of what they are learning and experiencing. Thus, the teacher has an important role to play in raising students' consciousness about the concepts and principles underpinning the simulations and their own reactions. In addition, the teacher has important managerial functions. With more complex games and issues, the teacher's activities are even more critical if learning is to occur. We have identified four roles for the teacher in the Simulation Model: *explaining, refereeing, coaching,* and *discussing.*

EXPLAINING   To learn from a simulation, the players need to understand the rules sufficiently to carry out most of the activities in the game and to understand the implications of each move they might make. However, it is *not* essential that the students have a complete understanding of the game at the start. As in real life, many of the rules become relevant only as the game is played. The player need know only enough of the mechanics to start playing the game. Thus, repeating the rules of the game and drilling the students is unnecessary; instead, explanation of the game should be kept to a minimum. Implications of various game moves are much clearer to students *after* they have played and are best discussed then.

REFEREEING   Simulations used in the classroom are designed to provide educational benefits. The teacher should control student participation in the game to assure that these benefits are realized. Before the game is played, the teacher must assign students to teams (if the game involves teamwork), matching individual capabilities with the roles in the game to assure active participation by all students. Shy and assertive students, for example, should be mixed on teams. One pitfall the teacher should avoid is assigning the apparently more "difficult" roles to brighter students and the more passive roles to less academically talented students. Many simulations call on a broader range of personal competencies than do typical classroom tasks. Besides, the more academically proficient students have already had experience in leadership roles. Simulations offer an opportunity to distribute such experiences more widely.

The teacher should recognize in advance that simulations are *active* learning situations and thus call for more freedom of movement and more talk among students than do other classroom activities. The teacher should act as a referee who enforces game rules but does his or her best not to interfere in the game activities.

COACHING   The teacher should act as coach when necessary, giving players advice that enables them to play better—that is, to exploit the game's possibilities more fully. As a coach, the teacher should be a supportive advisor, *not* a preacher or a disciplinarian. In a game, players have the opportunity to make mistakes and take consequences—and learn. Furthermore, a coach does *not* play. The coaching role of the teacher should consist of offering (but not insisting on) advice only when it is solicited by players, and perhaps making some unsolicited suggestions to players who seem shy.

DISCUSSING   During the game the teacher should explain, referee, and coach. After the game the teacher should be certain to lead the class in discussing how closely the game simulates the real world, what difficulties and insights the students had in playing the game, and what relationships can be discovered between the simulation and the subject matter that the game was meant to supplement. The class might also suggest ways to improve the game!

THE MODEL OF TEACHING

SYNTAX

The Simulation Model has four phases: orientation, participant training, the simulation itself, and debriefing (see Table 20-1). In the orientation (phase one), the teacher presents the topic to be explored, the concepts that are embedded in the actual simulation, an explanation of simulation if this is the students' first experience with it, and an overview of the game itself. This first part should not be lengthy but can be an important context for the remainder of the learning activity. In phase two the students begin to get into the simulation. At this point the teacher sets the scenario by introducing the students to the rules, roles, procedures, scoring, types of decisions to be made, and goals of the game. He or she organizes the students into the various roles and conducts an abbreviated practice session to ensure that students have understood all the directions and can carry out their roles.

Phase three is the actual game activity and administration. The students participate in the game or simulation, and the teacher functions in his or her role as referee and coach. Periodically the game may be stopped so that the students receive feedback, evaluate their performances and decisions, and clarify any misconceptions.

Finally, phase four consists of participant debriefing. Depending on the

Table 20-1   Syntax of Simulation Model

PHASE ONE: ORIENTATION	PHASE TWO: PARTICIPANT TRAINING
Present the broad topic of the simulation and the concepts to be incorporated into the simulation activity at hand. Explain simulation and gaming. Give overview of the simulation.	Set up the scenario (rules, roles, procedures, scoring, types of decisions to be made, goals). Assign roles. Hold abbreviated practice session.
PHASE THREE: SIMULATION OPERATIONS	PHASE FOUR PARTICIPANT DEBRIEFING (ANY OR ALL OF THE FOLLOWING ACTIVITIES)
Conduct game activity and game administration. Obtain feedback and evaluation (of performance and effects of decisions). Clarify misconceptions. Continue simulation.	Summarize events and perceptions. Summarize difficulties and insights. Analyze process. Compare simulation activity to the real world. Relate simulation activity to course content. Appraise and redesign the simulation.

outcomes of the game the teacher may help the students focus on (1) the events and their other perceptions and reactions; (2) analyzing the process; (3) comparing the simulation to the real world; (4) relating the activity to course content; and (5) appraising and redesigning the simulation.

SOCIAL SYSTEM

Because the teacher selects the simulation activity and directs the students through carefully delineated activities, the social system of simulation is rigorous. Within this structured system, however, a cooperative interactive environment can, and ideally should, flourish. The ultimate success of the simulation, in fact, depends partly on the cooperation and willing participation of the students. Working together, the students share ideas, which are subject to peer evaluation but not teacher evaluation. The peer social system, then, should be nonthreatening and marked by cooperation.

PRINCIPLES OF REACTION

The reactions of the teacher are primarily those of a facilitator. Throughout the simulation he or she must maintain a nonevaluative but supportive attitude. It is the teacher's task to first present and then facilitate understanding and interpretation of the rules of the simulation activity. In addition, should interest in the activity begin to dissipate or attention begin to focus on irrelevant issues, he or she must direct the group to "get on with the game."

SUPPORT SYSTEM

Simulation requires support materials ranging from simple teacher-made games, to marketed games (which sell for under $10 to more than $200), to specifically designed simulators such as car-driving or airplane-navigating simulators (whose costs can ascend into thousands of dollars). Simulations are gaining in popularity, and the number of published materials increases every year. The 1973 *Social Science Education Consortium Data Book* lists more than fifty simulations available for use in social studies alone. The teacher who is interested in using simulations is directed to publishers' catalogs; the aforementioned *Data Handbook* (1971, 1972, 1973); Ronald Kleitsch, *Directory of Educational Simulations, Learning Games, and Didatic Units* (1979); David Zuckerman and Robert Horn, *The Guide to Simulation Games for Education and Training* (1970); and Ron Stadsklev, *Handbook of Simulation Gaming in Social Education* (n.d.).

APPLICATION

There are two ways students learn from a simulation game. The first is a direct result of the experience in the simulation, and the second is a result of the activities or discussions that follow the game. A good point-of-departure for discussion is to ask the students to evaluate how their experiences in the game compare to what they believe to be true about the real world. According to William Nesbitt, the important thing is "for students to be explicit about their experience with and in the game and from there to examine their views of the real world or referent situation" (Nesbitt, 1971, pp. 38–39).

Simulation games can stimulate a variety of learning, such as learning about (1) competition; (2) cooperation; (3) empathy; (4) the social system; (5) concepts; (6) skills; (7) efficacy; (8) paying the penalty; (9) the role of chance; and (10) the ability to think critically (examining alternative strategies and anticipating those of others) and to make decisions (Nesbitt, 1971, pp. 38–53).

The Simulation Model is somewhat different from many other models of teaching in that it depends on the prior development of a simulation, either by research and development specialists, a commercial company, or a teacher or group of teachers. The simulation itself presents problems to the learners, and the learners deal with those problems as they carry out the simulation operations.

The number and range of simulation games is vast for both elementary and secondary students. The Social Science Education Consortium's 1973 *Databook* covers many topics—consumer education, political decision making, city planning, economics, ecology, family management and budgeting, and career planning. Over seventy games are described in that one book.

It is apparent that the Simulation Model can be used for a variety of teaching purposes. In the classroom, simulations are generally employed as part of a fairly extensive unit of study. They can be used to introduce a unit of work, to extend and deepen understandings as the unit progresses, or to pull ideas together and ensure their application to real-life problem situations. For example, the game of Hang Up can be used to begin a unit on personal values and racial stereotyping. Similarly, Bafá can be used to introduce the study of culture and cultural interchange. The Legislative Game can be used to bring together knowledge of the legislative process and caucusing.

Essentially, to apply simulation to a unit, the teacher develops a plan that specifies content and scope. Then he or she examines lists of simulations, searching for ones that might be applicable and sifting them for quality. It is wise to try a simulation with a small group of people, whether children or adults, before using it in the classroom.

Upper elementary, junior high, and high school students can be prepared for leadership roles through simulations. It is important to note, however, that if students are to be used as leaders, they have to be coached so that the essential point of the game is quite clear to them. Some game-type simulations have a tendency to go off on tangents if the leader loses focus.

Since simulations teach people to work within a system, it is important to identify the elements of the system that have to be mastered by the end of the game. Political games, for example, require the mastery of a political system, and economic games, the mastery of an economic system. This is, of course, why simulations are so good as introduction to and culminating activities of units of study.

Some simulations are good only for one operation; Bafá is such a game. Once you have learned its system, there is little incentive to learn it again. Other simulations, such as the Legislative Game, can be played more and more effectively as students acquire information, in this case, about the legislative process.

INSTRUCTIONAL AND NURTURANT EFFECTS

The Simulation Model, through the actual game and through discussions afterwards, nurtures and instructs a variety of educational outcomes, including: concepts and skills; cooperation and competition; critical thinking and decision making; empathy; knowledge of political, social, and economic systems; sense of effectiveness; awareness of the role of chance; and facing consequences (see Figure 20–1).

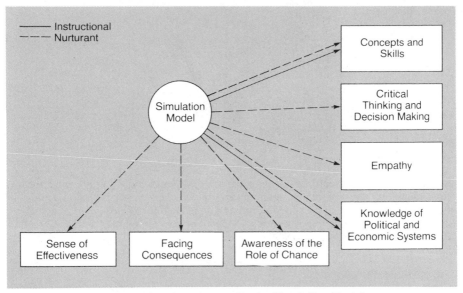

FIGURE 20-1 Instructional and nurturant effects: Simulation Model.

Summary Chart: Simulation Model

SYNTAX

Phase One:
Orientation
Present the broad topic of the simulation and the concepts to be incorporated into the simulation activity at hand.
Explain simulation and gaming.
Give overview of the simulation.

Phase Two:
Participant Training
Set up the scenario (rules, roles, procedures, scoring, types of decisions to be made, goals).
Assign roles.
Hold abbreviated practice session.

Phase Three:
Simulation Operations
Conduct game activity and game administration.
Feedback and evaluation (of performance and effects of decisions).
Clarify misconceptions.
Continue simulation.

Phase Four:
Participant Debriefing
(any or all of the following activities)
Summarize events and perceptions.
Summarize difficulties and insights.
Analyze process.
Compare simulation activity to the real world.
Relate simulation activity to course content.
Appraise and redesign the simulation.

SOCIAL SYSTEM

The social system is structured by the teacher through selecting materials and directing the simulation. The interactive environment of the class, however, should be non-threatening and marked by cooperation. The teacher has the role of managing the simulation (taking care of organization and logistics), explaining the game, maintaining the rules, coaching (offering advice, prompting), and conducting the debriefing discussion.

PRINCIPLES OF REACTION

1. Do not evaluate players' decisions and moves.
2. Facilitate student's understanding and interpretation of rules.
3. Encourage participation and help the students cope with unceratainty.
4. Tell students to "get on with the game" when necessary.

SUPPORT SYSTEM

Simulation requires a carefully structured base of resource materials.

21

ASSERTIVE TRAINING
Toward Integrative Communication

SCENARIO

Miss York's tenth grade social studies class has been studying social skills. As part of their study they've been examining ways that people either express themselves or hide their feelings. They have made a list of complimentary things that people might say to one another—for example, things that might be said to athletes after a good play or to actors after a performance, as well as compliments about clothing, hair, and other personal characteristics. They are now role playing the responses that individuals might make to those compliments. Two students engage in each enactment while the rest of the class watch. They then analyze the response. John Herndon draws the compliment, "Gee, that's a neat hat, Sally," and Sally Wilkins has to respond.

"Oh, it's just an old thing I found in the back of the closet," she says.

The class groans. "What's wrong with that?" says Sally.

"Well," says John, "it sure took the wind out of my sails."

"What do you mean?" says Sally.

"I was really getting all juiced up to tell you how great that imaginary hat you're wearing is, and I really wanted you to feel that I cared. And when you said, 'Oh, it's nothing,' I kind of was left pawing the air, if you know what I mean."

"How did you feel, Sally, when he said that?"

"I felt a little embarrassed. It isn't just that we're role playing—any time somebody says something to me like that, part of me wants to say thanks, and the other part wants to crawl in a little hole somewhere."

The class is engaged in assertiveness training. They are beginning to learn how we conceal and express our feelings. Now they're going to experiment with different ways of communicating.

In the desensitization and other behavioral models, we discussed the role of anxiety in inhibiting our behaviors and in producing physical tension. Anxiety also decreases our effectiveness in communicating how we feel to other people. Our fear of retaliation or of displeasing someone is likely to produce anxiety that inhibits directness. For example, when someone interrupts us repeatedly we may fail to inform that person that he or she is making us uncomfortable if we feel that he or she may retaliate in some way or like us less for our expression of discomfort. If we feel anxiety about saying something like, "I'd like to get my whole idea out. When I can't, I lose my train of thought and it flusters me," we will probably founder anyway and give mixed messages while feeling poorly about ourselves. The result is a loss of authentic contact with others. The list of areas in which many of us have difficulty expressing ourselves is very long indeed. Assertiveness training is a very direct training method for helping students acquire the social skills that will enable them to express themselves comfortably and smoothly in situations that have previously made them feel anxious and inhibited. Joseph Wolpe (Wolpe and Lazarus, 1966) and Andrew Salter (1949) laid the early base for its theory and practice, and there are a number of popularizers of the techniques (Alberti and Emmons, 1978; Fensterheim and Baer, 1975; Smith, 1975). The model presented here is based primarily on the descriptions of Rimm and Masters (1974) but draws on the work of Fensterheim and Baer and Alberti and Emmons.

ORIENTATION TO THE MODEL

ASSERTIVENESS, NONASSERTIVENESS, AND AGGRESSSION

Various definitions of assertiveness have been offered over the years. Wolpe refers to assertiveness as the proper expression of any emotion other than anxiety. Lazarus speaks in terms of "emotional freedom" and the recognition and expression of every emotional state. More recent sources refer to assertive behavior as simply the honest and straightforward expression to other people (and ourselves) of how we feel. It is characterized by openness, directness, spontaneity, and appropriateness. Contrary to some opinions, assertiveness is not a tool of aggression but a tool of contact. The hope is that one will feel better and be less anxious if he or she can assert his or her feelings to others, partly because this will result in a more satisfactory relationship with them and partly because social interactions will be accompanied by less anxiety.

Assertive behavior is generally distinguished from nonassertive behavior and aggressive behavior. People who are nonassertive in a given situation typically deny their true feelings and inhibit actions that would reflect these feelings. They often wind up feeling hurt. Because nonassertive people allow others to choose for them, they rarely achieve their goals. Aggressive people, on the other hand, accomplish their goals at the expense of other people. They are usually emotionally expressive, but in a way that dominates others and does not recognize their worth. When we are subjected to aggressive behavior, we often end up feeling hurt, rejected, and defensive. In contrast to nonassertive and aggressive behavior, assertiveness involves getting what one wants in a way that does not hurt others and that does not impose one's value system on them. People generally experience their own assertiveness as enhancing, honest expressions of their feelings. They believe that they have made choices about their actions. Generally in an assertive transaction, both parties feel they have achieved their goals. Examples of the three types of responses appear in the following vignettes.

DINING OUT

Mr. and Mrs. A are at dinner in a moderately expensive restaurant. Mr. A has ordered a rare steak, but when the steak is served Mr. A finds it to be very well done, contrary to his order. His behavior is:

Nonassertive: Mr. A grumbles to his wife about the "burned" meat and observes that he won't patronize this restaurant in the future. He says nothing to the waitress, responding "Fine!" to her inquiry "Is everything all right?" His dinner and evening are highly unsatisfactory, and he feels guilty for having taken no action. Mr. A's estimate of himself, and Mrs. A's estimate of him are both deflated by the experience.

Aggressive: Mr. A angrily summons the waitress to his table. He berates her loudly and unfairly for not complying with his order. His actions ridicule the waitress and embarrass Mrs. A. He demands and receives another steak, this one more to his liking. He feels in control of the situation, but Mrs. A's embarrassment creates friction between them, and spoils their evening. The waitress is humiliated and angry and loses her poise for the rest of the evening.

Assertive: Mr. A motions the waitress to his table. Noting that he had ordered a rare steak, he shows her the well done meat, asking politely but firmly that it be returned to the kitchen and replaced with the rare-cooked steak he originally requested. The waitress apologizes for the error, and shortly returns with a rare steak. The A's enjoy dinner, tip accordingly, and Mr. A feels satisfaction with himself. The waitress is pleased with a satisfied customer and an adequate tip.

SOMETHING BORROWED

Helen is a college sophomore, bright, attractive, a good student liked by teachers and peers. She lives in a residence hall with two roommates, in a suite arrangement with six other girls. All of the girls date quite regularly. One evening, as Helen's roommates are dressing for their dates (Helen plans a quiet evening working on a term paper), Mary says that she is going out with a "really special" young man, and she hopes to make a good impression. She asks Helen if she may borrow and wear a new and quite expensive necklace Helen has just received from her brother, who is overseas in military service. Helen and her brother are very close, and the necklace means a great deal to her. Her response is:

Nonassertive: She swallows her anxiety about loss or damage to the necklace, her feeling that its special meaning makes it too personal to lend, and says "Sure!" She denies herself, reinforces Mary for making an unreasonable request, and worries all evening (which makes little contribution to the term paper).

Aggressive; Helen shows her outrage by her friend's request, tells her "absolutely not," and proceeds to upbraid her severely for even daring to ask "such a stupid question." She humiliates Mary and generally makes a fool of herself. Later she feels uncomfortable and guilty, interfering with her work on the paper. Mary's hurt feelings show on her date, and she has a miserable time, puzzling and dismaying the young man. Thereafter the relationship between Helen and Mary becomes very strained.

Assertive: She explains the significance of the necklace to her roommate and politely but firmly observes that the request is an unreasonable one since this piece of jewelry is particularly personal. She later feels good for having asserted herself, and Mary, recognizing the validity of Helen's response, makes a big hit with the young man by being more honest herself.[1]

The areas of our lives that call for assertive communication or behavior are more numerous than most of us realize. We are usually aware of the person who won't get angry and won't prevent others from taking advantage, but we often are unaware that *feeling talk* of any kind, especially expressions of positive feelings, are difficult for many people. Some people find it difficult to give or receive a hug, to smile, to say "thank you," 'I'm so glad you're here," or "I've thought about you often." Nonassertive and aggressive people often have difficulty giving and receiving compliments. How many times have you heard someone deny a compliment, "Oh, it's nothing really. Anybody who can read can cook." Other areas, in addition to feeling talk, are the expression of *contradictory opinions* and *setting limits*. Sometimes we manage to disagree, but we cannot state what we are willing to do or not willing to have others do. Parents and teachers often have trouble setting limits—for example, with the adolescent who stays out late or the young child who eats too much junk food—and people of all ages who constantly watch television instead of doing their homework, their chores, or talking with their spouses have similar prob-

[1]From Robert E. Alberti, Ph.D., and Michael L. Emmons, Ph.D., *Your Perfect Right: A Guide to Assertive Behavior* (Third Edition). Copyright © 1978. Impact Publishers, Inc., San Luis Obispo, California. Reprinted by permission of the publisher.

lems. Limit setting is also very essential in landlord-tenant relations, consumer relations, and work relationships, especially between superiors and subordinates. A fourth area of assertions has to do with those situations that call for *self-initiation*. Generally these acts involve risks: the risk of being rejected if it is a social contact we are initiating; the risk of being turned down if we ask for a promotion; or the risk of failing if we try something new. Assertiveness trainers emphasize the skill of small talk, easy superficial conversation that is necessary to initiate new social contacts. Nonassertive and aggressive people often have difficulty with this type of social repartee, seeming either too forceful or too constricted.

Behavioral skills related to these four areas of assertion (feeling talk, contradictory views, limit setting, and self-initiation) have wide social utility as well as extreme importance for a sense of well-being and self-expression. Feeling talk provides a direct route to authentic and full contact with others. The ability to disagree comfortably and to set limits is essential to honest communication, comfortable social relations, and self-esteem. Again, at least from subjective evidence, it appears that the more one is able to engage in assertive behavior, the less will be one's anxiety in social situations (Rimm and Masters, 1974, pp. 82–83). Like muscle relaxation, the ability to assert oneself comfortably may inhibit anxiety. However, there is no direct evidence that assertion inhibits anxiety for physiological reasons.

COMPONENTS OF ASSERTIVE BEHAVIORS

The essential features of assertive behavior are nonverbal as well as verbal. Looking directly at other people when you speak to them (eye contact); facing them, leaning toward them, and sitting or standing relatively close and erect (body posture); maintaining a congruent facial expression—for example, not smiling when you are angry; and speaking in a firm, well-modulated manner, neither too soft nor too loud (voice tone) are nonverbal components of assertiveness (Alberti and Emmons, 1978, pp. 29–36). Some people routinely use nonwords, which take away from their assertiveness. Laughs, *uh*, and *you know* are examples of such nonwords. We have found that beginning teachers often add the expression *okay* after every request they make of their students, as if to ask permission to make their request.

Timing is another aspect of assertiveness. It is important to be spontaneous in your expression of feelings, not letting issues build until there is an explosion, and not withholding positive feelings until they are so distilled they lose their warmth. On the other hand, on certain occasions we must exercise judgment about when to speak our feelings. It may be more appropriate to express them privately or to wait until a particular set of stressful events for the recipient has passed. The danger, however, is that some people always use the latter as an excuse not to be assertive.

The third component of assertiveness has to do with the content of communication. A few guidelines are essential here. First, say what you are *feeling*, and *be honest*. If you are angry, say so. Second, accept responsibility for your feelings instead of putting someone else down. ("I'm very angry at your forgetting to pick up the check" instead of "You are so irresponsible.") Name calling and personality attributions are sure signs of aggressiveness. Third, emphasize the person's behavior, not his or her character. Be specific in your comments. ("I get nervous when you hover around the stove while I'm cooking" or "I really appreciate it when you surprise me with things I like" as opposed to "You are such a pest" or "You're so thoughtful.")

A fourth component concerns the appropriateness of the response. Most of us have been in situations in which a person overracts to a small gesture. If we accidentally bump someone's arm or step in his or her way, we are surprised to be grabbed by the collar or greeted by an angry, "What do you mean, *buddy?*" We may also have seen mouselike gestures made in highly volatile situations. Gauging the strength of one's response to a situation is another skill of assertiveness.

Other components of assertion include what we feel inside (emotional) and what we tell ourselves (cognitive). Proponents of assertiveness training maintain that changes in feeling will occur as a result of changes in behavior. By being assertive we will gradually reduce and eliminate anxiety in particular situations. Assertiveness training does not work directly on the cognitive component except that it requires people to subscribe to a new set of assumptions about how people should relate to one another, particularly in regard to the open expression of feelings, including anger. Manuel Smith has developed a Bill of Assertive Rights (Smith, 1975, pp. 24–71).[2] The articles include: You have the right to judge your own behavior, thoughts, and emotions and to take the responsibility for their initiation and consequences upon yourself; and you have the right to say "I don't care."

Some theorists on assertiveness have identified specific behavioral skills for handling various situations that call for assertive communication.[3] Probably the most basic skill in being assertive is using *I* instead of *you* or *it*. The assertive examples in this chapter begin with *I*, followed by a feeling word. When people use the word *I* they are automatically accepting responsibility for their feelings and are not likely to emit a put-down expression. For example, appropriate expressions of anger might be "I'm becoming very angry . . . " "I get mad when . . . " "I'm bothered by . . . " and "I disagree with you." *It* is a vague term that distances people from their feelings; *I* is more direct.

One way of thinking about the appropriateness of a communication is to

[2]Dr. Smith's version stresses self-defense techniques.

[3]Smith (1975) discusses several such situations: broken record (persistence); free information and self-disclosure (social conversation); fogging and negative assertion (criticism); negative inquiry.

distinguish levels of assertion. For instance, if in a theater the person in front of you is smoking and the smoke is traveling back to your face, you might first make a simple, polite *request*, "Could you please put out your cigarette?" If nothing happens, you might increase the strength of your request by *adding a feeling*: "I feel very uncomfortable when the smoke blows in my face, and I'd like you to put out your cigarette." Finally, if you get no results, *add a consequence*: "The smoke from your cigarette is making me very uncomfortable. I'd like you to put it out, and if you don't I will call the manager."

GOALS AND ASSUMPTIONS

Assertiveness training directly applies the general behaviorist assumption that learned behavior can be unlearned. More accurately, new behaviors can be learned and substituted for the others, which then gradually disappear from the behavior pattern. Thus, if one is timid about expressing feelings one can, by learning to express feelings, reduce that timidity. The pattern of assertive behavior will replace that of withholding feelings. Similarly the anxiety accompanying the inability to express oneself will probably be reduced. Some people are not assertive because their feelings and fears inhibit them. Others are not assertive because they have not acquired the skills through experience and practice.

Assertiveness training also assumes that our actions serve as the basis of our self-concepts. As we assert ourselves and move toward a goal, our self-concepts are enhanced. Related assumptions are that changes in our feelings will *follow* the changes in behavior, and that small behavioral changes may have a great impact on our social relationships and our own self-images. For example, simply using *I* statements in place of indirect expressions of feeling can make a great difference in our internal states and our effects on others.

As in all behavioral models, behaviorists assume that the past has little to do with acquiring new behavior patterns. People can get rid of undesirable behaviors and acquire new ones if they want to change.

Finally, assertiveness training implies a general set of principles, a philosophy of human relations. The essence of this philosophy is that the best relationships are characterized by a free expression of feelings. All feelings, especially anger, are legitimate simply because they exist. It is healthy to express feelings directly and honestly, and it is essential that we be in touch with our feelings as we experience them.

The Assertiveness Training Model is a powerful tool for facilitating behavior change and for improving self-image. The primary objectives are to: (1) increase the use of feeling talk, expressions both of positive feelings and negative feelings; (2) express contradictory feelings and set limits; and (3) increase self-initiative (risk-taking) behaviors. As skills in each of these areas are increased, we anticipate richer interpersonal relationships characterized by increased intimacy, genuineness, and fulfillment; more skillful ways of handling conflict; reduction of stress and anxiety in handling social situations; improvement in self-image, including more positive feelings about oneself and actions indicative of personal growth; and finally, few psychosomatic symptoms.

We believe that these objectives are well within the scope of general education. Whereas therapists deal with the person who is acutely unable to use feeling talk or disagree with others, educators may use assertiveness training to increase the general capability of children to discuss their feelings comfortably and to handle opinions in a socially acceptable way during interchanges with other people. Alberti and Emmons say that "assertiveness training has been shown to be highly valuable for students who wish to become better able to raise questions in class, to make presentations and reports, to respond to teacher questions, to express opinions, or to participate in group discussions. Similarly, assertiveness training is pertinent to helping students who seem to 'come on too strong' in asking questions, expressing opinions, and so on" (Alberti and Emmons, 1978, pp. 147–48).

Teachers too can profit from the incorporation of assertive skills into their classroom management of behavior. In fact, good teachers use them naturally. Both the philosophy of human relations that underlies this training and the assertive skills and methods of training are easily acquired and understood.

THE MODEL OF TEACHING

The model of teaching we present here integrates a certain amount of training in basic assertive skills with their use in more complex situations. Depending on the instructional setting and curriculum context, the teacher may want to go over the basic components of assertive behavior and the basic assertive skills ahead of time, or concurrent with but separate from the phases presented here. In any case, the instructor will surely want to be familiar with the conceptualizations of assertiveness and the basic skills to convey them to the students as the opportunity arises. As presently formulated the model has five phases: (1) identifying target behaviors; (2) setting priorities for situations and behaviors; (3) role playing the instances; (4) undertaking reenactments; and (5) transfer.

SYNTAX

Identifying target behaviors (phase one) can occur as teacher and students discuss situations in which they have some difficulty expressing feelings and identify the kinds of feelings they have trouble expressing. In a continuation of the discussion the situations and events can be ordered in terms of which ones occur most frequently and are most acute (setting priorities for situations and behaviors, phase two). The list should include both situations and the kinds of feelings that they have difficulty expressing. Rimm and Masters use the example of persons who have trouble saying "I'd really like you to go out with me," "I'd really like to go out with you," or "There is something I want to do. Can you join me in it?" and instead say things like "You wouldn't want to go out someplace on Saturday night would you?" which avoids expressing feelings and puts the burden on the other person. This list provides the basis for the students and teacher to select the situations and the feelings they will concentrate on first. As in the case of desensitization, moderate but persistent situations should be selected first.

Once the situations have been selected the students will engage in behavior rehearsal or role playing (phase three). At first the enactment will be carried out avoiding the expression of clear feelings and assertiveness, either through nonassertiveness or aggressive behaviors. The observers and role players then discuss the enactment, determining its fidelity to real life and the ways in which feelings were actively suppressed. After a discussion of how the role playing might be modified so that the expression of feelings would be both adequate and socially acceptable, role players again enact the situation, this time with some expression of feeling. This enactment is followed by several others in which the students (and perhaps the teacher) model for one another various ways in which feelings can be expressed adequately in the situation.

Especially when a contradictory feeling is to be expressed or when one needs to interfere with the behavior of someone else, the teacher can lead a discussion of various kinds of relatively unaggressive but effective responses that can be made in social situations. An example is trying to get the attention of a clerk in a store who appears to be deliberately ignoring one's presence. The students and teacher can practice responses to obtain the person's attention ("I'd like to be waited on, please.") but do not place one in the position of putting down the other person or escalating a conflict, such as "I've been waiting here a hell of a long time (Rimm and Masters, 1974, p. 98). In other words, at this point the teacher may choose to engage in assertive skill training and modeling.

In phase four, further enactments are undertaken. Students practice new behaviors and observe a variety of assertive styles. They give each other feedback on ways to be more effective, and gradually the elements of clear expression of feelings and assertiveness are made explicit.

The assumption of the model is that students will learn the new behaviors and begin to transfer them to their real-life situations. It is worthwhile, therefore, for the group to make a commitment to try out the expressive responses and to report to the group the consequences of their doing so (phase five). The teacher should be aware that not all the consequences will be positive. Some students will find they can more comfortably ask for dates.

Others will express their feelings with someone ("Gee, I'd like you to come to the dance with me on Saturday night.") and be turned down. In such cases, however, it is likely that the students will feel better because they have expressed their feelings directly. It should be pointed out that being turned down (or failing to get someone's attention) probably is not a consequence of expressing one's feeling directly, but is the result of some other reason (which very likely is a good one). (See Table 21-1.)

Helping students to transfer to real-life situations is extremely important, so that the instructor does not simply "get them out on a limb" with new behavior without helping them understand what is happening as they attempt those behaviors. The Assertiveness Training Model takes place in discussions and role-playing sessions held periodically over a considerable period of time. People do not learn to express their feelings quickly, and teachers should expect relatively slow but steady progress.

SOCIAL SYSTEM

It is essential that a social system of acceptance and cooperation be developed so this model can be successful and avoid possible damage and side effects. It is also important that individuals be accepted on their own terms,

Table 21-1   Syntax of the Assertiveness Training Model

PHASE ONE: IDENTIFYING TARGET BEHAVIORS	*PHASE TWO:* SETTING PRIORITIES FOR SITUATIONS AND BEHAVIORS
PHASE THREE: ROLE PLAYING THE SITUATION	*PHASE FOUR:* UNDERTAKING REENACTMENTS
Select role players and observers. Instruct observers. Enact with feelings suppressed and nonassertive behavior. Discuss components of nonassertiveness and validity of enactment. Enact again with feelings expressed and assertive behavior. Discuss enactment, especially component of assertiveness. Model assertive behavior, if necessary.	Reenact situation showing several assertive possibilities. Discuss the reenactment. Practice.
PHASE FIVE: TRANSFER TO REAL-LIFE SITUATIONS	
Identify specific situations. Try out responses. Discuss.	

and that everyone in the group share the responsibility for making the others comfortable. Most students will respond to this and work to make the group positive and supportive for others. Nearly everyone will recognize the potential benefits of becoming more effective in expressing feelings and can recognize easily the importance of a positive and humane social situation for everyone involved. The model has moderate to low structure, because it reflects situations the students themselves identify. The role of the teacher is to be a facilitator. Sometimes the teacher has an instructional function.

PRINCIPLES OF REACTION

The teacher should be very sensitive to the formation of groups for assertiveness training. To place a very shy, timid student within an already assertive clique of students, for example, could have poor side effects for everyone concerned. On the other hand, in any assertiveness training group (as probably in any instructional group), one of the teacher's major tasks is to help everyone to be comfortable and to have confidence that the reinforcement will be positive. The teacher should introduce cognitive aspects of assertiveness when appropriate, and should encourage group feedback.

SUPPORT SYSTEM

No special support system is necessary. However, a sensitive, skilled instructor is essential.

APPLICATION

We believe assertiveness training is greatly needed in schools, particularly at the secondary level. Fensterheim and Baer speak of levels of assertion, implying that training should begin with the lowest level. The three levels are:

1. *Nonverbal*: eye contact, standing straight, firm voice
2. *Basic assertive skills*: ability to say no and yes; ask favors; make requests; communicate feelings and thoughts in an open, direct way; handle put downs; control work habits
3. *Complex situations*: adaptive behavior in job situation, ability to form a social network, achieving close personal relations, parental relations (Fensterheim and Baer, 1975, p. 33)

We view this hierarchy as heuristic, but we do want to emphasize that the simple behaviors should not be overlooked. In an assertiveness training workshop, one of the authors was asked to practice making a simple request like "Raise the pencil, lower the pencil." It turned out that it is not so easy to make even a simple request of a stranger without a nonverbal gesture that stifles the power of the request—laughing, smiling, looking away. Each time one of these distractors appeared, the author was asked to "break" and begin the exercise again. It took fifteen minutes and a good deal of frustration to give a simple command with full power and intent. We believe that prior (or concurrent) training in individual assertive skills is an important instructive accompaniment to the basic Assertiveness Training Model.

Assertiveness training in groups has been particularly successful. Groups can provide various models and diverse feedback, and trainees are able to learn from one another. The general format in groups calls for a brief introduction to the philosophy of assertive behavior with many illustrations. Initially individuals may be asked to pair up, role play a particular situation or practice individual skills (meeting a new person, asking someone for a date, question a teacher's grade, ask someone to lower his or her voice, ask a person to stop cheating, give a command, say no to a request). Gradually, participants will be asked to identify for themselves areas of their lives that present difficulties and to describe particular problem situations that can be worked on, using the phases of the model as described earlier.

Gerald Lundquist and Gerald Parr (1978) conducted a study of assertiveness training with adolescents. Their findings confirmed that the three areas of need in the secondary schools are: talking to parents, teachers, and authority figures; talking to people of the opposite sex; and refusing unreasonable requests. The basic skills of assertive expression, of saying yes and no, and of making simple requests can begin much earlier than the secondary grades. We see them incorporated easily and unobtrusively into the elementary classrooms, where they may be used as principles of solving interpersonal issues or of self-expression in group sharing, a typical event in many elementary classrooms. As the backbone of an affective education curriculum, they may be trained for directly and taught.

Many studies of assertiveness training, such as the Lundquist and Parr study, focus on identifying the optimal format, particularly the value of modeling and behavioral rehearsal. Lundquist and Parr identified sixty eighth and ninth graders from a Denver-area junior high school, who were in the lower third of scores on an assertiveness questionnaire; thus, presumably, they identified students in need of training. The students were randomly assigned to situations using varieties of the general assertiveness training methodology. One group received modeling only, another rehearsal only, a third modeling plus rehearsal, a fourth counseling through scripts describing assertiveness behavior, and the others comprised a control group who received training after the period of study. The counselors worked with the students as individuals for forty-eight minutes, once a week, during a six-week period. At the end of the training a variety of measures were used, including an assertiveness questionnaire in which students rated themselves on how they responded to those situations, a role-playing test, a peer rating (by other students), a problem inventory, and a teacher rating.

The findings indicated that rehearsal "may be a more prudent treatment strategy than modeling" (Lundquist and Parr, 1978, p. 42). However, modeling did contribute to the effects of the training. The script counseling group, whose students corresponded with their counselors, was effective compared to the control group but less effective than the modeling, rehearsal, or combined modeling and rehearsal groups. The authors conclude that "script counseling apparently has potential for some students" (Lundquist and Parr, 1978, p. 42).

On the basis of their findings, Lundquist and Parr believe that the most feasible training model includes modeling early in the process, a good deal of behavioral rehearsal (including covert rehearsal where students "act out" behaviors in their minds without role playing), and "live tryouts of assertive behavior, starting with the least difficult or threatening situation and working toward threatening or difficult areas" (Lundquist and Parr, 1978, p. 43). The teacher should operate as coach, reinforcer, and assistant in goal setting.

Lundquist and Parr's study is thus helpful in its encouragement to use modeling, rehearsal (or role-playing stages), and live tryouts in real-life situations. Brown and Brown's (1980) review of the research does a good job of showing the acomplishments of the research to date and the directions we should take to increase our knowledge about how to conduct assertiveness training more effectively.

INSTRUCTIONAL AND NURTURANT EFFECTS

The direct outcome is the ability to express oneself in social situations, stating feelings and desires but avoiding aggressive behavior. Accomplishing this goal should nurture positive feelings about self, provide tools for dealing with conflict, and reduce stress and anxiety in social situations. As is the case of all three behavior-therapy models, a feeling of increased self-control and personal strength should emerge (see Figure 21–1).

Summary Chart: Assertiveness Training Model

SYNTAX

Phase One:
Identifying Target Behaviors

Phase Two:
Setting Priorities for Situations and Behaviors

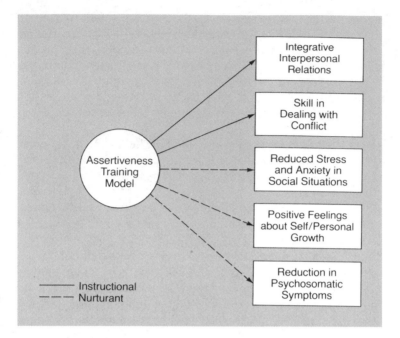

FIGURE 21-1   Instructional and nurturant effects:
Assertiveness Training Model.

Phase Three:
Role Playing the Situation

Select role players and observers.
Instruct observers.
Enact with feelings suppressed and nonassertive behavior.
Discuss components of nonassertiveness and validity of enactment.
Enact again with feelings expressed and assertive behavior.
Discuss enactment, especially component of assertiveness.
Model assertive behavior, if necessary.

Phase Four:
Undertaking Reenactments
Reenact situation showing several assertive possibilities.
Discuss the reenactments.
Practice.

Phase Five:
Transfer to Real-Life Situations
Identify specific situations.
Try out responses.
Discuss.

SOCIAL SYSTEM

The model has moderate to low structure. Initiative is shared between teacher and students. A sense of group cooperation and collaboration is established. The teacher serves as facilitator and, at times, may perform a brief instructional function.

PRINCIPLES OF REACTION

Acceptance of each person's behaviors and efforts is encouraged. The teacher should: (1) facilitate participation of everyone but accept the possibility that some students may need to hold back for awhile; (2) introduce or verbalize cognitive aspects of assertiveness whenever appropriate; and (3) encourage group feedback.

SUPPORT SYSTEM

No special support is necessary.

Part V

Educational Outcomes and Models of Teaching

INTRODUCTION

Until now we have examined specific models on their own terms, except for some stress on their "family" relationships. Now we turn to the consideration of the use of repertoire. How do we select models in order to achieve particular combinations of personal, social, and academic objectives? How do we combine them? How do we organize them so as to promote the development of hierarchies of skills, concepts, and ways of thinking.

In Chapter 22 we examine a framework for classifying educational objectives and models. In Chapter 23 we examine the types of thinking that various models promote. From our perspective, each model teaches a mode of thinking and, thus, models of teaching represent a framework for the teaching of thinking in schools. Finally, we examine the work of Robert Gagné, who has provided perhaps the most precise way of coordinating objectives and teaching strategies.

22

THE EFFECTS
OF MODELS
OF TEACHING
Academic, Personal, and Social Objectives

How do we reach into the storehouse of models and select a combination to use for a curriculum, a unit, or a lesson? This chapter explores a position on learning and teaching that provides a foundation for the selection of teaching models.

THE ASSUMPTIVE WORLD
THAT LINKS THEORY AND PRACTICE

The position rests on several theses about the available models of teaching. The first thesis is that there is a considerable array of alternative approaches to teaching. Many of these, including the ones in *Models of Teaching*, are practical and can be implemented in schools and classrooms in which students and teacher have the skills and willingness. Further, these models of teaching are sufficiently different from one another that they change the probability that various kinds of outcomes will result if they are used. Thus, the second thesis is that methods make a difference in what is learned as well as in how it is learned. The difference is probabilistic; particular methods boost certain outcomes and diminish others. Rarely do they guarantee some while obliterating the rest; often they can be combined to produce greater effects than they would if used alone.

Third, students are a powerful part of the learning environment, and students react differently to any given different teaching method. Combinations of personality, aptitudes, interpersonal skills, and previous achievements contribute to configurations of learning styles so that no two people react in exactly the same way to any one model of teaching. The power of any model resides in the ability of the students to use it.

Operating from this stance, the task of the school and the teacher is to equip themselves with a basic variety of models of teaching that they can bring into play for different purposes, employ and adapt for different learners, and combine artfully to create classrooms and learning centers of variety and depth. To do this requires clarity about what models exist, what they can accomplish, and how different students will react to them and will learn to use them.

CONTENT AND METHOD

Our focus in this chapter is on *method* and learning style. The strength of the learner is considered primarily in terms of the ways his or her characteristics interact with the variety of models of teaching available. Content and instructional material are also imporant, however, because they too interact powerfully with teaching method. For example, the content of an arithmetic course—the emphasis given to algorithms, number facts, mathematical concepts, and problem solving—can vary greatly from classroom to classroom, and selection from among the options within any content area to a large extent defines the opportunity to learn. Some physical education departments teach soccer as a sport; others do not. Some physics courses are slanted toward the applied whereas others emphasize the theoretical. In literature courses different weights can be given to poetry, short stories, and grammar, and different types of criticism can be emphasized. The continuous selection of content is an important function of teaching.

Similarly, materials have a powerful effect on the learning environment. In reading, for example, some teachers use a basal text without supplementary workbooks. Some teach through trade books and have the children choose what they will read. Other teachers build reading and language lessons from social studies and science materials. The materials themselves differ in structure and form. Audio-visual materials have properties vastly different from print materials and concrete objects.

Content and material for carrying content provide the raw, sensory data out of which learning is made. Teaching method transforms content and material through emphasis and process, and both vary according to the model used. For example, some models of teaching highlight the value implications of the content. Other models emphasize the retention of factual material. Still others emphasize concepts or methods of inquiry. Thus, the selection of method magnifies certain aspects of content and diminishes others.

PROCESS AND SOCIAL CLIMATE

The process of the method itself is also learned by the student as he or she practices learning in a particular way. Models based on ways of inquiring teach methods of thinking as well as the content that is mastered.

Finally, a model of teaching creates a certain social system within the classroom, and this social system is learned as well. Properly implemented models based on democratic process create a democratic social system and require students to learn the skills of negotiation. Those emphasizing competition provide competitive social systems that are experienced and learned by the student. Thus, method defines the emphasis given to content, provides a process to be learned, and provides a social climate that will greatly influence the behavior of learners toward one another and toward the teacher, and will in the future affect their behavior toward others. The effects of method, thus, are complex and multidimensional.

SIMILARITIES AND DIFFERENCES
IN PROCESS AND PURPOSE

When we compare several models of teaching we find that the degree of differences between them vary quite a bit. Some models resemble each other in process, others in the social climates they generate, and still others in the content they emphasize. By the same token, some are quite different in one or another of these aspects.

Very few models are good for one purpose only, although there are a few special-purpose models. Most have a primary purpose and one or more secondary purposes. We speak of the primary directions as the *instructional* effects of a model and the secondary directions as their *nurturant* effects. The picture is complex because many models can be directed toward a variety of purposes. Thus, selecting a model is not always synonymous with selecting a purpose.

Synectics is an example: It was constructed to boost creative thinking, and it can be applied to a number of content areas (science, social problems, creative writing). A side effect of synectics is group cohesion. The effect is so powerful that the model can be chosen just for that reason. Many other models have broad purposes. Group investigation, nondirective teaching, and behavior modification are appropriate for teaching parts of nearly every subject area.

Also, models are seldom used alone for long periods of time. Courses, units of work, learning centers, and curricula generally require a combination of models. Very few models of teaching alone are sufficient to define an entire curriculum, although one can serve as the core. Most models can be strengthened by being combined with a variety of others, both to be more effective in achieving any given set of desired learning outcomes and to increase stimulation and variety. Effects can be increased by an artful pyramiding of the power of several models. For example, inductive thinking (Taba) can be strengthened by adding creativity training (Gordon) and inquiry training (Suchman).

Almost any process, however attractive at first, becomes less exciting after repeated usage unless variety is provided within it. Through blending, models offer teachers the opportunity to increase the variety and to sustain the intensity of a course or unit, curriculum, or learning center.

Thus, our entire approach rests on the thesis that teachers can learn to select and blend models of teaching in such a way as to increase learning of various types. Various models can produce more of certain kinds of learning, and blends or combinations can ensure the probability of increasing learning even more.

At times it is argued that teaching methods are completely different with respect to their power. This is probably not the case. Each one is likely to boost certain kinds of learning for specific kinds of learners, but most have positive effects on several kinds of learning.

Models are not like a series of interchangeable parts with different effects so that we can plug one in to get one effect, another for another effect, and so on. Rather, each one increases the likelihood that students will learn certain kinds of things but does not depress other learning outcomes.

THE LEARNER DOES THE LEARNING

To begin with, it is the student who does the learning, and he or she is the most powerful person in the teaching/learning situation. His or her intelligence, adaptability, creativity, motivation, and general configurations of personality are much more important determiners of how much he or she will learn than anything the teacher or curricular system can do. Given the opportunity to learn certain kinds of material, the individual's capability will determine what will result more than will anything else. Teaching, however, can boost the likelihood that the student will develop in certain ways, and effective teaching can be very powerful if all teachers in a given school are devoted to the achievement of certain learning outcomes, such as creativity, and select models oriented toward creative thinking. The odds are increased that the learners will become more creative in the long run. However, the students will continue to learn facts, concepts, and interpersonal skills.

LEARNING OBJECTIVES
OVERLAP, TOO

The world would be much simpler if learning objectives did not overlap, if we sought only one at a time, and if models of teaching were completely objective-specific. In that case, we could generate a clean matrix and say, "If you want to accomplish objective X, use method X." However, life is not so simple. Various objectives not only overlap but also turn out in many cases to be embedded in one another. Also, we rarely seek one objective at a time. For example, consider some of the objectives of primary grade reading. The objective of increasing students' word-attack skills does not stand alone. It also relates to comprehension. Also, students' feelings about reading and understanding of what reading is used for probably affect the development of skills. Additionally, in every lesson, we are trying to help the student feel better as a reader and as a person. Finally, in every unit the teacher is helping a group of children to work together effectively as learners. That which appears at first to be a simple enough class of objectives—increasing students' ability to sound out words having certain kinds of characteristics—turns out to overlap with other objectives and is not an objective we would pursue in disregard of others. Consequently, as we select models, we want to choose ones that have a good chance of achieving not only the objective that happens to be the substantive core of a particular lesson (boosting word-attack skills, in this case) but also the objective that will be likely to pay off and not interfere with the other kinds of learning associated with it.

Any set of objectives is generally weighted in terms of general importance, and the weights vary from time to time. Helping a student achieve a positive self-concept has high priority some times and moderate priority at others. At certain times we concentrate heavily on helping children to work together, whereas at other times that objective is less prominent. Fortunately, most models of teaching are likely to produce more than one kind of learning at any given time. Counseling methods were derived to help the student understand himself or herself and become an independent, well-integrated personality and learner, but they can also be used to teach reading or almost any other subject. Ausubel's theory of verbal learning, which gives rise to the Advance Organizer Model of teaching, is designed to increase the mastery of verbal material by providing the students with sets of concepts within which they can store new material (Ausubel, 1963). Yet that model teaches the concepts that are at the core of the academic disciplines—as well as facilitating the retention of verbal material; it also implicitly encourages a certain attitude toward the nature of subject matter and what constitutes school learning.

Models of teaching can be modified and adapted to increase the likelihood that they will result in certain kinds of learning. For example, role playing, which is designed to make personal values accessible for study, can be combined with counseling approaches to help students acquire a strategy for analyzing values. Thus, the problem of selection is one of identifying the multiple learning objectives and determining which models are most likely, with any given group of students or any individual student, to boost the objectives most fervently sought, knowing that others will be reached as well.

ON ADDING, BLENDING, AND NOT BEING HEAVY-HANDED

The power of any given model of teaching is relative to any other model (and is affected by the style of the learner as well). Even when one model is clearly the most powerful with respect to the objective sought, one may not necessarily select that model at any given time because another model boosts other objectives deserving some priority or because a different model will reach the learner more clearly and effectively.

For example, a ski instructor may generally use very direct instructional models focusing on building skills. However, the instructor is also concerned with ensuring that the students will continue to instruct themselves, gradually overcome their fear of the mountain, and develop the spontaneity and integration of movements that make specific skills almost imperceptible from one another. Thus, at certain times the instructor may use methods more like those described in "inner tennis" or "inner skiing," which are designed to help the student "feel" the sport and free him or her from the constraints of fear, a self-image of awkwardness, and an overemphasis on performing individual skills in isolation from one another (Gallway, 1974, 1977).

Teaching method is often debated as if given methods were in opposition to one another. This is rarely the case, and we are suspicious of "overadvocacy" of any given method, even for a very specific purpose. One of the great teachers of tennis, Vic Braden, operates a tennis college that on the surface would appear to be very skill-oriented (Braden and Bruns, 1977). When teaching how to play doubles, however, Braden does not rely solely on the training models, for doubles is a matter of cooperation and mutual confidence. A good doubles team has to coordinate not only on an intellectual level but also on a personal level. Braden takes great pains to teach how to build team rapport and to help his students understand what harm disintegrative behaviors, such as deprecating one's partner, do to the team. The training model is clearly the most used and relied on, but there are strong elements of counseling and something of an atmosphere of a very lighthearted T-group in his approach to doubles. Nearly everyone, regardless of his or her level of tennis, comes away from the tennis college feeling good about himself or herself.

Similarly, even the most skilled use of models to help us inquire into English literature needs to be leavened by playful, enjoyable, and spontaneous reading without analytic overtones. On the other hand, if the only English instruction received were loose and playful, the students would not develop the concepts and analytical tools essential to a full comprehension of the subject. Thus, balance is important, and the arts of teaching require delicacy and restraint. Even though particular models of teaching will generally boost certain kinds of learning outcomes, they can be run into the ground with heavy-handedness or overuse.

In addition, the teachers' comfort with certain models will influence their effectiveness. Although a professional teacher has no excuse for not continuously struggling to improve his or her repertoire, there are certain approaches he or she will be most comfortable with or will simply enjoy the most. Within limits, one should relax and use what is most natural and spontaneous. A really good group-dynamics teacher can learn to blend techniques from other models that will help the students to master subject matter and learn tools of inquiry. The staple approach may be through group process augmented by other models that at first do not "feel as natural." Similarly, a good academic instructor can gradually learn the tools of the personal and social models to balance the teacher process.

Specific models can also have a particular personal appeal for short-term use. On certain days a teacher may have a terrific urge to clarify things or to express himself or herself and the way he or she thinks about the material. On those days he or she is likely to lecture with the use of advance organizers. On other days he or she would be bored by that same approach and would use another to stay lively and to help students stay with him or her. Pretending that we, as teachers, are not people would be a serious error in teaching, and our intuitions about what feels right on any given day should be listened to, even though we select models on an analytic basis much of the time.

PROBABLE EFFECTS
OF MODELS OF TEACHING

As stated earlier, each of the families of models of teaching comes from a somewhat different view of humans and how they learn, and each is weighted toward certain priorities. Within any of the families, however, there are models that have been used for virtually all of the purposes that are the primary focus of the other families. The difference is a matter of emphasis and degree.

There is no body of research that compares the range of models of teaching with respect to the spectrum of educational objectives, but there is a vast body of research about single models and a substantial body comparing two or three models with respect to two or three classes of objectives. From the intramodel research and the orientation of the models, we can justify statements about the probable relative effects of each family and the specific boosts to learning that are likely from the individual models.

MODELS, MISSIONS, AND OBJECTIVES

There are three types of missions in education:

1. We can attempt to reach the learner through the academic domain, by teaching academic skills and ways of dealing intellectually with the complexity of the world (as, for example, an attempt to teach mathematics). Information-processing and cybernetic models were developed for this purpose.
2. We can attempt to improve the capacity of the learner through intervention in the personal domain (as through an attempt to increase student self-direction). Personal models were developed for this purpose.
3. We can attempt to enter the social domain, to change the learner at the point of interaction with his or her fellows (as when an attempt is made to teach social or economic skills). Social models were developed to accomplish this.

POINT OF ENTRY:
THE STRATEGY OF THE SCHOLAR

Focuses from the academic disciplines are characterized by teaching ideas and techniques that have been developed by scholars. Probably more schools use academic content as their point of entry than any other approach. Mathematics is taught with the belief that the mathematician's ways of thinking and calculating will be useful in the life of the learner. History, or the historian's way of thinking, is taught with the hope that the sweep of history will help the growing student orient himself or herself in the flow of humanity. Content from the sciences is taught, or less frequently, the systems of thinking employed by scientists are introduced, to help the child learn the technologies of the modern world. Still less frequently, aesthetics, ethics, and humanitarian philosophies are taught to the child. More often than those, foreign languages, literature, or the social sciences are explored, although none of these areas is commonly taught in American public schools (see Table 22–1).

The accumulated knowledge of the human race is increasingly concentrated in the hands of professional scholars. In the humanities, sciences, and

Table 22-1   Alternative Objectives within the Academic Domain

1. Emphasize general symbolic proficiency (reading, writing, arithmetic, technical skills).
2. Emphasize information from selected disciplines (history, geography, literature).
3. Emphasize major concepts from the disciplines
   a. Treat broad, related fields together (social studies, language, arts, science).
   b. Treat a few disciplines separately (economics, physics, history, music).
4. Emphasize modes of inquiry (ways of thinking) of the disciplines.
5. Emphasize broad philosophical schools or problems (aesthetics, humanitarian issues, ethics).

social sciences, knowledge is produced systematically and at an explosive rate. And many pursuits that were at first the result of people's practical imaginations (such as marine architecture and agriculture) have become the objects of systematic scholarship. At the larger universities people presently study just about every conceivable human activity.

The school is the first formal link between this scholarly activity and the child. It can function to make the scholarly world accessible to the child and to prepare him or her for a lifelong relationship to scholarly material.

To many people, the school's primary functions should be in the academic domain. Some of these people simply see academic learning as the route to all development in all domains—they tend to brand any other function as "antiintellectual" and therefore bad. Others, however, are increasingly concerned with the complexity of the modern world and the need for every person who can to be able to handle this complexity conceptually. They too see the organized scholarly disciplines as the best possible source of this knowledge.

Far and away, the most common performance goal in education is to transmit the technical and symbolic systems that we use to communicate. That is, reading, writing, and arithmetic receive the greatest emphasis in today's elementary schools. The nursery, kindergarten, and primary school years especially, spanning from age 3 or 4 to about 9, are devoted almost exclusively to language and number development. In the middle grades we find map skills, study skills, information-location techniques, summary writing, and the like. In secondary schools the emphasis shifts to learning symbol systems of the various areas of knowledge, so that the technical language of biology, mathematics, or grammar can be more precisely utilized.

The fact that the technical-symbolic performance goal is so well established and so likely to be agreed on as one of the missions of the schools encourages the authors to minimize a discussion of it here—to spare the reader what he or she already knows. In general, that goal emphasizes precise mastery of reading, mathematics, writing, and the skills necessary to handle material in the academic areas.

When playing the role of instructional manager, the teacher emphasizes symbolic proficiency or competence. When playing the role of inquiry trainer, the teacher can take any of the last four emphases listed in Table 22-1, depending on the curriculum plan within which he or she is operating, the children with whom he or she is working, and the preference he or she shares with fellow teachers.

POINT OF ENTRY: PERSONAL CAPACITY

The human organism has many potential capacities for responding to its environment: intelligence, which includes the ability to solve problems, to analyze and synthesize information, and to build new ideas; creativity, or the

Table 22-2   Alternative Objectives within the Personal Domain

1. The developing organization of the self.
2. The development of productive thinking capacity (including creativity, flexibility, ability to produce alternatives).
3. The development of a personal meaning.
4. The development of self-teaching and problem-solving ability.
5. The development of aesthetic capacity.
6. The development of motivation to achieve.

capacity to do new and interesting things with the environment; the organization of the inner self, the feeling of adequacy or openness, and the ability to grow and face complexity; independence or autonomy, the capacity to respond fearlessly and on one's own terms; feelings of warmth and affiliation, which enable a comfortable and nonthreatening response (see Table 22-2).

In the role of counselor, the teacher tries to increase these capacities. He or she may emphasize creativity, for example, or may organize activities around the attempt to increase intelligence and rationality. Or he or she may focus on means of increasing the personality development of the individual.

A school that sees its mission as the development of personal capacity will emphasize the individual in everything it does, and thus, emphasize the role of person seeker for all of its teachers. The school will try to challenge pupils, to free them, to teach them how to teach themselves. Such a school will concentrate on the personal capacity of the individual and subordinate attention to social and academic demands in favor of personal roles.

In recent years a large number of educators and psychologists, many of them from schools of humanistic and personal psychology, have believed that a central mission of education should be the development of a strong self, the creation of a person who feels adequate and who reaches out warmly and integratively to others. These theorists believe that the function of the school lies in helping the child find and develop a healthy self, one with great capacity for personal and social development (Fromm, 1941, 1955, 1956). Education should help the child find direction rather than impose it on him or her.

Creative problem solving—the ability to produce alternatives and the capacity to integrate material into new forms—could be the means of allowing the individual to find new routes to self-fulfillment. Theorists like Torrance, Taylor, and Thelen have considered creative thinking to be the central purpose of the school. Psychologists like Hunt, Torrance (1965), Rokeach, and Wertheimer (1945) have studied the characteristics of creativity and the kinds of environments that stimulate it (see also Barron, 1963; Taylor, 1964).

Other theorists have emphasized the capacity to discover personal meaning in life and to avoid alienation through affiliation with people. Writers like Fromm and Phenix have described the process by which persons discover themselves and find meaning in a social world (Phenix, 1961). In so doing, they have defined another possible goal for the school.

Another avenue is to attempt to increase the student's capacity to direct his or her own learning, to solve problems independently, and to plan and organize independent lines of inquiry. This emphasis is found in the writing of Dewey (1910, 1920, 1946, 1956, 1960), Holt (1968), and Hullfish and Smith (1961), among others. Supporters of this goal assume that the self-directed individual will continue to grow and seek self-fulfillment throughout life.

Quite a different objective is to try to affect the students' aesthetic capacities—to change their response to beauty in the world and to imbue them with the drive to enhance the beauty in their lives and their physical and social environments. This approach is found in the works of Ducasse, Beittel, Eisner, Santayana, and again, Dewey.

Another distinct approach is to try to arouse the student's desire for self-improvement, the desire to master knowledge and skills. Described by psychologists McClelland and Atkinson, among others, this approach is recommended by educators like Hansen, and can be seen in the philosophy of many of the programs of compensatory education (Atkinson, 1966; Hansen, 1962, McClelland, 1953). Such programs frequently try to arouse the desire of inner-city children to develop themselves more fully.

These six possible alternative objectives can give focus to the role of person seeker. Any would serve well as the driving mission of a fairly vigorous school or classroom, yet these are only a few of the possible focuses of the role.

POINT OF ENTRY: SOCIAL INTERACTION

Teachers can seek, in their roles as group leaders, to enter the learners' lives in such a way as to directly affect their relations with groups, the society, and the culture (see Table 22-3). The school can help commit the student to a life of service and social activism. There are schools, for instance, in which the children are involved in social work from the middle elementary years and in which many of them take part in political activities and the affairs of international organizations. These activities reflect the focus of those schools on developing the social commitment of the students. The works of Kenworthy (1955), Preston (1956), and Cahm describe such a goal.[1]

Another societal focus was recommended by Dewey, who considered the school's role to be to commit the student to the *cooperative problem-solving* method. The school would be operated as a miniature democracy in

---

[1] The National Council for the Social Studies, *The Glens Falls Story* (Washington, D.C.: National Education Association, 1964) provides an interesting description of an entire community school's effort to carry out this objective.

Table 22-3   Alternative Objectives within the Social Domain

1. Enculturation: socializing the child to a culture and transmitting a cultural heritage.
2. Developing competence as an international citizen.
3. Developing cooperative problem-solving capacity (democratic-scientific approach, political and social activism).
4. Developing economic competence and social mobility.
5. Promoting nationalistic fervor.
6. Improving human relations: increasing affiliation and decreasing alienation.

which the young citizens would learn the arts of cooperative inquiry and would apply the scientific method to the problems that interested them as individuals and that confronted them as social beings. Dewey was the most formal and thorough spokesperson of this view, but it is also found today, though in quite different forms, in the works of Thelen (1961), Miel (Miel and Bregan, 1957), Michaelis (1963), and others. Recently, this has been expressed as an emphasis on social activism in some of the experimental schools of Washington, D.C., and other large cities.

Another objective in the social domain might be the development of *economic independence*. The school might emphasize the skills and knowledge that are essential for economic survival and development. This is a more common mission for technical junior and senior high schools than it is for elementary schools, but many people consider reading and arithmetic to be the central elementary school "subjects" because of their potential economic usefulness.

Schools in many nations have attempted to dominate children's social education with a commitment to *nationlistic ends*. William L. Shirer's *The Rise and Fall of the Third Reich* (1960) has an excellent description of the program to induct the youth of Germany during the 1930s into the service of the state. The nationalistic emphasis, in less extreme forms, still exists in schools.

Another approach to social education is to attempt to improve *human relations* directly. Such a mission characterized the school-improvement program of the Wilmington, Delaware, public schools in the late 1950s and early 1960s under the direction of Muriel Crosby (Crosby, 1965; see also Cook and Cook, 1954, 1957; Shaftel and Shaftel, 1967; Taba, 1952, 1964). The philosophy of the Bank Street School also reflected this emphasis (Mitchell, 1950).

The possible ways of approaching the student at the point of interaction with society are as numerous as the ways of attempting to develop personal ability. And, of course, personal and social development can and should be seen together. The attempt, for example, to develop a creative response might be combined with a focus on thinking creatively with respect to the society.

Similarly, the attempt to focus on personal problem-solving ability might be combined with a focus on cooperative problem solving.

The approach to personality development outlined by psychologists O. J. Harvey, David E. Hunt, and Harold M. Schroder (1961) describes the intellectual capacity to deal with complexity simultaneously with the capacity to handle interpersonal relations. Hence, their structure integrates a way of looking at intellectual and interpersonal complexity together.

In sum, educational objectives can be divided into the academic, personal, and social, but the categories are avenues and are not mutually exclusive. Personal growth, for example, can lead to academic growth. Most schools seek objectives in all three areas. Table 22–4 summarizes the objectives discussed here.

The array of broad goals is considerable. When described in terms of specific objectives the number becomes vast. Fortunately, the available array of approaches to teaching is large—there are more than enough methods to use, even for such a complex of purposes.

FAMILIES OF MODELS AND THEIR PROBABLE EFFECTS

The families of models have distinctive orientations that lend themselves to particular clusters of teaching missions. *However, it should not be assumed that the families are tailored only for specific domains of objectives.* Personal models,

Table 22–4   Selected Missions of Education

MISSIONS	ACADEMIC SKILLS	PERSONAL CAPACITY	SOCIAL INTERACTION
Alternative Objectives	1. Information from selected disciplines (commonly history, geography, and literature) 2. Structure of knowledge (concepts from disciplines) 3. Modes of inquiry (how scholars think) 4. Broad philosophical (aesthetics, ethics) Technical-symbolic skills (reading, arithmetic)	1. Self-organization 2. Productive thinking 3. Personal meaning 4. Self-teaching and problem solving 5. Aesthetic capacity 6. Motivation to achieve	1. Enculturation 2. Internationalism 3. Cooperative problem solving and social activism 4. Economic competence 5. Nationalism 6. Human relations; affiliation v. alienation

for example, can be employed to achieve social and academic goals. The issue of selection is one of relative emphasis and suitability for the learner.

INFORMATION-PROCESSING MODELS

These models focus directly on intellectual capability. Some work directly on teaching and thinking, some teach general or specific academic methods of inquiry, and others facilitate mastery of subject matter.

Information-processing models can be either inductive, deductive, or what is called "guided" discovery. Inductive models lead students through processes of inquiry. The students collect and analyze their data and form concepts about it. Deductive models provide students with frameworks for mastering subject matter and present the material to them. Guided discovery models lead students step by step through a series of tasks that represent intellectual processes.

The primary purposes are: (1) the mastery of methods of inquiry; (2) the mastery of academic concepts and facts; (3) the development of general intellectual skills, such as the ability to think more logically.

Since social and personal concerns can be the subject of intellectual inquiry, these models can also be used to nurture the development of social skills, understanding of values, and personal understanding.

PERSONAL MODELS

The emphasis of these models is on the unique character of each human being and his or her struggle to develop as an integrated, confident, and competent personality. The goal is to help each person to take responsibility for his or her own development and to achieve a sense of self-worth and personal harmony. Personalists emphasize the integration of the emotional and intellectual selves.

They attempt to help students understand themselves and their goals and to develop the means for educating themselves. Much reliance is placed on the students' self-understanding and on their becoming the active agents in learning. Many of the personal models of teaching have been developed by counselors, therapists, and other persons interested in stimulating individual creativity and self-expression. Motivation for learning comes from inside rather than outside, and these models are shaped to release the energy of the individual so that he or she can reach out to the knowledge that lies about him or her in experiential and symbolic form. Knowledge is seen, then, as possessed by individuals and transformed by them. Their unique frames of reference control the nature of knowledge as it resides within them. The mastery of academic content and skills is done by the individuals. As students understand themselves and reflect on their purposes and goals, they reach out for further development.

The teacher has to accept students as competent to direct themselves. He or she brings new ideas and interpersonal situations within range of the students, but the teacher trusts them to generate their own education with the help of the counselor, teacher, and fellow students. Teaching becomes helping students to teach themselves. Thus, the primary goals are: (1) to increase the students' sense of self-worth; (2) to help students understand themselves more fully; (3) to help students recognize their emotions and become more aware of the way emotions affect other aspects of their behavior; (4) to help them develop goals for learning; (5) to help students develop plans for increasing their competence; (6) to increase the students' creativity and playfulness; and (7) to increase the students' openness to new experience.

The student, with a counselor-teacher, reaches out to master academic content and skills. Thus, one can "teach" the goals toward the objectives of academic subjects, but it is through the learner and through his or her cooperation that one teaches. The teacher's academic expertise becomes available to the learner because of their cooperative relationship. Together the learner and teacher plan to use other models of teaching, drawing on the resources for learning that have originated from other stances. The personal models thus instruct the self and nurture the mastery of academic material.

SOCIAL MODELS

Social models draw on the energy of the group and capitalize both on common cause and the potential that comes from differing points of views and orientations. The core objective is to help students learn to work together to identify and solve problems, either academic or social in nature. Increasing ability in group organization, problem identification, clarification of values, and development of social skills are primary goals. As in the case of the personal models, academic content and skills are developed as a part of the inquiry. Problems and values are the focus, and the material is mastered in relation to them.

Some of the social family models are quite specific in their orientation (the Jurisprudential Inquiry Model, for example, focuses on public issues and clarifying values in relation to those issues), but many of them are quite broad and can be used to approach almost any academic subject matter.

The primary goals are: (1) to help students work together to identify and solve problems; (2) to develop skills in human relations; (3) to become aware of personal and social values. Secondary goals are derived from the direction of the group and can include the range of academic and social content.

CYBERNETICS AND
BEHAVIOR-MODIFICATION MODELS

The essence of these approaches is that the human being is an information-processing system that learns from obtaining feedback about the effects of behavior.

While both depend on feedback, the cybernetic approaches present students with tasks, provide them with feedback, and help them see the relationship between performance and the goals they are to achieve. As they succeed and err, they will notice the consequences and will experiment with their behavior until they reach a satisfactory level of performance. Cybernetic approaches may or may not use external rewards, but if they do, the rewards come at the end of a series of tasks when a major skill or concept has been mastered, and the students generally are permitted to reward themselves. Behavior modification approaches depend on the establishment of a contingency schedule in which correct performance is approved immediately. Sometimes this is accomplished by the development of programmed tasks designed to ensure errorless performance, under the assumption that knowledge of correct performance is satisfying and reinforcing in itself.

Cybernetic and behavior-modification approaches have been applied to nearly the entire range of personal, social, and academic skills, including skills in the psychomotor domain.

SPECIFIC MODELS
AND THEIR PROBABLE EFFECTS

Within the families, specific models have particular purposes. Some are designed for *very* special purposes and have little general use (the Jurisprudential Inquiry Model and the Relaxation Model are examples), whereas others, such as the Group Investigation Model, are very broad. Since there has been relatively little cross-model research, our data base for relative effects is slim, but research on specific models is generally positive. Most of the ones described in this book generally achieve the purposes for which they are designed.

Table 22–5 depicts the probability that ten models of teaching will boost several classes of learning outcomes directly or secondarily. The pattern of Table 22–5 indicates the relative breadth and narrowness of the direct and nurturant effects of several models of teaching. Most of the personal and social models are relatively specific but nurture a wide variety of learning objectives. The information-processing models are directed toward a larger span of objectives but chiefly function in the academic domain. Their nurturant effects are not as broad as those of the personal and social models. Generally, personal and social models are more nurturant in character, and information-

Table 22-5   Probable Outcomes Boosted by Ten Models of Teaching

MODELS (Family)		Self-Understanding	Awareness	Creativity	Interpersonal Skills	Social Values	Academic Inquiry	Concepts	Factual Material	Academic Skills	Psychomotor Skills
Nondirective Teaching	(P)	D	N	N	V	V	N	N	N	N	N
Group Investigation	(S)	D	N	N	D	N	D	N	N	N	N
Synectics	(P)	N	N	D	D	N	N	N	N	N	N
Gestalt (Awareness Oriented)	(P)	D	D	N	D	D					
Advance Organizer	(IP)						N	D	D	N	
Inductive Thinking	(IP)						D	D	D	D	
Inquiry Training	(IP)						D	D	D	D	
Cybernetic (Simulation)	(CBM)				V	V	V	D	D	D	D
Cybernetic (Training)	(CBM)				D(V)	V	D	D	D	D	D
Behavior Modification	(CBM)	V			V		V	D	D	D	D

D = Direct (primary)

N = Nurturant (secondary)

V = Variable, depending on focus (generally nurturant)

processing, cybernetic, and behavior-modification models are more directive. The probable cause for this is that the models that focus on the individual human being attempt not only to improve people's self-understanding and awareness but also to help them develop in a wide variety of ways.

Nondirective Teaching and Group Investigation are probably the broadest of all models. The first, developed from a counseling orientation, attempts to help the individual develop across the spectrum of possibilities. Group investigation, derived from a concern with broad societal development and the growth of the individual through the life of the group, also seeks to facilitate growth in many areas.

SELECTING LEARNING EXPERIENCES

Keeping in mind that this comparison is based on somewhat speculative reasoning and that the probable effects are relative, we have nonetheless arrived at the beginning of a clarified position from which to select and adapt models of teaching to increase the likelihood that various kinds of learning will take place. The position rests on the contention that there are real differences among the approaches to teaching and that these differences affect what is learned. Essentially, teaching is the creation of learning environments, and different environments are directed toward or nurture different kinds of learning. If we add to that contention Hunt's reformulation of Lewin's maxim that behavior is a function of a person / environment, then selected learning experiences are essentially a coordination of objectives, learner, and environment.

Objectives provide definitions of the behavior and content to be sought. Except for the most minute "lesson" or teaching episode, there are usually multiple objectives, with degrees of priority attached to them. As illustrated earlier, a large-scale unit of a course in reading includes a concern with skill, self-concept, and desire to read, among others. Thus, most complex units or courses require the use of several models.

Learners differ in myriad ways. Self-concept, achievement, personality, and cognitive development are but a few of the dimensions along which we can differentiate the people we teach. To complicate matters, differences among students are often not highly correlated. There are high achievers with poor self-concepts, and extroverts with good self-concepts and terrible study skills. We want to tailor learning environments to fit the learner as closely as possible, but we have practical limitations. A simple formula is to translate student characteristics into two dimensions: a need for and tolerance of *structure,* and a need for and tolerance of *task complexity. Structure refers to the degree of prescription in the environment.* The greater the structure the more detailed the plan and the less independence provided. *Task complexity refers to the intricacy of the process*—the more complex tasks require higher degrees of skill on the part of the learner.

Hunt suggests that we strive for an "optimal mismatch" between the present capacity of the learner and the model chosen so as to "pull" the student toward greater capacity but not overstress his or her capabilities. Environments can also be modified to accommodate learner needs, and model-relevant skills can be taught as necessary.

Hence, we can select models according to their appropriateness for the objectives we seek and their "fit" to learner preference for structure and varying degrees of task complexity. Compromise is obviously necessary. Nondirective teaching, for example, is appropriate for the objective of improving self-esteem but may be too unstructured for some learners. More structure may be introduced or a different model, such as awareness training, might be used because it has similar goals but can easily be employed with a fair amount of structure.

The personal, social, and information-processing models of teaching roughly correspond to personal, social, and academic missions, but as indicated earlier, the correspondence is not of the one-to-one variety. It is a question rather of emphasis and the extent to which objectives are pursued directly or nurtured. Also, as indicated earlier, we would seldom use a single model of teaching alone but rather would use combinations to boost the effects of one another. We would also modify them to reach learners who need different degrees of task complexity and structure. The models described in this book represent the capability to boost learning in nearly every domain and are characterized by a large range of degrees of structure and task complexity. Among them, they can reach nearly every learner. Careful selection should increase the probability of reaching nearly every learner in such a way as to boost the desired kinds of learning.

23

THE SKILLS OF THINKING
Teaching Students How to Learn

Old fencing masters used to tell their students that you grip the sword as you would hold a sparrow. If you hold it too tightly, it cannot breathe. If you hold it too loosely, it will fly way.

Good thinking bears analogy to the fencer's grip. It combines discipline with flexibility. If we are to nurture it we must master that paradox, and create environments that offer strength without strangulation.

We are dreaming about creating a school where the study of human thought is a central mission, where the cultivation of the intellect is comfortably woven with the study of values, the mastery of information, and training in the basic subjects.

In our school science and social science are taught with the methods of their parent disciplines. Reading, literary analysis, and writing draw on criticism and nurture productive thinking. Theatre introduces the craft and special metaphors of the stage. Domestic and international perspectives are illuminated by philosophy. The atmosphere draws talent into bloom as naturally and inexorably as springtime leads the daffodil toward its lovely fate.

The core of good thinking is the ability to solve problems. The essence of problem solving is the ability to learn in puzzling situations. Thus, in the school of these particular dreams, learning how to learn pervades what is taught, how it is taught, and the kind of place in which it is taught (Downey, 1967).

Through the ages our dream has had different forms in the minds of our most powerful thinkers. The variety of embodiments of just a few of them is wonderful to think about. Plato and Aristotle spun different webs around the subject. In the Middle Ages Acquinas created his version out of catholic philosophy; it was echoed later, in Renaissance terms, by John Amos Comenius. With secular logic Newton wove his discipline of thought. Martin Luther spoke for the Reformation, Jefferson, Franklin, and Rousseau for the democratic revolution. Dewey and James pulled the methods of science toward the psychology of thought. The distinctive orientations of Montessori, De Beauvoir, Hutchins, Adler, Bruner, Schwab, and the other academic reformers followed and are now mixed with the current arguments about how to bring electronic technology into play. The world views embraced by these people have a wide span. They emphasize different aspects of thinking and recommend different ways of teaching it. But they all agree that there is life after school and that learning to think (learning to learn) is what school is all about.

As we enter a period where this theme is again being made prominent, this time with an emphasis on the skills of thinking, we need to ponder why something so universally affirmed has so rarely become a dream fulfilled in the realities of education.

We believe that two bad habits share the majority of the blame. (The enemy, as usual, is us.) The first is the habit of setting different approaches against each other and persuading ourselves that they are incompatible. The second is by trying to reform the school without making the emotional and material investment to really change it, especially by investing in the education of its staff. By producing unnecessary argument and confusion, the first saps our strength. The second satisfies our nostalgic love of the old schoolhouse. By giving change a limp hand, we do not have to give up our old ways. Let's look at these habits in concrete terms.

THE UNNECESSARY DICHOTOMIES

The most familiar wrangles are between the emphasis on basic school subjects, most commonly the "basic skills," and on the direct teaching of thinking. The argument is usually carried on as if to do one would sacrifice the other. Otherwise reasonable people argue that if we teach the sciences inductively, we will lose coverage of the subjects, or that we will undermine values if we teach students to think about them, or even that drill and practice will always and surely dull the mind. These arguments reductio ad absurdo, riding on deeply felt emotions and expressed in hyerbole, are hangers-on from the poverty of our past, when it seemed almost too much to afford the barest education. Now, when any but the fullest education will deprive our children of important parts of the achievements of this new worldwide civilization, we must put away the childish toy of dichotomous thinking. The skills of reading, the study of values, the analytic tools of scholars, and the nurture of intuition are compatible, and we can and should teach them simultaneously or even together. As we enter this period of renewed emphasis on the teaching of thinking let us not pit the cultivation of the mind against the acquisition of skills and knowledge as if these goals were adversaries.

Our second bad habit, of trying to make educational changes without the pain of sufficient investment, must also be overcome as we renew emphasis on the teaching of thinking. We need to profit from our recent history with academic reform which, we must now acknowledge, paid sufficient attention to staff development, leadership training, and materials in only a few districts. In those it was very successful. In others, the implementation levels were so low as to make the study of effects a hopeless activity (Fullan, 1983; Fullan and Park, 1981; Fullan and Pomfret, 1977; Joyce, Hersh, and McKibbin, 1983). This time around, however, we have the advantage of knowing these mistakes and more about the process of innovation. We also have a rich storehouse of methods for teaching thinking on which we can build—we do not have to start from scratch. We have also much experience with the teaching of thinking from which we can profit.

Hence, let us now discuss that storehouse of models for teaching thinking and some of the experience we have had with them, especially how children acquire various modes of thinking and how teachers can acquire thinking-oriented teaching models.

ON NOT DOING THINGS HALF-WAY

Carl Bereiter has analyzed a variety of approaches that districts take to implement the teaching of thinking; he has identified two that are unlikely to work and a third that will. The first is to teach thinking as "enrichment." The second is to teach thinking as subject matter (Bereiter, 1984, pp. 75–77). When thinking is taught as enrichment, either special "thinking" exercises are developed and added to the curriculum or special classes on thinking are organized. In either case thinking is considered as something that is "added on," as if it were a curriculum area. Being separate from academic substance it is likely to have lower priority than the core school subjects and is thus likely to gradually disappear. Also, it is likely to be shallow because it is separated by content. It ends up in the same category as do reading skills taught separately from literature. The approach creates a false dichotomy between basic subjects and intellectual activity. Worse, it is a statement that it is all right to teach the core subjects in a manner that does not stretch the intellect so long as we stimulate it elsewhere. Then why would anyone take this approach? The reason is because it can be implemented administratively without rocking the educational boat. If teachers learn some thinking games that they can employ or they set up special workshops for thinking, then the curriculum as a whole is not touched. The hard task of learning to teach everything in an intellectually stimulating manner can be avoided.

Teaching thinking as content is the second approach. To do this, one first identifies the elements of "good thinking" and then teaches students what those elements are. (Examples are "making observations" and "drawing inferences.") What results is essentially a course in logic and problem solving. The problem is not that raising thinking to a conscious level cannot enhance it—it can. The problem is that the practice of thinking requires content if the students are to transfer use of the knowledge to outside of the "thinking laboratory."

However, it is not necessary to have separate activities or courses for thinking or to teach thinking abstractly without connection to the curriculum.

THE TREATMENT OF CHOICE— THE PERVASIVE APPROACH

As Bereiter points out, a third alternative, a "pervasive" approach, is available. It is possible to pervade the curriculum with intellectual activity so that the teaching of thinking is an important component of every activity. The reasons for adopting a pervasive approach are:

1. We have a substantial storehouse of models of teaching that directly teach both content and intellectual process. Although we always need to invent more, the existing storehouse is more than adequate to create programs that will develop many of the most powerful ways of thinking that have been discovered.
2. These models of teaching result in more effective teaching of the basic school subjects, both elementary and secondary, than the methods generally employed to teach them (Joyce, Showers, Beaton, and Dalton, 1984).
3. Teaching the basic subjects in such a way that thinking is enhanced avoids the traditional dichotomies between the content of education and intellectual activity.

There is no inherent conflict between teaching the fundamentals of citizenship in a democratic society, learning to read, write, analyze literature, engage in scientific inquiry, participate in the performing arts or athletics, on the one hand, and learning how to think on the other. The schools of thought identified earlier all have some educational truth in them and each is enhanced by the other. To teach the basic subjects without teaching thinking simultaneously not only neglects thinking, but is also inefficient. Students learn more traditional substance when mastery is generated by models that also produce intellectual growth. Similarly, the development of citizenship is enhanced by the analysis of social values and the clarification of social issues. Learning to be a committed and self-aware person is enhanced by learning to think about one's growing self and to analyze one's development and social milieu.

MODELS OF TEACHING, THINKING SKILLS, AND CURRICULUM

Various kinds of thinking are enhanced by particular models of teaching. Some models, for instance, are designed to teach students to:

> Attack problems inductively
> (Concept Formation Models)
> Attain concepts and analyze their thinking strategies
> (Concept Attainment Models)
> Analyze social issues and problems
> (Jurisprudential and Role Playing Models)
> Break set and think divergently
> (Synectics and Group Investigation Models)

Other models are designed to teach students to:

> Work together to generate and test hypotheses
> (Group Investigation and Scientific Inquiry Models)
> Reason causally
> (Inquiry Training, Scientific Inquiry, Synectics, Group Investigation, Simulation Models)
> Master complex bodies of information
> (Memory, Scientific Inquiry, Group Investigation Models)
> Analyze personal behavior and set personal goals and independent inquiry programs
> (Nondirective Teaching, Awareness Training Models)
> Analyze social situations and develop flexible social skills
> (Role Playing, Assertiveness Training, Simulation, Group Investigation, Nondirective Teaching Models)
> General intellectual complexity
> (Although all of the just-described models contribute heavily to general growth in thinking ability, the Cognitive Development and Conceptual Models are specifically designed to enhance cognitive growth.)

This is just part of the storehouse of models and the types of intellectual growth the models can stimulate. Some of them are designed to teach particular types of thinking; others are designed to teach thinking skills that are applicable in many types of situations. For maximum effect, they are generally used in combination; when they are, the results can be very impressive. Spaulding used a combination of social learning, scientific inquiry, and cognitive development with disruptive primary school students from economically deprived homes. Effects were evident on social behavior and on lower-order and higher-order achievement. Increases in general intelligence even occurred (Spaulding, 1973). Some single models, used intensively, have also had impressive results. Well-implemented Scientific Inquiry Models, for example, have achieved substantial informational and conceptual outcomes, have successfully taught methods of scientific inquiry, and have also produced increases in intelligence test scores (Bremer, 1984).

Models are combined not only to pyramid their effects but also to address the different kinds of objectives and thinking that we wish to engender. For example, learning how to memorize is an important intellectual skill but we do not expect a memory model to be the only foundation of creative thinking. Likewise, Creative Thinking Models, although they enhance memory, are not the only ones we would use to do so.

USING MODELS
TO TEACH THINKING TO CHILDREN

First of all, the core outcome of using a model of teaching is that students learn how to learn (reason) in a certain fashion. When we use a model to enhance memory, we teach students to think in such a way that they will increase their ability to memorize. Similarly, when we use inductive models we teach students how to learn inductively by thinking inductively. When we use group investigation we teach students to work together to gather information, set and test hypotheses, and balance one another's perspectives for approaching a problem area.

Second, to teach students how to think and learn in a certain way, we have to establish a program to use on a regular basis. If, in social studies, we wish to teach strategies for analyzing social issues, then we have to use the appropriate model over time and handle it in such a way that the students become increasingly able to analyze social issues independently. In other words, we teach the model to the students. This takes patience. The first time that students are exposed to a method for attaining concepts, they are likely to be inefficient. With practice and instruction they become more competent. Finally, they are able to attain concepts and analyze their thinking strategies effectively and comfortably. Teachers and administrators are often concerned that students first exposed to a model appear slow and uncomfortable with its processes. They worry that valuable instructional time is being lost. If they persist, however, they find that the students become more powerful. In the early stages, then, we provide more structure and explicit instruction in the skills necessary to learn from and use a model. As the students become more skillful, less and less instruction is necessary from us (Joyce, 1984).

Third, by teaching students how to reason independently we increase their power to teach themselves and thus to share power in the instructional situation. We cannot teach students to reason inductively and then reject the ideas they develop. We can guide them so that they develop better and better ideas. Encouraged to think creatively, students will develop solutions we have not thought of. We have to expect this and learn to love the uncertainty it creates for us.

Fourth, strategies for thinking do not come in fragments. We cannot teach their elements as isolated skills—for example, "how to observe objectively." Rather, we teach thinking strategies that include particular skills, such as how to observe, but the observations are used in relation to other skills.

Teaching thinking requires a commitment to solid instruction in the models of teaching that engender those types of thinking and the willingness to persist until the students become effective in their use. Thinking strategies are most effectively taught in conjunction with appropriate content. It is not difficult to use synectics to teach students to use metaphors and analogies more skillfully in their writing, unless we try to teach the use of metaphor separately from the acts of writing. It is not difficult to teach students to form concepts when they read, unless we separate concept formation from the act of reading.

Thus, teaching thinking requires that we teach the core subjects of the school in a different fashion, using the appropriate models systematically over time until they are a part of the students' natural repertoires.

LEARNING TO TEACH THINKING

The difficulty arises from the fact that models for teaching thinking are considerably different from the norms of instruction in most school settings. Studies of teaching and staff development reveal what any observer can easily discover: The recitation method dominates most schools and is the major item in most people's repertoires (Medley, 1981). Why is that a problem? Simply, because it means that most of our students and most of us have much more practice with recitation than with other methods of teaching. This is another way of saying that we would not have to worry about teaching thinking if we had been doing it all along. The students would be good at the appropriate models and we would be good at teaching them to use them.

24

THE CONDITIONS OF LEARNING
Focusing Instruction

One of the most important books on learning and teaching is Robert N. Gagné's *Conditions of Learning* (1965). Gagné does not provide a model of teaching as such but gives us a careful analysis of the key variables in learning and how instruction can be organized to take these variables into account. He has made a valuable contribution in developing a picture of the "varieties of change called learning," which enables us to classify and specify learning objectives and the relationships *between* various kinds of performances.

Gagné identifies six varieties of performances that can be the result of learning:

1. Specific responding;
2. Chaining;
3. Multiple discrimination;
4. Classifying;
5. Rule using;
6. Problem solving.

VARIETIES OF PERFORMANCE

Specific responding is making a specific response to a particular stimulus. An example occurs when a first grade teacher holds up a card (the stimulus) on which the word *dog* is printed, and the children say "dog" (the response).

Specific responding is an extremely important type of learning and is the basis for much of the information we possess. In order for the student to learn to make correct specific responses we must assume he or she has the ability to make connections between things. In the previous example, the printed word *dog* is associated, or connected, with the verbal statement "dog."

Chaining is making a series of responses that are linked together. Gagné uses the examples of unlocking a door with a key and of translating from one language to another. Unlocking a door requires us to use a number of specific responses (selecting a key, inserting it, turning it) in an order that will get the job done. When one takes the English words *How are you?* and translates them to *¿Como está ustéd?* in Spanish, one is chaining by taking a series of specific responses and linking them into a phrase.

Multiple discrimination is involved in learning a variety of specific responses and chains and in learning how to sort them out appropriately. For example, one learns to associate colors with their names under very similar conditions, but then has to sort out the colors and apply them to varieties of objects under different conditions, choosing the right responses and chains. Multiple discrimination, then, involves learning to handle previously learned chains of various sorts.

Classifying is assigning objects to classes denoting like functions. Learning to distinguish plants from animals, or automobiles from bicycles, involves classifying. The result of this process is *concepts,* ideas that compare and contrast things and events or describe causal relations among them.

Rule using is the ability to act on a concept that implies action. From example, in spelling we learn varieties of concepts that describe how words are spelled. Then we apply those concepts in rule form in the act of spelling itself. For example, one learns that in consonant-vowel-consonant words ending in *t,* such as *sit,* the consonant is doubled when *ing* is added. This becomes a rule (double the *t*) that one usually follows in spelling such words.

Finally, *problem solving* is the application of several rules to a problem not encountered before by the learner. Problem solving involves selecting the correct rules and applying them in combination. For example, a child learns several rules about balancing on a seesaw and then applies them when moving a heavy object.

FACILITATING THE CLASSES
OF LEARNING

Gagné believes that these classes of learning form an ascending hierarchy; thus, before one can chain one has to learn specific responses. Multiple discrimination requires prior learning of several chains. Classifying builds on multiple discrimination. Rules for action are forms of concepts learned through classification and the establishment of causal relations. Problem solving requires previously learned rules. Each level of learning requires certain conditions. The task of the instructor is to provide these conditions (by using the appropriate model of teaching).

To facilitate specific responding, a stimulus is presented to the student under conditions that will bring about his or her attention and induce a response closely related in time to the presentation of the stimulus. The response is then reinforced. Thus the teacher may hold up the word *dog*, say "dog," ask the children to say "dog," and then smile and say "good" to the students. If a teacher does this repeatedly, he or she increases the probability that the students will learn to recognize words and be able to emit the sounds that are associated with the symbols. The Memory and Training Models are approaches that facilitate specific responding.

To facilitate the acquisition of chaining, a sequence of cues is offered, and appropriate responses are induced. A language teacher may say, "How are you?" followed by "*¿Como se dice ustéd?*", inviting the students to say, "How are you?" and "*¿Como se dice ustéd?*" and provide sufficient repetition that the students will acquire the chain and achieve fluency. The Memory Model, Advance-Organizer, and Inductive-Thinking Models are appropriate to this area.

To facilitate multiple discrimination, practice with correct and incorrect stimuli is needed, so that the students can learn to discriminate. For example, suppose the students are learning the Spanish expressions for "How are you?", "good morning," and "hello"; they must learn to discriminate which one to use in a given situation. The instructor provides sets of correct and incorrect stimuli until the students learn the appropriate discrimination. Advance organizers and inductive reasoning are useful in this process.

Classification is taught by presenting varieties of exemplars and concepts so that the students can gradually learn bases for distinguishing them. Concept attainment and inductive thinking are appropriate, among others.

Rule using is facilitated by inducing the students to recall a concept and then apply it to a variety of specific applications. In the earlier spelling example, students recall the rule about doubling the final consonant when adding *ing* and are presented with examples they can practice. Inquiry training can help students move from concepts to rules.

Problem solving is largely done by the students themselves, because problem solutions are unique. It can be facilitated by providing sets of problems that the students can attempt to attack, especially when the instructor knows that the students have acquired the rules needed to solve the problem. Inquiry training, group investigation, synectics, simulation, and nondirective teaching can be used for problem-solving activities.

FUNCTIONS OF THE INSTRUCTOR

Gagné emphasizes that it is the learner's activity that results in the learning. It is the function of the instructor to provide conditions that will increase the probability that the student will acquire the particular performance. Practice is extremely important so that the learner makes the necessary connections, but it is the learner who makes the connections even when they are pointed out to him or her. The instructor cannot substitute his or her activity for that of the student. We agree completely with Gagné on this point.

The instructors (or perhaps an instructional system) operate through the following instructional functions:

1. Informing the learner of the objectives;
2. Presenting stimuli;
3. Increasing learner's attention;
4. Helping the learner recall what he or she has previously learned;
5. Providing conditions that will evoke performance;
6. Determining sequences of learning;
7. Prompting and guiding the learning.

Also the instructor encourages the student to generalize what he or she is learning so that the new skills and knowledge will be transferred into other situations.

Informing the learner of the performance expected is critical for providing him or her with a definite goal. For example, the teacher might say, "Today we're going to try to learn about three presidents of the United States. We'll learn about their names, when they lived, and what they are most known for."

The teacher then presents the pictures of Washington, Lincoln, and Theodore Roosevelt. Their names are printed under the pictures. Pointing to the pictures and names, and saying the names will draw the students' attention.

To recall previous learning, the teacher may say, "Do you remember that we discussed how the country has grown and changed in various ways? Can you tell me what some of those changes were?" The students can reach into their memories and stimulate themselves with material that will later be connected to the presidents.

To induce performance, a teacher may ask the students to name the three presidents and then read printed material describing the life of each. Then the teacher can ask them to tell him or her what they have learned.

A variety of sequences can be used, depending on the type of learning and the subject matter in question. Generally, however, presenting a stimulus, evoking attention, helping the learner understand the objectives, inducing performance, and then helping the learner to generalize are the major instructional tasks, which follow one another naturally.

Gagné has provided an instructional paradigm that is useful in defining learning outcomes and identifying the tasks of instruction. As indicated throughout this discussion, models of teaching, especially form the information-processing and cybernetic/behavior-modification families, can be used to design many of the conditions. Concept attainment, for example, provides ways of presenting stimuli, controlling attention, and evoking performance.

Gagne's paradigm also reminds us of a variety of important instructional functions not specifically dealt with in several of the models. For example, the importance of informing the learner of objectives and encouraging generalization is implicit in many models but is not spelled out in particular.

Although the instructional paradigm Gagné advocates is very direct and may appear at first to be highly controlling, he emphasizes that we cannot control learning but can only increase the probability that certain kinds of behavior will occur. We can present stimuli in close connection with others and ask the student to perform, but it is the *learner* who makes the connection between the printed and spoken word:

> It seems evident, then, that in controlling all of the aspects of external learning conditions described previously, instruction nevertheless can only make the occurrence of this crucial internal, idiosyncratic event more probable. So far is known now, instruction cannot directly control this eternal and internal event. The careful design of instruction can surely increase its probability, and, by so doing, make the entire process of learning more sure, more predictable and more efficient. But the individual nervous system must still make its own individual contribution. The nature of that contribution is, of course, what defines the need for the study of individual differences. (Gagné, 1967, pp. 291–313)

From this point of view, a model of teaching brings to the student environments that change the probability that he or she will learn certain things (see Chapter 23). The syntax presents tasks to the student, the reactions of the teacher pull him or her toward certain responses, and the social system generates a need for particular kinds of interaction with others. The net effect is to make it more likely that various kinds of learning will take place. In Table 24–1, several information-processing models and a few from other families are paired with the six varieties of performance that Gagné has identified.

The more complex models involve activities likely to increase the probability that several kinds of learning will take place. Gagné's hierarchy is useful in helping us select models appropriate for varieties of educational objectives. It also reminds us of the multiple types of learning promoted by individual models and the attention that must be given to the varieties of performance as the students engage in the study of any important topic. For example, students using inductive thinking (Chapter 3) to explore a problem in international relations, such as the balance of payments, will gather data (specific responding and chaining), organize it (multiple discrimination and classifying), and develop principles (rule using) to explore solutions to problems (problem solving).

Before beginning any extensive unit of instruction, it is worthwhile to

Table 24–1   Models Especially Appropriate for Varieties of Performance

TYPES OF PERFORMANCE		MODELS			
Specific responding	Memory	Phase one Inductive Thinking	Phase one of Concept Attainment	Advance Organizer	Group Investigation (data-gathering activities)
Chaining	Concept attainment	Inductive Thinking			
Multiple discrimination	Inquiry training				
Classifying	Concept attainment	Inductive Thinking	Advance Organizer		
Rule using	Inquiry training	Simulation			
Problem solving	Synectics	Scientific Thinking	Inquiry Training	Group Investigation	

identify the varieties of performance that will be sought, determine the appropriate models, and then analyze which kinds of learning will be emphasized in phases of the study and how they can be enhanced.

Part VI

The Student

INTRODUCTION

**AVOIDING THE MECHANICAL
TRUSTING YOUR INTUITION**

David Hunt's long experience with the problems of learning style allows him to provide us with wisdom as well as knowledge from research (Hunt, 1985).

He cautions us against rigid, mystical notions of learning style. The students we are dealing with are real, flexible people who share many elements of the same culture. As learners we differ in the ways we perceive the world, represent it, and respond to it (Kolb, 1976), but these are differences in degree and are not unbridgeable.

He cautions about trying the impossible in accommodating to individual differences. For example, it is not possible for teachers to assess the developmental levels of all their students and then create totally personalized curriculums exactly matching their levels. Nor would it be desirable to do so. Individual differences are productive in affirmative social climates.

Also, we can trust the students to adapt, if we will give them the chance. If we use combinations of words, diagrams, and dramatization when we present ideas, those who need the diagrams more can be counted on to use them more.

And, finally, the simplest way to discover the environments students progress best in is to provide them with a variety and observe their behavior. Cooperative learning will really "turn on" some of the students, but we will not learn that unless they have shared learning experiences as part of their educational diet.

We need to study our own styles, because we are likely to shade our teaching toward the modalities in which we learn best. If you find yourself using lots of diagrams it is probably because you naturally represent information that way. If you find yourself lecturing without diagrams it is probably because you favor symbolic forms of representation. Learning how you see things and respond to them you can increase your awareness about how to broaden the variety you use so that you can make it easier for your students.

The broader your repertoire of models of teaching the more you can ensure not only that you can select the combinations most fitted to your goals as a teacher but also use a range that will keep your students stimulated and adapting.

25

LEARNING STYLES AND MODELS OF TEACHING
Making Discomfort Productive

In this chapter and the one that follows we deal explicitly with the relations between styles of learning and models of teaching. First we present a general stance toward individual differences and how to teach students to learn productively from a variety of models. Then, in the following chapter, we describe a model to guide us as we coordinate learning environments and student characteristics.

Learning styles are important because they are the education-relevant expressions of the uniqueness of the individual. Individual differences are to be prized because they are the expression of the uniqueness of personalities. Individually, our configurations give us our personal identities; together, they also exemplify the richness of our society's culture.

We hope to provide our children with a common education that enhances their individuality and encourages their personalities, and simultaneously passes along our culture and its tools. As teachers we have to ask ourselves how we can use our teaching repertoires in such a way that we capitalize on and fit the development and characteristics of our students and help them achieve increasing control over their own growth.

With respect to models of teaching we can begin by avoiding two mistakes. The first is to assume that a model of teaching is a fixed, unadaptive formula for teaching that should be employed rigidly for best results. The second is to assume that each learner has a fixed style of learning that is unlikely to change or grow. Both mistakes lead us into an impossible dilemma, for if unyielding teaching methods are mismatched with rigid learners a destructive collision is inevitable. Fortunately, teaching methods have great flexibility, and students have great learning capacities and, hence, adaptability.

Consider the nature of the models of teaching we have been discussing. By its very nature, the personal family begins with the uniqueness of the learner and each personal model tries to help the students take charge of their own growth. The social models depend on the synergy caused by the interaction of heterogeneous minds and personalities. The Group Investigation Model, for example, explicitly generates the energy for learning from different perceptions of academic and social problems. The behavioral models build into instructional sequences the ability to adjust pace and complexity of tasks to the ability and prior achievement of the student. The information-processing models provide ways of adjusting instruction to cognitive development and style.

Then, perhaps most important to this discussion, we not only employ a model to teach information, concepts, skills, the analysis of values, and other content objectives, but we also teach the students to use the strategies of each model to educate themselves. In the previous chapter we cast each model as a way of teaching students to learn particular ways of thinking. From that perspective, each model of teaching can be seen as a model of learning—a way of helping students expand their styles of approaching problems now and in their futures.

Yet, as we expose students to content and learning styles that are new to them, we will inevitably cause varying degrees of discomfort. We have to deal with this by teaching our students to manage discomfort productively. The real dilemma we have to solve is that real growth often requires us to make our learners uncomfortable and we have to help them deal with the unfamiliar situations that we must create for them.

DISCOMFORT AND LEARNING

I[1] would like to begin on a personal note that explains why discomfort is so prominent in this discussion of learning styles and educational environments. Twenty years ago, at the University of Chicago, I ended a conversation with Herbert Thelen by borrowing a copy of his *Education and the Human Quest* (1960); I spent much of the night reading the book. The next day we had a chance to talk again. Among the powerful ideas Thelen had generated, one left me most stimulated and uncomfortable: Significant learning is frequently accompanied or impelled by discomfort. Sometimes he put it pungently: "The

[1] I refers to Bruce Joyce, who wrote this section.

learner does not learn unless he does not know how to respond" (Thelen, 1960, p. 61). Sometimes he put it in terms of the dynamics of the inquiry process in the approach to teaching he called "group investigation." Group investigation begins with "a stimulus situation to which students . . . can react and discover basic conflicts among their attitudes, ideas, and modes of perception" (Thelen, 1960, p. 81). Thelen challenges the effects of the "norms of comfort and accommodation" (Thelen, 1960, p. 80) that exist in so many classrooms and that mitigate against the abrasive argumentation and difficult, uncomfortable tasks that characterize effective instruction as he sees it.

My first reaction was confusion. Thelen's ideas appeared to conflict with what I had been taught regarding learners as fragile sets of concepts of self that had to be protected by a supportive environment, so that they would in fact feel *comfortable* enough to stretch out into the world. How can the learner be made comfortable and uncomfortable at the same time? I asked Thelen that question and he only smiled and replied, "That is a puzzling situation you will have to think about."

Psychologists from otherwise different orientations have dealt with the concept of discomfort for some time, albeit not always using the term as such. Personalistic psychologists are an example. Interpreters of Carl Rogers frequently concentrate on his argument for providing a safe place for learners to explore themselves and their environments. However, Rogers also emphasizes that our natural tendency as learners is to confine ourselves to those domains in which we already feel safe. A major task of counselor/teachers is to help the learner reach into those domains that are shrouded in fear. To grow, learners have to acknowledge discomfort and set tasks to help break the barriers of fear. The educator's task is not simply to unloose the environmental bounds that constrict the learners but to help them become active seekers after new development (Rogers, 1951).

Self-actualization, as described by Maslow (1959), is a state that not only enables people to venture and take risks, but also to endure the inevitable discomfort felt when attempting to use skills foreign to customary practice. Maslow's constructs apply to adults as well as children. In a four-year study of teachers exposed to a wide variety of staff-development activities, it appeared that the teachers' self-concepts were important predictors of their abilities to use new skills and knowledge in their classroom situations (Joyce and McKibbin, 1980).

The role of discomfort and the ability to manage it productively appears in a different guise when we consider developmental stage theories (see Erikson, 1950; Harvey, Hunt, & Schroder, 1963; Piaget, 1952). Most developmental stage theories emphasize not only the naturalness of growth through the stages, but the possibility of arrestation, and the accommodation that is necessary if higher levels of development are to be reached. Consider Piaget: Interpreters of Piaget are often most impressed by the naturalness of growth described from his stance—the position that the assimilation of new information will inevitably force the accommodations that lead to the success of stages of development. However, not everyone makes it upward through the Piagetian stages. Arrestation *is* possible. Accommodation sufficient to bring about the reconfiguration necessary to a new stage requires a "letting go" of the confines of one level so that the essentials of the next level can be reached. If the comfort of any given level of development is not challenged, the learner may happily forego the important leaps in cognitive structure.

In conceptual systems theory, Hunt (1971) stresses the relationship of the environment to development. He describes stages of development and the characteristics of environments that permit people to function effectively at each stage while progression to the next stage is facilitated. The next chapter presents synopses of the stages and environments that facilitate progression.

If the environment is perfectly matched to the developmental level of the learners the learners are likely to be arrested at that level. The very language that Hunt and his colleagues use is provocative. If the environment is too comfortable or "reliable" the learners may be satisfied at the stage of concrete thinking, where the ability to integrate new information and form new conceptual systems is limited indeed. To impel learners to diverge from the familiar sets of concepts that enable them to view the world in "blacks and whites," the environment must be dissatisfying in some ways. Although he approaches development from a very different perspective from Thelen, Hunt (1971) states explicitly that discomfort is a precursor to growth. To stimulate development, we *deliberately* mismatch student and environment so that the student cannot easily maintain the familiar patterns but must move on toward greater complexity. (But not too much so, for we seek an optimal mismatch where the learner's conceptual systems are challenged, but not overwhelmed.)

Research on teacher training has repeatedly uncovered a "discomfort factor" as teachers acquire new repertoires. Between 1968 and 1983 a series of investigations inquired into teachers' abilities to acquire the skills necessary to enable them to use widespread repertoires of teaching strategies (Joyce, Brown, and Peck, 1981; Joyce and Showers, 1981). Teachers could acquire skill by studying the theories of various models of teaching or skills, seeing them demonstrated a number of times (fifteen or twenty, the researchers came to believe), and practicing them about a dozen times with carefully articulated feedback. However, as teachers attempted to use approaches new to them they experienced considerable discomfort. Only a small percentage (about 5 or 10 percent) of the teachers who had learned teaching strategies new to their repertoires were able to handle the discomfort without assistance. Most teachers never tried an unfamiliar strategy at all unless support personnel were available to them. Even then, during the first half-dozen trials most teachers found the use of the new teaching strategies, whatever they were, to be extremely uncomfortable. The explanation was that the discomfort resulted in part because the teachers needed to adapt other, well-ingrained skills in order to use the new strategies, in part because students exposed to the new strategies needed to learn complementary skills so they could relate to them, and in part because the teachers felt less confident with any new strategy than they felt with their older repertoires.

The result was that most teachers withdrew from the use of strategies new to them, even after they had had careful training that brought them to the ability to produce the teaching strategy with relative ease, from a skill point of view alone. However, after a number of trials with the new strategies, they became more comfortable with and developed power in the use of the new approaches. Conceptual Level (CL) is a predictor of the ability to acquire new repertoires. The higher CL teachers mastered sets of new models more fully and also tended to use them more (Joyce et al., 1981). The relationship between conceptual level and the ability to learn new teaching strategies is partly related to how one manages feelings of discomfort attendant to learning the new repertoire. The more conceptually flexible teachers managed the process of discomfort more effectively. They incorporated the new information from their students, accommodated the discomfort of their students, and most important, learned how to live through their periods of learning until the new teaching strategies worked in their classrooms.

It also became apparent that a critical part of a teacher's task in learning to use a new teaching strategy has to do with helping the learners acquire the skills necessary to relate to the new approach to teaching. Hunt and his associates initiated a series of studies to investigate the process by which learners responsed to unfamiliar teaching strategies (Hunt, Joyce, Greenwood, Noy, Reid, and Weil, 1981). Hunt et al. identified students of varying conceptual levels and exposed them to teaching strategies that were matched and mismatched to their levels of development. Nearly all learners were able to respond to a wide variety of teaching strategies, but there were considerable individual differences in their responses. Students with a high need for structure (low CL) were more uncomfortable with teaching strategies that provided low degrees of structure, whereas learners who preferred independent direction were more uncomfortable with teaching strategies that provided higher structure.

Moreover, the students "pulled" the behavior of the teachers toward their preferred styles. Those who required the higher degrees of structure "asked" for that structure and the teachers responded by adapting the strategies to conform to the personalities of the students. Curiously, the more a given model of teaching was mismatched with the natural learning style of the student, the more it presented a challenge to the student to take an affirmative stance so as to pass through the period of discomfort and develop skills that permit a productive relationship with the learning environment.

For example, gregarious students are initially the most comfortable with social models and can profit from them quickly. However, the less gregarious students were in the greatest need of the models least comfortable for them. Hence, the challenge is not to select the most comfortable models but to enable the students to develop the skills to relate to a wider variety of models, many of which appear, at least superficially, to be mismatched with their learning styles.

The formulation gradually developed that significant growth requires discomfort. If the environment and the student are too much in harmony, the student is permitted to operate at a level of comfort that does not require the challenge of growth. To help students grow we need to generate what we currently term a "dynamic disequilibrium." Rather than matching teaching approaches to students in such a way as to minimize discomfort, our task is to expose the students to new teaching modalities that will, for some time, be uncomfortable to them.

MARGINALITY IN LEARNERS

Most of the literature about learners and educational environments emphasizes explicit matching, the adjustment of environments to the optimal "comfort level" of the students. The comfort-level matching concept appears frequently in most discussions of learning styles (hemispheric dominance, sensing modalities, cognitive levels, etc.). To consider the productive possibilities of discomfort, let us now discuss the "marginal" learners—students who experience great discomfort in the environments in which they find themselves.

Currently many educators are concerned with what are called "marginal" learners and are seeking ways to make the school environment more productive for the people who are regarded as marginal in the environment. If we consider the concept of marginality we can join the issues of discomfort and growth directly. When learners relate only marginally to educational environments, we tend to change the environments and reestablish the "norms of comfort." In fact, the discomfort they feel may be a clue to how we should behave to help them reach new plateaus of growth.

Marginality is a condition that exists when a learner has difficulty relating to an educational environment and profiting from it. Learners may relate marginally to some environments but not others. The theoretically possible range of marginality is from none (when the learner relates productively to all of the environments to which he or she is exposed) to all (when the learner experiences virtually no environments that are productive for him or her.) Educators create environments but they clearly cannot do the learning, which is why the condition of the learner accounts for so much of the variance when we consider the productivity of any given environment. If the learner is marginal with respect to a particular environment, then educational productivity for that learner is likely to be depressed; worse, if the marginality is acute, serious side effects are likely to occur. The learner becomes frustrated and, very likely, "learns" that he or she cannot be productive in that environment. If the learner generalizes from enough frustrating experiences a likely derivative lesson may be that the process of education is hopeless (from the perspective of that particular person).

Let us begin by stating a number of assumptions about learners, learning environments, and our culture.

ASSUMPTIONS ABOUT LEARNERS

ENCULTURATION   The first assumption is that our learner has been enculturated to a certain degree, having been exposed to the behavior patterns, artifacts, and cognitions that make up American culture. The learner may (or may not) have a smaller vocabulary than the average person but does possess a vocabulary, has internalized the basic linguistic properties of our language, has been a participant in the cultural process, and has been an observer of adults as they behave in our society. In other words, our learner is not culturally different from the rest of us although, within the cultural boundaries, the learner may be relatively unsophisticated. This may seem like an obvious point, but much language about marginal learners connotes, if it does not actually denote, that the people who relate marginally to the common educational environments are essentially members of a subculture so different from the mainstream that they have to be treated as foreigners. That is rare indeed. Human beings are born with the capacity to learn a culture and it is the rare person who develops cultural patterns that do not in some way match the major configurations of our society.

INTELLECTUAL CAPACITY AS A TEMPORAL FACTOR   Second, the position about intellectual differences articulated by Carroll (1971) and Bloom (1971) has considerable validity. Specifically, this position is that differences in intellectual ability as we currently measure them translate substantially into temporal differences with respect to the mastery of particular learning objectives. This second assumption relates to the first, for one way of restating Carroll and Bloom's position is that the less "intelligent" learner is not culturally different with respect to what can be learned, but may require more time, perhaps *considerably* more time, to acquire a particular cognition that resides within the culture. In other words, the learner is one of us. Some of us are slower than others to acquire some of the elements of the culture in given educational situations. We can make the optimistic assumption that our marginal learner is capable of learning but may require more time than some people do, given the situation.

STIGMATIZATION   A third assumption is that the inability to relate to a given educational environment productively has social stigma attached to it. The learner who does not fit in will be socially stigmatized by other people and, probably more damaging, will internalize the norms of the culture; failing to fit in with these norms, the learner will stigmatize him- or herself. Education, as manifested in formal institutions, is largely a public activity and the full power of the society comes down on the learner when a marginal condition exists—hence, the latent side effects. The marginal learner is punished twice: first, by being frustrated and, second, by being stigmatized by others (or by self-stigmatization).

LEARNERS ARE FLEXIBLE   A final assumption about learners is that learners are flexible. They are not fixed, but they are growing entities and have considerable adaptive capabilities. Nearly all learners have the potential to relate to a wide variety of learning environments, provided they are not made *too* uncomfortable and that they are provided with assistance to relate productively to any given environment.

ASSUMPTIONS ABOUT LEARNING ENVIRONMENTS

ENVIRONMENTS AS WITHIN-CULTURE VARIATIONS   Learning environments, viewed from a cultural perspective, are variations on our basic cultural theme. That is, all of the approaches to teaching that have dominated our literature for the last twenty-five years have had their origins in Western societies. They belong well within the cultural mainstream. Put another way, all of our models of teaching represent variety within the culture but they are not culturally different. They have originated with scholars and teachers who belong not only to the same genus and species but to the same normative configuration. Thus, both teaching models and learners have the same cultural roots.

INDIVIDUATION AND ENVIRONMENTS   Every learning environment produces a range of responses by students, expressed in terms of the efficiency and comfort with which the learners are able to interact with the environment. Loosely speaking, we can say that learning styles and environments designed to produce learning will interact differentially. No given learning environment will produce exactly the same effects on all students.

ENVIRONMENTS CAN BE ADAPTIVE   Learning environments can be adaptive, potentially at least, if we design them with flexibility in mind. An appropriate model of teaching does not simply bore into the learner in an unyielding and unforgiving fashion. Properly constructed, a learning environment fits soft rather than hard metaphors. It curls around the students, conforming to their characteristics just as, properly treated, learners also fit better soft rather than hard metaphors and can curl around the features of the learning environment.

ALTERNATIVE ENVIRONMENTS AND EDUCATIONAL OUTCOMES   Finally, there exist a good number of approaches to teaching (the construction of learning environments) that are likely to produce different effects on learners. Certain approaches to teaching increase the probability that certain kinds of learning outcomes will eventuate and, probably reciprocally, decrease the probability that others will happen. For example, contrast the Role Playing Model with the Inquiry Training Model. Shaftel's model of role playing (Shaftel and Shaftel, 1967) is designed to enable students' values to become available for examination by those students. Suchman's (1962) model of inquiry training is designed to increase the probability that students will build capability to make causal inferences. As such, all things being equal, if Shaftel's model is used to design a learning environment, it will increase the probability that students' social values will be made available to them. Suchman's model will increase the probability that the students will become more able to reason causally. We are not dealing with an orthogonal world, however. The examination of values *can* improve causal reasoning, and, vigorously conducted, *ought* to do so. Similarly, there is no law that dictates that Suchman's model cannot be used to increase the ability to reason causally about values. At any given moment it is conceivable that Shaftel's model might be more effective in teaching causal reasoning than Suchman's or that Suchman's might be more effective as an approach to social values. Over the long term, however, each model is more likely to pay off in the direction for which it was designed than it is in the direction for which it was not designed. Thus, it is wise for educators to have in their repertoires the models of choice for given learning objectives.

DEALING WITH MARGINALITY

Returning now to marginal learners, our problem is to consider what to do when a learner has a marginal reaction to any given learning environment. To keep the discussion within some kind of boundaries, let us imagine two learners who are exposed to Shaftel's and Suchman's models. Each learner responds positively to one environment and not to the other. What do we do?

In this example, both learners are marginal in one environment but not in the other. We can predict that one will engage in the study of values in a relatively comfortable way and that the other will increase the capability to engage in causal reasoning. If we do nothing the differences between the two learners will probably increase. One will get better and better at the study of values and the other better and better in reasoning ability.

For the time being, let us put aside the question of explanation—that is, let us not begin by sorting out the reasons *why* each learner responds to one environment and not to the other; instead, let us concentrate on what we can do.

SOLUTIONS FOR CORRECTING MARGINALITY

First, we reject the "do nothing" approach. We do not want to leave either of our learners in an unproductive, frustrating, and, perhaps, phobia-producing situation. A second approach is to remove the learner from the offending environment, thus eliminating the frustration. For each learner we identify the models of comfort. For each learner we eliminate the models of discomfort and choose the ones of greatest comfort. On the positive side, enough models of teaching exist that we can be relatively sure that almost any learner can relate productively to some of them. In our example we already have an initial diagnosis.

THE INDUSTRIAL SOLUTION   In what Hunt (1971) calls the "industrial" solution, we search for the approaches to teaching in which our learners are least marginal, and then we employ them. This approach makes a certain amount of pragmatic sense. Its obvious difficulty is that it eliminates for certain learners the instructional models of choice for the achievement of various kinds of objectives. Consider the case of our two learners. Since Shaftel's model is elegantly constructed to promote the study of values, our eliminating it for the learner who is marginal in it means that we are going to have to use a model less elegantly appropriate for the study of values. For any given learner that might be only a moderate loss of efficiency but if we consider large numbers of learners over a long period of time, the industrial solution has a built-in efficiency factor.

However, this is certainly a more efficient solution than ignoring the problem. It also reduces the likelihood that the most damaging side effects of mismatching will occur. The success of the industrial model depends on the assumption that we can find enough industrial models that accommodate both our students and our objectives.

ADAPTATION OF THE MODELS OF CHOICE   Another solution is to adapt the models to conform to the characteristics of the learners. We identify the reasons why a given learner has trouble relating to a particular learning environment and then modulate the features of that environment to make it easier for the learner to fit in. For example, suppose that we are using inquiry training in elementary science. It is possible that our learner who is not comfortable with the model may be reacting to the ambiguity of inductive reasoning. Our learner may like a direct route to the correct answer and may be uncomfortable asking questions that may be wrong and that, surely, do not provide quick resolution. We could moderate the task complexity of the inquiry training exercises by providing puzzlements for which there are plainly only two or three possible avenues of inquiry and to which the learner can bring considerable knowledge.

Our learner who has trouble relating to role playing may be somewhat embarrassed during enactments of the puzzling situations, may have difficulty taking the role of the "other," or may find the discussion of values to be uncomfortable. To compensate we can guide the enactments to make them relatively simple and straightforward or we can provide practice in the skills necessary to analyze values. Hunt (1971) has pointed out that if we "drill" a model "through" the learner we exacerbate our problem. If we take the trouble to find out what is bothering the learner we have many options for modifying the environment. We can increase the structure of unstructured models, decrease the structure of highly structured ones, modulate the degree of learner control, manipulate task complexity, and in other ways make the learning environment a safe one for the person who would otherwise be marginal in it.

The merits of this solution are that it permits us to continue to use the "models of choice" for given objectives—that is, the ones likely to produce certain kinds of learning—and that it reduces the likelihood that the student will be acutely uncomfortable. It depends on the assumption that the natural mismatch between the learner and the model is not too great to overcome. Because learners are members of the same culture from which the models of teaching came, we can have some confidence that they will bring some developed tools to the environment. Relatively few learners should have no capacity at all to function within a fairly wide range of models.

Much research is needed in this area. We need to study how to adapt a wide spectrum of models to learners who, on first contact with them, display varying degrees of marginality. Without such knowledge, we are left with uncertainty about how far we can go. One of the major findings of the match-mismatch studies mentioned earlier was the extent to which the students exerted modifying influences on the environment. Students who needed more structure asked more questions about procedures and literally forced instructors to provide them with more explicit information about what they were doing, even in the open-ended models. They required teachers to interrupt themselves periodically and to reexplain what was going on. They made teachers break up the model into bite-sized chunks that better fit their intellectual mouths. Other learners vied for control of the procedures, lowering the degree of imposed structure annd actually increasing the amount of ambiguity in task complexity. I was the teacher in some of these studies, and I came away from that work with the feeling that many learners will help us out if we let them. They would like to have a productive learning environment and will work with us to adapt the environment if we will give them the opportunity.

LEARNER FLEXIBILITY TRAINING A third solution for correcting marginality is to attempt to teach the learners to relate to a wide spectrum of learning environments. Maintaining our earlier example, we teach one learner the skills necessary to relate to role playing and the second learner the skills necessary to relate to inquiry training. Again, Hunt's (1971) experiments with direct model-relevant skills training have contributed significantly to our knowledge in this area. To provide skill training requires diagnosing what it is about the learner that makes for a marginal relationship to the instructional model. This training is provided to help that learner become more powerful in that kind of environment. Some of the recent studies in teacher training are instructive on this point. The more a model of teaching is different from the developed and customary teaching style of given teachers, the more uncomfortable they are when beginning to use it. Practice with the model combined with model-relevant skill training appears to make a difference. As we coach teachers who are trying to learn a new model, they identify the particular areas where they are having difficulty and we provide direct training adapted to their particular learning problems (Showers, 1982).

We need to learn much about helping learners develop environment-relevant skills. It is interesting to observe students in schools that have distinctive approaches to learning and that pay attention to helping their learners become effective in the environments they are creating. Schools that emphasize self-directed activity need to teach students how to engage in self-direction. Learning laboratories with highly sequenced activities need to help students learn to receive diagnoses and prescriptions and relate to those highly sequenced activities. Again, some of my own clinical experience is relevant. When I was the director of the laboratory at Teachers College, Columbia University, we built a set of learning centers that operated on very different models, and the students contracted for activities within those centers. We became convinced that nearly all of our learners were increasing their capabilities to learn in a variety of ways and that they adapted their learning styles to the requirements of the different centers to which they were exposed (Joyce and Morine, 1977).

If we take the skill-training approach seriously, then we devote substantial energy to teaching students to relate to an appropriate variety of learning environments. We help them master the skills of learning that will enable them to master facts, concepts, and skills, and to solve problems collectively. We include the skills of learning as basic skills in the curriculum and we measure our success as teachers partly by our abilities to help the students become more effective as learners.

From this perspective, we see individual differences in relating to learning environments in a fresh light. When a learner is uncomfortable with a particular learning environment, we know we have identified an objective—to help the learner become competent to relate to that environment. Rather than giving up, we proceed to give that learner protected practice and the special help necessary for a productive relationship to develop between learner and environment. Thus, our learner who has trouble relating to role playing is not viewed as immutably unable to study values using that technique but as someone who, through practice, can develop competence. We also modify pace, using Carroll's (1971) and Bloom's (1971) formulations as a heuristic. We assume that all learners can become able to profit from a variety of environments but that some need more time than others to become productive in specific environments. One reason learners become marginal is because they are asked to work at a faster pace than will permit them mastery of the environment. Even though most of the applications of mastery learning have been within the basic skill areas of the elementary school, we suggest that the principles would apply to the ability to master all manner of learning objectives. Hence, some learners will be slower profiting from a Rogerian environment. Others will be slower working their way through the models that are appropriate to generate divergent thinking. Others will be slower attaining concepts with the models appropriate to concept learning.

There are no special models for marginal learners. All learners are part of this culture and practically all can learn to relate to a considerable array of environments provided the environments are adapted to the learners' characteristics and we pay attention to teaching them how to learn more effectively. Experience with persons with very severe sensory handicaps provides us with a case in point. From a models-of-teaching point of view, there are no special models for the blind or the deaf. They can learn to relate to a great variety of environments and, more important, to profit from them. To fail to help them do this productively is to deny them opportunities for growth in many areas. Learning to relate to an increasing variety of environments is, in itself, growth. That kind of growth leads to a pyramiding array of possibilities for more learning.

THE INTELLIGENCE OF GROWTH

Our nature as learners contains an interesting contradition: Important growth requires change. We have to give up our comfortable ways of thinking and survive the buffets of taking on unfamiliar ideas, skills, and values. The need to grow is built into the fiber of our being. We are impelled upward in a developmental sense. Paradoxically, however, we have an ingrained tendency to conserve our beings as they are or were. Nostalgia is, in fact, a yearning not to have grown or changed. We would like to go on and see things the way we could when we were young and untutored. Curiously, the answer is to produce disequilibrium—to create environments that impel us to change, not discarding what we were at any given stage, but learning to build on it productively. Thelen's advice to us is corect: The learner needs to confront problems and diverse opinions in order to reach beyond the present stage and develop the constructs that will sustain growth at another level.

When we are infants, the process of change is built into us. We do not intend to learn language, but we do so and in so doing we change. We do not expect to walk, but walking leads us where we could not go before. Not very many years later we learn our culture and begin to function at a level so satisfying that we can stay there "forever." The purpose of education is to generate the conditions that will enable us to acknowledge the disequilibrium of change as a fundamental of the continuance of growth so that we can reach beyond ourselves toward richer understanding and accept the wisdom that lies within ourselves—that discomfort is our lot if we are not to be arrested along our road.

26

A MODEL
FOR MATCHING
ENVIRONMENT
TO PEOPLE
Conceptual Systems
Theory

SCENARIO

Terry Dorphman, a fifth grade teacher, has been studying the learning styles of his students using a system devised by Professor Robert Spaulding of San Jose State University. This sytem compares the ways that students cope with different kinds of learning situations. It describes students along a continuum from being actively involved, to being passive participants, to being actively disruptive. One of Terry's students, Mary Baker, appears to be passive most of the time, but during the last week became more active when Terry organized activities in which the students worked in pairs to solve difficult arithmetic problems. Working with another student, Mary became much more active and animated. Terry set up an observation schedule in which he recorded Mary's response to different kinds of learning situations for a period of two weeks. He then decided to praise Mary whenever she became more active and to put her into more situations in which she would work in tandem with other students. Her greater activity in the team-learning situations, he hoped, would begin to carry over into other learning activities. He also decided to reinforce her greater activity. He took care during the next month to put her into as many two-student situations as he could, and whenever possible he rewarded her when she showed greater involvement.

Sure enough, after about a week, Mary began to participate, albeit somewhat tentatively, in a group discussion. Terry praised her and took time to comment on her performance in the group settings. After class he commented on her performance and discussed it with her. Gradually, she began to reach out in a variety of situations, and other students began to respond to her. He also reinforced them when they responded to her. By the end of the month Mary was contributing to some extent in nearly every learning situation. Knowing that she would be likely to withdraw unless she received satisfaction from reaching out, Terry took pains to continue to reinforce her and was careful for some time afterward not to place her in situations in which she would have to contribute in too large a student-directed group.

Several schools of thought directly address learning styles and educational environments. Rita and Kenneth Dunn (1983) have developed a system that describes many aspects of student behavior and ways of adjusting the classroom to them. Anthony Gregoric has an interesting system for classifying thinking styles and modulating instruction to accommodate them. Robert Spaulding (1971) has built an intricate (and *very* effective) system based on social learning theory.

We are describing conceptual systems theory in this chapter for several reasons: First, there is a body of research directly exploring conceptual development and various models of teaching. Second, the theory is in itself an interesting source of approaches to child development, parenting, counseling, and teaching. Third, conceptual development is in itself a goal of education.

We feel that a general framework to accommodate learning styles is extremely important if the models are to be considered together in a coherent decision-making framework. For example, granting that nondirective teaching is designed to focus on personal development, we still need to ask the questions, "Does it provide the best environment for everyone?" "Is it possible that some people need more structure than nondirection provides?" Similarly, we may grant the efficiency of operant conditioning, but we may ask, "Are there some people who need less external control?" "Do some people need a mixture of controlling environments and situations that give them responsibility for directing their activities?" "Should we modify models for individuals, and if so, how should we go about making appropriate changes?"

Conceptual-systems theory was developed by David Hunt and his associates (Harvey, Hunt, and Schroder, 1961; Schroder, Driver, and Streufert, 1967). The theory describes human development in terms of increasingly complex systems for processing information about people, things, and events. Growth is "an interactive function of the person's level of personality development (or stage) and the environmental conditions he encountered" (Hunt, 1970, p. 4). Optimal development occurs when the environment facilitates the "conceptual work necessary for the person's conceptual growth. When environmental conditions are not optimal, then some form of arrestation is assumed to occur" (Hunt, 1970, p. 4). In other words, as the individual becomes more complex, the environment needs to change with him or her if growth is to continue at an optimal rate. One of Hunt's purposes is to help us plan environments to keep people growing conceptually. Second, since people at different stages of development respond differently, he wants to help us shape teaching strategies to match the learner's development. Theoretically, the closer a teaching strategy is tailored to the learner's conceptual level, the more learning will take place (Hunt, 1970, p. 2).

As mentioned earlier, the focus of conceptual systems theory is on the learner's cognitive complexity (the complexity of his or her information-processing system). Since the original work, Hunt and his associates have also studied other learner characteristics that affect their information-processing capacities, such as their motivational orientations (what turns them on), their value orientations (their preferred beliefs), and their sensory orientations (do they learn better through some senses than they do through others?) (Hunt, 1970, p. 2). Because work on the conceptual level (cognitive orientation) is by far the most developed aspect of conceptual systems theory, we concentrate on it here, bearing in mind the need to consider the other learner characteristics and their interrelationships at some later point.

Our first task is to examine the construct of conceptual level (CL). Then we explore its implications for the identification of optimal training environments. Finally, we discuss how to select and modify models of teaching according to the theory.

ORIENTATION TO THE MODEL

An information-processing view of personality development focuses on the structures—that is, the programs or sets of rules—by which individuals relate to their environment. For example, whereas some psychologists are concerned with the *content* of personality development (how a child feels about himself or herself) or the content of a person's political or social beliefs (preferences in political or social values), the conceptual systems theorist is concerned with the structure of the system.

Harvey, Hunt, and Schroder focus on the integrative complexity of the conceptual structure. Some individuals, for example, relate to the environment through relatively few lenses—they see fewer dimensions of a situation, and those few are not very well integrated with one another. At the opposite end of the continuum are individuals who view the environment through many dimensions and manifest a high level of integrative complexity in their relationships to it. The number of dimensions with which a person relates is not necessarily correlated with the degree of integrative complexity in his or her system (relationships among the dimensions), but there probably is some relationship. That is, the more dimensions one has, the more likely integration is present. Highly integrated information-processing systems have many more conceptual connections between rules—that is, "they have more schemata for forming new hierarchies, which are generated as alternative perceptions, or further rules for comparing outcomes. High integration structures contain more degrees of freedom, and are more subject to change as complex changes occur in the environment" (Schroder, Driver, and Streufert, 1967, p. 7).

By the conceptual systems view, therefore, we can discriminate individuals in terms of the number of dimensions they use for relating to the environment and the interrelationships of these dimensions. For example, Figure 26–1 illustrates the relationships among rules in situations of low and high integration (Schroder, Driver, and Streufert, 1967, p. 8). Individual A obtains information through three dimensions but reduces them to one integrated dimension. Individual B also uses three dimensions but processes the data he or she receives in complex ways.

To illustrate concretely, let us consider an interpersonal-relations situation. Person A would tend to respond to ideas that conflict with his or hers either by incorporating them into his own as if there were no difference, or by rejecting them completely. Person B would dissect the ideas, balancing them against his or her own, perhaps rejecting portions and accepting others, perhaps modifying his or her own.

FOUR LEVELS OF INTEGRATIVE COMPLEXITY

Particular behavior patterns are characteristic of different levels of integrative complexity. Schroder, Driver, and Steufert identify and describe four levels: low complexity, moderate complexity, moderately high complexity, and high complexity.

LOW COMPLEXITY

Let us look at the behavioral characteristics of individuals of low complexity:

1. Categorical, black-white thinking. The discrimination of stimuli along dimensions is minimally graduated; for example, if a person holds an extremely concrete attitude toward Negroes, and "Negroes" are categorized in a single way, it follows that all Negroes will tend to be lumped into one category (for example, "bad") and contrasted with others. A structure that depends upon a single fixed rule of integration reduces the individual's ability to think in terms of relativeness, of "grays" and "degrees."

A. Low Integration Index B. High Integration Index

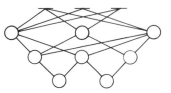

FIGURE 26-1 Variation in level of conceptual structure. (From Schroder, Driver, and Streufert, *Human Information Processing* © 1967 by Holt, Rinehart & Winston. Reprinted by permission of the publisher and authors.)

2. Minimizing of conflict. Stimuli either fit into a category or are excluded from consideration. There is no conceptual apparatus that can generate alternatives; the result is fast "closure" in choice or conflict situations (Shroder, Driver, and Streufert, 1967, pp. 16–17)

MODERATE COMPLEXITY

The major characteristics of this second structural level are: The presence of a conceptual apparatus that is able to generate alternate organizations of dimensions. That is, if there are three dimensions, such a structure would provide at least two possible rules for combining these dimensions.

This moderately low level of organization is characterized by the delineation of several alternative ways of structuring the world. Although such conceptual properties are not effective for relating or organizing differentiated sets of rules for decision-making processes, they do usher in the problem of choice and probability.

Some of the consequences of moderately low structural properties include: A movement away from absolutism. Because of the availability of alternate schemata, "right" and "wrong" are not fixed as they were in structures with low integration index (Schroder, Driver, and Streufert, 1967, p. 19)

A good deal of negativism is also present, because the individual is struggling against his or her old rules and, hence, against those who expose them. He or she especially resents parents and authority figures or any other controlling figures.

MODERATELY HIGH COMPLEXITY

Moderately high complexity is described as follows:

The system is less deterministic. Combining and using two alternate systems of interpretation greatly increase the number of alternative resolutions that can be generated. Even when the individual closes on a particular decision, he is still open to a number of alternative pressures. At this level, abstractness (that is, lack of fixity) becomes a formal rule of the system . . . .

The environment can be tracked in many more ways. While moderately low integration index structure permits different ways of tracking or interpreting an environment at different times, moderately high integration index structure can vary combinations of alternate schemata. A person who is functioning at this level may view a social situation in terms of two points of view, see one in relationship to the other, perceive the effects of one upon the other. He is able to generate strategic adjustment processes, in which the effects of behavior from one standpoint are seen as influencing the situation viewed from another vantage point. This implies, for example, that a person can observe the effects of his own behavior from several points of view; he can simultaneously weigh the effects of taking different views. The adaptive utilization of alternate schemata here is much less compartmentalized than at moderately low levels. (Schroder, Driver, and Streufert, 1967, pp. 21, 23)

HIGH COMPLEXITY

High level structure includes additional and more complex potentialities for organizing additional schemata in alternate ways. At the fourth level, comparison rules can be further integrated. Alternate complex combinations provide the potential for relating and comparing different systems of interacting variables. As with other system differences, the difference between the moderately high and the high levels is one of degree. In the latter, the potential to organize different structures of interacting schemata opens up the possibility of highly abstract function . . . .

This very abstract orientation should be highly effective in adapting to a complex, changing situation. It is certainly much more effective than a structure that is dependent upon external conditions for building rules and upon past experiences for predicting events. (Schroder, Driver, and Streufert, 1967, pp. 22, 23)

OPTIMAL TRAINING ENVIRONMENTS

According to Harvey, Hunt, and Schroder, the best procedure for inducing an individual to progress toward complexity and flexibility is to match that person's present stage of personality development to the training environment tailored to the characteristics of that stage, but in such a way as to pull the individual toward the next stage of development (Harvey, Hunt, and Schroder, 1961). The following chart summarizes the four conceptual levels described earlier and indicates in general terms the matching training environment:

Characteristics of Stage
I. This stage is characterized by extremely fixed patterns of response. The individual tends to see things evaluatively—that is, in terms of rights and wrongs—and he or she tends to

Optimal Training Environment
In order to produce development from this stage, the training environment needs to be reasonably well structured, because this kind of person will become even more concrete and rigid in an

Characteristics of Stage

categorize the world in terms of stereotypes. He or she prefers unilateral social relationships—that is, those which are hierarchical and in which some people are on top and others are on the bottom. He or she tends to reject information which does not fit in with his or her present belief system or to distort the information in order to store it in his or her existing categories.

II. In this stage the individual is characterized by a breaking away from the rigid rules and beliefs which characterized his or her former stage. He or she is in a state of active resistance to authority and tends to resist control from all sources, even nonauthoritative ones. He or she still tends to dichotomize the environment. He or she has difficulty seeing the points of view of others, and difficulty in maintaining a balance between task orientation and interpersonal relations.

III. At this stage, the individual is beginning to reestablish easy ties with other peole and to take on the point of view of the other. In his or her new-found relationships with other people he or she has some difficulty maintaining a task orientation because of his or her concern with the development of interpersonal relations. He or she is, however, beginning to balance alternatives and to build concepts which bridge differing points of view and ideas which apparently contradict each other.

IV. The individual is able to maintain a balanced perspective with respect to task orientation and the maintenance of interpersonal relations. He or she can build new constructs and beliefs, or belief systems, as these are necessary in

Optimal Training Environment

overly open social system. At the same time, however, the environment has to stress delineation of the personality in such a way that the individual begins to see him- or herself as distinct from his or her beliefs and begins to recognize that different people, including him- or herself, have different vantages from which they look at the world, and that the rights and wrongs in a situation, and the rules in a situation, can be negotiated. In summary, the optimal environment for him or her is supportive, structured, and fairly controlling, but with a stress on self-delineation and negotiation.

The delineation of self which is suggested is now taking place, and the individual needs to begin to reestablish ties with others, to begin to take on the points of view of others, and to see how they operate in situations. Consequently, the training environment needs to emphasize negotiation in interpersonal relations and divergence in the development of rules and concepts.

The training environment at this point should strengthen the reestablished interpersonal relations, but an emphasis should also be placed on tasks in which the individual as a member of the group has to proceed toward a goal as well as maintain him- or herself with other individuals. If the environment is too protective at this point, the individual could be arrested at this stage, and although he or she might continue to develop skills in interpersonal relations, would be unlikely to develop further skill in conceptualization or to maintain himself or herself in task-oriented situations.

Although this individual is adaptable, he or she no doubt operates best in an interdependent, information-oriented, complex environment.

Characteristics of Stage

order to accommodate to changing situations and new information. In addition, he or she is able to negotiate with others the rules or conventions that will govern behavior under certain conditions, and can work with others to set out programs of action and to negotiate with them conceptual systems for approaching abstract problems.

CONCEPTUAL DEVELOPMENT AND THE MODELS OF TEACHING

The models of teaching in this book have been substantially different in structure. This should facilitate matching for conceptual complexity, because models of high structure are generally most appropriate for individuals of *low* complexity, and models of low structure are most appropriate for individuals of *high* complexity. Table 26–1 characterizes each of the models in terms of its degree of structure. It should be remembered, however, that each model can be modified substantially. Low-structure models can be "tightened" and high-structure models can be "loosened."

Hunt hypothesizes the following:

> Given the characteristics of low CL learners—categorical, dependent on external standards, and not capable of generating their own concepts—the prediction follows they will profit more from educational approaches providing a high degree of structure. Given the characteristics of high CL learners—capable of generating new concepts, having a greater degree of internal standards, and being capable of taking on different perspectives—they should profit more from approaches which are low in structure, or degree of structure may not affect their performance. Thus, the heart of the CL matching model is a generally inverse relation between CL and degree of structure: *Low CL learners profiting more* from high structure and high CL learners profiting more from low structure, or in some cases being less affected by variations in structure. (Hunt, 1970, p. 19)

Thus, we can search for the amount of structure the student needs and select models closest to the needed degree—or, equally, *we can modify models to increase or decrease their structure to fit the level at which the student operates best.*

CLASSROOM APPLICATION

The teacher has three important tasks in relation to the conceptual system of the child. First, he or she can learn to discriminate children according to levels of development. Second, inasmuch as individuals of varying levels of in-

Table 26-1   Classification of Models by Amount of Structure

NAME OF MODEL	AMOUNT OF STRUCTURE	APPROPRIATE CONCEPTUAL LEVEL
1. Inductive (Taba)	Moderate	Moderate
2. Inquiry Training (Suchman)	High	Low
3. Scientific Inquiry (Schwab)	Moderate	Moderate
4. Jurisprudential Teaching (Oliver and Shaver)	High	Low
5. Concept Attainment (Bruner)	Moderate	Moderate
6. Developmental (Piaget)	Can vary from low to high (usually high)	Low
7. Advance-Organizer (Ausubel)	High	Low
8. Group Investigation (Thelen)	Low	High
9. Social Inquiry (Massialas and Cox)	Moderate	Moderate
10. Laboratory Method (National Training Laboratory)	The T-group is exceedingly *low* structure, whereas the exercises can be *moderately* structured	High
11. Nondirective Teaching (Rogers)	Low	High
12. Classroom Meeting (Glasser)	Moderate	Moderate-high
13. Synectics (Gordon)	Moderate	Moderate-high
14. Awareness Training (Shutz)	Moderate to low	High
15. Conceptual Systems (Hunt)	Varies from low to high	_____
16. Operant Conditioning (Skinner)	High	Low

tegrative complexity perform very differently in different environments, the teacher must create an environment that is *matched* to the complexity of the student. Third, environmental prescriptions can be made to *increase* the integrative complexity of the individual—that is, the optimal environments for *growth* in personality can be identified.

Let us look closely at each of these three tasks. Discriminating the conceptual level of individuals is extremely important because of the effect of conceptual level on the perceptual world. The "real" world of a person of low complexity (who regards his or her environment as fixed, prefers hierarchical relationships, is evaluative, and becomes rigid under even moderate stress) is very different from the real world of a person of high complexity (who can generate many alternative avenues for dealing with stress and opposition, accepts the responsibility for creating rules in new situations, and can easily build conceptual bridges between himself or herself and problem situations). The first individual is not likely to be adaptive or flexible, whereas the latter individual is likely to have the capacity to generate new solutions to problems and to adapt to changing conditions. This would be true whether the individual is young or old. For example, mature physicists of about equal knowledge who differ greatly in integrative complexity could be expected to face problem situations very differently. Similarly, an elementary school youngster of very low complexity would be expected to perceive civil disorder differently from an individual of high complexity (Hunt and Hardt, 1967).

The very different performance of individuals who differ in conceptual complexity under different conditions makes the second task—creating an environment matched to the student's complexity—an interesting challenge for the teacher. For example, when Hunt divided groups of culturally deprived youngsters in Syracuse according to their levels of integrative complexity, teachers found that the groups of low complexity had difficulty carrying on discussions. A discussion technique simply was not appropriate for individuals who view the world as fixed and rules as unchanging and permanent. On the other hand, individuals of moderate structure who were engaged in delineating themselves sharply from authority were very easy to engage in debate, although the debate was terribly vigorous and difficult to control.

In other words, for optimal growth in complexity, the student needs to be exposed to an environment matched to the characteristics of his or her world. An environment in which a complex individual will flourish would create unbearable stress for a person of low complexity. There are considerable implications here for educational theory and practice. Many theorists, for example, advocate specific democratic forms—process teaching and Rogerian methods of teaching for all learners (Rogers, 1951). Under conceptual systems theory, however, we would postulate that Rogerian teaching methods could be threatening, stressful, and possibly even destructive if they are rigidly applied to individuals of very low complexity, although they might be optimal for individuals of moderate to high complexity.

Hunt's research on the Upward Bound programs in the United States validated the position that personality and training environment should be related. Hunt examined a sample of Upward Bound prgrams and found that when environment and trainee personality were matched (high structure with low complexity, and vice versa) the greatest growth took place (Hunt and Hardt, 1967).

The third task is to provide environments that will help individuals become more complex, and the hypothesis that makes the most sense at this time is to attempt to lead the person's present state of development slightly—that is, when an individual is at a low level of complexity, one would want to have a moderate amount of complexity in the environment, but not too much. The tasks presented to the individual, for example, should involve some negotiating about rules, but not total negotiation as, for example, under Rogerian conditions.

Hunt's model is really a plan for changing social systems to match the complexity of the learner. As such, none of the stage-prescribed environments really has a syntax in the sense that we have been speaking of it—that is, it suggests principles for behaving in relation to the student, depending on the kind of person he or she is. For students of low conceptual level, tasks or educational approaches of low complexity, with high sequence and a clear establishment of the rules, would be indicated. For students of high complexity, a very emergent structure, with higher task complexity and an interdependent social system, would be indicated.

The teacher is considered to be the agent responsible for developing the training environment appropriate to the student. He or she is to radiate a variety of environments, depending on the students with whom he or she deals. For students of low conceptual level, the instructor is to be fairly controlling, clear in his or her directions, supportive, but fairly direct. When dealing with students of high conceptual level, the teacher needs to be much more interdependent and mutual, placing much more of the burden for learning on the students and helping them develop their own structure.

APPLICABILITY AND RESEARCH

Hunt's paradigm has been developed to produce changes in the personality dimension of the individual's general information-processing capacity. It represents a frontal approach to personality development. This contrasts with approaches aimed at specific behaviors, rather than at the generic behavior of individuals. For instance, Margarite Warren (1966) has applied Hunt's work in counseling delinquents in San Francisco. She has attempted to change the ways in which delinquents process information from their environment—the very ways they relate to the environment—and has tried to produce training environments likely to do this. A probation officer, on the other hand, is likely to try simply to keep track of a delinquent, making sure that he or she observes the rules and does not engage in any delinquent behaviors. As Warren applied the Hunt model, however, the probation officer's task became one of attempting to change the delinquent's general behavior rather than to suppress specific undesirable behaviors. If this same principle were applied to mathematics teaching, the teacher would attempt to match the environment to the student in such a way as to improve his or her general capacity for handling information. This would be regarded as much the task of the instructor as would be the task of teaching specific mathematical devices to process information.

Thus, a social studies teacher who can match students and environment should be more effective at teaching the social studies and have a more comfortable time in managing the students than a teacher who does not make such a match. For example, students with a high preference for structure could be very uncomfortable under conditions of low structure and might not learn as much as they would in highly structured environments. This notion is especially brought out in Hunt's work in the evaluation of Upward Bound. No one type of training program appeared to be more effective than any other, but when students were matched with the appropriate program, greater growth seemed to occur. Presumably, if there is validity to this type of theory, the same should be true in any classroom situation.

Hunt, Joyce, and others have engaged in a series of investigations to determine the relationship between conceptual level and student response to a variety of teaching models. These are described in some detail in a series of papers by Hunt and in a lengthy review (Joyce, Peck, and Brown, 1979). In most of the investigations students who varied considerably in conceptual level were taught using models of teaching representing different structures. It was expected, for example, that the high CL students would perform more effectively in the relatively unstructured models such as group investigation than would the low CL students. Generally speaking, the results of Hunt's theories were confirmed by these investigations. Conceptual level definitely affects student behavior when different models of teaching are used, and the directions of the differences in behavior generally confirmed conceptual systems theory. Student learning from various models of teaching is also affected by conceptual level. For example, in experiments with the Inductive Thinking Model, students of higher conceptual level formed more concepts, but factual learning was about equal. Apparently more flexible students function more effectively as the cognitive demands of the model increase, resulting in the development of greater conceptual activity and hence increased numbers of concepts learned.

Hunt modified his theory considerably in the 1970s and is presently experimenting with ways of helping low CL students compensate by acquiring skills that will enable them to relate to models of teaching otherwise beyond their grasp. He generally takes the optimistic view that even though conceptual level may predict student responsiveness, the differences in responsiveness can be compensated for to some extent by effective training and by modifying the teaching strategy. From this point of view differences in conceptual level help to identify needed types of training rather than prohibit students from participating in certain kinds of education (see Hunt and Sullivan, 1974).

There are a great many other theoretical positions from which matching models have been developed. Piaget considers the kinds of models developed to match learning with the cognitive development of the learner. Thelen has emphasized the compatibility of students and teachers, recommending that a teachable group be composed of students bearing similarities of certain types, who work with a teacher well suited to respond to that kind of student (Thelen, 1967).

Kohlberg has recommended that moral education take into account the kind of approach used by the teacher and the stage of development of the student: "There is also an important problem of match between the teacher's level and the child involved in affective moral communication. Conventional moral education never has had much influence on children's moral judgment because it has disregarded this problem of developmental match (Kohlberg, 1966, pp. 1–30).

A differential training model can be used as a blueprint for describing a wide variety of teaching strategies as they are appropriate to given individuals. Looking over the models of teaching described here, one may feel that some of them will have great effectiveness with some learners, and very little with others unless they are modified to fit the learner's personality. Possibly any science of behavior that ultimately emerges will require us to learn about the differentiation among human beings as well as the regularities to which we are all subject.

SKILL TRAINING FOR SPECIFIC MODELS OF TEACHING

Hunt's optimism led us to consider how we can increase the range of models from which students can profit. It is surely true that students react quite differently to various models of teaching, and everybody finds that there are certain ways of learning most comfortable for him or her. But nearly everyone learns something from each model of teaching; there are very few students whose characteristics are so pronounced that they cannot profit to some extent from any given model.

Some students, however, are extremely uncomfortable in relatively chaotic social situations that often prevail in group-investigation and encounter groups. Other students are somewhat uneasy if there is too much control of their behavior, such as the conditions that prevail in game-type simulations and training models.

Rather than excluding students from experiences with those models, we find that we can adapt the teaching strategy so that most students can be relatively comfortable using them. We should be optimistic about students' abilities to learn from a variety of models of teaching: A major goal of education is to help students develop the skills they need to react productively to an increasingly broad spectrum of approaches to learning.

Thus, a considerable portion of our energy when we are teaching is directed toward helping students learn "how to learn" so that they will become increasingly independent, versatile, and productive. We take the position that the ability to respond productively to any model of teaching is more a matter of skills on the part of the learner than it is a matter of any kind of immutable characteristic. Our task as teachers is to identify the skills necessary to use the model productively, find out which ones our students possess, and teach them the others. For example, role playing requires the ability to analyze a problem situation, to take the part of another in the enactment, and to empathize with alternative points of view. In addition it requires skill in expressing one's value position and in developing concepts that build bridges between one's own values and those of others.

Some of the instruction in model-relevant skills can take place in the course of using a given model. Inquiry training, for example, is built on the premise that students need to learn skills of inquiry. We do not expect a high level of performance the first time students attempt to engage in the inquiry process. However, those early attempts provide us with the opportunity to learn which skills the students need so that we can teach them directly. Also, students learn through practice. For example, when engaging in the enactments of role playing for the first time, students are often "stagey" and artificial. With successive enactments, however, they learn that role playing depends on involvement, and they begin to overcome their awkwardness and shyness and play the roles more spontaneously.

Generally speaking, the more complex the social action required by a model and the more demanding its intellectual tasks, the more initial difficulty students will have with that approach to teaching. Unfamiliarity also increases initial difficulty. For example, students who have never engaged in directing their own learning activities will have considerable difficulty with the Nondirective Model in which the teacher relinquishes control and increasingly asks the students to direct their own educational activities. After a time, however, the students will become more accustomed to taking directions and learn the skills of setting their own objectives, reflecting on their own experiences and accepting feedback from the teacher. Thus, practice with the model gives the students a chance to learn some of the skills it requires. Those not acquired by practice we can teach directly.

Table 26–2 outlines the skills directly related to the four families of teaching models. Personal models, for example, emphasize the individual as the primary actor in his or her own education. Thus, the skills involved in accepting responsibility for growth, such as setting goals, making personal plans, and reflecting on them are critical. Similarly, skills in stating needs are crucial, for if individuals are unable to make their needs known, it is difficult for them to set goals or make realistic plans. At the same time, the skill of analyzing one's own behavior has to be developed if the student is to come to the increasing self-awareness necessary to conduct his or her own education.

The skills in the social models include practical interpersonal skills such as negotiating goals and plans with others, but also include the far more complex skills necessary to clarify one's values, analyze one's role in group situations, and take the view of others. There are also substantive skills involved in debating alternatives and in negotiating goals and plans. Until the learner has skill in perceiving his or her own behavior in the group, social models are not very satisfying.

The skills important to the information-processing family have to do primarily with collecting and organizing information, generating and testing

Table 26-2   Student Skills for Families of Models of Teaching

PERSONAL	SOCIAL
Accepting responsibility for growth (setting goals, making plans)	Negotiating goals
Stating needs	Negotiating plans
Reflecting on self	Clarifying values
Analyzing one's behavior	Debating alternatives
	Understanding oneself as transactor
	Analyzing roles
	Taking view of other

INFORMATION PROCESSING	BEHAVIOR MODIFICATION
Collecting data	Identifying objectives
Organizing data	Receiving feedback
Generating hypotheses	Providing self with feedback
Relating data to hypotheses	Studying one's progress
Stating concepts	
Relating data to concepts	
Stating theories	
Relating data to theories	

hypotheses and theories, and moving back and forth from data to more abstract concepts and ideas. Unless these skills are developed, the student is extremely dependent on the teacher.

Finally, effective participation in behavior-modification programs requires that the students understand clearly what they are to learn and that they develop skill in receiving feedback, including providing themselves with information about their progress. Without becoming a student of his or her own behavior and developing a keen awareness of the relationships between tasks and outcomes, the student is a helpless victim of the behavioral system.

This list of skills is by no means exhaustive, but it does illustrate the kinds of skills that can be taught systematically.

TEACHING STUDENTS THE MODEL-RELEVANT SKILLS

At certain times within teaching episodes, skills are concentrated on and practiced. With inquiry training, for example, students need to develop the skills of listening to one another and tracking down the facts involved in the problem situation. At first many students lack these skills, and students are likely to ask their own questions without regard for the line of inquiry being pursued by others. It is not difficult to present the students with relatively simple problems and then demonstrate to them how one follows up another person's line of inquiry. Many basic skills can be taught simply by interrupting the sequence of activities and concentrating on a particular skill.

Training sessions can be organized for students who have special skill needs. An experiment to verify a hypothesis in inquiry training, for example, may be easy for some students and not others. We can provide time to work more closely with the students whose skill deficits are greatest and ease them through the early stages of training.

ADAPTING THE MODEL

Similarly, the teacher can take a more active role in structuring activities in the areas in which students are having difficulty. Nearly all learners, from children to adults, are unaccustomed to engaging in the problem-solving activities characteristic of group investigation. Thus, when students are first learning to engage in group investigation we can provide more structure, taking a more active leadership role, so that students are not asked to engage in activities beyond their independent capabilities. As they become more familiar with the model, we simply loosen the structure, turning increasing amounts of control over to the learners.

In the Scientific-Inquiry Models many students have considerable difficulty engaging in lengthy series of experiments. We can modulate the model by selecting relatively simple problems, helping students identify experiments that are fairly easy to perform, and providing greater leadership for them. As the students learn to engage in the inquiry, we simply increase the complexity of the problems, provide more independence in the identification of experiments, and turn over greater degrees of the leadership to them. Throughout the process, we continuously adjust the activities to the ability levels of the students as they gradually learn the model.

In all models, the teacher should be open with the students. Part of their task is not simply to learn the material under consideration but to become increasingly capable of directing their own activities. The students, in other words, gradually learn the model itself.

LEVELS OF STRUCTURE

In general, then, we work to help students develop the skills necessary to profit from the approaches to teaching that we use, and we gradually teach them to assume control. The first time that students are exposed to game-type simulation, we make elaborate preparations to acquaint them with the game, its purpose, and its rules, and we lead them step by step through the simulation. After several such experiences, students should take an active role in orienting themselves, identifying the goals and rules, and governing their own activities.

"Classroom discipline" is thus a matter of teaching students how to relate to instruction and helping them assume greater responsibility for their own learning. In the "best-disciplined" classrooms, students know what they are doing, how to go about it, and how to govern themselves. Until this stage has been achieved, we cannot say that "discipline" is complete, in any sense of the word that relates to the purposes of the school. Thus, we begin with relatively high levels of structure, both external control and assistance. Gradually we reduce that control as the students become increasingly capable of governing their own affairs.

As indicated earlier, the best way to identify the skills students need is to let them practice with the method and observe their behavior. In inductive teaching, for example, if students are having trouble collecting data, instruction can be provided to help them become more effective. Similarly, students working with group investigation may be relatively good at negotiating goals and fairly poor at clarifying values. We can teach much more effectively if we take the time to diagnose the skills our students need to carry out the models of instruction being employed.

Part VII

Professional Skill
and Knowledge

Despite our attempts to illustrate in practical terms what the alternative approaches to teaching look like in classroom practice, this book is not intended to provide the instruction necessary for a complete practical application. By using it and the sources from which it draws, a highly skilled teacher can begin to explore some of the approaches, and working together, teachers can bring themselves to a considerable level of expertise. The companion books, *Information-Processing Models of Teaching*, *Social Models of Teaching*, and *Personal Models of Teaching*, contain the relatively complete instructional systems to help people acquire competence in eight models selected from those three families. If used with their accompanying video tapes, which demonstrate ways of carrying on each of the eight models, nearly every motivated person can learn to carry on those models in a reasonably powerful form.

In this part we explore a few of the questions about how to learn a repertoire of models, including how many to acquire, how to choose them, how to go about learning them, and how the repertoire chosen will very likely affect one's teaching style. For a relatively complete review of the research into learning a repertoire of models of teaching, the reader is referred to "The 'Models of Teaching' Community: What

Have We Learned?" in the *Texas Tech Journal of Education* (Joyce, 1975); *Flexibility in Teaching* (Joyce, Peck and Brown, 1975), and *Power in Staff Development* (Joyce and Showers, 1983).

27

HOW TO LEARN A TEACHING REPERTOIRE
Training Ourselves

It is plain from the research on training that teachers can be wonderful learners. They can master just about any kind of teaching strategy or implement almost any kind of sensible curriculum—if the appropriate conditions are provided. It is also clear that those who critize the motivations of teachers, worry about their willingness and ability to learn, or believe that the only way to improve the teaching profession is to change its personnel are fundamentally wrong. High-quality training will give excellent results. Important new learning involves pain, and teachers are well able to withstand the discomfort. In many quarters teachers have been undersold as learners simply because inadequate training has been provided.

Let us consider the case of a new member of the Inland School faculty:

Sharlene Daniels is in her fifth year of teaching. During her first four years she worked in Rolling Hills, a suburb of a small city. Rolling Hills had a reputation as a very good district and a fine place to work. The district inservice program in Rolling Hills consisted of three one-day workshops, and the board of education was proud that they had been able to persuade the community that the two days that they closed school each year for the workshops would pay off for the district in the long run.

The first staff development day took place just before school opened, the second in November, and the third in March. Rolling Hills hired well-known consultants, who generally brought a complete day's set of activities with them. Sometimes, however, they would start things off with an inspirational speaker in the morning and then have consultants for the elementary, middle, and high school for the rest of the day. Sharlene heard several fine speeches and watched a host of performers present their methods for teaching the various elementary and secondary subjects.

When she tried their ideas in her classroom, however, she became very frustrated. What had sounded so good and looked so reasonable didn't work out very well in her hands.

Her principal looked in on her regularly and praised her orderly, attractive classroom and her good ideas for teaching reading.

At the end of her first year she enrolled in a reading clinic at a nearby university. For eight weeks, she studied with the team of teachers that operated the clinic and took courses in the diagnosis and remediation of reading disabilities. Sharlene thought that her strengths were in the content areas of social studies, science, and literature, but her principal was concerned with how she taught reading and arithmetic and didn't seem particularly interested in her ideas for teaching reading through the content areas.

Nonetheless, by the end of her fourth year of teaching, Sharlene was comfortable. She had learned the role of teacher as it was acted out at Rolling Hills. Still, she was able to back off from the role a bit and reflect on the school and the education it was providing its students. She wondered how the school could be regarded as one of the best in the area when science, mathematics, social studies, creative writing, and literature were missing from the curriculum. She realized that she was working in a very pleasant, but very limited environment where the skills of reading and arithmetic were dominant, but where the reading and writing was not very literary and the arithmetic not very mathematical.

At a weekend science workshop she became acquainted with some of the members of the Inland School faculty in another school district. She noticed that they had come to the workshop as a team and that they were gathering materials and making plans for their workshops back at Inland. They let her join them. Later, she visited the Inland school and watched that team and others at work, teaching before each other, offering advice and experimenting together.

When an opening at Inland appeared, Sharlene applied for it on an impulse, was interviewed, and accepted. The members of the team to which she was assigned explained that she would have a "coaching partner" and that she and that partner would visit each other, watch each other teach, and give each other assistance. They also had to agree on one or two teaching strategies that they would focus on each year and make a commitment to master them and experiment with them in the classroom.

Before the first workshop, Sharlene was given curriculum materials and an explanation of the rationale behind the teaching strategy approach that was to be used. The first workshop was devoted almost entirely to a discussion of the uses of the strategy, the theory behind it, and how various children responded to it. Sharlene was surprised, because she thought the workshop would be devoted to demonstrations. However, those were reserved for the workshop's second session: The Inland consultant demonstrated the teaching strategy, teaching the teachers the same kinds of lessons they would later be teaching to children. Several of the team members were uncomfortable with science, so the consultant decided that it was important for those persons to become familiar with the learner's role in the teaching strategy because they would soon be teaching their children those same roles. At the end of the workshop, the consultant did a careful demonstration with a group of children. She explained the teaching strategy to both the children and the teachers and, after the children had gone, they discussed the lesson and how it could be adapted to various groups of children. For the next workshop, Sharlene found that *she* was expected to prepare a lesson and teach it to her fellow teachers.

At that workshop, Sharlene and the rest of her team took turns teaching one another. Thus, she got to see the other teachers practice the strategy. Her team then made plans to try a couple of prototype lessons for their students over the next two weeks. Those two weeks were very uncomfortable ones for Sharlene. Things did not go quite as planned. She found herself thinking she already had developed several fine ways of teaching and wondering why she should go to the trouble of learning these new methods, especially if it was going to be painful to learn them. Her coaching partner laughed when Sharlene shared her thoughts and explained that everyone felt the same way. They had learned that it wasn't too hard to understand any new teaching strategy and to develop a certain skill with it, but until they had tried it a dozen or so times, they all felt varying degrees of discomfort. "The better you are," explained her partner, "the worse you feel, because you're used to having things go well. Actually, things probably are going well, but you just don't feel as comfortable as you did teaching in the ways that have become familiar to you."

Sure enough, after five or six tries with the children Sharlene began to feel much more comfortable. She was actually able to get the children to engage in inductive thinking and it excited them. Then the teachers began to demonstrate for one another. Soon she found herself in the library after school teaching a group of her students surrounded by a ring of her fellow teachers. She had watched the other teachers occupy the same position, but this was her first time and she felt like a child on the first day of school. After the children left, she was surprised that no one made critical comments. Then she suddenly realized that none of them ever made critical comments to one another. Instead, they offered suggestions. More important, most of the discussion that followed came after a comment by one of the teachers whom Sharlene had felt looked the most confident and even nonchalant in the workshop settings. "You just showed me a new level of that lesson," she said. "I've been doing all right and thought I had it right, but the way you handled that teaching strategy gave me a lot of ideas that I can use to make it a lot stronger than I believed it was."

Sharlene was learning what it meant to go from a school with a minimal curriculum and a minimal inservice program to a school whose faculty had learned how to train themselves to make curriculum changes for the school as a whole and to add new teaching techniques to their individual repertoires.

After a couple of months, during which each teacher tried the new strategies a dozen times or more, they began to feel "possession" of the strategies. Then initial discomfort passed to feelings of strength and power. They owned a new tool and it became part of their "natural" repertoires.

The Inland team is engaged in the serious study of alternative models of teaching (Joyce and Weil, 1980), using training procedures that enable them to bring almost any approach to teaching within their grasp. The elements they use include:

The study of the theoretical basis or the rationale of the teaching method;

The observation of demonstrations by persons who are relatively expert in the model;

Practice and feedback in relatively protected conditions (such as trying out the strategy on each other and then on children who are relatively easy to teach);

Coaching one another as they work the new model into their repertoires, providing companionship, helping one another to learn to teach the appropriate responses to their students and to figure out the optimal uses of the model in their courses, and providing one another with ideas and feedback.

In previous reviews (Joyce and Showers, 1981, 1982), we have accumulated reports of research into the effects of each of these components on the development of skill in the use of a new approach to teaching and on the transfer of that approach into one's active teaching repertoire. The study of theory, the observation of demonstrations, and practice with feedback, taken together (provided they are of high quality), are sufficient to enable most teachers to develop skill to the point where they can, when called upon to do so, use the model fluidly and appropriately. However, the development of skill alone does not ensure transfer. Relatively few persons, having mastered a new teaching skill, will then transfer that skill into their active repertoires. *In fact, few will use it at all* (Showers, 1982). Continuous practice, feedback, and coaching are essential to enable even *highly motivated* persons to bring additions to their repertoires under effective control.

To master a single teaching strategy, the Inland team uses procedures that are much more complex and extensive than common staff development procedures. Yet anything short of that effort will, for most people, fall short of its objective. Why is this so? We think the answer is in the nature of the process of transfer—of building competence in complex teaching skills to the point that they are incorporated into the teaching repertoire.

HORIZONTAL AND VERTICAL TRANSFER

Classically, transfer refers to the effect of learning one kind of material or skill or the ability to learn something new. When practice in one kind of athletic skill increases ability to learn another, *transfer* is occurring. Teaching, by its nature, requires continuous adaptation; it demands new learning in order to solve the problems of each moment and situation. Teaching skills and strategies are designed to help teachers solve problems—to reach students more effectively. To master a new teaching strategy, a teacher needs first to develop *skill* in the strategy. This can be accomplished in a training setting, such as a workshop. Then, the teacher needs to acquire executive control over the strategy, including the ability to use it appropriately and to adapt it to the students and classroom setting. Sometimes the achievement of executive control requires extensive amounts of new learning that can only be accomplished through practice in the classroom. It is at this phase of the mastery of the new strategy that the distinction between horizontal and vertical transfer becomes important.

Horizontal transfer refers to conditions in which a skill can be shifted directly from the training situation in order to solve problems. *Vertical* transfer refers to conditions in which the new skill cannot be used to solve problems unless it is adapted to fit the conditions of the workplace—that is, an extension of learning is required *before* problems can be solved effectively. Vertical transfer is more likely when: the context of training and the conditions of the workplace are different; a given skill is different from one's existing repertoire and does not fit easily into it; or additional understanding is needed to achieve executive control over the skill.

When the work and training settings are virtually identical, a skill often can be transferred from the training setting to the workplace "as is" with little additional learning on the job (horizontal transfer). For example, carpenters who learn to use a handsaw in a woodshop can, on the job, recreate the conditions of the shop almost exactly and apply their skill very much as they learned it in the training setting. When a new technique is introduced, carpenters can add it to their repertoires without much additional learning. The chief problem is integrating the new skill into existing patterns of behavior. Vertical transfer, however, involves differences in context so sufficient that new learning has to take place as the skill is transferred into the work situation. The additional learning has to occur in the work setting. In a real sense, the trainee must repossess the skill in the work context.

Examples of the vertical transfer problem abound in fields like counseling and teaching. In training settings, counselors can be introduced to the theory of an approach, they can see a demonstration of it, and they can practice it under simulated conditions. However, when they try to apply this skill in the workplace, they have the clients' needs, characteristics, and course of therapy to contend with. Counselors cannot simply go out and practice skill "X" whether or not the client needs it; they have to wait for the appropriate opportunity and exercise judgment about when and how to employ the skill. In addition, although the counselor can be taught to recognize variations in clients and general principles for adapting the skill to different clients, clients come in very great variety. The use of the skill requires counselors to learn about their clients, enter their frames of reference, and adjust the skill to their needs. In other words, to use the skill effectively, it must be transformed to "fit" the situation.

The distinction between horizontal and vertical transfer refers to the amount of learning and repossession of the skill that is necessary if it is to be functional in the work situation. When the skill just "slides" from training place to workplace, we say that the process is horizontal. When additional learning is required to transfer the skill, we speak of the process as vertical.

An important factor is the degree to which the new skill disrupts existing patterns of performance. Familiarity is the key here. The greater the degree to which a new skill fits into already familiar patterns, the less adjustment is needed. For example, imagine a primary teacher who employs Cuisenaire rods to teach mathematics concepts and definitions and who organizes the students into small groups to work with the rods. If that teacher is then introduced to the use of the abacus, he or she will need much less adjustment than a teacher who never uses concrete aids. The nonuser will have fewer existing behaviors to draw on and may have to develop a new pattern of organization as well (such as organizing groups of students to use the new material). In other words, the second teacher will probably have more skills to develop and more adjustments to make in order to be able to use the skill effectively.

DEVELOPING EXECUTIVE CONTROL

The conditions of performance can be divided into two categories—those in which the circumstances of performance *demand* the utilization of the skills and those in which the skills are brought into play as a consequence of a judgment made by the performer. In military and industrial settings, considerable effort has been expended in the development of "standard operating procedures"—that is, sequences of skills that have been previously organized for each worker. For example, during the training of infantry platoons procedures are developed for dispersing personnel, for organizing them to bring their fire to bear on given targets, for developing clear fields of fire, and for advancing on a target while keeping dispersed and under cover.

As much as possible, standard operating procedures include directions about when to bring to bear a cluster of relevant skills. In other words, a shifting and changing scene of events is reduced as much as possible to sets of operations that can be brought into play when the appropriate cues appear in the environment. General principles are formulated and taught so as to activate the skills. In training pilots, sets of skills are clustered around the elements of a flight plan and are brought to bear on demand. Entering the cockpit, the flight personnel know what to do to check out the equipment and instruments in the aircraft, communicate with the control tower, and leave the parking space. Another set of skills is brought into play to bring the aircraft to the edge of the runway, yet another to obtain clearance and propel the aircraft into flight. Other sets of closely monitored skills are brought to bear to carry out the flight plan and bring the aircraft to a safe landing.

The more closely the skills are identified and the principles governing their use defined, the less the trainees are permitted to use their own discretion. For example, factory workers are organized to the point where judgment is exercised as little as possible and breakdowns are referred to supervisory personnel.

Teaching personnel operate with relatively little surveillance and few standard operating procedures. For example, a teacher of English has considerable latitude about the literary works that will be studied, the concepts that will be emphasized, the relationship between the study of literature and the study of writing, the teaching strategies that will be used, and the methods of evaluation that will be exercised. As presently organized, the tasks of teaching are not composed, as are the tasks of factory workers, of sets of objective-related activities to be called up in sequence according to predetermined principles. Consequently, the content of teacher training cannot be organized just by referring to a set of standard operating procedures. When a teacher is taught a range of teaching strategies and the appropriateness of those strategies to various kinds of objectives and students, the transfer of those skills into the workplace is largely under the governance of that individual teacher.

Teaching behavior *can* be more closely prescribed when highly detailed curriculum plans and elaborate training programs have been designed to prepare teachers to engage in highly standardized activities. However, in most phases of their work, teachers have wide latitude and work under little surveillance (Miles, 1981). Their training must provide them with usable repertoires, not simply prepare them to implement sets of predefined operations.

In the phases of work where competence is derived from one's judgment-controlled repertoire, the effective use of a skill depends on what we term "executive control." Executive control consists of understanding the purpose and rationale of the skill and knowing how to adapt it to students, apply it to subject matter, modify or create instructional materials attendant to its use, organize students to use it, and blend it with other instructional approaches to develop a smooth and powerful whole.

Showers' (1982) recent study of teachers learning to use several models of teaching previously unfamiliar to them has provided new insight into the process of developing executive control during the period when vertical transfer is being accomplished. Showers' teachers were able to develop skill in the training situation with little apparent difficulty . . . . As they began to practice the strategies in their classrooms it became apparent that they needed help less with the observable skills for implementing the models than with the thinking processes necessary to use them effectively. The attainment of executive control became the major content of the coaching process that assisted them to transfer their skills to the workplace.

Teachers otherwise positive toward the content and process of their training and willing to practice the new teaching models in their classrooms, but who could not think conceptually about what they taught, and how and why, were apparently unable to use the new models successfully during the teaching of the experimental unit used as a transfer task for all teachers.

Teachers who did not, or could not, use the new strategies during the transfer task (a social studies unit focused on the town of Roussillon, France) rarely cited difficulty in thinking of ways to use the models as the reason for their failure to do so. Instead, they tended to mention time pressures or technical deficiencies. An examination of the lesson plans and interview data, however, revealed interesting differences in the organizational approaches taken to the material. While "low-transfer" teachers aimed toward mastery of factual lists (the climate, crops, occupations, and so on of Roussillon), "high-transfer" teachers focused on objectives, such as a "comparison of social mores in Roussillon-Eugene" and the "effects of Roussillon's economic system on politics and family life." Apparently, the high-transfer teachers could readily find appropriate uses for teaching strategies that stressed conceptual and analogic student thinking. The executive control they developed with the new teaching strategies appeared to be an essential ingredient in the successful navigation of transfer.

DISCOMFORT: A PROBLEM
CREATED BY EFFECTIVE TRAINING

During transfer, many teachers experience some degree of discomfort for several reasons. To begin with, learning to use new skills involves greater effort than using old ones. Second, new skills "feel" more awkward and less neutral than familiar ones for some time. Third, the use of an important new skill involves some risk. Instruction may go less smoothly until the new skill is mastered. Until executive control is achieved, the use of the skill can be confusing and laborious. The more important the skill, the more powerful it is, the greater the discomfort will be because it disrupts more behavior than a trivial skill.

Discomfort reduces the pleasure of practice and leads to avoidance because using the new skill can be more painful than continuing familiar ones. Thus, the teacher who needs the most practice—the one for whom the vertical path will be steepest—is the one most likely to avoid that practice.

ATTACKING THE TRANSFER PROBLEM

We believe that the "problem" of transfer is actually a new stage of learning that becomes a problem only if it is not recognized. The learning process does not stop once a teaching skill has been obtained. That skill must be transformed when it is transferred into one's active teaching repertoire. The conditions of the classroom are sufficiently different from training situations that one cannot simply walk from the training session into the classroom with the skill completely ready for use. It has to be changed to fit classroom conditions. The appropriate use of the skill in its context also requires that an understanding of the students, subject matter, the objectives to be achieved, and the dimensions of classroom management all be under "executive" control—that is, clearly understood so that skill can be used appropriately and forcefully.

All of us are less skillful with a model of teaching that is new to us than we are with the ones we have been using for some time. Successful transfer requires a period of labor during which the skill is practiced in its context until it is tuned to the same level of fluidity as the rest of one's repertoire. To confound things somewhat further, sets of teaching behaviors that surround and make one's existing repertoire function well may actually prove dysfunctional when new models of teaching are added to the storehouse of skills.

For example, suppose a teacher who is accustomed to running brisk and pointed "drill-and-practice" sessions begins to learn how to work inductively with students. The swift pace of the drill and practice, the directive feedback to the students, and the ability to control the content and movement of the lesson are at first somewhat dysfunctional as the teacher assumes a less assertive stance, relies more on the students' initiative, probes their understanding, and helps them to give one another feedback. The new teaching strategy seems awkward. Its pace seems slow. The teaching moves that served so well before now appear to retard the progress of the new kind of lesson. After a while, however, practice in context smooths off those rough edges and the new strategy gradually comes to feel as comfortable and "under control" as the old one did.

Of course, for some people the process of transfer is easy, but for no one is it effortless. For most of us, vertical transfer requires substantial assistance. Let us see what we can do to attack the problem, to create conditions that will enable teachers to achieve vertical transfer with as much ease and power as possible.

EXPERIENCE OUTSIDE
OF EDUCATION

In military, industrial, and medical applications trainers traditionally attack the problem of transfer in three ways. First, they attempt to bring training conditions as close as possible to an approximation of the work situation and emphasize the "overlearning" of skills. Second, they attempt to design the work situation to bring about demand conditions in which the routines of skills can be applied very much as they are learned. Third, they try to simplify the problem frame of the workplace whenever a repertoire of new skills has to be learned.[1]

BRINGING TRAINING IN LINE WITH THE CONDITIONS OF THE WORK-PLACE With the use of devices such as simulators, designers of training have attempted to provide circumstances in which skills can be practiced in situations as close as possible to those encountered in the workplace. In these training contexts, the study of theory, the use of modeling, and opportunities for practice with careful feedback are mixed in such a way as to bring the trainees to the highest possible levels of skill. Then they are taught to apply the skill under realistic conditions.

The idea is to *minimize* the amount of new learning that has to take place during the process of transfer. Obviously, if the training conditions can be made exactly equal to the conditions of the workplace, and the trainee brought to the point at which he or she can exercise a high level of skill in those training conditions, then the new learning required to bridge the gap to the workplace will be minimized. "Overlearning" means that supervised practice is continued *after* the point where an acceptable criterion of performance is achieved in order to develop really smooth processes that are very much under control.

CONTROLLING THE CONTEXT OF THE WORKPLACE: CREATION OF "DE-MAND" CONDITIONS In military, industrial, and commercial applications, considerable effort is exerted to provide *predictable* conditions of work so that the skills learned in training can be put into place with minimum disruption. Assembly lines, for example, are organized in such a way as to minimize unpredictable events. Detailed work plans are developed and control mechanisms put in place to ensure that they will be carried out. In a curious kind of way, this serves to make the workplace an extension of the training setting, and in fact training is used as one of the mechanisms for controlling the workplace.

Pilot training is a good example. Pilots are taught how and when to behave in certain kinds of ways in training and are not expected to invent different kinds of sequences capriciously in the course of their work. They are, in fact, to make the workplace conform to the routines that have been learned during training. This again minimizes the problem of transfer—that is, it reduces it to one of horizontal rather than vertical transfer. Every possible behavior is in a sense programmed, and the necessary skills for exercising those behaviors are taught in the training situation. Of course, pilots do face unpredictable conditions sometimes, and for these they are taught general principles involving the exercise of judgment and new learning as problems are being solved.

Similarly, business procedures are routinized. Accountants are not only taught how to set up accounting procedures but to exert control in the workplace so that those accounting procedures can in fact be implemented.

[1]For a discussion of occupational differences in conceptions of training and its practice, see Joyce and Clift, 1983.

CONTROLLING THE PROBLEM SETTING WHERE A JUDGMENT-APPLIED REPERTOIRE IS NECESSARY   Most intricate, perhaps, are the attempts to simplify the setting for application when it is not possible to create a complete approximation of the workplace in the course of training.

Medicine provides a good example. Physicians are prepared with sets of skills and strategies for solving problems, many of them highly standardized. A mixture of practical experience and lectures, readings, demonstrations, and practice under close supervision is used to develop skills in those routines. However, the medical profession has no managers who attempt to provide a complete system for the practice of medicine or for its application in the workplace. Physicians make judgments about what skills in their repertoire they will apply in a particular work setting and when, and they assemble that repertoire as they deem it necessary in order to solve their problems.

What *is* done is to provide conditions under which the exercise of judgment can occur under optimal conditions. Generally speaking, physicians contact one patient at a time so they can concentrate on the symptoms of that patient. When working under emergency conditions, they can call on laboratories and deploy other personnel to carry out treatment. If puzzled, they can call on colleagues. These conditions do not eliminate the problem of transfer from the training situation into the workplace, but they do simplify it.

In emergency circumstances, doctors behave very much like workers in very complex factories, applying routines that have been organized well in advance to stop bleeding, restore breathing, and provide assistance to stabilize the human organism. In most of their practice, however, doctors work in problem-simplifying situations that give them the time to apply their repertoires in a relatively deliberate and judgmental fashion. Similarly, counselors work with one patient at a time or with small groups to establish programs that give them an opportunity to observe their clients and make decisions about which treatments to apply.

In contrast, teaching is a very confusing and difficult setting. The circumstances of young teachers are cases in point. There has been much attention recently to the stress beginning teachers experience in their early months and years of teaching. From a training point of view, this stress is not surprising at all. Even assuming that their training has been excellent, beginning teachers are thrust into a situation in which they have to organize up to six classes of children. They select the content to be taught and the teaching strategies and instructional materials to be used; they learn to manage children, handle behavior problems, and relate to parents, and they struggle to get along with both administrators and peers—all of this in circumstances in which they meet their clients in large groups where the stimuli for individuals are mixed with those of many others.

Moreover, they work in a field where many types of problems and situations are not approached systematically through training, so they have to manufacture solutions to many problems on the spot. Under these conditions, transfer is extremely difficult. Excellent training may have provided them with fine teaching strategies, but these will be good for only certain purposes. They have to decide on an appropriate occasion for using the strategy, adjust it for not one but twenty to thirty clients, and gain their on-the-job practice while engaging in a large number of other complex tasks.

MAKING TRAINING MORE EFFECTIVE

The basic problem is the acquisition of ideas and skills and obtaining executive control over them—the expansion of professional competence and its application in a complex situation.

What can be done? We propose that the following elements be included in training programs:

1. Forecasting the problem of transfer throughout the training process;
2. Developing very high degrees of skill prior to classroom practice;
3. Providing explicitly for executive control;
4. Providing for practice in the workplace immediately following skill development;
5. Providing for "coaching" by peers as vertical transfer is being accomplished;
6. Generating a "learning how to learn" effect.

These should not be implemented separately and, as we see, require a quite different attitude toward training than has been common in the past. But, each element contributes distinctively to the achievement of our goal.

FORECASTING THE PROBLEM OF TRANSFER

The first step is to teach everyone involved in training about the problem of transfer and what they can do to overcome it. The trainees must be made aware of what is involved in horizontal transfer. Failure to forecast transfer is one of the reasons why teacher candidates develop the view that the first components of their training programs are "theoretical" and useless. It is a mistake for teachers to believe that if they attend a workshop, even where a skill is explained, demonstrated, and practiced, that they will need no further learning to bring the skill under control.

Teacher trainees must be mentally and emotionally prepared to engage in the practice necessary to permit new learning to take place. Even experienced teachers will find themselves uncomfortable with new skills for some time for the reasons we have already described. They will have much less control over the new skills than the skills in their existing repertoires, and consequently they will feel less competent with them. The skills that surround the new skills in action will also need to be adjusted or "reprogrammed" in order to minimize interference from them.

The teacher must accept responsibility for the struggle to achieve transfer. To ease the struggle, the first step is to develop an understanding of the process of transfer and accept the challenge it presents. The experience of the approximately 5 percent of teachers who have managed to incorporate new teaching strategies into their repertoires without assistance has much to tell us. Several who we have interviewed indicate that they are well aware of what is involved. They forecast the problem for themselves and consciously push themselves through the period of discomfort, deliberately altering customary patterns to accommodate the new skills and viewing the dislocation of familiar skills as a challenge to be overcome.

DEVELOPING A HIGH DEGREE OF SKILL

A major part of the attack is the development of a *high degree* of skill in the training setting. Quite simply, it is not reasonable to expect poorly developed skills to be transferred. Thorough training conducted in an adequate time frame is essential. While there are quite a number of formulations of training elements, four conditions appear to be both necessary to and adequate for the development of job-related skills in most vocations and professions. The first of these is the exploration of the theory of the skill through lectures, discussions, readings, and so forth. The trainee is brought to an understanding of the rationale behind the skill, why it is constructed as it is, how it is used in the workplace, and the principles that govern its use. Study of theory facilitates skill acquisition by increasing one's discrimination of the demonstrations, by providing a mental image to guide practice and clarify feedback, and by promoting the attainment of executive control.

Second is the demonstration of the skill (modeling). Although the mechanisms by which modeling works are not clearly understood, skill development is greatly facilitated by seeing demonstrations of it. Skills can be demonstrated in settings that stimulate the workplace, mediated through film or videotape, or conducted live in the training setting. Demonstrations can be mixed with explanation; the theory and modeling components need not be conducted separately. In fact, they have reciprocal effects. Mastery of the rationale of the skill facilitates discrimination, and modeling facilitates the understanding of underlying theories by illustrating them in action.

The third component is practice of the skill under simulated conditions. The closer the training setting approximates the workplace the more transfer is facilitated. Considerable amounts of skill can be developed, however, in settings far removed from and different from the workplace. "Peer-teaching," practice with other teachers, even has advantages. It provides experience as a "student," enables trainees to profit from one another's ideas and skills, and clarifies mistakes. It also is a good arrangement in which to develop the skills of peer coaching. Peer teaching and practice with small groups of children are safer settings for exploration than a full classroom. How much practice is needed depends, of course, on the complexity of the skill. The more simple skills, or those most similar to previously developed ones, will require less practice than those that are more complex or different from the teacher's current repertoire.

Finally, feedback about performance greatly facilitates skill development. Trainees can learn to provide feedback to each other and, utilizing audio or video recordings, can critique themselves once they have a clear idea of the skill and how to use it.

Mediated packages have been developed that provide presentations of theory, demonstrations, and instructions on how to practice and obtain feedback. A motivated trainee can learn a relatively simple skill on his or her own. Complex skills or models of teaching, however, generally require training staff to demonstrate, provide feedback, and help the trainees visualize implementation.

When a new skill fits easily into a trainee's existing repertoire, the development of a high degree of skill is in itself sufficient to bring about transfer by a motivated learner. When the skill involves an expansion of one's repertoire, however, further training in the workplace is necessary for most trainees if they are to gain control of the skill. Even horizontal transfer demands the attainment of a much higher degree of skill than has been customary in most training applications in teacher education.

Our current rule of thumb is that trainees learning a new teaching strategy probably need fifteen to twenty demonstrations over the course of the training sequence and a dozen or more opportunities to practice the skill. Sharan and Hertz-Larowitz (1982), in a program designed to teach a new and complex teaching strategy to a group of Israeli teachers, provided sixty hours of theory, demonstration, practice, and feedback in one year before instituting a combination consultant and peer-coaching treatment to facilitate transfer of the new strategy to the workplace in the following year. One- or two-day workshops simply do not provide enough time to develop the degree of competence necessary for most trainees to be able to apply a new skill in the work setting.

EXECUTIVE CONTROL

Important skills cannot be used mindlessly, and principles need to be developed in the training setting concerning the appropriate use of the skill, how to modify it to fit the students, how to tell when it is working, and how to read one's own behavior and the behavior of the students to determine the degree to which it is effective. Principles for executive control provide teachers with the intellectual scaffolding necessary to understand the skill and its appropriate use and to discriminate elements of the skill from one another. During practice in the workplace, the teacher uses these principles to judge appropriate use and decides how to modify behavior to accommodate the students. Not until the teacher can select the strategy when it is appropriate to do so, modify it to fit the characteristics of the students, implement it, and assess its effectiveness can we say he or she has achieved an adequate degree of executive control. A deep rather than superficial understanding is necessary both for the effective use and durability of new skills in one's repertoire. (See Fullan's [1982] discussion of the importance of deep rather than surface understanding.)

PRACTICE IN THE WORKPLACE

The more new learning that is necessary to transfer the skill into the active repertoire the more the trainee has to be prepared to practice the skill (preferably, as we see in the next section, with assistance from experts in the skill or from other trainees who are also attempting to integrate it into their active repertoires). We can set forth a number of principles to guide the practice. The first is that practice must follow *immediately* after the attainment of the new skill. If a teacher is learning a new teaching strategy in workshop settings, he or she should practice the new strategy several times under classroom conditions right after the skill has been obtained. If much time elapses before practice in workplace conditions, there will be a serious loss of skill and understanding.

Second, the first practices provide *some* new learning, but the major outcome will be a clear understanding by the teacher of the amount of new learning that is going to be required to achieve full transfer: teaching students to respond to the new strategy, modulating the strategy to accommodate differences in learning styles, changing classroom patterns, and so forth.

Teachers conduct their classrooms by establishing sets of activities and socializing the students to partake in them. They read cues from the students and adjust their behavior in accord with the requirement for that activity flow. A new teaching strategy requires that the teacher obtain new information from the students and modify long-standing patterns of behavior that have become relatively automatic. We estimate that fifteen or twenty trials are necessary before this integration takes place to the point that teachers feel nearly as comfortable with fresh strategies as with their older repertoires.

Both thought processes and deeply ingrained behaviors are triggered by events in the classroom. To the extent that these long-standing behaviors are appropriate to the use of a new skill, they will encourage its integration. However, to the extent that they are not, the teacher will feel uneasy and familiar and comfortable skills will be dislocated as the new strategy is used. After about fifteen or twenty trials, a more comfortable state will be reached, however, as greater understanding and skill with the new behaviors provides competence in integrating new repertoire with old.

THE PROCESS OF COACHING

Setting up arrangements for the trainees to develop a self-help community to provide coaching is regarded as essential if transfer is to be achieved. Ideally, "coaching teams" are developed during training. If we had our way, *all* school faculties would be divided into coaching teams—that is, teams who regularly observe one another's teaching and provide helpful information, feedback, and so forth. In short, we recommend the development of a "coaching environment" in which all personnel see themselves as one another's coaches. For now, however, the primary function of coaching is to assist in the acquisition of new teaching skills. Thus, most of the illustrations that follow are of teachers organized into coaching teams . . . .

What does the process of coaching actually involve? We think it has four major functions:

1. The provision of companionship;
2. The provision of technical feedback;
3. The analysis of application (extending executive control and attaining "deep" meaning);
4. Adaptation to the students.

THE PROVISION OF COMPANIONSHIP   The first function of coaching is to provide interchange with another human being over a difficult process. The coaching relationship results in the possibility of mutual reflection, the checking of perceptions, the sharing of frustrations and successes, and the informal thinking through of mutual problems. Two people, watching each other try a new model of teaching for the first time, will find much to talk about. Companionship provides reassurance that the problems are normal. Both trainees find that their habitual and automatic teaching patterns create awkwardness when they practice the new procedures. Concentrating on unfamiliar moves and ideas, they forget essential little odds and ends. The companionship not only makes the training process technically easier, it enhances the quality of the experience. It is a lot more pleasurable to share a new thing than to do it in isolation. The lonely business of teaching has sorely lacked the companionship that we envision for our coaching teams.

THE PROVISION OF TECHNICAL FEEDBACK   In the course of training, our team members learn to provide feedback to one another as they practice their new models of teaching. They point out omissions, examine how materials are arranged, check to see whether all parts of the teaching strategies have been brought together, and so on. "Technical" feedback helps ensure that growth continues through practice in the classroom. The pressures of the context tend to diffuse the teaching experience and draw attention away from the new teaching strategies. The provision of technical feedback helps keep the mind of the teacher on the business of perfecting skills, polishing them, and working through problem areas. Nearly any teacher who has been through a training process can learn to provide technical feedback to another teacher.[2]

The act of providing feedback is also beneficial to the person doing it. The coaching partner has the privilege of seeing a number of trials of the new model by another skilled teacher. It is often easier to see problems of confusion and omission when watch-

---

[2]Technical feedback should not be confused with general evaluation. Feedback implies no judgment about the overall quality of teaching but is confined to information about the execution of model-relevant skills.

ing someone else teach than when attempting to recapture one's own process. Ideas about how to use the model are also collected through observation. When a group of four or six teachers observes each other regularly, they not only can give technical feedback to each other, they can receive it vicariously while watching others on the team provide it. Among them, they will also produce a number of fine practices that constitute further demonstrations and from which they can obtain ideas for maximizing their use of the model.

ANALYSIS OF APPLICATION: EXTENDING EXECUTIVE CONTROL   One of the most important things one learns during the transfer period is when to use a new model appropriately and what will be achieved by doing so. Selecting the right occasions to use a teaching strategy is not as easy as it sounds. Nearly everyone needs help in learning to pick the right spots. Unfamiliar teaching processes also appear to have less certain outcomes than do the familiar ones. From the early trials, one often has the impression that one has "worked all day and not gotten very far." Most of us need help to find out how much we have, in fact, accomplished and, of course, how much we might accomplish by making adjustments in the way we are using the model. During training, the coaching teams need to spend a considerable amount of time examining curriculum materials and plans and practicing the application of the model that they will be using later. Then, as the process of transfer begins, practice in the classroom is intensified, with closer and closer attention given to appropriate use.

ADAPTATION TO THE STUDENTS   As we have already mentioned, much of the energy expended in learning to use a new model of teaching is consumed in the process of learning how to teach it to the children. Successful teaching requires successful student response. Teachers are familiar with the task of teaching students how to engage in instructional activities that are common. A model that is new to a group of students, however, will cause them trouble. *They* will need to learn new skills and to become acquainted with what is expected of them, how to fulfill the task demands of the new method, and how to gauge their own progress. In addition, the model of teaching needs to be adapted to fit different groups of students. More training must be provided for some, more structure for others, and so on. In the early stages, adaptation to the students is relatively difficult and usually requires a lot of direct assistance and companionship.

One of the major functions of the coach is to help the "players" to "read" the responses of the students so that the right decisions are made about what skill training is needed and how to adapt the model. This is especially important in the early stages of practice when one's hands are full managing one's own behavior and it is more difficult to worry about the students than it will be later on.

When practicing any new approach to teaching, one is surely less competent with it than with the approaches in one's existing repertoire. When trying a new model, nearly all of us feel bad about ourselves as we fumble around. The students sense our uncertainty and let us know in not so subtle ways that they are *aware* we are less certain and sure-footed than usual. At such times, we tend to become easily discouraged. The expression "I tried that method and it didn't work" refers as much to the sense of dismay we feel during the early trials as it does to the actual success or failure of the method itself.

The fact is, successful use of a new method requires practice. The early trials just are not perfect, or even close to our normal standards of adequacy. One of the principal jobs of the coaching team, then, is to help its members feel good about themselves during the early trials. It is tragic that teaching currently provides so little interpersonal support and close contact with other teachers, because classrooms are terribly isolated places. Coaching reduces the isolation and offers genuine support.

A question often asked is, who should coach? We're not really sure about that. On a practical basis, most coaching should be done by teams of teachers working together to study new approaches to teaching and to polish their existing teaching skills. There is, of course, no reason why administrators or curriculum supervisors or college professors cannot be effective coaches, too. But if only as a matter of logistics, teachers are closer to one another and in an excellent position to do most of the coaching necessary.

In summary, there are several types of new learning involved in the transfer process. To accomplish these kinds of learning in such a way that they will effectively attack or, better yet, prevent the transfer problem, five techniques are available. These techniques are:

To forecast the transfer process throughout the training cycle;

To reach the highest possible level of skill development during training;

To develop what we term "executive control"—that is, an understanding of the appropriate content for the model and how to adapt it to different types of students—a "metaunderstanding" about how the model works, how it can be fitted into the instructional repertoire, and how it can be adapted to students;

To practice in the workplace;

To institute a process of coaching during practice in the work setting.

PARALLELS WITH ATHLETIC TRAINING

We are beginning to discover parallels between the problem of transfer in teaching and the problem of transfer in athletic skills.

There are going to be so many things in your head that your muscles just aren't going to respond like they should for awhile . . . . You've got to understand that the best way to get through this is to relax, not worry about your mistakes, and come to each practice and each meeting anxious to learn. *We'll generally make you worse before we make you better.*[3]

Coach Brooks' recent admonition to his freshmen highlighted the parallels for us. Intrigued, we approached Coach Brooks and asked him to talk with us about training and the problems of transfer. The resulting interveiw revealed striking similarities in the training problems faced by teachers, football players, and their coaches.

> **Q:** Coach Brooks, I'm interested in how you approach skill development in football training and if you consider the transfer of those skills to game conditions to be a separate training problem.
>
> **A:** Although our players come to us with skills, we reteach and refine those skills as though we were starting from scratch. We teach them our way of doing it, because all those skills have to fit together into one team. They're all interdependent.
>
> **Q:** Could you tell me your approach to skill development?
>
> **A:** We use a part/whole/part method. All skills are broken down into discrete steps. We work on each segment, then combine them into whole skills, then into plays, etc., then go back and work on the specifics of skills that are giving problems.
>
> **Q:** Could you give me an example of a specific skill and how you would approach the training for that skill?

[3]Coach Rich Brooks of the University of Oregon to his incoming freshman football players, in The Eugene Register-Guard, August 14, 1981.

A: The fundamentals of blocking and tackling—bending the knees and striking a blow. All positions need this skill. The trick is to get the player to visualize, to have a mental picture of how it looks and how it feels. Otherwise, feedback isn't effective. We can tell them where it's wrong, but they can't correct it till they know.

Q: How do you get them "to know" what the skill is?

A: We tell them, show them, demonstrate with people and with film, show them films of themselves, have them practice with the _____ .

Q: The what?

A: It's a mechanical dummy they practice with. We have them practice each move separately, then put the moves together, first one, then two, then three—how their knees should be bent, where their arms should come up, where they strike, what all the muscles should be doing. We diagnose problems with the dummy and keep explaining how it should work, over and over again, in sequence.

Q: In teacher training, we believe that theoretical understanding is important to later performance. How important is it in football skills?

A: It's essential. They must understand how their bodies work, why certain muscle groups in certain combinations achieve certain effects. We never stop explaining.

Q: After they have mastered blocking to your satisfaction with the dummy, then what?

A: Moving from the machine to a live test is difficult; moving from practice to a game is also very difficult. Some people have all the physical ability in the world, all the moves, but can't play because they can't grasp the entire concept, can't fit in with the whole picture.

Q: We have problems with transfer of training, too. Do you coach them differently after they've mastered the "basic skills" of football? What will you be doing differently next month after the season has started? How do you work on transfer?

A: Fear of failure is a factor. My job is to create confidence and success situations. Skills have to be overlearned so that they're past conscious thinking. I can't have someone thinking of how to throw a block in a game. They have to be thinking of who and when and what the guy on their left or behind them is doing.

Q: So specifically, how do you coach transfer of skills to a game situation?

A: First, we reemphasize skill training to everyone—the second, third, fourth year guys as well. We're always working for improved execution. Then we work hardest on integration, which is just a new kind of teaching. Coaching is really just teaching. We work on confidence by putting them in situations where they can see the improvement. If a guy was lifting 300 pounds two weeks ago and is lifting 350 now, no one has to tell him he's getting stronger.

Q: How does the training break down for your players right now, before school starts?

A: We spend three hours in the classroom and two hours on the field. On their own, they spend a couple of hours in the weight room and working out and another couple of hours with the trainers, working out their bumps and bruises.

Q: And after school starts?

A: We'll spend 45 minutes a day in class, two hours on the practice field, plus whatever they can manage on their own after studies.

Q: How does that differ from pro football players' training regimen?

A: They meet two-three hours daily in position meetings, offensive and defensive meetings, watching films of themselves and their opponents, then practice two to four hours a day depending on their coaches, then their personal work and time with the trainers. They have more time to get into the complexities of the game.

Changing what we do, even slightly, can unbalance the rest of our "game." Whether we are adjusting the grip on a golf club or initiating an inquiry procedure for science teaching, the new behavior does not fit smoothly with our existing practice. The fact that the new skill may have been perfected in parts and practiced thoroughly in simulated conditions does not prevent the transfer problem. Surrounding behaviors must be adjusted to the presence of a different approach, and the resulting discomfort is often enough to ensure a return to the former smooth, if less efficient, performance.

Perhaps the most striking difference in training between athletes and teachers is the initial assumptions held by each. *Athletes do not believe mastery will be achieved quickly or easily.* They understand that enormous effort will result in small (and not always linear) increments of change. We, on the other hand, have often behaved as though teaching skills were so easily acquired that a simple presentation, one-day workshop, or single videotaped demonstration were sufficient to ensure successful classroom performance. To the extent that we have communicated this message to teachers, we have misled them. Learning to use an inductive strategy in the classroom is surely at least as difficult as learning to throw a block properly.

Coach Brooks' description parallels the argument we have tried to make. The task of learning new skills and integrating them, the knowledge that "we'll generally make you worse before we make you better," and the importance of continuing to try when the results are discouraging eloquently forecast the transfer process. The necessity of overlearning skills to the point that they become automatic if they are to be useful in a more complex setting is also reflected in Brooks' training regimen. "Executive control" is sought in the frequent and ongoing emphasis on theory and the classroom work on "plays," "game plans," and analysis of films.

The elements of coaching in teaching—the provision of companionship and technical feedback, study of application, study of students (or opposing teams) and personal facilitation—are also clear in the interview with Coach Brooks. Football players, however, have a built-in advantage when undertaking this process: Their training is *organized* as a group activity with continuous feedback from coaches. We came away from this interview feeling more strongly than ever that teachers must also organize *themselves* into groups for the express purpose of training themselves and each other and to facilitate the transition from skill development to transfer.

INCREASING LEARNING APTITUDE

To increase one's repertoire is to develop the aptitude to teach: the ability to coordinate objectives, students, and learning environments with increasing skill and effectiveness. Moreover, the more we develop our repertoires, the more we develop the ability to *add* to those repertoires *at will*.

The most important outcome of any educational exercise is an increase in aptitude— the ability to learn in new situations and to solve problems as they arise. Academic subjects provide us with examples. As a student learns skills in arithmetic, those skills represent an increased aptitude to solve problems, including sizing them up, sorting out the important features of the situation, selecting which skills to use, and applying them. Learning new skills increases one's aptitude to solve problems. Similarly, the well-developed reader has the aptitude to read new things—that is, material not previously encountered. Previously acquired knowledge of literature is brought to bear on new literary works. The primary importance of instruction in reading is not the material read in class but the increased aptitude it gives the students to handle new material.

The purpose of training for teachers is to increase the aptitude to learn in new situations—that is, to comprehend and solve goal-related problems. We try to increase our repertoires of teaching strategies so we can more effectively select objectives, pick appropriate models of teaching, and adjust them to the learning requirements of our students (Hunt, 1971). As we organize training, it is our goal not only to provide environments that maximize teachers' opportunities to expand their repertoires but also to increase their abilities to learn new skills and apply them as they teach. Essentially, the more we learn the easier it becomes.

We believe that the research on training conducted in the last twenty years has yielded enormous dividends. We understand better both the nature of transfer and the problem of achieving it, and we are able to outline procedures to enable nearly all teachers to learn the most powerful teaching strategies to the point that they can use them comfortably in the classroom. Working in teams committed to the coaching process, teachers can explore the theory behind any given teaching strategy, examine demonstrations, practice and provide one another feedback, and coach one another through the process of application.

An optimal training program is also organized so that the tasks of adding to the teaching repertoire become easier and easier—that is, the teachers not only acquire new teaching strategies but become better and better at the process of learning them. We are beginning to understand something about how to do this and have developed a series of propositions to guide program construction when increasing one's aptitude to learn is an objective.

PRINCIPLE 1: LEARNING NEW TEACHING STRATEGIES IN ITSELF INCREASES THE ABILITY TO LEARN OTHER ONES
In other words, engaging in the training process itself has beneficial effects. When teachers participate in a program designed to teach them several new teaching strategies, the first one is the hardest, the second one somewhat easier, and the third and fourth much easier than the first two. We can discover why this is true by considering a group of typical experienced teachers engaging in a program designed to help them learn new teaching strategies for the first time.

As the first model of teaching is presented, some members of the group are relatively indifferent to the theory of the model, while others watch the demonstration somewhat critically and spend much of the discussion time questioning whether the teaching strategy will, in fact, be of value to them. Still others resist the practice sessions, believing that a few demonstrations and a little explanation are "all we need" in order to use the teaching strategy. A few others are resistant to feedback and, finally, some of the coaching teams are slow getting started and some members of the coaching teams are slow to begin the necessary practice.

By the time the second model rolls around, however, the value of the theory is more clear and the demonstrations are watched more closely because everyone knows that practice will follow soon thereafter. Feedback is more welcome, practice less resisted, in fact, they have discovered that the process of teaching for one another is rather enjoyable and not nearly as threatening as it seemed. Feedback is also welcomed because the importance of a high level of skill development has become clear. The coaching teams have also become organized, and the importance of early practice is now apparent to everyone. In other words, practice in the training process increases one's skill in engaging in it. In fact, when teams stay together, they often work out ways to make the process more efficient. For all these reasons, experience with the training process increases the aptitude to profit from it.

PRINCIPLE 2: THE HIGHLY SKILLED LEARNERS UNDERSTAND THE PROCESS OF TRANSFER BETTER
Hence, the study of the process of transfer should become part of the content of training.

In our own training, we incorporate the content of this piece directly into the training program. As the coaching teams are organized, the process of transfer is discussed—forecast, as we put it above—and the research base for the training program is laid out in detail.

We find that the analogies from the sports, business, and military worlds are useful because they help teachers visualize the transfer problem as a general one rather than something specific to teaching. Direct experience with the transfer problem, however, remains the most useful teacher, and we try to acomplish this in two ways. First, we organize the training so that the first goal is to acquire a relatively simple teaching skill, and the training components are employed to help the trainees acquire that skill. The skill of "explaining" is a useful example, and the following sequence is generally employed.

First, each teacher is given a written passage about an unfamiliar topic and is provided some time to study it and prepare a brief (two- or three-minute) explanation of the topic for a group of peers. Working in small groups, each trainee explains the major points in the passage he or she has been given with a time limit placed on the explanation. Nearly everyone finds that it is much harder to explain a topic than they first believed. The skills for explaining are then described and some brief demonstrations are given. Then the process is repeated. Each person receives a new written passage, studies it, and then again attempts to explain it to a small group of peers. Performance increases, but nearly everyone is still dissatisfied with his or her explanation. The cycle is then repeated two or three times with further explanations of explaining and more practice. By the end of a single day, nearly all of the teachers are surprised at their increase in skill and comfort, although prior to the day nearly every one of them would probably have asserted that he or she was a relative expert at "explaining."

Exercises such as these are persuasive, but they are not enough. The more powerful experience occurs as the first model of teaching is taught, and the coaching teams find themselves engaged directly in the problem of transfer. They find that the research does indeed accurately depict the problem and that nearly everyone has to work very hard through a serious period of discomfort before gradually beginning to achieve some mastery of the model.

PRINCIPLE 3: THE PROCESS IS SIMPLIFIED BY CONCENTRATING ON OVERLEARNING: FIRST THE NEW SKILL, THEN "FIRST-STAGE" APPLICATION, AND THEN "EXPANDED CONTROL"

The entire training process is not satisfying to teachers until complete mastery has been achieved. Most teachers are quite frustrated until that point has been reached. Once teachers understand the training problem, however, they become much more comfortable with focusing first on the essential skills of the new teaching approach, then on finding opportunities to initially apply it without expecting full mastery, and only after that on getting assistance to help them achieve full control.

For most of us, the attempt to reach full control in the first stage is simply unrealistic. We need to concentrate on the basics, get enough experience with the new skills so they become relatively comfortable, and then concentrate on understanding how to use the model and adapt it to students. With increasing experience, teachers become much more comfortable concentrating on each of these levels of control in turn and become less frustrated when the last level cannot be achieved completely.

This also helps teachers overcome what we call a "batting away" reflex at the onset of discomfort during training. For many trainees, the first reaction to the use of a new skill is the relative awkwardness of that skill in comparison with long-standing ones. There is a tendency to reject the skill at that point and to begin to resist the training. But with experience and the acquisition of new skills, teachers become more understanding of their own discomfort and more receptive to attempts to help ease their passages through the initial stages of training.

Trainers need to understand that this discomfort is normal and accept it. Many good training programs have been discarded because the trainers, having discovered a really fine approach to teaching, mistakenly lose faith in the idea when it meets with resistance from the trainees. But the idea itself is seldom being rejected. The trainees are going through a normal process of discomfort that will gradually disappear as the training is consolidated.

PRINCIPLE 4: THE GREATEST NEW LEARNING OCCURS WITH ENGAGE-MENT WITH UNFAMILIAR SKILLS There is a perverse law of training that everyone needs to understand. It is simply that the more important an addition to one's repertoire a given model of teaching is, the greater the discomfort it will cause. The greatest opportunity for all of us as teachers is to learn skills that are quite unfamiliar to us but which have the most potential when we apply them in the classroom. We stretch ourselves by reaching out beyond the edges of our contemporary repertoires. Teachers and trainers alike have a tendency to seek the teaching skills that will be most easily acquired—that is, ones adjacent to or well within our contemporary ranges. But as training progresses, we come to understand that the greatest new learning pulls at the edges of our current range of skills and takes us to places where our initial discomfort will be succeeded by a true addition to our aptitude to solve the problems of teaching.

STATES OF GROWTH

Nothing is more important to a human being's health than his or her ability to continue to grow and adapt. No profession magnifies that truth more than education. The teacher's life is one of changing conditions: new students, new ideas, and social ferment. Adaptation is essential. There is no endeavor for which lack of growth is more clearly and desperately damaging than teaching.

While the enormous importance of personal and professional states of growth has long been recognized, in the ebb and flow of research and practice it has received varying degrees of attention. In the last few years, however, it has again begun to receive a lot of attention, partly because of concern about the nature of "adult learners," partly through studies of adult continuing education, and partly as a result of recent studies of teachers' self-concepts and interactions with their environments.

Recent studies (McKibbin and Joyce, 1982) have begun to identify clear differences among teachers when they interact with the formal system of staff development, with one another, and with the environments of their personal lives. As is the case with all other groups of people, some teachers are in states of very active interchange with their environments while others are less active, isolated from, and even resistant to, opportunities for growth.

The mastery of complex academic content and new teaching strategies requires an active state of interchange. Experiencing periods of discomfort, continuing to interact with colleagues, and learning to coach others require active learning states. Collaborative governance of training directly increases motivation and involvement and generates several conditions conducive to achievement (Joyce, 1978). Critical is the creation of a productive social system so that those in the most active states of growth help others to reach out more powerfully into their environments. The key is in the development of an energizing environment within the workplace of teachers.

In McKibbin and Joyce's (1982) recent study of the growth states of more than 200 teachers, it became clear that a substantial portion of them were heavily influenced by the environment of their school, some positively, some negatively. Many teachers who would otherwise have been "passive consumers" were propelled into more active states because the social climate of their school was active and compelling. In less active environments, some of the most energized teachers worked in relative isolation, generating their own social climate with small groups of peers. Many of those in less active states became withdrawn and in some cases resistant. Sharan and Hertz-Lazarowtiz (1982) have documented clearly the effect of resistance on training. In a loose and disorganized social climate without clear goals, reticent teachers may actually subvert elements of the training process not only for themselves but also for others.

Unquestionably, principals can have a substantial effect on the social climates of their schools, both by direct leadership and by freeing the energy of the more active teachers and increasing their influence within the social systems of the schools. Powerful training of the type we have been describing is exceptionally difficult to implement except in energized environments.

ADAPTATION OF TRAINING TO THE LEARNING STYLES OF TEACHERS

Training need not be seen as a monolithic series of steps. Teachers have preferences for varying degrees of control over their own activities. Their conceptual levels and self-concepts interact with their training (Showers, 1982). Training that is inflexible will perforce generate negative energy by depressing motivation and creating dissidence between trainees and trainers. Caring and considerate instructional designers and trainers can create settings in which training is modulated to the learning styles of the teachers. The energizing qualities of the environment and the states of growth of the teachers involved enormously influence both one's satisfaction with training and its likelihood of success. Responsive environments permit teachers to influence the process of training and adapt it to significant differences in their learning styles.

We are confident that effective training procedures exist. They should be implemented in such a way that the social environment of teaching becomes more adoptive and energizing, pulling teachers toward more active states of growth, providing avenues that release the power of individual styles of learning, and enabling teachers to increase their own personal technologies for acquiring fresh ideas and skills (Joyce, 1983, pp. 2–32).

28

EDUCATIONAL THEORY, RESEARCH, AND PRACTICE
Creating an Art and Science of Education

We have repeatedly voiced our hope that the coming decade will see a renewal of vigorous and humble dialogue on approaches to education. There is much quackery abroad in educationland—much selling of models as panaceas with little evidence that they can achieve even limited goals. On the other hand, there is as yet so little certain evidence available to us that to wait for a complete picture from research would require us to cease most educational activity for a generation or more.

What is needed is a proper recognition of our ignorance, combined with acceptance of the stance that we have many reasonable bases to use for present action. In fact, so many and different approaches are available that the likelihood that any one of us has opened the way to all the truth is ridiculously unlikely. Vigorous examination and lively debate appear very much in order.

DIMENSIONS FOR DEBATE

Any debate in educational theory should be directed toward action. To analyze, debate, and experiment with models of teaching requires that we identify classes of activity to which the models can be related. The educational environment has three dimensions to which models of teaching can be related: the personal dimension, involving the individual's quest for meaning and development; the social dimension, involving both the interpersonal aspects of teaching and the obligation to the larger society, the need to improve society and find meaning in relation to it; and the intellective dimension, relating to sources for improved problem-solving strategies.

We can discuss models for teaching in terms of their relevance to each of these aspects. In the first place, some models emphasize one or more of the dimensions. In group investigation, for example, the social system is specified in detail and dominates the others. Similarly, the nondirective-teaching and laboratory methods are primarily social models. The information-based models, on the other hand, are generally curricular in nature, for they specify type and nature of learning activities. The Conceptual-Systems Model is designed to generate differential systems that relate environments and students. If an educational environment is designed solely in terms of one of these models, then one system or dimension of the environment is likely to be emphasized and the others to be deemphasized.

Thus we find that models differ with respect to the dimensions they emphasize and can provide specifications for (Figure 28–1). There are two implications of this finding: One is that some models need to be augmented so that all three dimensions are filled in; the other is that in the creation of environments models will have varying utility, some providing help in some areas, others in different ones.

As a comparison of models proceeds on this basis, dialogue should emerge on the philosophical implications of differences in the environments derived from the models. Part of the debate can center on learning output and

FIGURE 28–1   Relationship of three hypothetical models to three dimensions of teaching.

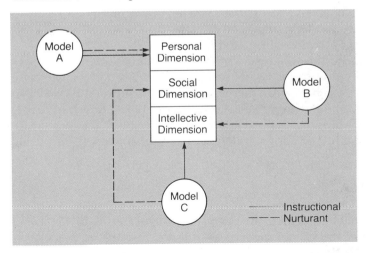

involve questions about what different models are good for and how efficient they are. For example, people may feel that some of the *less* efficient models in terms of skill and knowledge outcomes are preferable because of desirable social effects. (There are two sides to that debate!)

Probably a more significant set of questions concerns the long-range implications of a model. What are the relatively permanent effects on students of living in a client-centered environment, an environment steeped in group analysis, or one centered on academic debate? Does a student come to construct reality in a way that reflects his or her educational environment? In an environment characterized by instructional systems, would a student become production-oriented and utilitarian, whereas in an awareness training environment would he or she become more humanistic and personal? In short, does experiencing a model, aside from intended outcomes, also affect student personality in terms of skills developed, knowledge acquired, and attitudes formed?

We believe the answer to these last questions is resoundingly yes, and we offer the following propositions for discussion:

1. That the major significant differences between models are less in their efficiency for achieving particular instructional goals than in the effects of their internalization by the student. Educationally speaking, one becomes what he or she experiences. It is the differences in nurturant effects that are important.
2. That there are significant differences between models. Exposed to a particular environment for a reasonable time, one begins to construct reality in ways similar to that environment.
3. That every environment has a ceiling of growth. Thus, a pluralistic environment, one reflecting several models, is necessary if the student is to go beyond the limits of his or her mentors and create new syntheses.

Thus, students will benefit most from teachers and schools that manifest multiple ways of educating, not because educational pluralism offers something for everyone, but because the exposure to several vigorous ways of teaching will induce greater complexity of growth and ward off those great subverters of education—dogmatism and boredom.

We *could* extend this discussion into a long exhortation, but the issues should be worked out in dialogue, not in one-sided exposition—so we close with the hope that teachers and other educators will continue the dialogue through word and, far more important, through action. The glassy homogeneity of our schools at present simply cries out for more models that are actualized, and schools with vigorously developed, unique characters.

NEED FOR RESEARCH

There is a great need for research into the dimensions of the instructional and nurturant effects of the various models. Most of the research on models has taken place within the framework of one model rather than in a cross-disciplinary framework. There are some notable exceptions, such as Almy's (1970) study of the effect of teaching the structures of the disciplines on the logical thinking of young children. Oliver and Shaver (1968) examined recitative and dialogue-based approaches to teaching the jurisprudential framework. Roberts (1969) examined the use of laboratory method in social studies teaching. Sohunk (n.d.) studied the use of forms or organizers on learning within the BSCS framework. Romberg and Wilson (1970) examined a variety of forms of organizers with respect to various learning outcomes. Hawkes (1971) studied the effects of operant conditioning on students' inductive activity in studying important social problems.

All of these studies represent the type of cross-disciplinary framework that is necessary if the nurturant and instructional effects of the models are to be studied in productive relationship with one another.

CODA

Our final word is one of caution and hope intermingled. Models of teaching are often deliberate and theoretical; those are the kinds we have emphasized in this book. Others are patterns that emerge from intuition. Some of the latter are very attractive; others are not so pleasant. By analyzing practice, using a framework for describing and clarifying its meaning, we can see more clearly what the teacher is up to. For example, let us look at an educational practice that is truly horrifying but that has elements not uncommon in real schools.

A MODEL NOBODY WILL LOVE

The following is partly comic, partly serious, and intended to provoke discussion of the value issues in teaching:

BRAINWASHING MODEL

BASIC ORIENTATION

The model is designed to make the students docile. They are to be alienated from their fellow students and then provided with an ideology that will direct their behavior.

If they learn their lessons well, they are rewarded with privilege and responsibility. If they do not, they are subjected to scorn and to physical and social deprivation. Then, when they beg for relief, they are given the opportunity to practice their ideology until they are ready for responsibility.

This process is repeated until they lose their sense of egoistic self and are ready to submerge themselves in the discovery of the true way to fulfillment.

The family of the model is, of course, the antiperson, antisocial, antiin-formational family, a category especially created for this illustration.

SYNTAX

In the first phase, the subject is housed with a group of fellow subjects in a hut on a campus removed from ordinary social activities. Any in the group who show signs of leadership are removed from the group until only the apathetic remain. Group members are interviewed daily and asked to relate defects in the characters or behavior of the others. The interviewer lets each individual know what he or she has heard about them, and once a day the in-formation gleaned about each is publicly narrated to all in a group meeting. If this phase is successful, members of the group become increasingly suspicious of one another, interact less, and become unable to respond to initiative from their peers.

Contact with the outside world is discontinued in phase two. No letters, telephone calls, or mass media are permitted. The members receive tranquiliz-ing drugs at breakfast and at night. Rote lessons on the evils of old social systems and the advantages of the new social ideology are begun. If any members resist, all are punished by deprivation of food, warmth, and clothing.

In addition, each member publicly states his own defects at group meetings. All members correct him if he falters or defends himself or herself in any way.

In phase three the conditions of phase two are maintained, and indoc-trination progresses. Rote lessons now concentrate on the defects of the United States imperialist system and remedies proposed by the International Committee on World Social Improvement.

Lessons learned well are rewarded with food, clothing, or shelter. These are removed if resistance or inadequate learning occurs. The group is en-couraged to deal in this way with any members who cause deprivation.

The conditions of phase three are maintained in phase four, while subversion of the old order gets underway. Interviews are initiated with in-dividuals, who are offered the opportunity to serve the new ideology in a number of ways. They may make radio broadcasts or write news stories de-nouncing the old ideology and praising the new. They can defect from the old country to the new. They can return to the old country to initiate revolu-tionary activity or to carry on espionage activities.

When judged ready, they can leave the campus and rejoin society in these roles.

PRINCIPLES OF REACTION

Trainers are to be alert for signs of leadership and are to be ready to remove it when it is found. In the early stages they are to humiliate the students and drive them from each other. In the later phases, they should encourage individuals who have become completely docile or who eagerly seize the new ideology and wish to serve it. They should punish severely those who wish personal profit or privilege, however, by depriving their group of clothing and shelter until they confess their egoism and recant their personal desires.

SOCIAL SYSTEM

Leadership is to be entirely with the trainers. Social control is to be punitive, and mass punishment, with consequent retaliation by group members on the offender, is to be employed.

Members are to become alienated from one another until they become totally dependent on the mediators of the new ideology. They are to become completely subservient to the ideology.

CLASSROOM IMPLEMENTATION

Generally, the model is not designed for use in the classroom, and its use in American classrooms will be left to the reader's imagination.

GENERAL APPLICABILITY

The most famous application of this model was, of course, in prison camps in Korea during the period 1950 to 1953, in the so-called brainwashing

FIGURE 28-2 Instructional and nurturant effects: Brainwashing Model.

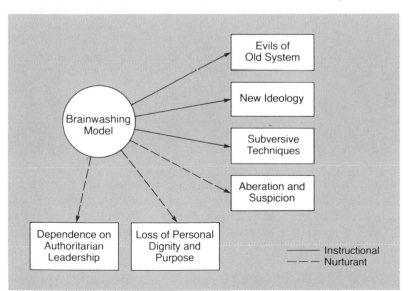

of the Americans imprisoned by the Chinese People's Republic. The direct purpose was to produce turncoats who would provide propaganda for the Communists' public-relations arm. The latent effects, of course, were to destroy ego-mediation and to produce people incapable of acting as individuals or of relating warmly to their fellows (see Kincaid, 1959). The instructional and nurturant effects of the model are shown in Figure 28–2.

Summary Chart: Brainwashing Model

SYNTAX

Phase One
Deprivation of privacy and dignity.
Establishment of physical punishment.

Phase Two
Development of group pressure and alienation.
Introduction of ideology.

Phase Three
Indoctrination to new ideology.

Phase Four
Preparation for subversion of old order.

WARNING!

The frightening thing is the similarity of elements of the Brainwashing Model to common educational practices. For example, competition is common in some schools. It tends to isolate students from each other and to alienate them from themselves. Public self-criticism is not uncommon in circumstances less harsh than those just described. Repetition of doctrine is by no means rare in schools, and adherence to particular ideologies is certainly not unexpected (nor should it be, considering the function of schools in the society). Some opinions, if expressed, are punished in many schools.

To live with truth and dignity as educators we must teach so that our models have moral validity. When we select practices we nurture not only the short-term growth but also the testing of our students and our society. Deciding what to instruct and nurture and how to instruct and nurture are decisions made by each of us in our classrooms. These humble decisions, each affecting only a few students, operate to shape the reality of humanity, for all of us are created in some part by our teachers and by the models they use.

REFERENCES

ADKINS, D. C., F. D. PAYNE, and J. M. O'MALLEY, "Moral Development," in *Review of Research in Education*, eds. F. N. Kerlinger and J. B. Carroll. Itasca, Ill.: F. E. Peacock Publishers, Inc., 1974.

ADLER, MORTIMER, *The Paideia Proposal*. 1983.

ALBERTI, R. E. and M. L. EMMONS, *Your Pefect Right: A Guide to Assertive Behavior* (3rd ed.), San Luis Obispo, Calif.: Impact Publishers, 1978.

ALMY, M., *Logical Thinking in Second Grade*. New York: Teachers College Press, 1970.

ANDERSON, HAROLD H., and J. E. BREWER, *Studies of Teacher Classroom Personality II*. Stanford, Calif.: Stanford University Press, 1946.

ANDERSON, L., C. EVERTSON, and J. BROPHY, "An Experimental Study of Effective Teaching in First-grade Reading Groups," *Elementary School Journal*, 79, 1979, 192–223.

ANDERSON, L. W., C. SCOTT, and N. HUTLOCK, "The Effects of a Mastery Learning Program on Selected Cognitive, Affective, and Ecological Variables in Grades 1 Through 6." Paper presented at the annual meeting of the American Educational Association, San Francisco, 1976.

APPLE, MICHAEL, *Ideology and Curriculum*. London: Routledge and Kegan Paul, 1979.

AQUINAS, THOMAS, *The City of God*, trans. John Healy. London: J. M. Dent, 1931.

ARGYRIS, CHRIS, AND E. SCHON, *Theory Into Practice: Increasing Professional Effectiveness*. San Francisco: Jossey Bass, 1974.

ARISTOTLE, *The Works of Aristotle*, ed. J. A. Smith and W. D. Ross. Oxford: Clarendon Press, 1912.

ARLIN, M., "Time Variability in Mastery Learning," *American Educational Research Journal*, 21, 1984, 103–20.

ARLIN, M., and J. WEBSTER, "Time Costs of Mastery Learning," *Journal of Educational Psychology*, 75, 1983, 187–96.

ASPY, DAVID N., and FLORA ROEBUCK, "An Investigation of the Relationship Between Student Levels of Cognitive Functioning and the Teacher's Classroom Behavior," *Journal of Educational Research*, 65, 1973, 365–368.

ASPY, DAVID N., FLORA ROEBUCK, M. A. WILLSON, and O. B. ADAMS, "Interpersonal Skills Training for Teachers." Interim Report #2 for NIMH Grant Number 5 PO 1 MH 19871, Monroe, La.: Northeast Louisiana University, August, 1974.

ATKINSON, J. W., *Achievement Motivation*. New York: John Wiley & Sons, Inc., 1966.

ATKINSON, RICHARD C., "Mnemotechnics in Second Language Learning," *American Psychologist*, 30, 1975, 821–28.

AUSUBEL, D., *Educational Psychology: A Cognitive View*. New York: Holt, Rinehart & Winston, 1968.

AUSUBEL, D. P., *The Psychology of Meaningful Verbal Learning*. New York: Grune & Stratton, Inc., 1963.

AUSUBEL, DAVID, "Schemata, Cognitive Structure, and Advance Organizers: A Reply to Anderson, Spiro, and Anderson," *American Educational Research Journal*, 17, 3, Fall, 1980, 400–04.

AUSUBEL, D. P., "The Use of Advance Organizers in the Learning and Retention of Meaningful Verbal Material," *Journal of Educational Psychology*, 51, 1960, 267–72.

AUSUBEL, D. P., and FITZGERALD, "Organizer, General Background and Antecedent

Learning Variables in Sequential Verbal Learning," *Journal of Educational Psychology,* 53, 1962, 243–49.

AUSUBEL, D. P., M. STAGER, and A. J. H. GAITE, "Retroactive Facilitation of Meaningful Verbal Learning," *Journal of Educational Psychology,* 59, 1968, 250–55.

AXELROD, S., *Behavior Modification for the Classroom Teacher.* New York: McGraw-Hill, 1977.

BAKER, E., and A. SALOUTOS, "Evaluating Instructional Programs," Washington, D.C.: Department of Health, Education, and Welfare, National Institute of Education, 1974.

BANDURA, A., "Psychotherapy Based on Modeling Principles," in *Handbook of Psychotherapy and Behavior Change.* eds. A. S. Bergin and S. L. Garfield, New York: John Wiley & Sons, Inc., 1971.

BANDURA, ALBERT, *Social Learning Theory.* New York: General Learning, 1971.

BANDURA, A., *Principles of Behavior Modification.* New York: Holt, Rinehart & Winston, 1969.

BANDURA, A., and B. PERLOFF, "Relative Efficacy of Self-monitored and Externally Imposed Reinforcement Systems," *Journal of Personality and Social Psychology,* 7, 1967, 111–16.

BANGERT, R. L., and J. A. KULIK, "Individualized Systems of Instruction: A Meta-analysis of Findings in Secondary Schools." Paper presented at the annual meeting of the American Educational Research Association. New York, March, 1982.

BANY, M., and L. V. JOHNSON, *Classroom Group Behavior: Group Dynamics in Education.* New York: Macmillan, Inc., 1964.

BARNES, BUCKLEY R., and ELMER V. CLAUSON, "Do Advance Organizers Facilitate Learning? Recommendations for Further Research Based on an Analysis of 32 Studies," *Review of Educational Research,* 43, 4, Fall, 1975, 637–59.

BARNES, B. R., and E. V. CLAUSON, "The Effects of Organizers on the Learning of Structured Anthropology Materials in the Elementary Grades," *Journal of Experimental Education,* 42, 1973, 11–15.

BARRON, F., *Creativity and Psychological Health: Origins of Personal Vitality and Creative Freedom.* Princeton: Von Nostrand, 1963.

BARRON, R. R., "The Effects of Advance Organizers upon the Reception, Learning, and Retention of General Science Concepts," DHEW Project No. 1B-030 ERIC Document Reproduction Service, ED 061554, 1971.

BECK, A. T., *Cognitive Therapy and the Emotional Disorders.* New York: International Universities Press, 1976.

BECKER, WESLEY C., "Teaching Reading and Language to the Disadvantaged—What We Have Learned from Field Research," *Harvard Educational Review,* 47, 1978, 518–543.

BECKER, WESLEY, *Classroom Management.* Chicago: Science Research Associates, 1975.

BECKER, W., and D. CARNINE, (1980). "Direct Instruction: An Effective Approach for Educational Intervention with the Disadvantaged and Low Performers," in *Advances in Child Clinical Psychology,* eds. B. Lahey and A. Kazdin. (pp. 429–473). New York: Plenum, 1980.

BECKER, WESLEY C., and RUSSELL GURSTEN, "A Follow Up of Follow Through: The Later Effects of the Direct Instruction Model on Children in the Fifth and Sixth Grades," *American Educational Research Journal,* 19, 1, Spring, 1982, 75–92.

BENCKE, W. N., and M. B. HARRIS, "Teaching Self-control of Study Behavior," *Behavior Research and Therapy,* 10, 1972, 35–41.

BENNIS, W. G., and H. A. SHEPARD, "A Theory of Group Development," in *The Planning of Change: Readings in the Applied Behavioral Sciences,* eds. W. G. Bennis, K. D. Benne, and R. Chin. New York: Holt, Rinehart & Winston, 1964.

BEREITER, C., "How to Keep Thinking Skills from Going the Way of All Frills," *Educational Leadership,* 42, 1, September 1984.

BEREITER, C. and S. ENGLEMANN, *Teaching the Culturally Disadvantaged Child in the Preschool.* Englewood Cliffs, N.J.: Prentice-Hall, Inc., 1966.

BEREITER, CARL, and M. KURLAND, "Were Some Follow Through Models More Effective than Others?" *Interchange*, 12, 1981–82, 1–22.

BERGER, P., and T. LUCKMAN, *Social Construction of Reality.* Garden City, N.Y.: Doubleday & Co., Inc., 1966.

BLOCK, JAMES. *Mastery Learning: Theory and Practice.* New York: Holt, Rinehart, and Winston, 1971.

BLOCK, J. W., and L. W. ANDERSON, *Mastery Learning in Classrooms.* N.Y.: Macmillan, 1975.

BLOCK, J. W., "Success rate," in *Time to Learn*, eds. C. Denham and A. Lieberman. Washington, D.C.: Program on Teaching and Learning, National Institute of Education, 1980.

BLOOM, B. S., *Human Characteristics and School Learning.* New York: McGraw-Hill, 1976.

BLOOM, B. S., "Mastery Learning," in *Mastery Learning: Theory and Practice*, ed. J. H. Block. New York: Holt, Rinehart, & Winston, 1971.

BLOOM, B. S., "Time and Learning," *American Psychologist*, 29, 1974, 682–688.

BLOOM, B. S., et al. *Taxonomy of educational objectives. Handbook I: Cognitive domain.* New York: David McKay Co., 1956.

BODE, B., *Modern Educational Theories.* New York: Macmillan, Inc., 1927.

BOOCOCK, S. S. "The School as a Social Environment for Learning Social Organization and Micro-social Process in Education," *Sociology of Education*, 1973.

BOOCOCK, S., and E. O. SCHILD, *Simulation Games in Learning.* Beverly Hills, Calif.: Sage Publications, Inc., 1968.

BOUTWELL, C., *Getting It All Together.* San Rafael, Calif.: Leswing Press, 1972.

BRADEN, V., and B. BRUNS, *Vic Braden's Tennis for the Future.* Boston: Little, Brown & Company, 1977.

BRADFORD, L. P., J. R. GIBB, and K. D. BENNE, eds. *T-Group Theory and Laboratory Method.* New York: John Wiley & Sons, Inc., 1964.

BREDDERMAN, T., "Elementary School Process Curricula: A Meta-analysis," ERIC Ed. 1981, 170–333.

BROOKOVER, W., J. H. SCHWITZER, J. M. SCHNEIDER, C. H. BEADY, P. K. FLOOD, and J. M. WISENBAKER, "Elementary School Social Climate and School Achievement," *American Educational Research Journal*, 15 (2), 1978, 301–318.

BROPHY, J., "Teacher Praise: A Functional Analysis." *Review of Educational Research*, 51, 1981, 5–32.

BROPHY, J. E. "Stability of Teacher Effectiveness," *American Educational Research Journal.* 10, 1973, 245–252.

BROPHY, J., and C. EVERTSON, "The Texas Teacher Effectiveness Project: Presentation of Nonlinear Relationships and Summary Discussion." Report No. 74-6, Research Development Center for Teacher Education, University of Texas, 1974.

BROPHY, J., and THOMAS GOOD, "Teacher Behavior and Student Achievement." Chapter Eleven. *The Third Handbook of Research on Teaching.* M. Wittrock, ed., in press.

BROUDY, H., "Historic Exemplars of Teaching Methods," in *Handbook of Research on Teaching*, ed. N. L. Gage. Chicago: Rand McNally & Company, 1963.

BROWN, G., *Human Teaching for Human Learning.* New York: Viking Penguin, Inc., 1971.

BROWN, G., "Humanistic Education." Report to the Ford Foundation on the Ford-Esallen Project, "A Pilot Project to Explore Ways to Adapt Approaches in the Affective Domain to the School Curriculum." 1968.

BRUNER, J., *The Process of Education.* Cambridge, Mass.: Harvard University Press, 1961.

BRUNER, J., J. J. GOODNOW, and G. A. AUSTIN, *A Study of Thinking*. New York: Science Editions, Inc., 1967.

BURGESS, E. W., and D. J. BOGUE, "The Delinquency Research of Clifford R. Shaw and Henry D. McKay and Associates," in Urban Sociology, eds. Burgess and Bogue. Chicago: University of Chicago Press, 1962.

BUSHELL, D. JR., *The Behavior Analysis Classroom*, Lawrence, Kansas, Univ. of Kansas Dept. of Human Development, 1970.

CANFIELD, L. H., and H. B. WILDER, *The Making of Modern America*. Boston: Houghton Mifflin Co., 1966.

CANTER, L., and M. CANTER. *Assertive Discipline: A Take-Charge Approach for Today's Educator*. Seal Beach, Calif.: Canter and Associates, 1976.

CARROLL, J. B., "A model of school learning," *Teachers College Record*, 64, 1963, 722–733.

CARROLL, J. B., *Language and Thought*. Englewood Cliffs, N.J.: Prentice-Hall, 1964.

CARROLL, J. B., "A Revisionist Model of School Learning," *Review of Education*, 3, 1977, 155–167.

CARROLL, J. B., "Problems of Measurement Related to the Concept of Learning for Mastery," in *Mastery Learning: Theory and Practice*. ed. J. H. Block, New York: Holt, Rinehart & Winston, 1971.

CHAMBERLIN, C. D., and E. S. CHAMBERLIN, *Did They Succeed in College?* New York: Harper and Row, 1943.

CHARLES, C. M., *Building Classroom Discipline: From Models to Practice*. White Plains: Longman Inc., 1985.

CHESLER, M., and R. FOX, *Role-Playing Methods in the Classroom*. Chicago: Science Research Associates, Inc., 1966.

CLAUSON, E. V., and M. G. RICE, "The Changing World Today," *Anthropology Curriculum Project Publication 72-1*. Athens, Ga: The University of Georgia, 1972.

CLAUSON, E. V., and B. R. BARNES, "The Effects of Organizers on the Learning of Structured Anthropology Materials in the Elementary Grades," *Journal of Experimental Education*, 42, 1973, 11–15.

COHEN, M., "Effective Schools: Accumulating Evidence." *American Education*, January/February 1982, pp. 13–16.

COLEMAN, J. S., E. Q. CAMPBELL, C. J. HOBSON, J. McPORTLAND, A. M. MOOD, E. D. WEINFIELD, and R. L. YORK, *Equality of Educational Opportunity*. Washington, D.C.: Government Printing Office, 1966.

COLLINS, K., "The Importance of Strong Confrontation in an Inquiry Model of Teaching," *School Science and Math*, 69, (7), 1969, 615–617.

COOK, L., and E. COOK, *Intergroup Education*. New York: McGraw-Hill, 1954.

COOK, L., and E. COOK, *School Problems in Human Relations*. New York: McGraw-Hill, 1957.

COPPEL, CAROL, and IRVING E. SIGEL, *Educating the Young Thinker. Classroom Strategies for Cognitive Growth*. Krieger, 1981.

COUNTS, G., *Dare the School Build a New Social Order?* New York: The John Day Company, 1932.

CROSBY, M., *An Adventure in Human Relations*. Chicago: Follet Corporation, 1965.

DAMON, W., *The Social World of the Child*. San Francisco: Jossey-Bass, 1977.

DAMON, W., "Studying Early Moral Development: Some Techniques for Interviewing Young Children and for Analyzing Results," Unpublished paper. Worcester, Mass.: Clark University, n.d.

Data Handbook. Boulder, Colo.: Social Science Consortium, 1971, 1972, and 1973.

DEAN, V. M., *The Nature of the Non-Western World*. New York: New American Library of World Literature, Inc., 1960.

DECKER, R. E., and R. ALPERIN, *Emotional Rating Supplement*. Palo Alto, Calif.: Unpublished manual, n.d.

DENHAM, C., and A. LIEDERMAN (eds.), *"Times to Learn,"* Washington, D.C.: Program on Teaching and Learning, National Institute of Education, 1980.

DEWEY, J., *The Child and the Curriculum*. Chicago: University of Chicago Press, 1960.

DEWEY, J., *Democracy and Education*. New York: Macmillan, Inc., 1916.

DEWEY, J., *Experience and Education*. New York: McMillan, Inc., 1937.

DEWEY, J. *How We Think*. Boston: Heath, 1910.

DEWEY, J., *Reconstruction in Philosophy*. New York: Henry Holt, 1920.

DEWEY, J., *The School and Society*. Chicago: University of Chicago Press, 1956.

DREIKURS, R., *Psychology in the Classroom*. New York: Harper and Row, 1968.

DREIKURS, R., B. GRUNWALD, and F. PEPPER, *Maintaining Sanity in the Classroom*. (2nd ed.). New York: Harper and Row, 1982.

EDMONDS, R., "Some Schools Work and More Can," *Social Policy*, 9 (5), 1979, 28–32.

EL-NEMR, M. A., "Meta-analysis of the Outcomes of Teaching Biology as Inquiry." Unpublished doctoral dissertation, University of Colorado, Boulder, 1979.

ELEFANT, EMILY. "Deaf Children in an Inquiry Training Program," *The Volta Review*, 82, 1980, 271–279.

ELIOT, T. S. "The Waste Land," in *Collected Poems 1909–1962*. New York: Harcourt, Brace Jovanovich, Inc.

ELLIS, A., and R. HARPER, *A New Guide to Rational Living*. Englewood Cliffs, N.J.: Prentice-Hall, Inc., 1975.

EMMER, E., C. EVERTSON, and L. ANDERSON, "Effective Classroom Management at the Beginning of the School Year," *The Elementary School Journal*, 80, 1980, 219–231.

ENGLEMANN, S., J. OSBORN, and T. ENGLEMANN, *DISTAR Language Program*. Chicago: Science Research Associates, Inc., 1972.

ERIKSON, ERIK. *Childhood and Society*. New York: Norton, 1950.

ESTES, W. E., ed. *Handbook of Learning and Cognitive Processes, Vol. IV: Attention and Memory*. Hillsdale, N.J.: Lawrence Erlbaum Associates, 1976.

ESTES, W. K., ed. *Handbook of Learning and Cognitive Processes, Vol. II: Conditioning and Behavior Theory*. Hillsdale, N.J.: Lawrence Erlbaum Associates, 1975.

EVERTSON, C., "Differences in Instructional Activities in Higher and Lower-Achieving English and Math Classes," *The Elementary School Journal*, 82 (4), 1982, 329–350.

FEELEY, THEODORE, "The Concept of Inquiry in the Social Studies." Doctoral dissertation, Stanford University, 1972.

FENSTERHEIM, H., and J. BAER, *Don't Say Yes When You Want to Say No*. New York: Dell Publishing Co., Inc., 1975.

FESTINGER, C. L., "Behavior Support for Opinion Change," *Public Opinion Quarterly*. 28, 1964, 404-17.

FISHER, C. W., D. C. BERLINER, N. N. FILBY, R. MARLIAVE, L. S. GHEN, and M. M. DISHAW, "Teaching Behaviors, Academic Learning Time, and Student Achievement: An overview," in *Time to learn*, eds. C. Denham and A. Lieberman. Washington, D.C.: National Institute of Education, 1980.

FLANDERS, N., *Analyzing teaching behavior*. Reading, Mass: Addison-Wesley, 1970.

FLAVELL, J. H., *The Developmental Psychology of Jean Piaget*. Princeton, N.J.: Van Nostrand Reinhold, 1963.

FROMM, E., *The Art of Loving*. New York: Harper, 1956.

FROMM, E., *Escape from Freedom*. New York: Farrar and Rinehart, 1941.

FROMM, E., *The Sane Society*. New York: Rinehart, 1955.

FULLAN, MICHAEL, "The Meaning of Educational Change," Toronto: Ontario Institute for Studies in Education, 1983.

FULLAN, M., and A. POMFRET, "Research on Curriculum and Instruction Implementation," *Review of Educational Research*, 47 (1), 1977, 335–397.

FURTH, H. G., *Piaget and Knowledge*. Englewood Cliffs, N.J.: Prentice-Hall, 1969.

GAGE, N. L., *The Scientific Basis for the Art of Teaching*. New York: Teachers College Press, 1979.

GAGNÉ, R., "Military Training and Principles of Learning," *American Psychologist*, 17, 1962, 46–67.

GAGNÉ, R., *Conditions of Learning.* New York: Holt, Rinehart & Winston, 1965.

GAGNÉ, ROBERT, "The Learning of Concepts," *The School Review,* 75, 1965, 187–196.

GAGNÉ, R., "Instruction in the Conditions of Learning," in *Instruction: Some Contemporary Viewpoints,* ed. Laurence Siegel. New York: Harper & Row, Publishers, Inc., 1967.

GAGNÉ, R., et al. *Psychological Principles in Systems Development.* New York: Holt, Rinehart & Winston, 1962.

GAGNÉ, ROBERT, and LESLIE BRIGGS, *Principles of Instructional Design.* New York: Holt, Rinehart and Winston, 1979.

GALL, MEREDITH D., and JOYCE P. GALL, "The Discussion Method," "Psychology of Teaching Methods," *Seventy Fifth Yearbook of the National Society for the Study of Education.* Chicago: University of Chicago Press, 1976, 166–216.

GALLWAY, W. T., *Inner Skiing.* New York: Random House, Inc., 1977.

GINOTT, H., *Teacher and Child.* New York: Macmillan, 1971.

GLASS, G., "Primary, Secondary, and Meta-analysis of Research," *Educational Researcher,* 7, 1978, 3.

GLASS, G. V., L. S. CAHAN, M. L. SMITH, and N. N. FILBY, *School class size: Research and Policy.* Beverly Hills, Calif.: Sage, 1982.

GLASSER, W., *Reality Therapy.* New York: Harper & Row, Publishers, Inc., 1965.

GLASSER, WILLIAM, *Schools Without Failure.* New York: Harper and Row, 1969.

GLASSER, WILLIAM, and WILLIAM T. POWERS, *Stations of the Mind: New Directions for Reality Therapy.* New York: Harper and Row, 1981.

GLASSER, WILLIAM, *Take Effective Control of Your Life.* New York: Harper and Row, 1984.

GOLEMIEWSKI, R. T., and A. BLUMBERG, *Sensitivity Training and the Laboratory Approach.* Itaska, Ill.: F. E. Peacock Publishers, Inc., 1970.

GOOD, T., D. GROUWS, and H. EMEIER, *Active Mathematics Teaching.* New York: Longman, Inc., 1982.

GOOD, T., and D. GROUWS, "Teaching Effects: A Process-product Study in Fourth-grade Mathematics Classrooms," *Journal of Teacher Education,* 28, 1977, 49–54.

GOODLAD, J., and F. KLEIN, *Looking Behind the Classroom Door.* Worthington, Ohio: Charles E. Jones, 1970.

GOODLAD, JOHN, *A Place Called School.* New York: McGraw Hill, 1983.

GOODMAN, P., *Compulsory Miseducation.* New York: Horizon Press, 1964.

GORDON, WILLIAM J. J., "The Integration of Creative Persons," paper delivered to Sloan Fellows, MIT, November, 1952.

GORDON, WILLIAM J. J., "Some Environmental Aspects of Creativity," paper delivered to the Department of Defense, Fort Belvior, Va., December, 1955.

GORDON, WILLIAM J. J., "Creativity as a Process," paper delivered at the First Arden House Conference on Creative Process, October 10–12, 1956.

GORDON, WILLIAM J. J., "Operational Approach to Creativity," *Harvard Business Review,* Vol. 34, No. 6 (November–December, 1956), pp. 41–51.

GORDON, WILLIAM J. J. (with Jerome Bruner), "Motivating the Creative Process," paper delivered at the Second Arden House Conference on Creative Process, May 7–10, 1957.

GORDON, WILLIAM J. J., "The Role of Irrelevance in Art and Invention," paper delivered to the Third Arden House Conference on Creative Process, November 1–4, 1957.

GORDON, WILLIAM J. J., *SYNECTICS.* New York: Harper & Row, 1961.

GORDON, WILLIAM J. J., "Director of Research," *The New Yorker,* November 4, 1961.

GORDON, WILLIAM J. J., "The Pures," *The Atlantic Monthly,* May, 1962.

GORDON, WILLIAM J. J., "The Nobel Prizewinners," *The Atlantic Monthly,* August, 1962.

GORDON, WILLIAM J. J., "How to Get Your Imagination Off the Ground," *Think* (IBM Press), March, 1963.

GORDON, WILLIAM J. J., "Mrs. Schyler's Plot," *The Atlantic Monthly,* April, 1963.

GORDON, WILLIAM J. J., "The Metaphorical Way of Knowing," *Education of Vision,* Gyorgy Kepes, editor. New York: George Braziller, 1965.

GORDON, WILLIAM J. J. (Poze, T., project director), *Making it Strange, Books 1 and 2.* Evanston: Harper & Row, 1968.

GORDON, WILLIAM J. J. (Poze, T., editor), *Making it Strange, Books 3 and 4.* Evanston: Harper & Row, 1969.

GORDON, WILLIAM J. J., "The Metaphorical Development of Man," *The Changing World and Man,* Chandler McC. Brooks, editor. New York: NYU Press, 1970.

GORDON, W. J. J., *The Metaphorical Way of Learning and Knowing.* Cambridge, Mass.: S.E.S. Press, 1970.

GORDON, WILLIAM J. J. (Poze, T., research editor), *The Metaphorical Way of Learning and Knowing.* Cambridge: Porpoise Books, 1971.

GORDON, WILLIAM J. J. (Poze, T., research editor), *What Color is Sleep?* Cambridge: Porpoise Books, 1971.

GORDON, WILLIAM J. J., and POZE, T., *The Basic Course in Synectics.* Cambridge: Porpoise Books, 1971.

GORDON, WILLIAM J. J., and POZE, T., *The Art of the Possible.* Cambridge: Porpoise Books, 1971.

GORDON, WILLIAM J. J., and POZE, T., *Invent-o-rama.* Cambridge: Porpoise Books, 1971.

GORDON, WILLIAM J. J., and POZE, T., *Facts & Guesses.* Cambridge: Porpoise Books, 1971.

GORDON, WILLIAM J. J., and POZE, T., *Making it Whole.* Cambridge: Porpoise Books, 1971.

GORDON, WILLIAM J. J., "Architecture—the Making of Metaphors," *Main Currents in Modern Thought,* Vol. 28, No. 1 (September–October, 1971).

GORDON, WILLIAM J. J., "Use of Metaphor Increases Creative Learning Efficiency," *Trend,* Spring 1972, pp. 11–14.

GORDON, WILLIAM J. J., and POZE, T., *Strange & Familiar, Book VI.* Cambridge: Porpoise Books, 1972.

GORDON, WILLIAM J. J., and POZE, T., *Activities in Metaphor.* Cambridge: Porpoise Books, 1972.

GORDON, WILLIAM J. J., and POZE, T., *Teaching is Listening.* Cambridge: Porpoise Books, 1972.

GORDON, WILLIAM J. J., and POZE, T., *Introduction to Synectics (Problem-Solving).* Cambridge: Porpoise Books, 1972.

GORDON, WILLIAM J. J., "On Being Explicit About Creative Process," *Journal of Creative Behavior,* Vol. 6, No. 4 (Spring 1973), pp. 295–300.

GORDON, WILLIAM J. J., and POZE, T., "Learning Is Connection-Making," *Professional Report* (Croft Publications), February, 1974.

GORDON, WILLIAM J. J., and POZE, T., *From the Inside.* Cambridge: Porpoise Books, 1974.

GORDON, WILLIAM J. J., and POZE, T., "Creative Training in an Occupational Context," *Technical Education Reporter,* Vol. 1, No. 1 (May–June, 1974), pp. 52–57.

GORDON, WILLIAM J. J., "Some Source Material in Discovery-by-Analogy," *Journal of Creative Behavior,* Vol. 8, No. 4 (Fall, 1974), pp. 239–257.

GORDON, WILLIAM J. J., "Training for Creativity," *International Handbook of Management Development and Training.* London: McGraw Hill, 1975.

GORDON, WILLIAM J. J., and POZE, T., *Strange & Familiar, Book III.* Cambridge: Porpoise Books, 1975.

GORDON, WILLIAM J. J., and POZE, T., *Strange & Familiar, Book I.* Cambridge: Porpoise Books, 1975.

GORDON, WILLIAM J. J., and POZE, T., *The Art of the Possible.* Cambridge: Porpoise Books, 1976.

GORDON, WILLIAM J. J., "Toward Understanding 'the Moment of Inspiration'," paper delivered at the Creativity Symposium for the American Association for the Advancement of Science, February 21, 1977.

GORDON, WILLIAM J. J., "Connection-Making is Universal," *Curriculum Product Review,* Vol. IX, No. 4 (April, 1977).

GORDON, W. J. J., and T. POSE, *Teaching Is Listening*. Cambridge, Mass.: Synectics Education Systems, n.d.

GUETZKOW, H., et al. *Simulation in International Relations*. Englewood Cliffs, N.J.: Prentice-Hall, Inc., 1963.

GUETZKOW, HAROLD, and JOSEPH J. VALADEZ, eds. *Simulated International Processes: Theories and Research in Global Modeling*. Beverly Hills: Sage Publications,

HANSEN, C., *Amidon*. Englewood Cliffs, N.J.: Prentice-Hall, Inc., 1962.

HARVEY, O. J., D. E. HUNT, and H. M. SCHRODER, *Conceptual Systems and Personality Organization*. New York: John Wiley & Sons, Inc., 1961.

HAWKES, E., "The Effects of an Instruction Strategy on Approaches to Problem-Solving." Unpublished doctoral dissertation, Teachers College, Columbia University, 1971.

HEARD, S., and B. WADSWORTH, "The Relationship between Cognitive Development and Language Complexity." Unpublished paper, Mount Holyoke College, 1977.

HERSH, R. H., *"What Makes Some Schools and Teachers More Effective?"* Eugene, Oregon Center for Educational Policy and Management, University of Oregon, 1984.

HOETKER, J., and W. AHLBRAND, "The Persistence of the Recitation," *American Educational Research Journal*, 6, 1969, 145–167.

HOLMS, T. H., and R. H. RAHE, "The Social Readjustment Rating Scale," *Journal of Psychomatic Research*, 11, 1967, 213–18.

HOPKINS, K., "The Unit of Analysis: Group Means Versus Individual Observations," *American Educational Research Journal*, 19, 1982, 5–18.

HULLFISH, H. G., and P. G. SMITH, *Reflective Thinking: The Method of Education*. New York: Dodd, Mead & Company, 1961.

Human Relations Laboratory Training Student Notebook. ED 018 834. Washington, D.C.: U.S. Office of Education, 1961.

HUNT, D. E., "A Conceptual Level Matching Model for Coordinating Learner Characteristics with Educational Approaches," *Interchange: A Journal of Educational Studies*. 1(2), 1970.

HUNT, D. E., "Adaptability in Interpersonal Communication Among Training Agents." *Merrill Palmer Quarterly*, 16, 1970, 325–344.

HUNT, D. E., *Matching Models in Education*. Toronto: Ontario Institute for Studies in Education, 1971.

HUNT, D. E., "Person-Environment Interaction: A Challenge Found Wanting before It Was Tried," *Review of Educational Research*, 45, 1975, 209–230c.

HUNT, D. E., "Teachers' Adaptation to Students: Implicit and Explicit Matching." Stanford, Calif.: Research and Development Memorandum No. 139, SCRDT, 1975a.

HUNT, D. E., "The B-P-E Paradigm in Theory, Research, and Practice." *Canadian Psychological Review*, 16, 1975, 185–197b.

HUNT, D. E., "Teachers Are Psychologists, Too: On the Application of Psychology to Education," *Canadian Psychological Review*, 1976.

HUNT, D. E., J. GREENWOOD, R. BRILL, and M. DEINEKA, "From Psychological Theory to Educational Practice: Implementation of a Matching Model," Symposium presented at the annual meeting of the American Educational Research Association, Chicago, 1972.

HUNT, D. E., and R. H. HARDT, "The Role of Conceptual Level and Program Structure in Summer Upward Bound Programs." Paper presented to the Eastern Psychological Association, Boston, 1967.

HUNT, D. E., and E. V. SULLIVAN, *Between Psychology and Education*. Hinsdale, Ill.: Dryden, 1974.

HUNT, D. E., and E. V. SULLIVAN, *Between Psychology in Education*. Hinsdale, Ill.: Dryden, 1974.

HUNT, J. McV., *Intelligence and Experience*. New York: Ronald Press, 1961.

HUNTER, I. M. L., *Memory*. Middlesix, England: Penguin Books, 1964.

HUNZIKER, J. C., "The Use of Participant Modeling in the Treatment of Water Phobias." Unpublished Master's thesis, Arizona State University, 1972.

"Individually Prescribed Instruction," Philadelphia: Research for Better Schools. Unpublished manuscript, 1966.

"Individually Prescribed Instruction: Mathematics Continuum." Pittsburgh: University of Pittsburgh, Learning Research and Development Center, 1968.

IVANY, GEORGE, "The Assessment of Verbal Inquiry in Elementary School Science," *Science Education*, 53 (4), 1969, 287–293.

JACOBSON, E., *Progressive Relaxation*. Chicago: University of Chicago Press, 1979.

JACKSON, P. W., *Life in classrooms*. New York: Holt, Rinehart and Winston, 1968.

JOHNSON, D., and R. JOHNSON, "Instructional Goal Structure: Cooperative, Competitive, or Individualistic," *Review of Educational Research*, 44, 1974, 213–240.

JOHNSON, D. W., R. T. JOHNSON, J. JOHNSON, and D. ANDERSON, "The Effects of Cooperative vs. Individualized Instruction on Student Prosocial Behavior, Attitudes Toward Learning, and Achievement," *Journal of Educational Psychology*, 68, 1976, 446–452.

JOHNSON, D. W., R. T. JOHNSON, and L. SCOTT. "The Effects of Cooperative and Individualized Instruction on Student Attitudes and Achievement," *Journal of Social Psychology*, 104, 1978, 207–216.

JOHNSON, D. W., R. T. JOHNSON, and L. SKON, "Student Achievement on Different Types of Tasks Under Cooperative, Competitive, and Individualistic Conditions," *Contemporary Educational Psychology*, 4, 1979, 99–106.

JOHNSON, D. W., and S. JOHNSON, "The Effects of Attitude Similarity, Expectation of Goal Facilitation, and Actual Goal Facilitation on Interpersonal Attraction," *Journal of Experimental Social Psychology*, 8, 1972, 197–206.

JOHNSON, D. W., G. MARUYAMA, R. T. JOHNSON, D. NELSON, and L. SKON, "Effects of Cooperative Competitive, and Individualistic Goal Structures on Achievement," *Psychological Bulletin*, 89, 1981, 47–62.

JOYCE, BRUCE, ed. "Involvement: A Study of the Shared Governance of Education," Washington, D.C.: The Eric Clearinghouse on Teacher Education, 1978.

JOYCE, B. R. "The 'Models of Teaching' Community: What Have We Learned?", *Texas Tech Journal of Education*. 2(2), 1975, 95-106.

JOYCE, B. R. and B. HAROOTUNIAN, *The Structure of Teaching*. Chicago: Science Research Associates, Inc., 1967.

JOYCE, BRUCE, RICHARD HERSH, and MICHAEL McKIBBIN. *The Structure of School Improvement*. New York: Longman, Inc., 1983.

JOYCE, B. K., M. McKIBBIN, and N. BUSH, "The Seasons of Professional Life: The Growth States of Teachers." Paper presented at the annual meeting of the American Education Research Association, Montreal, Canada, April, 1983.

JOYCE, B. R., L. PECK, and C. BROWN, eds. *Flexibility in Teaching*. New York: Longman Green, 1979.

JOYCE, B. R., and B. SHOWERS, "The Coaching of Teaching." *Educational Leadership*, 40 (1), 1982, 4–16.

JOYCE, BRUCE and BEVERLY SHOWERS. *Power in Staff Development Through Research on Training*. Washington, D.C.: Association for Supervision and Curriculum Development, 1983.

JOYCE, B. R., and B. SHOWERS, "Teacher Training Research: Working Hypothesis for Program Design and Directions for Further Study." Paper presented at the annual meeting of the American Education Research Association, Los Angeles, 1981.

JOYCE, B., B. SHOWERS, C. BEATON, and M. DALTON, "The Search for Validated Objectives of Teacher Education: Teaching Skills Derived From Naturalistic and Persuasion Oriented Studies of Teaching." Paper presented at the annual meeting of the American Educational Research Association, New Orleans, April 23–27, 1984.

JOYCE, BRUCE, BEVERLY SHOWERS, MICHAEL DALTON, and COLIN BEATON. "The Search for Validated Skills of Teaching: Four Lines of Inquiry." A paper presented to the annual meeting of the American Educational Research Association. Chicago, 1985.

JUDD, C. H., *Education and Social Progress.* New York: Harcourt Brace Jovanovich, Inc., 1934.

KAHN, S. B., and J. WEISS, "The Teaching of Affective Responses," in *The Second Handbook of Research on Teaching,* ed. R. M. W. Travers. Chicago: McNally & Company, 1973.

KAMII, C. and R. DeVRIES, "Piaget-Based Curricula for Early Childhood Education," in *The Preschool in Action,* (rev. ed.), ed. Ron Parker, Boston: Allyn & Bacon, Inc., 1974.

KENWORTHY, L. S., *Introducing Children to the World.* New York: Harper, 1955.

KILPATRICK, W. H., *The Project Method.* New York: Teachers College Press, 1919.

KINCAID, E., *In Every War But One.* New York: W. W. Norton, Inc., 1959.

KLAUSMEIER, H. J., and C. W. HARRIS, *Analysis of Concept Learning.* New York: Academic Press, Inc., 1966.

KLEITSCH, R. G., *Directory of Educational Simulations, Learning Games, and Didactic Units.* St. Paul, Minn.: Instructional Simulations, 1969.

KOHLBERG, L., "The Cognitive Developmental Approach to Moral Education," in *Moral Education . . . It Comes with the Territory,* ed. D. Purpel and K. Ryan. Berkeley, Calif.: McCutchan Publishing Corporation, 1976.

KOHLBERG, L., "Moral Education and the Schools," *School Review,* 74, 1966, 1–30.

KOHLBERG, LAWRENCE, *The Philosophy of Moral Development.* Harper & Row, Pub., 1981.

KOHLBERG, LAWRENCE, *The Psychology of Moral Development.* Harper & Row, Pub., 1983.

LAVATELLE, C., *Piaget's Theory Applied to an Early Childhood Education Curriculum.* Boston: American Science and Engineering, 1970.

LAWSON, A. E. et al., "Proportional Reasoning and Linguistic Abilities Required for Hypothetico-deduct Reasoning," *Journal of Research in Science Teaching,* 21(4), 1984, 377–384.

LAWTON, J. T. "The Use of Advance Organizers in the Learning and Retention of Logical Operations in Social Studies Concepts," *American Educational Research Journal.* 14 (1), 1977, 24–43.

LAWTON, JOSEPH T., and SUSAN K. WANSKA, "The Effects of Different Types of Advance Organizers on Classification Learning," *American Educational Research Journal,* 16, 3, Summer, 1979, 223–39.

LAWTON, JOSEPH T., "Effects of Advance Organizer Lessons on Children's Use and Understanding of the Causal and Logical 'Because'," *Journal of Experimental Education,* 46, 1, Fall, 1977, 41–6.

LAZARUS, A. A., *Behavior Therapy and Beyond.* New York: McGraw-Hill, 1971.

LEDERMAN, J., *Anger and the Rocking Chair.* New York: The Viking Press, 1973.

LEITHWOOD, K. and D. MONTGOMERY, "Assumptions and Uses of a Procedure for Evaluating the Nature and Degree of Program Implementation." Paper presented at the annual meeting of the AERA, 1983.

LEVIN, JOEL R., C. McCORMICK, H. MILLER, and J. BERRY, "Mnemonic versus nonmnemonic strategies for children," *American Educational Research Journal,* 19 (1), 1982, 121–136.

LEVIN, J., L. SHUBERG, and J. BERRY, "A Concrete Strategy for Remembering Abstract Prose," *American Educational Research Journal,* 20 (2), 1983, 227–290.

LEVY, D. V., and J. STARK, "Implementation of the Chicago Mastery Learning Reading Program at Inner-city Elementary Schools." Paper presented at the annual meeting of the American Educational Research Association, New York, 1982.

LEWIS, H., and H. STREITFELD, *Growth Games.* New York: Harcourt Brace Jovanovich, Inc., 1970.

LINDVALL, C. M., and J. O. BOLVIN, "The Project for Individually Prescribed Instruction," Oakleaf Project. Unpublished manuscript, University of Pittsburgh, Learning Research and Development Center, 1966.

LIPPITT, R., R. Fox, and L. SCHAIBLE, "Cause and Effect," *Social Science Resource Book.* Chicago: Science Research Associates, Inc., 1969.

LIPPITT, R., R. Fox, and L. SCHAIBLE, *Social Science Laboratory Units.* Chicago: Science Research Associates, 1969.

LOCKE, J., *Some Thoughts Concerning Education,* ed. R. H. Quick. Cambridge: Cambridge University Press, 1927.

LORAYNE, H., and J. LUCAS, *The Memory Book.* Briercliff Manor, N.Y.

LUCAS, S. B., "The Effects of Utilizing Three Types of Advance Organizers for Learning a Biological Concept in Seventh Grade Science," Doctoral Dissertation, Pennsylvania State University, 1972.

LUDLUM, R. P., et al. *American Government.* Boston: Houghton Mifflin Company, 1969.

LUITEN, J., W. AMES, and G. ACKERSON, "A Meta-analysis of the Effects of Advance Organizers on Learning and Retention," *American Educational Research Journal,* 17, 1980, 211–218.

LUNDQUIST, G., and G. PARR, "Assertiveness Training with Adolescents," *Technical Journal of Education,* 5, 1978, 37–44.

MAYER, RICHARD F., "Can Advance Organizers Influence Meaningful Learning?" *Review of Educational Research,* 49, 2, Summer, 1979, 371–83.

McCLELLAND, D. C., *The Achievement Motive.* New York: Appleton-Century-Crofts, 1953.

McDONALD, F. J., and P. ELIAS, "Beginning Teacher Evaluation Study: Phase II, 1973–74," Executive Summary Report. Princeton, N.J.: Educational Testing Service, 1976.

McKINNEY, C., A. WARREN, GUY LARKINS, MARY JANE FORD, and JOHN C. DAVIS, III, "The Effectiveness of Three Methods of Teaching Social Studies Concepts to Fourth-Grade Students: An Aptitude-Treatment Interaction Study," *American Educational Research Journal,* 20, 1983, 663–670.

MADDEN, N. A., and R. E. SLAVIN, "Cooperative Learning and Social Acceptance of Mainstreamed Academically Handicapped Students," *Journal of Special Education,* 17, 1983, 171–182.

MAHONEY, M., and CARL THORENSEN. "Behavioral Self-Control—Power to the Person," *Educational Researcher,* 1, 1972, 5–7.

MARCUSE, H., *Eros and Civilization.* Boston: Beacon Press, 1955.

MASLOW, ABRAHAM, *Toward a Psychology of Being.* New York: Van Nostrand, 1962.

MASSIALAS, B., and B. COX, *Inquiry in Social Studies.* New York: McGraw-Hill, 1966.

MEDLEY, D., *Teacher Competence and Teacher Effectiveness,* 1977, Washington, D.C.: American Association of Colleges of Teacher Education.

MEDLEY, D., "Teacher Effectiveness," in *Encyclopedia of Educational Research,* ed. H. Mitzel, 1982, 1894–1903.

MEDLEY, D. M., and H. E. MITZEL, "Measuring Classroom Behavior by Systematic Observation," in *Handbook of Research on Teaching,* ed. N. L. Gage. Chicago: Rand McNally and Co., 1963, 247–328.

MELAMED, B., and L. SIEGEL, "Reduction of Anxiety in Children Facing Hospitalization and Surgery by Use of Filmed Modeling," *Journal of Consulting and Clinical Psychology.* 43, 1975, 511–520.

MERRILL, M. D., and R. D. TENNYSON, *Concept Teaching: An Instructional Design Guide.* Englewood Cliffs, N.J.: Educational Technology, 1977.

MEYER, L., "Long-Term Academic Effects of the Direct Instruction Project Follow Through," *Elementary School Journal,* 84, 1984, 380–394.

MICHAELIS, J. U., *Social Studies for Children in a Democracy.* Englewood Cliffs, N.J.: Prentice-Hall, Inc., 1963.

MIEL, A., and P. BREGAN, *More Than Social Studies: A View of Social Learning in the Elementary School.* Englewood Cliffs, N.J.: Prentice-Hall, Inc., 1957.

MITCHELL, L. S., *Our Children and Our Schools.* New York: Simon & Schuster, Inc., 1950.

MORE, SIR THOMAS, *Utopia.* New York: E. P. Dutton & Co., Inc., 1965.

"The National Council for the Social Studies, The Glen Falls Story." Washington, D.C.: National Education Association, 1964.

NESBITT, W. A., *Simulation Games for the Social Studies Classroom.* New York: Foreign Policy Association, 1971.

OLIVER, D., and F. NEWMAN, *Taking a Stance: A Clear Guide to Discussion of Public Issues.* Middletown, Conn.: American Education Publishers, 1967.

OLIVER, D., and J. P. SHAVER, *Cases and Controversy: A Guide to Teaching the Public Issues Series.* Middletown, Conn.: American Education Publishers, 1971.

OLIVER, D., and J. P. SHAVER, *Teaching Public Issues in the High School.* Boston: Houghton Mifflin Company, 1966.

OLIVER, D. W., and J. P. SHAVER, "The Effect of Student Characteristics and Teaching Method Interactions on Learning to Think Critically." Paper presented to the American Educational Research Association, 1968.

OLSON, D. R., *Cognitive Development: The Child's Acquisition of Diagonality.* New York: Academic Press, Inc., 1970.

ORME, M., and R. PURNELL, "Behavior Modification and Transfer in an Out-of-Control Classroom" Monograph publ. by Harvard R & D Center on Educational Differences, 1968.

ORNSTEIN, R., *The Psychology of Consciousness.* New York: The Viking Press, 1972.

PALOMARES, U., G. BALL, and H. BESSELL, "Magic Circle: Human Development Program." La Mesa, CA: Human Development Institute, 1972–76.

PAVLOV, I., *Conditioned Reflexes: An Investigation of Physiological Activity of the Cerebral Cortex,* trans. G. V. Anrep. London and New York: Oxford University Press, 1927.

PERLS, F., *Gestalt Therapy Verbatim.* Lafayette, CA: Real People Press, 1968.

PERLS, F., R. HEFFERLINE, and P. GOODMAN. *Gestalt Therapy.* New York: Julian Press, 1951.

PERSING, P., W. C. BAILEY, and M. KLEG, "Life Cycle," Anthropology Curriculum Project, Publication 49. Athens, GA: The University of Georgia, 1969.

PETERSON, P. L., and C. M. CLARK, "Teachers' Reports of Their Cognitive Processes During Teaching," *American Educational Research Journal,* 15(4), 1978, 555–565.

PETERSON, P. L., R. W. MARX, and C. M. CLARK, "Teacher Planning, Teacher Behavior, and Student Achievement," *American Educational Research Journal,* 15(4), 1978, 417–432.

PHENIX, P., *Education and the Common Good.* New York: Harper, 1961.

PIAGET, J., *The Origins of Intelligence in Children.* New York: International University Press, 1952.

PIAGET, JEAN, *The Child's Conception of the World.* Atlantic Highlands, N.J.: Humanities Press, Inc., 1960.

PLATO, *The Republic.* McDonald Cornford. New York: Oxford University Press, Inc., 1945.

POLLACK, G. K., *Leadership of Discussion Groups.* Jamaica, N.Y.: Spectrum Publications, 1975.

PREMACK, D., "Reinforcement Theory," in Nebraska Symposium on Motivation, ed. D. Levine. Lincoln, Neb: University of Nebraska Press, 1965.

PRESSLEY, MICHAEL, "Children's Use of the Keyword Method to Learn Simple Spanish Vocabulary Words," *Journal of Educational Psychology,* 69 (5), 1977, 465–472.

PRESSLEY, MICHAEL, and JANICE DENNIS-ROUNDS, "Transfer of a mnemonic keyword strategy at two age levels," *Journal of Educational Psychology,* 72 (4), 1980, 575–582.

PRESSLEY, MICHAEL, JOEL R. LEVIN, "Developmental Constraints Associated with Children's Use of Keyword Method of Foreign Language Learning," *Journal of Experimental Child Psychology,* 26 (1), 1978, 359–372.

Pressley, Michael, Joel R. Levin, and Howard D. Delaney, "The Mnemonic Keyword Method," *Review of Educational Research*, 52 (1), 1982, 61–91.

Pressley, Michael, Joel R. Levin, and Christine McCormick, "Young Children's Learning of Foreign Language Vocabulary: A Sentence Variation of the Keyword Method," *Contemporary Educational Psychology*, 5, 1980, 22–19.

Pressley, M., G. Miller, and J. Levin, "How Does the Keyword Method Affect Vocabulary Comprehension and Usage?", *Reading Research Quarterly*, 16, 1981, 213–226.

Preston, R. C., *Improving the Teaching of World Affairs*. Englewood Cliffs, N.J.: Prentice-Hall, Inc., 1956.

Purkey, S. C., and M. S. Smith, "Effective Schools: A Review," *Elementary School Journal*, 4, 1983, 427–452.

Ralphy, J. H., and Fennessey. "Science or Reform. The effective schools model," *Phi Delta Kappan*, June, 1982, 689–696.

Resnick, L., "Design of an Early Learning Curriculum." Pittsburgh, Pa: University of Pittsburgh Learning Research and Development Center, 1967.

Rhine, W., ed. *Making Schools More Effective: New Questions From Follow-through.* New York: Academic Press, 1981.

Rimm, D. C., and J. C. Masters, *Behavior Therapy: Techniques and Empirical Findings.* New York: Academic Press, Inc., 1974.

Roberts, J., "Human Relations Training and Its Effect on the Teaching-Learning Process in Social Studies." Final Report, New York State Education Department, Division of Research, Albany, New York, 1969.

Robinson, F. P., *Effective Study.* New York: Harper and Bros., 1946.

Roebuck, F., J. Buhler, D. Aspy, "A Comparison of High and Low Levels of Humane Teaching/Learning Conditions on the Subsequent Achievement of Students Identified as Having Learning Difficulties." Final Report: Order No. PLD 6816 - 76 re. the National Institute of Mental Health. Denton, Texas: Texas Woman's University Press, 1976.

Rogers, C., *Client Centered Therapy.* Boston: Houghton Mifflin Co., 1971.

Rogers, Carl, *Freedom to Learn.* Columbus: Charles E. Merrill, 1969.

Rogers, Carl, *A Way of Being.* Boston: Houghton Mifflin, 1981.

Rogers, Carl, *Freedom to Learn for the 80s.* Columbus: Charles E. Merrill, 1982.

Romberg, T. A., and J. Wilson, "The Effect of an Advance Organizer, Cognitive Set, and Post Organizer on the Learning and Retention of Written Materials." Paper presented at the annual meeting of the American Educational Research Association, Minn., 1970.

Rosenshine, B., "The Stability of Teacher Effects Upon Student Achievement," *Review of Educational Research*, 40, 1970, 647–662.

Rosenshine, B., *Teaching behaviors and student achievement.* London: National Foundation for Educational Research, 1971.

Rosenshine, Barak, "Direct Instruction," *International Encyclopedia of Education*, Eds. Torsten Husen and T. Neville Postlethwaite. Oxford: Pergamon Press, Vol. 3, 1985, 1395–1400.

Rousseau, J. J. *Emile*, New York: E. P. Dutton, 1983.

Rowen, Bossert, Dwyer, "Research on Effective Schools: A Cautionary Note," *Educational Researcher*, April, 1983, 24–31.

Rutter, M., B. Maughan, P. Mortimore, and J. Ouston, *15,000 Hours: Secondary Schools and Their Effects on Children.* Cambridge, Mass.: Harvard University Press, 1979.

Salter, A., "The Theory and Practice of Conditioned Reflex Therapy," in *Conditioning Therapies: The Challenge in Psychotherapy*, eds. A. Salter, J. Wolpe, and L. J. Reyna, New York: Holt, Rinehart & Winston, 1964.

Salter, A., J. Wolpe, and J. Reyna, eds. *The Conditioning Therapies: The Challenge in Psychotherapies.* New York: Holt, Rinehart & Winston, 1964.

Scanlon, R., and M. Brown, "In-Service Education for Individualized Instruction." Philadelphia: Research for Better Schools. Unpublished manuscript, n.d.

SCHAEFER, ROBERT, *The School as a Center of Inquiry.* New York: Harper and Row, 1967.

SCHEIN, E. H., and W. G. BENNIS, *Personal and Organizational Change Through Group Methods.* New York: John Wiley & Sons, Inc., 1965.

SCHRENKER, G., "The Effects of an Inquiry Development Program on Elementary School Children's Science Learning." Doctoral dissertation, N.Y.U., 1976.

SCHRODER, H. M., M. J. DRIVER, and S. STREUFERT, *Human Information Processing: Individuals and Groups Functioning in Complex Social Situations.* New York: Holt, Rinehart & Winston, 1967.

SCHRODER, H. M., M. KARLINS, and J. PHARES, *Education for Freedom.* New York: John Wiley, 1973.

SCHUTZ, W., *Firo.* New York: Holt, Rinehart & Winston, 1958.

SCHUTZ, W., *Joy: Expanding Human Awareness.* New York: Grove Press, Inc., 1967.

SCHUTZ, W., and EVELYN TURNER, *Body Fantasy,* Irvington Press, 1983.

SCHWAB, J. J., supervisor. *Biological Sciences Curriculum Study, Biology Teachers' Handbook.* New York: John Wiley & Sons, Inc., 1965.

SCHWAB, JOSEPH J., *Science, Curriculum and Liberal Education. Selected Essays.* Chicago: University of Chicago Press, 1982.

SHAFFER, J. B. P., and J. D. GALINSKY, *Models of Group Therapy and Sensitivity Training.* Englewood Cliffs, N.J.: Prentice-Hall, 1974.

SHAFTEL, F., and G. SHAFTEL, *Role Playing for Social Values: Decision Making in the Social Studies.* Englewood Cliffs, N. J.: Prentice-Hall, 1967.

SHAFTEL, FANNIE, and GEORGE SHAFTEL, *Role Playing in the Curriculum.* Englewood Cliffs, N.J.: Prentice-Hall, 1982.

SHANE, HAROLD, "Curriculum Change: Toward the 21st Century," Washington, National Education Association, 1977.

SHARAN, S., and Y. SHARAN, *Small-Group Teaching.* Englewood Cliffs, N.J.: Educational Technology Publications, 1976.

SHARAN, S., "Cooperative Learning in Small Groups: Recent Methods and Effects on Achievement, Attitudes, and Ethnic Relations," *Review of Educational Research,* 50, 1980, 241–71.

SHARON, S., and R. HERTZ-LAZAROWITZ, "Academic Achievement of Elementary School Children in Small Group versus Whole-class Instruction," *Journal of Experimental Education,* 48 (2), 1980, 120–129.

SHAVER, JAMES P., and WILLIAM STRONG, *Facing Value-Decisions: Rationale-Building for Teachers.* New York: Teachers College Press, 1982.

SHEPARD, H. A., "The T-Group as Training in Observant Participation," in *The Planning of Change: Readings in the Applied Behavioral Sciences,* ed. W. G. Bennis, K. D. Benne, and R. Chin. New York: Holt, Rinehart & Winston, 1964.

SHIRER, W. L., *The Rise and Fall of the Third Reich.* New York: Simon & Schuster, Inc., 1960.

SHOWERS, B., "Coaching: A Training Component for Facilitating Transfer of Training." Paper presented at the annual meeting of the American Educational Research Association, Montreal, Canada, April, 1983.

SHOWERS, B., "Peer Coaching and Its Effect on Transfer of Training." Paper presented at the annual meeting of the American Educational Research Association in New Orleans, Louisiana, April 23–27, 1984.

SHOWERS, B., "A study of Coaching in Teacher Training." Eugene: University of Oregon, Center for Educational Policy & Management, 1982.

SHOWERS, BEVERLY, "Teachers Coaching Teachers: The Dynamics of Staff Development." Educational Leadership, 42 (7), 1985.

SHULMAN, L. S., and E. R. KEISLAR, (eds.) *Learning by Discovery: A Critical Appraisal.* Skokie, Ill: Rand McNally & Company, 1966.

SIGEL, F. E., *The Piagetion System and the World of Educational Studies in Cognitive Development,* eds., David Elkind and John Flavell. New York: Oxford University Press, 1969.

SIGEL, IRVING E., ED., *Advances in Applied Developmental Psychology.* Ablex, 1984.

SIGEL, I. E., and F. H. HOOPER, *Logical Thinking in Children.* New York: Holt, Rinehart, & Winston, 1968.

SIROTNIK, K. A., "What You See is What You Get—Consistency, Persistency, and Mediocrity in Classrooms," *Harvard Educational Review,* 53 (1), 1983.

SKINNER, B. F., *Beyond Freedom and Dignity.* New York: Knopf, 1971.

SKINNER, B. F., *Reflections on Behaviorism and Society.* Englewood Cliffs: Prentice-Hall, 1978.

SKINNER, B. F., *Science and Human Behavior.* New York: Macmillan, Inc., 1953.

SKINNER, B. F., *The Technology of Teaching.* Englewood Cliffs, N.J.: Prentice-Hall, Inc., 1968.

SKINNER, B. F., *Verbal Behavior.* New York: Appleton-Century-Crofts, 1957.

SLAVIN, R., *Cooperative learning.* New York: Longman, 1983.

SLAVIN, R. E., "Classroom Reward Structure. An Analytic and Practical Review," *Review of Educational Research,* 47(4), 1977(a), 633–650.

SLAVIN, R. E., "How Student Learning Teams Can Integrate the Desegregated Classroom." *Integrated Education,* 15(6), 1977(c), 56–58.

SLAVIN, R. E., "Student Learning Team Techniques: Narrowing the Achievement Gap Between the Races," Center for Social Organization of Schools, The Johns Hopkins University, Report No. 228, 1977(b).

SLAVIN, R. E., "A Student Team Approach to Teaching Adolescents with Special Emotional and Behavioral Needs." *Psychology in the Schools,* 14(1), 1977(d), 77–84.

SLAVIN, R. E., "Separating Incentives, Feedback, and Evaluation: Toward a More Effective Classroom System," *Educational Psychologist,* 13, 1978(a), 97–100.

SLAVIN, R. E., "Student Teams and Achievement Divisions," *Journal of Research and Development in Education,* 12, 1978(b), 39–49.

SMITH, K. U., and M. F. SMITH, *Cybernetic Principles of Learning and Educational Design.* New York: Holt, Rinehart & Winston, 1966.

SMITH, LOUIS and PAT KEITH, Anatomy of an Innovation. New York: Wiley, 1971.

SMITH, M. J., *When I Say No I Feel Guilty.* New York: Bantam Books, Inc., 1975.

SMITH, M. L., "Effects of Aesthetics Educations on Basic Skills Learning." Boulder, Colorado: Laboratory of Educational Research, University of Colorado, 1980.

SOAR, R. S., "Follow Through Classroom Process Measurement and Pupil Growth (1970–71): Final Report." Gainesville, Fla.: College of Education, University of Florida, 1973.

SPAULDING, R. L., "Educational Intervention Program: Final Report." Durham, N.C.: Duke University, 1970.

SPAULDING, R. L., and M. R. PAPAGEORGIO, "Observation of the Coping Behavior of Children in Elementary Schools." Unpublished manuscript, San Jose State University, 1975.

SRI International. "Evaluation of the Implementation of Public Law 94-142." Menlo Park, Calif.: Sri International, 1982.

SPRINTHALL, M. A., and THIES-SPRINTHALL, L., "Teachers as Adult Learners," in The eighty-second yearbook of the National Society for the Study of Education, *Staff Development,* pp. 13–25, ed. Gary Griffin. Chicago: U of Chicago Press, 1981.

STADSKLEV, R., "Handbook of Simulation Gaming in Social Education, I (Textbook) and II (Directory)." University, Ala.: University of Alabama, Institute of Higher Education Research and Services, n.d.

STALLINGS, J., "Allocating Academic Learning Time Revisited Beyond Time on Task," *Educational Researcher,* 9, 1980, 11–16.

STALLINGS, J., "Implementation and Child Effects of Teaching Practices in Follow Through Classrooms." *Monographs of the Society for Research in Child Development,* 4D (7–8, serial No. 163), 1975.

STALLINGS, J. A., and D. H. KASKOWITZ, "Follow Through Classroom Observation Evaluation 1972–1973," SRI Project URU-7370, Stanford Research Institute, August, 1974.

STALLINGS, J., M. NEEDELS, and N. STAYROOK, "How to Change the Process of Teaching

Basic Reading Skill in Secondary Schools." Menlo Park, Calif.: Stanford Research Institute International, 1979.

"Stanford Program on Teaching Effectiveness," A factorially designed experiment on teacher structuring, solicting and reacting. Stanford, Calif.: Stanford Center for Research and Development in Teaching, 1976.

STARR, J., *Programmed Modern Arithmetic: Introduction to Sets*. Boston: D. C. Heath and Company, 1965.

STEPHENS, W. B., "The Development of Reasoning, Moral Judgment and Moral Conduct in Retardates and Normals: Phase II." Unpublished manuscript, Temple University, 1972.

STONE, CAROL LETH, "A Meta-Analysis of Advance Organizer Studies," *Journal of Experimental Education*, 51, 4, Summer, 1983, 194–99.

SUCHMAN, J., "Studies in Inquiry Training," in *Piaget Reconsidered*, eds. R. Ripple and V. Bookcastle. Ithaca, N.Y.: Cornell University, 1964.

SUCHMAN, J. R., "The Elementary School Training Program in Scientific Inquiry." Report to the U. S. Office of Education, Project Title VII. Urbana: University of Illinois, 1962.

SUCHMAN, RICHARD J., *Idea Book for Geological Inquiry*. Trillium Press, 1981.

SULLIVAN, E., "Piaget and the School Curriculum: A Critical Appraisal," *Bulletin No. 2*. Toronto: Ontario Institute for Studies in Education, 1967.

SULLIVAN, M. S., *Programmed English: A Modern Grammar for High School and College Students*. New York: Macmillan Publishing Co., Inc., 1963.

SULLIVAN, EDMUND V., *A Critical Psychology: Interpretations of the Personal World*. Plenum, 1984.

TABA, H., *Teacher's Handbook for Elementary Social Studies*. Reading, Mass: Addison-Wesley Publishing Co., Inc., 1967.

TABA, H., "Teaching Strategies and Cognitive Functioning in Elementary School Children," Cooperative Research Project 2404. San Francisco, Calif.: San Francisco State College, 1966.

TABER, J., R. GLASER, and H. S. HALMUTH, *Learning and Programmed Instruction*. Reading, Mass: Addison-Wesley Publishing Company, Inc., 1967.

TAYLOR, C., ed. *Creativity: Progress and Potential*. New York: McGraw-Hill, 1964.

THELEN, H., *Dynamics of Groups at Work*. Chicago: University of Chicago Press, 1954.

THELEN, H., *Classroom Grouping for Teachability*. New York: John Wiley & Sons, Inc., 1967.

THELEN, H., *Education and the Human Quest*. N.Y.: Harper and Row, 1960.

THELEN, HERBERT A., *The Classroom Society: The Construction of Education*. Halsted Press, 1981.

THORESON, C. E., and M. J. MAHONEY, *Behavioral Self-Control*. New York: Holt, Rinehart & Winston, 1974.

THORNDIKE, E. L., "Animal Intelligence: An Experimental Study of the Associative Process in Animals," in *Psychological Review*, Monograph Supplement 2, no. 8. New York: Macmillan, Inc., 1911.

THORNDIKE, E. L., *The Psychology of Learning, Vol II: Educational Psychology*. New York: Teachers College, 1913.

TORRANCE, E. P., *Gifted Children in the Classroom*. New York: Macmillan, Inc., 1965.

TORRANCE, E. P., *Guiding Creative Talent*. Englewood Cliffs, N.J.: Prentice-Hall, Inc., 1962.

TORRANCE, E. P., *Torrance Tests of Creative Thinking*. Normal Annual, Research Edition, Princeton, N.J.: Personnel Press, 1966.

TYLER, R. W., *Basic Principles of Curriculum and Instruction*. Chicago: University of Chicago Press, 1950.

"The Urban Simulator." Washington, D.C.: Washington Center for Metropolitan Studies, 1972.

VARENHORST, B. B., "The Life Career Game: Practice in Decision-Making," in *Simulating Games in Learning*, ed. S. Boocock and E. O. Schild. Beverly Hills, Calif.: Sage Publications, Inc., 1968.

512

Voss, B. A., "Summary of Research in Science Education." Columbus, Ohio: ERIC Clearinghouse for Science, Mathematics, and Environmental Education, November, 1982.

Wadsworth, Barry, *Piaget for the Classroom Teacher.* New York: Longman, Inc., 1978.

Walberg, Herbert, "Why Japanese Productivity Excels." A paper presented to the annual meeting of American Educational Research Association, Chicago, 1985.

Warren, M., "The Classification of Offenders as an Aide to Efficient Management and Effective Treatment," Community Treatment Project. Prepared for the President's Commission on Law Enforcement and the Administration of Justice, Task Force on Corrections, 1966.

Watson, J. B., "The Place of Conditioned Reflex in Psychology," *Psychological Review,* 23, 1916, 89–116.

Watson, J. B., and R. Rayner, "Conditioned Emotional Reactions," *Journal of Experimental Psychology,* 3, 1921, 1–14.

Weikart, D., et al. "The Cognitively Oriented Curriculum: A Framework for Preschool Teachers," Washington, D.C.: National Association for Education of Young Children, 1971.

Weil, M., B. Joyce, and B. Kluwin, *Personal Models of Teaching.* Englewood Cliffs, N.J. Prentice-Hall, Inc., 1978.

Weil, M., B. Marshalek, A. Mitman, J. Murphy, P. Hallinger, and J. Pruyn, "Effective and Typical Schools: How Different are They?" Paper presented at the annual meeting of the American Educational Research Association, New Orleans, La., April, 1984.

Weinstein, G., and M. Fantini, eds. *Toward Humanistic Education: A Curriculum of Affect.* N.Y.: Praeger, Inc., 1970.

Wertheimer, M., *Productive Thinking.* New York: Harper, 1945.

Wilson, Craig, *The Open-Access Curriculum.* Boston: Allyn Bacon, 1971.

Wing, R., "Two Computer-Based Economic Games for Sixth Graders." Yorktown Heights, N.Y.: Center for Educational Services and Research, Board of Cooperative Educational Services, 1965.

Wolpe, J., *The Practice of Behavior Therapy.* Oxford: Pergamon Press, 1969.

Wolpe, J., *Psychotherapy by Reciprocal Inhibition.* Stanford, Calif.: Stanford University Press, 1958.

Wolpe, J., and P. Lang, "Fear Survey Schedule." San Diego: Educational and Industrial Testing Service.

Wolpe, J., and A. A. Lazarus, *Behavior Therapy Techniques: A Guide to the Treatment of Neuroses.* Oxford: Pergamon Press, Inc., 1966.

Wolpe, Joseph, and David Wolpe, *Our Useless Fears.* Boston: Houghton Mifflin, 1981.

Worthen, B. R., "A Study of Discovery and Expository Presentation: Implications for Teaching," *Journal of Teacher Education,* 19, 1968, 223–242.

Wrenn, C. G., and R. P. Larsen, *Studying Effectively.* Stanford, Calif.: Stanford University Press, 1955.

Young, D., "Team Learning: An Experiment in Instructional method as Related to Achievement," *Journal of Research in Science Teaching,* 8, 1971, 99–103.

Zaltman, G., R. Duncan, and J. Holbek, *Innovation and Organization,* New York: John Wiley, 1973.

Ziegler, S., "The Effectiveness of Cooperative Learning Teams for Increasing Cross-ethnic Friendship: Additional Evidence," *Human Organization,* 40, 1981, 264–268.

Zuckerman, D. W., and R. E. Horm, *The Guide to Simulation Games for Education and Training.* Cambridge, Mass.: Information Resources, Inc., 1970.

INDEX

ACKNOWLEDGMENTS *(continued from p. ii)*

Excerpts from *Elementary School Training Program in Scientific Inquiry* by J. Richard Suchman, on pp. 58–60, © 1962 by The University of Illinois. Excerpts from *The Changing World Today* by Elmer V. Clauson and Marion G. Rice, The University of Georgia, 1972. Excerpts from *The Memory Book* by Harry Lorayne and Jerry Lucas, copyright © 1974 by Harry Lorayne and Jerry Lucas. Reprinted with Permission of Stein and Day Publishers. Excerpts from "Piaget and the School Curriculum: A Critical Appraisal" by Edmund Sullivan, Bulletin No. 2 of the Ontario Institute for studies in education, (Toronto, 1967). Reprinted by permission. Excerpts from *Piaget for the Classroom Teacher* by Barry J. Wadsworth, copyright © 1978 by Longman Inc. Excerpts from *Moral Education: It Comes with the Territory* by David and Kevin Kohlberg et al, Berkeley, McCutchan publishing Corporation © 1976. Permission granted by the publisher. Excerpts from *BSCS, Biology Teacher's Handbook* (New York: John Wiley and Sons, Inc., 1965) reprinted by permission of the Biological Sciences Curriculum Study. Excerpts from Carl Rogers, *Freedom to Learn*, (Columbus, Ohio: Charles E. Merrill Co., 1969). Reprinted by permission of Charles E. Merrill. Excerpts from *The Structure of School Improvement* by Bruce R. Joyce, Richard H. Hersh and Michael McKibbon, copyright © 1983 by Longman Inc. Excerpts from William J. J. Gordon *Metaphorical Way of Learning and Knowing*, (Cambridge, Mass: S.E.S. Press, 1970). Excerpts from *Growth Games* by Howard Lewis and Harold Strietfield reprinted by permission of Harcourt, Brace, Javonovitch, Inc. Excerpts from George Brown, *Humanistic Education Report to Ford Foundation* on the Ford-Esalen Project, "A Pilot Project to Explore Ways to Adapt Approaches in the Affective Domain to the School Curriculum," 1968. Excerpts from Wiliam C. Schutz, *Joy*, (New York: Grove Press, Inc.). Reprinted by permission. Excerpts from Herbert Thelen, *Education and the Human Quest* (New York: Harper & Row, Publishers, Inc., 1960). Excerpts from Fannie R. Shaftel, George Shaftel, *Role-Playing for Social Values: Decision-Making in the Social Studies*, © 1967, pp. 67, 69, 71. Reprinted by permission of Prentice-Hall, Englewood Cliffs, New Jersey. Excerpts from Donald W. Oliver and James P. Shaver, *Teaching Public Issues in the High School*, Logan, UT: Utah State University Press, 1974 (first edition published by Houghton Mifflin, 1966). Excerpts from Leland P. Bradford, "Developing Potentialities through Class Groups." *Human Forces in Teaching and Learning* Leland P. Bradford, ed. (Washington D.C.: National Training Laboratory, National Education Association, 1961). p. 30. Reprinted by permission of John Wiley & Sons, Inc. Excerpts from *Models of Group Therapy and Sensitivity Training* by John B. Shaffer and M. David Galinsky reprinted by permission of Prentice-Hall © 1974, pp. 194–95. Excerpts from *Inquiry in Social Studies* by Byron Massialas and Benjamin Cox. Copyright © 1966, by McGraw–Hill Book Company. Used by permission of McGraw–Hill Company. Excerpts from Leon H. Canfield and Howard B. Wilder. *The Making of Modern America*. Copyright © 1966, 1950 by Houghton Mifflin Company. Reprinted by permission of the publisher. Excerpts from *The Nature of the Non-Western World* by Vera Micheles Dean. Copyright © 1957, 1963, 1966 by Vera Micheles Dean. Reprinted by arrangement with The New American Library, Inc., New York, NY. Excerpts from Robert E. Alberti, Ph.D. and Michael L. Emmons, Ph.D., *Your Perfect Right: A Guide to Assertive Behavior* (Third Edition). Copyright © 1978. Impact Publishers, Inc., San Luis Obispo, California. Reprinted by permission of the publisher. *Behavior Modification and Transfer in an out-of-control Classroom* by Orme and Purnell used with permission of the Center for Research and Development on Educational Differences, Harvard University, Cambridge, MA. *Programmed English* by M. W. Sullivan reprinted with permission of Macmillan Publishing Company. Copyright © by M. W. Sullivan Associates 1963. Excerpts from *Human Information Processing* by Harold M. Schroder, Michael J. Driver, and Siegfried Streufert. Copyright © 1967 by Holt, Rinehart & Winston, Inc. Reprinted by permission of CBS College Publishing. Excerpts from David C. Rimm and John C. Masters, *Behavior Therapy: Techniques and Empirical Findings* (New York: Academic Press, Inc., 1974), pp. 284–85. Excerpts from George Brown, *Human Teaching for Human Learning*, pp. 143–45, 150–51. Copyright 1971 by George Brown. An Esalen Book. All rights reserved. Reprinted by permission of Viking Press, Inc. Excerpts from *The Structure of School Improvement* by Bruce R. Joyce, Richard H. Hersh and Michael McKibbon. Copyright © 1983 by Longman Inc.